Human Communication in Society

Third Custom Edition for San Francisco State University

Taken from:
Human Communication in Society, Third Edition
by Jess K. Alberts, Thomas K. Nakayama, Judith N. Martin

Communication Principles for a Lifetime: Volume 4 Presentation Speaking,
Portable Edition
by Steven A. Beebe, Susan J. Beebe, and Diana K. Ivy

Communication Counts: In College, Career, and Life, Second Edition
by David Worley, Debra Worley, and Laura Soldner

Cover Art: Courtesy of PhotoDisc/Getty Images

Human Communication in Society, Third Edition
by Jess K. Alberts, Thomas K. Nakayama, Judith N. Martin
Copyright © 2012, 2010, 2007 by Pearson Education, Inc.
Published by Allyn and Bacon
Boston, Massachusetts 02116

Communication Principles for a Lifetime: Volume 4 Presentation Speaking, Portable Edition
by Steven A. Beebe, Susan J. Beebe, and Diana K. Ivy
Copyright © 2009 by Pearson Education, Inc.
Published by Allyn and Bacon

Communication Counts: In College, Career, and Life, Second Edition
by David Worley, Debra Worley, and Laura Soldner
Copyright © 2012, 2008 by Pearson Education, Inc.

Pearson Learning Solutions, 501 Boylston Street, Suite 900, Boston, MA 02116
A Pearson Education Company
www.pearsoned.com

Printed in the United States of America

3 4 5 6 7 8 9 10 V011 17 16 15 14 13 12

000200010271303149

CB

ISBN 10: 1-256-74310-0
ISBN 13: 978-1-256-74310-1

Contents

7

Communication Across Cultures   150

8

Practicing Effective Interpersonal Communication   174

13

Organizing and Outlining Your Presentation   320

14
Delivering Your Presentation   340

15
Speaking to Inform   366

16
Speaking to Persuade   384

17
Presenting with Technology   412

Chapters 1–7, 9–11, Glossary, References, Credits, and Index were taken from *Human Communication in Society*, Second Edition by Jess K. Alberts, Thomas K. Nakayama, and Judith N. Martin.

Chapter 8 was taken from *Communication Counts: In College, Career, and Life*, Second Edition by David Worley, Debra Worley, and Laura Soldner.

Chapters 12–16 and the Appendix were taken from *Communication Principles for a Lifetime, Volume 4 - Presentation Speaking*, Portable Edition by Steven A. Beebe, Susan J. Beebe, and Diana K. Ivy.

Introduction to Human Communication

On her way to class, Adela called her father to let him know what time she would meet him that afternoon; she then texted a friend to arrange to meet at the cafeteria for lunch. Taking her seat in class, she checked her email and chatted with classmates. When the class began, she turned off her phone and listened attentively.

Most people, like Adela, exist in a sea of communication. They watch television; spend time (perhaps too much time) on Facebook; attend class lectures; phone, email, and text message their friends and family; and are inundated by messages over loudspeakers as they shop for groceries or use public transportation. Given all of this, it is hard to imagine that only seventy-five years ago most communication occurred either face to face or via "snail" mail. But in fact, throughout much of human history, individuals lived very close to the people they knew. They conducted commerce and maintained relationships primarily with the same small group of people throughout their lives. Today, people maintain relationships with individuals thousands of miles away, and they buy and sell products halfway around the globe on eBay. This instant and widespread access to the world has its benefits, but it also has its costs.

With so many communication options, people need a wider range of communication knowledge and skills than ever before. Successful communicators must converse effectively face to face; correspond clearly via email; learn when it is appropriate to use text messaging; and absorb the norms and etiquette surrounding cell phones, chat rooms, video conferencing, and Facebook posts. Becoming an effective communicator involves both understanding the components and processes of communication and putting them into practice. As you work in this course to improve your communication knowledge and skills, you may see positive changes in your relationships, your career, your engagement in civic life, and even your identity. How many other courses can claim all that?

Once you have read this chapter, you will be able to:

- Discuss the importance of studying human communication.
- Define communication.
- Name and explain the seven primary components of communication.
- Explain the Synergetic Model of Communication.
- Understand the ethical responsibilities of speakers and listeners.
- Formulate your own communication ethic.

THE IMPORTANCE OF STUDYING HUMAN COMMUNICATION

As you begin this book, several questions may arise. First, you may wonder exactly how the study of human communication differs from other studies of humans, such as psychology. Communication differs from other social science disciplines because it focuses exclusively on the exchange of messages to create meaning. Scholars in communication explore what, when, where, and why humans interact (Emanuel, 2007). They do so to increase our understanding of how people communicate and to help individuals improve their abilities to communicate in a wide variety of contexts. In addition, unlike most social sciences, the study of communication has a long history—reaching back to the classical era of Western civilization when Isocrates, Plato, and Aristotle wrote about the important role of communication in politics, the courts, and learning (National Communication Association, 2003; Rogers & Chafee, 1983). However, the ability to speak effectively and persuasively has been valued since the beginning of recorded history. As early as 3200–2800 BCE, the Precepts of Kagemni and Ptah-Hopte commented on communication (NCA, 2003).

Second, you may question why anyone needs to study communication; after all, most people have probably been doing a reasonably good job of it thus far. And isn't most communication knowledge just common sense? Unfortunately, it is not. If good communication skills were just common sense, then communication would not so often go awry. We would live in a world where misunderstandings rarely occurred; conflicts were easily resolved; and public speakers were organized, clear, and engaging. Instead, communication is a complex activity influenced by a variety of factors, including cultural differences, cognitive abilities, and social norms. (If you would like to discover how much you already know about communication, go to **http://www.mindtools.com/pages/article/newCS_99.htm** and take the fifteen-item Communication Quiz located on that page.) Good communication is not a cure-all for every relationship and career ill, but it can help attain goals, establish relationships, and develop one's identity.

Finally, you may think of communication as a set of skills that are easily learned and wonder why there is an entire course (even a major!) that focuses on communication. Although it is true that every day people use communication to accomplish practical goals such as inviting a friend to see a movie, resolving a conflict with a colleague, or persuading the city council to install speed bumps in their neighborhood, communication is more than just a set of skills, like baking, that one can use in a variety of contexts and settings with little alteration. Rather, communication is a complex process whose effective performance requires an in-depth understanding of how it works and the ability to apply one's critical thinking skills to communication experiences to learn from and improve them.

Critical Thinking: A Key to Successful Communication

Critical thinking requires that one become a critic of one's own thoughts and behavior. That is, rather than responding automatically or superficially, critical thinkers reflect upon their own and others' communication, behavior, and ideas before responding (Paul & Elder, 2008). Scholars have proposed various definitions of critical thinking; the one we advocate describes it as a process that involves the following steps (Passer & Smith, 2004):

1. Identify the assertion or action.
2. Ask, "what is the evidence for and against the assertion or action?"
3. Ask, "what does the bulk of evidence point to?"

4. Ask, "what other explanations or conclusions are possible?"

5. Continue to keep an open mind for new evidence and new ways of evaluating the assertion.

How might one apply this process to communication interactions? Let's explore this with a simple and common example. Imagine that you send a text message to your romantic partner on a Friday evening, but hours later have not heard back (Step 1: identify the action). How should you interpret the lack of reply and, consequently, how should you respond? If you were thinking non-critically, you might interpret the behavior negatively (my partner is cheating on me!) even though you have little or no evidence to support this interpretation. You then might respond by dashing off an accusatory text.

However, more critical thinkers evaluate their interpretations and beliefs before responding by asking themselves, "what evidence do I have for this belief or interpretation?" (Step 2). Thus, if their first impulse was to doubt their partner, they would ask themselves, "what evidence exists that my partner is cheating?" (Does failing to return a text necessarily mean the partner is intentionally refusing to respond? Even if the partner is purposely refusing to respond to a text, does that mean the reason for refusing is unfaithfulness?)

The critical thinker would then question whether this interpretation is supported by sufficient evidence and experience (Step 3: What does the bulk of the evidence point to—for example, has my partner cheated before? Does my partner usually respond quickly to texts? Is my partner normally trustworthy?). Next he or she would consider what other explanations are possible. (Step 4: What other conclusions are possible—for example, my partner's phone battery ran down; my partner fell asleep early and didn't receive my texts; my partner is studying and turned off his or her phone.)

If your romantic partner doesn't answer a text message, it could be because she is studying and has turned off her phone.

Only after following this process would a critical thinker settle on a likely interpretation and response. Even then, the critical thinker would continue to keep an open mind and evaluate new information as it was presented (Step 5). Thus, even if you decided there was no evidence that your partner was cheating, you might reevaluate your conclusion if your partner repeatedly failed to reply to texts on Friday nights.

Advantages of Studying Human Communication

Studying human communication conveys a number of advantages. Individuals use communication to meet people, to develop professional and personal relationships, and to terminate dissatisfying ones. Communication scholar Steve Duck argues that relationships are primarily communicative (1994). Moreover, the relationships we have with others—including how we think and feel about one another—develop as we communicate. Through communication interactions, relationship partners develop shared meanings for events, explanations for their shared past, and a vision of their future together (Alberts, Yoshimura, Rabby, & Loschiavo, 2005; Dixon & Duck, 1993). So, if you tell your romantic partner, "I have never loved anyone as much as I love you, and I never will," you are simultaneously redefining your past romantic relationships, creating shared meaning for the present relationship, and projecting a vision of your romantic future together. Similarly, through communication with friends, coworkers, and acquaintances, we all define and redefine our relationships.

Perhaps most fundamentally, your communication interactions with others allow you to establish who you are to them (Gergen, 1982; Mead, 1934). As you communicate, you attempt to reveal yourself in a particular light. For example, when you are at work, you may try to establish yourself as someone who is pleasant, hardworking, honest, and competent. With a new roommate, you may want your communication behavior to suggest you are responsible, fun, and easygoing. However, at the same time that your communication creates an image of who you are for others, *their* communication shapes your vision of yourself. For example, if your friends laugh at your jokes, compliment you on your sense of humor, and introduce you to others as a funny person, you probably will see yourself as amusing. In these ways, communication helps create both our self-identities and our identities as others perceive them.

Communication has the potential to transform your life—both for the better and for the worse. (To read how one student's communication created a transformation, see *It Happened to Me: Chelsea*). As many people have discovered, poor or unethical communication can negatively affect lives. How? Communicating poorly during conflict can end relationships, inadequate interviewing skills can result in unemployment, and negative feedback from conversational partners can lessen one's self-esteem. Sometimes communication can have even more significant effects. In 2004, author and television hostess Martha Stewart was sent to jail not for insider trading but for lying (and thereby obstructing justice) when her case was being investigated. Thus she was imprisoned for a specific unethical (and illegal) communication act (McCord, Greenhalgh, and Magasin, 2004).

It Happened to Me: *Chelsea*

When the professor asked us to identify a time when communication was transformative, many examples came to mind. Finally, I settled on one involving a negative relationship. In high school there's usually one person you just don't get along with. Boyfriend drama, bad-mouthing, you name it. I remember dreading seeing this one girl, and I'm sure she felt the same about me. Graduation came and went, and I completely forgot about her. A year later, I came across her Web page as I was searching for old classmates online. As I thought about how petty our arguments were and how cruel we were to each other, I felt smaller and smaller. So I decided to end it. I used email to apologize for my bad behavior because with email I felt safer. I could compose my thoughts, avoid a direct confrontation, and give her time to respond. A couple days later I received an email from her saying she felt the same way and was also sorry for the way she acted. Next week we're going to have a cup of coffee together to really put the past behind us. Maybe to some people that doesn't seem all that life changing, but after hating this girl for two years, it's an amazing transformation for me.

As you can see from Chelsea's story, developing excellent communication skills also can transform your life for the better. The three authors of this book have all had students visit months or years after taking our communication classes to tell us what a difference the classes have made in their lives. A student in a public-speaking class reported that, because of her improved presentation skills, she received the raise and promotion she had been pursuing for years; another student in a conflict and negotiation class revealed that her once-troubled marriage became more stable once she learned to express disagreements better. A third student felt more confident after he took a persuasion class that taught him how to influence people.

TEST YOUR KNOWLEDGE

- How does the study of communication differ from other social science disciplines?
- Why is communicating a complex activity?
- The process of critical thinking involves what five steps?

WHAT IS HUMAN COMMUNICATION?

Even though you have been communicating for your entire life, you probably have not given much thought to the process. You may question why we even need to provide a definition for something so commonplace. Although communication is an everyday occurrence, the term covers a wide variety of behaviors that include talking to friends, broadcasting media messages, and emailing coworkers. Because the term *communication* is complex and can have a variety of definitions, we need to acquaint you with the definition we will use throughout this text.

Broadly speaking, human communication can be defined as a process in which people generate meaning through the exchange of verbal and nonverbal messages. In this book, however, we emphasize the influence of individual and societal forces and the roles of culture and context more than other definitions do. Because we believe these concepts are essential to understanding the communication process completely, we developed a definition of human communication that included them. Accordingly, we define **human communication** as a *transactional process in which people generate meaning through the exchange of verbal and nonverbal messages in specific contexts, influenced by individual and societal forces and embedded in culture.* In the following sections, we will illustrate our definition of human communication and explore the meaning of each these concepts and their relationships to one another. To do so, we first look at the basic components of communication as highlighted in current definitions. Then, we examine the way these components serve as the building blocks of our own model of human communication in society, the Synergetic Model. Finally, we explain how individual and societal influences as well as culture and context contribute to an understanding of the communication process.

Components of Human Communication

Consider the following scenario:

Adela grew up in the United States; her parents are from Mexico, where her grandparents and many other relatives still live. Adela needed to talk to her father about her desire to live in the dorms at college rather than commuting from home. She was worried; she was the first member of her family to attend college and would be the first single family member to live away from home before marriage. She hoped to convince her father that it was a good idea for her to live in the dorms while also displaying respect for him as her father as well as her commitment to her family. To ensure that the conversation would go well, she decided they should meet at his favorite neighborhood café in the early afternoon so they could talk privately. She rehearsed how she would convey information that he might not be happy to hear and practiced responses to the objections she expected him to raise.

As this example reveals, communication is a complex process that can require considerable thought and planning. The complexity inherent in communication is due in part to the variety of factors that compose and influence it. The seven basic components of communication to consider in planning an interaction are *message creation, meaning creation, setting, participants, channels, noise,* and *feedback.* Each of these features is central to how a communication interaction unfolds. To help you understand this process, we analyze Adela's experiences with her father.

Message Creation

Messages are the building blocks of communication, and the process of taking ideas and converting them into messages is called **encoding** (receiving a message and interpreting its meaning is referred to as **decoding**). Depending on the importance of a message, people are more or less careful in encoding their messages. In our example above, Adela was very concerned with how she encoded messages to her father (and that is why she rehearsed what she would say). She particularly wanted to communicate to her father that they would remain close, both to persuade him that she should live on campus and to assure him that her leaving would not change her relationship with their family. To accomplish this, she decided to encode this idea into

human communication
a process in which people generate meaning through the exchange of verbal and nonverbal messages in specific contexts, influenced by individual and social forces, and embedded in culture

messages
the building blocks of communication events

encoding
taking ideas and converting them into messages

decoding
receiving a message and interpreting its meaning

symbol
something that represents something
else and conveys meaning

her message: "I'll still be able to come over to the bakery whenever you need me; you'll see me all the time!"

When we communicate, we encode and exchange two types of messages—verbal and nonverbal—and most of these messages are symbolic. A **symbol** is something that represents something else and conveys meaning (Buck & VanLear, 2002). For example, a Valentine's Day heart symbolizes the physical heart, it represents romantic love, and it conveys feelings of love and romance when given to a relational partner. The verbal system is composed of linguistic symbols (that is, words) while the nonverbal message system is composed of nonlinguistic symbols such as smiles, laughter, winks, vocal tones, and hand gestures.

When we say *communication is symbolic,* we are describing the fact that the symbols we use—the words we speak and the gestures we use—are arbitrary, or without any inherent meaning (Dickens, 2003). Rather, their meaning is derived as communicators employ agreed-upon definitions. For instance, putting up one's hand palm forward would not mean "stop" unless people in the United States agreed to this meaning, and the word *mother* would not mean a female parent unless speakers of English agreed that it would. Because communicators use symbols to create meaning, different groups often develop distinct words for the same concept. For instance, the common word for a feline house pet is *cat* in English, but *neko* in Japanese. Thus, there is no intrinsic connection between most words and their meanings—or many gestures and their meanings.

Because human communication is predominantly symbolic, humans must agree on the meanings of words. Consequently, words can, and do, change over time. For example, the term *gay* typically meant happy or carefree from the seventeenth century through much of the twentieth century. Although the term was occasionally used to refer to same-sex relationships as early as the 1800s, it has come to be used widely only since the late 1990s, when users agreed to this meaning and usuage. Nonetheless, people may have different meanings for specific symbols or words, especially if they come from different ethnic or national cultures. Read about one student's difficulties communicating while on a trip to Europe in *It Happened to Me: Alyssa.*

It Happened to Me: Alyssa

Recently I traveled in Europe; I had no idea how difficult it would be to communicate, even in England. I spent the first few days navigating London on my own. It was so hard! People tried to help, but because of the differences in word choice and accents I couldn't fully understand their directions. After London I went to Italy, where I had an even harder time communicating due to the language barrier. So I resorted to using nonverbal gestures such as pointing, smiling, and thumbs up and down. However, I ran into problems doing this. One night I ordered wine for a friend and myself. The bartender looked uncertain when he brought the two glasses of wine I'd ordered, so I gave him a "thumbs up" to mean okay, that he had it right. However, to him the gesture meant "one," so he thought I only wanted one glass, and he took the other away. It took us a while to get the order straight.

As Alyssa's experience reveals, though most people recognize that cultures vary in the words they use for specific ideas and items, they don't always realize that nonverbal gestures can have varied meanings across cultures as well. Creating messages is the most fundamental requirement for communication to occur, but it certainly is not enough. Messages also create shared meanings for everyone involved in the interaction.

Meaning Creation

The goal of exchanging symbols—that is, of communicating—is to create meaning. The messages we send and receive shape meaning beyond the symbols themselves. We also bring to each message a set of experiences, beliefs, and values that help shape specific meanings. This is why people can hear the same message but understand it differently. Adela was aware of this as she planned the conversation with her father. She knew they didn't always have precisely the same meanings for every word.

For example, the word "independent" carried positive meanings for her, but she knew it carried more negative and potentially upsetting meanings for her father. Therefore, when talking to her father, she would never argue that living in the dorm was a good idea because it would make her more independent.

Meaning is made even more complex because, as the example above suggests, each message carries with it two types of meaning—content meaning and relationship meaning. **Content meaning** includes denotative and connotative meaning. Denotative meaning is the concrete meaning of the message, such as the definition you would find in a dictionary. Connotative meaning describes the meanings suggested by or associated with the message and the emotions triggered by it. For example, denotatively the word *mother* refers to one's female parent, while connotatively it may include meanings such as warmth, nurturance, and intimacy. **Relationship meaning** describes what the message conveys about the relationship between the parties (Robinson-Smith, 2004; Watzlawick, Beavin, & Jackson, 1967). For example, if a colleague at works told you to "run some copies of this report," you might become irritated, but you probably wouldn't mind if your boss told you to do the same thing. In both cases the relationship message may be understood as "I have the right to tell you what to do," which is appropriate if it comes from your supervisor—but not if it comes from a peer.

Finally, communication helps create the shared meanings that shape families, communities, and societies. Specifically, the meanings we have for important issues including politics, civil behavior, family, and spirituality—as well as for less important concerns such as what food is tasty or what type of home is desirable—are created through people's interactions with one another. For example, if you were asked what your family "motto" is (that is, what is important in your family) what would you say? Some people might say it is "family first" while others declare it is "do the right thing." How do families come to have these shared beliefs and meanings? They do so through the countless interactions they have with one another; through these conversations and everyday experiences they create a meaning for what is important to their family. What do you think happens when two people marry, one of whom believes "family first" and another who thinks "do the right thing" is more important than even family? Like the families they grew up within, they will interact, live together, and jointly develop shared meanings for their family beliefs. A similar process occurs when people come together to form groups, organizations, communities, and societies. In sum, our relationships, our understanding of the world, and our beliefs about life and death are created through the interactions we have with others.

Setting

The physical surroundings of a communication event make up its setting. **Setting** includes the location where the communication occurs (in a library versus a bar), environmental conditions (including the temperature, noise, and lighting), time of day or day of the week, and the proximity of the communicators. Together these factors create the physical setting, which affects communication interaction.

Why do you think Adela chose to meet in midafternoon at her father's favorite café as the setting for their conversation? She did so for several reasons. First, her father would be more likely to feel relaxed and in a good mood in a familiar location that he liked. Second, she selected the middle of the afternoon because it was the most relaxed time of day for him; she knew that the family bakery business involved strenuous morning preparation and evening cleanup. Finally, she chose a public setting because she believed her father would remain calmer in public than in a private setting, such as at home; it would also give them more privacy and fewer interruptions. As you can see, Adela carefully selected a comfortable setting that she believed would enhance her chances of being successful.

content meaning the concrete meaning of the message, and the meanings suggested by or associated with the message and the emotions triggered by it

relationship meaning what a message conveys about the relationship between the parties

setting the physical surroundings of a communication event

participants
the people interacting during communication

channel
the means through which a message is transmitted

noise
any stimulus that can interfere with, or degrade, the quality of a message

Participants

During communication, **participants**—two or more people—interact. The number of participants, as well as their characteristics, will influence how the interaction unfolds. Typically, the more characteristics participants share (cultural, values, history), the easier they will find it to communicate, because they can rely on their common assumptions about the world.

As Adela planned her conversation, she recognized that she and her father shared a number of important characteristics—commitment to family, concern with finances, and a desire for harmony. However, she also realized that they differed in important ways. Although she was close to her family, she desired more independence than her father would want for himself or for her. In addition, she believed it was acceptable for young, single women to live away from their families, a belief she was sure her father didn't share.

The type of relationship communicators have and the history they share also affect their communication. Whether communicators are family members, romantic partners, colleagues, friends, or acquaintances affects how they frame, deliver, and interpret a message. Since Adela was talking with her father rather than her boyfriend, she focused on displaying respect for his position as her father and asking (rather than telling) him about wanting to live on campus.

As we have suggested already, the moods and emotions that communicators bring to and experience during their interaction influence it as well. Since Adela wanted to increase the likelihood that the conversation with her father would go well, she tried to create a situation in which he would be in a calmer and happier frame of mind.

Text messaging is one channel of communication. What other channels do you often use?

Channels

For a message to be transmitted from one participant to another, it must travel through a channel. A **channel** is the means through which a message is conveyed. Historically, the channels people used to communicate with one another were first face to face, then written (for example, letters and newsprint), and yet later electronic (for example, telephone calls, radio, and television). Today, thanks to technology, we have many more communication channels—email, instant messaging, mobile instant messaging, social networks such as Facebook and MySpace, and videophones, to name just a few.

The channel a person selects to communicate a message can affect how the message is perceived and its impact on the relationship. For example, if your romantic partner broke up with you by changing his or her Facebook relationship status instead of by talking to you face to face, how would you respond? Because Adela was sensitive to the importance of the communication channel she used with her father, she elected to communicate with him face to face because it was a channel her father was familiar with and would find appealing.

Noise

Noise refers to any stimulus that can interfere with, or degrade, the quality of a message. Noise includes external signals of all kinds: not only loud music and voices, but also distracting clothing or hairstyles, uncomfortably warm or chilly temperatures, and so on. Noise can also come from internal stimuli, such as hunger or sleepiness. Semantic interference, which occurs when speakers use words you do not know or use a familiar word in an unfamiliar way, is another form of noise. If you have ever tried to have a conversation with someone who used highly technical language in a noisy room while you were sleepy, you have experienced a "perfect storm" of noise.

How did the noise factor affect Adela's choices? She chose to meet at a café in the middle of the afternoon, avoiding the crowded lunch and dinner hours. There would be fewer competing voices and sounds, and the wait staff would be less likely to interrupt with meal service, so there would be fewer distractions. By choosing a setting that minimized interference, she improved the chances that her message would be clear.

Feedback

Finally, the response to a message is called **feedback**. Feedback lets a sender know if the message was received and how the message was interpreted. For example, if a friend tells you a joke and you laugh heartily, your laughter serves as feedback, indicating that you heard the joke and found it amusing. Similarly, if you fall asleep during a lecture, you provide feedback to your professor that either you are very tired or you find the lecture boring. Thus your feedback serves as a message to the sender, who then uses the information conveyed to help shape his or her next message.

Although Adela wasn't sure what type of feedback her father would provide or what type she would need to give him, she did spend time anticipating what they each would say. She also knew that she would need to be sensitive to his messages and be prepared to offer feedback that was both supportive and persuasive.

TEST YOUR KNOWLEDGE

- How do the authors define human communication?
- What are the seven basic components of the communication process?
- In what ways does communication create meaning?

A MODEL OF HUMAN COMMUNICATION: THE SYNERGETIC MODEL

To help people understand complex processes, scientists and engineers, among others, create visual models to show how how all components of a process work together. Scholars of human communication have done the same. They have developed models to reveal how the seven components described above work together to create a communication interaction.

The first such model of human communication depicted communication as a linear process that primarily involved the transfer of information from one person to another (Eisenberg, Goodall, & Trethewey, 2010; Laswell, 1948; Shannon & Weaver, 1949). In this model, communication occurred when a sender encoded a message (put ideas into words and symbols) that was sent to a receiver who decoded (interpreted) it. Then, the process was believed to reverse: The receiver became the sender, and the sender became the receiver (Laswell, 1948). This model (see Figure 1.1) also included the components of "noise" and "channel." Since that time other, more complex models, such as our Synergetic Model, have been created to show a greater variety of factors that interact with one another to influence the communication process.

The **Synergetic Model** is a transactional model that, like most previous models, depicts communication as occurring when two or more people create meaning as they respond to each other and their environment. In addition, it is based on a belief in the important roles of individual and societal forces, contexts, and culture in the communication process. We discuss each of these topics in detail below, and to help clarify the the concepts, we revisit Adela's interaction with her father once again to illustrate how they function during the communication process.

After carefully planning for the interaction with her father about her desire to leave home to go to graduate school, Adela engaged in the following conversation with him:

feedback
the response to a message

Synergetic Model of Communication
a transactional model based on the roles individual and societal forces, contexts, and culture play in the communication process

FIGURE 1.1: A Linear Model of Communication

Early models depicted communication as a linear process that primarily involved the transfer of information from one person to another.

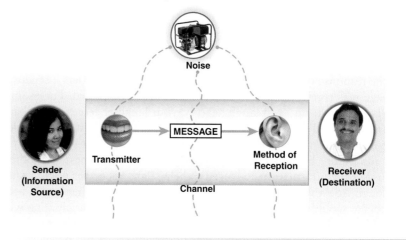

Adela: Dad, guess what! Purdue, Illinois, ASU, and Texas all let me in. (Then, noticing a quizzical look on her father's face, she continues) *I mean, they all admitted me to their undergraduate programs.*

Father: Oh. How many did you apply to?

Adela: Just four. They all accepted me.

Father: I always knew I had a smart daughter! But (frowning, speaking uncertainly), *what does that mean for next year?*

Adela (cautiously): *Well, I was thinking of staying here and attending ASU.*

Father (smiling): *Good! So it won't be any different from having you in high school—you'll still be at home when you're not in class.*

Adela (hesitantly): *Well, that is something I wanted to talk to you about. I would like to live in one of the dorms on campus instead of living at home.*

Father (firmly, shaking his head): *Oh. No, I don't think that is a good idea. We can't afford to pay for room and board, and we need you to help out with the accounts for our bakery.*

Adela: Well, what I didn't mention before is that I've been offered a scholarship to cover my room and board, so we'll actually save money if I live on campus—plus I won't have to have a car to commute to school.

Father (looking doubtful): *Well, this is something to think about. But what about your responsibility to do the accounts for the bakery?*

Adela: I'll still be able to come over to the bakery whenever you need me; you'll see me all the time! I can take the light rail near campus. If I live on campus I can still be here when you need me, plus I'll save money and will have more time to study since I won't be stuck in traffic during my commute.

Father: I guess you make some good points. But I don't know if I am ready to see you move out of the house.

Communication Is Transactional

To say that *communication is a transaction* (see Figure 1.2) captures the fact that (1) each communicator is a sender and receiver *at the same time*, (2) meaning is created as people communicate together, (3) communication is an ongoing process, and

FIGURE 1.2: Communication Is Transactional
Transactional models express the idea that meaning is created as people communicate.

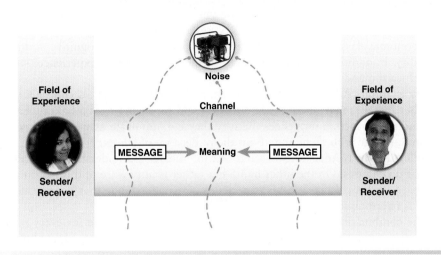

(4) previous communication events and relationships influence its meaning (Warren & Yoder, 1998; Watzlawick, Beavin, & Jackson, 1967). What does this mean?

First, all participants in a communication event both receive and send messages simultaneously, even if those messages are sent only nonverbally. As you may have noted, as Adela explained that she was "let in" to four universities, she realized from her father's nonverbal behavior that he was confused. That is, she received his message even as she talked, and he sent a message even as he listened.

Second, as the example above suggests, meaning is not something one person creates and then sends to another person via a message. If that were true, Adela's father would not have been confused by the expression "let in"; Adela's initial message would have been sufficient. Rather, meaning was created as Adela and her dad communicated together; she made a statement, he showed his lack of understanding, and Adela offered more information until they shared similar understandings or meaning.

Third, describing communication as ongoing highlights the fact that it is a process whose specific beginnings and endings can be difficult to discern. All the interactions one has had with individuals in the past influence one's communication in the present, just as a person's current communication affects his or her expectations for and experiences of future interactions. For instance, Adela planned her interaction and communicated with her father based on her previous experiences with him. Specifically, she knew he would disapprove of her living on campus, so she was prepared to offer arguments for why living in the dorms was a better choice. Her experiences with her father, then, affected the messages she crafted for their conversation. In addition, she recognized that their conversation would influence how they communicated with each other in the future. If he became angry, he likely would communicate with her less or more negatively. This, in turn, would influence her future messages to him, and so on.

Finally, because communication is ongoing and interactive, when people communicate, they and their conversational partner(s) reaffirm or alter their identities and relationships. Thus, Adela's conversation with her father is likely to change how they see each other. He might see her as more adult and independent because of her desire to leave home, or he may now perceive her as a less loving child. Similarly, she may view him as less of an authority figure and more of a peer, or she might believe he is even more authoritarian and rigid than she previously thought.

field of experience
the education, life events, and cultural background that a communicator possesses

Communication Is Influenced by Individual Forces

The individual is a primary focus in communication. Many separate individual forces or characteristics contribute to your identity, and these in turn affect your communication. Individual forces include your demographic characteristics such as age, race, ethnicity, nationality, gender/sex, sexual orientation, regional identity, and socioeconomic class, as well as such factors as personality and cognitive and physical ability. In addition, individual forces include your **field of experience**, such as your education and experiences.

For example, Adela is female, eighteen, and about to become a college student, while her father is male, is in his late forties, and owns and runs a bakery. Each of these individual factors influences the way they communicate as well the ways others communicate with them and about them. Because of her experiences as a potential college student, Adela knows what "let in" means and understands the benefits of living on campus. On the other hand, her father is not aware of this information, and based on his culture and his experiences, he understands that commitment to family is paramount.

The combination of these individual characteristics is unique for every person, so people communicate in distinctive ways. However, every society places limits on the variations that are deemed acceptable. For example, not all men speak assertively, enjoy talking about sports, or "high five" one another. In mainstream U.S. culture, though, many people consider these behaviors as normal for males. Speaking in a more "female" style, such as speaking very quietly or politely, talking about fashion, or using "effeminate" nonverbal gestures, is typically considered inappropriate for men and boys. Those who veer somewhat from the norm may be seen as odd, or they might be shunned; those who veer too far from the norm may be labeled as mentally ill. So while we are each individuals, society places constraints on the range of our individualism, a topic we will explore later.

Communication Is Influenced by Societal Forces

As we suggested just above, individual differences are not value free. They are arranged in a hierarchy in which some individual characteristics are more highly valued than others. For example, being white is often advantageous in U.S. society, being young has advantages over being old, and being physically able is more advantageous than having a disability. How society evaluates these characteristics affects how we talk to—and about—people who display them.

The political, historical, economic, and social structures of a society influence this value hierarchy and affect how we view specific individual characteristics. The historical conditions under which many U.S. racial and ethnic groups arrived in the United States, for instance, continue to affect their identities. For example, many of the earliest Vietnamese immigrants who moved to the United States during and shortly after the Vietnam War had very strong work ethics but were not fluent in English, so they created businesses of their own—as restaurant owners, nail technicians, and other service professionals. Consequently, many people still fail to realize that Vietnamese Americans also work as lawyers, professors, and physicians. Similarly, even though Barack Obama was elected President of the United States, the fact that many African Americans are descendants of people who came to the United States as slaves continues to influence the ways people think and talk about him.

The values attributed to individual characteristics such as age, sexual orientation, and sex also come from these larger societal forces—whether communicated to us through the media, by our friends and family, or by organizations such as schools, religious institutions, or clubs. For example, the teachings of religious groups shape many people's views on sexual orientation, and because most societies historically have been patriarchal, they continue to value women in the public realm less than they do men.

In Adela's case, two societal forces at work in her interaction with her father are how society views women and parent/child interactions. Her father was raised in a culture where males held considerably more power than females, and parents were assumed to know what was best for their children even when the children were grown. Consequently, he tends to hold the belief that fathers should have considerable decision-making power over their children, especially their unmarried female children. On the other hand, Adela grew up in a culture where men and women are seen as more equal and parents exert less control over their children's lives as the children grow up.

Social hierarchies wherein men are more valued than women, or older people's opinions are considered more worthwhile than younger people's, arise from the meanings that societal structures impose on individual characteristics, and communication maintains these hierarchies. For example, cultures that value maleness over femaleness have many more stereotypes and negative terms for women than they do for men. Moreover, these cultures value certain types of communication over others. Thus men in leadership positions are expected to communicate decisively and avoid appearing "weak" by apologizing or admitting mistakes, while the same is not usually true for women. We will explore social hierarchies in more detail in later chapters.

Communication Is Influenced by Culture

Communication also is embedded in culture. **Culture** refers to the learned patterns of perceptions, values, and behaviors shared by a group of people. Culture is dynamic and heterogeneous (Martin & Nakayama, 2005), meaning that it changes over time and that despite commonalities, members of cultural groups do not all think and behave alike. You probably belong to many cultures, including those of your gender, ethnicity, occupation, and religion, and each of these cultures will have its own communication patterns.

When you identify yourself as a member of a culture defined by age, ethnicity, or gender, this culture-group identity also becomes one of your individual characteristics. For example, as people move from their teen years into young adulthood, middle age, and old age, they generally make a transition from one age-related culture to another. Since each cultural group has a unique set of perceptions, values, and behaviors, each also has its own set of communication principles. As you become an adult, then, you probably stop using language you used as a teenager. And even though changing your language is an individual decision, it is influenced by cultural and societal expectations as well.

Culture affects all or almost all communication interactions (Schirato & Yell, 1996). More specifically, participants bring their beliefs, values, norms, and attitudes to each interaction, and the cultures they belong to shape each of these factors. Cultural beliefs also affect how we expect others to communicate. As we discussed above, because he is Mexican, Adela's father values family closeness, loyalty, and the role of the father as head of the family. Because she is Mexican American, Adela holds many of these same beliefs, but she also values independence and individuality in ways that her father does not.

In addition to participants' cultural backgrounds, the culture in which a communication event takes place influences how participants communicate. In the United States, politicians routinely mention religion in their public addresses and specifically refer to God; however, in France, because of a stricter separation between church and state, politicians typically do not mention religion or deities in their public communication and would be criticized if they did. Regional culture can also affect participants' expectations for appropriate communication behavior. For instance, southerners in the United States tend to be more nonverbally demonstrative and thus might hug others more than do northeasterners (Andersen, Lustig, &

culture
learned patterns of perceptions, values, and behaviors shared by a group of people

Being gay is both an individual and cultural factor.

Andersen, 1990). Of course, other cultural differences (ethnic background, religious background) might influence these nonverbal behaviors as well.

Communication Is Influenced by Context

Each communication interaction occurs in a specific context. Context includes the setting, or aspects of the physical environment, in which an interaction occurs. It also includes which and how many participants are present, as well as the specific occasion during which the interaction unfolds (for example, a Sunday dinner or a birthday party). Context can exert a strong influence on how people communicate with one another. For example, you could argue with your close friend in private when just the two of you are present, during a social event when you are part of a group, during a staff meeting at work, on a television talk show about feuding friends, or in the mall. Can you imagine how each of these contexts would influence your communication? You might be more open if the two of you are alone and in private; you may try to get others involved if you are with friends; you could be more subdued at the mall; you might refrain from mentioning anything too negative on television; or you might be more hostile in an email. It is because context strongly affects individuals' interactions that Adela arranged to talk with her father at his favorite café in the afternoon.

The tensions that exist among individual forces, societal forces, cultures, and contexts shape communication and meaning. To help clarify this tension, let's return yet again to Adela's conversation with her father. Their conversation was influenced by the context (a restaurant), multiple individual forces (each person's age, sex, cultural background, and education), multiple societal forces (the value placed on education, family, sex, and age) as well as their cultures (the meanings of independence, loyalty, and family). Thus, in the conversation between Adela and her father, the context in which the conversation occurred, their individual experiences with higher education, and the cultural meaning of the parent-child relationship all came together to influence the communication interaction. These components and their relationships to one another are depicted in Figure 1.3, the Synergetic Model.

FIGURE 1.3: The Synergetic Model

The Synergetic Model presents communication as a transactional process in which meaning is influenced by cultural, societal, and individual forces.

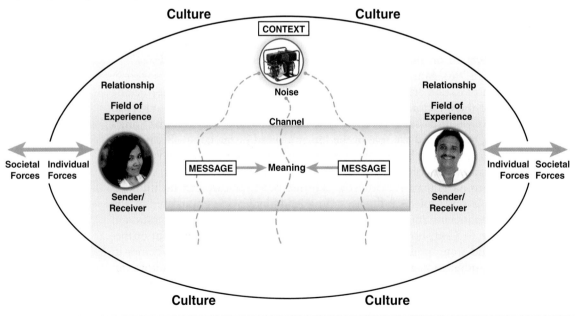

As we stated at the beginning of the chapter, and as is revealed in our model, for us, communication is a transactional process in which people generate meaning through the exchange of verbal and nonverbal messages in specific contexts, influenced by individual and societal forces and embedded in culture. This is the definition and model of communication that will guide you as you explore the remainder of this book. After you complete this course, we recommend that you return to this section to assess how your own understanding of the communication process has changed and deepened.

Our goal in developing this model is to provide a framework for students to organize, read, and understand this complex process we call communication. However, before moving on, we need to discuss one more essential concept that frames and guides all of your communication efforts—ethics.

TEST YOUR KNOWLEDGE

- How does the linear model of communication depict the communication process?
- What does it mean that communication is a transactional process?
- According to the Synergetic Model, what are the individual factors that influence the communication process?
- According to the Synergetic Model, what are the social factors that influence the communication process?

COMMUNICATION ETHICS

In the United States, we appear to be in the midst of a crisis with regard to ethical communication. In the business world, investment executive Bernard Madoff was found guilty of running a Ponzi scheme in 2008 (Leventhal, 2011), and Red Cross CEO Mark Everson was dismissed from his job in 2009 when he was accused of having a personal relationship with a subordinate (Jones & Koppel, 2010). The world of politics does not seem to be faring much better: In 2010 former presidential candidate John Edwards admitted to fathering a child with a campaign worker while still married to his ill (now deceased) wife; and former U.S. House Majority Leader Tom DeLay was convicted of money laundering (FoxNews.com, 2010).

Individuals' personal lives are apparently in a state of ethical disarray as well: Approximately 85 percent of surveyed daters admitted having lied to their partners in the previous two weeks (Tolhuizen, 1990), while 74 percent of students admitted to cheating on exams and 84 percent to cheating on written assignments (McCabe & Trevino, 1996). And it isn't only college students who admit to deceiving their partners. In a survey conducted by the National Endowment of Financial Education, 31 percent of respondents confessed to lying to their marital and living partners about money, often with disastrous consequences. To discover the five most common money lies, see *Did You Know? Breakdown of Money Lies*.

Given examples such as these, one may wonder if a communication ethic still exists. We strongly believe that it does. Even if unethical communication is widespread, and some people get away with their misbehavior, most people are still held responsible for the messages they create (Barnlund, 1962; Christians & Traber, 1997; Johannesen, 1990). If you spread gossip about your friends, lie to your employer, or withhold information from your family, justifying your behavior by pointing to the ethical failures of others will not excuse you. Those who know you and are close to you still expect you to meet basic standards for ethical communication.

Why are communication ethics so important? First, they sustain professional success. Yes, unethical people may prosper in the short run, but over time unethical practices catch up with the people who engage in them. To a great extent, your reputation as a person of integrity determines whether others want to hire you, work

Did You Know?

Breakdown of Money Lies

Financial infidelity may be the new normal. In a recent survey, one in three Americans (31%) who have combined their finances admitted lying to their spouses about money, and another one-third of these adults said they'd been deceived.

The online poll, commissioned by ForbesWoman and the National Endowment for Financial Education (NEFE) and conducted by Harris Interactive, surveyed 2,019 U.S. adults. [Among the couples who experienced] financial infidelity, 67% said the deception led to an argument and 42% said it caused less trust in the relationship. Perhaps most alarming, 16% of these respondents said the money lie led to a divorce and 11% said it led to a separation" (Goudreau, 2010).

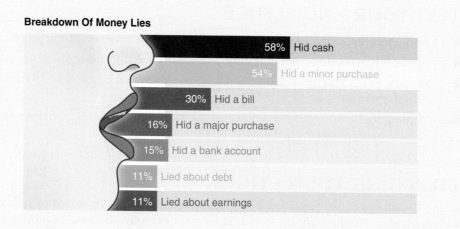

Breakdown Of Money Lies

58%	Hid cash
54%	Hid a minor purchase
30%	Hid a bill
16%	Hid a major purchase
15%	Hid a bank account
11%	Lied about debt
11%	Lied about earnings

Source: Goudreau, J. (2010, January 13). Is your partner cheating on you financially? Financially fit. Retrieved February 17, 2011, from http://shine.yahoo.com/event/financiallyfit/is-your-partner-cheating-on-you-financially-31-admit-money-deception-2439792

What are three specific communication behaviors you believe are unethical? What principles guide your decisions regarding whether a given communication behavior is ethical or unethical?

for you, or conduct business with you. Once that reputation is damaged, it can be difficult if not impossible to regain; consequently, communicating and behaving ethically is just good business.

Communication ethics are vital to personal relationships as well. Maintaining intimate and caring relationships can be difficult, but they become virtually impossible if one communicates unethically by lying, manipulating, or verbally abusing friends and lovers. Intimate relationships are grounded in trust. Without trust, people can't be open and vulnerable with one another, behaviors which are essential to intimacy. When one person abuses that trust by his or her unethical conduct, the other party often is deeply wounded and finds it difficult to ever again be intimate within the relationship. Imagine, for example, how Adela's father would have reacted to her proposal to live in the dorms if in the past she had been caught lying to him about spending the night at a friend's house. Far too many people have learned the hard way that a lack of ethics destroys relationships.

As a communicator, you will face many ambiguous and difficult choices of both a professional and a personal nature. If you develop your own set of communication ethics you will be better prepared to face these difficult choices. Therefore, in this section we provide some basic principles of ethical communication for you to consider as you critically review your own ethical standard.

Fundamentally, individuals, groups, and communities develop ethical codes to reflect their beliefs and values. Clearly the guidelines we offer reflect our own communication ethics. We do not expect you to adopt our beliefs wholesale. Rather, we present this information so that you can analyze it critically to determine to what extent it reflects your own beliefs and behavior, what evidence supports it, and what other guidelines may be as useful or more useful for you. Thus, we want you to use your critical thinking skills specifically to critique our claims here and to use that analysis to form your own ethical code.

Defining Your Communication Ethic

Ethics can be defined in a variety of related ways. Most basically, it refers to a system of moral principles by which actions are judged as good or bad, right or wrong. It also has been defined as the rules of conduct recognized by a group, class, or individual; and as a belief system in which the determination of what is right is based on what promotes the most good or the common good. After reading these definitions, which one do you believe is the best explanation? Which one most closely reflects your current perspective?

Communication ethics describes the standards of right and wrong that one applies to messages that are sent and received. When you hear the term *communication ethics*, you might think we are simply referring to whether messages are truthful. Although truthfulness is one of the most fundamental ethical standards, communicating ethically requires much more than simply being truthful. It also involves deciding what information can and should be disclosed or withheld, and assessing the benefit or harm associated with specific messages. Individuals have a responsibility to evaluate the ethics of their own and others' communication efforts. Similarly, corporations ought to weigh the ethics of sharing or withholding information that might affect the value of their stock shares, and media companies should decide whether it is ethical to report private information about individuals. Let's look at some of the issues you need to reflect on as you develop your code of ethics.

Truthfulness

Truthfulness plays a fundamental role in ethical communication for two reasons: First, others expect messages to be truthful, and second, messages have consequences. Because people inherently expect speakers to be truthful, we actually may make it easier for them to deceive us (Buller & Burgoon, 1996). If an audience is not suspicious, they probably won't look for cues that the speaker is lying (McCornack & Parks, 1986). However, because of the implicit contract to be honest, discovery of deception can severely damage relationships. The more intimate the relationship, the greater the expectation people have that their partners will be truthful, and the more damaging any deception will be.

As we've implied, people rely on messages to be truthful because they have consequences. One's communication can influence the beliefs, attitudes, and behaviors of others. For example, an individual's communication could persuade a customer to purchase an item, a friend to lend money, or an acquaintance to become romantically involved with him or her. The more consequential the outcome of your message, the more likely you will be held accountable to the truth. You might not be criticized too harshly for exaggerating your salary during a flirtation with a stranger, but an employer will most likely consider it unethical if you lie about your salary on a job application.

Sharing or Withholding Information

A related fundamental principle of ethical communication concerns what information should be divulged and what can be withheld. When is withholding information a matter of legitimate privacy, and when is it a matter of inappropriate secrecy? Thus, you have to determine whether to tell your romantic partner how many sexual partners you have had; media organizations have to decide whether to reveal the

ethics
standards of what is right and wrong, good and bad, moral and immoral

communication ethics
the standards of right and wrong that one applies to messages that are sent and received

COMMUNICATION IN SOCIETY
Young Job Seekers Hiding Their Facebook Pages

Justin Gawel says there's nothing too incriminating on his Facebook page.

"There are a lot of pictures of drinking [but] nothing naked or anything—at least I don't think so," he said jokingly.

Even so, the Michigan State University junior recently changed his Facebook display name to "Dustin Jawel" to keep his personal life from potential employers while applying for summer internships.

Although Gawel ditched his rhyming alias after two weeks when he realized Facebook users also can be searched by e-mail address, school and network, he is not alone in his efforts to scrub his online résumé. Many students and recent graduates say they are changing their names on Facebook or tightening privacy settings to hide photos and wall posts from potential employers.

And with good reason.

A recent survey commissioned by Microsoft found that 70 percent of recruiters and hiring managers in the United States have rejected an applicant based on information they found online.

What kind of information? "Inappropriate" comments by the candidate; "unsuitable" photos and videos; criticisms of previous employers, co-workers, or clients; and even inappropriate comments by friends and relatives, according to the survey report, titled "Online Reputation in a Connected World."

Such prying into his online life makes Gawel uncomfortable.

"I understand that when [employers look] at someone's Facebook page, they're just trying to paint a bigger picture of the people they're hiring—so they're not just a name on a résumé," he said. "But that doesn't demonstrate whether they can do the job. It shouldn't matter what someone does when they're not in the office."

Gawel said he's not sure that employers would object to the information on his Facebook page. For him, it's more about personal privacy.

"Too many people take pictures of you. I didn't want to go through and 'untag' all of them," he said. "There's nothing illegal or too ridiculous in the photos…but people don't take pictures of people studying or doing school work. They take pictures of people at parties and doing silly things."

For better or worse, online screenings may be a permanent part of the 21st-century hiring process. The Microsoft survey found that 79 percent of U.S. hiring managers have used the Internet to better assess applicants.

SOURCE: Goldberg, S. (2010, March 29). CNN Tech. Retrieved February 21, 2011, from http://articles.cnn.com/2010-03-29/tech/facebook.job-seekers_1_facebook-hiring-online-reputation?_s=PM:TECH

identity of confidential news sources; and physicians have to choose how much information to tell patients about the possible side effects of a prescribed drug.

In our view, a message can be considered legitimately private when other parties have no right to expect access to it. Inappropriate secrecy, on the other hand, occurs when other parties might legitimately expect access to a message that is withheld. This distinction is important because it is generally ethical to maintain privacy, but it may be unethical to engage in secrecy.

What's the difference between privacy and secrecy? We believe communicators have an ethical responsibility to share information that other people require to make informed decisions. For example, if you have only dated someone once or twice, you may choose to keep private that you have a sexually transmitted disease. However, if the two of you consider becoming sexually intimate, you probably have an ethical obligation to reveal the information. Without this information, your partner cannot make an informed decision about whether to engage in sexual contact. What will happen to your relationship if you withhold the information and your partner contracts your disease—and finds out later that you withheld the information? Similarly, your friends may not need to know why you were fired from your last job, but your new boss may have a legitimate need for access to this information.

On the other hand, revealing information can sometimes be unethical. For example, if you have agreed to maintain confidentiality about a topic, it could be considered unethical to reveal what you know. However, if you violate a confidence because of a higher ethical principle, most people would likely consider your behavior ethical. For example, if you have a duty of confidentiality to your employer, but your company engages in illegal toxic dumping, it likely would be more ethical to break this confidence. Here, the ethic of protecting the public health likely supersedes the ethic of keeping a confidence. These are not easy decisions, but they reflect the type of complex ethical choices that people have to make.

Now that you have read our guideline for differentiating secrecy and privacy, do you find yourself agreeing or disagreeing with it? Can you think of situations in which it would not apply? Can you think of a better principle one could use to make decisions about whether to withhold or reveal information? Again, it is not important that you adopt our guideline but that you think through and develop one that is in line with your own ethical code.

You can begin to think through your position on this issue by exploring an important trend in job searches—the growing use of Internet searches by corporations to gather information on potential or current employees as well as the practice of potential or current employees hiding Facebook information from employers. To *do so, see Communication in Society: Young Job Seekers Hiding Their Facebook Pages.*

When individuals hide information on Facebook, do you believe they are engaging in secrecy or privacy attempts? How would you defend your position to someone who disagrees with you? That is, what evidence and examples would you use to argue for your belief? What arguments might someone make who disagrees with you? To what extent does the context of Facebook communication influence your response?

Benefit and Harm of Messages

To determine the most ethical choice, you also should consider the benefit or harm associated with your messages. A classic example concerns whether it is right to lie to a potential murderer about the whereabouts of the intended victim. A principle of honesty suggests that you should tell the truth. But in this case, once you evaluate the potential harm of sharing versus withholding the information, you might well decide to withhold the information.

More typically, issues of harm and benefit are less clear. For example, if you discover your best friend's romantic partner is being unfaithful, should you share that information? Will it result in more harm or more benefit? If you know that a relative cheated on her taxes, should you report her to the IRS?

Think again about Adela's conversation with her father. If she had told her father that she wasn't accepted at ASU, then he would think she would have to live away from home to go to college. In that scenario, she wouldn't have had to worry as much that he would try to persuade her to live at home. However, because honesty in close relationships is part of her ethical standard and she understands the consequences that unethical behavior can have on relationships, she chose to be open and honest with her father regarding her options.

Because many communication events are complex and the underlying ethical principles are not definitive, you will need to gradually develop your own philosophy of ethical communication and apply it on a case-by-case basis. This is one requirement of being an effective communicator. However, just as you develop your own ethical standards and decisions, others will do so as well, which means you and others in your life may not always agree.

Absolutism versus Relativism

A fundamental decision in communication ethics concerns how **absolute** or **relative** your ethical standards will be. Will you use the same absolute standards for every communication interaction, or will your ethical choices be relative and depend on each situation? The Greek philosopher Plato and the German philosopher Immanuel Kant conceptualized the absolutist perspective (Kant, 1949), and both believed there is a rationally correct, moral standard that holds for everyone, everywhere, every

absolute
pertaining to the belief that there is a single correct moral standard that holds for everyone, everywhere, every time

relative
pertaining to the belief that moral behavior varies among individuals, groups, and cultures and across situations

time. Relativists such as French philosopher Jean-Paul Sartre, on the other hand, hold the view that moral behavior varies among individuals, groups, and cultures. They argue that since there is no universal standard of morality, there is no rational way to decide who is correct (Sartre, 1973).

If you hold to the absolutist perspective that lying is always wrong, then in the earlier example regarding the potential murderer, you would be obligated not to lie about the whereabouts of the intended victim. But if you adhere to a relativistic position regarding truth and deception, you would decide in the moment what the most ethical choice is based on the specific circumstances. You might tell a lie to save a life.

In reality, few people develop an ethical standard that is completely absolute or relative. Instead, absolutism and relativism are the opposite ends of a continuum, and most people's standards lie somewhere along that continuum.

The issue for you is to decide how absolute or relative your ethical standards will be. If you strongly believe that deception is wrong, you may choose the path of deception only when you believe the truth will cause great harm—a standard that falls toward the absolutist end of the continuum. However, if you favor a more relative view, you will consider a variety of factors, in addition to harm, as you make your decisions.

Communication Ethics in Practice

In this discussion of ethics, we have offered guidelines for creating your own communication ethics. However, in practice many situations arise that are ambiguous, complex, and multilayered. At times you may not see how you can be ethical and accomplish important goals at the same time. For example, if you know that a friend and classmate has plagiarized a paper, what should you do? Should you keep quiet and maintain your friendship, or should you maintain your personal ethics and tell the instructor? Similarly, if you are a salesperson, how do you respond if a potential client asks whether a competitor's product is as good as yours, and you believe it is? Do you tell the truth and thus jeopardize a potential sale? People who tend toward an absolutist view say that you must always tell the truth, so you should only sell a product you truly believe is superior. Others may tell you that no one expects salespeople to be completely truthful in this context; therefore, you are not bound to share your opinion (Diener, 2002; Wokutch & Carson, 1981).

We believe that all communicators need to create an ethical stance based on their own beliefs, values, and moral training. Once you've established your ethical stance, you will be prepared to make thoughtful and deliberate communication choices.

Should a salesperson admit that a competitor's product might be as good as the product he or she is selling?

For further guidance in creating your own communication ethic, please see *Communication in Society: Making Ethical Decisions.*

TEST YOUR KNOWLEDGE

- Why is developing one's own code of communication ethics important?
- What are the three definitions offered for ethics?
- What is the difference between privacy and secrecy?
- What is the difference between an absolutist versus a relativistic view of ethics?

COMMUNICATION IN SOCIETY
Making Ethical Decisions

Making good ethical decisions requires a trained sensitivity to ethical issues and a practiced method for exploring the ethical aspects of a decision and weighing the considerations that should impact our choice of a course of action. Having a method for ethical decision making is absolutely essential. When practiced regularly, the method becomes so familiar that we work through it automatically without consulting the specific steps.

The more novel and difficult the ethical choice we face, the more we need to rely on discussion and dialogue with others about the dilemma. Only by careful exploration of the problem, aided by the insights and different perspectives of others, can we make good ethical choices in such situations.

We have found the following framework for ethical decision making a useful method for exploring ethical dilemmas and identifying ethical courses of action.

A Framework for Ethical Decision Making

Recognize an Ethical Issue

1. Could this decision or situation be damaging to someone or to some group? Does this decision involve a choice between a good and bad alternative, or perhaps between two "goods" or between two "bads"?

2. Is this issue about more than what is legal or what is most efficient? If so, how?

Get the Facts

3. What are the relevant facts of the case? What facts are not known? Can I learn more about the situation? Do I know enough to make a decision?

4. What individuals and groups have an important stake in the outcome? Are some concerns more important? Why?

5. What are the options for acting? Have all the relevant persons and groups been consulted? Have I identified creative options?

Evaluate Alternative Actions

6. Evaluate the options by asking the following questions:
   - Which option will produce the most good and do the least harm? (The Utilitarian Approach)
   - Which option best respects the rights of all who have a stake? (The Rights Approach)
   - Which option treats people equally or proportionately? (The Justice Approach)
   - Which option best serves the community as a whole, not just some members? (The Common Good Approach)
   - Which option leads me to act as the sort of person I want to be? (The Virtue Approach)

Make a Decision and Test It

7. Considering all these approaches, which option best addresses the situation?

8. If I told someone I respect—or told a television audience—which option I have chosen, what would they say?

Act and Reflect on the Outcome

9. How can my decision be implemented with the greatest care and attention to the concerns of all participants?

10. How did my decision turn out and what have I learned from this specific situation?

SOURCE: Markkula Center for Applied Ethics (2010). A framework for thinking ethically. Retrieved March 9, 2010, from http://scu.edu/ethics/practicing/decision/framework.html. This framework for thinking ethically is the product of dialogue and debate at the Markkula Center for Applied Ethics at Santa Clara University. Primary contributors include Manuel Velasquez, Dennis Moberg, Michael J. Meyer, Thomas Shanks, Margaret R. McLean, David DeCosse, Claire André, and Kirk O. Hanson.

SUMMARY

Studying human communication can enrich and transform your life professionally and personally. *Critical thinking*, which involves reflection and weighing evidence, is a key to successful communication. Communication skills are crucial in developing relationships, establishing identity, and opening career doors.

The *process of communication* involves seven basic components: message creation, meaning creation, setting, participants, channels, noise, and feedback. Communication has been described in the past as a linear process between sender and receiver; more recently a transactional model was introduced. The *Synergetic Model* views communication as a transactional process; it emphasizes that all communication interactions are influenced by the intersection of individual and societal forces, that they are embedded in culture, and that they occur in specific contexts.

The *ethics* of individual communication choices are another essential feature of communication. This is a topic we will return to throughout the book. Key aspects of communication ethics to consider as you make decisions include truthfulness, decisions regarding sharing or withholding information, and the benefit and harm associated with one's choices. Communicators' ethical choices are affected by their position on the continuum of absolutism versus relativism, which in turn influences their language use and how they receive and how they respond to others' communication efforts.

HUMAN COMMUNICATION IN SOCIETY ONLINE

To review this chapter, use the MyCommunicationLab Web site to test your understanding of the following key terms, record your answers to the chapter review questions, and complete the suggested activities. Expand your learning and understanding of chapter concepts by completing additional activities and exercises online. Access code required. Go to www.mycommunicationlab.com for more information or to purchase standalone access.

KEY TERMS

human communication 6	setting 9	field of experience 14
messages 7	participants 10	culture 15
encoding 7	channel 10	ethics 19
decoding 7	noise 10	communication ethics 19
symbol 8	feedback 11	absolute 21
content meaning 9	Synergetic Model	relative 21
relationship meaning 9	of Communication 11	

APPLY WHAT YOU KNOW

1. **Guidelines for Responding to Electronic Communication**

   Much debate has raged over whether it is appropriate to talk on one's cell phone in restaurants, in front of friends, or in the car. The Federal Aviation Administration is considering whether to allow airline passengers to use their cell phones during flights—and many people are already complaining about the possibility. The widespread use of instant text messaging and the ability to access our email almost anywhere have made the issues surrounding the appropriate use of electronic communication even more complex. To focus the discussion and guide your own decisions regarding your responses to these types of electronic communication, develop a list of rules for how, when, and with whom it is appropriate to use the various types of electronic communication.

2. **Creating a Communication Ethic**

   Interview three people and ask them to describe the underlying ethic(s) that guide their communication choices. Then write a brief statement that describes your own communication ethic.

3. **Communication Ethics in the Media**

   Watch television for one evening and observe the number of ethical dilemmas related to communication that people and characters confront. Note their response to each dilemma. How many people/characters make choices that you consider ethical? How many do not? What justifications or reasons do people/characters give for their choices? What consequences, if any, are portrayed? What conclusions can you draw about the portrayal of communication ethics on television?

EXPLORE

1. Make a list of all of the careers that you believe require good communication skills. Then, locate a list of careers from a university career center, such as North Carolina Wilmington's Career Center or Western Washington University Department of Communication's Career Information page, and examine the site's list of careers for which a communication degree prepares students. What careers did you list that are not listed on a university's career website? Why do you think the differences exist? Finally, create a list of careers you would post if you were responsible for creating such a site for your university.

2. Go to the National Communication Association's "Famous People with Degrees in Communication" site. After reading the page, develop a list of at least 10 different careers that famous people have pursued after obtaining degrees in communication.

   Locate a website that discusses how to develop authentic communication skills, such as the site Authentic Communication or Hodu.com. After reading the suggestions and strategies described on the website, answer the following questions: When are you most likely to lie? What benefits do you think you will accrue if you lie? What can you do to increase how authentic you are when you communicate with others?

2

Perspectives on Human Communication

chapter outline

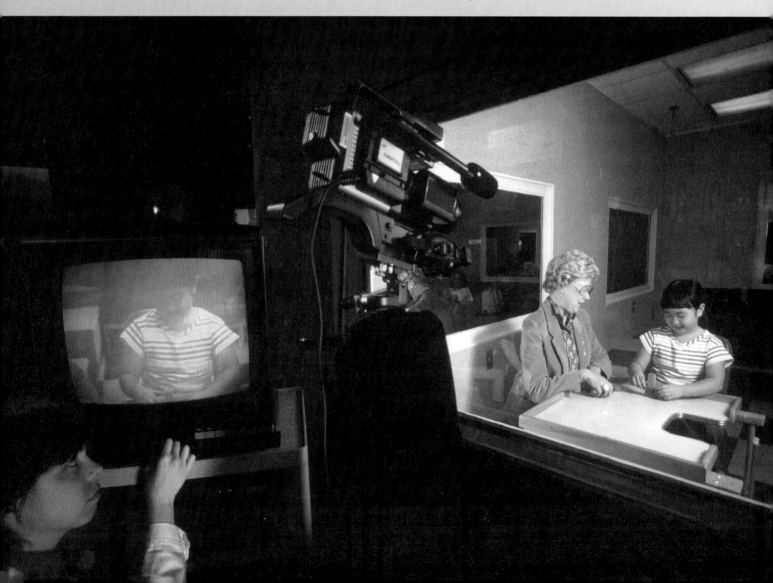

"Communication theories, then, are not just academic exercises; they explain and offer insight into one's own and others' communication."

Nadia and Ben have been together for about a year. While they get along really well most of the time, Nadia has noticed that whenever they have serious disagreements about something, like future plans or how much time they spend with each other's friends, Ben gets really quiet and just doesn't say much. This frustrates Nadia. The more she tries to get him to talk, the quieter he gets. It's getting to the point where they don't seem to even talk about anything where they might have disagreements; as a result, the relationship seems less satisfying for both of them.

Nadia is a communication major, and she's started to wonder about their pattern of conflict communication. Why does Ben get so quiet? Why does it bother her that he doesn't seem to engage in disagreements? Is it because they come from different family backgrounds and each learned different ways of dealing with conflict? Is it a reaction to Nadia, specifically? Are they having more conflict because, with midterms coming up and no employment yet for summer, they both are having a lot of other stresses in their lives?

Nadia does not want her relationship with Ben to end. She starts to think about how best to approach this communication dilemma. She wonders if any of the communication experts and theorists might have suggestions to help her and Ben communicate more effectively.

Believe it or not, these are the types of real-life dilemmas that lead communication professors and scholars to develop theories about everyday communication. Theories are sets of statements that explain a particular phenomenon. In this case, as we'll see in this chapter, there are communication theories that can explain Ben's and Nadia's relationship challenges and could ultimately help them work through their conflicts. In fact, research shows that learning how to manage conflict effectively leads to more satisfying relationships. Communication theories, then, are not just academic exercises; they explain and offer insight into one's own and others' communication (Craig, 1999; Milburn, 2010).

In this chapter, we will explore how communication scholars approach the study of communication and how this systematic study of communication differs from just making theories up out of thin air, or making generalizations from a few personal experiences. You will see that communication scholars do not all agree on how to best approach the study of communication! We'll also address larger questions, such as: how do we know what we know about communication? and how do communication scholars decide what to study in the first place? We want to introduce material that will show you the broad range of communication theories and lead to an exploration of the role of societal and individual forces in the communication process.

In this chapter we'll explain three major theoretical approaches in the communication discipline: the social science, interpretive, and critical approaches. As you will see, social science and interpretive theories take a more individual approach to the study of communication, while the critical takes a more societal approach. To help you understand these three approaches and how they arose, we'll also incorporate some description of the development of the communication discipline.

Once you have read this chapter, you will be able to:

- Describe the underlying assumptions of three contemporary approaches to the study of communication.
- Identify theories and methods of each of the three approaches.
- Identify ethical concerns of each approach.
- Describe the strengths and limitations of each of these three approaches.
- Understand the role of paradigm, theory, and methods in communication studies.
- Describe the major historical influences in communication studies: rhetoric and behaviorism.

CONTEMPORARY APPROACHES TO STUDYING HUMAN COMMUNICATION

How might different communication experts investigate Nadia's communication dilemma? What type of expert information is out there that explains Nadia and Ben's pattern of communication, taking into consideration the larger contexts and forces that might influence their relationship? What type of expert information would *you* trust to provide insight and guidance about interpersonal relationships and the larger contexts?

Communication researchers use various approaches and methods to understand human communication.

There are a number of ways to investigate the topic of interpersonal conflict. One might systematically interview men and women about their behavior during conflict, or observe cross-sex couples during conflict in natural settings or laboratories. Or one could even create and test some hypotheses—perhaps speculating that men physically react more negatively to conflict or just can't deal with it. To test this hypothesis, one could measure couples' heart rates, blood pressure, and cortisol levels during conflict interactions. Or one could take a step back and examine Nadia's and Ben's family and cultural backgrounds to discover if these conflict patterns lie not in their individual personalities, but rather in the ways they were each socialized. Or one could study the contexts in which these disagreements occur and identify situational elements that seem to trigger or exacerbate the conflict.

The ways of investigating we have just described represent three contemporary approaches to studying human communication: the social science approach, the interpretive approach, and the critical approach. Each of these approaches to understanding the situation is actually represented by contemporary scholars conducting real research. Each approach also reflects very different assumptions about the nature of human behavior and the best way to obtain insights and build knowledge about human behavior. And each represents a particular historical tradition, some hundreds of years in the making.

Paradigms, Theories, and Methods

Before we discuss the various approaches to studying human communication, we need to answer a basic question: What do we mean by an *approach*? Each approach represents a belief system, much like a religious system or faith does. In the academic world we call these belief systems **paradigms** (Burrell & Morgan, 1988). Each approach or paradigm carries with it a set of assumptions about knowledge, the nature of reality, and human nature; these assumptions guide research and theory development (Mumby, 1997). For example, most social scientists endorse a paradigm which assumes that reality is external to individuals, that it persists across time and groups, and that one can predict future behavior based on observations of past or

paradigm
belief system that represents a particular worldview

present behavior. Therefore, they believe knowledge can be best acquired through observing the behavior of a group of individuals and generalizing from it. Using this approach, one might predict, for example, that males and females will consistently use different strategies to manage conflict across many different conflict situations. Interpretivists, in contrast, assume that reality is socially constructed and, therefore, is internal to individuals and groups; thus it may not be consistent from group to group. They believe they can best acquire knowledge by understanding the perspectives and experiences of individuals and groups, although such knowledge may not be generalizable.

A **theory** is a set of statements that explains a particular phenomenon. Scholars develop theories in an attempt to explain why people communicate as they do. **Methods** describe the specific ways in which scholars collect and analyze data, the results of which are used to test their theories. For example, if researchers wanted to test whether men and women used different types of conflict communication strategies, a method could be to place males and females in conversational groups and ask them to discuss a very controversial topic. Researchers could observe their behaviors over a period of time and determine whether there was a difference in the way males and females approached conflict management. Another method would be to ask the men and women to imagine a conflict situation and then ask them to complete a survey containing questions about how they would prefer to approach the conflict situation. Researchers also use many other types of methods, including interviews, focus groups, and analyses of texts (such as speeches).

How does a researcher decide which method to use? The method depends on her paradigm or approach to the study of human communication. For example, if she believes the best explanations (or theories) of communication behavior come from examining the behaviors of many people, a survey would be the most likely method, allowing her to collect information or data from a lot of people. Scholars often disagree about the virtues or faults of a particular method. Thus, some claim that survey studies have limited usefulness, as they can only tell us how *most* people behave, and not much about an individual person. Others find interview methods inadequate because one cannot easily interview large numbers of people, making universal generalizations very difficult. Like religious belief systems, these paradigms also include ethical beliefs about the right (and wrong) ways to study communication. For example, some scholars find it objectionable to conduct large-scale surveys because they feel that researchers are usually too distant and unfamiliar with the groups they are studying and often do not understand the individuals well enough to adequately interpret the results.

Why do communication experts disagree about the best way to study communication? Part of the reason lies in the fact that the communication discipline is interdisciplinary in nature—its paradigms, theories, and methods have been influenced by different disciplines over the years. The earliest influence was from the study of rhetoric (public speeches), whereas later influences came from the fields of sociology and psychology.

As a way of understanding the differences among the three contemporary approaches, let us examine how each might view Nadia and Ben's communication dilemma. Before we begin, however, we would like to offer an important caveat. Although we believe that by clearly differentiating each of these three paradigms from the others, we make it easier for you to understand them, the reality is a bit more complex and fluid. Many communication scholars' work does not fit neatly and precisely into just one of the research paradigms; nor does it follow a single set of research methods. And although these paradigms may have been more clearly differentiated from one another in the early stages of their development, they have evolved over time. Scholars have borrowed from one another, their understanding of the research process has changed, and the differences among the paradigms have become less clearly defined. Some of the paradigms have more in-

theory
a set of statements that explains a particular phenomenon

methods
the specific ways that scholars collect and analyze data which they then use to prove or disprove their theories

social science approach
contemporary term for the behaviorist approach

behaviorism
the focus on the study of behavior as a science

naturalistic
relating to everyday, real-life situations, such as a classroom, cafe, or shopping mall

quantitative methods
methods that convert data to numerical indicators, and then analyze these numbers using statistics to establish relationships among the concepts

demand-withdrawal
an interaction pattern in which one partner criticizes or tries to change the other partner, who responds by becoming defensive and then disengaging—either psychologically or physically

ternal variations today than when they were originated. To highlight the underlying principles of these three paradigms in our discussion, let's look now at what each approach might have to offer Ben and Nadia.

TEST YOUR KNOWLEDGE

- What are three contemporary approaches to studying communication?
- What is a theory?
- What is a research paradigm?
- Why don't communication scholars agree on the best way to study communication?

THE SOCIAL SCIENCE APPROACH

The **social science approach** in communication originally focused on the individual or, less frequently, the dyad (a pair of people, like Nadia and Ben, who interact with each other). Because the social science approach grew out of the fields of psychology and sociology, communication scholars typically relied on some of the same research methods used by these social scientists.

Assumptions

Early social science researchers were oriented to **behaviorism**, a branch of psychology that focuses on observable behavior. They believed that the aim of communication research was to describe, predict, and explain human behavior with the ultimate goal of discovering universal laws that apply across situations and contexts. They believed predictions were possible because they saw reality as both observable and describable. So in Nadia's case, the behaviorist view would involve making observations and then formulating predictions for why Ben seems to withdraw. There are a number of social science theories that might explain their conflict patterns. Let's see how this works.

Theories and Methods

Social science researchers generally focus on causality. Thus they seek to determine what factors influence communication behavior. They first make predictions (hypotheses) that came from theories, and then they test these predictions by gathering data through various methods. Common methods include observing subjects in either a laboratory or a **naturalistic** setting (that is, in everyday, real-life situations, such as a classroom, café, or shopping mall), using surveys, and conducting focused interviews.

Once social science researchers collect their data, they use it to confirm or disconfirm their hypotheses about human communication behavior, most frequently through **quantitative methods**. These methods can be used to answer questions such as "how many?" and "what proportion?" That is, researchers convert their data into numerical indicators, and then analyze these numbers using statistics to establish relationships among the concepts.

One area of research that might help explain Nadia and Ben's conflict communication pattern is the **demand-withdrawal** interaction pattern, which has been investigated by communication researchers for more than 50 years. This pattern occurs when one partner criticizes or tries to change the other partner, who responds by becoming defensive and then disengaging—either psychologically or physically (Christensen, 1987; Eldridge & Christensen, 2002).

Communication scholars have conducted many studies that attempted to explain, and predict, how and why this pattern occurs. Whereas most of the research has focused on dyads composed of heterosexual romantic couples, the pattern seems to extend to many different relationships and contexts, and it seems that, as with

Nadia and Ben, women are statistically more likely to be the "demanders" who request change from their male partners, while men are more likely than women to withdraw (Christensen, 1987; Christensen & Heavey, 1990; Eldridge, Sevier, Jones, Atkins, & Christensen, 2007).

A variety of explanations have been offered for the observed sex differences in demanding and withdrawing behaviors in relationship conflict, including differences in how men and women are socialized (Christensen, 1987, 1988). However, some scholars disagree and speculate that it's not a question of sex difference, but rather a function of who wants the other person to change. The person who asks for change will be the "demander," which sometimes influences the other person to withdraw.

John Caughlin and Anita Vangelisti (1999) are among a number of communication scholars who have tested this hypothesis. In their study, they asked 57 married couples to discuss some common topics. In previous studies, the conflicts were not naturally occurring, as the couples were often asked to simply recall or speculate how they *might* react in a conflict. To ensure that the interactions in their study were as natural as possible, Caughlin and Vangelisti observed conversations that took place in each couple's home. The topics of conversation were common conflict issues: criticism of the other spouse's lifestyle or beliefs, the amount and type of affection in their marriage, disagreements about spending money, how to spend leisure time together, and so on. For each topic, each spouse was asked to indicate how much they would like their partner to change.

The researchers measured the demand/withdrawal behaviors of each spouse in two ways. First, they observed the couple and rated their demands or pressure to change (blaming, demands, nags) and their avoidance/withdrawal behaviors (hesitating, changing topics, diverting attention, and so on) and then converted their observations into numerical data. Second, they asked each spouse to rate their own and their partner's communication on a numerical scale using the same dimensions (demands and pressure to change; avoidance and withdrawal). Third, participants completed a "Communication Patterns Questionnaire" that asked them to make an overall (numerical) assessment of how often they engaged in demand/withdrawal behavior, and how often their spouse did so. Finally, the researchers conducted a statistical analysis on the numerical data and found that gender was not an important factor in the demand/blame interaction pattern. Rather, whoever (male or female) desired the change on a particular topic was also the one blaming and pressuring the other to change; in response, the other spouse would sometimes withdraw.

More recently, other researchers decided to test the same hypothesis using different methods aimed at a more comprehensive view of the problem. This team of researchers asked 116 couples to keep "conflict diaries," recording each instance of marital conflict over a period of two weeks and then returning the diary to the researchers at the end of that time (Papp, Kouros, & Cummings, 2009). The participants were trained to record in great detail exactly what occurred in each conflict episode, with respect to demanding, blaming, and withdrawal behaviors. In addition, they also completed several questionnaires measuring their overall conflict resolution level and their sense of well-being in the relationship. After gathering and coding all the information, converting into numerical data, and conducting statistical analyses, these researchers found results similar to those in the earlier study: when one partner raised a conflict issue, made a demand, or cast blame, this resulted in the other partner withdrawing. The results also indicated that this type of communication pattern (demand-withdrawal) is particularly problematic in close relationships—it seems to go hand in hand with negative emotions and destructive tactics that can eventually lead "to a cycle of increasingly negative and hostile conflicts" (p. 298). Additional research even suggests that these negative communication patterns have larger societal implications in the form of higher divorce rates (see *Communication in Society: Can Communication Styles Predict Divorce?*).

COMMUNICATION IN SOCIETY
Can Communication Styles Predict Divorce?

According to a national research project called "The Early Years of Marriage Study," the patterns spouses use to communicate when a conflict arises may have a bearing not only on the quality of their relationship, but on whether the couple ends up divorcing early in the marriage.

A particularly toxic pattern [occurs] when one spouse deals with conflict constructively, by calmly discussing the situation, listening to their partner's point of view, or trying hard to find out what their partner is feeling, for example—and the other spouse withdraws.

"This pattern seems to have a damaging effect on the longevity of marriage," said [University of Michigan] researcher Kira Birditt, first author of a study on marital conflict behaviors and implications for divorce published in the current issue (October 2010) of the *Journal of Marriage and Family*. "Spouses who deal with conflicts constructively may view their partners' habit of withdrawing as a lack of investment in the relationship rather than an attempt to cool down."

The data are from the Early Years of Marriage Study, supported by funding from the National Institute of Aging and the National Institute of Child Health and Human Development. It is one of the largest and longest

research projects to look at patterns of marital conflict, with 373 couples interviewed four times over a 16-year period, starting the first year of their marriages. The study is also one of just a few to include a high enough proportion of Black couples that researchers can assess racial differences in conflict strategies and their effects.

Overall, husbands reported using more constructive behaviors and fewer destructive behaviors than wives. But over time, wives were less likely to use destructive strategies or withdraw, while husbands' use of these behaviors stayed the same through the years.

"The problems that cause wives to withdraw or use destructive behaviors early in a marriage may be resolved over time," Birditt said. "Or, relationships and the quality of relationships may be more central to women's lives than they are to men. As a result, over the course of marriage, women may be more likely to recognize that withdrawing from conflict or using destructive strategies is neither effective nor beneficial to the overall well-being and stability of their marriages."

"We hope this study will lead to additional research on the complex dynamics of conflict between husbands and wives, and the potential explanations for changes versus stability in conflict behaviors over time," Birditt said.

SOURCE: Source: Provided by University of Michigan (news : web:) Retrieved March 10, 2011, from http://www.physorg.com/news204909834.html

Is stonewalling or withdrawal in romantic relationships related to a generally avoidant attachment style?

attachment
an emotional tie, such as the closeness young children develop with their caregivers

Other communication theories can help Nadia and Ben understand their conflict patterns. For example, some communication experts believe there is a relationship between the type of **attachment** infants have with their caregivers and their communication patterns later in life. The idea here is that as children interact with their caregivers (parents and others who care for them), they develop expectations for future interactions in relationships in general. Through these initial interactions, they come to see themselves as worthy (or unworthy) of love and affections from others (Bartholomew, 1990; Bowlby, 1982; Rholes et al., 2007). In a recent study, communication scholars Craig Fowler and Megan R. Dillow (2011) predicted that individuals who engage in specific types of conflict communication in close romantic relationships—criticism, defensiveness, contempt and stonewalling (withdrawal)—would also have a history of "avoidant attachment." In order to test this prediction, they gave survey questionnaires to 170 individuals who were in romantic relationships, measuring their orientations toward anxiety and avoidance and also their criticalness, defensiveness, contemptuousness, and stonewalling.

Their hypotheses were confirmed; the researchers concluded that individuals whose attachment history includes fears of abandonment and rejection also tend to engage in ineffective conflict behaviors with their loved ones that actually increase the chances of their fears of abandonment becoming reality.

There are many other communication studies that could help Nadia and Ben understand their communication patterns. For example, Guerrero, Farinelli, and McEwan (2009) predicted that satisfaction in relationships would be related to partners' particular attachment style and their emotional communication. They gave questionnaires to 581 couples asking about their attachment style, their relationship satisfaction, and how they expressed emotion in the relationship. They found, as predicted, that individuals were most satisfied in relationships with a partner whose attachment style was "secure" and who also tended toward positive emotional communication. Conversely, participants were less satisfied in relationships with partners who had "dismissive" or "preoccupied" attachment styles and who also expressed destructive negative emotions or detached emotional communication, respectively. It is possible, then, that Nadia and Ben might explore or reflect on their attachment pattern history or how they express emotions in their relationship to understand their communication during conflict situations.

Communication researchers interact with those being researched during the research process.

Jess Alberts (1988) studied the effect of couples' relationship satisfaction on their complaint behavior. In her study, she analyzed the types of complaints that happy and unhappy couples made to each other, such as complaints about behavior and complaints about personal characteristics. She then counted how many of each complaint type happy couples used and how many unhappy couples used. Finally, she applied statistical analyses to the resulting numbers to determine which couple type was more likely to use which complaint type. She discovered that happy couples made more complaints about behavior and their partners often responded in agreement, whereas unhappy couples made more personal complaints and their partners tended to respond with countercomplaints. Perhaps Nadia and Ben could examine their own complaint behavior to see if the type of complaints they make lead to conflict or influence their own satisfaction (or dissatisfaction).

As you can see, researchers in the social science approach to understanding communication often use quantitative analysis of surveys and observation; they may also use experiments and focused interviews to gather data. However, they also sometimes use qualitative methods such as conversation analysis, where they examine naturally occurring conversation to understand better the sequences and functions of everyday talk. Here, they do not use statistical analysis or count the number of times a conversational element occurs (as in Jess Alberts' study); rather they are interested in identifying patterns and providing examples of these patterns.

Ethical Issues

Researchers in all three approaches are concerned about the ethical issues involved in conducting communication research—although they may disagree on which issues are the most important (Martin & Butler, 2001). For example, communication researchers in the social science paradigm often follow the long-standing, very specific ethical guidelines of the American Psychological Association—which in turn are based in ethical guidelines established by the medical profession. This code of ethics emphasizes that no harm should be done to research participants. Specifically, all participants must be informed about all aspects of the research process, including the expected duration of the research, the exact procedures, the right to decline, and all foreseeable consequences of declining, any potential risks, discomfort, or adverse effects of participating in the research, and any potential research benefit. They must also be informed that their privacy and confidentiality will be maintained; they must be told of any limits of confidentiality, if there are any incentives for participation, and who they can contact for additional information or clarification (http://www. apa.org/ethics/code/index.aspx).

For the most part, these guidelines are followed without any problems; however, there are some areas of communication research that involve challenges to these guidelines. For example, some communication researchers study deception in interpersonal relationships—why people choose to deceive their partners and the potential consequences for that deception. Imagine how difficult it is to study deception without deceiving participants involved in the study—something that is explicitly forbidden by the research code of ethics!

Strengths and Limitations

You can see that social science research can be useful in identifying and explaining communication patterns and predicting their effects. However, the social science approach has its limits (as do the other approaches we will discuss). As you probably have realized, human communication is not always predictable, and in particular, predictions based on laboratory research may not hold true outside the lab. Although surveys can provide insight into individuals, beliefs, and attitudes, survey questions cannot fully assess individuals' thoughts and feelings, which are based on a multiplicity of factors and influences, as we described in Chapter 1. In addition, answers to survey questions may be inadequate, particularly for complex issues, because people often provide only short, superficial responses to predetermined questions. One might also argue that when surveys provide a set of answers from which respondents can choose, they are even less likely to tap into their true behaviors, beliefs, and emotions. Critics argue that researchers cannot obtain a full picture if they only measure behavior or if they assess thoughts and feelings only through survey questions.

The social science approach typically has focused on individual forces and their impact on communication without regard for societal forces. However, critics say that the social science approach tends to ignore the bigger picture, such as whether relational issues (like interpersonal conflict) are related to particular contexts or are influenced by large societal issues, like structural inequalities (racism, sexism), socioeconomic issues, cultural differences, and forces of globalization, like immigration. Essential elements of the social science approach are shown in *Visual Summary 2.1: Three Contemporary Approaches to the Study of Communication.*

TEST YOUR KNOWLEDGE

- What are the underlying assumptions of the social science approach?
- Identify at least two social science theories that address interpersonal conflict.
- What is the overall guideline for ethical research, according to social science scholars?
- What are the strengths and limitations of the social science approach?

THE INTERPRETIVE APPROACH

interpretive approach
contemporary term for humanistic (rhetorical) study

rhetoric
communication that is used to influence the attitudes or behaviors of others; the art of persuasion

humanism
a system of thought that celebrates human nature and its potential

Scholars who developed the **interpretive approach** were influenced by the ancient Greek tradition of **rhetoric,** or the art of persuasion, and by **humanism,** a branch of philosophy that celebrates human nature and its potential. Like the social science approach, the interpretive approach focuses on the individual, but interpretive communication researchers have goals and assumptions that differ from those who use the social science paradigm.

Three Contemporary Approaches to the Study of Communication

	SOCIAL SCIENCE (Behaviorism)	INTERPRETIVE (Humanism)	CRITICAL
Goal of Research	To describe, predict, and explain behavior	To describe, explain, and understand behavior in context	To describe, explain, and understand society in order to affect change
View of Reality	External and describable	Subjective	Subject and material
View of Human Behavior	Complex but predictable	Creative and voluntary	Resistive
Primary Methods	Quantitative analysis of surveys, **observation**, experiments, focused interviews	Qualitative analysis of rhetorical texts and ethnographic data (such as **participant observation**, observation, interviews)	Textual analysis, **media analysis**
Contributions	Identifies communication patterns and associations among variables	Emphasizes in-depth study of communication	Emphasizes power relations in communication interactions; recognizes societal impacts on communication
Limitations	Does not focus on the influence of power or societal forces	Limited number of participants; does not focus on power or societal forces	Does not focus on face-to-face communication

VISUAL SUMMARY 2·1

qualitative methods
methods in which researchers study
naturally occurring communication
rather than assembling data and
converting it to numbers

content analysis
approach to understanding
communication that focuses on specific
aspects of the content of a text or
group of texts

Assumptions

The goal of interpretive researchers is to understand and describe individual human communication behavior in specific situations, from the perspective of the communicator. Originating with the ancient Greek rhetoricians, and then the humanists, the interpretive approach has emphasized the creativity, instead of the predictability, of human behavior. Interpretive researchers assume that humans construct their own reality and that researchers must tap into these constructions for a full understanding of human communication.

Theories and Methods

Interpretive researchers generally use qualitative methods for analysis. Rather than reducing data to numbers as quantitative researchers do, interpretivists use qualitative data and/or tests to understand how communicators and receivers understand a communication event (Denzin & Lincoln, 2005; Lindlof & Taylor, 2002). These methods—which can answer questions like "what is it like?" and "how does it feel?"—are called **qualitative methods**, as they assess the quality of communication interactions. And rather than manipulating the research situation as one might do in a lab, they tend to study naturally occurring communication.

What type of interpretive studies might help Nadia and Ben understand their communication patterns better? One recent study investigated the nature of defensive communication in romantic relationships. As we will describe in Chapter 5 (Verbal Communication), defensive communication occurs when an individual perceives a threat from another person perhaps due to feelings of inadequacy; the person who feels threatened then may lash out, criticize, and blame the other. In general, defensive communication is unproductive, as it can lead to a cycle of conflict that results in very unsatisfying personal relationships. In order to better understand defensive communication in romantic relationships, communication scholars Jennifer Becker, Barbara Ellevold, and Glen Stamp (2008) conducted in-depth interviews with 50 participants, asking them to recall a conversation with their romantic partner in which they became defensive. The researchers conducted individual interviews with each partner as well as joint interviews with both partners.

In order to analyze the information, they transcribed all the interviews, which totaled 108 single-spaced pages! Unlike researchers in the social science paradigm who categorize the conversational elements and conduct statistical analyses to confirm (or disconfirm) their hypotheses, Becker and her colleagues searched for recurring themes and categories in the interviews in an effort to build a theory of defensive communication that would reflect the reality of the participants' everyday communication. This effort to build a theory based directly on participants' experiences and words is often used by interpretivists; it is called a grounded theory approach (Glaser & Strauss, 1967; Strauss & Corbin, 1998).

This grounded theory approach is a type of **content analysis**—a technique for objectively and systematically identifying specified characteristics of communication messages. For Becker and her colleagues, it involved carefully reading and listening to the interviews over and over again, then developing a framework of categories that grouped, labeled, and summarized particular acts of communication in the data. The researchers systematically compared and contrasted the categories, continually refining them, always with the goal of capturing the actual experiences and views of the participants. Eventually, they developed a theory that outlined the components of defensive communication, as well as what contributes to, and resulted from, defensive communication, and the context of defensive communication.

One of the most useful aspects of the Becker theory for Ben and Nadia (and anyone in close relationships) is a set of four suggestions for how to repair the potential damage caused by defensive communication. These strategies can be used uniquely or in combination.

1. Metacommunication: partners engage in supportive communication by indicating that they understand the other's perspective, relating common experiences, forgiving each other, and engaging in intimacy and behaviors or humor.

2. Apologetic communication: the offending partner apologizes and admits wrongdoing after seeing the damage to the other partner.

3. Partner-centered preventive communication: focuses on preventing future defensive communication—in contrast to metacommunication that involves discussion of a past defensive communication.

4. Avoidance: partners have a brief period of physical or verbal withdrawal to give the couple some time to regain their composure and clarify their thoughts.

Studying communication can help to identify and understand employee-manager interactions.

Here it is easy to see how theories are not just abstract notions, but also sources of useful insights for improving everyday communication in important relationships.

Ethnographic, or field study, methods are common in interpretive research. In an ethnographic study, researchers actively engage with participants; methods include participant observation, observations, and ethnographic interviewing. During participant observations, the researcher joins the group or community under study. These methods are often used by researchers who are investigating cultures different from their own. For example, communication expert Sheryl Lindsley (1999) spent a year and half in several *maquiladoras* (manufacturing businesses on the Mexican-U.S. border) investigating intercultural interaction and conflicts between Mexican workers and managers and U.S. American managers in the organizations. She spent many hours in the factories, observed the interactions of managers and workers, and conducted in-depth interviews. Her data, then, included her notes and transcriptions, which she analyzed (using content analysis) to discover the themes and categories that characterized the employee interactions. She found that many of the misunderstandings and conflicts were due to cultural differences.

In contrast, during purely observational research as in some the studies described earlier, the researcher maintains distance, simply observing participants (for example, couples in conflict) without actually spending a lot of time with the couples.

Communication scholar Donal Carbaugh has conducted a number of interpretive studies in which he describes the communication patterns of Finnish people, Blackfeet Indians, and U.S. residents in varying contexts. For example, using in-depth analyses of ethnographic observations and interviews, he describes the role of silence and listening in Blackfeet communication, the tendency of Finns to be reserved in communication, and the emphasis many in the United States place on speaking for themselves. More importantly, he shows how these communication patterns are inextricably tied to cultural identities in each community (Carbaugh, 1990; 1999; Carbaugh & Berry, 2001). We'll see more examples of these types of cross cultural studies in Chapter 7 (Communication across Cultures).

An important interpretive method is **rhetorical analysis**, in which researchers examine and analyze texts or public speeches as they occur in society. The earliest rhetorical scholars were interested in understanding how a speech affected audiences. These researchers sought to determine the best ways for speakers to construct and deliver speeches so they could affect their audiences in particular ways. Modern researchers also focus on interpreting what texts mean in the settings in which they occur. What do we mean by "the settings in which they occur"? We mean the physical space (e.g., classroom or place of worship) as well as broader environments (e.g.,

ethnographic
relating to studies in which researchers actively engage with participants

rhetorical analysis
used by researchers to examine texts or public speeches as they occur in society with the aim of interpreting textual meaning

educational versus social; historical versus contemporary) in which the speech or text is delivered.

Researchers who do rhetorical analysis typically do not interact with the speakers or authors of the texts they study, and therefore face different ethical concerns than do ethnographic researchers. Rhetoricians must be especially attentive to accuracy in their depictions of the text and the historical period in which the text occurred.

While rhetoricians typically do not study interpersonal communication, there are some rhetorical studies that relate to gender issues—rhetorical studies that analyze women's contributions through public communication, many of which were unnoticed at the time they were delivered (Borda, 2002; Campbell, 1994; Zaeske, 2002). There are other rhetorical studies related to the issues of interpersonal conflict. One such study was conducted by Jeremy Engels (2009), who focused on the role of "uncivil speech" (invective) and how it functions, then and today, in a democratic society. Engels begins by analyzing a famous speech given by Robert Owen, a well-known philanthropist, on July 4, 1826—the 50th anniversary of the fledgling United States. In this speech, Owen railed against many social institutions, including religion, slavery, and marriage—arguing that all three were a cover for a system of oppression. His speech, "The Declaration of Mental Independence," created so much antagonism and outrage that it is only in retrospect that rhetorical scholars recognized its contribution to society. Owen stated that marriage enslaved women by making them private property of men; he even championed divorce—utterly unheard of at the time. He was denounced and reviled, called a foreigner and an atheist. However, rhetoric scholar Engels points out that his speech in fact served an important function, as citizens were already anxious about slavery and women's rights and the speech allowed them to transform their guilt into blame on Owen. The "uncivil speech" also provided a common bond, uniting citizens and ultimately affirming a national identity.

Engels goes on to argue that "uncivil speech," which is often used by politicians and commentators on both the conservative and liberal ends of the political spectrum, is central to democracy throughout U.S. history and even today. It fulfills a democratic purpose because it is open to anyone and everyone, and it serves as a way of managing cultural anxiety by making it difficult for people to focus their rage on the real systemic problems in society.

Ethical Issues

For interpretive researchers, particularly those doing ethnographic research, ethical issues go beyond the concern for not harming research participants. Ethnographic researchers strive for equality and reciprocity, a mutual respect in their relationships with participants. Some researchers suggest that an ethical relationship with participants involves being friendly but at the same time maintaining sufficient scholarly distance and disengaging appropriately from participants after the research is completed. Others acknowledge that researchers and participants may become friends during the course of a study and that this relationship then involves a special set of "relational ethics"—a challenge to "act in a "humane, nonexploitative way, while being mindful of our role as researchers" (Ellis, 2007, p. 5).

Another important ethical concern is presenting findings in a way that accurately reflects the views of the participants (González, 2000; Tanno, 1997). To ensure this, researchers often share their interpretations and conclusions with the study participants, a procedure called member-checking (Miller & Crabtree, 2005; Lindlof & Taylor, 2002). Some include their participants in various stages of the research and describe them as co-researchers, rather than subjects or participants (Tanno, 1997).

Strengths and Limitations

The strengths of the interpretive approach include the in-depth understanding it provides of communication in specific situations and the insight it offers into the purposes of those messages. The limitation is that it usually involves few research participants—or none—as is the case in rhetorical analyses of texts. From a social science perspective, its utility is limited because researchers cannot generalize conclusions from such small samples. Thus, it does not help us discover broader laws about human behavior. A second limitation is that the researchers often are outsiders to the communities they study, which means that they may not accurately interpret the communication patterns they see. For example, some studies have concluded that the Amish avoid dealing with conflict, whereas an Amish person might explain that they do deal with conflict, but in a different way—by actively strengthening relationships so that they do not reach the point of open conflict (Kraybill, 2001; Kraybill, Nolt, & Weaver-Zercher, 2010). Essential elements of the interpretive approach are presented in *Visual Summary 2.1* on page 35.

critical approach
an approach used not only to understand human behavior but ultimately to change society

TEST YOUR KNOWLEDGE

- What are the underlying assumptions of the interpretive approach?
- Identify and describe at least two interpretive research methods.
- What is the overall guideline for ethical concerns of interpretive researchers?
- What are the strengths and limitations of the interpretive approach?

THE CRITICAL APPROACH

Both the social science approach and interpretive approach focus on individual behavior, whereas the **critical approach** is much more concerned with how societal forces influence and interact with individual forces—with the ultimate goal of changing society.

The critical approach examines power differences such as those between refugees and aid workers.

Assumptions

In order to reach the ultimate goal of changing society, critical researchers believe that one must understand the societal forces that shape how people come into contact and communicate. The roles that power and hierarchy play in these exchanges must be understood as well. For example, a critical scholar might consider the power differences that exist in everyday interactions between the school custodian and the principal, the refugee and the Red Cross worker, the student and the professor. Critical scholars believe that by examining such interactions and writing about how power functions in them, people gain the awareness they need to resist societal forces of power and oppression.

Cultural studies is one research approach that arises from the critical paradigm. This approach attempts to reveal the complexities of culture and the ways that people actively participate in their culture and resist its powerful influences. Cultural studies scholars believe such resistance might be expressed in a number of ways. For example, factory workers can resist the authority structure of management in many ways, some subtle (e.g., work slowdowns, extending their autonomy) and some more obvious (e.g., whistleblowing) (Mumby, 2005). Communication scholar Angela Trethewey (1997) conducted a critical ethnographic study of a social service organization and found that clients resisted the confining authority structure of the organization in a number of ways, including breaking some of the rules, bitching, and re-visioning, or re-framing, client-social worker relationships. In all these ways of resisting, people find ways to meet their needs and struggle to make relationships and contexts more equitable.

Like interpretivists, critical scholars believe that reality is subjective, or that we each construct our own reality. However, they also stress that these realities have corresponding material, or physical, consequences—meaning that they have real consequences in people's lives. For example, in the United States we socially construct a reality in which professional athletes are accorded high salaries and power while schoolteachers are not. These social constructions result in real differences in how each group is treated, what each group can buy, and what sacrifices each group must make.

Theories and Methods

Critical scholars generally use qualitative methods in their research, including both field observation, which we have discussed earlier, and **textual analysis**, a method of analyzing cultural "products" such as media (TV, movies, journalistic essays) and public speeches (in which case they may be called critical rhetoricians). Some critical researchers use ethnographic methods, as in the case of the study by Trethewey described above. With these analyses critical scholars seek to understand the influence of societal forces such as the economic, government, and cultural institutions that produce, circulate, and profit from these cultural products. In addition, they may use ethnograhic methods (observation, interviews) to understand how power and privilege affect people's lives. For example, one research project features collaboration between scholars and community members to raise awareness and find solutions to health disparities in minority communities (see *Did You Know? Engaging Through Art and Performance*).

How would critical scholars study interpersonal gender conflict? They would take a broad societal perspective (Litwin & Hallstein, 2007) and might suggest that

Did You Know?
Engaging Through Art and Performance

Communication scholar Olga Idriss Davis is part of a research team that works through partnership with community leaders and members with the goal of decreasing health disparities in minority communities in Arizona. Her responsibility is to engage the community in raising awareness and finding ways to promote better health.

Davis, who is trained in rhetoric and theatrical performance, saw an opportunity to combine her two fields of study into one educational and engaging event addressing the weighty issues of "cultural processes in risk and resilience" in minority groups. She put together an event that blended artists and performers (dancers, drummers, singers) with local healthcare professionals using visual and performance art. As she describes it, "The expression of public art is sometimes a better, or alternative, way of educating. Performance art has a way of dispelling boundaries of race, gender, sexuality, class…It's a way of universally connecting humans to humans."

Davis worked closely with some of the artists who performed at this event, helping them to better understand both this concept and the interrelation of art and health. "I had them reflect on the social, political, and cultural issue of health disparities," she said. "Many of them connected through story. They're communicating their life experiences, their relationships, through their visual and performance talents."

In another research project, Davis showed how barbers in African American neighborhoods can serve as information and even intervention centers in the efforts to reduce high blood pressure and heart disease, which are often prevalent in minority communities. The Barbershop Hypertension Screening Program is designed to increase health literacy and knowledge of Black males through high blood pressure screening and referrals.

These projects are both good examples of how scholars, comingling knowledge and action, can work for social change at the grass-roots level.

SOURCES: Engaging through Art and Performance. Retrieved April 20, 2011, from http://community.uui.asu.edu/features/art.asp

Davis, O. I., & Marsiglia, F. F. (2011, June). Cultural catalysts for community dialogues: Black barbers as interventionists in cardiovascular health of African American men. Poster presented at the annual meeting of the Society for Prevention Research, Washington, D.C.

a female-demand/male-withdrawal pattern is expected in heterosexual romantic relationships because men have traditionally occupied a more privileged position in society and in marriage relationships and therefore would be less likely than women to want to change (Noller, 1993). Conversely, women benefit less from marriage and so are more likely to be the ones to ask for change (more help with household chores, child care, and so on) (Jacobson, 1989, 1990). In one critical study, Elizabeth Suter (2004) explored why, given U.S. women's historical struggle to gain legal and social acceptance, the overwhelming majority of women continue to follow tradition and adopt their husbands' names. In a similar vein, critical scholars Bernadette Calafell and Fernando Delgado (2004) examined the messages that are communicated about Latino identity in *Americanos*, a published collection of photographs of Latina/Latino life in the United States.

Many critical scholars look to popular texts like films and television to understand male and female roles in society. For example, some Disney characters (the princesses) have been criticized for depicting women in passive roles. On the other hand, Lisa Lazard (2009) analyzes the female characters in horror movies and makes the argument that women in this film genre are often strong.

Some critical scholars have traced the changing roles of men in contemporary U.S. society by analyzing popular movies and books, showing how these movements are responses to societal forces and "crises in masculinities." For example, there was the backlash against the women's movement exemplified by some Michael Douglas films (e.g., *Falling Down*, 1993; *Disclosure*, 1994). Wendy Sommerson (2004) analyzes John Sayles's (1996) film *Lone Star* to explore how a new positive white male type was developing in the 1990s, and notes how this type was represented by Bill Clinton who functioned as the father figure-leader during his presidency. She argues that Clinton's masculinity, open to cultural, national, and racial differences in a positive way, mirrored the political and social realities of the time, as the country was changing to a more transnational multicultural position.

More recently, Helen Shugart (2008) explores the cultural trend of metrosexuality represented by *Queer Eye for the Straight Guy* and the book *The Metrosexual Guide to Style: A Handbook for the Modern Man*—showing that this trend performed a specific, important role in "redressing anxieties inherent in commercial masculinity" as men came to grips with increasing gay social presence, increasing power of women, and decreasing acceptances of traditional macho masculinity.

Dana Cloud has researched the gender power relationships that are seen in reality TV shows

Another recent critical study examined gender roles portrayed on one of the most popular types of television, the reality show. Asking "how real is reality TV?" critical scholar Dana Cloud (2010) examines male/female role portrayal on one season of *The Bachelor*—where bachelor Brad refused to choose a love interest at the end, which disappointed and irritated a lot of viewers. Cloud shows how this show both reinforces very traditional, retro images of women and men (even the commercials show men as active, women just "there" as objects) and, at the same time, invites the audience to not really take it seriously—as aspects of the show are campy and humorous.

Cloud, like many critical scholars, is not interested in predicting communication or describing communication behavior. Rather, she hopes to educate and illuminate communicators so that, ultimately, they might understand the larger societal impacts (like media) on communicators' attitudes and practices and transform communication to become more just and equitable—a lofty goal for a scholar. Critical scholars look at the larger picture, attempting to see communication in the context of social, political, religious, and historical contexts (Hill, 2010). To do this, they use a variety of methods, but they often look to media texts. Unlike an interpretivist, who might focus on the specific communication patterns of men and women in various types of relationships and settings, or a social scientist, who might survey large groups of men and women as part of theoretical predictions, a critical scholar always explores the communication in the larger societal contexts.

What insights would these studies contribute to Nadia and Ben's dilemma? How could they help Nadia and Ben understand their relationship better? All these studies attempt to show the relationship between cultural gender roles as represented in popular culture and the political realities—focusing on the intersections of the individual and society. Perhaps Nadia and Ben might gain insights by stepping back and exploring how their own relationship is influenced by societal and cultural gender role expectations and pressures.

Ethical Issues

In analyzing popular texts, critical researchers may have a rather distant relationship to the objects of their study, but they are especially concerned about the way in which they and other scholars present the worldview of others. A key ethical question for them is whether they have the right to study, analyze, and represent other people's views, particularly when crossing racial/ethnic and class boundaries. They point out that many cultural groups—such as Native Americans and the poor—have been exploited and misrepresented by researchers who stood to gain academic rewards by portraying them in certain ways. In the meantime, the communities being researched gained little from their participation (Alcoff, 1991/1992).

Strengths and Limitations

The strength of the critical approach is its emphasis on the importance of economic, political, and historical forces in communication. These factors are largely ignored by the social science and interpretive approaches. A second strength inherent in the critical approach is its acknowledgment of the role of power in communication encounters.

However, a limitation of this approach is the lack of attention to face-to-face interaction by critical researchers who focus primarily on public and media communication such as film, TV, music videos, magazine advertisements, and speeches. So, although critical textual research may help us understand the historical and contemporary roots of sex roles and how contemporary gender images perpetuate stereotypes and may contribute to gender discrimination, it may not help us communicate better in our interpersonal relationships.

Like the interpretive approach, the critical approach relies on qualitative research methods and does not tend to generate generalizable conclusions. For example, in the popular cultural analyses described above, the researchers did not measure viewers' reactions to the various movies and then generalize about all viewers' attitudes toward gender roles. Rather, *their* essays present their analysis of the images and portrayals on the screen, and the validity of their conclusions is based only on the strength of their arguments. The essential elements of the critical approach are presented in *Visual Summary 2.1* on page 35.

TEST YOUR KNOWLEDGE

- What are the underlying assumptions of the critical approach?
- Identify at least two critical methods that address conflict.

- What are two ethical concerns of critical researchers?
- What are the strengths and limitations of the critical approach?

A MULTIFACETED APPROACH

We hope that this review of the three major contemporary approaches gives you an idea of the varied viewpoints you will encounter within the field of communication studies. Rather than emphasizing one of the three in this text, we draw from all of them. This is our position: If you only view a sculpture from one perspective, you can never fully appreciate the work. The same goes for the field of communication studies.

Three Perspectives on Communication

If you want to be able to view the communication process, like a sculpture, from various perspectives, you need to understand and be able to recall the essential contributions each research approach offers. Here is a brief explanation of each approach:

1. The social science approach seeks snapshots of certain communication phenomena and from them attempts to find universal laws that explain human communication.
2. The interpretive approach uses content analysis, ethnographic field studies, and rhetorical analysis to take a more individualized, specific look at human communication.
3. The critical approach seeks to uncover the element of power that exists in every interaction and to use communication analysis to effect social change.

This review of the research paradigms illustrates the way that these three approaches have guided communication research. Our understanding of the communication process flows from all three research approaches, and from this we have formulated the synergetic model of communication, which we presented in Chapter 1. The synergetic model's focus on societal factors evolved from the critical approach, whereas its inclusion of individual forces reflects the influence of the social science and interpretive approaches.

Despite differences in the various communication models and research approaches, individual communicators play a key role in all of them. Therefore, like Nadia and Ben, in order to have a complete understanding of communication, communicators need to understand how individuals' identities influence and are influenced by communication. They also need to understand how individual and societal forces act together to affect identity development. Each communicator is unique because of the ways in which individual and social forces together create individual identities. In turn, these identities influence how individuals communicate and how others communicate with them. We explore the question of identity and communication in Chapter 3.

TEST YOUR KNOWLEDGE

- Why is it important to draw from all three research approaches in studying communication?
- What does each research approach contribute to the synergetic model of communication?

SUMMARY

Currently there are three research paradigms (belief systems) in communication research today. Each approach or paradigm carries with it a set of assumptions about knowledge, the nature of reality, and human nature, and these assumptions guide research methods and theory development. Theory is a set of statements that explains a particular phenomenon. Methods describe the specific ways in which scholars collect and analyze data, the results of which are used to test their theories. The social science approach emphasizes individual forces, seeks to predict human behavior, emphasizes universal theories, and generally uses quantitative research methods. This approach can be useful in identifying and explaining communication patterns and predicting their effects. However, human communication is not always predictable, and in particular, predictions based on laboratory research may not hold true outside the lab.

The interpretive approach also emphasizes individual social forces but seeks to understand, not predict, human behavior. Interpretive researchers assume that humans construct their own reality and that researchers must tap into these constructions for a full understanding of human communication. Interpretive researchers generally use qualitative methods. The strengths of the interpretive approach include the in-depth understanding of communication in specific situations, but it is limited in that it usually involves few research participants—or none—as is the case in rhetorical analyses of texts. A second limitation is that the researchers often are outsiders to the communities they study, which means that they may not accurately interpret the communication patterns they see.

The critical approach is very different from the social science and interpretive perspectives as it is much more concerned with how societal forces influence and interact with individual forces—with the ultimate goal of changing society. In order to change society, critical researchers believe that one must understand the societal forces that shape how people come into contact and communicate. The role that power and hierarchy play in these exchanges must be understood as well. The strength of the critical approach is its emphasis on the importance of economic, political, and historical forces in communication and its acknowledgment of the role of power in communication encounters.

Critical scholars generally use qualitative methods, often conducting textual analysis in which they analyze cultural "products" such as media (TV, movies, journalistic essays) and even speeches (in which case they may be called *critical rhetoricians*). In addition, they may use observations or ethnographic methods to better understand how power and privilege affect people's lives. A limitation of this approach is the lack of attention to face-to-face interaction by critical researchers who focus primarily on public and media communication; as such it may not help us communicate better in our interpersonal relationships.

These three approaches combine to form the foundation for our synergetic model of communication. The synergetic model's focus on societal factors evolved from the critical approach, whereas its inclusion of individual forces reflects the influence of the social science and interpretive approaches.

HUMAN COMMUNICATION IN SOCIETY ONLINE

To review this chapter, use the MyCommicationLab Web site to test your understanding of the following key terms, record your answers to the chapter review questions, and complete the suggested activities. Expand your learning and understanding of chapter concepts by completing additional activities and exercises online. Access code required. Go to www.mycommunicationlab.com for more information or to purchase standalone access.

KEY TERMS

paradigm 28
theory 29
methods 29
social science approach 30
behaviorism 30
naturalistic 30

quantitative methods 30
demand-withdrawal 30
attachment 32
interpretive approach 34
rhetoric 34
humanism 34

qualitative methods 36
content analysis 36
ethnographic 37
rhetorical analysis 37
critical approach 39
textual analysis 40

APPLY WHAT YOU KNOW

1. Find five examples of the word *communication* in popular magazines and newspapers. How is the word being used in those forms? What are some of the different meanings for communication?
2. Identify a common communication topic (e.g., deception, teamwork, intimacy, credibility). How would researchers from the three different paradigms investigate this topic? What would be the general goal of each researcher? What would each emphasize in the investigation? What type of research methods might each use to conduct her or his investigation? What might be the ethical concerns of each? (Hint:

Use the information presented in *Visual Summary 2.1: Three Contemporary Approaches to the Study of Communication.*)
3. Locate a journal article and an article in a popular magazine that report on the same communication issue from a social science perspective. How was the issue presented in each? What are the strengths and weaknesses of each article? What are the strengths and weaknesses of a social science approach to this topic? (Hint: Use the information presented in *Visual Summary 2.1: Three Contemporary Approaches to the Study of Communication.*)

3
Communicating Identities

When I'm talking with Americans and ask about their nationality, the answer is usually about ethnicity: "I'm Swedish" or "I'm Polynesian and French." Rarely does anyone answer, "I'm American." In my many travels around the world, I have noticed that the U.S. is the only country whose people fail to understand that their national identity is, in fact, U.S. American. I am nationally an American, and ethnically I am Chinese, Syrian, and Ukrainian. As an Asian American who grew up in New Jersey, I feel culturally tied to my national identity, whereas I merely feel influenced by my ethnic cultural identities.

—*Mike*

When you think about identity, you may be pondering who you "really" are and how you got to be that way. Do you feel, like Mike, that your national identity is a major determinant of who you are? Or do you feel that your ethnic identities are also a strong influence? What about your gender, religious, and social class identities? Mike notes that he is an "Asian American"; it's true that China, Syria, and Ukraine are all in Asia, but do you think of those ethnicities when you think of Asian Americans? Mike also says he is from New Jersey. How do our regional identities influence who we "really" are? Can you choose to be whomever you want, or do your background and social environment determine who you are? In this chapter we address these identity questions as well as the important role communication plays in them.

As we discussed in Chapter 1, communication is a deeply cultural process. In this chapter we explore how individual characteristics, such as gender and age and the societal meanings associated with them, interact to create cultural identities—and the important role communication plays in that development. Within cultures, communication patterns, habits, values, and practices develop around specific individual characteristics such as race, gender, sexuality, age, social class, and religion. For example, in the United States, people commonly understand that it is not acceptable to tell racist or sexist jokes, particularly in the workplace, at job interviews, and in other formal settings. This understanding exists because people are aware of the impact of this type of communication on people's identities. We all possess many cultural identities, as we identify with genders, races, ethnicities, religions, organizational affiliations, schools, and so on. Some of these identities affect our communication experiences more than others. In this chapter we explain which identities are most influential and why. We also examine how societal forces influence identity and discuss ethical issues associated with communication and identities. We conclude by looking at some skills for communicating about identities.

⬖ Once you have read this chapter, you will be able to:

- Identify five reasons identity is important to communication.
- Define *identity*.
- Clarify how reflected appraisals, social comparisons, self-fulfilling prophecies, and self-concept contribute to identity development.
- Describe how social forces influence the communication of identity.
- Identify examples of racial, national, ethnic, gender, sexual, age, social class, disability, and religious identities.
- Discuss three ethical considerations for communicating in a sensitive manner to and about others' identities.
- Explain three ways to communicate more effectively about identities.

THE IMPORTANCE OF IDENTITY

Identity has a tremendous impact on the communication process in a number of ways. How we communicate, as well as how our communication is received by others, can be shaped by our identities and the identities of others. Let's look at some of the ways that identity influences communication. First, because individuals bring their self-images or identities to each communicative encounter, every communication interaction is affected by their identities. For example, when elderly people converse with teenagers, both groups may have to accommodate for differences in their experiences and language use.

Second, communication interactions create and shape identities (Hecht, 1993). If older adults treat teenagers with respect and admiration during their conversations, these young people may view themselves as more mature and more valuable than they did previously. Conversely, communication can also be used to denigrate other identities and create tension between groups. It is always important to think about the impact of communication on various identity groups.

Third, identity plays an important role in intercultural communication, something that has become increasingly common in our global, technology-based world. As more and more businesses have international branches and subsidiaries, workers are increasingly likely to have contact with people from other cultures. The more familiar they are with the values related to identity in these cultures, the better prepared they will be to succeed in today's society.

Fourth, understanding identity is useful because so much of U.S. life is organized around and geared toward specific identities (Allen, 2004). In the United States we have television stations such as *Black Entertainment Television* and *Telemundo* and magazines like *Ebony* and *More*, which are targeted to groups based on their race, age, and/or sex. We also have entertainment venues such as Disneyland and Club Med that are developed specifically for families, romantic couples, and singles. In this identity-based climate, individuals often communicate primarily with others who share their identities. Consequently, learning how to communicate effectively with individuals whose identities vary from yours may require considerable thought and effort.

Finally, identity is a key site where individual and societal forces come together to shape communication experiences. Although we each possess identity characteristics such as social class or nationality, the society where our communication takes place will define the meanings of those characteristics. For example, depending on whether you are in the United States or visiting a country where anti-American sentiment is common, what it means to be an "American" can have different nuances. Moreover, we cannot separate our identities—as individuals or as members of society—from our communication experiences. Identity is vital to how meaning is created in communication (Hecht, 1993). We explain this interaction more fully throughout this chapter.

TEST YOUR KNOWLEDGE

- List five advantages to understanding the relationship between communication and identity.

WHAT IS IDENTITY?

When you enrolled in college, you were most likely required to provide a piece of identification, such as a birth certificate, passport, or driver's license. Identity is tied closely to identification; it refers to who you are and the specific characteristics that make you different from other individuals. In communication studies, *identity* includes not only who you are but also the social categories you identify yourself with and the categories that others identify with you. Society creates social categories such as *middle aged* or *college student*, but they only become part of one's identity when one identifies with them or others identify you in these categories. For example, you may think of yourself as short, but others may classify you as being of average height. Many young people in their late teens and early twenties identify with the category *college student*, but a growing number of people in their thirties, forties, and even older are also returning to school and identifying with this category. The many social categories that exist can be divided into two types; *primary* and *secondary* identities (Loden & Rosener, 1991; Ting-Toomey, 1999). Primary identities are those that have the most consistent and enduring impact on our lives, such as race, gender, and nationality. Secondary identities, such as college major, occupation, and marital status, are more fluid and more dependent on situation.

To help define the term **identity**, let's examine its essential characteristics. The first characteristic is that identities exist at the individual and the societal levels. Jake Harwood (2006) explains this concept: "At the individual (personal identity) level, we are concerned with our difference from other individuals, and the things that make us unique as people. At the collective (social identity) level, we are concerned with our group's differences from other groups, and the things that make our group unique" (pp. 84–85). For example, if you are an athlete, and you are thinking about how you are different and unique from others who are not athletic, then you are focusing on part of your individual identity. If you are focusing on how your sports team is different and unique from other sports teams, then you are focusing on your social identity.

We should note that identities are not necessarily only individual or social; they can be both, depending on the situation. How is this contradiction possible? Let's look at an example. Many readers of this text are U.S. Americans, and their national identity is part of their social identity. Because they are surrounded by others from the United States, they may not be conscious of this as being part of their individual identity. But if they travel abroad, their national identity becomes part of their individual identity because this significant characteristic will differentiate them from others.

A second important aspect of identity is that it is both fixed and dynamic. Again, this seems like a contradiction. If you think about it, however, you will realize that certain aspects of our identities, although stable to some extent, actually do change over time. For instance, a person may be born male, but as he grows from an infant to a boy to a teenager to a young man to a middle-aged man and then to an old man, the meanings of his male identity change. He is still a male and still identifies as a male, but what it means to be male alters as he ages, and social expectations change regarding what a boy or a man should be (Kimmel, 2005).

identity
who a person is; composed of individual and social categories a person identifies with, as well as the categories that others identify with that person

Our relationships with others help us understand who we are and how others perceive us.

A third characteristic of identity is that individual and social identities are created through interaction with others. The relationships, experiences, and communication interactions we share with others shape how we see ourselves. For example, people who travel abroad and then return home may experience stress, but they also experience growth and change—and communication with those they meet as they travel plays a key role in both (Martin & Harrell, 1996). As another example, in the 1960s and '70s, many American women became more aware of, and dissatisfied with, their social identity as wives and mothers. This prompted them to become involved in a larger social movement known as feminism, in which women organized and attended "consciousness raising" groups designed to alter how they perceived and performed their identities as females. Women in these groups were encouraged to think of themselves not primarily as wives and mothers but as the professional and social equivalents of men. This type of mobilization of women also occurred earlier in history, when they organized to gain the right to vote. It also happened for others—both women and men—who organized to protest against racial discrimination. In these instances a common social identity brought people together into communities, and these communities in turn acted to improve the position of the particular social identity in society.

A fourth consideration is that identities need to be understood in relation to historical, social, and cultural environments. The meaning of any identity is tied to how it has been viewed historically and how people with that identity are situated in a given culture and society (Hecht, Jackson, & Ribeau, 2003; Johnson, 2001). For instance, throughout history, we have had varied notions of what it means to be female (Bock, 1989).

Although Cleopatra was an Egyptian Pharaoh and Joan of Arc led the French army into battle in the fifteenth century, these individual women were significant exceptions to the rule. In their times and for much of history, women have been perceived as intellectually inferior, physically delicate, and/or morally weak when compared to men. Because of these beliefs, in many cultures women were denied voting and property rights and even custody of their children in the event of divorce. For example, until 1881, upon marriage, English women's legal identities were subsumed by their husbands such that all of their property and wealth transferred to their spouses as well as their right to enter into any contracts (Erickson, 1993). In the United States, women didn't win the right to vote until 1920—and, more recently, Supreme Court Justice Antonin Scalia has argued that the U.S. Constitution "does not, in fact, bar sex discrimination" (Cohen, 2010).

Contemporary U.S. American women have all of the legal rights of men, yet historical conceptions of women still affect how they are positioned in society today. For example, on average women earn 82.8 percent of men's median weekly pay (Cauchon, 2010). While this gap is closing because the recent recession has had a greater impact on men's jobs than on women's, the gap reflects the lower value traditionally placed on women's work. Moreover, a number of religions still remain opposed to women serving as ministers and priests. The situation for women in other cultures can be even more challenging. In Saudi Arabia, although women make up 70 percent of those enrolled in universities, they compose just 5 percent of the workforce; their testimony in court is treated as presumption rather than fact; and they live mostly segregated lives (Azuri, 2006). Thus, a hierarchy exists across cultures in which one identity (male) is preferentially treated over another (female). You can probably think of other examples in which preferential treatment was given—or denied—based on race, sexuality, religion, social class, or age (Allen, 2004).

In sum, identity is key to understanding communication, and communication is key to understanding identity. As Abrams, O'Connor, and Giles have stated, "identity and communication are mutually reinforcing" (2002, p. 237).

Alternative VIEW
Census in India Includes a Third Gender Choice

As the official record of a nation's population, what information should any census seek? What categories should the census use?

The United States is just one of many countries that conduct a census at regular intervals. Census forms typically ask for basic personal data like age, race, and gender. In 2000, the U.S. census made history by allowing respondents to check multiple race/ethnicity categories. In the 2010 census, the form was designed to "give the nation's more than 308 million people the opportunity to define their racial makeup as one race or more" (El Nasser, 2010).

The 2011 census in India also made history, as its new census form gave respondents the option of answering the question about their gender identity with either "Male," "Female," or "Other." In India, individuals who are biologically male and adopt female gender identity are considered a third gender known as hijra; they face severe discrimination in mainstream Indian society (Venkat, 2008). The 2011 census will "give India a firm count for its 'third-gender' hijra community—the origins of which go back millennia to a time when transsexuals, eunuchs and gays held a special place in society backed by Hindu myths of their power to grant fertility" (Daigle, 2011).

To view a copy of the 2011 census form for India, see: http://www.censusindia.gov.in/2011-Schedule/Shedules/English_Household_schedule.pdf

To view a copy of the 2010 census form for the United States, see: http://2010.census.gov/2010census/about/interactive-form.php

TEST YOUR KNOWLEDGE

- How do individual and societal forces influence our understanding of identity?

THE INDIVIDUAL AND IDENTITY

Although it can be tempting to boil a person's identity down to one word—say, *nerd*, *jock*, or *sorority girl*—in reality, everyone is more complex than that. If you had to pick only one word to describe yourself and you had to use it in every situation—personal and professional—what word would you choose? For most people this task is impossible, for we all see ourselves as multidimensional, complex, and unique. People in the United States, especially, are invested in the notion that they are unique. Twins often go to great lengths to assure people that they are *not* the same. Perhaps the most famous example of this is the Olsen twins, Mary-Kate and Ashley. Mary-Kate dyed her hair dark so she would look less like her sister, and when the sisters received a star on Hollywood's Walk of Fame, they requested that they be given separate stars (a request that was denied). Like almost everyone, they recognize and value their uniqueness—and they would like others to do so as well.

How is it possible that people who are as much alike as twins can still have distinct identities? It is possible because of the ways in which identities are created and how these identities are "performed" in daily life—the topics we take up in the next section.

Identity Development Through Communication

In communication, our understanding of identity development arises out of a theory called symbolic interactionism (Blumer, 1969; Mead, 1934). According to this theory, individuals' meanings for the objects, actions, and people around them arise out of social, or symbolic, interaction with others. What you define as beautiful, ethical, and even edible is based on what you have heard and experienced during your interactions with others. You likely learned through observing and communicating

reflected appraisals
the idea that people's self-images arise primarily from the ways that others view them and from the many messages they have received from others about who they are

looking-glass self
the idea that self-image results from the images others reflect back to an individual

particular others
the important people in an individual's life whose opinions and behavior influence the various aspects of identity

with others that eating lobster is a luxury but that eating bugs is disgusting. We develop and reveal identities through communication interactions in much the same way. In this section we describe three communication processes involved in identity development—*reflected appraisals*, *social comparison*, and *self-fulfilling prophecies*—and explore how they shape one's sense of self, or self-concept.

Reflected Appraisals

A primary influence on identity development is a communication process called **reflected appraisals** (Sullivan, 1953). The term describes the idea that people's self-images arise primarily from the ways that others view them and from the many messages they have received from others about who they are. This concept is also often referred to as the **looking-glass self** (Cooley, 1902; Edwards, 1990), a term that highlights the idea that your self-image results from the images others reflect back to you.

The process of identity development begins at birth. Although newborns do not at first have a sense of self (Manczak, 1999; Rosenblith, 1992), as they interact with others, their identities develop. How others act toward and respond to them influences how infants build their identities. For example, as infants assert their personalities or temperaments, others respond to those characteristics. Parents of a calm and cheerful baby are strongly drawn to hold and play with the infant, and they describe the child to others as a "wonderful" baby. On the other hand, parents who have a tense and irritable baby may feel frustrated if they cannot calm their child and might respond more negatively to the infant. They may engage in fewer positive interactions with their baby and describe the child as "difficult." These interactions shape the baby's identity for him or herself and for the parents, as well as for others who have contact with the family (Papalia, Olds, & Feldman, 2002).

A study of shy and reticent male toddlers explored the influence that parents can have on their sons' interactions (Phelps, Belsky, & Crnic, 1998). The researchers found that parents who encouraged their sons to interact with others and to take social risks became less reserved over time; when parents did not encourage their sons in this way, however, the children maintained their shy and reticent nature. As this study shows, parental communication influences how children behave and ultimately how they, as well as others, view them.

The reflected appraisal process is repeated with family, friends, teachers, acquaintances, and strangers as the individual grows. If as a child you heard your parents tell their friends that you were gifted, your teachers praised your classroom performance, and acquaintances commented on how verbal you were, you probably came to see yourself those ways. However, if family, friends, and acquaintances commented on how you couldn't "carry a tune in a bucket" and held their ears when you sang, then over time you likely came to view yourself as someone who couldn't sing. Through numerous interactions with other people about your appearance, your abilities, your personality, and your character, you developed your identities as a student, friend, male or female, or singer, among others. To read about one student's experiences with reflected appraisals, see *It Happened to Me: Bianca*.

Interaction with two types of "others" influences this process of identity development. George Herbert Mead (1934) described them as *particular others* and the *generalized other*. **Particular others** are the important people in your life whose opinions and behavior influence the various aspects of your identity. Parents, caregivers, siblings, and close friends are obvious particular others who influence your identity. Some particular others may strongly influence just one of your identities or one aspect of an identity. If you perceive that your soccer coach believes you have no talent, then you may see yourself as a poor soccer player even if friends and family tell you otherwise.

Your sense of yourself is also influenced, however, by your understanding of the **generalized other**, or the collection of roles, rules, norms, beliefs, and attitudes endorsed by the community in which you live. You come to understand what is valued and important in your community via your interactions with significant others, strangers, acquaintances, various media such as movies, books, and television, and the social institutions that surround you. For example, if you notice that your family, friends, and even strangers comment on people's appearances, that the media focus on people's attractiveness, that certain characteristics consistently are associated with attractiveness, and that people who look a certain way seem to get lighter sentences in criminal proceedings, get more attention at school, and are hired for the best jobs, then you develop an internalized view of what the generalized other values and rewards with regard to appearance. You then will compare yourself to others within your community to see if you fulfill the norms for attractiveness, which then affects how this aspect of your identity develops.

It Happened to Me: *Bianca*

I really relate to the concept of reflected appraisals. I was born in Brazil with an Italian mother and a Brazilian father. When I attended an all-girls private school in Cleveland, Ohio, I had a very difficult time blending in. After spending so much time with these other students, however, I gradually began feeling like one of them. I was speaking English all the time, even at home with my parents (whose first language is not English). I felt like I was an American. People communicated to me as an American. In my junior year, I moved back to Brazil. Being Brazilian and speaking Portuguese fluently, their reflections of me made me feel completely Brazilian and I began to lose my sense of American identity. Even today, at a U.S. college, I feel confused about my selfhood because of the different ways I am reflected off of people depending on which nationality group I am hanging out with.

Gradually, you begin to see yourself in specific ways, which in turn influences your communication behavior, which further shapes others' views of you, and so on. Thus, individual identities are created and re-created by communication interactions throughout one's life.

However, reflected appraisals aren't the only type of communication interaction that shapes identity. Each of us also engages in a process called *social comparison*, which influences how we see and value our identities.

Social Comparisons

Not only do we see ourselves as possessing specific characteristics, we also evaluate how desirable those characteristics are. As we discussed, the generalized other becomes the basis for our understanding of which characteristics are valued. For example, Amish children learn through their interactions with family, friends, the church, and their community that aggression is a negative trait that one should minimize or eliminate (Kraybill, 1989). In contrast, in gangs, aggression is valued and encouraged, and community members learn this as well (Sanders, 1994).

Children's self-images are affected by their teachers' reflected appraisals.

Once we understand what characteristics are valued (or disdained) in our communities, we assess whether we individually possess more, or less, of them than do others in our communities. We compare ourselves to others to determine how we measure up, and through this social comparison, we evaluate ourselves. In this way the groups we compare ourselves to—our reference groups—play an important role in shaping how we view ourselves.

We compare ourselves to others in our identity group and decide how we rate. A woman might say, "I look good for my age," comparing herself to others in her reference group, which in this case is other women her age. Similarly, classmates often want to know each other's test scores and grades so that they can decide how to view their own performances. For example, how would you feel if you earned a 78 on an exam and your grade was the highest in the class? What if 78 were the lowest

generalized other
the collection of roles, rules, norms, beliefs, and attitudes endorsed by the community in which a person lives

We compare ourselves with others in our reference group and decide how we measure up.

grade in the class? Thus, your evaluation of yourself and your abilities is shaped not only by a specific trait but also by how it compares to the traits of others in your reference group. However, your self-evaluation can vary depending on what you use as a reference group. If you compare your appearance to that of your friends, colleagues, and classmates, you may feel pretty good. However, if you use the idealized images of actors and models in magazines and movies, you may not feel as positively about your attractiveness.

Self-Fulfilling Prophecy

Communication interactions can also influence one's identity through a process known as the **self-fulfilling prophecy**, meaning that when an individual expects something to occur, the expectation increases the likelihood that it will. For example, if you believe you can perform well on an exam, you are likely to study and prepare for the exam, which typically results in your doing well. Others also have expectations for you that can influence your behavior. For example, if your sales manager believes you are a poor salesperson, she may assign you to a territory where you won't have access to big accounts, and she may refuse to send you to sales conferences where your skills could be honed. If you still succeed, she may believe that you just got lucky. However, because you have a poor territory, don't have the opportunity to enhance your sales skills, and receive no rewards for your successes, you probably will not be a very good salesperson.

Thus, the belief in a particular outcome influences people to act and communicate in ways that will make the outcome more likely; in turn, the outcome influences how we perceive ourselves. For example, parents often unwittingly influence how their children perform in math and how their children perceive themselves as mathematicians. If a child hears her mother complain about her own poor math skills and how unlikely it is that her child will do better, the child is unlikely to succeed in math classes. When the child encounters difficulty with math, the messages she heard from her mother may increase the likelihood that she will give up and say, "Well, I'm just not good at math." On the other hand, if a child hears messages that she is good at math, she is more likely to keep trying and work harder when faced with a difficult math problem. This, in turn, will influence her to see herself as a competent mathematician.

Self-fulfilling prophecies can have a powerful effect on an individual's performance, especially when they are grounded in stereotypes of one's identity. For example, stereotypes exist that Asian students excel at math, that African American students are less verbally competent than white students, and that females are worse at math and spatial reasoning than males. Studies have shown that even subtly or implicitly reminding individuals of these stereotypical expectations can impact their performance, a concept called **stereotype threat**.

In one study, African Americans who were simply reminded of race performed significantly worse on a verbal exam than when the issue of race was not mentioned (Steele & Aronson, 1995); and in another study, Asian American students performed better on a math test when reminded of their race (Shih, Pittinsky & Ambady, 1999). In a similar study, females who were cued to think about gender performed worse on math and spatial ability tests than when the issue of gender was not raised (McGlone & Aronson, 2006). Yet another study found that white male engineering students solved significantly fewer problems when told that they were part of a study to examine why Asian Americans perform better in math than when told it was simply a timed test (Smith & White, 2002).

These studies reveal that individuals' performances can be enhanced or hampered when they are reminded, even implicitly, of expectations related to important identities. This is true not only of sex and gender but also has been shown to be true of socioeconomic status (Croizet & Claire, 1998) and age. These findings remind us that we need to be careful about creating self-fulfilling prophecies for others and allowing others' expectations to become self-fulfilling prophecies for us.

self-fulfilling prophecy
when an individual expects something to occur, the expectation increases the likelihood that it will

stereotype threat
process in which reminding individuals of stereotypical expectations regarding important identities can impact their performance

Through repeated communication interactions such as reflected appraisals, social comparisons, and self-fulfilling prophecies, we come to have a sense of who we are. This sense of who we are is referred to as one's *self-concept*.

Self-Concept

As we have suggested, identity generally continues to evolve; at the same time, individuals also have some fairly stable perceptions about themselves. These stable perceptions are referred to as self-concept. **Self-concept** includes your understanding about your unique characteristics as well as your similarities to, and differences from, others. Your self-concept is based on your reflected appraisals and social comparisons. However, reflected appraisals only go so far. When someone describes you in a way that you reject, they have violated your self-concept. For example, if you think of yourself as open and outgoing, but a friend calls you "a very private person," you are likely to think the friend doesn't know you very well. Thus, your self-concept is an internal image you hold of yourself. It affects the external image you project to others, and in turn, your self-concept influences your communication behavior. If you think of yourself as ethical, you may correct others or assert your views when they behave in ways you believe are unethical.

Self-esteem is part of an individual's self-concept. It describes how you evaluate yourself overall. It arises out of how you perceive and interpret reflected appraisals and social comparisons. Like identity, self-esteem can alter over time. It functions as a lens through which we interpret reflected appraisals and social comparisons, which may make it hard to change. For example, if you have relatively high self-esteem, you may discount negative reflected appraisals and overgeneralize positive ones. So, if a student with high self-esteem fails an exam, he may attribute the failure to external factors (e.g., the test was unfair) rather than to himself. On the other hand, a person with low self-esteem may see negative reflected appraisals where none exist and may consistently compare herself to unrealistic reference groups. In addition, this person is more likely to attribute a failure to the self (I'm not smart enough) than to external factors.

Because self-esteem is such a powerful lens through which you see the world, your self-concept may not be entirely consistent with how others see you. Several additional factors can create a mismatch between how you see yourself and how others do. First, your self-image and the feedback you receive may be out of synch because others don't want to hurt your feelings or because you respond negatively when faced with information that contradicts your self-image. Few people tell their friends and loved ones that they are not as attractive, talented, smart, or popular as they themselves think they are. Why? They don't want make others feel bad and/or they don't want to deal with the recipient's feelings of anger or sadness.

Second, if you hold onto an image of yourself that is no longer accurate, you may have a distorted self-image—or one that doesn't match how others see you. For example, if you were chubby in grade school, you may still think of yourself as overweight, even if you are now very slim. Similarly, if you were one of the brightest students in your high school, you may continue to see yourself as among the brightest students at your college, even if your GPA slips.

Finally, people may not recognize or accept their positive qualities because of modesty or because they value self-effacement. If your social or cultural group discourages people from viewing themselves as better than others, you may feel uncomfortable hearing praise. In such cases, the individual may only compare himself to exceptionally attractive or talented people or may refuse to acknowledge his strengths in public settings. In Japanese culture the appearance of modesty (*kenkyo*) is highly valued (Davies & Ikeno, 2002). A similar trait of "yieldedness to others" (*glassenheit*) leads the Amish to downplay their accomplishments (Kraybill, 1989). As you can see, both culture and identity are deeply embedded in our communication.

self-concept
the understanding of one's unique characteristics as well as the similarities to, and differences from, others

self-esteem
part of one's self-concept; arises out of how one perceives and interprets reflected appraisals and social comparisons

Yet another aspect of self-concept is self-respect. While self-esteem generally refers to feeling good about one's self, **self-respect** describes a person who treats others—and expects themselves to be treated—with respect (Rawls, 1995). Self-respect demands that individuals protest the violation of their rights and that they do so within the boundaries of dignity and respect for others. However, people with high self-esteem may not necessarily have self-respect (Roland & Foxx, 2003). For example, some people with high self-esteem may not treat others with respect or respond to violations of the self with dignity. Many atrocities, such as those committed by Saddam Hussein against his people, have been waged by those who, because of their sense of superiority, thought they had the right to dominate and harm others.

Throughout this discussion of identity development we have focused on four separate constructs: reflected appraisals, social comparison, self-fulfilling prophecy, and self-concept. However, identity development is a circular process in which these constructs are interrelated. For example, reflected appraisals influence your self-concept, which affects your communication behavior, which in turn shapes how others see you and, ultimately, what they reflect back to you. Then the process starts all over again. To view an illustration of this process, see *Visual Summary 3.1: Identity Development Through Communication*. The issue of identity goes beyond this complex process of development, however. In everyday life we enact or "perform" these identities. Let's see how this process works.

Performance of Individual Identity

The **performance of identity** refers to the process or means by which we show the world who we think we are. For example, many Green Bay Packers fans express their identity by wearing team colors, calling themselves Cheeseheads, and wearing plastic cheese wedges on their heads. In contrast, Pittsburgh Steelers fans often wave "the terrible towel" to cheer on their team. People also perform their identities in more subtle ways every day—with the type of clothing or jewelry (including wedding rings) that they choose to wear or the name they use. Some celebrities have taken stage names that the public is more familiar with than their legal, birth names. For example, Larry King was born Larry Zieger. Charlie Sheen's name is Carlos Estevez. Lady Gaga's real name is Steffani Germanotta. What do these different names communicate to the public? How do these names help these celebrities perform their public identities?

Communication style is another way people perform, or enact, their identities. For example, do you speak to your mother in the same way that you speak with your friends? If you bring a friend home, do you feel like a different person as he watches you communicate with your family? If so, you're not alone. Most people adapt their communication to the identity they wish to perform in a given context.

In fact, the branch of communication studies called performance studies focuses on the ways people perform, or communicate, their various roles. In other words,

self-respect
treating others, and expecting to be treated, with respect and dignity

performance of identity
the process or means by which we show the world who we think we are

Identity Development Through Communication

Reflected Appraisal (The Looking-Glass Self)

Social Comparisons

Self-Fulfilling Prophecies

How I see myself is developed through communication with others . . .

- Interactions with parents and others shape our early identity and sense of self.
- The process is repeated with family, friends, teachers, acquaintances, and strangers.
- **Particular others** are important people in our lives who influence aspects of our identity.
- **Generalized others** are the collection of roles, rules, norms, beliefs, and attitudes endorsed by our community.

and how I compare myself to others . . .

- Through our interactions with others, we learn what characteristics are valued (or disdained) by others.
- Then, we assess whether we have more or fewer of those characteristics to determine how we measure up to others in our **identity group**.

each of which affects my evaluation of myself.

affects how I communicate with them and they with me . . .

- When we expect something to occur, that expectation increases the likelihood that it will.
- A belief in a particular outcome influences people to act and communicate in ways that make the outcome more likely.
- Others can also cause their prophecies about us to come true by communicating with us as though they will come true.

Self-Concept

Self-Concept

- Self-concept is composed of the fairly stable perceptions we have of ourselves.
- It includes our understanding of similarities and differences between ourselves and others.
- It is an internal image we have of ourselves and affects the external image we project to others.
- It influences our communication behavior.
- **Self-esteem** is the part of self-concept that is the internal valuation of what we see in the looking glass.
- **Self-respect** the extent to which one feels entitled to regard and respect from self and others.

enacting identities
performing scripts deemed proper for particular identities

role expectations
the expectation that one will perform in a particular way because of the social role occupied

mutable
subject to change

people **enact identities** by performing scripts that are proper for those identities. In his analysis of how tourists tell stories about their trips, Chaim Noy of the Hebrew University of Jerusalem identifies the ways that tourists perform their identities. As a part of this performance of identity, tourists emphasize the ways that their travels have changed their identities and how they view the world. While tourists are often viewed as consuming or watching other cultural identities on performance, Noy underscores the ways "that tourists are in effect acting protagonists who perform on the stages of tourism" (2004, p. 116). For example, in his study, Noy tells the story of a backpacker who tells others of his adventures and performs a form of tourism: "I told everyone of my adventures and so I was a kind of an attraction. It was nice" (qtd. in Noy, p. 130). Through the use of narrative in his communication, this backpacker is able to perform an identity of a tourist who has seen and experienced something special.

Nadene Vevea (2008) analyzed how people use tattoos and body piercing to perform their identities. In her interviews, she found that people use body art for many different reasons, to communicate many different feelings. For example, "some of the fraternity brothers who responded to my survey all got matching tattoos to signify their membership but use body art as a positive connection between friends to show loyalty to one another" (p. 22).

Sometimes we enact family roles; other times we enact occupational roles. The enactment of identity is closely tied to one's movements into and out of different cultural communities and one's expectations regarding particular roles. Police officers, physicians, and teachers also enact particular roles in performing their occupations. If one of these professionals—say, a teacher—steps out of the appropriate role and tries to be the best friend of her students, problems can arise. In Minnesota, a physician "has been reprimanded for allegedly touching 21 female patients inappropriately during what were described as 'unconventional' medical exams" (Lerner, 2008). In this case, "Dr. Jed E. Downs, 51, reportedly would close his eyes and make 'unusual sounds or facial expressions' while examining female patients, according to an investigation by the Minnesota Board of Medical Practice" (Lerner, 2008). In this case, we expect physicians to communicate—verbally and nonverbally—in professionally appropriate ways. When the physician does not do this, problems can arise.

Thus, we perform various roles and communicate with others based on **role expectations**. If you are pulled over for a traffic violation, you expect the police officer to perform in a particular way. In turn, you communicate with the officer based on a prescribed script. If you do not enact the expected role or if the police officer does not enact the prescribed role, then confusion—or worse—can occur. Everyone carries many scripts with them into all kinds of interactions. For example, the authors of this book are all pet owners. When we speak to our pets, we sometimes repeat communication patterns that our parents used with us when we were children. Pets are not children, yet we often communicate to them as if they were because the script is familiar to us.

As we noted earlier, identities are **mutable**, or subject to change. When people change identities, they also change the way they perform them. For example, as people age, if they perform the "grown-up" role appropriately, they hope others will treat them more like adults. If they don't change the way they behave, then they might be told to "stop acting like a child."

Because identities are not fixed, sometimes you see mismatches between the performance of identity and any one identity category. Sometimes the difference between identity performance and identity category can be rather benign. For example, if we say that someone is young at heart, we are saying that we perceive that person's identity performance to resemble that of someone much younger in years. Thus, two people may be the same chronological age, but one may listen to contemporary music, watch current films and television shows, and dress according to the latest fashion trends. The other may listen to oldies radio stations and dress as she did years ago.

Sometimes this disconnect is viewed much more negatively. When people enact a gender identity at odds with the cultural identity category, such as when males perform identity scripts that are typically female, they may be ridiculed, ostracized, or worse. Still, how do particular identity categories, or ways of performing them, acquire meaning? How do you know what a particular category is supposed to "look like" or how it is to be performed? The answer has to do with societal forces, the subject we take up next.

TEST YOUR KNOWLEDGE

- What are the key concepts in identity development?
- How is identity performed?

THE INDIVIDUAL, IDENTITY, AND SOCIETY

The development of individual identities is influenced by societal forces. Therefore, you cannot understand yourself or others without understanding how society constructs or defines characteristics such as gender, sexuality, race, religion, social class, and nationality. For example, as a child, you were probably told (some of) the differences between boys and girls. Some messages came from your parents, such as how boys' and girls' clothing differs or how girls should behave as compared with boys. Other messages came from your schoolmates, who may have told you that "they" (either boys or girls) had "cooties." You may also have picked up messages about gender differences, or about any of the identity categories mentioned, from television or other media. By combining messages from these various sources you began to construct images of what is considered normal for each identity category.

Communication scholars are particularly interested in how identities are communicated, and created, through communication. For example, in his work focusing on communication interactions, Donal Carbaugh (2007) is particularly interested in studying intercultural encounters, and he focuses on how communication interaction reveals insights into cultural identities.

When people enact identities that are contrary to social expectations, they may be pressured to change their performance. Thus, boys and girls who do not perform their gender identities in ways prescribed by society can be called "sissies" or "tomboys." People who do not perform their racial identities in ways that are expected are sometimes called "oreos," "apples," "coconuts," "bananas," or "race traitors." Although the Church of Jesus Christ of Latter Day Saints has banned the use of alcohol, those Mormons who do drink are sometimes called "Jack Mormons." Similarly, a person who does not perform heterosexuality as expected might be seen as gay or lesbian. Chaz Bono, son of Cher and Sonny Bono, has spoken publicly about his decision to transition from female to male starting in 2009. In 2011, the film, *Becoming Chaz*, and the book, *Transitions*, both were released and tell Chaz's story of gender change from Chastity Bono.

Those who do not conform to expected social communication or performance patterns may become victims of threats, name-calling, violence, and even murder (Sloop, 2004). These aggressive responses are meant to ensure that everyone behaves in ways that clearly communicate appropriate identity categories. For example, after a lengthy lawsuit, Shannon Faulkner became the first woman to enroll at the Citadel, South Carolina's formerly all-male military college. During the time she attended the school, she received death threats and had to be accompanied by federal

Many parents choose clothes that communicate the gender of their babies.

Did You Know?

Performing Identity: Chaz Bono

What difference does it make who you think you are and who others think you are? How much of your identity is a feeling that you have about who you are?

In his own words, Chaz Bono describes the difficult journey of transitioning from female to male. Communication plays a key role in this transition.

> I always felt like the male from the time I was a child. There wasn't much feminine about me. I believe that gender is something between your ears not between your legs. That is something I discovered in the early 90s. It was just a long process of being comfortable enough to do something about it. I was turning 40 and I thought it's now or never. I want to still feel vibrant and be able to enjoy my life in a male body and not wait until I am an old man.... I will be changing for about four to five years in total but I'll be on testosterone for the rest of my life.... The nice thing about this process is it is slow. I am literally going through puberty.... The most important thing about this for me is that my outsides are finally starting to match my insides. I feel like I'm living in my body for the first time and it feels really good (Chaz Bono opens up, 2009).

marshals (Bennett-Haigney, 1995). Thus, some groups in society have strong feelings regarding how identities should be performed, and they may act to ensure that identities are performed according to societal expectations.

In this section of the chapter we will look at a range of primary identity categories. (See *Visual Summary 3.2: Dimensions of Self* to review the most salient identity categories for most people.) Note that each is a product of both individual and societal forces. Thus, whatever you think your individual identity might be, you have to negotiate that identity within the larger society and the meanings society ascribes to it.

Racial Identity

Despite its frequent use, the term *race* is difficult to define. Historically, races were distinguished predominantly by physical aspects of appearance that are generally hereditary. A race was defined as a group with gene frequencies differing from those of other groups. However, many physical anthropologists and other scholars now argue that because there is as much genetic variation among the members of any given race as between racial groups, the concept of race has lost its usefulness (Hirschman, 2003).

Despite the difficulty in accurately delineating the various races, race is still a relevant concept in most societies, and individuals still align themselves with specific racial groups, which we discuss next.

Racial identity, the identification with a particular racial group, develops as a result of societal forces—because society defines what a race is and what it is called. This means that racial categories are not necessarily the same from country to country. For example, unlike the United States, the United Kingdom does not include people of Chinese origin in the category it calls Asian. For those in the United Kingdom, only those of Indian, Pakistani, and Bangladeshi origin are considered to be Asian. The Office for National Statistics has established racial categories for England and Wales and posted them on its Web site at **www.ons.gov.uk/about-statistics/classifications/archived/ethnic-interim/presenting-data/index.html.**

Even within the United States the categorization of racial groups has varied over time. The category *Hispanic* first appeared on the U.S. census form as a racial category

racial identity
identification with a particular racial group

Dimensions of Self

Social Meanings of these dimensions

Self

RACE
What are racial categories in my society? Another society?

GENDER
What are the gender categories in my society? What are gender expectations in another society?

ETHNICITY
What are ethnic groups in m society? What is their status in society?

AGE
Which ages are more valued in my society? What difference does age make in my society?

NATIONALITY
What does citizenship mean in my country? How do we view those without it?

RELIGION
Which religions are common in my society? How are varius religions viewed in society?

SEXUAL IDENTITY
Are all sexualities valued and treated equally in my society?

SOCIAL CLASS
How does my society organize social class? What are the characteristics of social class?

in 1980. In the 2000 census, however, Hispanic was categorized as an ethnicity, which one could select in addition to selecting a racial identity. Therefore, one could be both *Asian* (a race) and *Hispanic* (an ethnicity), or one could be both *white* (a race) and *Hispanic* (again, an ethnicity). Similarly, as Susan Koshy (2004) has noted, people from India were once labeled "non-white Caucasians," but today are categorized with Asian Americans on the U.S. census. These categorizations are important because historically they have affected the way people are treated. While discrimination based on race is no longer legal, we continue to live with its consequences. For example, although slavery ended almost 150 years ago in the United States, many churches, schools, and other social institutions remain racially segregated (Hacker, 2003).

Although people often think of racial categories as scientifically or biologically based, the ways they have changed over time and differ across cultures highlight their cultural rather than their biological basis. How cultures describe and define specific races affect who is considered to belong to a given race and, consequently, how those individuals are treated. As anthropologist Gloria Marshall explains: "Comparative studies of these popular racial typologies show them to vary from place to place; studies of these popular racial classifications also show them to vary from one historical period to another" (1993, p 117). Moreover, communication is a strong factor in furthering, affecting, or altering racial categories and identities to serve different social needs. For example, Guzman and Valdivia (2004) studied the media images of three Latinas—Salma Hayek, Frida Kahlo, and Jennifer Lopez—to see how gender and Latinidad are reinforced through the media (see Chapter 10). Face-to-face communication also influences peoples' ideas about racial identities. If individuals have little contact with people of a different racial group, it is especially likely that one or two encounters may lead them to draw conclusions about the entire group.

Beginning with the 2000 census, the U.S. government has allowed people to claim a **multiracial identity** (Jones & Smith, 2001). This category recognizes that some people self-identify as having more than one racial identity. So, how should we categorize Barack Obama? While "there is much to celebrate in seeing Obama's victory as a victory for African Americans," writer Marie Arana (2008) also thinks that "Obama's ascent to the presidency is more than a triumph for blacks." She feels that "Barack Obama is not our first black president. He is our first biracial, bicultural president." What difference does it make if we see Obama as our first African American president or as our first biracial president? As you think through this issue, you can see the complexities of race and racial politics within a culture.

National Identity

Racial identity can often be confused and conflated with **national identity**. We often misuse the notion of nationality when we ask someone "What's your nationality?" but what we really want to know is their ancestry or ethnic background. *Nationality* or national identity refers to a person's citizenship. In other words, Madonna's nationality is not Italian, but U.S. American, as she holds U.S. citizenship. John F. Kennedy's nationality was not Irish; he was a U.S. citizen. Many U.S. Americans did not actively choose their national identity; they simply acquired it by being born in the United States. Although many of us have not actively chosen our national identity, most of us are content with—or even proud—of it.

Like our other identities, the importance placed on national identity can vary, depending on many factors. In their study of national identity, John Hutcheson et al. (2004) found that U.S. Americans communicated a much stronger sense of national identity after September 11, 2001. Do you remember seeing many U.S. flags flying in your neighborhood after September 11? This resurgence of national identity was reflected in the media as well.

Because the ability to travel has made the world seem so much smaller and borders seem more permeable, old ideas of national identity may no longer apply. For example, what does it mean to be Irish? In one study, Vera Sheridan (2004) traced the journey of Vietnamese refugees who moved to Ireland to become Irish citizens. Although they may not meet our expectations of what Irish people look like, their nationality is now Irish.

However, as communication scholars Laura Lengel and John T. Warren (2005, p. 5) remind us, "nation does not equal culture or cultural identity; it is merely one facet." Thus, identifying someone's nationality provides a glimpse of only one aspect of their cultural identity, which is both communicated to them, communicated by them, and communicated about them.

Ethnic Identity

Although race and ethnicity are related concepts, the concept of ethnicity is based on the idea of social (rather than genetic) groups. Ethnic groups typically share a national or tribal affiliation, religious beliefs, language, and/or cultural and traditional origins and background. A person's **ethnic identity** comes from identification with a particular group with which they share some or all of these characteristics. Thus, some U.S. citizens say that they are Irish because they feel a close relationship with Irish heritage and custom, even though they are no longer Irish citizens—or perhaps never were. Likewise, in the United States many U.S. Americans think of themselves as Italian, Greek, German, Japanese, Chinese, or Swedish even though they do not hold passports from those countries. Nonetheless, they feel a strong affinity for these places because of their ancestry. Unlike national identity, ethnic identity does not require that some nation's government recognizes you as a member of its country. It is also unlike racial identity, in that any racial group may contain a number of ethnic identities. For example, people who are categorized racially as white identify with a range of ethnic groups, including Swedish, Polish, Dutch, French, Italian, and Greek.

In other parts of the world, ethnic identities are sometimes called tribal identities. For example, "in Kenya, there are 50 tribes, or ethnic groups, with members sharing similar physical traits and cultural traditions, as well as roughly the same language and economic class" (Wax, 2005, p. 18). Tribal identities are important not only across Africa, but also in many nations around the world, including Afghanistan (Lagarde, 2005). In some societies, tribal or ethnic identity can determine who is elected to office, who is hired for particular jobs, and who is likely to marry whom. In Malaysia the three major ethnic groups are Malay, Indian, and Chinese. Since the Malay are in power and make decisions that influence all three groups, being Malay gives one an important advantage. In the United States, however, the ethnic identities of many white Americans are primarily symbolic, as they have minimal influence in everyday life (Waters, 1990). Even if ethnic identity does not play an important role in your life, it can carry great significance in other parts of the world.

Gender Identity

Similar to race, gender is a concept constructed through communication. *Gender* refers to the cultural differences between masculinity and femininity, while *sex* refers to the biological differences between males and females. Gender describes the set of expectations cultures develop regarding how men and women are expected to look, behave, communicate, and live. For example, in U.S. culture women (who are biologically female) are expected to perform femininity (a cultural construction) through activities such as nurturing, crossing their legs and not taking up too much room when sitting, speaking with vocal variety and expressivity, and wearing makeup. How do people respond to women who cut their hair in a flattop, sit sprawled across the couch, speak in an aggressive manner, and refuse to wear makeup? Often, they call them names or ridicule them; occasionally they even

ethnic identity
identification with a particular group with which one shares some or all of these characteristics: national or tribal affiliation, religious beliefs, language, and/or cultural and traditional origins and background

In many families in the United States, gender roles follow a cultural rule about inside versus outside activities or chores.

mistake them for males because these behaviors are so culturally attached to notions of masculinity.

Gender identity refers to how and to what extent one identifies with the social construction of masculinity and femininity. Gender roles and expectations have changed enormously over the centuries, and cultural groups around the world differ in their gender expectations. How do we develop our notions of gender, or what it means to be masculine or feminine? We learn through communication: through the ways that people talk about gender, through the media images we see, and through observing the ways people communicate to males and females. For example, while crying is acceptable for girls, young boys receive many messages that they are not supposed to cry.

A leading scholar on gender, Judith Butler (1990, 1993) was one of the first to argue that gender identity is not biological but based on performances. She asserted that people's identities flow from the ways they have seen them performed in the past. In other words, a man's performance of male identity rests on previous performances of masculinity. Because the performances of traditional masculinity have been repeated for so long, individuals come to believe that masculine identity and behaviors are natural. However, some people choose to enact their identity in nontraditional ways, and their performances will be interpreted against the backdrop of what is considered acceptable and appropriate.

In many families in the United States, gender roles follow a cultural rule about inside versus outside activities or chores. Those activities that take place inside the house are widely viewed as feminine and, therefore, should be performed by a female. Activities that take place outside are seen as masculine and are expected to be performed by a male.

The case of South African runner Caster Semenya underscores the complexity of gender. After Semenya achieved some very fast running times, accusations about her gender arose. If she was not a woman, then she could not compete in women's track events. The IAAF (International Association of Athletics Federations), the governing body of track and field events, decided to test her gender through a series of tests. While the "details of the medical testing that Semenya underwent will remain confidential" (Zinzer, 2010), the difficulty in knowing Semenya's gender highlights the complexity of categorizing people. After 11 months in limbo, the IAAF finally cleared her to compete in women's track events again. The issue of identifying males and females can be problematic (see Table 3.1 for the relative numbers of people who are intersex).

Sexual Identity

Sexual identity refers to which of the various categories of sexuality one identifies with. Because our culture is dynamic, it has no set number of sexual identity categories, but perhaps the most prominent are heterosexual, gay or lesbian, and bisexual. Although most people in our culture recognize these categories today, they have not always been acknowledged or viewed in the same ways. In his *History of Sexuality*, French historian and theorist Michel Foucault (1988) notes that over the course of history, notions of sexuality and sexual identities changed. In certain eras and cultures, when children were born with both male and female sexual organs, a

gender identity
how and to what extent one identifies with the social construction of masculinity and femininity

sexual identity
which of the various categories of sexuality one identifies with

Table 3.1 Statistics on Intersex Births, 2000	
People whose chromosomal pattern is neither XX nor XY	1 in 1,666 births
People whose bodies differ from standard male or female	1 in 100 births
People receiving surgery to "normalize" genital appearance	1 or 2 in 1,000 births

Source: Intersex Society of North America (2005). How common is intersex? Retrieved June 12, 2006, from www.isna.org/faq/frequency

condition referred to as *intersexuality*, they were not necessarily operated on or forced to be either male or female.

Many people think of sexuality or sexual identity as private, but it frequently makes its way into the public arena. In everyday life, we often encounter people who will personally introduce us to their husbands or wives, a gesture that shares a particular aspect of their sexual identity. However, our society often exposes an individual's sexual identity to public scrutiny. For example, in 2006, U.S. Representative Mark Foley resigned from Congress amid questions that he sent inappropriate text messages and instant messages to male teenagers who had been congressional pages. The scandal led him to publicly disclose that he was gay (Candiotti et al., 2006). Senator Larry Craig's arrest for solicitation of sex in a men's restroom at the St. Paul–Minneapolis Airport became national news in 2007. Media coverage drew attention to that particular restroom—although by the end of 2008 it began to lose its appeal as a tourist destination (Sen. Craig restroom, 2008). In contrast to Representative Foley, Senator Craig insisted, "Let me be clear: I am not gay. I never have been gay" (Milbank, 2007). Because identity categories are social constructions, there is not always agreement about what they mean. Clearly, in the public arena, people manipulate these identity categories to help retrieve their reputations when their sexual activities become public.

In daily life, a person's sexual identity plays a role in such mundane matters as selecting which magazines to read and which television shows and movies to watch, as well as choosing places to socialize, people to associate with, and types of products to purchase. Television shows, magazines, books, Internet sites, and other cultural products are targeted toward particular sexual identities, or they assume a certain level of public knowledge about sexual identities and groups. For example, *Gary Unmarried*, *Millionaire Matchmaker*, and *Real Housewives of Orange County* presume an understanding of U.S. heterosexual culture. In contrast, Logo cable channel is specifically geared to gay and lesbian viewers. *Modern Family* and *Brothers and Sisters*, in contrast, include gay characters. These communication texts can reinforce, confirm, or challenge our notions of various categories of sexual identity.

Age Identity

Age, when thought of strictly as the number of years you've been alive, is an important identity for everyone. But your **age identity** is a combination of how you feel about your age as well as what others understand that age to mean. How old is "old"? How young is "young"? Have you noticed how your own notions of age have changed over the years? When you were in first grade, did high school students seem old to you? While *age* is a relative term, so are the categories we use for age groups. Today, for example, we use the terms *teenager*, *senior citizen*, *adult*, and *minor*, but these terms have meaning only within our social and legal system. For example, the voting age is 18, but people have to wait until they are 21 to buy liquor. Someone who commits a heinous crime can be charged as an adult, even if he or she is not yet 18. Still, whether a person feels like an adult goes beyond what the law decrees and comes from some set of factors that is far more complex.

Other age-related concepts are culturally determined as well. For example, the notion of "teenager" has come into use only relatively recently in the United States, and it is certainly not a universal category (Palladino, 1996). The notion that people have "midlife" crises is not a universal cultural phenomenon, either. Moreover, these age categories are relatively fluid, meaning that there are no strict guidelines about where they begin and end, even though they do influence how we think about ourselves (Trethewey, 2001). For example, because people today generally live longer, the span of years thought of as middle age comes later in our lives. These changes all illustrate the dynamic nature of age identity and the categories we have for it.

You probably feel your age identity when you shop for clothes. How do you decide what is "too young" for you? Or what is "too old"? Do you consciously consider the messages your clothing communicates about your age? As you reflect on

age identity
a combination of self-perception of age along with what others understand that age to mean

social class identity
an informal ranking of people in a culture based on their income, occupation, education, dwelling, child-rearing habits, and other factors

your shopping experiences, think about the tensions between what you like (the individual forces) and what others might think (societal forces). Here you see the tension that drives all social identities, including age.

Social Class Identity

Social class identity refers to an informal ranking of people in a culture based on their income, occupation, education, dwelling, child-rearing habits, and other factors (Online Glossary, 2005). Examples of social classes in this country include working class, middle class, upper middle class, and upper class. Most people in the United States identify themselves as middle class (Baker, 2003). However, there is no single agreed-upon definition for each of the classes. For example, the Census Bureau describes the middle class as being composed of the 20 percent of the population who earn between $40,000 and $95,000 (Baker, 2003), while the Drum Major Institute for Public Policy (2005) reports that the middle class conventionally has come to include families with incomes between $25,000 and $100,000. However, even 16.8 percent of those with incomes over $110,000 self-identify as middle class (Baker, 2003).

In his work on social class, French sociologist Pierre Bourdieu (1984) found that people of the same social class tended to view the world similarly: They defined art in similar ways, and they enjoyed similar sports and other aspects of everyday life. Moreover, based on his study of social class, Paul Fussell (1992) noted that U.S. Americans communicate their social class in a wide variety of ways, some verbal and some nonverbal. For example, middle-class people tend to say "tuxedo," while upper-class people are more apt to say "dinner jacket." In the category of nonverbal elements that express social class identity, he included the clothes we wear, the way we decorate our homes, the magazines we read, the kinds of drinks we imbibe, and the ways we decorate our automobiles. We will discuss more about class and verbal and nonverbal communication in the next two chapters.

Those in occupations such as nursing, teaching, and policing soon may no longer be considered middle class. What other occupations have fallen or might fall from middle-class status? In their study *The Fragile Middle Class*, Teresa Sullivan and her colleagues noted the increasing numbers of bankruptcy filings (2001), especially among those in occupations that we consider securely middle class, such as teachers, dentists, accountants, and computer engineers. In the wake of the recent recession, there has been increasing public discussion about income inequality and its toll on the middle class. The recession has drawn attention to the very wealthy and the increasing wealth they are amassing while unemployment remains stubbornly high. These discussions may portend a new focus on social class identity.

How does your own speech reveal your social class background and identity? Can you identify aspects of your family's home, yard, interior decorating, and clothing that reveal social class identity?

One reason people in the United States avoid discussing social class is because they tend to believe that their country is based on *meritocracy*, meaning that people succeed or fail based on their own merit. This idea leads to claims such as "anyone can grow up to be president." However, this has not proven to be true. For example, until the election of Barack Obama in 2008, every president in the United States has been white, male, and, in all cases but one, Protestant. Social identity and class have a powerful impact on one's life, as they can determine where you go to school (and what quality of education you receive), where you shop (and what quality of resources you have access to), which leisure activities you participate in (on a scale from constructive and enriching to destructive and self-defeating), and who you are most likely to meet and with whom you are mostly likely to socialize. In this way, social class identity tends to reproduce itself; the social class one is born into is often the same as the social class one dies in. People who are working class tend to live around other working-class people, make friends with working-class people (who influence their expectations and behavior), and attend schools that reinforce working-class values. In an early study that showed how communication was used to perform social class identity in conjunction with gender and race, Gerry Philipsen (1992) noted that men tended to speak much less than women and rarely socialized

Did You Know?
Social Class ID Check

U.S. Americans often do not think much about their social class. Many U.S. Americans identify as "middle class," and many others don't really think about their social class. The questions below are meant to help you think through your social class and how it has shaped you and your communication experiences

1. What is your social class?
2. How important is your social class to you?
3. What and who have been the primary sources of socialization for you about your social class? Name specific persons. If relevant, identify the organizations or types of organization with which they were affiliated.
4. How, if at all, do you express your social class—through language, communication style, dress, accessories, music?
5. Does your awareness of your social class ever facilitate your communication with others? Explain.
6. Does your awareness of your social class ever hinder your communication with others? Explain.
7. What situations, if any, do you avoid because of apprehensions related to your social class?
8. What situations, if any, do you seek because of your social class?
9. What advantages, if any, do you enjoy based on your social class?
10. Do you know of any stereotypes about your social class? If so, list them.
11. Are you ever aware of stereotypes about your social class as you interact with others? Explain.
12. How do the media tend to depict your social class? Do media depictions correspond with your sense of your social class? Explain.

SOURCE: Reprinted by permission of Waveland Press, Inc., from Brenda J. Allen, *Difference Matters: Communicating Social Identity* (Long Grove, IL: Waveland Press, Inc., 2004). All rights reserved.

outside their working-class community, which he called "Teamsterville." More recently, Kristen Lucas (2011) studied how family is an important site for communication messages that "both encourage and discourage social mobility" (p. 95). By examining how families reproduce their working-class identity, we can see how there are contradictory messages sent to the children about social class and moving toward white-collar occupations.

In our earlier example of the 2011 census in India, the census form does not ask people about their caste. In that cultural context, "census officials worried the sensitive subject of caste in multicultural and secular India could upset the results of the population count" (Daigle, 2011). Social class can be a very sensitive topic in many cultures. To better understand your own social class identity, see *Did You Know? Social Class ID Check*.

Disability Identity

People can identify with or be identified as disabled for many different reasons. **Disability Identity** is often defined as having an impairment of some kind. Some people experience differences in hearing, sight, and/or mobility. Not all disabilities are visible or evident to others. In 1990, the United States passed the Americans with Disabilities Act, which recognized disability as an important identity that needed federal protection from discrimination. This act also defines "disability" in Section 12102:

The term "disability" means, with respect to an individual

(A.) a physical or mental impairment that substantially limits one or more major life activities of such individual;

(B.) a record of such an impairment; or

disability identity
identification with physical or mental impairment that substantially impact everyday life

(C.) being regarded as having such an impairment (Americans with Disabilities Act, 1990, 2008).

While this legal definition may be helpful to some, it does not tell us what this identity means and how it is performed by those who identify as disabled, nor does it tell us how disability is viewed by others.

It is through communication that "disability" as an identity gains its meaning in our society. As Deanna Fassett and Dana L. Morella explain,

> while someone might have a medical or physical condition that structures her/his experience, it is in her/his interactions with others that that condition takes on meaning and becomes what our collective social environment would consider disability, with all the punishments and privilege that entails. We build this social environment in our own mundane communication, in classrooms and faculty meetings; we learn and reiterate, often unknowingly, as institutional members, what is normal and what is not and what that means (p. 144).

If we are swimming in a sea of communication, the many meanings that we generate in everyday communication give meaning to "disability."

Like other identities, disability is performed; it is "always in the process of becoming, then disability is something we do, rather than something we are" (Henderson and Ostrander, 2008, p. 2). For example, in his study on disabled athletes who play wheelchair rugby, Kurt Lindemann found that "performances of disability, especially in a sport context, can subvert the stigma associated with physical disability in surprisingly effective ways" (2008, p. 113). By focusing on athletic activities, disabled people attempt to challenge stereotypical views of those with disabilities

People who are not disabled can become disabled and then develop this new identity as a part of their larger configuration of identities. For example, many people, as they grow older, may experience increasing hearing loss, reduced visual acuity, or other physical or mental impairments that can render them disabled. But disability, of course, is not limited to older people. How we talk about disability, see it in media images, and experience it in everyday life are all part of how we communicate about and construct the meanings of disability as an identity. In her study on autobiographical narratives of those growing up with chronic illness or disability, Linda Wheeler Cardillo found that "communication at all levels has a powerful impact on these persons and their experiences of difference. A deeper understanding of this experience and how it is shaped by communication can lead to more sensitive, respectful, affirming, and empowering communication on the part of health-care providers, parents, teachers, and others" (2010, p. 539).

Religious Identity

In the United States today, **religious identity** is becoming increasingly important. Religious identity is defined by one's spiritual beliefs. For example, although Jim hasn't been to a Catholic church in decades, he still identifies himself as Catholic due to his upbringing and the impact the religion has had on his outlook. Most researchers and writers agree that "religion is certainly one of the most complex and powerful cultural discourses in contemporary society, and religion continues to be a source of conflict between nations, among communities, within families, and . . . within one's self" (Corey, 2004, p. 189). While you may believe that your religious identity is part of your private life and irrelevant outside your family, this is not true. For example, in the aftermath of the 2001 September 11 attacks, Muslim identity has been viewed with particular suspicion. A 2004 study done by researchers in the Department of Communication at Cornell University found the following attitudes about Muslim Americans:

About 27 percent of respondents said that all Muslim Americans should be required to register their location with the federal government, and 26 percent said they think that mosques should be closely monitored by U.S. law enforcement agen-

religious identity
aspect of identity defined by one's spiritual beliefs

cies. Twenty-nine percent agreed that undercover law enforcement agents should infiltrate Muslim civic and volunteer organizations in order to keep tabs on their activities and fund-raising. About 22 percent said the federal government should profile citizens as potential threats based on the fact that they are Muslim or have Middle Eastern heritage. In all, about 44 percent said they believe that some curtailment of civil liberties is necessary for Muslim Americans (Cornell University, 2004).

Religious identity also takes on public significance because it correlates with various political views and attitudes (Corey & Nakayama, 2004). For example, the 2004 Cornell study found that Christians who actively attend church were much more likely to support differential treatment of Muslim Americans. In contrast, the nonreligious, or those less active in their churches, were less likely to support restrictions on civil liberties of Muslim Americans.

However one responds to other people's religious beliefs, most U.S. Americans feel a very strong need to embrace and enact personal religious identities (Corey & Nakayama, 2004). In 2000, for example, 46 percent of U.S. Americans belonged to religious groups, and approximately 40 percent of U.S. Americans claimed to attend religious services regularly (Taylor, 2005). Thus, in their article on "Religion and Performance," Frederick Corey and Thomas Nakayama (2004) write that individuals feel a "tremendous need to embody religious identities and reinforce those identities through spirited, vernacular performances" (p. 211).

We've shown throughout this chapter that aspects of our personal identity such as race, nationality, ethnicity, gender, age, social class, and religion develop through the tension between individual and societal forces. While we may assert a particular identity or view of ourselves, these views must be negotiated within the larger society and the meanings that the larger society communicates about that identity. See *Alternative View: Respecting Religious Differences* for an example of how one individual's religious identity became a public issue whose meaning was discussed and negotiated within the larger society. In the next section, we discuss the role of ethics in communication about identity.

How would you describe your religious identity? How do you communicate it to others? Do you ever conceal it? If so, when and why?

Alternative VIEW
Respecting Religious Differences

Should Americans care about the religious identity of their elected leaders, or is someone's religion a private matter? Should elected leaders be guided by their religious beliefs to a greater or lesser extent than ordinary citizens? Explain your answers.

When any society has multiple religions, difficult issues can arise. As we look back upon the media coverage of the 2008 U.S. presidential election, "much of the coverage related to false yet persistent rumors that Obama is a Muslim" (Pew Forum on Religion and Public Life, 2008). Concerns about John F. Kennedy's religion (Catholicism) also circulated when he ran for the presidency. In a society that values religious freedom, what difference does it make what religion (if any) a political candidate follows?

How should we deal with these claims in a society that wants to respect and tolerate different religious beliefs? In response to the claims that Obama is a Muslim, former Secretary of State Colin Powell stated:

Well, the correct answer is, he is not a Muslim, he's a Christian. He's always been a Christian. But the really right answer is, what if he is? Is there something wrong with being a Muslim in this country? The answer's no, that's not America. Is there something wrong with some 7-year-old Muslim American kid believing that he or she could be president? Yet I have heard senior members of my own party drop the suggestion. 'He's a Muslim and might be associated with terrorists.' This is not the way we should be doing it in America.

SOURCE: Robinson, E. (2007, August 29). The power of Powell's rebuke, *Washington Post*, p. A17. Retrieved December 31, 2000, from www.washingtonpost.com/wp-dyn/content/article/2008/10/20/AR2008102002393.html

TEST YOUR KNOWLEDGE

1. What are the primary identity categories? Define each.
2. Give an example of how identity might be performed for each primary identity category.

⊠ ETHICS AND IDENTITY

As you are probably aware, a person's sense of identity is central to how he or she functions in the world. Moreover, because identities derive their meanings from society, every identity comes with values attached to it. The ways we communicate may reflect these values. If you wish to be sensitive to other people's identities, you should be aware of at least three key ethical issues that can impact your communication with others.

One issue you might consider is how you communicate with people whose identities are more, or less, valued. What do we mean by more or less valued? You probably already know. In the United States, for example, which of the following identities is more highly valued: White or multiracial? Male or female? Lawyer or school bus driver? Still, these rankings are not necessarily consistent across cultures. In Denmark, for example, work identities do not follow the same hierarchical pattern as those in the United States (Mikkelsen & Einarsen, 2001). Thus, Danes are more likely to view street sweepers and doctors as social equals because they don't place as high a value on the medical profession nor as low a value on service jobs as many U.S. Americans do. In the United States, in contrast, many service workers complain that most of the people they serve either ignore them or treat them rudely—even with contempt. Consequently, you might ask yourself, "Do I communicate more politely and respectfully with high- versus low-status people?" If you find yourself exhibiting more respect when you communicate with your boss than you do with the employees you manage, then you might want to consider the impact of your communication on your subordinates' identities.

The second ethical point to reflect on involves language that denigrates or puts down others based on their identities. Such language debases their humanity and shuts down open communication. Examples of unethical communication and behavior related to identity occur if men yell sexual slurs at women on the street, or straight people harass individuals they believe are gay, or when White people are disrespectful to people of color. Although you probably don't engage in such obvious insults to people's identities, do you denigrate them in other, more subtle ways? For example, have you ever referred to someone as "just a homemaker" or "only a dental assistant"?

Third, think about whether you tend to reduce others to a single identity category. As we pointed out earlier, each of us is composed of multiple identities, and even within a specific identity group, individuals may differ widely from one another. Thus, individuals may be offended when others respond to them based on only one of their identities, especially one that is not relevant to the situation at hand. For example, managers in some organizations will not promote mothers of small children to highly demanding positions. They justify this by claiming the women won't be able to fulfill both their family and their professional roles competently. Although these women may be mothers, their identities as mothers likely are not relevant to their workplace identities and performances—just as men's identities as fathers are rarely seen as relevant to their jobs. Each person is a complex of identities, and each person desires others to recognize his or her multiple identities. You are more likely to communicate ethically if you keep this fact in mind.

TEST YOUR KNOWLEDGE

1. What are three key ethical concerns related to identity?

SKILLS FOR COMMUNICATING ABOUT IDENTITIES

Related to our discussion about ethical issues, we offer three guidelines for communicating more effectively about identities. The first guideline concerns the self-fulfilling prophecy we discussed earlier: How you communicate to someone and *about* someone can influence how they perform their identity or how it develops. If a parent continually communicates with the child as if she were irresponsible, then the child is likely to act irresponsibly. To communicate effectively, be aware of the ways you create self-fulfilling prophecies through your own communication.

Second, there are many ways to perform a particular identity. You can improve your ability to communicate if you are tolerant of the many variations. For example, even if you believe that "real men" should act in certain ways, you are likely to communicate more effectively if you do not impose your beliefs on others. For example, you should not assume that because someone is male, he enjoys watching football, baseball, and other sports; wants to get married and have children; or eats only meat and potatoes. If you do, you are likely to communicate with some men in ways they will find less interesting than you intend.

Third, remember that people change over time. If you have been out of touch with friends for a period of time, when you encounter them again you may find that they have embraced new identities. Sometimes people change religious identities, or sometimes they change occupations. You can increase your communication effectiveness if you recognize that people change and that their new identities may be unfamiliar to you.

TEST YOUR KNOWLEDGE

1. What are three strategies you can use to communicate more effectively with regard to identities?

SUMMARY

Learning about identities and communication is important for at least five reasons: (1) we bring our identities to each communication interaction, (2) communication interactions create and shape identities, (3) identity plays a key role in intercultural communication, (4) much of our life is organized around specific identities, and (5) identity is a key site in which individual and societal forces come together.

Identities are defined social categories, and each of us is made up of many of them. They may be primary or secondary. Primary identities (race, ethnicity, age) are the focus in this chapter and have the most consistent and enduring impact on our lives; secondary identities, such as occupation and marital status, are more changeable over the life span and from situation to situation. Our identities exist at both the individual and social level, are both fixed and dynamic, and are created through interaction. Furthermore, identities must be understood within larger historical, social, and cultural environments. Important communication processes that influence personal identity development include reflected appraisals, self-concept, and self-fulfilling prophecies.

The primary identity categories—race, nationality, ethnicity, gender, sexuality, age, social class, disability, and religion—are constructed between individual and social forces and what society communicates about those identities. Individuals perform their identities, and these performances are subject to social commentary. Straying too far from social expectations in these performances can lead to disciplinary action.

Ethical concerns center on how people are treated based on their identities. Guidelines to ethical communication include learning to value and respect people within all identity groups, to avoid using denigrating language or reducing people to a single identity category. Guidelines for more effective communication about identities involve being aware of the ways you create self-fulfilling prophecies through your communication and being tolerant of different ways of enacting various identities.

HUMAN COMMUNICATION IN SOCIETY ONLINE

To review this chapter, use the MyCommunicationLab Web site to test your understanding of the following key terms, record your answers to the chapter review questions, and complete the suggested activities. Expand your learning and understanding of chapter concepts by completing additional activities and exercises online. Access code required. Go to www.mycommunicationlab.com for more information or to purchase standalone access.

KEY TERMS

identity 49
reflected appraisals 52
looking-glass self 52
particular others 52
generalized other 53
self-fulfilling prophecy 54
stereotype threat 54
self-concept 55

self-esteem 55
self-respect 56
performance of identity 56
enacting identities 58
role expectations 58
mutable 58
racial identity 60
multiracial identity 62

national identity 62
ethnic identity 63
gender identity 63
sexual identity 64
age identity 65
social class identity 66
disability identity 67
religious identity 68

APPLY WHAT YOU KNOW

1. List the identities that are most important to you. Some of these identities may not have been discussed in this chapter. Note some situations in which the identities not discussed in the chapter become most relevant and some situations where other identities dominate.

2. Which of your identities are shared by a majority of people in society? What are some of the stereotypes of those identities? To answer this question, you may need to ask people who do not share that identity.

3. Interview someone who is at least twenty years older than you. Ask the person how her or his identities have changed over the years and what those changes entailed. Then reflect on changes in your own identity as you have grown up. How many of these changes were motivated by individual forces and how many might have been due to social forces?

4
Communicating, Perceiving, and Understanding

chapter outline

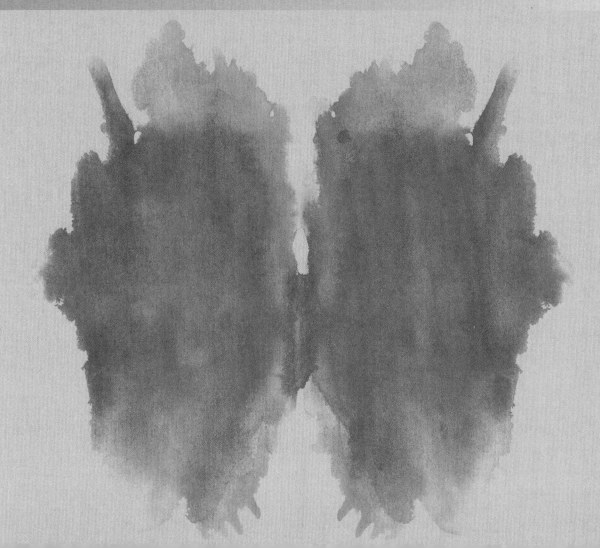

After the first hall meeting in their dorm, Travis and Samantha went out for coffee to discuss their experiences. They soon found themselves sharing their impressions of Bo, the dorm Resident Assistant (R.A.).

TRAVIS: What did you think of Bo?

SAMANTHA: I suppose he's okay. He seemed a little, I don't know, bossy. He was funny, but I don't know if I am going to like having him as my dorm resident; he seems like he might be hard to talk to.

TRAVIS : Really? I liked him a lot. I thought Bo was cool and would be really easy to talk to. He is someone I think I could hang out with.

SAMANTHA : He seemed kind of distant to me. I guess we'll have plenty of chances to find out what he is really like during the semester.

As the conversation between Travis and Samantha illustrates, our perceptions of others strongly influence how we respond to and communicate about them. If we perceive people as friendly, fun, and similar to ourselves, we tend to be drawn toward them and want to communicate with them. If we view individuals as distant, controlling, and quite unlike ourselves, we may try to minimize contact. However, not everyone perceives and responds to people and events the same way. Our perceptions are affected by individual factors, such as age, gender, genetics, and experience, as well as by societal forces including culture, historical events, and social roles.

For instance, on average females experience pain more intensely than do males (Hurley & Adams, 2008), so a touch that feels uncomfortable to a man may feel painful to a woman. (It can be helpful to remember this difference when we are shaking hands with others.) But how can societal forces affect perception? Among other things, societies teach us what foods and beverages are tasty and how they should be served. One example of this is the difference in how soft drinks are served in the United Kingdom versus how they are served in the United States. In most parts of the United Kingdom, cold beverages include a few pieces of ice, while in the United States a glass of soda may be half ice. Because of this, people in the two cultures have very different perceptions of what a "good" cold drink should taste like.

In this chapter we will first explore the importance of perception and the perception process. Next we'll examine how individuals' attributes and experiences affect their perceptions, and we will consider societal influences on perception. We also will discuss how people can evaluate their perceptions through an ethical lens. Finally, we will end the chapter with suggestions for sharpening your perception skills.

⊠ Once you have read this chapter, you will be able to:

- ▣ Explain why understanding perception is important.
- ▣ Define what we mean by perception.
- ▣ Name three individual factors that affect one's perceptual processes.
- ▣ Understand how power, culture, and historical time period influence perception.
- ▣ Explain why ethics is a relevant consideration for one's perceptions.
- ▣ Offer three ways to improve one's perception skills.

THE IMPORTANCE OF PERCEPTION

How individuals respond to people, objects, and environments depends largely on the perceptions they have about them. For example, when we perceive people as being polite, we are more likely to agree to their requests (Kellerman, 2004). When we communicate, we don't just respond to others' words; we respond to our perceptions of the way they look, sound, smell—and sometimes how they feel. For example, considerable research has established that when people perceive others as attractive, they treat them better than those viewed as less attractive (Chaiken, 1986; Wilson & Nias, 1999). This may explain the popularity of makeover shows like *The Biggest Loser* and *What Not to Wear*.

In addition, some research suggests that sexual attraction is influenced by the body odor of a potential partner (McCoy & Pitino, 2002; Singh & Bronstad, 2001). So, the next time someone breaks off a relationship by saying, "It's not you; it's me," they may be telling the truth. You just may not smell right to that person! Interestingly, women may be more likely to make this statement than are men since on average they have a keener sense of smell than do men (Estroff, 2004; Herz & Inzlicht, 2002). Overall, women may be more positively influenced by smells they find attractive and negatively by smells they dislike. For more information on the influence of smell on perception, see *Communication in Society: Sex Difference in Smell.*

As we noted in Chapter 3, identities play an important role in communication. They also influence and are influenced by perception. Thus, just as our perceptions of others impact how we communicate with them, our perceptions and communication impact how they see themselves. Let's take our scenario above as a case in point. How might Travis's or Samantha's perceptions affect Bo's perception of himself? If most people perceive Bo as Travis does—as amusing and open—and, therefore, respond to him by laughing and including him in activities, then Bo probably sees himself positively. On the other hand, if most people respond as Samantha did, and consequently choose to have little contact with him, Bo may perceive himself more negatively.

As you might expect, then, perception and identity are powerfully intertwined. On the one hand, Samantha's perceptions of Bo affect his identity. At the same time, how Bo views himself and others impacts how he perceives and responds to the world around him. If he has a positive self-image, Bo may perceive that others like him, he might be more optimistic and see the positive aspects of a situation more readily, and he could be less aware of others' negative reactions to him.

As you read this chapter, you are receiving considerable sensory input. An air conditioner or heater might be running, cars and people may be moving past you, and the temperature where you sit likely fluctuates over time. In addition, you may feel hungry or tired, you might detect the scent of cleaning products, and the chair you are sitting on could be uncomfortable. How are you able to manage all the information your senses bring to you so that you can focus on your reading? How are you able to make sense of all this sensory input? The answer is that you continuously engage in a variety of processes that limit and structure everything you perceive (Kanizsa, 1979; Morgan, 1977). Let's look at how this works.

COMMUNICATION IN SOCIETY
Sex Differences in Smell

Have you noticed a difference in sense of smell between the sexes?

Why do you think women typically have a keener sense of smell?

A variety of studies suggest that, on average, women are better at identifying odors than are men. Some researchers have found that women of all ages and in a variety of cultures are better than men of the same age and culture at identifying and remembering smells. However, other researchers claim that this sex difference is most pronounced during the period when women are fertile, especially during ovulation, and that their superior smelling ability fades with age. These scholars believe that women's higher levels of estrogen are likely responsible for this sex difference.

Experiments that have examined men's and women's scent ability reveal that both sexes are able to recognize others from their body odor alone. In an experiment at Hebrew University, Jerusalem, childless women held an unrelated baby in their arms for an hour. When tested later to see if they could recognize the baby they had held by scent, most of them were successful. This study did not test men, so it isn't clear if men possess similar smell recognition ability for unfamiliar others. However, other tests have determined that men and women both can recognize their own children or spouses by their scent. Typically in these studies, participants' children or spouses wore a T-shirt for several days, then the participants were asked to use scent to recognize the T-shirt belonging to their family member.

SOURCES: Doty, R. L., Applebaum, S., Zusho, H., & Settle, R. G. (1985). Sex differences in odor identification ability: A cross cultural analysis. *Neuropsychologia*, 23(5), 667–72.
Doty, R. L. (1984). Smell identification ability: Changes with age. *Science*, 226(4681), 1441–1443.
Maccaby, E. E., & Jacklin, C. N. *The psychology of sex differences*. Palo Alto, CA: Stanford University Press.

TEST YOUR KNOWLEDGE

■ Why is perception important to the communication process?

WHAT IS PERCEPTION?

Perception refers to the processes of **selection**, **organization**, and **interpretation** of the information we collect through our senses: what we see, hear, taste, smell, and touch. The sensory data we select, the ways we organize them, and the interpretations we assign to them affect the ways we communicate (Manusov & Spitzberg, 2008). Although these processes tend to happen concurrently and unconsciously, researchers separate them to better explain how they function.

Selection

Because people experience more sensory information than they can process, they selectively focus on and remember only part of it. In every interaction, each communicator has a field of perception. In this field some objects, symbols, or words are at the center, while others are on the periphery, and still others are outside the field altogether. Consciously or unconsciously we attend to just a narrow range of the full array of sensory information available and ignore the remainder. This process is called **selective attention**.

Suppose your friend is telling you a very interesting story about a mutual acquaintance while the two of you are seated in a crowded cafeteria. Most likely, your friend will have your full attention. Peripherally you may notice the sights and sounds of the other people in the room, the smells of food, and the glare of sunlight coming through the window; however, none of this will distract your focus. You probably will not even notice who is sitting at the table next to you, the color of the walls, the type of flooring, or the storm clouds gathering in the sky. Your attention will be devoted to the center of your field: your friend.

selection
the process of choosing which sensory information to focus on

organization
the process by which one recognizes what sensory input represents

interpretation
the act of assigning meaning to sensory information

selective attention
consciously or unconsciously attending to just a narrow range of the full array of sensory information available

Take a moment to remember the nicest comment anyone has made to you in the past 24 hours. Next, recall the unkindest remark anyone has made to you in that time period. Which remark did you find easiest to remember? Was your most memorable comment positive or negative? Did your most memorable comment violate your expectations? What were you doing when you heard the comment? To what extent does your experience fulfill or violate the claim that people are more likely to remember negative than positive comments?

The sensory input we select, however, is not random (Greenough, Black, & Wallace, 1987). When a range of sensory experiences accost you, various factors affect your selection, including your identity, features of the person or object you have encountered, and your experiences and values. For example, at large social events you are likely to attend to only one or a few people because you cannot focus on everyone at once. Who captures your focus depends on:

- aspects of your identity (e.g., if you are Native American, you may find your attention drawn more to participants who also are Native American)

- features of the person (e.g., someone dressed differently from everyone else will likely attract your attention)

- your goals (e.g., if you would like to meet a potential romantic partner, you may pay special attention to attractive men or women in your age range)

Researchers have also found that people are most likely to pay attention to and remember comments that are negative, violate their expectations, and are made in situations that are important to them (Siu & Finnegan, 2004). For example, a comment like "What on earth did you do to your hair?" is more likely to remain prominent in your mind than "Nice haircut." Similarly, when an instructor says, "This will be on the test," students usually pay close attention to what the instructor says next. Comments that violate our expectations also become more salient and gain more attention. Suppose you meet someone new and ask "How are you?" Instead of the expected, "Fine, thanks," the person explains in detail all the misfortunes that have befallen him or her in the past year. You not only will be surprised, you will remember the event. You may even decide that this new person is highly negative, or strange, and that you should avoid future interactions with him or her.

Organization

After selecting the sensory input we will attend to, we need to be able to recognize *what* it represents. To do this, we must organize the information into a recognizable picture that has meaning. If you are awakened in the middle of the night by a loud noise, you will certainly attend to that noise and little else. However, you also must be able to make sense of the sound in order to respond. Is it a mechanical sound or an animal one? Is it human? You can make judgments like these because you possess organizational structures or templates that tell you what information belongs together and how to "read" or understand what you perceive (Kanizsa, 1979). How does this work? In this section we examine two primary cognitive principles—cognitive representation and categorization—which help people organize and respond to their perceptions.

Cognitive Representation

The term **cognitive representation** describes the human ability to form mental models, or cognitive maps, of the world we live in (Levinthal & Gavetti, 2000; Weick, 1995). We create these maps and then refer to them later when circumstances call for them. For example, people know that a fire alarm communicates danger; furthermore, they know how to respond to a fire alarm because they have a cognitive map for alarms. Schools and workplaces have fire drills, in fact, to help people create cognitive maps that are familiar and enable them to act appropriately in an emergency.

People also develop and use cognitive maps when they communicate. As we grow up, we learn cognitive maps or models for engaging in many types of communication acts, such as complaining, apologizing, and asking for a favor. Many people learn quite early that it is useful to be nice to someone before asking them for a favor, and this information becomes part of the map for requesting favors. Remem-

cognitive representation
the ability to form mental models of the world

ber that maps are *representations* of things, not the things themselves. Thus cognitive maps consist of general outlines; they are not fixed sets of utterances that are memorized.

Two specific types of cognitive representations, or maps, that individuals use to organize their perceptions about people and communication are called prototypes and interpersonal scripts.

Communication behavior is strongly influenced by idealized **schemas** called prototypes. A **prototype** is the most typical or representative example of a person or concept. For example, many people's prototypical idea of a professor is a person who is male, has white hair (and perhaps a beard), and wears a tweed jacket with leather patches. Although a few professors fulfill this prototype, many more do not. (Just look around your campus.) Nonetheless, this prototype persists, in part because of how media depict college professors.

Prototypes are important because people compare specific individuals to their prototype and then communicate with them based on the degree to which they perceive that the individual conforms to that prototype. This often happens when it comes to the issue of gender. People have prototypical ideas of what a "man" or a "woman" is. These prototypes represent idealized versions of masculinity and femininity. The more an individual resembles one's prototype, the more likely one is to communicate with that person in a stereotypical (or prototypical) manner. For example, men who are muscular and tall and have facial hair are often perceived to be very masculine. Consequently, people tend to communicate with them as if these men embody typical masculine characteristics, such as having an interest in sports, a heterosexual sexual orientation, and a lack of interest in topics such as fashion, interior design, or personal relationships. Similarly, a man who possesses none of those characteristics may be viewed as not masculine and be communicated with accordingly.

An interpersonal **script** is a relatively fixed sequence of events expected to occur; it functions as a guide or template for how to act in particular situations (Burgoon, Berger, & Waldron, 2000; Pearce, 1994). We develop scripts for activities we engage in frequently. Most people have a script for how to meet a new person. For example, when you first encounter a student you'd like to get to know, you probably introduce yourself, tell the person a basic fact about yourself such as "I live across the hall from you," and then ask a question such as "How do you like living on campus?" "What is your major?" or "Where is your home town?" Thus, you follow a routine of sorts (Douglas, 1990).

We enact scripts because we find them comfortable, they are efficient, and they keep us from making too many social mistakes. Although many of the scripts we use will be familiar to others, we also tailor them to fit our own expectations for a situation. Our choice of script or the way we alter a script depends on our perceptions of others. We may use a different script to initiate a conversation with someone we perceive as friendly, attractive, and fun than with someone we perceive as shy, quiet, and withdrawn.

As this discussion suggests, cognitive representations help people navigate through the physical and social world. These maps provide guidelines that shape how we communicate with others through the prototypes and interpersonal scripts we develop as we grow up and mature.

Categorization

Another type of cognitive process we use to organize information is **categorization**. Categorization is inherent to all languages. The linguistic symbols (or words) we use represent the groupings we see around us. Because it is impossible to remember

How does the script for obtaining food in a fast-food restaurant differ from scripts for obtaining food in other situations?

schemas
cognitive structures that represent an individual's understanding of a concept or person

prototype
an idealized schema

script
a relatively fixed sequence of events that functions as a guide or template for communication or behavior

categorization
a cognitive process used to organize information by placing it into larger groupings of information

label
a name assigned to a category based
on one's perception of the category

stereotyping
creating schemas that overgeneralize
attributes of a specific group

everything, we use groupings that represent larger categories of information or objects (Lakoff, 1987).

For example, we lump a lot of information under the category of *restaurant*. What did you think of when you read the word *restaurant*? You probably envisioned a subcategory, such as a café or a pancake house. However, the concept of *restaurant* has certain features that apply to all subcategories, so that you know what is meant and what to expect when you go to one. You understand that *restaurant* refers to a place to eat and not a place to worship or attend classes. Forming and using categories allows us to understand and store information and makes us more efficient communicators.

Although grouping is a natural cognitive and perceptual process, it also can lead to misperceptions. Categorizing can cause one to reduce complex individuals to a single category or to expect them to behave in ways consistent with the category, regardless of the circumstance. For instance, you might categorize an individual based on your perception that the person is responsible and serious, or silly and fun. Once you reduce people to a category, you may communicate with them as if they possess no other characteristics. For example, if you categorize the students in your biology class as serious, you may never joke around with them or allow them to be silly or fun.

When people categorize others, they typically also assign them a **label**. The two activities tend to go hand in hand. Thus, groups of people and the individuals within those groups may be labeled or described as jocks, sorority girls, emo, or goth. Although labeling others can function as a useful shortcut, it also can lead to negative outcomes (Link & Phelan, 2001). When we label people, we run the risk of viewing them only through the lens of the label. The label also influences our expectations, evaluations, and responses to them. Labeling can cause problems even when the labels are positive, as was the case in *It Happened to Me: Lin Sue.*

When you were growing up, did your family have a label they used to describe you? Were you the smart one or the well-behaved one or the goof-up? If you were labeled the goof-up, you may not have been given many opportunities to disprove the label, and your ideas may have been discounted even when they were valid. Because of such a label, you may have come to discount the value of your own ideas. This effect can be magnified when entire groups of people are labeled in ways that create problems, such as the labeling of British people as snobbish or Muslims as terrorists.

As you may have guessed, labeling is related to stereotyping. **Stereotyping** occurs when schemas overgeneralize attributes of a group to which others belong (Fiske & Taylor, 1991). A stereotype is an assumption that every member of the group possesses certain characteristics. For example, you may assume that most females enjoy talking about fashion trends, so, you initiate a conversation with an unfamiliar woman by discussing the *Style Network*. But not every member of a group fits the stereotype—if you use the fashion opener with every woman you meet, you may encounter some women who give you a blank stare in response.

While grouping individuals makes it easy to remember information about them, it often leads to inaccurate beliefs and assumptions. Overgeneralizing a group's attributes makes it difficult to see the individuality of the people we encounter. Thus, a reliance on stereotypes can get those who use them into trouble.

How do you perceive these two males? Do any stereotypes come to mind?

It Happened to Me: Lin Sue

Because I am Chinese American, people often assume that I am some kind of whiz kid in academics. Well, I'm not. I was hit by a car when I was little, and I have residual brain impairment because of it. I have to study hard just to make passing grades. I get both angry and embarrassed when people assume I am this great student and imply that I will surely go to graduate school. I will feel fortunate if I just get out of undergraduate school. I really wish people wouldn't do this to me. They think they are being nice and complimentary, but they are still stereotyping me.

Interpretation

After you perceive and organize sensory information, you assign meaning to it (Bruner, 1958, 1991). Returning to our earlier example, imagine that you are awakened late at night. You hear a loud noise, which you determine is caused by a banging on your bedroom window. You now have to interpret what this means. Is it a tree branch? A shutter? Is it someone trying to break in?

We all assign meaning to the information we perceive, but we do not all necessarily assign the same meaning to similar information. One of the factors that influences how we interpret information is the frame through which we view it.

Frames

Structures that shape how people interpret their perceptions are called **frames**. An individual's understanding of an event depends on the frame used to interpret it (Dillard, Solomon, & Samp, 1996). For example, if you are someone who frames the world as a dangerous place rife with criminals, you are likely to interpret that banging on your window as an indication of someone trying to break in. In essence, individuals view the world through interpretive frames that then guide how they make sense of events (Dijk, 1977; Fisher, 1997).

Individuals' frames develop over time, based on experience, interaction with others, and innate personality (Neale & Bazerman, 1991; Putnam & Holmer, 1992). Since we cannot perceive every aspect of an experience, frames also direct our attention toward some features of an episode and away from others. A bad mood, for example, directs attention to the negative aspects of an event. Usually, people don't become aware of frames until something happens to force them to replace one frame with another. If a friend points out that you are focusing only on the negative, you will become more aware of how your mood is framing, or focusing, your perceptions and interpretations. Your frame can change, then, as new information is introduced.

How should you use this information about framing? Now that you are aware that interpretations of people, events, and objects are influenced by an individual's specific frames, you should be more critical of your own interpretations. It is helpful to recognize that your interpretations (as well as others') do not necessarily represent the "truth"—but simply represent a particular way of viewing the world.

Frames are important elements of interpretation because they function as lenses that shape how observers understand people and events. But bear in mind that interpretation involves more than just framing; when individuals interpret events, they also offer explanations for them. When we develop explanations for our own and others' behaviors, we are engaged in making attributions. Let's see how this process works.

Attribution

How often do you wonder "why did she (or he) do that?" As we observe and interact with others, we spend considerable energy attempting to determine the causes of their behavior. For example, if your friend ignores you before class, you try to figure out why. At heart, most of us are amateur psychologists who search for the reasons people behave as they do.

Attribution theory explains the cognitive and verbal processes we use to judge our own and others' behavior (Manusov & Spitzberg, 2008). Fritz Heider (1958), a psychologist and professor, said that attribution is the process of drawing inferences. When individuals observe others, they immediately draw conclusions that go beyond mere sensory information. When someone cuts you off in traffic, what conclusion do you usually draw? What attribution would you make if you called your romantic partner at 3 a.m. and he or she wasn't home? Although we're constantly being told we shouldn't judge others, attribution theory says we can't help it (Griffin, 1994).

frame
a structure that shapes how people interpret their perceptions

attribution theory
explanation of the processes we use to judge our own and others' behavior

attributional bias
the tendency to attribute one's own negative behavior to external causes and one's positive actions to internal states

self-serving bias
the tendency to give one's self more credit than is due when good things happen and to accept too little responsibility for those things that go wrong

fundamental attribution error
the tendency to attribute others' negative behavior to internal causes and their positive behaviors to external causes

One attribution we often make is whether the cause of an individual's behavior is internal or external. An *internal* cause would be a personality characteristic, while an *external* cause would be situational.

We are particularly likely to make internal attributions when the behavior is unexpected—that is, when it is something that most other people would not do (Kelley, 1973). For instance, if someone laughs during a sad scene in a movie, people are more likely to attribute this unexpected reaction to a personality trait—for example, rudeness or insensitivity. But when the behavior fits our expectations, we are likely to attribute it to external causes. Therefore, if someone cries during a sad movie scene, people are likely to attribute the behavior to the movie.

Besides expectations, attributions may also depend on whether we are the actor or observer of the behavior. We are more likely to attribute our own negative behavior to external causes and our positive actions to internal states (Jong, Koomen, & Mellenbergh, 1988). This is referred to as an **attributional bias**. If you are polite, it is because you have good manners; if you are rude, it is because others mistreated you. These attributions are examples of a **self-serving bias**. Operating under this bias, we tend to give ourselves more credit than is due when good things happen, and we accept too little responsibility for those things that go wrong.

Most individuals are harsher judges of other people's behavior than they are of their own. We tend to attribute others' negative behavior to *internal* causes (such as their personality) and their positive behavior to *external* causes (such as the situation). This tendency is referred to as the **fundamental attribution error** (Ross, 1977). For example, when you are driving during rush hour traffic and someone cuts in front of you abruptly as two lanes merge, what attribution do you make about the other driver? According to fundamental attribution error, people are more likely to attribute the behavior to some trait internal to the other driver ("That driver is a jerk and is deliberately trying to get ahead of me") rather than to something external ("That driver is distracted by a child in the car and doesn't realize the lane is merging"). But if the other driver slows down to let you enter the merged lane first, most people might assume the driver was simply following the rules of the road rather than deliberately attempting to be thoughtful.

Attributional biases have implications for the way people communicate and conduct relationships. For example, the types of attributions spouses make are linked to their feelings of marital satisfaction (Sillars, Roberts, Leonard, & Dun, 2000; 2002). Those in unhappy relationships tend to assume the spouse's negative behaviors are internal, or personality-based, and difficult to change. Unfortunately, they also tend to view their spouse's positive behaviors as situational and temporary (Bradbury & Fincham, 1988). Thus, unhappy spouses often feel helpless to change their partner's negative characteristics. This pessimistic outlook can then increase negative communication within the relationship.

Interestingly, when people make attributions about others, they tend to trust the negative information they hear more than the positive information (Lupfer, Weeks, & Dupuis, 2000). If you hear both positive and negative information about a classmate, you tend to remember and rely on the negative rather than the positive information to formulate your attributions. However, you are not confined to these faulty attributional processes; you can work to overcome them.

First, remember that none of us is a mind reader and that the attributions we make are not always accurate. Remain aware that attributions are really just guesses (even if they are educated guesses). It also helps if one remains aware of the self-serving bias and works to minimize it. Recognize that we all have a tendency to attribute our own positive actions to ourselves and others' negative actions to themselves. Look for alternative explanations for your own and others' behavior. Last, avoid overemphasizing the negative. People have a tendency to remember and to highlight the negative, so try to avoid the negative in your own comments and balance the positive against the negative in your evaluations of others. For an example of a mistaken attribution, see *It Happened to Me: Danika.*

TEST YOUR KNOWLEDGE

- How important is the role of interpretation in the perception process? What factors most influence how individuals interpret events?
- What two cognitive processes help us organize what we perceive?
- Why is stereotyping "normal"? When is it helpful? When is it harmful?

It Happened to Me: Danika

I was at a party recently when I went up to this attractive guy and stood next to him. When he didn't seem to notice me, I introduced myself and tried talking to him. But he completely ignored me! I was so put off that I stomped away and started complaining to my friend Amira. I told her that the guy might be good looking, but he sure was a snob. She looked puzzled. "Oh, were you standing on his left side?" she asked. When I told her yeah, she explained that he was deaf in his left ear and probably hadn't heard me. I felt bad that I had jumped to a negative attribution so quickly. Later, I approached him on his right side and talked to him; I found out he was a really nice guy.

PERCEPTION AND THE INDIVIDUAL

Thus far we have explained how perceptions are formed: Individuals engage in selective attention, use a variety of organizational processes, and assign meaning to their perceptions. Thus, if you hear a loud noise in the street, you will turn your attention to the street; and if you see a car stopped and a person lying in the road with her motorcycle, you will categorize the event as an accident. Finally, you likely will decide (interpret) that the car hit the motorcycle rider. However, a variety of individual factors influence people's perceptual processes and affect their selection, organization, and interpretation of sensory input. For example, those who often ride motorcycles may attribute fault for the accident to the car driver (since they have frequently experienced inattentive auto drivers) while people who only drive cars my attribute blame to the motorcyclist (because they observed cyclists driving between lanes of cars on the road). The individual factors that influence our perceptual processes generally fall into three categories: physical, cognitive, and personality characteristics. Let's begin with the physical factors.

Physical Differences

Each person's unique physical capabilities affect what they perceive and how they understand it. Some people have more acute hearing than others. Others have more acute sight or taste than others do. For example, professional wine tasters have a very highly developed sense of taste, pilots are required to have 40/40 vision, and musicians must possess the ability to identify various pitches and notes. As mentioned earlier, age can influence perception, and an individual's sex can affect the sensory input they notice.

Synesthesia is another individual physical difference that affects perception, which has only recently been recognized and studied. Synesthesia is a rare cognitive and physical trait that influences people's perception and, to some extent, their communication. To learn what synesthesia is (and whether you have it!), refer to *Alternative View: Hearing Colors, Tasting Shapes.*

Cognitive Complexity

As we discussed earlier, the process of categorization helps us to organize information. Scientists refer to the categories we form as **constructs. Cognitive complexity**

constructs
categories people develop to help them organize information

cognitive complexity
the degree to which a person's constructs are detailed, involved, or numerous

Alternative VIEW

Hearing Colors, Tasting Shapes

People with synesthesia—those whose senses blend together—provide valuable clues to understanding the organization and functions of the human brain.

What does synesthesia reveal about how the brain affects perception? How can these differences in perceptual abilities affect how individuals interact with one another?

When Matthew Blakeslee shapes hamburger patties with his hands, he experiences a vivid bitter taste in his mouth. Esmerelda Jones (a pseudonym) sees blue when she listens to the note C sharp played on the piano; other notes evoke different hues—so much so that the piano keys are actually color-coded, making it easier for her to remember and play musical scales. And when Jeff Coleman looks at printed black numbers, he sees them in color, each a different hue. Blakeslee, Jones, and Coleman are among a handful of otherwise normal people who have synesthesia; they are part of the estimated 1 percent of people worldwide who are synesthetic. They experience the ordinary world in extraordinary ways and seem to inhabit a mysterious no-man's-land between fantasy and reality. For them the senses—touch, taste, hearing, vision, and smell—get mixed up instead of remaining separate.

Modern scientists have known about synesthesia since 1880, when Francis Galton, a cousin of Charles Darwin, published a paper in *Nature* on the phenomenon. But most have brushed it aside as fakery, an artifact of drug use (LSD and mescaline can produce similar effects), or a mere curiosity. About four years ago, however, we and others began to uncover brain processes that could account for synesthesia. Along the way, we also found new clues to some of the most mysterious aspects of the human mind, such as the emergence of abstract thought, metaphor, and perhaps even language.

Overview/Synesthesia

- Synesthesia (from the Greek roots *syn*, meaning "together," and *aisthesis*, or "perception") is a condition in which otherwise normal people experience the blending of two or more senses.

- For decades, the phenomenon was often written off as fakery or simply memories, but it has recently been shown to be real. Perhaps it occurs because of cross activation, in which two normally separate areas of the brain elicit activity in each other.

- As scientists explore the mechanisms involved in synesthesia, they are also learning about how the brain in general processes sensory information and uses it to make abstract connections between seemingly unrelated inputs.

SOURCE: "Hearing Colors, Tasting Shapes," by S. Vilayanur, V. S. Ramachandran, & E. M. Hubbard, *Scientific American*, May 2003. Copyright © 2003 Scientific American, Inc. All rights reserved.

refers to how detailed, involved, or numerous a person's constructs are (Burleson & Caplan, 1998). But how does cognitive complexity affect perception?

First, people tend to be more cognitively complex about—and have more constructs for—those things that interest them or with which they have had experience. If you like music, you have a wide range of constructs, such as rap, hip hop, alternative, progressive, and neocountry, and these are constructs that others may not possess at all. This high number of constructs affects your perceptions of music. As you listen, you can distinguish between multiple forms of music, and you recognize when an artist is employing a specific form or fusing two or more. In addition to these sets of personal constructs that help you interpret the world, you also possess *interpersonal constructs* that you use to make decisions and inferences about other people (Deutsch, Sullivan, Sage, & Basile, 1991).

From an early age, everyone possesses simple constructs that help them explain their perceptions of others. These constructs tend to be bipolar, or based on opposing categories of characteristics, such as funny or serious, warm or cold, and responsible or careless. One's age, intellectual ability, and experiences influence how complex or detailed such constructs are. For example, very young children typically describe others with only a few constructs, such as nice or mean; most adults, however, have a much more involved set of constructs that allows them to describe others in more varied and specific ways.

In addition, when you have cognitively complex construct systems, you tend to have many ways of explaining and understanding interpersonal interactions. Suppose, for example, that your friend Laura was almost an hour late meeting you for a dinner date. If you are cognitively complex, you might come up with a number of reasons to explain this behavior: Laura (a) was in a traffic accident, (b) forgot about the date, (c) was detained by an unforeseen event, (d) decided not to keep the date, and so on. These are all plausible explanations; without further information you will not know which one is correct. The point is that cognitively complex individuals can develop a large set of alternative explanations.

Cognitively complex individuals can develop a large number of explanations for the late arrival of a dinner date.

In turn, your degree of cognitive complexity influences your perceptions and thus your communication behavior. For example, if you can only explain Laura's lateness by deciding that she is thoughtless, you will likely perceive her negatively and use a hostile communication style when you meet. Individuals' levels of complexity influence a broad range of communicative issues, such as how many persuasive messages they can generate (Applegate, 1982) and how well they can comfort others (Samter & Burleson, 1984).

Personality and Individual Characteristics

Each person's unique mix of personality, temperament, and experience influences how they interpret and respond to sensory information. Elements that make up this mix include emotional state, outlook, and knowledge.

Emotional State

If you are feeling happy or optimistic, you will tend to interpret and respond to sensory input differently than if you are feeling depressed, angry, or sad (Planalp, 1993). For instance, if you feel angry, you may perceive music, other people's voices, or background noise as irritating. On the other hand, if you are in a positive mood, you may behave more helpfully toward others. In one experiment, researchers tested 800 passersby (Gueguen & De Gail, 2003). In half the cases, researchers smiled at the passersby, and in half they did not. A few seconds after this interaction, the passersby had the opportunity to help another researcher who dropped his or her belongings on the ground. Those who were exposed to the smile in the first encounter were more likely to be helpful in the second. Thus, even a small impact on your emotional state can influence how you communicate and interact with others.

Outlook

One's outlook refers to a tendency to view and interpret the world in consistent ways. Research shows that people tend to have a natural predisposition to either optimism or pessimism, based on genetics and experience (Seligman, 1998). People who are optimistic by nature may expect more positive experiences and make fewer negative attributions. These positive expectations can have an influence on their behavior—but not always for the best. For example, young people with an optimistic bias tend to believe that they are less likely than others to experience negative consequences from health behaviors. Therefore, they may be more likely than others to engage in sexual risk-taking (Chapin, 2001).

Knowledge

People frequently interpret what they perceive based on what they know of an event. If you know that your friend has a big exam coming up, you may interpret his or her irritability as due to nervousness. Our knowledge of specific topics also influences

Do you wonder how cognitively complex your interpersonal constructs are? To find out, think of a person you know well. Then for the next sixty seconds, write down as many terms as you can think of to describe that person. How many terms were you able to generate? How many different categories of terms were you able to list? (For example, nice, kind, thoughtful would group into one category as would athletic, physically fit, sporty.) Typically, the more terms and categories of terms you can generate, the more cognitively complex your interpersonal constructs are believed to be.

our perceptions, communication, and decision making. For instance, a study on organ donation revealed that members of families that discussed the subject were twice as likely to donate their organs as were members of other families (Smith, Kopfman, Lindsey, Massi, & Morrison, 2004). The researchers concluded that once people communicate and know more about the topic of organ donation, they perceive it in a more positive light.

Your perceptions strongly shape your communication and your actions. If you strike up a conversation with someone new who looks physically attractive but whose voice reminds you of someone you dislike, you may choose to end the conversation and move on. However, if you meet someone who reminds you of someone you like, you might invest energy in getting to know that person. If you interpret a new friend's teasing as a sign of affection, you may decide to increase your involvement with her. In these ways, your perceptual processes influence your interactions and relationships. In addition, broader societal factors also play a role in what you perceive, how you organize it, and the meanings you attach to it. We discuss these societal influences next.

TEST YOUR KNOWLEDGE

- How do physical differences influence the perception process?
- What is cognitive complexity, and how does it influence the perception process?

✖ THE INDIVIDUAL, PERCEPTION, AND SOCIETY

How do societal factors affect perception? As we will explain in this section, the position individuals hold in society and the cultures in which they live affect what they perceive and how they interpret these perceptions. As you read this section, we encourage you to consider the societal forces that affect your perceptions as well as how they might affect the perceptions of others.

The Role of Power

Every society has a hierarchy, and in a hierarchy some people have more power than others. Your relative position of power or lack of power influences how others perceive you, how you perceive others, and how you interpret events in the world. Moreover, those in power largely determine a society's understandings of reality. For example, in the United States, the dominant perception is that everyone can move up in society through hard work and education ("Middle of the Class," 2005). However, individuals who are born poor and who live in deprived areas with few resources can find it very difficult, no matter how hard they try to follow the path to "success" as defined by mainstream U.S. culture. Thus the perceptual reality of these people is likely to differ from that of those higher in the power hierarchy. Nonetheless, a specific view of reality dominates U.S. culture because it is communicated both explicitly and implicitly through media messages, public speeches, schools, and other social institutions.

One's individual experiences within that hierarchy may lead one to accept or reject that dominant perception. For example, middle-class people may believe that if they work hard they will get ahead in society, whereas poor people may perceive that it takes a lot more than hard work and education (Ehrenreich, 2001). Similarly, if a you grew up relatively wealthy, you may believe that your admission to a highly selective college is largely due to your intelligence, hard work, and skills, whereas someone who grew up relatively poor may believe that social connections and family money better explain this achievement (Douthat, 2005).

Your position in the racial hierarchy also influences your perceptions about the reality of racial bias. It is well documented that White Americans and African Americans have very different perceptions regarding the role of race in the United States (Hacker, 2003). A study conducted after Hurricane Katrina devastated the Gulf Coast revealed a broad divergence in perceptions: When asked whether racial inequality remains a major problem, 71 percent of African Americans replied yes, compared to only 32 percent of Whites (Pew Research Center for the People and the Press, 2005).

The Role of Culture

Culture strongly influences individual perception. One way it does so is through its *sensory model*. Every culture has its own sensory model, which means that each culture emphasizes a few of the five senses (Classen, 1990). Moreover, what a culture emphasizes affects what its members pay attention to and prefer. People in the United States, for example, tend to give primacy to the visual; thus, we have sayings such as "seeing is believing," and students almost demand that professors use PowerPoint slides in the classroom. On the other hand, people living in the Andes Mountains of South America tend to place more emphasis on what they hear than on what they see. In their culture, important ideas are transmitted through characters in stories and narratives (Classen, 1990). Knowing this, how do you think students in the Andes prefer to learn? You might imagine that they would prefer elaborate stories rather than a list of brief terms and concepts on PowerPoint slides.

A culture is composed of a set of shared practices, norms, values, and beliefs (Brislin, 2000; Shore, 1996), which in turn helps shape individuals' thoughts, feelings, perceptions, and behaviors. For example, individuals in East Asian cultures often are highly interdependent and emphasize the group over the individual. Consequently, they don't approve of bragging and encourage greater self-criticism than some other cultures. By encouraging self-criticism (and then working on self-improvement), the thinking goes, they are contributing to the overall strength of the group (Heine & Lehman, 2004; Markus, Mullally, & Kitayama, 1997). In the United States, however, the emphasis is often on the individual, and most people are encouraged to distinguish themselves from others. For example, current books on dating and work success teach U.S. Americans how to "brand" themselves like a product. The dominant culture in the United States also encourages people to talk about their success and to refrain from self-criticism. As a result, someone from East Asia may see U.S. Americans as braggarts, while a person from the United States may see East Asians as overly modest (Kim, 2002).

Cultural background also influences how people expect to talk to one another (Scollon & Wong-Scollon, 1990). In some Native American cultures, for example, individuals perceive strangers as potentially unpredictable, so they may talk little—if at all—until they have established familiarity and trust with the newcomer (Braithwaite, 1990). This approach differs considerably from the customs of some European American cultures, in which people view strangers as potential friends and strike up conversations to become acquainted with them (Krivonos & Knapp, 1975).

Now imagine a Native American and a European American from these different communication cultures meeting for the first time. How is each likely to behave? The Native American may remain relatively quiet while observing the new person. The European American will most likely try to engage in a lively conversation and may ask a number of questions to draw the other person out. As a result, the Native American may view the European American as nosy, pushy, and overly familiar, while the European American may see the Native American as unfriendly or shy (Braithwaite, 1990). Each perceives or evaluates the other based on expectations that were shaped by his or her own cultural perceptions, values, and the meanings typical for his or her own culture (Scollon & Wong-Scollon, 1990).

Cultural norms, values, and expectations provide a backdrop of familiarity. When we travel or when we meet people from other cultures close to home, we can learn from exposure to our differences. However, sometimes these differences are upsetting, frustrating, or baffling. For example, one of our students, Simone, was taken aback when she was offered *chapulines* (fried grasshoppers) during her trip to Oaxaca, Mexico. Interestingly, most of us not only value the ways of our own culture, we often feel that others' cultural norms are less desirable—or even wrong—an issue we discuss next.

The Role of Social Comparison

As we discussed earlier, categorizing groups of objects, information, or people is a basic quality of perception. *Social* categorization—or categorizing people—leads us to specific expectations about how others should or should not behave. These social categories and the expectations associated with them typically arise out of our culture and where we are positioned in the culture. For example, in the United States, middle- and upper-middle-class people often perceive individuals who receive government subsidies for food or housing as people who do not want to work hard, and they may therefore categorize them as lazy or dependent. However, people who are in the working class or among the working poor may have a different perception, asserting that those who rely on these government subsidies work hard but are underemployed or have to live on a salary that is not a living wage ("Middle of the Class," 2005; Ehrenreich, 2001). As you can see, the perceptions and categories that we develop tend to be tied to stereotypes and prejudice, which both flow from ethnocentrism, the perceptual concept at the core of social comparison.

Ethnocentrism

Most people view their own group as the standard against which they evaluate others. Thus, one's own ethnic, regional, or class group is the one that seems right, correct, or normal. This tendency to view one's own group as the standard against which all others are judged is described as **ethnocentrism**. It comes from the Greek words *ethnos*, which means nation, and *kentron*, which refers to the center of a circle (Ting-Toomey, 1999). People behave ethnocentrically when they view their own values, norms, or modes of belief and behavior as better than those of other groups.

While it is normal to be proud of one's national, cultural, racial, or ethnic group, one becomes ethnocentric when he or she engages in polarized thinking and behavior. This occurs when people believe that if "we" are right, correct, normal, and even superior, then "they" must be wrong, incorrect, abnormal, and inferior. Such thinking can seriously interfere with our ability to communicate effectively with those outside our group.

Stereotypes

Earlier in the chapter, we described stereotypes as broad generalizations about an entire class of objects or people, based on some knowledge of some aspects of some members of the class (Brislin, 2000; Stephan & Stephan, 1992). When you stereotype computer programmers as smart but socially inept, you likely are basing your beliefs on your interactions with a few programmers—or perhaps on no interactions at all. Stereotypes may be based on what you have read, images in the media, or information you have obtained from others, as you'll see was the case with one college student in *It Happened to Me: Damien.*

If you develop a stereotype, it tends to influence what you expect from the stereotyped group. If you believe that someone is a lesbian, you may also believe she engages in specific types of communication behavior, dress, or interests. When you hold these types of beliefs and expectations, they tend to erase the stereotyped person's individual characteristics. In addition, you are likely to communicate with her as if your stereotypes were accurate rather than basing your messages on her actual interests and behavior (Snyder, 1998).

ethnocentrism
the tendency to view one's own group as the standard against which all other groups are judged

Stereotyping is an understandable and natural cognitive activity; in fact, stereotypes can serve as useful shorthand to help us understand the world. If you are interviewing for a job in the Southern United States, it may be helpful for you to know that many Southerners prefer to engage in social interaction before getting down to business (though this is certainly not always true). However, when stereotyping leads to polarized understandings of the world as "between me and you, us and them, females and males, Blacks and Whites," then it can cause problems (Ting-Toomey, 1999, p. 149). In turn, polarized thinking frequently leads to a rigid, intolerant view of certain behavior as correct or incorrect (Ting-Toomey, 1999). For example, do you believe it is more appropriate for adult children to live on their own than with their parents before they marry? People with polarized thinking assume that their own cultural beliefs regarding this issue are right or correct instead of recognizing that cultures differ in what is considered appropriate.

It Happened to Me: Damien

Shortly after school started, I decided to join a fraternity and began going to parties on the weekends. Often when people heard me mention that I was a part-time computer programmer, they would first look shocked and then crack some kind of joke about it, like, "Bill Gates, Jr., eh?" I guess it surprises people that I don't have glasses, that I venture out into the sunlight once in a while, and that I engage in some social activities! I realize that their preconceived notions about "techies" have come from somewhere, but, since at least half of my fellow "computer geeks" are far from the nerdy stereotype, it would be nice if people would recognize that we aren't all pale, glasses-wearing, socially awkward nerds!

Prejudice

Stereotypes and feelings of ethnocentrism often lead to prejudice. **Prejudice** occurs when people experience aversive or negative feelings toward a group as a whole or toward an individual because she or he belongs to a group (Rothenberg, 1992). People can experience prejudice against a person or group because of his or her physical characteristics, perceived ethnicity, age, national origin, religious practices, and a number of other identity categories.

Given the negative associations most people have with the concept of prejudice, you may wonder why it persists. Researchers believe that prejudice is common and pervasive because it serves specific functions, the two most important of which are *ego-defensive functions* and *value-expressive functions* (Brislin, 2000). Let's explore these concepts.

The **ego-defensive function** of prejudice describes the role it plays in protecting individuals' sense of self-worth. For example, an individual who is not financially successful and whose group members tend not to be financially successful may attribute blame to other groups for hoarding resources and preventing him or her from becoming successful. The less financially successful individual may also look down on groups that are even less financially successful as a way to protect his or her own ego. These attitudes may make people feel better, but they also prevent them from analyzing reasons for their own failure. Moreover, they negatively affect the ways people talk to and about the targeted groups. People who look down on groups that are less financially successful may describe them and talk to them as if they were lazy, incompetent, or not very bright.

Prejudice serves its **value-expressive function** by allowing people to view their own values, norms, and cultural practices as appropriate and correct. By devaluing other groups' behavior and beliefs, these people maintain a solid sense that they are right. Unfortunately, this same function causes group members to denigrate the cultural practices of others. You may have seen many examples of the value-expressive function of prejudice, as when individuals engage in uncivil arguments and personal attacks over issues such as men's and women's roles, abortion, and politics.

prejudice
experiencing aversive or negative feelings toward a group as a whole or toward an individual because she or he belongs to a group

ego-defensive function
the role prejudice plays in protecting individuals' sense of self-worth

value-expressive function
the role played by prejudice in allowing people to view their own values, norms, and cultural practices as appropriate and correct

The Role of Historical Time Period

In addition to a person's place in the power hierarchy, their culture, and their awareness of social comparison, the historical period in which one grows up and lives influences perception and communication (U.S. National Research Council, 1989). For example, this author is writing this chapter on September 11, 2010. Anyone living in the United States who was older than five or six on September 11, 2001, likely has had their perceptions altered by events of that day. They may feel less safe, perceive air travel as riskier, and feel more patriotic than they did before the terrorist attacks on that day. These perceptions may in turn influence how they talk about the United States; or how they communicate, for example, with individuals who are Muslim.

Other historical events have affected the perceptions of individuals who lived through them. For instance, people who lived through the Great Depression may perceive resources as being scarcer than others do; those who were young during the Vietnam War likely believe that collective action can influence political policy; and those who grew up watching *The Real World* and other reality TV programs probably view privacy differently than do prior generations. As you might expect, these perceptions influence how, and about what, the various generations communicate, a process called the **cohort effect**. Thus those who came of age after 2000 may feel comfortable discussing a wide range of topics previously considered taboo, such as sexual conduct or family dysfunction. Similarly, women who grew up when sexual discrimination was more prevalent might object to the use of "girls" when referring to women.

Social Roles

The roles one plays socially also influence one's perception and, consequently, communication. **Social role** refers to the specific position or positions an individual holds in a society. Social roles include job positions, familial roles (such as mother or father), and positions in society. For example, Teri holds a variety of roles, including mother, religious leader, soccer coach, and community activist. The fact that she holds these social roles affects how people perceive and communicate with her in several ways. First, society defines specific expectations for her various social roles (Kirouac & Hess, 1999). Many people, for example, expect that religious leaders will be especially moral, selfless, and well intentioned. In turn, these expectations affect the ways that religious leaders interact with others. If you expect Teri, as a religious leader, to be highly moral, she may work to communicate with you in ways that fulfill your expectations.

Second, the education, training, and socialization Teri undergoes for her social roles influence her perceptions. In much of U.S. culture it is expected that women will become mothers and that they will behave in specific ways as they fulfill that role. As they grow up, girls are socialized and taught, by both word and example, how mothers are supposed to communicate. Because Teri is a parent, she may perceive different issues as important. For example, she may be more concerned with the quality of schools, the safety of her neighborhood, and access to health care than a nonparent might. Similarly, when individuals receive education and training, their perceptions of the world around them are affected. A person trained as a police officer, for example, may perceive the world as populated with more criminals than the average person does; whereas a person trained as a nurse may be more aware of how to prevent illnesses and injuries.

Each individual's perceptions are unique, based on his or her own roles and characteristics. However, individuals also share certain perceptual realities with others in their power position in society's hierarchy as well as with others in their cultures and social role groups. Because of these differing realities and power positions, your perceptions may lead you into prejudicial and intolerant thinking and

cohort effect
the process by which historical events influence the perceptions of people who grew up in a given generation and time period

social role
the specific position or positions one holds in a society

communication. In the concluding section of this chapter, we suggest strategies for improving your perception processes and communication.

TEST YOUR KNOWLEDGE
- What is social comparison? How is it related to ethnocentrism and prejudice?

ETHICS AND PERCEPTION

As we've discussed throughout this chapter, the ways people communicate to and about others are connected to their perceptions and cognitions about them. That is, what we select to attend to, what categories we put people in, and the attributions we make about them all strongly influence what we believe, say, and do. For example, Sharina was driving home late one night and stopped at a traffic light when she notice a young man of color in the car next to hers. She reached over and locked her door. As she looked up, she saw the man smile slightly then lean over and lock *his* door. In this case, Sharina was responding based on stereotypical perceptions and cognitions, and the other driver was gently reminding her of that fact.

A common example of a time when perception, ethics, and communication intersect occurs when speakers perceive and label other groups of people negatively and then use derogatory terms to refer to them. Unfortunately, using such terms can reinforce and even intensify one's own as well as others' negative responses to these groups. In addition, if what individuals attend to and perceive about people first is their skin color, their sex, or their relative affluence, they may find themselves communicating with those people stereotypically and failing to recognize other roles they fulfill. Doing so may lead one to assume and communicate as if all adult women are mothers (or there is something wrong with them if they are not) or to refer to a physician as nurse because she happens to be female. Each of these behaviors is problematic in that it denies others their right to legitimate identities. Consequently such behaviors are ones that are usefully examined through an ethical lens. That is, when tempted to create stereotypes of others and to communicate with them based on that stereotype, it helps to ask yourself if doing so fits within your own ethical framework.

Although social factors such as power and position can impact many aspects of your life, you do have control of, and responsibility for, your perceptions and cognitions. Even though your social circle and your family may engage in problematic perceptual, cognitive, and communicative processes, once you become an adult you are responsible for how you interpret the world. To help you think about your perceptions and cognitive processes through an ethical lens, below we discuss some guidelines to assist you in this process.

TEST YOUR KNOWLEDGE
- How is ethics relevant to the perception process?

IMPROVING YOUR PERCEPTION SKILLS

You probably realize now that perceptions are subject to variance and error because of the variety of steps one goes through in forming them (selection, organization, and interpretation) and the range of factors that influence the perception process (individual characteristics, cognitive complexity, power, culture, historical time period, and social roles). However, certain cognitive and communication behaviors can improve one's ability to perceive and understand the world.

First, one can engage in *mindfulness* to improve perception and understanding. Mindfulness refers to a clear focus on the activity one is engaged in, with attention to as many specifics of the event as possible (Langer, 1978). People tend to be most mindful when they are engaged in a new or unusual activity. Once an activity becomes habitual, they are likely to overlook its details. Mindfulness requires that one bring the same level of attention and involvement to routine activities as one does to novel ones.

In addition, before assuming your perceptions are accurate, you might ask yourself a few questions to help you check those perceptions:

- Have you focused too narrowly and missed relevant information due to selective attention? For example, did you focus on what the person was wearing rather than what he or she was saying?

- What type of organizational pattern did you use? For example, just because two people are standing next to one another does not mean they are together.

- To what extent have you considered all possible interpretations for the information you perceived, using the full range of your cognitive complexity? For example, if you did poorly on a test, was it due to poor test construction, your lack of sleep, the teacher's failure to prepare you, or your own failure to study sufficiently?

- How might your physical condition have influenced your perceptions? For example, are you tired, hungry, or frightened?

- How has your cultural background influenced your perceptions? For example, are you perceiving politeness as deception?

- How has your social role influenced your perception? For example, have you begun to perceive all elderly people as infirm because you work in a nursing home?

- How has your social position influenced your perception? For example, have you considered how others with different positions might perceive the same issue?

Another way to improve one's perception and understanding is to clearly separate *facts* from *inferences*. Facts are truths that are verifiable based on observation. Inferences are conclusions that we draw or interpretations we make based on the facts. Thus, it may be a fact that Southerners speak more slowly than do people from other regions of the United States, but it is an inference if you conclude that their slow speech indicates slow thought processes.

Finally, one communication act in particular will greatly improve anyone's perception skills: perception checking. That is, checking with others to determine if their perceptions match your own. If they do not, you may need to alter your perceptions. For example, Rosario once had an extremely negative reaction to a job candidate who interviewed at her company. She perceived him as arrogant and sexist. However, when she talked with her colleagues she discovered that no one else had a similarly strong negative response to the candidate. She decided that her perceptions must have been influenced by something in her own background; for example, he may have reminded her of someone she had once known who did display those negative traits. In revising her opinion of the candidate, Rosario demonstrated a well-developed sensitivity to the perception side of communication. All of us can benefit from greater awareness of the assumptions and attributions we make.

TEST YOUR KNOWLEDGE

- What one skill could you develop that would most improve your perception processes? Why does it help?

SUMMARY

Perception plays an important role in everyday communication. People use three perceptual processes to manage the vast array of sensory data in their environments: selection, organization, and interpretation. From all the sounds, sights, smells, tastes, and textures available, people choose only a few to focus on. Once we attend to particular sensory information, we organize it to make sense of it. Two of the cognitive processes we use to organize information are cognitive representations and categorization. Finally, after we perceive and organize sensory information, we assign meaning to it using frames and attributions.

In addition, the sensory data we select to attend to, how we organize it, and the interpretations we assign are all influenced by our individual characteristics, such as physical abilities and differences, cognitive complexity, and any personality and individual differences. In addition, perception processes are affected by one's position in the power hierarchy, culture, historical events during one's lifetime, and social roles.

Because people vary so much in their perceptions, no one should assume that what he or she perceives is the same as what others perceive. Instead, we all must carefully check our perceptions on a regular basis and expend energy to overcome errors in processing as well as any attributional biases.

HUMAN COMMUNICATION IN SOCIETY ONLINE

To review this chapter, use the MyCommunicationLab Web site to test your understanding of the following key terms, record your answers to the chapter review questions, and complete the suggested activities. Expand your learning and understanding of chapter concepts by completing additional activities and exercises online. Access code required. Go to www.mycommunicationlab.com for more information or to purchase standalone access.

KEY TERMS

selection 77
organization 77
interpretation 77
selective attention 77
cognitive representation 78
schemas 79
prototype 79
script 79

categorization 79
label 80
stereotyping 80
frame 81
attribution theory 81
attributional bias 82
self-serving bias 82
fundamental attribution error 82

constructs 83
cognitive complexity 83
ethnocentrism 88
prejudice 89
ego-defensive function 89
value-expressive function 89
cohort effect 90
social role 90

APPLY WHAT YOU KNOW

1. **Examining Stereotypes**
   For each of the words below, write down your beliefs about the group represented. In other words, provide a list of specific characteristics you believe are typically displayed by members of these groups.

   a. fraternity members
   b. politicians
   c. models
   d. rap stars
   e. body builders
   f. religious leaders

   After you have done so, compare your list to the lists created by other members of your class. What characteristics for each group did you have in common?

What characteristics differed? Can you think of at least one person from each group who does not display the characteristics you listed? What information and perceptions helped shaped your stereotypes? How valid do you think your stereotypes are?

2. **Attributional Biases**

As this chapter explains, people have a tendency to attribute their own positive behavior to internal traits and their negative behavior to external factors. However, they are also more likely to attribute others' positive behavior to external conditions and others' negative behavior to internal traits. In this exercise we want you to indicate how the attributional bias would cause you to describe each of the following behaviors, depending on who had performed it.

Example: Forgetting to make a phone call

I'm busy. You're thoughtless.

Example: Earning a good grade

I'm intelligent. You were lucky.

Do the exercise for each of the following behaviors/ events:

a. Receiving a raise
b. Breaking a vase
c. Arriving late
d. Winning an award
e. Burning a meal
f. Making a group laugh

Compare your responses with those of others in your class. What terms were used to describe one's own experiences? What terms were used to describe others' experiences? What is it about the perception process that makes attribution bias so common?

Although this is just an exercise, remember that the attributional bias is quite common. Pay attention to your own thoughts and comments the next time something bad happens to you or others.

3. **Ethics and Perception**

The authors argue that ethics is relevant to our perceptual processes. To what extent do you agree or disagree with this statement? Provide three arguments for each position. Now that you have considered arguments for both positions, is your opinion the same as it was before or has it altered?

EXPLORE

1. Go to a website that features perception exercises and information, such as the Hanover College Sensation and Perception Tutorials or the Encyclopedia of Psychology's Sensation and Perception tutorial. After experiencing at least two of the tutorials, write a paragraph in which you explain what you have learned about perception.

2. Go to a website such as Gestalt Laws or Perceptual Grouping and read the information regarding the Gestalts laws of grouping. In a brief paper, provide an explanation of the Gestalt laws then describe how

these laws might influence how we view and communicate with others.

3. Go to a website such as Harvard University's Interpersonal Perception Communication Lab or Tufts University's Interpersonal Perception and Communication page and read a description of at least one interpersonal perception and communication research project. Write a paragraph summarizing what the project you reviewed explains about the relationship between perception and communication.

5

Verbal Communication

chapter outline

> ## "The verbal elements of communication are the foundation on which meaning is created."

When I took a trip to Britain, I thought people would speak with a "British accent." I didn't realize that there are many different accents and the differences are not just pronunciation, but also vocabulary. In order to get my message across, I learned to avoid using slang words as much as I could. I didn't realize how much American slang I use in my everyday speech! Despite the many different ways of speaking English across the UK, I felt the way that I speak English made me stick out as an American.

When we think of "communication," we tend to think about the verbal elements of communication: the words people choose, the accents they speak with, and the meanings they convey through language. We frequently don't consider the ways in which verbal communication assists or hinders relationship development, as illustrated in the opening example, or its effect on the creation of identities.

In this chapter we will explore the verbal elements of communication and how people use verbal communication to accomplish various goals. First we discuss the importance of verbal communication and its value as a topic of study. We then describe how individuals use verbal communication, including the functions it serves and the components of language that make it possible. Next we explore individual characteristics such as gender, age, regionality, ethnicity and race, and education and occupation that influence verbal communication. We investigate the societal forces that influence verbal communication by examining the relationships among language, perception, and power. Finally, we provide suggestions for communicating more ethically and more effectively.

Once you have read this chapter you will be able to:
- Identify three reasons for learning about verbal communication.
- Describe the functions and components of language.
- Identify and give an example of each of the influences on verbal communication.
- Describe the relationships between language, perception, and power.
- Identify and give examples of confirming communication, disconfirming communication, and hate speech.
- Discuss ethical issues in verbal communication.
- Discuss ways to improve your own verbal communication skills.

THE IMPORTANCE OF VERBAL COMMUNICATION

Children from families who converse and eat meals together on a regular basis have higher self-esteem and interact better with their peers.

Although the nonverbal aspects of communication are important, the verbal elements of communication are the foundation on which meaning is created. If you doubt that this is the case, try this simple test. Using only nonverbal communication, convey this message to a friend or roommate: "I failed my exam because I locked my keys in my car and couldn't get my textbook until well after midnight." How well was your nonverbal message understood? If you have ever traveled in a country where you didn't speak the language, no doubt you already knew before trying this experiment that nonverbal communication can only get you so far. We will touch on the importance of nonverbal communication here and discuss it in depth in Chapter 6. In this section we propose that to be a highly effective communicator you need to understand the verbal elements of communication.

Verbal communication is also important because of the role it plays in identity and relationship development. As you might remember from our discussion in Chapter 3, individuals develop a sense of self through communication with others. More specifically, the labels used to describe individuals can influence their self-concepts and increase or decrease their self-esteem. People's verbal communication practices also can impede or improve their relationships. Research by four psychology professors at Emory University supports our claims about the relationship between verbal communication and an individual's identity development and relationship skills. These scholars found that families that converse and eat meals together on a regular basis have children who not only are more familiar with their family histories but also tend to have higher self-esteem, interact better with their peers, and be better able to recover from tragedy and negative events (Duke et al., 2003).

In addition, the very language people speak is tied to their identities. Studies of bilingual and multilingual speakers show that their perceptions, behaviors, and even personalities alter when they change languages (Ramírez-Esparza, Gosling, Benet-Martínez, Potter, & Pennebaker, 2006). Why does this occur? The answer is that every language is embedded in a specific cultural context, and when people learn a language, they also learn the beliefs, values, and norms of its culture (Edwards, 2004). So speaking a language evokes its culture as well as a sense of who we are within that culture. Thus the language you use to communicate verbally shapes who you are, as you will see in *It Happened to Me: Cristina.*

It Happened to Me: Cristina

I was teaching an adult education class composed primarily of Mexican immigrants when I first noticed that the language people speak affects how they behave. I'm bilingual, so even though we normally spoke English in my class, sometimes we switched to Spanish. Over time, I noticed that several male students were respectful and deferential when we spoke English; however, when we switched to Spanish, they became more flirtatious and seemed less willing to treat me as an authority figure. Now I understand that these differences probably were related to how men and women interact in the two cultures.

WHAT IS VERBAL COMMUNICATION?

Verbal communication generally refers to the written or oral words we exchange; however, as our opening example shows, verbal communication has to do with more than just the words people speak. It includes pronunciation or accent, the meanings of the words used, and a range of variations in the way people speak a language, which depend on their regional backgrounds and other factors.

Language, of course, plays a central role in communication. Some argue that it is our use of language that makes us human. Unlike other mammals, humans use symbols that they can string together to create new words and with which they can form infinite sets of never-before-heard, -thought, or -read sentences. This ability allows people to be creative and expressive, such as when they coin terms like "Googleganger"—nominated by the American Dialect Society as one of the most creative words for 2007—meaning a person with your name who shows up when you google yourself. This is a play on words with the German word "Doppelgänger," which refers to a double of someone (especially a ghostly double). Even small children who are unschooled in grammar create their own rules of language by using innate linguistic ability together with linguistic information they glean from the people around them. For example, young children often say "mouses" instead of "mice" because they first learn, and apply broadly, the most common rule for pluralizing—adding an *s*.

To help you better understand the role of language in the communication process, the next section explores seven communicative functions of language as well as four components of language use.

Functions of Language

We all use language so automatically that we usually don't think about the many roles it plays. However, language helps us do everything from ordering lunch to giving directions to writing love poems. Moreover, a single utterance can function in a variety of ways. For example, a simple "thank you" not only expresses gratitude, it also can increase feelings of intimacy and liking. Consequently, understanding the ways language functions can help you communicate more effectively. As we discuss next, language can serve at least seven functions: instrumental, regulatory, informative, heuristic, interactional, personal, and imaginative.

- The most basic function of language is **instrumental**. This means we can use it to obtain what we need or desire. For instance, when you invite friends to dinner, the invitation is instrumental in that you want your friends to come to dinner and the invitation helps make that happen.

- A second (and closely related) language function is **regulatory**, meaning that we can use it to control or regulate the behaviors of others. In your invitation, you may ask your friends to bring a bottle of wine or a dessert, as a way of regulating their behavior.

- Another basic function of language is to **inform**—to communicate information or report facts. When you invite your friends to dinner, you usually include the date and time to inform them of when you want them to come.

- We also use language to acquire knowledge and understanding, which is referred to as a **heuristic** use. When you want to invite friends to dinner, you may ask them if they are available at that date and time to learn if your dinner is going to occur as scheduled or if you need to change the date.

- When language is used in an **interactional** fashion, it establishes and defines social relationships in both interpersonal and group settings. Thus, when you invite your friends to dinner, you engage in a behavior that helps maintain your relationship with them as friends.

- **Personal language** expresses individuality and personality and is more common in private than in public settings. When you invite your friends to dinner you might jokingly say, "Don't bring that cheap bottle of wine, like you did last time." In this way, you use language to express your sense of humor.

- A final way you can use language is **imaginatively**. Imaginative language is used to express oneself artistically or creatively, as in drama, poetry, or stories. Thus,

instrumental
use of language to obtain what you need or desire

regulatory
use of language to control or regulate the behaviors of others

informative
use of language to communicate information or report facts

heuristic
use of language to acquire knowledge and understanding

interactional
use of language to establish and define social relationships

personal language
use of language to express individuality and personality

imaginative
use of language to express oneself artistically or creatively

if on the cover of your invitation to dinner you wrote "A loaf of bread, a jug of wine, and thou," you would be using the imaginative function of language.

As our discussion thus far indicates, language has seven basic functions, and speakers use them to accomplish specific goals or tasks. Note that these functions overlap and that one utterance can accomplish more than one function at the same time. For example, when inviting your friends to dinner, if you jokingly said, "James, our butler, will be serving dinner promptly at eight, so don't be late!" your utterance would both be imaginative (unless you actually have a butler named James) and regulatory. That is, you would be using language creatively while also attempting to regulate your guests' behavior to ensure they arrived on time.

Now that we have summarized the essential functions that language can serve, let's examine the basic components that allow us to use language as a flexible and creative tool of communication.

Components of Language

Scholars describe language use as being made up of four components: *phonology* (sounds), *syntax* (structure or rules), *semantics* (meaning), and *pragmatics* (use), as shown in *Visual Summary 5.1: Components of Language*. Every language has its own rules of **grammar**—the structural rules that govern the generation of meaning in that language. In this section, we examine the role each plays in the communication process.

Phonology: Sounds

Phonology is the study of the sounds that compose individual languages and how those sounds communicate meaning. Basic sound units are called phonemes. They include vowels, consonants, and diphthongs (pairs of letters that operate as one, such as *th*). Different languages can use different phonemes. For example, French does not have the *th* sound. As a result, many native French speakers find it difficult to pronounce "this" or "that." Similarly, in Japanese, a phoneme that is between *r* and *l* is the closest equivalent to the English *r* sound. For more information about phonology, see www.langsci.ucl.ac.uk/ipa/, the home page of the International Phonetic Association.

Syntax: Rules

Syntax refers to the rules that govern word order. Due to the English rules of syntax, the sentences "The young boy hit the old man" and "The old man hit the young boy" have very different meanings, even though they contain identical words. Syntax also governs how words of various categories (nouns, adjectives, verbs) are combined into clauses, which in turn combine into sentences. Whether or not we are conscious of them, most of us regularly follow certain rules about combining words—for example, that the verb and subject in a sentence have to agree, so people say "the pencil *is* on the table," not "the pencil *are* on the table." Because of these rules, people combine words consistently in ways that make sense and make communication possible.

Semantics: Meaning

Semantics is the study of meaning, which is an important component of communication. To illustrate the effect of syntax compared with the effect of meaning, Noam Chomsky (1957), an important scholar in the field of linguistics, devised this famous sentence: "Colorless green ideas sleep furiously" (p. 15). This sentence is acceptable in terms of English grammar, but on the semantic level it is nonsensical: Ideas logically cannot be either colorless or green (and certainly not both!), ideas don't sleep, and nothing sleeps furiously (does it?).

As a student, which functions of language do you use most frequently? Which do you use most often in your professional life? If you use different functions in each of these roles, why do you think this is true?

grammar
the structural rules that govern the generation of meaning in a language

phonology
the study of the sounds that compose individual languages and how those sounds communicate meaning

syntax
the rules that govern word order

semantics
the study of meaning

As you remember from Chapter 1, a central part of our definition of communication is the creation of shared meaning. For any given message, a number of factors contribute to the creation of its meaning. Perhaps most important are the words the speaker chooses. For example, did you have a friend in high school who always gave the right answer in class, got excellent grades, and always seemed to have a wealth of information at his fingertips? What word would you use to describe this friend: *smart, intelligent, clever, wise,* or *brilliant?* Because each word has a slightly different meaning, you try to choose the one that most accurately characterizes your friend. However, in choosing the "right" words, you have to consider the two types of meaning that words convey: *denotative* and *connotative*—terms that we also discussed in Chapter 1.

The **denotative meaning** refers to the dictionary, or literal, meaning of a word and is usually the agreed-upon meaning for most speakers of the language. Referring back to our description of your friend: The dictionary defines wise as "Having the ability to discern or judge what is true, right, or lasting; sagacious" and *intelligent* as "Showing sound judgment and rationality" ("American Heritage Dictionary," 2000). Does either word exactly capture how you would describe your friend? If not, which word does?

Words also carry **connotative meanings**, which are the affective or interpretive meanings attached to them. Using the previous example, the connotative meaning of the word *wise* implies an older person with long experience, so it might not be the best choice to describe your young friend.

Pragmatics: Language in Use

Just like phonology, syntax, and semantics, the field of pragmatics seeks to identify patterns or rules people follow when they use language appropriately. In the case of pragmatics, however, the emphasis is on how language is used in specific situations to accomplish goals (Nofsinger, 1999). For example, scholars who study pragmatics might seek to understand the rules for communicating appropriately in a sorority, a faculty meeting, or an evangelical church. They would do this by examining communication that is successful and unsuccessful in each setting. The three units of study for scholars of pragmatics are *speech acts, conversational rules,* and *contextual rules.* Let's examine what each contributes to communication.

Speech Acts.   One branch of pragmatics, **speech act theory**, looks closely at the seven language functions described previously and suggests that when people communicate, they do not just say things, they also *do* things with their words. For example, speech act theorists argue that when you say, "I bet you ten dollars the Yankees win the World Series," you aren't just saying something, you actually are doing something. That something you are doing is making a bet, or entering into an agreement that will result in an exchange of money.

One common speech act is the request. A recent study examined one type of request that occurs primarily in U.S. family contexts—the common practice of "nagging" (Boxer, 2002). Nagging (repeated requests by one family member to another) often concerns household chores and is usually a source of conflict. The researcher found that nagging requires several sequential acts. First, there is an initial request, which is usually given in the form of a command ("Please take out the garbage") or a hedged request ("Do you think you can take out the garbage this evening?"). If the request is not granted, it is repeated as a reminder (after some lapse of time), which often includes an allusion to the first request. ("Did you hear me? Can you please take out the garbage?") When a reminder is repeated (the third stage), it becomes nagging and usually involves a scolding or a threat, depending on the relationship, for example, whether the exchange is between parent/child ("This is the last time I'm going to ask you, take out the garbage!") or between relational partners ("Never mind, I'll do it myself!").

denotative meaning
the dictionary, or literal, meaning of a word

connotative meaning
the affective or interpretive meanings attached to a word

pragmatics
field of study that emphasizes how language is used in specific situations to accomplish goals

speech act theory
branch of pragmatics that suggests that when people communicate, they do not just say things, they also *do* things with their words

Components of Language
Phonology, Syntax, Pragmatics, Semantics

I Love You

Phonobgy

ī lŭv yōō

What do the words sound like?

Syntax

I love you

Subject   Verb   Object

How are the words arranged?

Pragmatics

What is really going on here for the people involved? What are the implications of these words for their everyday lives?

Semantics

What do the words mean?

The researcher found that men were rarely involved in nagging, and she suggests that this is because men are perceived as having more power and are therefore able to successfully request and gain compliance from another family member without resorting to nagging. She also notes that children can have power (if they refuse to comply with a request despite their lack of status) and a parent can lack power despite having status. The researcher also found that nagging mostly occurs in our intimate relationships. She concludes that, by nagging, we lose power—but without power, we are forced into nagging; thus it seems to be a vicious cycle! The study shows that what we *do* with words affects our relationships.

Understanding the meaning of various speech acts often requires understanding context and culture (Austin, 1975; Sbisa, 2002). For this reason, people may agree on what is said but disagree on what is *meant*. For example, the other day Katy said to her roommate Hiroshi, "I have been so busy I haven't even had time to do the dishes." He replied, "Well, I'm sorry, but I have been busy, too." What did he think Katy was "doing" with her utterance? When they discussed this interaction, Katy explained that *she* was making an excuse, while Hiroshi said *he* heard a criticism— that because she hadn't had time to do the dishes, he should have. Thus, messages may have different meanings or "do" different things, from different persons' viewpoints. This difference lies in the sender's and receiver's interpretations of the statement. Most misunderstandings arise not around what was said—but around what was done or meant.

As we have seen, speech acts may be direct or indirect. That is, speech acts such as requests can be framed more (or less) clearly and directly. Let's suppose that you want your partner to feed the dog. You may directly ask: "Would you feed the dog?" Or you could state an order: "Feed the dog!" On the other hand, you may communicate the same information indirectly: "Do you know if the dog was fed?" or "I wonder if the dog was fed." Finally, you may make your request very indirectly: "It would be nice if someone fed the dog," or "Do you think the dog looks hungry?"

Which do you think is better—to communicate directly or indirectly? This is actually a trick question. The answer is: It depends—on the situation and the cultural context. Although direct requests and questions may be clearer, they also can be less polite. Ordering someone to feed the dog makes one's desire clearly and unequivocally known, but at the same time, it can be seen as rude and domineering.

Recent research shows that U.S. Americans tend to be more indirect in their requests, when compared to Mexicans (Pinto & Raschio, 2007), but probably not as indirect as many Asians (Kim, 2002). However, when expressing disagreement, most U.S. Americans tend to be more direct than most Asians. A recent study investigated how Malaysians handled disagreements in business negotiation and concluded that the Malays' opposition was never direct or on record, but always indirect and implied. Despite their disagreements with the other party, they honored the other, always balancing power with politeness (Paramasivam, 2007). A pragmatic approach reminds us that how language is used always depends on the situation and cultural context. We'll discuss more cross-cultural differences in communication practices further in Chapter 7.

Conversational Rules.   Conversational rules govern the ways in which communicators organize conversation. For example, one rule of conversation in U.S. English is that if someone asks you a question, you should provide an answer. If you do not know the answer, others expect you to at least reply, "I don't know" or "Let me think about it." However, in some cultures and languages, answers to questions are not obligatory. Among Warm Spring Indians of Oregon, for example, questions may be answered at a later time (with little reference to the previous conversation) or not answered at all (Philips, 1990).

Nagging is one common type of speech act that occurs in U.S. family contexts.

Conversational rules—such as turn-taking—govern the way we communicate and vary somewhat from context to context.

Perhaps the most researched conversational rules involve turn-taking. The most basic rule for English language speakers, and many others, is that only one person speaks at a time. People may tolerate some overlap between their talk and another's, but typically they expect to be able to have their say without too much interruption (Schegloff, 2000). Still, as a refinement of this point, Susanna Kohonen (2004) found in her cross-cultural study of turn-taking that conversationalists were more tolerant of overlaps in social settings, such as at parties or when hanging out with friends, than in more settings. Thus, sometimes the context influences conversational rules. We discuss contexual rules next.

Other rules for turn-taking determine who is allowed to speak (Sacks, Schegloff, & Jefferson, 1978). For example, if you "have the floor" you can generally continue to speak. When you are finished, you can select someone else. You can do this either by asking a question, "So Sue, what is your opinion?" or by looking at another person as you finish talking. If you don't have the floor but wish to speak, you can begin speaking just as the current speaker completes a turn.

The turn-allocation system works amazingly well most of the time. Occasionally, however, people do not follow these implicit rules. For example, the current speaker could select the next speaker by directing a question to her, but someone else could interrupt and "steal" the floor. Also, some speakers are quicker to grab the talk turn, which allows them more opportunities to speak. Then, speakers who are slower to begin a turn or take the floor have fewer opportunities to contribute to the conversation. They may feel left out or resent the other speakers for monopolizing the conversation.

Pragmatics involves understanding the implicit communication rules that apply in one setting or another.

Contextual Rules. No matter what language or dialect you speak, your use of language varies depending on the communication situation (Mey, 2001). For example, you probably wouldn't discuss the same topics in the same way at a funeral as you would in a meeting at your workplace, in a courtroom, or at a party. What would happen if you did? For example, telling jokes and laughing at a party is typically acceptable, whereas those same jokes and laughing might be interpreted very negatively in a courtroom or at a funeral. One challenge for pragmatics scholars, then, is uncovering the implicit communication rules that govern different settings. As noted earlier, communication pragmatics also vary by culture. For example, in some houses of worship, appropriate verbal behavior involves talking very quietly or not all, acting subdued, and listening without responding—but in others, people applaud, sing exuberantly, and respond loudly with exclamations like "Amen!" Neither set of communication rules is "right"; each is appropriate to its own setting and cultural context.

As you can see, verbal language is far more than the words people use; it also includes the sounds and meanings of those words, and the rules individuals use for arranging words and for communicating in particular settings. Moreover, speakers differ in the ways they use language to communicate. They also differ in the ways they enunciate their words and how they present their ideas. For example, Southerners "drawl" their vowels while New Englanders drop the r after theirs; some speakers are extremely direct, while others are not. What accounts for these differences? We explore the answers in the next section.

TEST YOUR KNOWLEDGE

- What are the seven functions of language? Give an example that illustrates how each works.

- What is phonology? Syntax? Semantics? How do they work together to facilitate effective communication?

- What do pragmatics scholars study? How do they determine pragmatics in specific communication contexts?

- What is the difference between connotative and denotative meaning?

INFLUENCES ON VERBAL COMMUNICATION

As we saw in Chapter 3, our communication is influenced by our identities and the various cultures to which we belong. In turn, our communication helps shape these identities. When identities influence several aspects of language, we say that speakers have a distinct **dialect**, a variation of a language distinguished by its **lexical choice** (vocabulary), grammar, and pronunciation. In other instances, the influence of identity is less dramatic, and speakers vary only in some pronunciations or word choices. In this section we examine how identities related to gender, age, regionality, ethnicity and race, and education and occupation shape language use.

Gender

Growing up male or female may influence the way you communicate in some situations, because men and women are socialized to communicate in specific ways. In fact—as exemplified in the popularity of books like *Men Are from Mars, Women Are from Venus* (Gray, 1992)—many people believe that English-speaking men and women in the United States speak different dialects. These beliefs are reinforced by media depictions that tend to present stereotypical depictions of men and women in magazines, on television, and in movies (Wood & Dindia, 1998). For example, one team of researchers reviewed how journal articles talked about gender differences in the past fifty years and found that because people are more interested in hearing about differences than similarities, shows and books that emphasize these differences tend to sell better and receive wider recognition (Sagrestano, Heavey, & Christensen, 1998).

Even scholarly research tends to focus on, and sometimes exaggerate, the importance of sex differences; some researchers have reported that women's verbal style is often described as supportive, egalitarian, personal, and disclosive, while men's is characterized as instrumental, competitive, and assertive (Mulac, Bradac, & Gibbons, 2001; Wood, 2002). But although these and other studies suggest that men and women do use different language and communication styles, other research refutes this claim. A recent review of studies comparing males and females on a large array of psychological and communication differences, including self-disclosure and interruptions, revealed very few significant differences (Hyde, 2006). In fact, the differences in men's and women's communication patterns are estimated to be as small as 1 percent, or even less (Canary & Hause, 1993).

How can these contradictory findings be explained? To begin, many studies of gender differences ask participants to report on their perceptions or ask them to recall men's and women's conversational styles (e.g., Aylor & Dainton, 2004). This approach can be problematic because people's perceptions are not always accurate. For example, Nancy Burrell and her colleagues (1988) argue that persistent, stereotypical, gender-based expectations likely influence people's perceptions that men and women behave or communicate differently even when few behavioral differences exist. More recently, Heilman, Caleo, and Halim (2010) found that gender stereotypes were invoked even more strongly when workers were told they would communicate using computer-mediated communication rather than face to face.

How do these faulty perceptions arise about communication differences between men and women? Two important contributors are a person's perceptions of his or her own gendered communication and media representations of men's and women's communication. Knott and Natalle (1997) and Margaret Baker (1991) explain that indi-

dialect
a variation of a language distinguished by its vocabulary, grammar, and pronunciation

lexical choice
vocabulary

viduals who see themselves as being very feminine or masculine tend to view others in the same light, and they tend to have rigid views of the sexes and their communication behavior (Canary & Emmers-Sommer, 1997).

Carol Rose (1995) asserts forcefully that such gender-based perceptions are hard to change, whether or not the perceptions are true. For example, the negative stereotype of the talkative woman is very persistent. In one recent study, students were shown a videotaped conflict between a man and a woman and were asked to rate the two on likability and competence. In different versions of the video, the researchers varied how much the man and woman each talked. As the researchers expected, viewers rated the couple as less likable when they saw the woman doing more of the talking. And the man who talked more was rated as most competent (Sellers, Woolsey, & Swann, 2007). Even though this negative stereotype persists, many studies have shown that not only do women generally not talk more than men, actually the opposite is true—men tend to be more talkative in many situations (Leaper & Ayres, 2007; Wiest, Abernathy, Obenchain, & Major, 2006). In addition, the stereotype persists that women are more "kind, helpful, sympathetic, and concerned about others" while men are seen as "aggressive, forceful, independent, and decisive" (Heilman, 2001, p. 658). Furthermore, these gender stereotypes can create differential treatment in the workplace.

Laurie Coltri (2004) also claims that the gender of the communicator heavily influences people's perceptions of her or his communication behavior. In her study of gender stereotypes in mediation, or informal dispute resolution, she manipulated transcripts of mediations so that half the time Person A was identified as male and Person B as female, and half the time the reverse occurred. In each case, the person labeled as female was rated more negatively than when that same person was labeled as male. Considering the influence of perception and gender stereotypes, you can see how difficult it can be to objectively evaluate communication differences between the sexes.

Another factor that makes it difficult to pinpoint the impact of gender differences in communication is that researchers sometimes overlook the influence of situation and relationship on individuals' language use and communication styles. For example, imagine that a researcher observes communication in two situations: (1) groups of men talking among themselves and (2) groups of women talking among themselves. After coding the communication behaviors observed in the two types of groups, the researcher concludes that men and women communicate differently. What is wrong with this conclusion? It ignores the possibility that these same men and women might communicate in much more similar ways when they are talking in mixed-gender groups (Aries, 1996). The researcher has failed to consider that they may adapt their communication style to their audience.

When people adapt to a specific audience, they are often adjusting to the communication style of the more powerful members of that audience. Thus, if powerful members of the audience use more direct or task-focused language, so might the speaker. In addition to adapting their communication style, people also often use more deferential or tentative language when communicating with more powerful people. Both men and women adapt to these power differences; thus both groups are more likely to use tentative language with their bosses than with their siblings. Women use language that is more tentative overall because generally they have lower status, and people with lower status are not typically expected to make strong, assertive statements (Reid, Keerie, & Palomares, 2003). Similarly, women tend to use more "filler words" (such as *like* or *well*) and more conditional words (*would, should, could*) (Mehl & Pennebaker, 2003).

Researchers have wondered whether gender differences in conversations are a consequence of interacting with a partner who uses a particular style of communication. For example, if you encourage another person to talk by nodding your head in agreement, asking questions, or giving supportive linguistic cues (such as "uh-huh," or "yes …"), you are using a facilitative style of communication. To explore this question, social psychologists Annette Hannah and Tamar Murachver assigned male and female partners who were strangers to each other to meet and talk several times. After the first conversation, their communication styles were judged by outside observers to be either facilitative or nonfacilitative; and the researchers found that, regardless of gender, participants responded to each other in ways that mirrored their partner's style (Hannah & Murachver, 2007).

Over time, however, in subsequent conversations, the women and men shifted their speech toward more stereotypically gendered patterns; that is, the men talked more, for longer times, while women increased their use of minimal responses, reduced the amount they spoke, and asked more questions. In other words, the women increased their facilitative style of speech while the men decreased theirs. Discussing their findings, the researchers pose several questions: Why are women more facilitative in their speech? Why do they talk less when talking with men? Do they feel threatened or insecure? Are they less comfortable in talking more than men? Perhaps women feel that dominating conversations with men has negative social consequences and, therefore, they encourage men to do the talking—an explanation that would be confirmed by the earlier study we mentioned, where students negatively evaluated couples in which the women talked more than the men. The researchers provide no definitive explanation, but note, as do we, that gender differences are complicated (Hannah & Murachver, 2007).

In conclusion, women and men do show differences in their communication styles, and much of this difference likely is attributable to differences in power, status, and expectations in communication situations.

Age

You may not think of age as affecting language use, but it does, particularly when it comes to word choice. For example, you might have talked about "the cooties" when you were a child, but you probably don't now. Moreover, children have a whole vocabulary to describe "naughty topics," especially related to bodily functions. Yet, most adults do not use those words. Adolescents also develop vocabulary that they use throughout their teenage years and then drop during early adulthood. Adolescents have described highly valued people and things as "cool," "righteous," "bad," "hot," and "phat," depending on the generation and context. This distinct vocabulary helps teenagers feel connected to their peers and separate from their parents and other adults.

The era in which you grew up also influences your vocabulary. As you age, you continue to use certain words that were common when you were growing up, even if they have fallen out of use. This is called the **cohort effect** and refers to common denominators of a group that was born and reared in the same general period. For example, your grandparents and their contemporaries may refer to dancing as "cutting a rug," while younger speakers rarely use this term. However, recent research suggests that young girls may be becoming the trendsetters in language use both for their own and other cohorts. Some linguists argue that girls in southern California are influencing young men's—and even older women's—language use; they call it the "California vowel shift." For example, "Like, what dew you mean, tha-yt I hayve an accent?" At a recent meeting of a high school club in southern California called Girls for a Change, teen girls gathered to discuss ways to fix cultural ills; they talked about social action as "something important to *dew*." Among different approaches, they considered "tew-toring." There is evidence that young men and some older women are beginning to adopt some of the sounds started by teenage girls. As new ways of saying things find their way in the general language, a regional—or even statewide—dialect emerges (Krieger, 2004).

People's communication skills and the meanings they attribute to concepts also vary due to their age. Why? Older people are more cognitively developed and have had more experiences; therefore they tend to view concepts differently than do younger people, especially children (Pennebaker & Stone, 2003). For example, children typically engage in egocentric speech patterns (Piaget, 1952). This means that

cohort effect
the influence of shared characteristics of a group that was born and reared in the same general period

they cannot adapt their communication to their conversational partners nor understand that others may feel or view the world differently. Children lack the number of constructs adults have. For example, very young children have little concept of future or past time, so understanding what might happen next week or month is difficult for them. Consequently, parents usually adapt their communication when trying to help children understand some event in the future.

Regionality

Geographical location also strongly influences people's language use. The most common influence is on pronunciation. For example, how do you pronounce the word "oil"? In parts of New York it is pronounced somewhat like "earl," while in areas of the South it is pronounced more like "awl," and in the West it is often pronounced "oyl" as in "Olive Oyl." Sometimes regionality affects more than just accent, leading to regional dialects. Why do these differences arise?

Historically, verbal differences developed wherever people were separated by a geographical boundary—whether it was mountains, lakes, rivers, deserts, oceans—or some social boundary, such as race, class, or religion (Fromkin & Rodman, 1983). Moreover, people tended to speak similarly to those around them. For example, in the eighteenth century, residents of Australia, North America, and England had relatively little contact with one another; consequently, they developed recognizably different dialects even though they all spoke the same language. Typically, the more isolated a group, the more distinctive their dialect.

In the United States, dialectical differences in English originally arose because two groups of English colonists settled along the East Coast. The colonists who settled in the South, near present-day Virginia, primarily came from Somerset and Gloucestershire—both western counties in England—and they brought with them an accent with strongly voiced s sounds and with the r strongly pronounced after vowels. In contrast, the colonists who settled in the north, what we now call New England, came from midland counties such as Essex, Kent, and London, where people spoke a dialect that did not pronounce the r after vowels, a feature still common to many New England dialects (Crystal, 2003). See Figure 5.1 for an interesting outgrowth of U.S. local dialects.

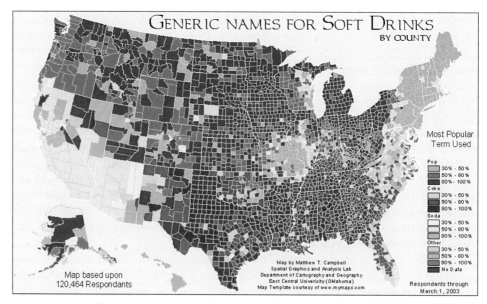

FIGURE 5.1: The terms we use to refer to soft drinks also vary by region in the United States.

Alternative VIEW
The Northern Cities Vowel Shift

Conventional wisdom says that dialects should be disappearing, due to increasingly transient populations, immigration from other countries, and the influence of pervasive mass media. However, University of Pennsylvania linguist William Labov and his colleagues published a phonological atlas (2005) showing that across the country, regional dialects are stronger than ever. In a radio interview, he described some these specific changes.

In what ways do you think regional accents influence communication between people from different areas of the United States? Do you see regional accents as a positive or negative influence on American society?

The most important differences have developed in this huge area around the Great Lakes region which we call the Inland North, extending westward from Syracuse through Buffalo, Cleveland, Detroit, Chicago, and Milwaukee. Those great cities occupied by about 35 million people are all moving in a very different linguistic direction from the rest of the United States.

Now what happens here is that the short-a becomes "ai" [like in "yeah"] in every single word, so that people have, say, "theaht" and "feahct." In the meantime, the short words spelled with short-o like "socks" or "block" or "cot" move into the position that was formerly occupied by "ah." So the man's name [John becomes] "Jahn"—that's man's name, "Jahn." And the girl's name [Jan] becomes "Jain"… This example of a sound change in the United States called the "Northern Cities Shift."

SOURCES: Adapted from Voice of America (VOA) radio interview with William Labov on January 12, 2005. Retrieved June 2, 2008, from http://www.voanews.com/specialenglish/archive/2005-01/a-2005-01-11-5-1.cfm. And from Labov, W. (Ed.). (2005). *Atlas of North American English*. New York: Walter De Gruyter, Inc.

Other waves of immigration have occurred over the past four hundred years, increasing dialectical diversity in the United States. Each group of immigrants brings a distinctive way of speaking and culture-specific communication rules. Some groups, especially those who have remained somewhat isolated since their arrival, maintain much of their original dialect; an example is the inhabitants of Tangier Island in the Chesapeake Bay (Crystal, 2003). Other groups' dialects have assimilated with the dialects of their neighbors to form new dialects. Thus, the seventeenth-century "western" English dialect of Virginia has become the southern drawl of the twenty-first century.

Today the world is a global village, so people all over the country (and, for that matter, all over the world) are able to speak frequently with one another and have access to similar media. Nonetheless, according to a recent comprehensive study, local dialects are stronger than ever (Labov, 2005; Preston, 2003). This is due in large part to the fact that people tend to talk similarly to the people they live around and hear speak every day. Thus, dialectic differences originally occurred because of patterns of isolation, but they persist because of exposure. As people have increasing contact and access to a range of language models, dialectic differences may become less pronounced, but it will be a long time—if ever—before they completely disappear. For an example of an increasingly distinct regional dialect, see *Alternative View: The Great American Vowel Shift.*

Ethnicity and Race

One's ethnicity can influence one's verbal style in a number of ways. In the United States, English is a second or colanguage for many citizens. This, of course, influences syntax, accent, and word choice. For example, if one is Latino/Latina and learns Spanish either before or at the same time as one learns English, one may use the same syntax for both. Thus, Spanish speakers may place adjectives after nouns (*the house little*) when they are speaking English because that is the rule for Spanish. The reverse can also occur: When English speakers speak Spanish, they have a tendency to place adjectives before nouns (*la pequeña casa*), which is the rule for English but not for Spanish.

Speakers' ethnicity can also influence their general verbal style. For example, Jewish Americans may engage in a style of talking about problems that non-Jews perceive as complaining (Bowen, 2003); some Native American tribes use teasing as a form of public rebuke (Shutiva, 2004); and some Chinese Americans who live in the southern United States are particularly likely to let other speakers choose conversational topics (Gong, 2004). When two ethnic or racial groups speak the same language but use different syntax, lexical items, or verbal style, one or both of the groups may view the other's verbal style as incorrect, as a failed attempt at proper speech rather than as a dialect with its own rules (Ellis & Beattie, 1986).

These views can have important real-life implications—political and monetary. Take the controversy about **Ebonics**—a version of English that has its roots in West African, Caribbean, and U.S. slave languages. There is no agreed-upon definition of Ebonics; some linguists emphasize the international nature of the language (as a linguistic consequence of the African slave trade); others stress that it is a variety of English (e.g. , the equivalent of Black English) or as different from English and viewed as an independent language. Yet we should also keep in mind that "there is no single and correct way to be 'African American.' These identities are negotiated in context and situationally emergent" (Hecht et al., 2003, p. 2). The controversy over definition has had important real-life consequences. A few years ago the Oakland, California, school board passed a resolution that recognized Ebonics as a separate language, not just a dialect. The resolution instructed teachers to "respect and embrace the language richness of Ebonics." But more important, they required schools to provide English as a second language instruction to students who spoke Ebonics as their first "language." A number of teachers and policymakers viewed Ebonics as simply substandard English, not even a dialect, and were not willing to recognize it as a legitimate language nor provide funds for English language instruction (Wolfram, Adger, & Christian, 1999). This language controversy had far-reaching implications—involving not only teachers and parents, but also linguists and policymakers.

Education and Occupation

We will discuss education and occupation together because they are often mutually influencing. For example, medical doctors speak a similar language because they share a profession, but also because they were educated similarly. Typically, the more educated people are, the more similarly they speak (Hudson, 1983). Thus, larger dialect differences occur between easterners and midwesterners if they have not been to college than if they have doctoral degrees. This does not mean that all lawyers talk the same or that all professors speak similarly; rather, it suggests that differences become less pronounced as people receive more education.

Education affects dialect in part because any given university or college attracts people from different parts of the country. Therefore, college students have contact with a variety of dialects. At the same time, as students attend college they develop similar vocabularies from their shared experiences and learn similar terms in their classes. For example, you may never have used the term *dyad* to refer to two people before you went to college, but this is a term you might

Physicians, like members of other professions, develop specialized terms called jargon.

encounter in a range of courses, including psychology, sociology, anthropology, and communication.

Your occupation also influences the specialized terms you use to communicate. The specialized terms that develop in many professions are called **jargon**. Professors routinely speak of *tenure, refereed journals,* and *student credit hours.* Physicians speak of contusions (bruises), sequelae (results), and hemorrhagic stroke (a stroke where a blood vessel bursts). In fact, most occupations have their own jargon. In addition to influencing your lexical choices, your occupation may also influence your overall communication style—including tone of voice and some nonverbal behaviors. For example, nursery school teachers are often recognizable not only by their vocabulary but also by the rhythm, volume, and expressivity of their communication style.

To sum up, then, various features of language—phonology, syntax, semantics, and pragmatics—contribute to the development of meaning in verbal communication. These features combine with individual influences in language use, such as gender, age, and level of education, to create one's specific communication style. However, we have not yet covered every aspect of verbal communication. We now turn to the influence of societal forces on verbal communication.

TEST YOUR KNOWLEDGE

- How do regional dialects develop?
- How do our gender, age, ethnicity and race, and education and occupation influence the way we speak?

THE INDIVIDUAL, VERBAL COMMUNICATION, AND SOCIETY

How do societal forces influence verbal communication? Culture and power are two of the most important influences. Culture impacts verbal communication primarily through its influence on language and perception. As we saw in Chapter 4, perception plays a key role in communication. Power is connected to verbal communication because within society, some language styles are viewed as more powerful, with consequences for both the powerful and the powerless.

Language and Perception

Scholars have long argued about the influence of language and culture on perception. The central issue they have debated is whether the words a culture has available to it influence how its members see and perceive the world around them. For example, the English language expresses action in the past, present, and future. Thus, English speakers may say "Alan went to the library" (past), "Alan is at the library" (present), or "Alan will be going to the library" (future). In contrast, Japanese makes no distinction between the present and future. Although the verb for "went" is *ikimashita*, the verb used for both "is" and "will be going" is the same, *ikimasu*. Because English and Japanese have two different verb structures, scholars have questioned whether English speakers and Japanese speakers think about present and future actions in different ways. Scholars who have debated this relationship between language and perception generally fall into two camps: the *nominalists* and the *relativists.*

Nominalists claim that any idea can be expressed in any language and that the structure and vocabulary of the language do not influence the speaker's perception of the world. According to nominalists, English and Japanese may express present and future in different ways, but English speakers and Japanese speakers still understand the distinction.

In contrast, the relativists argue that language serves not only as a way for us to voice our ideas but that, in addition, it "is itself the shaper of ideas, the guide for the individual's mental activity" (Hoijer, 1994, p. 194). This idea is the basis for the

jargon
the specialized terms that develop in many professions

nominalists
those who argue that any idea can be expressed in any language and that the structure and vocabulary of the language do not influence the speaker's perception of the world

relativists
those who argue that language serves not only as a way for us to voice our ideas but "is itself the shaper of ideas, the guide for the individual's mental activity"

Surfers have many more words for the types of waves in the ocean than do nonsurfers.

Sapir-Whorf hypothesis. The Sapir-Whorf hypothesis argues that the language people speak determines the way they see the world. Adherents to this hypothesis believe language is like a prison, as it constrains the ways individuals can perceive the world (Koerner, 2000). According to this hypothesis, the distinction between the present and the future is not as clear-cut for Japanese speakers as it is for English speakers. As another example, surfers have many more words for the types of waves in the ocean than do nonsurfers (Scheibel, 1995); the Sapir-Whorf hypothesis argues that, because of this, surfers perceive more types of waves than do others.

So how much does language influence perception? The Sapir-Whorf hypothesis position has been challenged by a number of scholars who investigate the connection between language and how we think (Kenneally, 2008). They represent a modified relativist position on the relationship between language and perception. For example, Steven Pinker (2007), a renowned cognitive scientist, cautions against assuming a simplistic connection between language and thought, and rejects the Sapir-Whorf assumption that the particular language we speak compels us to perceive the world in a particular way or prevents us from thinking in different ways. He uses the example of applesauce and pebbles to argue that we naturally categorize (and therefore label) these two substances differently (as "hunk" and "goo"). By looking at language from the perspective of our thoughts, Pinker shows that what may seem like arbitrary aspects of speech (the hunk–goo distinction) aren't arbitrary at all, but rather that they are by-products of our evolved mental machinery. In sum, all languages have the formal and expressive power to communicate the ideas, beliefs, and desires of their users. From this vast range of possibilities, human communities select what they want to say and how they want to say it (Li & Gleitman, 2002, p. 291). This view allows for more freedom than indicated by the Sapir-Whorf hypothesis.

Language and Power

In many ways, language and power are inextricably connected. People in power get to define what languages and communication styles are appropriate. In addition, people who use language and communication according to the rules of the powerful may be able to increase their own power. This view of the relationship between language and power is explained by *cocultural theory*. **Cocultural theory** explores the role of power in daily interactions using the five following assumptions:

1. In each society, a hierarchy exists that privileges certain groups of people; in the United States, these groups include men, European Americans, heterosexuals, the able-bodied, and middle- and upper-class people.

2. Part of the privilege these groups enjoy, often subconsciously, is being able to set norms for what types of communication are acceptable or not acceptable (Orbe, 1998). Consequently, communication patterns of the dominant groups (in the United States, rich, male, White, educated, straight) tend to be more highly valued. For example, the preferred communication practice in many large corporations is that used by White males—direct, to the point, task oriented, and unemotional (Kikoski & Kikoski, 1999).

3. Language maintains and reinforces the power of these dominant groups, again, mostly subconsciously. Thus, people whose speech does not conform to what is valued in society may be excluded and/or negatively stereotyped. As we noted

Sapir-Whorf hypothesis
idea that the language people speak determines the way they see the world (a relativist perspective)

cocultural theory
explores the role of power in daily interactions

earlier, commentators sometimes characterize women's speech as sounding more tentative than male speech. Because society values male speech styles at work, women aspiring to corporate leadership positions may undertake a special effort to make their speech direct or tough enough, or to avoid being too cooperative or nurturing in their communication practices.

4. In the relationship realm, society tends to value a more female communication style, and men may be criticized for failing to communicate appropriately with their intimates. Remember that none of these language variations is inherently good or bad, powerful or powerless; it is the societal hierarchies that teach us how to view particular communication practices. Of course, not every White male is direct, to the point, and task oriented, nor does every woman speak tentatively at work. Nor is every woman supportive and self-disclosive and every man distant and terse in close relationships. These generalizations can help explain communication practices, but they should not solidify into stereotypes.

5. These dominant communication structures impede the progress of persons whose communication practices do not conform to the norms. For example, what are the consequences for women who do not conform to "male" communication norms in a corporation? Or for African Americans who do not conform to "White" communication norms of the organizations in which they work? Or for students who do not conform to the "middle-class" communication norms at a university? They may risk being labeled negatively ("not serious enough," "soft," "doesn't have what it takes") and marginalized.

We explore these ideas further in Chapter 7. Now, let's look at how these societal hierarchies affect attitudes toward words, accents, and dialects, and how they impact identity labels.

Power and Words

Attitudes about power can be built into language by certain roots or by the very structure of the language. Consider words like *chairman*, *fireman*, or the generic use of "he" and "man" to refer to people. In the past it was widely believed that it didn't matter whether we used masculine words to mean *human*, but in recent decades researchers discovered that people didn't think *human* when someone mentioned the word *man*—they thought about a man. Similarly, awareness of the inequality inherent in terms such as *Mr.* (not designating marital status) and *Mrs.* (which does) has resulted in the use of new, more equal terms like *Ms.* and *he/she*.

While some languages, such as Japanese or Korean, are strongly gendered (meaning that traditionally, men and women used almost a separate language), English is somewhat gendered, or androcentric. *Androcentrism* is the pairing of maleness with humanity and the consequent attribution of gender difference to females—often to women's disadvantage. Scholars recently reviewed fifty years of psychology articles for androcentric bias. While they found few uses of "he" for *human*, information was still portrayed in a way that emphasized male as the norm. Male data was placed first in tables, and gender differences were often described as female—subconsciously assuming that male is the norm and female is different. Researchers point out that being different is not necessarily harmful but probably reflects some of the underlying stereotypes (and societal hierarchies) we have discussed earlier (Hegarty & Buechel, 2006).

What are the implications for students? We argue that it's not about freedom of speech or being overly politically correct, but rather about audience and awareness. Gender-neutral language has gained support from most major textbook publishers, and from professional and academic groups, as well as major newspapers and law journals. As an English professor suggested, "You need to be able to express yourself according to their guidelines, and if you wish to write or speak convincingly to people who are influenced by the conventions of these contexts, you need to be conscious of their expectations."

Specific suggestions for avoiding this kind of built-in bias are presented in *Did You Know? Avoiding Bias in Language*.

Did You Know?
Avoiding Bias in Language

The American Psychological Association (APA) provides suggestions for avoiding gender and heterosexual bias in writing. Which view of language is represented here, nominalist or relative? What are the reasons for or against following these suggestions? Which groups of people do you think would be more in favor of these changes—those with or without power in U.S. society? What do you think of the "further alternatives"? Would you use them?

Using Gender-Neutral Language

■ **Use "they" as a singular.** Most people, when writing and speaking informally, rely on singular "they" as a matter of course: "If you love somebody, set them free" (Sting). If you pay attention to your own speech, you'll probably catch yourself using the same construction yourself. Some people are annoyed by the incorrect grammar that this solution necessitates, but this construction is used more and more frequently.

■ **Use "he" or "she."** Despite the charge of clumsiness, double-pronoun constructions have made a comeback: "To be black in this country is simply too pervasive an experience for any writer to omit from her or his work," wrote Samuel R. Delany. Overuse of this solution can be awkward, however.

■ **Use pluralizing.** A writer can often recast material in the plural. For instance, instead of "As he advances in his program, the medical student has increasing opportunities for clinical work," try "As they advance in their programs, medical students have increasing opportunities for clinical work."

■ **Eliminate pronouns.** Avoid having to use pronouns at all; instead of "a first grader can feed and dress himself," you could write, "a first grader can eat and get dressed without assistance."

■ **Further alternatives.** "He/she" or "s/he," using "one" instead of he, or using a new generic pronoun (thon, co, E, tey, hesh, hir).

Avoiding Heterosexual Bias in Language

■ **Use "sexual orientation" rather than "sexual preference."** The word "preference" suggests a degree of voluntary choice that is not necessarily reported by lesbians and gay men and that has not been demonstrated in psychological research.

■ **Use "lesbian" and "gay male"** rather than "homosexual" when used as an adjective referring to specific persons or groups, and lesbians and gay men. The word "homosexual" perpetuates negative stereotypes with its history of pathology and criminal behavior.

■ **Such terms as "gay male" are preferable** to "homosexuality" or "male homosexuality" and so are grammatical reconstructions (e.g., "his colleagues knew he was gay" rather than "his colleagues knew about his homosexuality"). The same is true for "lesbian" over "female homosexual," "female homosexuality," or "lesbianism."

■ **Bisexual women and men, "bisexual persons," or "bisexual"** as an adjective refer to people who relate sexually and affectionally to women and men. These terms are often omitted in discussions of sexual orientation and thus give the erroneous impression that all people relate exclusively to one gender or another.

Did You Know? *(continued)*

■ **Use "gender" instead of "sex."** The terms "sex" and "gender" are often used inter-changeably. Nevertheless, the term "sex" is often confused with sexual behavior, and this is particularly troublesome when differentiating between sexual orientation and gender.

SOURCES: Adapted from "Some notes on gender-neutral language." Retrieved May 23, 2008, from http://www.english.upenn.edu/~cjacobso/gender.html. And from "Avoiding heterosexual bias in language." Retrieved May 23, 2008, from http://www.apastyle.org/sexuality.html

Power and Accent

Where did people learn that an English accent sounds upper crust and educated? Or that English as spoken with an Asian Indian accent is hard to understand? Why do communicators often stereotype Black English as sounding uneducated? While these associations come from many sources, they certainly are prevalent in the media. People have become so accustomed to seeing and hearing these associations that they probably don't even question them. In fact, William Labov, a noted sociolin-guist, refers to the practice of associating a dialect with the cultural attitudes toward it as "a borrowed prestige model." For example, until the 1950s, most Americans thought that British English was the correct way to speak English (Labov, 1980); even today, people con-

It Happened to Me: *Bart*

I recently had a course taught by an Asian Indian professor, and it took me some time to understand his accent and form of speaking. Sometimes I thought he was mumbling, and sometimes his speech sounded so fast that I couldn't understand it. After a couple of classes, my hearing disciplined itself to understand him better. In the end, I realized he was a fine teacher.

tinue to think that an English accent sounds very refined and educated. On the other hand, Southern drawls and Black English have become stigmatized so that today, people who speak them are often perceived negatively. For similar reasons, people often find the English accent of people from India (where English often is a first language) difficult to understand—as reported by our student in *It Happened to Me: Bart.*

Such language stereotypes can be "set off" in one's head before a person even speaks, when one *thinks*, generally because of the person's appearance, that she or he will not speak Standard English (Ruben, 2003). This is probably what happened to our student, Bart. Once he adjusted to the Indian English accent, he found he could understand his Indian professor just fine. (For examples of accents from many different language backgrounds, go to classweb.gmu.edu/accent/.)

How does language cause one group to become elevated and another denigrated? The answer lies partly in understanding the social forces of history and politics. The positive and negative associations about African American, White, and British English developed during the nineteenth and twentieth centuries when European Americans were establishing themselves as the powerful majority in the United States, while passing legislation that subjugated African Americans and other minority groups. Thus it is not surprising that the languages of these groups were viewed so differently. Similarly, the English spoken by people from India was negatively stereotyped as the aberrant language of the colonized, since England was the colonial power in India until the mid-twentieth century. Similar attitudes can be seen toward immigrant groups today; their accented English is often stigmatized, sometimes leading to language discrimination and lawsuits, as illustrated in *Did You Know? Language Discrimination.*

Power and Identity Labels

The language labels that refer to particular identities also communicate important messages about power relations. Members of more powerful groups frequently in-

Did You Know?

Language Discrimination

Should language discrimination be illegal? Are there jobs where speaking English with an accent would impair someone's ability to do the job? Does language discrimination happen outside of employment as well?

Language discrimination includes inter-language discrimination and intra-language discrimination. Inter-language discrimination happens when people are treated differently because of the languages that they speak. In countries with an official language, discrimination can occur against those who do not speak the official language(s). Intra-language discrimination happens when people are treated differently because they speak in a way that is not considered "proper" or the dominant language. In the U.S., for example, someone who speaks Hawaiian pidgin, or Ebonics, may be treated differently than someone who speaks standard American English. Both kinds of discrimination can happen in job situations where someone is not hired or promoted because of an accent, or is treated differently from other employees. Language discrimination can also happen in schools when students are forbidden to speak certain languages. In the U.S., for example, some schools require students to speak English, not only in class but also outside of class. Language discrimination can also happen in social settings when someone is rebuffed because of the way they speak.

In contrast, some accents are preferred. For example, some U.S. Americans find a British or French accent to be attractive. Others like the Irish accent or accents from Australia or New Zealand. Some people like or dislike Southern accents, New England accents, and other varieties of English. Do you find yourself treating others with different accents in different ways?

Attempts to impose languages on others can be a legacy of colonialism. English, French, and Spanish are widely spoken around the world, largely due to a history of colonialism. Does requiring people to speak a particular language raise a human rights issue? Some languages that used to be more widely spoken are now marginalized, such as Irish; and some others have become extinct, such as Susquehannock (spoken by the Native Americans along the Susquehanna River). When we discriminate against people who speak in certain ways or speak certain languages, we are discriminating against the individuals, not just the accents or languages.

voke labels for members of other groups without input from those group members. For example, straight people label gays but rarely refer to themselves as straight. White people use ethnic and racial labels to refer to others (*people of color*, *African American*, or *Black*), but rarely refer to themselves as White. This power to label seems "normal," so most people don't think twice about specifying that a physician is a "woman doctor" while never describing one as a "male doctor." Or they might identify someone as a gay teacher, but not a White teacher (even if this teacher is both). People usually don't think about the assumptions that reflect societal power relations; in sum, individuals feel the need to mark minority differences, but they tend not to identify majority group membership.

Not only do the more powerful get to label the less powerful—they may also use language labels to stigmatize them. However, the stigma comes from the power relations, not from the words themselves. For example, in the Polish language, the word *Polack* simply means "a man from Poland," but the stigma associated with the term comes from the severe discrimination practiced against Eastern Europeans in the early twentieth century, which led to jokes and stereotypes that exist to this day. The term *Oriental* originated when Western countries were attempting to colonize, and were at war with, Asian countries—and the connotative meaning was *exotic* and *foreign*. Today, many Asians and Asian Americans resent this label. Read about one of our student's opinions on the topic in *It Happened to Me: Hiroko*.

This resentment can make communication more difficult for Hiroko and those who use this term to refer to her. As this example reveals, understanding the dictionary meanings of words does not always reveal the impact of identity labels. Members of minority communities are the best informants on the communicative power of specific labels.

Not everyone in an identity group has the same denotative meaning for a particular label. For example, some young women do not like to be called "girl"; they find it demeaning. Others are comfortable with this term.

Moreover, the power of labels can change over time. In an earlier age, many viewed the term *WASP* (White, Anglo-Saxon, Protestant) as a descriptor or even a positive label; now, however, it is seen as

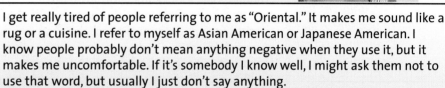

It Happened to Me: *Hiroko*

I get really tired of people referring to me as "Oriental." It makes me sound like a rug or a cuisine. I refer to myself as Asian American or Japanese American. I know people probably don't mean anything negative when they use it, but it makes me uncomfortable. If it's somebody I know well, I might ask them not to use that word, but usually I just don't say anything.

rather negative (Martin, Krizek, Nakayama, & Bradford, 1999). The shift probably reflects the changing attitudes of Whites, who are now more aware of their ethnicity and the fact that they are not always the majority. Similarly, the term *Paddy* as in "paddy wagon" (a term for a police wagon) originally was a derogatory term; some older Irish Americans may still find it offensive. It reflected a stereotype, widely held one hundred years ago, of Irish men as drunks who had to be carted off to jail. Now that discrimination (and stereotyping) against the Irish has all but disappeared, this term has lost much of its impact.

In summary, language, power, and societal forces are closely linked. The societal environment profoundly influences the way people perceive the world and the language choices available to them. Those in power set the language and communication norms, often determining what verbal communication style is deemed appropriate or inappropriate, elegant or uneducated. They frequently get to choose and use identity labels for those who are less powerful. Those whose language does not fit the standard, or who are the recipients of negative labels, may feel marginalized and resentful, leading to difficult communication interactions.

TEST YOUR KNOWLEDGE

- What is the difference between the nominalist and relativist perspectives on the relationship between language and perception?
- How does power influence language, words, accent, and labels?
- Can you give examples of the role of power in language, words, accent, and labels?

ETHICS AND VERBAL COMMUNICATION

We have already discussed a number of ethical issues related to verbal communication in this book. In Chapter 1, we argued that ethical communicators consider the benefit and/or harm associated with their messages. In this section, we examine one specific type of language whose use may harm individuals or relationships.

Hate Speech

In the United States, we place a high value on freedom of speech. We have codified this value into our legal system, beginning with the First Amendment to the Constitution. However, freedom of speech is always balanced by competing societal interests. As the familiar saying goes, freedom of speech does not include the right to shout "fire!" in a crowded theater. But what about the right to express negative opinions about others? In the 1980s and '90s, as American society became more aware of the ethics of minority rights, the term hate speech began to be used (ACLU, 1994). Hate speech, or the use of verbal communication to attack others based upon some social category such as race, ethnicity, religion, or sexuality, is seen as threatening an entire group and/or inciting violence against members of these groups. In the U.S., the first-amendment guarantee of free speech is generally used to protect against laws that would make hate speech illegal (Liptak, 2008). However, many argue that even if hate speech is legal, it is unethical.

Many countries view the use of verbal communication to attack, demean, and degrade other groups of people as not only unethical, but also illegal. Canada's criminal code, for example, forbids speech, writing, and Internet postings that advocate genocide or that publicly incite hatred (Media Awareness Network, n.d.). As another example, in some European countries it is illegal to deny that the Holocaust occurred. In 2008, a Belgian court sentenced two people to prison for denying the Holocaust in print (Prison ferme, 2008).

Whether illegal or unethical, the use of verbal communication to attack others based on their group membership is often seen as an attack on the whole group, not just the person who is the receiver of such messages.

Confirming and Disconfirming Communication

While hate speech may be obviously unethical, there are other, less obvious types of communication that can be unethical because of the harm they can cause. One of these is *disconfirming communication*. **Disconfirming communication** occurs when people make comments that reject or invalidate a self-image, positive or negative, of their conversational partners (Dance & Larson, 1976). Consider the following conversation:

> **Tracey:** Guess what? I earned an A on my midterm.
>
> **Lou:** Gee, it must have been an easy test.

Lou's response is an example of disconfirming communication, because it suggests that Tracey could not have earned her A because of competence or ability. Consequently, his message disconfirms Tracey's image of herself. You can disconfirm people either explicitly ("I've never really thought of you as being smart") or implicitly (as Lou did).

How can messages such as these cause harm? Imagine that you received numerous disconfirming messages from people who are important to you. How might it affect you? Such messages not only can negatively influence your self-image, but they also can impair your relationships with the people who disconfirm you. For instance, Harry Weger, Jr. (2005) and John Caughlin (2002) have found that when couples engage in disconfirming behavior, their marital dissatisfaction increases. Disconfirming messages can harm both individuals and relationships and may be considered unethical as well as ineffective because they focus on the person.

If you want to avoid sending disconfirming messages, what should you do instead? You can provide others with confirming messages. Confirming messages validate positive self-images of others, as in the following example of **confirming communication.**

> **Tracey:** Guess what? I earned an A on my midterm.
>
> **Lou:** That's great. I know it's a tough class; you deserve to be proud.
>
> **Or Lou might say:** Congratulations! I know you were studying very hard and you deserve that grade.

As ethical communicators, where should we draw the line between free speech and unethical verbal communication?

hate speech
use of verbal communication to attack others based upon some social category

disconfirming communication
comments that reject or invalidate a positive or negative self-image of our conversational partners

confirming communication
ccomments that validate positive self-images of others

Confirming messages are not only more ethical, they are usually more effective. Most people enjoy communicating with those who encourage them to feel good about themselves. Although engaging in confirming communication will not guarantee that you will be instantly popular, if you are sincere, it will increase the effectiveness of your communication and ensure that you are communicating ethically. If using confirming communication does not come naturally to you, you can practice until it does.

You might be wondering how you can provide negative feedback to people without being disconfirming. We discuss how to do this in the next section.

IMPROVING YOUR VERBAL COMMUNICATION SKILLS

When considering the ethics of language use, you should think about the effectiveness of your verbal choices. What are some guidelines for engaging in more effective verbal communication? We describe two ways in which you might improve: You can work on using "I" statements and also become more aware of the power of language.

"I" Statements

One type of disconfirming message involves making negative generalizations about others. Although you recognize that people are complex and variable, have you nevertheless found yourself making negative generalizations such as those listed here?

"You are so thoughtless."

"You are never on time."

As you can see, negative generalizations (which also are called "you" statements) are typically disconfirming. But, in the real world everyone lives in, some people *are* thoughtless, and some *are* consistently late. So is there an ethical and effective way to make your dissatisfaction known? Yes. You can use a type of message called an "I" statement. "I" statements allow you to express your feelings (even negative ones) by focusing on your own experiences rather than making negative generalizations (or "you" statements) about others.

"I" statements are conveyed through a three-part message that describes

1. the other person's behavior,
2. your feelings about that behavior, and
3. the consequences the other's behavior has for you.

Taking the examples just given and rewriting them as "I" statements, you could come up with:

"When you criticize my appearance (behavior), I feel unloved (feeling), and I respond by withdrawing from you (consequence)."

"I think I must be unimportant to you (feeling) when you arrive late for dinner (behavior), so I don't feel like cooking for you (consequence)."

"You" statements often lead recipients to feel defensive and/or angry because of the negative evaluation contained in the message and because the listener resents the speaker's position of passing judgment. "I" statements can lead to more constructive resolution of conflicts because they arouse less defensiveness. They also are more effective than "you" statements because the receiver is more likely to listen and respond to them (Kubany, Bauer, Muraoka, Richard, & Read, 1995). In addition, in order to make "I" statements, speakers have to explore exactly what they are dissatisfied with, how it makes them feel, and what the consequences of the other person's behavior are. "I" statements prevent speakers from attacking others in order to vent their feelings.

While many communication scholars believe in the value of "I" statements, a recent study found that people reacted similarly to *both* "I" and "you" statements involving negative emotions. However, the authors point out that their study involved written hypothetical conflict situations. They admit that their results might have been different if they had studied real-life conflict situations (Bippus & Young, 2005).

Although "I" statements can be very effective in a variety of contexts, this does not mean they are *always* appropriate. Situations may arise where others' behavior so violates what you believe is decent or appropriate that you wish to state your opinions strongly. Thus, if your friend abuses alcohol or takes illicit drugs, you may need to say "You should not drive a car tonight" or "You need to get help for your addiction." The effectiveness of one's verbal communication must always be evaluated in the context of the situation, the relationships one has with others, and one's goal.

Become Aware of the Power of Language

As we noted in Chapter 1, language is a powerful force that has consequences and ethical implications. Wars have been started, relationships have been ruined, and much anger and unhappiness has resulted from intentional and unintentional verbal messages. The old adage "Sticks and stones can break my bones, but words will never hurt me" is not always true. Words *can* hurt, as shown *Communication in Society: Mind Your (Terror) Language* describing language offensive to many Arabs and Muslims.

When a speaker refers to others by negative or offensive identity terms, the speaker not only causes harm, he or she also denies those labeled individuals their identities—even if it isn't intentional. For example, one of our students, Cynthia, told us how bad she felt when she realized that some of her gay coworkers were offended by her use of the term "homosexual" (instead of gay). They explained that "homosexual" was used as a description of a psychiatric disease by the American Psychiatric Association's list of mental disorders until 1973, and has a connotation of this sexual orientation as a cold, clinical "condition." Using her embarrassment as a learning experience, she initiated an enlightening discussion with her coworkers. She learned that often the best way to discover what someone "wants to be called" is to ask. However, a conversation of this nature can only occur in the context of a mutually respectful relationship—one reason to have a diverse group of friends and acquaintances.

COMMUNICATION IN SOCIETY
Mind Your (Terror) Language

Words like "terrorist," "terrorism," and "war on terror" are frequently used, but how often do we think about what they actually mean?

It is often said that one group's "terrorist" is another group's "freedom fighter"—the difference depends on whether the person in question is perceived as being on the side of "us" or "them." Similarly, whether a leader in a foreign culture is described as a "warlord" or a "tribal elder" often depends on whose side we believe the individual supports.

In the 21st century, Muslims and Arabs are particularly sensitive to such language. Referring to someone as a "moderate Muslim" implies that the norm is extremism, not moderation. Equating the term *fatwa* with a threat to someone's life gives the word an inaccurate-ly extreme meaning; it actually refers to a legal pronouncement or judgment to settle a question not covered by Islamic law. The Islamic term *jihad* translates as "striving" or "struggle," not "holy war" as some non-Muslims have rendered it.

When a violent incident occurs in which many people who were going about their business in a public place are injured or killed, it is easy to rush to judgment and use words like "terrorist," "suicide bomber," and "extremist." As a thoughtful communicator, choose to use language that describes what happened—a bomb exploded, several people were shot, or a truck ran through a checkpoint—and refrain from language that characterizes who is responsible and what their motives are before an incident can be investigated.

SUMMARY

Verbal communication plays a significant role in people's lives, assisting in relationship development, creating identities, and accomplishing everyday tasks. Language is the foundation of verbal processes and it functions in at least seven ways: instrumental, regulatory, informative, heuristic, interactional, personal, and imaginative. The four components of language study are phonology, the study of sounds; syntax, the grammar and rules for arranging units of meaning; semantics, the meaning of words; and pragmatics, the rules for appropriate use of language.

Individual influences on language include speakers' memberships in various identity groups (gender, age, regionality, ethnicity and race, education and occupation). When identities influence several aspects of language (vocabulary, grammar, and pronunciation), these speakers have distinct dialects. In other instances identity groups' language variations may be minor, involving only some pronunciation or word choices.

Societal forces affect verbal processes because they shape our perceptions and the power relationships that surround us. The language used in a given society influences its members' perceptions of social reality, while power relationships affect how its members' verbal patterns are evaluated.

Communicating more ethically involves avoiding hate speech and using confirming rather than disconfirming language. To improve your verbal communication skills, learn to use "I" statements when expressing dissatisfaction, and recognize the power of language.

HUMAN COMMUNICATION IN SOCIETY ONLINE

To review this chapter, use the MyCommunicationLab Web site to test your understanding of the following key terms, record your answers to the chapter review questions, and complete the suggested activities. Expand your learning and understanding of chapter concepts by completing additional activities and exercises online. Access code required. Go to www.mycommunicationlab.com for more information or to purchase standalone access.

KEY TERMS

instrumental 99
regulatory 99
informative 99
heuristic 99
interactional 99
personal language 99
imaginative 99
grammar 100
phonology 100

syntax 100
semantics 100
denotative meaning 101
connotative meaning 101
pragmatics 101
speech act theory 101
dialect 105
lexical choice 105
cohort effect 107

Ebonics 110
jargon 110
nominalists 111
relativists 111
Sapir-Whorf hypothesis 112
cocultural theory 112
hate speech 118
disconfirming communication 118
confirming communication 118

APPLY WHAT YOU KNOW

1. For each scenario, write a paragraph describing a typical communication exchange. For each, think about the various elements of verbal communication: sounds, grammar, meaning (word choice), conversational rules, and contextual rules.

   - an informal family outing

   - a meeting with your advisor

   - a bar, where you are trying to impress potential partners

   Hint: Working in a small group, see whether you and your classmates can come up with some shared contextual rules for communication in these various situations. Give some reasons why you can or cannot come up with shared rules.

2. Take three sheets of paper and write one of the following words on each sheet: *garbage*, *milk*, *mother*. Take the first piece of paper and crumple it up and then stomp on it. Do the same with the second and third pieces. How did you feel crumpling up and stomping on the first piece of paper? The second? The third? What does this say perhaps about the difference between denotative and connotative meanings?

3. Think about two accents or dialects you've heard, either in a personal encounter or on radio or television. For each one, answer the following questions:

   - Do you have a negative or positive association for this dialect/accent?

   - Where did these associations (negative or positive) come from?

   - How might these associations (negative or positive) influence the way you communicate with a person who uses this accent or dialect?

   Share your answers with your classmates. Do you have similar reactions and associations for the same accent or dialect? What does this say about the power of society in influencing perceptions about communication and language use?

4. For each of the examples that follow, create an "I" statement that expresses your feelings about the situation:

   - Once again your roommate has borrowed some of your clothes without asking and has returned them dirty and/or damaged.

   - For the third time this semester, your instructor has changed the date of an exam.

   - Your good friend has developed a habit of canceling plans at the last moment.

   - Your romantic partner embarrasses you by teasing you about personal habits in front of friends.

   Form a group with two or three of your classmates. Take turns reading your "I" statement for each situation. Discuss the strengths and weaknesses of each statement. As a group, develop an "I" statement for each situation above that best expresses the group's feelings without encouraging defensiveness in the receiver.

5. Locate five people who either grew up in different parts of the United States or who grew up in different countries. Try to include both men and women and people of different ages in your sample. Ask each person to answer the following questions:

- What do you call a carbonated beverage?

- How do you pronounce "roof"?
- What expressions do you use that some other people have had trouble understanding?
- What does the term *feminist* mean?
- Who do you think talks "different"?

6 Nonverbal Communication

Recently a colleague took her four-year-old daughter with her to a business meeting. After observing the interaction for a few minutes, her daughter Anna whispered, "When it's your turn to talk, you have to make your mad face."

Even though Anna is only four years old, she is sensitive to the nonverbal behavior of others. She readily reads others' facial expressions and assigns meaning to them. From a very early age, all children learn the basics of nonverbal communication (Boone & Cunningham, 1998); in fact, infants from an early age imitate others' nonverbal behavior. For example, when newborns observe caregivers sticking out their tongues, they imitate them and do the same (Als, 1977; Meltzoff & Prinz, 2002).

In this chapter, we take a close look at the intricacies of nonverbal communication and the many factors that shape nonverbal messages and their interpretation. First, we describe the importance of nonverbal communication, provide a definition, and explore how it differs from nonverbal behavior. We then give you an overview of the various types of nonverbal codes, and we examine the functions that nonverbal messages serve. We next explore how societal forces intersect with individuals' nonverbal communication. We conclude the chapter by discussing ethical issues in nonverbal communication and providing you with suggestions for improving your nonverbal communication skills.

Once you have read this chapter, you will be able to:

- Explain the important role of nonverbal communication in social interaction.
- Identify four factors that influence the meaning of nonverbal communication.
- Define five nonverbal codes and discuss the five functions of nonverbal messages.
- Articulate the role of power in nonverbal communication.
- Understand how nonverbal communication can trigger, and express, prejudice and discrimination.
- Discuss six guidelines for ethical nonverbal communication.
- Name five ways to improve your ability to interpret nonverbal behavior.

THE IMPORTANCE OF NONVERBAL COMMUNICATION

Nonverbal communication plays an important role in social interaction. It helps us express and interpret the verbal aspects of communication—such as when a person:

- smiles to *reinforce* an expression of thanks;
- uses the "OK" sign to *substitute* for saying "I am all right";
- laughs flirtatiously to *contradict* the words, "I hate you";
- puts his fingers close together to *illustrate* how thin his new computer is.

125

Even young children understand and use nonverbal communication.

Nonverbal communication also influences how individuals interpret messages, especially those related to feelings, moods, and attitudes. Nonverbal cues are important to the expression of emotion because communicators are often more comfortable expressing their feelings nonverbally (such as by smiling or glaring) than they are stating them more explicitly through words (Mehrabian, 2007). For example, how often do you flatly tell a friend or colleague, "I am mad at you"? If you are like most people, this is a relatively rare event; instead, you probably rely on some type of nonverbal cue to indicate your dissatisfaction.

However, nonverbal communication can be complex and ambiguous—both for senders of messages to convey and for receivers of messages to interpret. Even though we begin learning nonverbal communication as children, we often have difficulty interpreting others' nonverbal communication. Why is this so? One reason is the fact that humans express a wide array of nonverbal behaviors, many of which can be quite subtle. Consequently, understanding nonverbal communication requires knowledge and skill.

However, beware of books, Web sites, and magazine articles that promise to teach you to "read a person like a book": there is no such thing as a key to decoding or interpreting every **nonverbal behavior** in every context. Why not? Because understanding nonverbal communication requires interpreting behavior and assigning meaning to it, and we don't always have the information we need to do that. If you are sitting in the library and notice a stranger staring at you, what does the stare mean? Does the person think he knows you? Is he interested in meeting you? Is he being aggressive? Or is the person simply lost in thought and only *appearing* to be gazing at you? As this example illustrates, nonverbal cues can be ambiguous. Because the meaning of nonverbal behavior is determined by a variety of factors, including context, culture, and even intentionality, it can be tricky to interpret a specific behavior.

In addition, nonverbal cues are continuous, meaning that people exhibit nonverbal behaviors virtually all the time they are conscious, and multiple behaviors act in concert to create a given message—or different messages, even unrelated ones. For example, imagine that Joan is talking to her husband about their need to spend time together to strengthen their marriage. Just as her husband asks, "What do you want to do about our marriage?" Joan happens to look over his shoulder at her computer screen and sees it displaying an error message. In frustration, she throws up her hands and sighs heavily. Joan was responding to her computer failure, but her husband thought she was responding to his question. He became very upset, assuming she was expressing a wish to give up on their marriage.

Nonverbal communication also can be difficult to interpret because nonverbal cues are multi-channeled; that is, they can be transmitted in a variety of ways simultaneously. Speakers can convey nonverbal messages through their facial expressions, voice qualities, eye gaze, posture, and gestures and by other channels we will discuss throughout this chapter. Moreover, because a variety of cues may occur at the same time, it can be difficult and confusing to keep up with everything (Schwartz, Foa, & Foa, 1983). If, for example, you are focusing on someone's face, you may miss important messages conveyed by the body.

"Pop psychology" treatments of nonverbal communication typically assume that each behavior has one meaning regardless of the context or who is performing it. Such explanations don't distinguish between nonverbal behavior and nonverbal communication; nor do they consider context, culture, individual variations in behavior, or the relationship that exists between the people being observed. All these factors, and more, can influence the meaning of a nonverbal behavior in a specific instance. So don't believe that just because someone has her arms crossed over her body, it means she is closed off to you. It may simply mean she needs a sweater.

nonverbal communication
nonverbal behavior that has symbolic meaning

nonverbal behavior
all the nonverbal actions people perform

Nonverbal messages are not only complex and ambiguous—they are also key components of communication. Understanding nonverbal communication can make you a better *verbal* communicator. In addition, nonverbal communication can help you navigate everyday life. For example, humans rely on nonverbal cues to determine whether other humans are a threat. In the television show *Going Tribal*, journalist Bruce Parry visited the remote Suri tribe in Ethiopia. As he approached the first tribal member, Parry carefully observed the tribesman thrust his bow and arrow at him and pace quickly back and forth while averting his eye gaze. Although many of the Suri's nonverbal behaviors communicated belligerence, the fact that he did not stare aggressively influenced Bruce to approach him slowly with a gift—which was accepted.

Similarly, on a daily basis people need to be able to read subtle nonverbal behaviors in order to assess how friendly or hostile others may be. This is especially true for individuals whose identities are less valued culturally or whose societal position makes them more vulnerable. Because of this vulnerability, such individuals tend to become quite adept at reading and interpreting nonverbal communication. For example, if Gary's boss walks into the office frowning and shaking her head, Gary may interpret this as meaning that she is in a bad mood; consequently, he may try to be especially helpful and avoid doing anything to provoke her. In a study that compared African Americans' and White Americans' ability to read the nonverbal behaviors of Whites, researchers found that African Americans were far better at detecting prejudicial attitudes as expressed in subtle nonverbal behavior than Whites (Richeson & Shelton, 2005). Similarly, a study of heterosexual and gay men found that gay men were better able to identify the sexual orientation of unfamiliar men when watching videos of them (Shelp, 2002).

Nonverbal communication also is important because it can affect public policy decisions. For example, after several years of allowing students to wear just about anything they wished to school, many public schools now institute dress codes. Although some schools primarily regulate clothing that they see as "inappropriate" or too revealing, others require school uniforms. The supporters of this latter policy argue that school uniforms "help erase cultural and economic differences among students" (Isaacson, 1998) and improve student performance and attendance. Regulating school dress rests on the assumption that one form of nonverbal communication, attire, should be regulated because it can be distracting or even disruptive. Other examples of public policy attempts to regulate nonverbal expression include efforts to ban flag burning and to forbid the wearing of Muslim headscarves. Countries would not engage in efforts to control nonverbal expression if it were not so important.

Public policy seeks to regulate nonverbal expression, such as what type of clothing people can wear.

TEST YOUR KNOWLEDGE

1. Why is it impossible to "read a person like a book"?
2. What features of nonverbal communication make it challenging for us to interpret it easily?

WHAT IS NONVERBAL COMMUNICATION?

The nonverbal components of communication include all the messages that people transmit through means other than words. More specifically, communication scholar Valerie Manusov and psychologist Miles Patterson define nonverbal communication as "encompassing the sending and receiving of information through appearance, objects, the environment and behavior in social settings" (Manusov & Patterson, 2006, p. xi). Thus, they argue that we communicate nonverbally when we blow a kiss, scratch our arm, or wear clothing that signals our group membership. Even more frequently, nonverbal and verbal aspects of communication combine to convey messages, as when we indicate anger by turning our backs and saying "I don't want to talk with you right now."

However, not every scholar believes that all nonverbal behavior is communicative. These researchers argue that nonverbal communication occurs only when nonverbal behavior has symbolic meaning and is communicated intentionally (Burgoon, Buller, & Woodall, 1996). That is, they believe nonverbal communication stands for something, while nonverbal behavior may not. For example, from this perspective, scratching one's arm usually isn't intended by the scratcher, nor understood by the observer, to convey a particular message. Although it may provide information (that one's arm itches), it doesn't necessarily signal an *intentional* message. Rather, it would be considered an involuntary bodily "output." However, these scholars would argue that in baseball when a manager scratches his arm to signal that a runner on base should steal home, scratching the arm is symbolic and, therefore, an instance of nonverbal communication.

Nonetheless, these scholars acknowledge that some nonverbal communication does lack the element of intentionality. For example, a smile may be understood as an expression of pleasure even if the smiler is unaware that he is smiling. Thus, if a behavior typically is used communicatively, then that behavior is understood to be part of our nonverbal "vocabulary" and will be interpreted as such, regardless of one's own conscious use of it (Burgoon, Buller, & Woodall, 1996).

However, scholars who prefer a broader definition of nonverbal communication argue that many actions one might consider just a "bodily output" can still convey messages nonverbally. For example, people usually cough because of a scratchy throat or yawn because they are tired, and when they engage in these behaviors others interpret their meaning. Of course, they also believe that when a person coughs as a signal to capture someone's attention or yawns to indicate he is bored, he is engaging in nonverbal communication.

As our discussion thus far suggests, most nonverbal behaviors have a variety of meanings—just as scratching one's arm can have multiple meanings. Therefore neither we, nor anyone else, can provide you with interpretations for specific nonverbal actions. Perhaps in part because of this difficulty, we cannot accurately estimate the amount of meaning that nonverbal communication contributes to the overall meaning in an interaction. This inability is revealed in *Did You Know? How Much Does Nonverbal Communication Contribute to Meaning?* where you can see why it can be difficult to estimate how much meaning nonverbal components convey in any message.

TEST YOUR KNOWLEDGE

1. What is nonverbal communication?
2. How do some scholars differentiate nonverbal behavior from nonverbal communication?

NONVERBAL COMMUNICATION AND THE INDIVIDUAL

If a smile is viewed as communicating pleasure even when the smiler doesn't intend to do so, then why don't all behaviors that are part of our nonverbal vocabulary always convey the same meaning? The answer is that assigning one simple meaning to

Did You Know?
How Much Does Nonverbal Communication Contribute to Meaning?

How much of the meaning of a message do you think is conveyed by its nonverbal components? Fifty percent? Seventy-five percent? One of the most common beliefs about communication is that over 90 percent of the meaning of a message is transmitted by its nonverbal elements. However, in truth, we do not know! So where did this belief originate?

In 1967, psychologist Albert Mehrabian(along with Morton Wiener) wrote that 93 percent of the meaning of the utterances he examined was conveyed through the nonverbal aspects of communication. Specifically, he argued that 38 percent of meaning in his study was derived from paralinguistic cues (tone of voice, etc.) and 55 percent from facial expressions, leaving only 7 percent of meaning to be provided by the verbal message. After he published his findings, other people, researchers and non-researchers alike, began to generalize his claims about his one study to all communicative interactions.

However, a variety of scholars have contradicted this claim, either arguing for a different percentage (Birdwhistell, 1985) or suggesting that one cannot accurately determine how much words, context, nonverbal messages, and other factors actually contribute to the meaning of an utterance. Those who critique Mehrabian's analysis argue that his study exhibited several problems. First, it examined how people interepreted the meaning of single tape-recorded words, which is not how we naturally communicate. Second, he combined the results of two studies that most scholars believe should not be combined. Further, he did not consider the contributions to meaning made by gestures and posture. Also, he tried to estimate the contribution of particular nonverbal behaviors—for example, gesture versus facial expression. In practice, however, no one behavior is particularly useful in determining meaning. In other words, inferences made about the meaning of any given action are not all that reliable, nor are estimates of what percentage of the total message a single nonverbal cue communicates.

a nonverbal behavior ignores the multiple meanings that may exist, depending on the context in which the behavior occurs. For example, you will read in this chapter that when a person leans toward another (called a *forward body lean*), this is often a sign of interest or involvement. Does that mean that the forward body lean always indicates interest? Absolutely not! A person might lean forward for a variety of reasons: her stomach hurts, the back of her chair is hot, or her lower back needs to be stretched.

To understand the meaning of a nonverbal behavior you have to consider the entire behavioral context, including what the person might be communicating verbally (Jones & LeBaron, 2002). Therefore, interpreting others' nonverbal behavior requires that you consider a variety of factors that can influence meaning. To interpret nonverbal communication, you also need to know the codes, or symbols and rules, that signal various messages. Finally, you will benefit from a familiarity with the variety of ways that nonverbal messages function. These are topics we take up next.

Influences on Nonverbal Communication

Culture is one of the more important factors that influence the meaning of nonverbal communication. This is not to say that many nonverbal cues and signals aren't shared; in fact, research shows that gaze is used to communicate aggression, dominance, and power as well as connection and nurturance across cultures (and even species) (Matsumoto, 2006); however, the specific manner in which gaze is used to communicate these messages can vary. For example, in many Arabic cultures, eye gaze during social interaction is more direct than is typical in the United States

(Watson & Graves, 1966); thus, eye gaze that might be interpreted as friendly and involved in an Arabic culture could be perceived as somewhat aggressive by a U.S. American. Similarly, within the United States, gaze and visual behavior differ across sexes and ethnic groups, with women tending to gaze more than men (Briton & Hall, 1995) and African Americans often using more continuous eye gaze while talking and less while listening than many Whites (Samovar & Porter, 2004).

Some nonverbal cues are used widely across cultures, such as nodding to mean yes—though this is not true in every culture. However, many nonverbal gestures have vastly different meanings in different cultures. In the United States, for instance, the "thumbs up" signals success and the "hitchhiker's thumb" asks for a ride, but these nonverbal signs carry potentially vulgar meanings in several other cultures. In East Africa, instead of pointing with fingers, people often point with their lips—a gesture that is completely unfamiliar to most people in the United States. Differences in gestures also occur across ethnic groups in the United States. For example, historically Korean Americans tended to reserve smiling, shaking hands, and saying hello for friends and family; however, many immigrants changed this pattern of behavior once they recognized its meaning and importance in the United States (Young, 1999). Thus, the meaning of any nonverbal behavior is defined by the cultures of those interacting (Axtell, 1993; Segerstrale & Molnár, 1997).

In addition to culture, the relationship between the people interacting affects the meaning of nonverbal behaviors (Manusov, 1995). If a husband takes his wife's arm as they are crossing the street, the meaning likely is some mixture of care and affection; if a police officer were to do so, one probably would interpret it as an aggressive or controlling gesture. However, if a boss were to do the same with a subordinate, the meaning is more complex and potentially confusing or troubling. One might wonder whether she is being friendly, controlling, affectionate—or maybe too affectionate? How we interpret others' nonverbal behavior, then, is highly dependent on the type of relationship we have with them.

Third, the meaning we attribute to someone's nonverbal behavior varies based on how well we know the communicator. For example, if a stranger smiles at you, you might interpret it as a gesture of friendliness, since that is the meaning most often associated with this facial expression. However, if you know your best friend tends to smile when she is angry, then you will be more accurate at interpreting that her smile is a sign of her displeasure than would someone who did not know her well. Once we know people, then, we can usually read their nonverbal behavior and interpret its associated messages with more accuracy, as Abbad explains in *It Happened to Me: Abbad*.

It Happened to Me: *Abbad*

I am from the Middle East, and I arrived in the United States in 2000 with a couple of my friends. On a school break, we decided to travel to Washington, D.C. On the road, we stopped at a McDonald's to eat and to pray. As Muslims, we have to pray five times a day, and during the prayer we cannot talk at all. While in the middle of our prayer, a McDonald's employee approached and asked what we were doing. Since we could not talk, one of my friends used a hand gesture that in our culture means "wait for a minute." This hand gesture is expressed by holding one's fingers together like a pyramid. For some reason, the employee understood the gesture as an invitation for a fight. I guess this is what it means in some parts of the United States. That's when the employee called 911. By the time the police officer arrived, we were done with our prayer. We explained we were new to this country and that the hand gesture we used means something else in our culture. We apologized to the employee for the misunderstanding and continued on our trip.

Finally, we tend to interpret individuals' nonverbal behavior based on their sex. For example, when women toss their hair, the behavior often is read as flirtatious—and therefore communicative. However, if a man does the same, we are more likely to believe he is just trying to get his hair out of his eyes—a nonverbal behavior that is not necessarily communicative. As we discuss throughout this book, sex differences in nonverbal and verbal communication are due to biological as well as social and cultural influences.

Nonverbal Codes

Nonverbal codes or signals are distinct, organized means of expression that consist of both symbols and rules for their use (Cicca, Step, & Turkstra, 2003). Although we describe a range of such codes in this section, we do not mean to imply that any one code occurs in isolation. Generally, a set of behaviors and codes together determines the meaning or significance of an action. For our purposes, we isolate a specific kind of behavior for analysis; in the real world, without knowing the context, interpretations about any behavior may be questionable or even wrong (Patterson, 1983). In this section, we'll look at the five aspects of nonverbal codes—*kinesics, paralinguistics, time and space, haptics,* and *appearance and artifacts*—to see how this system of nonverbal codes works.

Kinesics

Kinesics is the term used to describe a system of studying nonverbal communication sent by the body, including gestures, posture, movement, facial expressions, and eye behavior. For clarity we group kinesic communication into two general categories, those behaviors involving the body and those involving the face.

The Body.   Our bodies convey many nonverbal messages. For example, we use gestures such as pointing, waving, and holding up our hands to direct people's attention, signal hello, and indicate that we want to be recognized. Communicators use four types of nonverbal gestures: *illustrators, emblems, adaptors,* and *regulators.* **Illustrators** are signals that accompany speech to clarify or emphasize the verbal messages. Thus when people come back from a fishing trip they hold their hands far apart to indicate the size of the fish that got away. **Emblems** are gestures that stand for a specific verbal meaning; for example, raising one's hand in class indicates that one wishes to speak. **Adaptors** are gestures we use to manage our emotions. Many adaptors are nervous gestures such as tapping a pencil, jiggling a leg, or twirling one's hair. Finally, people use **regulators** to control conversation; for example, if you want to prevent someone from interrupting you, you might hold up your hand to indicate that the other person should wait. In contrast, if you wish to interrupt and take the floor, you might raise a finger to signal your desire.

Gestures contribute a lot to our communication efforts; even their frequency can signal meaning. For instance, how much gesturing we do while speaking can indicate how involved we are in a conversation. Typically, people who are excited indicate their involvement by using many and varied gestures; those who have little involvement may indicate their lack of interest by their failure to gesture.

We also use our bodies to convey meaning through our posture and our movement. In general, posture is evaluated in two ways: by how *immediate* it is and by how *relaxed* it appears (Mehrabian, 1971; Richards, Rollerson, & Phillips, 1991). **Immediacy** refers to how close or involved people appear to be with each other. For example, when people like someone they tend to orient their bodies in the other person's direction, lean toward them, and look at them directly when they speak. How do people act when they wish to avoid someone? Typically, they engage in the opposite behavior. They turn their backs or refuse to look at them, and if they are forced to stand or sit near the person they dislike, they lean away from them. To understand this, imagine how you would behave if you were attempting to reject an unwanted amorous advance.

Relaxation refers to the degree of tension one's body displays. When you are at home watching TV, for instance, you probably display a relaxed posture: lounging in a chair with your legs stretched out in front of you and your arms resting loosely on the chair's arms. However, if you are waiting at the dentist's office, you may sit hunched forward, your legs pressed tightly together, and your hands tightly grasping the chair arms.

---

nonverbal codes
distinct, organized means of expression that consists of symbols and rules for their use

kinesics
nonverbal communication sent by the body, including gestures, posture, movement, facial expressions, and eye behavior

gestures
nonverbal communication made with part of the body, including actions such as pointing, waving, or holding up a hand to direct people's attention

illustrators
signals that accompany speech to clarify or emphasize the verbal messages

emblems
gestures that stand for a specific verbal meaning

adaptors
gestures used to manage emotions

regulators
gestures used to control conversation

immediacy
how close or involved people appear to be with each other

relaxation
the degree of tension displayed by one's body

What nonverbal messages might be understood from this photo? Remember that a nonverbal behavior can have multiple meanings.

The way you walk or move also can communicate messages to others, particularly about your mood or emotional state. Sometimes you use movement deliberately to communicate a message—such as when you stomp around the apartment to indicate your anger. At other times, your movement is simply a nonverbal behavior—that is, you move naturally and unconsciously without any clear intentionality. Even when your movement is not intentional, observers can and do make judgments about you. One study found that observers could identify when pedestrians were sad, angry, happy, or proud, just from the way they walked (Montepare, Goldstein, & Clausen, 1987). However, some emotional states (anger) were easier to identify than others (pride), and some individuals were easier to classify than others. So although people consciously communicate a great deal with their body movements and gestures and observers interpret others' movements, some messages are more clearly transmitted than others. It should also be noted that many of the same factors discussed earlier, such as culture, context, background knowledge, and gender, can affect the ability to interpret kinesic behavior.

The Face.   Facial expressions communicate more than perhaps any other nonverbal behavior. They are the primary channels for transmitting emotion, and the eyes, in particular, convey important messages regarding attraction and attention. Some research suggests that facial expressions of happiness, sadness, anger, surprise, fear, and disgust are the same across cultures and, in fact, are innate (Ekman & Friesen, 1969, 1986), although not all scholars agree. Through observations of deaf, blind, and brain-damaged children, researchers have concluded that commonality of facial expressions among humans is not due to observation and learning but rather to genetic programming (Eibl-Eibesfeld, 1972; Ekman, 2003). (To better understand the role of facial expressions in the communication of emotion, go to http://www.persuasive.net/blog/it-is-written-all-over-your-face-understanding-facial-expressions/)

The ability to accurately recognize others' emotions gives individuals an edge in their interpersonal actions. For example, people with greater emotional recognition accuracy are effective in negotiations and are able to create more value for all parties and to achieve more favorable outcomes (Elfenbein, Maw, White, Tan, & Aik, 2007). If you are not very adept at recognizing others' emotions, however, you can improve your ability to do so. A variety of studies show that individuals who are trained in emotion recognition and then receive feedback on their performance can improve their ability to recognize others' emotional expressions, especially if their targets are from different cultures than their own (Elfenbein, 2006).

Of course, people don't display every emotion they feel. Individuals learn through experience and observation to manage their facial expressions, and they learn which expressions are appropriate to reveal in what circumstances. In many cultures expectations of appropriateness differ for men and women. For example, in the United States, males are often discouraged from showing sadness, while females are frequently criticized for showing anger. In addition, women are routinely expected to smile, no matter how they feel, while relatively few men receive the same message. Whether or not they are conscious of such cultural expectations, men and women generally learn to manage their facial expressions so as not to reveal emotions that they believe they shouldn't feel or that they don't want others to see.

Eye behavior is especially important in conveying messages for humans as well as animals. For example, both humans and dogs use prolonged eye gaze (a stare) to communicate aggression, and they avert their gaze when they want to avoid contact. Furthermore, eye behavior interacts with facial expressions to convey meaning. Thus, most people believe a smile is genuine only when the eyes "smile" as well as the lips. Actors such as Julia Roberts and Tom Cruise are particularly gifted at this; they can, at will, express what appears to be a genuine smile.

Like other types of nonverbal communication, context and culture shape the meanings people attach to eye behavior. For example, cultures differ significantly in how long one is supposed to engage in eye contact and how frequently. Many Native Americans such as Cherokee, Navajo, and Hopi engage in minimal eye contact compared to most White U.S. Americans (Chiang, 1993). Swedes tend to gaze infrequently but for longer periods of time, while southern Europeans gaze frequently and extensively (Knapp & Hall, 1992, 2001). Your relationship with others affects how you interpret their eye behavior. Thus, you may find it very appealing when a romantic partner gazes into your eyes but find the same behavior threatening when exhibited by a stranger. For an example of how differences in eye contact and facial expression can affect communication, see *Communication in Society: When You Smile on the Job.*

paralinguistics
all aspects of spoken language except the words themselves; includes rate, volume, pitch, stress

voice qualities
qualities such as speed, pitch, rhythm, vocal range, and articulation that make up the "music" of the human voice

Paralinguistics

The vocal aspects of nonverbal communication are referred to as **paralinguistics**, which include rate, volume, pitch, and stress, among others. Paralinguistics are those aspects of language that are *oral* but not *verbal*. That is, paralinguistics describe all aspects of spoken language except the words themselves. For example, typically you recognize other speakers' voices in large part through their paralinguistics, or how they sound, rather than the specific words they say. Thus, when you call a close friend or relative, you may expect them to recognize you just from hearing your voice on the telephone. If someone close to you has ever failed to recognize your voice on the phone, you may have felt hurt or offended, and the simple phone call may have turned into an anxiety-producing quiz. Paralinguistics are composed of two types of vocal behavior—*voice qualities* and *vocalizations*.

Voice Qualities. **Voice qualities** include speed, pitch, rhythm, vocal range, and articulation; these qualities make up the "music" of the human voice. We all know people whose voice qualities are widely recognized. For example, President Barack Obama's vocal qualities are frequently remarked upon. One critic (Dié, 2008) described it as resembling that used by preachers, arguing that if you listen only to how the President speaks (rather than what he says), you would feel as if you were sitting in a small church in any black neighborhood in the U. S. He uses the same

COMMUNICATION IN SOCIETY
When You Smile on the Job

Do you think it is reasonable for a retail store to require women cashiers to smile and make eye contact with all customers? Why or why not? Why do you think the female Safeway employees believed their smiles were the cause of the men's attention?

Have you noticed the smiles and greetings you receive when you shop at major grocery store chains such as Walmart and Safeway? Grocery stores weren't always such welcoming places. This friendly behavior, often called the "supermarket mandatory smile" began in the U. S. in the late 1990s. Although many stores encouraged this behavior, Safeway actually required its employees to greet customers with a smile and direct eye contact. However, some female employees lodged complaints over this policy because they argued that male customers repeatedly propositioned them and asked them out on dates when they acted so friendly. Although Safeway denied that their policy was the cause of the men's behavior, they did eventually end it. If the organization had consulted nonverbal research on flirting, they might never have instituted the policy in the first place. One of the most common behaviors women use to signal their interest in men is a smile combined with eye contact and a slight tilt of the head (Trost & Alberts, 2009).

"ebb and flow" or rhythms and intonations that are common to ministers' rhetorical style. To compare the vocal qualities of various presidents, go to www.presidentsusa.net/audiovideo.html and listen to audio and video recordings of many presidents.

Speakers whose voices vary in pitch and rhythm seem more expressive than those whose voices do not. For example, actor Keanu Reeves is criticized by some as boring and inexpressive because they perceive his delivery as monotonous. (This worked to his advantage, however, during his role as Klaatu in *The Day the Earth Stood Still*.) Speakers also vary in how they articulate sounds, some pronouncing each word distinctly and others blurring their words and sounds. We tend not to notice this paralinguistic feature unless someone articulates very precisely or very imprecisely. If you have difficulty understanding a speaker, usually the fault lies not with how fast the person talks but with how clearly he or she articulates. When combined, the qualities of pitch and rhythm make your voice distinctive and recognizable to those who know you. Think back to the last time you encountered someone you could tell was truly happy to see you. How could you tell? What nonverbal behaviors communicated the other person's happiness to you?

Vocalizations.   **Vocalizations** are the sounds we utter that do not have the structure of language. Tarzan's yell is one famous example. Vocalizations include vocal cues such as laughing, crying, whining, and moaning, as well as the intensity or volume of one's speech. Also included are sounds that aren't actual words but that serve as fillers, such as "uh-huh," "uh," "ah," and "er."

The paralinguistic aspects of speech serve a variety of communicative purposes. They reveal mood and emotion; they also allow us to emphasize or stress a word or idea, create a distinctive identity, and (along with gestures) regulate conversation.

Time and Space

How people use time and space is so important to communication that researchers have studied their use and developed specialized terms to describe them. **Chronemics**, from the Greek word *chronos*, meaning "time," is the study of the way people use time as a message. It includes issues such as punctuality and the amount of time people spend with each other. **Proxemics** refers to the study of how people use spatial cues, including interpersonal distance, territoriality, and other space relationships. Let's see how these factors influence communication and relationships.

Chronemics.   People often interpret others' use of time as conveying a message, which removes it from the realm of behavior and places it in the realm of communication. For example, if your friend consistently arrives more than an hour late, how do you interpret her behavior? Culture strongly influences how most people answer this question (Hall & Hall, 1987). In the United States, time typically is valued highly; we even have an expression that "time is money." Because of this, most people own numerous clocks and watches. Events are scheduled at specific times and typically begin on time. Therefore, in the United States, lateness can communicate thoughtlessness, irresponsibility, or selfishness. A more positive or tolerant view might be that the perpetually late person is carefree.

Not all cultures value time in the same way, however. In some Latin American and Arab cultures, if one arrives thirty minutes or even an hour after an event is scheduled to begin, one is "on time." When people come together from cultures that value time differently, it can lead to conflict and a sense of displacement. This happened when one of our colleagues taught a class in Mexico. On the first class day, she showed up at the school shortly before the class was scheduled to begin. She found the building locked and no one around. And even though she knew that people in Mexico respond to time differently than she did, during her stay she never was comfortable arriving "late," and routinely had to wait outside the building until someone showed up to let her in.

vocalizations
uttered sounds that do not have the structure of language

chronemics
the study of the way people use time as a message

proxemics
the study of how people use spatial cues, including interpersonal distance, territoriality, and other space relationships, to communicate

Did You Know?
Expectancy Violations

Think of a time when someone violated your expectations for nonverbal behavior. How did you interpret the behavior? Did you see it as a positive or negative violation? Why? How did you respond? How can a person use expectancy violation theory to increase liking?

Our expectations are one factor that influences our interpretations of others' nonverbal behavior. *Expectancy violation theory* states that when people violate our expectations, we tend to notice, become aroused, and attribute meaning to the violation, resulting in increased scrutiny and appraisal of the violator's behavior. For example, if you expect a stranger to shake your hand upon being introduced, you likely will search for an explanation if she or he hugs you instead.

However, we don't necessarily interpret and respond to these violations negatively. Judee Burgoon and her colleagues repeatedly have shown that responses to another's violation of our expectations are influenced by how we perceive the violator. In other words, we judge a violation as positive or negative depending largely on whether we view the violator as someone with whom we'd like to interact. Thus, if the stranger who hugs you is very attractive and you are single, you may evaluate this violation positively. This judgment shapes your response to the violation; in this case, if you interpret the hug positively, you may respond by hugging back (Burgoon & Hale, 1988; Burgoon & LePoire, 1993).

The timing and sequencing of events convey a variety of messages. For example, being invited to lunch carries a different meaning than being invited to dinner, and being asked to dinner on a Monday conveys a different message than being asked to dinner on a Saturday. Events also tend to unfold in a particular order; so we expect first dates to precede first kisses and small talk to precede task talk. When these expectations are violated, we often attribute meaning to the violations, as shown in *Did You Know? Expectancy Violations.*

In addition, some people use time **monochronically**, while others use it **polychronically**, and the differences can be perceived as transmitting a message (Hall, 1983; Wolburg, 2001). Individuals who use time monochronically engage in one task *or* behavior at time—one reads *or* participates in a conversation or watches a movie. If you engage in multiple activities at the same time, you are using time polychronically. Historically in the United States, people have used time monochronically; however, now that technology is so pervasive, more people are using time polychronically as they listen to their iPods, talk on cell phones, and cruise the Web while they interact with others. Unfortunately, people who use time monochronically may be insulted by those who use it polychronically, leading to comments such as "Put down that iPhone and pay attention to me when I talk to you!"

Whenever an individual's use of time differs from that of others, miscommunication is possible. If you tend to value punctuality more than others do, you may arrive at events earlier than expected and irritate your host, or you may be perceived as too eager. Similarly, if you don't value punctuality, you may discover that others won't schedule activities with you or are frequently annoyed with you for disrupting their plans. Relationships and communication benefit when the people involved understand how the others value and use time.

Proxemics. As we mentioned earlier, proxemics is the study of how one uses space and how this use of space can serve a communicative function. Thus, the distance people stand or sit from one another often symbolizes physical and/or

monochronically
engaging in one task or behavior at a time

polychronically
engaging in multiple activities simultaneously

psychological closeness. If a longtime friend or partner chose not to sit next to you at a movie theatre, you probably would be perplexed, perhaps even hurt or angry. Research by Edward T. Hall, a well-known anthropologist, has delineated four spheres or categories of space that humans use (Hall, 1966). Let's take a look at each.

Intimate distance (0 to 18 inches) tends to be reserved for those whom one knows very well. Typically, this distance is used for displaying physical and psychological intimacy, such as lovemaking, cuddling children, comforting someone, or telling secrets. **Personal distance** (18 inches to 4 feet) describes the space we use when interacting with friends and acquaintances. People in the United States often use the nearer distance for friends and the farther one for acquaintances, but cultures and personal preference strongly influence this choice. When others prefer closer distances than you do, you may find their closeness psychologically distressing; comedian Jerry Seinfeld has referred to these people as "close talkers." One of our students details her encounters with such a person in *It Happened to Me: Katarina*.

Social distance (4 to 12 feet) is the distance most U.S. Americans use when they interact with unfamiliar others. Impersonal business with grocery clerks, sales clerks, and coworkers occurs at about 4 to 7 feet, while the greatest distance is used in formal situations such as job interviews. **Public distance** (12 to 25 feet) is most appropriate for public ceremonies such as lectures and performances, though an even greater distance may be maintained between public figures (such as politicians and celebrities) and their audiences.

It Happened to Me: Katarina

I have a friend whom I like very much but who makes me really uncomfortable sometimes. She tends to lean in very close when she talks, especially if she has been drinking. One night, we were sitting together at a party. I sat in the corner of a couch while she leaned in to talk with me; I kept trying to pull my face away from hers while she talked until I was almost leaning over the back of the couch.

One's culture, gender, relationship to others, and personality all influence whether one feels most comfortable at the near or far range of each of these spheres. In the United States, two unacquainted women typically sit or stand closer to each other than do two unacquainted men, while many men are more comfortable sitting or standing closer to unknown women than they are even to men they know (Burgoon & Guerrero, 1994). However, people in other cultures may prefer the closer ranges. Cultural disparities can result in a comedic cross-cultural "dance," where one person tries to get closer to the other and that person, made uncomfortable by the closeness, moves away.

What does the space between interactants in a given culture reveal? It can communicate intimacy or the lack of it; it also can communicate power and dominance. If person A feels free to enter person B's space without permission but refuses to allow B the same privilege, this lack of reciprocity communicates that A is dominant in the relationship. This situation is common between supervisors and subordinates and may exist in some parent–child relationships as well.

All humans, as well as animals, have strong feelings of territoriality. We exhibit territorial behavior when we attempt to claim control over a particular area. A primary way we attempt to claim and maintain control of a space is through personalization or marking, especially by use of artifacts. Thus we alter spaces to make them distinctly our own through activities such as placing a fence around a residence or displaying family photos in an office. These markers are a form of nonverbal communication that specifies territorial ownership or legitimate occupancy (Becker, 1973). Markers function mainly to keep people away, thereby preventing confrontational social encounters. An unexpected manifestation of territoriality is described in *Did You Know? Territoriality: Maintaining Private and Public Spaces*.

Primary territories (areas under private control, such as houses and the bedrooms within them) serve as extensions of the owner's sense of identity, so that

intimate distance
(0 to 18 inches) the space used when interacting with those with whom one is very close

personal distance
(18 inches to 4 feet) the space used when interacting with friends and acquaintances

social distance
(4 to 12 feet) the distance most U.S. Americans use when they interact with unfamiliar others

public distance
(12 to 25 feet) the distance used for public ceremonies such as lectures and performances

markers there often include personally meaningful symbols reflecting the owner's style and taste (name plates, art objects, flower gardens). Public territories are less central to our self-concepts and, therefore, we tend to mark them with objects that are less personalized and/or that represent explicit claims to the space (for example, "reserved parking" signs). When someone violates a public territory, we tend to react with verbal retaliation, for example, asking the violator to leave. In contrast, we are likely to react strongly when someone violates our primary territory, for example, by seeking physical retaliation and legal sanctions (Abu-Ghazzeh, 2000).

Haptics

Although researchers in communication know that touch, or **haptics**, is important, it is among the least studied forms of nonverbal communication. Nonetheless,

haptics
the study of the communicative function of touch

Did You Know?
Territoriality: Maintaining Private and Public Spaces

Do you have bumper stickers or decals on your car? If so, do you think the research findings below describe you? Do they describe people you know? How do you mark your other personal and public territories? What do you think your markers say about you?

Watch out for cars with bumper stickers.

That's the surprising conclusion of a recent study by social psychologist William Szlemko. Drivers of cars with bumper stickers, window decals, personalized license plates, and other "territorial markers" not only get mad when someone cuts in their lane or is slow to respond to a changed traffic light, but they are far more likely than those who do not personalize their cars to use their vehicles to express rage—by honking, tailgating, and other aggressive behavior.

It does not seem to matter whether the messages on the stickers are about peace and love—"Visualize World Peace," "My Kid Is an Honor Student"—or angry and in your face—"Don't Mess With Texas," "My Kid Beat Up Your Honor Student."

Szlemko and his colleagues found that people who personalize their cars acknowledge that they are aggressive drivers, but usually do not realize that they are reporting much higher levels of aggression than people whose cars do not have visible markers on their vehicles.

"The more markers a car has, the more aggressively the person tends to drive when provoked," Szlemko said. "Just the presence of territory markers predicts the tendency to be an aggressive driver."

The key to the phenomenon apparently lies in the idea of territoriality. Drivers with road rage tend to think of public streets and highways as "my street" and "my lane"—in other words, they think they "own the road." Why would bumper stickers predict which people are likely to view public roadways as private property?

Social scientists such as Szlemko say that people carry around three kinds of territorial spaces in their heads. One is personal territory—like a home, or a bedroom. The second kind involves space that is temporarily yours—an office cubicle or a gym locker. The third kind is public territory: park benches, walking trails—and roads.

Drivers who individualize their cars using bumper stickers, window decals, and personalized license plates, the researchers hypothesized, see their cars in the same way as they see their homes and bedrooms—as deeply personal space, or primary territory.

"If you are in a vehicle that you identify as a primary territory, you would defend that against other people whom you perceive as being disrespectful of your space," Bell added. "What you ignore is that you are on a public roadway—you lose sight of the fact you are in a public area and you don't own the road."

FROM: Vendantam, S. (2008, June 16). Looking to avoid aggressive drivers? Check those bumpers. *The Washington Post.* © 2008 The Washington Post. Reprinted with permission.

professional touch
type of touch used by certain workers, such as dentists, hairstylists, and hospice workers, as part of their livelihood; also known as *functional touch*

functional touch
the least intimate type of touch; used by certain workers such as dentists, hairstylists, and hospice workers, as part of their livelihood; also known as *professional touch*

social-polite touch
touch that is part of daily interaction in the United States; it is more intimate than professional touch but is still impersonal

friendship touch
touch that is more intimate than social touch and usually conveys warmth, closeness, and caring

love-intimate touch
the touch most often used with one's romantic partners and family

demand touching
a type of touch used to establish dominance and power

research does indicate that infants and children need to be touched in order to be physically and psychologically healthy (Field, 2002). Also, although people vary considerably in how much or what type of touch they prefer, most enjoy being touched by those they care about.

Touch can be categorized into several general types (Givens, 2005), but people rarely notice the types unless a discrepancy occurs between their expectations and their experience. **Professional, or functional, touch** is the least intimate; people who must touch others as part of their livelihood, such as medical and dental caregivers, hairstylists, and tailors, use this type of touch. Because touch often conveys intimacy, people who must use professional touch have to be careful of their interaction style; for example, they may adopt a formal or distant verbal communication style to counteract the intimacy of their touch. **Social-polite touch** is part of daily interaction. In the United States, this form of touch is more intimate than professional touch but is still impersonal. For example, many U.S. Americans shake hands when greeting acquaintances and casual friends, though in many European countries, such as France and Italy, hugging and kissing are appropriate forms of social touch. Even within the United States, people have different ideas about what types of touch are appropriate socially.

Friendship touch is more intimate than social touch and usually conveys warmth, closeness, and caring. Although considerable variation in touch may exist among friends, people typically use touch that is more intimate with close friends than with acquaintances or strangers. Examples include brief hugs, a hand on the shoulder, or putting one's arm loosely around another's waist or shoulders. **Love-intimate touch** most often is used with one's romantic partners and family. Examples are the long kisses and extended hugging and cuddling we tend to reserve for those with whom we are closest.

As is true of other forms of nonverbal communication, sex, culture, and power strongly influence patterns of touch. In the United States, heterosexual males are more likely to reserve hand-holding for their romantic partners and small children, while females touch other women more frequently and hold hands with older children, their close female relatives, and even female friends. In general, women tend to touch other women more frequently than men touch other men, and in cross-sex interactions, men are more likely to initiate touch than do women (Hall & Hall, 1990). However, in cross-sex interactions, the nature of the relationship influences touch behavior more than does the sex of the participants. Across all stages of heterosexual romantic relationships, partners reciprocate touch, so they do not differ in amount of touch (Guerrero & Andersen, 1991). However, men respond more positively to their partners' touch than do women (Hanzal, Segrin, & Dorros, 2008). In addition, men initiate touch more in casual romantic relationships, while women do so more often in married relationships (Guerrero & Andersen, 1994).

Each form of touch we have discussed thus far has a "positive" quality; but, of course, people also use touch to convey negative messages. For example, one study revealed that individuals (especially parents) use aggressive touch and withdrawal of affectionate touch with children to signal their displeasure (Guerrero & Ebesu, 1993). Aggressive touch can include grabbing, hitting, and pinching, while withdrawal of affection involves rejecting the touch attempts of others, as when one pushes another's arm away or refuses to hold hands. Both children and adults use aggressive touch with their peers as well, though in none of these instances is aggressive touch considered an appropriate or competent way to communicate.

Another type of touch that can be perceived negatively is **demand touching**, a type of touch used to establish dominance and power. Demand touching increases in hierarchical settings, such as at work. One significant characteristic of demand touching is that touchers typically have higher status and have more control over encounters than do receivers; this allows them more freedom of movement and more visual contact. An everyday example of demand touch occurs when a supervisor stands behind a subordinate and leans over to provide directions, placing his or her hand on the subordinate's shoulder. The subordinate can't move easily or look directly at the supervisor, and the subordinate may feel both physically and psychologically constrained (Kemmer, 1992).

artifacts
clothing and other accessories

Appearance and Artifacts

In all cultures, individuals' appearance matters, as do their **artifacts**, or the clothing and other accessories they choose. Let's first consider appearance and how it operates as a nonverbal code.

In general, people's looks are believed to communicate something about them, and people develop expectations based on how others look. Hairstyle, skin color, height, weight, clothing, accessories such as jewelry, and other aspects of appearance all influence how we are perceived and how we perceive others. And in the United States, appearance is seen as especially important (Newport, 1999).

What is considered attractive, however, is influenced by one's culture and the time period in which one lives (Grammer, Fink, Joller, & Thornhill, 2003). Many people find it hard to believe that the Mona Lisa was considered a great beauty in her day, and even more people wonder who could ever have liked the clothes and hairstyles their own parents wore when they were young. Although the global village we live in now means the media transmit images that can be seen all over the world, cultures still vary in what they consider most attractive. The current ideal body type for women in the United States, as portrayed in the media, for example, is considered too thin and unfeminine by many African Americans (Duke, 2002). While some American women get collagen injections to achieve full lips, our Japanese students tell us that such thick lips are not considered attractive in Japan. Some Europeans also dislike the defined musculature favored for males in magazines and television ads in the United States.

In the United States, people invest considerable time, money, and energy adapting their appearance to cultural ideals of attractiveness. They diet, color and style their hair, frequent gyms and tanning booths, and even undergo extreme makeovers to be more attractive. People engage in all these efforts because the U.S. culture generally equates beauty with happiness, success, goodness, and desirability.

While people face certain limits in reshaping their bodies and other physical attributes, they also have great flexibility in using clothing and other artifacts to convey important messages about themselves. In most business contexts, a suit is perceived to be authoritative and an indication of status. This is especially true of men; evaluations of their status often are based on their appearance and clothing (Mast & Hall, 2004). People also use artifacts to signal their occupations and identities. Nurses, flight attendants, and police officers wear uniforms to help others identify them and to send specific messages about their jobs (Gundersen, 1990). Thus, police officers wear paramilitary uniforms not only to allow us to easily identify them but also to reinforce their role in maintaining social order.

Individuals also choose their accessories and artifacts, such as purses, watches, jewelry, sunglasses, and even cars, to communicate specific messages about status, personality, success, and/or group membership. A student who carries a leather briefcase on campus creates a different image than one who carries a canvas backpack. On a typical college campus, it is fairly easy to differentiate the communication professors from the business professors and the engineering students from the theater majors based on their dress and artifacts. We might argue that in the United States, where it is not considered polite to announce one's status or success, people often use artifacts to make those announcements for them (Fussell, 1992).

As you can see from the preceding discussion, multiple categories of nonverbal behavior influence communication; these include kinesics, paralinguistics, chronemics and proxemics, haptics, and appearance and artifacts. These categories are, in turn, influenced by multiple individual and cultural factors. In the next section we explore how these categories work together to influence how we send and interpret messages.

What artifacts are important to you in terms of communicating your identity or status? If you had only one means of communicating high status, would you drive an expensive car, wear designer clothes, or live in an upscale neighborhood? What do you think your choice reflects about you?

The Functions of Nonverbal Messages

As mentioned earlier, when people interpret nonverbal behaviors they don't isolate kinesics from haptics or proxemics from appearance; rather, they observe an integrated set of behaviors, consider the context and the individual, and then attribute meaning. If you see two people standing closely together in a public place, you wouldn't necessarily assume they were being intimate. Rather, you would examine how relaxed or tense their bodies appeared, evaluate their facial expressions and eye gaze, and consider the appropriateness of intimate displays in this public space (for example, a bar versus a church). Only then might you make an attribution about the meaning or function of the couple's behavior.

In general, scholars have determined that nonverbal behaviors serve five functions during interaction (Patterson, 1982, 2003). Those five functions are communicating information, regulating interaction, expressing and managing intimacy, establishing social control, and signaling service-task functions. The most basic function is to communicate information, and this is the one we examine first.

Communicating Information

Most fundamentally, nonverbal message are used to **communicate information**. From the receiver's point of view, much of a sender's behavior is potentially informative. For example, when you meet someone for the first time you evaluate the pattern of the sender's behavior to assess a variety of factors. First, you might evaluate the sender's general disposition to determine if it is warm and friendly or cool and distant. You likely will also assess her more fleeting nonverbal reactions to help you decide if she seems pleased to meet you or is just being polite. Finally, of course, you evaluate the person's verbal message. For example, does the speaker say, "I've really been looking forward to meeting you," or does she say, "I'd love to chat, but I've got to run"? You then combine all these pieces of information to ascribe meaning to the encounter.

Nonverbal communication helps individuals convey and interpret verbal messages. They can do this in five ways:

1. By repeating a message (winking while saying "I'm just kidding");
2. By highlighting or emphasizing a message (pointing at the door while saying "Get out!");
3. By complementing or reinforcing a message (whispering while telling a secret);
4. By contradicting a message (saying "I love your haircut" while speaking in a hostile tone and rolling one's eyes);
5. By substituting for a message (shaking one's head to indicate disagreement).

As these examples illustrate, using nonverbal communication effectively can make you a better *verbal* communicator.

Regulating Interaction

Nonverbal communication also is used to **regulate interaction**. That is, people use nonverbal behaviors to manage turn-taking during conversation. Thus, if you want to start talking, you might lean forward, look at the current speaker, and even raise one finger. To reveal that you are finished with your turn, you may drop your volume and pitch, lean back, and look away from and then back toward the person you are "giving" your turn to. The regulating function tends to be the most automatic of the five, and most of us rarely think about it. The behaviors you use in this way include the more stable ones such as interpersonal distance, body orientation, and posture, as well as more fluid behaviors like gaze, facial expression, volume, and pitch, which are important in the smooth sequencing of conversational turns (Capella, 1985).

Expressing and Managing Intimacy

A third function of nonverbal communication, and the most studied, involves **expressing and managing intimacy**. The degree of your nonverbal involvement

communicating information
using nonverbal behaviors to help clarify verbal messages and reveal attitudes and moods

regulating interaction
using nonverbal behaviors to help manage conversational interaction

expressing and managing intimacy
using nonverbal behaviors to help convey attraction and closeness

with another usually reflects the level of intimacy you desire with that person. If you are on a date and notice your partner is leaning toward you, gazing into your eyes, nodding his head, and providing many paralinguistic cues such as "uh huh" as you talk, your date is revealing a high degree of nonverbal involvement, which often signals attraction and interest. Of course, people can manipulate these behaviors to suggest attraction and involvement even if they are not experiencing these feelings. For example, in the workplace when subordinates talk with their supervisors, they often display fairly high levels of nonverbal involvement, regardless of their true feelings for their bosses.

Establishing Social Control

People also use nonverbal communication to exert or **establish social control**, or to exercise influence over other people. Individuals engage in the social control function when they smile at someone they want to do them a favor or when they glare at noisy patrons in a theater to encourage them to be quiet. You can use either positive or negative behaviors (or both) in your efforts to control others. People who are "charming" or very persuasive typically are extremely gifted at using nonverbal behavior to influence others.

Sports coaches, tailors, and other professionals use nonverbal communication that has a service-task function.

When expressing and managing intimacy people tend to respond in similar, or reciprocal, ways to one another's nonverbal behavior. On the other hand, when engaging in social control, people tend to respond in complementary ways to one another's nonverbal behavior.

Signaling Service-Task Functions

Finally, nonverbal communication has a **service-task function**. Behaviors of this kind typically signal close involvement between people in impersonal relationships and contexts. For example, golf pros often stand with their arms around a novice golfer to help her with her golf swing and massage therapists engage in very intimate touch as part of their profession. In each of these cases, the behavior is appropriate, necessary, and a means to a (professional) end.

Accurately interpreting nonverbal messages is a complex endeavor, requiring awareness of a number of elements—factors that influence individuals' communication patterns, nonverbal communication codes and signals, and the communicative functions that nonverbal messages fulfill. However, in some senses, we have only shown you one piece of the picture, as we have thus far focused primarily on nonverbal communication as performed by individuals. In the next section, we expand the frame to explore how societal forces influence both the performance and interpretation of nonverbal messages and behavior.

TEST YOUR KNOWLEDGE

- What is a nonverbal code?
- What five functions does nonverbal communication serve?

✕ THE INDIVIDUAL, NONVERBAL COMMUNICATION, AND SOCIETY

Nonverbal communication, like all communication, is heavily influenced by societal forces and occurs within a hierarchical system of meanings. One's status and position within the societal hierarchy, as well as one's identity, are all expressed nonverbally. However, the more powerful elements in society often regulate these expressions. In

establishing social control
using nonverbal behavior to exercise influence over other people

service-task functions
using nonverbal behavior to signal close involvement between people in impersonal relationships and contexts

addition, nonverbal communication can trigger and express prejudice and discrimination. Let's see how this operates.

Nonverbal Communication and Power

Nonverbal communication and power are intricately related—especially via the nonverbal codes of appearance and artifacts. In the United States, power is primarily based on an individual's access to economic resources and the freedom to make decisions that affect others. Economic resources are typically revealed or expressed through nonverbal codes. People display wealth through the clothing and accessories they wear, the quality of their haircuts, and the value of their homes and cars. Whether one can afford to buy the latest designer fashions, or only to shop in discount stores, communicates clearly one's social class and power. English professor Paul Fussell (1992) provides an extensive description of how nonverbal messages communicated in our everyday lives reveal class standing. Consider, for example, the messages communicated by one's home. Fussell notes that the longer the driveway, the less obvious the garage, and the more manicured the grounds, the higher is one's socioeconomic class.

People use nonverbal cues to communicate their own status and identities, and to evaluate and interpret others' status and identities. Based on these interpretations, people—consciously and unconsciously—include and exclude others, and approve or disapprove of others. For example, in wealthy communities, people who don't look affluent may be stopped and questioned about their presence or even be asked to leave. More overtly, gated communities offer clear nonverbal messages about who belongs and who does not belong to a community. Of course, it isn't just the wealthy who use artifacts to convey their identity and belonging. Gang members, NASCAR fans, football fans, and many others also use attire as well as gestures to signal their individual and group identities.

The use of nonverbal cues to communicate social class extends beyond the use of appearance and artifacts. For example, psychology professors Michael Kraus and Dach Keltner (2009) examined individuals' use of nonverbal communication while interacting with a stranger. In these interactions they found that people with high socioeconomic status were more likely to display nonverbal signs of disengagement, such as doodling, and fewer signs of engagement, such as smiling and nodding, than people with lower socioeconomic status. In addition, people who observed these interactions could correctly guess the participants' social class from their nonverbal behavior. Thus, nonverbal communication reproduces—or re-creates—the society and social classes in which we live.

Although all groups use nonverbal communication to convey identity, more powerful segments of society typically define what is allowed. For example, many corporations have dress codes designed to communicate a particular professional image to the public. For the same reason, they may also have rules that regulate nonverbal expression of men's facial hair. The military and many police organizations have policies on tattoos as well (Zezima, 2005). Because these organizations are hierarchical, the decisions made by those in power in the organization must be followed by those who wish employment there.

In 2005, the National Basketball Association issued rules governing the off-court dress of NBA players: They are to dress in "business casual" whenever engaged in team or league business, and they are specifically excluded from wearing sleeveless shirts, shorts, T-shirts, headgear of any kind, chains, pendants, and sunglasses while indoors. See http://worklaw.jotwell.com/does-the-nbas-dress.code-violate-title-vii/ for more information on this topic. Through these dictums, the organization is attempting to regulate not only the players' clothing, but their expression of their identities as well. Of course, not all players support these regulations (Wise, 2005). Some NBA players feel that the ban on chains and other jewelry was racially motivated. In short, this new policy "called attention to a generational chasm between modern pro-

The NBA issued rules governing NBA players' off-court dress to help shape the images they present to the public.

fessional athletes, many of whom are Black, and their mostly White paying customers" (Wise, 2005, p. A-1).

The number and range of dress codes and regulations on appearance underscore the powerful impact that nonverbal cues can have. The more powerful segments of society also define what is most desirable and attractive in our culture. For example, cosmetic corporations spend $231 billion annually on the development of beauty products and advertising to persuade consumers to buy them. The largest cosmetic companies have recently expanded to China where the nation's 451 million women are of great interest to the cosmetic market—which has doubled in the past five years to $8 billion (Carvajal, 2006). The media broadly communicate to us the definitions of beauty. This is why many U.S. Americans believe that blonde hair is better than brown, thin is better than fat, large breasts are better than small, and young is better than old—beliefs that are not shared universally. Messages promoting a specific type of youth and beauty might seem rather harmless, until one considers the consequences for those who are not thin and blonde, especially those who have no possibility of meeting the dominant standards of beauty. How does this hierarchy of attractiveness affect their communication with others? Do people respond to them negatively because of their appearance? Might they feel marginalized and resentful—even before they interact with others who more clearly meet the dominant standards?

Nonverbal expressions also are an important part of cultural rituals involving societal expectations. For example, in U.S. culture it is traditionally considered unacceptable to wear white to a wedding unless one is the bride, while black or other dark colors are considered appropriate to wear to funerals. Aspects of dress are very important in the United States at other cultural events, particularly for women. The outfits worn to the Academy Awards and other "show business" honor ceremonies are reviewed and evaluated and are a topic of great interest for many people. Similarly, what the President's wife wears on Inauguration Day and at subsequent parties is a subject of conversation; in fact, the First Lady's wardrobe is discussed and critiqued every day on TV, in blogs, and in magazines. The interest (and evaluation) of these nonverbal expressions, like clothing, is driven by societal forces. In all of these cases, women know that their nonverbal messages will be carefully scrutinized and evaluated.

Nonverbal Communication, Prejudice, and Discrimination

At the intersection of societal forces and nonverbal communication are prejudice and discrimination. Both can be triggered by nonverbal behavior and are also expressed through nonverbal behavior. Let's look at how this works. First, one's race and ethnicity, body shape, age, or style of dress—all of which are communicated nonverbally—can prompt prejudgment or negative stereotypes. How often do people make a snap judgment or generalization based on appearance? Second, prejudice and discrimination are expressed nonverbally. In some extreme cases, nonverbal signals have even triggered and perpetrated hate crimes. For example, one night in Phoenix, Arizona, Avtar (Singh) Chiera, a small-business owner and a Sikh, waited outside his business for his son to pick him up. Two White men pulled up in a small red pickup truck, yelled at him, and then opened fire on him. Because of anger over the events of 9/11, the two men likely targeted him as an Arab because of his turban and beard, even though Sikhs are neither Arab nor Muslim (Parasuram, 2003). In this encounter, nonverbal messages were the most important; the words spoken (if any) were of minimal impact.

Although the example of the shooting of Mr. Chiera is extreme, there are many other more subtle ways that prejudice can be communicated nonverbally—for instance, averting one's gaze or failing to reciprocate a smile. It can be as subtle as shifting your gaze, leaning your body away, or editing your speech. Sociologist A. G.

This antigroping sign from Japan illustrates a common problem in many parts of the world. What are the ethical issues in this nonverbal behavior?

Johnson (2001, pp. 58–59) gives a list of specific nonverbal behaviors that can be interpreted as prejudicial. These are mostly noticed only by the person experiencing them and often happen unconsciously and unintentionally:

- Not looking at people when we talk with them;
- Not smiling at people when they walk into the room, or staring as if to say, "What are you doing here?," or stopping the conversation with a hush they have to wade through to be included in the smallest way;
- Not acknowledging people's presence or making them wait as if they weren't there;
- Not touching their skin when we give them something;
- Watching them closely to see what they're up to;
- Avoiding someone walking down the street, giving them wide berth, or even crossing to the other side.

Given the potential consequences of nonverbal communication, you may find it helpful to consider how your nonverbal communication reflects your own ethical stance. To guide you in making appropriate and ethical choices, in the next section we explore the ethics of nonverbal communication.

TEST YOUR KNOWLEDGE

1. How does power influence nonverbal communication norms?
2. How does status influence one's nonverbal communication?

ETHICS AND NONVERBAL COMMUNICATION

The ethics of nonverbal communication are actually quite similar to the ethics of communication in general. When people engage in behavior such as deceiving or threatening others or name-calling, their nonverbal behavior typically plays a central role in their messages. For instance, liars use nonverbal behavior to avoid "leaking" the deception, and they may also use it to convey the deceptive message. Moreover, deceivers may feel that lying nonverbally—for example, by remaining silent—is less "wrong" than lying with words. In the Old Testament, Joseph's brothers were very jealous of their father's affection for him, so they sold Joseph into slavery. When they returned without him, however, they didn't "tell" their father what happened; instead they gave him Joseph's bloody coat and let their father draw the conclusion that wild animals had killed Joseph. In this way, they deceived their father without actually speaking a lie. What do you think? Is it better, or less unethical, to lie nonverbally than it is to do so verbally?

When communicators use nonverbal cues that ridicule, derogate, or otherwise demean others, they run the risk of their behavior being viewed by others as unethical. For example, if someone speaks in a patronizing vocal tone, screams at the less powerful, or touches others inappropriately, would you view this behavior as unethical? What if people respond to others' communication in a way that misrepresents how they actually feel? For instance, if they laugh at a racist or sexist joke even though they dislike it, would you see that behavior as unethical?

Since these are the types of decisions you have to make routinely throughout your life, here are some guidelines for ethical nonverbal communication to help you make those decisions. Consider whether:

- your nonverbal behaviors reflect your real attitudes, beliefs, and feelings;
- your nonverbal behaviors contradict the verbal message you are sending;
- your nonverbal behaviors insult, ridicule, or demean others;
- you are using your nonverbal behavior to intimidate, coerce, or silence someone;
- you would want anyone to observe your nonverbal behavior;
- you would want this nonverbal behavior directed to you or a loved one.

Although there is no litmus test for evaluating the ethics of every nonverbal message in every situation, if you keep these guidelines in mind, they will help you make better, more informed decisions.

TEST YOUR KNOWLEDGE

- Describe some ways in which it is possible for people to engage in unethical nonverbal communication.

IMPROVING YOUR NONVERBAL COMMUNICATION SKILLS

By now you may be wondering how to decide what a set of behaviors means. How do you decide, for example, if your sports coach's touch is appropriately intimate (service-task) or just intimate? In the workplace, how can you determine whether your subordinate genuinely likes you and your ideas (nonverbal involvement) or is merely trying to flatter you (social control)?

One way you can assess your own and others' nonverbal communication is to examine how it interacts with verbal messages (Jones & LeBaron, 2002). That is, how congruent (similar) are the two sets of messages? When the two types of messages are **congruent**, they are often genuine (and/or we assume them to be so). For example, a positive verbal message ("I like you") combined with a positive nonverbal message (smile, forward body lean, relaxed posture) usually conveys a convincing positive message. However, it is also possible that people who are very good at deception are able to offer congruent messages while lying, and those who are less adept at communicating may unintentionally offer contradictory messages when telling the truth. Given all of this, what other factors could you rely on to help you decide whether a congruent message is truthful?

congruent
verbal and nonverbal messages that express the same meaning

contradicting
verbal and nonverbal messages that send conflicting messages

The meaning of this nonverbal behavior is strongly affected by the context.

Of course, verbal and nonverbal messages can also purposely **contradict** one another. When using sarcasm, people intentionally combine a positive verbal message ("what a nice pair of shoes") with a contradictory or negative nonverbal message (a hostile tone). However, at other times people offer contradictory messages unintentionally or carelessly. Caretakers often confuse children (and encourage misbehavior) by telling a child to stop a particular behavior while smiling or laughing. How does a child interpret this message? Most children will accept the nonverbal aspect of the message and ignore the verbal (Eskritt & Lee, 2003.)

In addition to assessing the congruence of the verbal and nonverbal components of a message, you improve your comprehension of nonverbal messages by analyzing the context, your knowledge of the other person, and your own experiences. For example, if you are playing basketball and a teammate slaps you on the rear and says "good going," the message may be clear. Given the context, you may read it as a compliment and perhaps a sign of affection or intimacy. But what if the slap on the rear occurs at work after an effective presentation? Given that such behavior is generally inappropriate in a business context, you probably will (and should) more closely assess its meaning. You might ask yourself whether this person simply lacks social skills and frequently engages in inappropriate behavior. If so, the message may be inappropriate but still be meant in a positive fashion. In contrast, if the person knows better and has touched you inappropriately at other times, the behavior may be intentionally designed to express inappropriate intimacy or social control.

Here are a few more suggestions to keep in mind:

- Recognize that others' nonverbal messages don't always mean the same as yours.
- Be aware of individual, contextual, and cultural factors that influence meaning.
- Ask for additional information if you don't understand a nonverbal message or if you perceive a contradiction between the verbal and nonverbal messages.
- Remember that not every nonverbal behavior is intended to be communicative.
- Don't place too much emphasis on fleeting nonverbal behaviors such as facial expression or vocal tone; rather, examine the entire set of nonverbal behaviors.

TEST YOUR KNOWLEDGE

- What are some specific strategies you can use to improve your ability to communicate nonverbally?

SUMMARY

Nonverbal messages are an important component of communication. They help you interpret and understand verbal messages and, in doing so, help you more effectively navigate your everyday life. Studying nonverbal communication is particularly important because they are complex and ambiguous.

Nonverbal communication is defined as all the messages that people transmit through means other than words. To understand the meaning of a nonverbal messages, you have to consider the entire behavioral context, including culture, relationship type, background knowledge, and gender. Nonverbal communication occurs through five codes or types of signals: kinesics, paralinguistics (vocal qualities), chronemics and proxemics (time and space), haptics (touch), and appearance and artifacts. These codes can combine to serve one of five functions, such as communicating information, regulating interaction, expressing and managing intimacy, exerting social control, and performing service-task functions.

Power relationships as well as societal norms and rules influence the range of nonverbal behaviors we are allowed to perform and how those behaviors are interpreted. In addition, everyone needs to be aware that nonverbal communication can trigger and express prejudice and discrimination. Thus, nonverbal communication has ethical aspects one must consider when composing one's messages.

You can become more effective in interpreting others' nonverbal communication by assessing the congruence of the verbal and nonverbal components of a message; analyzing the context, your knowledge of the other person, and your own experiences; recognizing that others' nonverbal messages don't always mean the same as yours do; asking for additional information if you don't understand a nonverbal message; and remembering that not every nonverbal behavior is intended to be communicative.

HUMAN COMMUNICATION IN SOCIETY ONLINE

To review this chapter, use the MyCommunicationLab Web site to test your understanding of the following key terms, record your answers to the chapter review questions, and complete the suggested activities. Expand your learning and understanding of chapter concepts by completing the exercises and activities available online. Access code required. Go to www.mycommunicationlab.com for more information or to purchase standalone access.

KEY TERMS

nonverbal communication 126	vocalizations 134	friendship touch 138
nonverbal behavior 126	chronemics 134	love-intimate touch 138
nonverbal codes 131	proxemics 135	demand touching 138
kinesics 131	monochronically 135	artifacts 139
gestures 131	polychronically 135	communicating information 140
illustrators 131	intimate distance 136	regulating interaction 140
emblems 131	personal distance 136	expressing and managing
adaptors 131	social distance 136	intimacy 140
regulators 131	public distance 136	establishing social control 141
immediacy 131	haptics 137	service-task functions 141
relaxation 131	professional touch 138	congruent 145
paralinguistics 133	functional touch 138	contradicting 146
voice qualities 133	social-polite touch 138	

APPLY WHAT YOU KNOW

1. **Waiting Times**

   How long is the "appropriate" amount of time you should wait in each of the following situations? Specifically, after how long a period would you begin to feel angry or put out?

   Estimate waiting times for:
   a. your dentist
   b. a checkout line in a department store
   c. a movie line
   d. a friend at lunch
   e. a friend at dinner
   f. being on hold on the telephone
   g. your professor to arrive at class
   h. a stop light
   i. your romantic partner at a bar
   j. your professor during office hours.

   Do you see any patterns in your expectations for waiting times? What influences your expectations most—your relationship with the other party? The comfort of the waiting area? Your ability to control events? Compare your waiting times with others' to see how similar or different they are.

2. **Violating Norms for Proximity**

   For this exercise we would like you to violate some of the norms for spacing in your culture. Try standing slightly closer to a friend or family member than you normally would, then note how they react. If you have a romantic partner or very close friend, sit much farther from them than you normally would. For example, in a theater, sit one seat away from him or her, or sit at the opposite end of the couch if you would typically sit closer. Pay attention to the reactions you elicit. Finally, when talking with an acquaintance, increase the distance between you each time the other person tries to decrease it and see how the other person responds. What do these responses to your space violations reveal to you regarding the importance of spacing norms in the United States?

   NOTE: Be careful in your selection of people with whom you violate norms of space, and be prepared to explain why you are behaving so oddly

3. **Cultural Differences in Nonverbal Communication**

   Go to a search engine such as Google, and look for a Web site that explains the rules for nonverbal communication and behavior in a culture outside the United States with which you are not familiar. What rules surprised you? What rules were similar to the ones you use? What do you think would happen if you used your "normal" rules for nonverbal behavior in this culture?

EXPLORE

1. Go to a website such as Michigan State University's Presidential Audio Recordings or Archer Audio Archives and compare the vocal qualities of four presidents–two presidents who served before the widespread use of television and two who have served since. What role do you think vocal versus visual cues played in the popularity of each president? Are there presidents whose appearance you find more appealing than their vocal qualities? Are there presidents whose vocal qualities you find more appealing than their appearance?

2. The study of facial expressions of emotion is complex and ongoing. Recently, researchers have begun studying the effect of Botox (which paralyzes facial muscles) on facial expressions and emotional response. Go to a website such as PsychCentral's *Facial Expressions Control Emotions* or WebMD's *Botox May Affect Ability to Feel Emotions* and read the articles. Based on what you read, write a brief paper in which you hypothesize how the use of Botox could affect interpersonal interaction.

7
Communication Across Cultures

chapter outline

> *Many, if not most, of your daily interactions are intercultural in nature."*

In my first semester in the United States, I lived in the dorm and made many friends from different countries. One day I was eating lunch when my Korean and Turkish friends started arguing loudly. The issue was the value of our school. The Turkish girl didn't like our school and was thinking of transferring. The Korean student defended our school vehemently.

The Korean and Turkish students wouldn't talk to each other after the argument, and the conflict created a very uncomfortable climate. I was concerned about both of them because we were all friends. So I asked some of my American friends what they thought about the issue. They said, "It's not your problem, Kaori. It's their problem. Stay away from it." I was shocked that my American friends didn't seem to care about the conflict and its negative influence, and it took me a while to understand what the phrase "it's their problem" actually means in this highly individualistic American society. I've been in the States seven years, and now I use the phrase myself. Do I think it's good? I don't know. At least, I know I am adapting better to American culture. Do I like it? I don't know. It's just how it is here. But I know that I would never ever say that to my family or friends in Japan.

Kaori's story illustrates a number of points about intercultural communication. First, intercultural contact is a fact of life in today's world, and second, as Kaori's story shows, while intercultural contact can be enriching, it also can bring conflict and misunderstandings. In Kaori's case, the clash between her American friends' individualistic belief and her more collectivistic orientation led her to believe that Americans did not value friendships as much as she did. Finally, the story illustrates that it is very common now for individuals, like Kaori, to live "on the border"—between two cultures—and like Kaori, to have to negotiate conflicting sets of cultural values.

In today's world, we typically have many opportunities to meet people from different cultures. You may sit in class with students who are culturally different from you in many ways—in nationality, ethnicity, race, gender, age, religion, and sexual orientation. In addition, today's widespread access to communication technologies and foreign travel provide many opportunities for intercultural encounters beyond the classroom. But the many political and ethnic conflicts around the globe may inspire doubt about the ability of people from different cultures to coexist peacefully. Interethnic violence in Sudan and other African nations, in the former Yugoslavia, and in the Middle East; clashes between Buddhists and Hindus in India; and tension in the United States between African Americans and Whites may lead people to believe that cultural differences necessarily lead to insurmountable problems. However, we believe that increased awareness of intercultural communication can help prevent or reduce the severity of problems that arise due to cultural differences.

In this chapter, we'll first explore the importance of *intercultural communication* and define what we mean when we use this term. Next, we will describe the increasingly common experience of individuals who must negotiate different cultural realities in their everyday lives. Then we'll examine how culture influences our communication and present a dialectical perspective on intercultural communication. Finally, we'll discuss how society affects communication outcomes in intercultural interactions and provide suggestions for how one can become a more ethical and effective intercultural communicator.

✕ Once you have read this chapter, you will be able to:

- Identify four reasons for learning about intercultural communication.
- Define *intercultural communication*.
- Identify six cultural values that influence communication.
- Describe the dialectical approach to intercultural communication.
- Understand the role of power and privilege in communication between people from different cultural backgrounds.
- Give three guidelines for communicating more ethically with people whose cultural backgrounds differ from your own.
- Discuss three ways to improve your own intercultural communication skills.

THE IMPORTANCE OF INTERCULTURAL COMMUNICATION

How many reasons for studying intercultural communication can you think of? If you are like many students, entering college has given you more opportunities than ever before for intercultural contact, both domestically and internationally. You will communicate better in these situations if you have a good understanding of intercultural communication. In addition, increased knowledge and skill in intercultural communication can improve your career effectiveness, intergroup relations, and self-awareness. Let's look at each of these reasons more closely.

Increased Opportunities for Intercultural Contact

Experts estimate that twenty-five people cross national borders every second—1 billion journeys per year ("Numbers," 2008). People leave their countries for many reasons, including national revolutions and civil wars (Afghanistan, Yugoslavia, Congo, Sudan) and natural disasters (floods in Pakistan, earthquake in Haiti). Experts estimate there are currently 36 million displaced persons (United Nations High Commissioner for Refugees, 2009). Sometimes, in a process called **diaspora**, whole groups of people are displaced to new countries as they flee genocide or other untenable conditions or are taken forcefully against their will. Disaporic groups often attempt to settle together in communities in the new location while maintaining a strong ethnic identity and a desire to return home. Historically, diasporic groups include slaves taken from Africa in the 1700s and 1800s, Jews persecuted throughout centuries and relocating around the world, Chinese fleeing famine and wars in the 19th and 20th centuries, and Armenians escaping Turkish genocide in early 1900s (Pendery, 2008; Waterston, 2005). More recent diasporas include Cubans fleeing their homes during the revolution in 1959; Afghans fleeing the Soviet invasion and Iranians leaving when the Shah was deposed, both in 1979; and in the 1990s, Eritreans from Ethiopia, Albanians from Kosovo, and Chechnyans from Russia (Bernal, 2005; Koinova, 2010). Some experts refer to the current Latino diaspora (increasing numbers of Latin Americans who settle outside their homelands) or the Katrina diaspora (the thousands of Hurricane Katrina survivors who are still unable to return home) (Anderson, 2010).

Increasing numbers of people travel for pleasure, some 880 million in 2010 ("Tourism Highlights," 2010). Many people, like the student Kaori in the opening story, also travel for study. According to the Institute of International Education,

diaspora
group of immigrants, sojourners, slaves, or strangers living in new lands while retaining strong attachments to their homelands

approximately 700,000 international students study in the United States each year and approximately 250,000 U.S. students study overseas (IIE, 2010a, 2010b).

Another source of increased opportunity for intercultural contact exists because of the increasing cultural diversity in the United States. Preliminary information from the 2010 census shows continuing dramatic increases in ethnic and racial diversity (Yen, 2011). As shown in Figure 7.1, the Hispanic population will triple in size and constitute approximately 30 percent of the population by 2050; in the same time period, the Asian American population will double in size and will constitute about 10 percent of the total population. African Americans will remain approximately the same in numbers and compose 13 percent of the population; Whites will continue to be a smaller majority as minority populations increase in number. The nation's elderly population will more than double in size from 2005 through 2050, as the baby-boom generation enters the traditional retirement years. The number of working-age Americans and children will grow more slowly than the elderly population, and will shrink as a share of the total population (Passel & Cohn, 2008).

Of course, the Internet also provides increased opportunity for intercultural encounters. You could play chess with an opponent in Russia on a game site, debate rock climbing techniques with climbers from Norway to New Zealand on a sports discussion forum, or collaborate with students from around the country for a virtual team project in one of your classes. In the next sections of this chapter, we will discuss the opportunities that these types of contacts offer—and the benefits to be had from learning more about the intricacies of intercultural communication.

Enhanced Business Effectiveness

Studying intercultural communication can lead to greater success in both domestic and international business contexts. In the domestic context, the U.S. workforce is becoming increasingly diverse as the general population does the same. Furthermore, businesses are becoming more multinational as virtual communication makes it faster and cheaper to collaborate with vendors and customers around the globe. Many industries are also outsourcing services overseas to countries where wages are lower (e.g., Latin and South America, China, Vietnam) and sometimes to former colonies where the

How multicultural is your circle of friends? How many of your friends differ from you in nationality, religion, class, gender, age, sexual orientation, or physical ability?

FIGURE 7.1: Population by Race and Ethnicity, Actual and Projected: 1960, 2005, and 2050 (percentage of total)

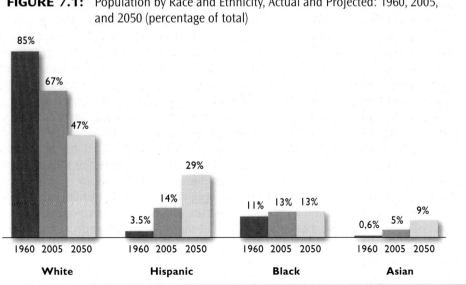

colonizer's language is already firmly established. For example, British and U.S. businesses have outsourced services to Ireland and India, and French businesses have sent jobs to Tunisia and Morocco (Bertrand, 2011).

Even though the trend toward globalization is no longer a new phenomenon, a primary cause for international business failures is still lack of attention to cultural factors. For example, when Disney Corporation established its Euro Disney outside Paris, the venture almost failed, in part because Disney executives mistakenly assumed they could transfer their U.S. cultural practices lock, stock, and barrel to the French context. French workers rebelled at the Disney dress code that mandated their hair and fingernail length; they also rebelled at being told they had to smile and act enthusiastic (also part of Disney code), and eventually they took their displeasure to court (Schneider & Barsoux, 2003).

What cultural differences prompted this displeasure? According to intercultural communication experts, the Disney policies went against French people's fundamental distrust of conformity and disrespect for mandated procedure (Hall & Hall, 1990, p. 106). Also, the notion of smiling constantly at work offended the French—contrary to the U.S. service industry's expectation for workers. The company seemed to learn from these cross-cultural challenges; it relaxed its rules on personal grooming for cast members and park employees, not only in France but in other countries. The most recent Disney venture in Hong Kong takes Chinese culture into consideration: green hats are not sold (green is associated with marital infidelity) and there are few clocks (the phrase for giving a clock sounds similar to that of attending the recipient's funeral) (Tai & Lau, 2009).

Improved Intergroup Relations

While we cannot blame all the world's political problems on ineffective intercultural communication, the need for better communication and understanding between countries and ethnic groups is clear. A case that is particularly important to U.S. citizens is improving relationships with people in the Middle East. Many experts think that to facilitate better relationships in this region the United States should establish meaningful contact with average citizens in the Muslim world, something that cannot be accomplished through military force or traditional diplomacy. One way to do this is to acquire intercultural knowledge and skills through learning the language, culture, and history of a country or region and being able to listen (Finn, 2003). U.S.-sponsored programs such as the Peace Corps and the Fulbright scholarship were designed with this kind of intercultural exchange and understanding in mind.

Intercultural communication expertise also can facilitate interethnic relations, which have frequently involved conflict. Consider the ethnic struggles in Bosnia and the former Soviet Union; the war between Hutus and Tutsis in Rwanda (Africa); the continued unrest in the Middle East; and the racial and ethnic struggles and tensions in neighborhoods of many U.S. cities. These conflicts often call for sophisticated skills of intercultural communication and **mediation**, or peaceful third-party intervention (Bercovitch & Derouen, 2004). For example, communication scholar Benjamin Broome (2004) has successfully facilitated interethnic relations on the island of Cyprus, one of the most heavily fortified regions in the world. Through his efforts, small groups of Greek and Turkish Cypriots have worked together to identify communication barriers and propose suggestions for improved relations between their two groups. It should be acknowledged, however, that even with **mediation**, miscommunication and intercultural conflicts can persist: witness the long-standing conflicts in the Middle East, where mediation has long been part of the attempts at resolution. In some cases, people are not motivated to resolve intergroup conflict. Although we must admit that there is no easy cure-all for intercultural tensions and misunderstandings, intercultural communication skills are certainly valuable in this area.

mediation
peaceful third-party intervention

Enhanced Self-Awareness

The final reason for studying intercultural communication is to increase self-awareness. This may seem like a contradiction, but it is not. Psychologist Peter Adler (1975) says that intercultural exploration begins as a journey into the cultures of others but often results in increased self-knowledge and understanding. People often learn more about themselves and their own cultural background and identities by coming into contact with people whose cultural backgrounds differ from their own, as our student discovered during her stay in South Africa (see *It Happened to Me: Susan*).

It Happened to Me: Susan

I rarely ever thought about being White or an American until my family and I spent a year in South Africa. Then, I thought about both every day, especially about my being White. The official language of South Africa is English, but even though we technically spoke the same language as the South Africans, my family and I had problems. It started when we were to be picked up from the airport in a *combie*, but I didn't know what that was. It turned out to be a van! Small pick-up trucks were *bakkies*, traffic signals were *robots*, and friends wanted to collect my *contact details*, which meant that they simply wanted the number of my *mobile*, better known as a cell phone, and our address. I felt that every time I opened my mouth, everyone *knew* I was American. The Black/White thing was even more pronounced. When we went down to the flea market or to the Zulu mass at the church we attended, we stood out like "five white golf balls on a black fairway" as my husband liked to say. I wondered if the self-consciousness I felt being White was the same as an African American has walking down the street in America.

What you learn about intercultural communication may depend on your social and economic position. For example, individuals from minority racial and ethnic groups in the United States may learn to be a bit wary of intercultural interactions and expect some subtle slights—like a Chinese American colleague who is sometimes approached at professional meetings by White communication professors who assume she is a waitress and ask them to take their drink order!

On the other hand, White and middle-class individuals may find that intercultural learning includes an enhanced awareness of privilege—like a White colleague who tells of feeling uncomfortable staying at a Caribbean resort, where he was served by Blacks whose ancestors were brought there as slaves by Europeans colonizers. While he realized that it was his relative privilege that allows him to travel and experience new cultures and places, he also wondered whether this type of travel simply reproduces those same historical post-colonial economic patterns.

With these reasons for studying intercultural communication in mind, we need to define precisely what we mean by intercultural communication and culture, which is the subject we turn to next.

TEST YOUR KNOWLEDGE

- What are four reasons for studying intercultural communication?
- Of the reasons given, which do you think are most important? Can you think of other reasons?

WHAT IS INTERCULTURAL COMMUNICATION?

Generally speaking, **intercultural communication** refers to communication that occurs in interactions between people who are culturally different. This contrasts with most communication studies, which focus on communicators in the same culture. Still, in practice, intercultural communication occurs on a continuum, with communication between people who are relatively similar in cultural backgrounds on one end and people who are extremely different culturally on the other. For example, your conversations with your parents would represent a low degree of "interculturalness" because while you and your parents belong to two different cultural (age) groups, you probably have much in common—nationality, religion, and language. On the other hand, an

intercultural communication communication that occurs in interactions between people who are culturally different

interaction with a foreign teaching assistant who has a different nationality, language, religion, age, socioeconomic status, and gender would represent a high degree of interculturalness. While these two examples represent different ends on the continuum, they are both intercultural interactions. So you can see that many, if not most, of your daily interactions are intercultural in nature.

The two essential components of intercultural communication are, of course, culture and communication. Having read this far in your text, you should have a good understanding of communication. However, we think it is worthwhile to review our definition of **culture**. In Chapter 1, we defined culture as *learned patterns of perceptions, values, and behaviors shared by a group of people*. As we also mentioned, culture is dynamic (it changes), **heterogeneous** (diverse), and operates within societal power structures (Martin & Nakayama, 2008, p. 28). Next we explore how these features of culture impact individuals' intercultural interactions.

TEST YOUR KNOWLEDGE
- What is a definition of intercultural communication?
- What is meant by the phrase "culture is dynamic, heterogeneous, and operates within societal power structures"?

INTERCULTURAL COMMUNICATION AND THE INDIVIDUAL

However, not all cultural differences have equal impact on one's interactions. For example, while your parents may sometimes seem to come from a very different culture, age differences generally have a less dramatic effect on people's interactions than do ethnic and national differences. Here we will examine some of the cultural differences that affect individuals' interactions with one another. We begin by exploring three types of intercultural interactions that can occur when individuals from different cultures coexist. We then explore specific cultural values that shape individuals' communication experiences, and we conclude this section by examining the ways that individuals within a culture can be both similar to and different from one another.

Intercultural Communication on the Borders

Because of increased opportunities for cultural contact, more people find themselves living a multicultural life. Travelers, racial/ethnic groups that live in proximity, immigrants, and people whose intimate partners come from other cultural backgrounds are only some of the groups that live between cultures, or as **border dwellers**. Here we refer to people who live on cultural borders as border dwellers because they often experience contradictory cultural patterns; thus, they may have to move between ethnicities, races, religions, languages, socioeconomic classes, or sexual orientations. One can become a border dweller in one of three ways: through travel, through socialization (cocultural groups), and through participation in an intercultural relationship. Let's look at each in turn.

Border Dwellers Through Travel

Individuals travel between cultures both voluntarily and involuntarily, and for both long and short periods. **Voluntary short-term travelers** include study-abroad students, corporate personnel, missionaries, and military people. **Voluntary long-term travelers** include immigrants who settle in other locations, usually seeking what they perceive is a better life, as is the case for many immigrants who come to the United States. **Involuntary short-term travelers** include refugees forced into cultural

culture
learned patterns of perceptions, values, and behaviors shared by a group of people

heterogeneous
diverse

border dwellers
people who live between cultures and often experience contradictory cultural patterns

voluntary short-term travelers
people who are border dwellers by choice and for a limited time, such as study-abroad students or corporate personnel

voluntary long-term travelers
people who are border dwellers by choice and for an extended time, such as immigrants

involuntary short-term travelers
people who are border dwellers not by choice and only for a limited time, such as refugees forced to move

migration because of war, famine, or unbearable economic hardship. For example, many people fled Iraq during the first Gulf War and then returned when it was safe to do so (UNHCR, 2009). **Involuntary long-term travelers** are those who are forced to permanently migrate to a new location, including the many diasporic groups referred to earlier.

When people think of traveling or living in a new culture, they tend to think that learning the language is key to effective intercultural interaction; however, intercultural communication involves much more than language issues. Most sojourners find there are two types of challenges: (1) dealing with the psychological stress of being in an unfamiliar environment (feeling somewhat uncertain and anxious) and (2) learning how to behave appropriately in the new culture, both verbally (e.g., learning a new language) and nonverbally (e.g., bowing instead of shaking hands in Japan) (Kim, 2005).

The first of these two challenges is often called *culture shock*. **Culture shock** is a feeling of disorientation and discomfort due to the unfamiliarity of surroundings and the lack of familiar cues in the environment. When travelers return home to their own country, they may experience similar feelings, known as reverse **culture shock** or **reentry shock**—a sort of culture shock in one's own country. After being gone for a significant amount of time, aspects of one's own culture may seem somewhat foreign, as the student Maham discovered on his return home to Pakistan after living in the United States for four years (see *It Happened to Me: Maham*).

Most travelers eventually adapt to the foreign culture to some extent if they stay long enough and if the hosts are welcoming. This is often the case for northern Europeans who visit or settle in the United States. Sometimes people even experience culture shock when they move from one region of the United States to another, such as someone who moves from Boston to Birmingham or from Honolulu to Minneapolis. The evacuation of tens of thousands of African American southerners from New Orleans after Hurricane Katrina highlighted this experience. Some of the evacuees were sent to stay in the mostly White state of Utah; a number of them said that Utah was so different from what they were used to that the experience seemed unreal.

There are many reasons why an individual may be more, or less, successful at adapting to a new culture. Younger people who have had some previous traveling experience seem to be more successful than older people and first-time travelers. On the other hand, if the environment is hostile or the move is involuntary, adaptation may be especially difficult and the culture shock especially intense. For example, many evacuees from Hurricane Katrina were forced to relocate. In some instances, they were greeted with great sympathy and hospitality in the new locations; in other instances they were subjected to considerable racism ("Rabbi: My radio," 2005). Asian, African, and Latino students in the United States tend to have a more difficult adaptation due to experiences of discrimination and hostility based on their race/ethnicity (Jung, Hecht, & Wadsworth, 2007; Lee & Rice, 2007). While we may think that anti-immigrant attitudes are a recent phenomenon in the United States because of the number of immigrants or where they come from, one writer suggests that today's immigrants have much in common with earlier immigrants—including anti-immigrant attitudes (see *Alternative View: Immigrants*).

involuntary long-term travelers
people who are border dwellers permanently but not by choice, such as those who relocate to escape war

culture shock
a feeling of disorientation and discomfort due to the lack of familiar environmental cues

reverse culture shock/reentry shock
culture shock experienced by travelers upon returning to their home country

It Happened to Me: Maham

I would say that I experienced culture (reentry) shock when I visited Pakistan after moving away from there four years ago. In those four years I had basically forgotten the language and became very unfamiliar with the culture back home. Even though I enjoyed my visit to Pakistan a lot, I had problems adjusting to some of the ways of life. I was not familiar with the bargaining system ... where people can go to the store and bargain for prices. I felt very out of place.... As I spent more time there, I got adjusted and used to how people did things there.

Alternative VIEW
Immigrants

Why do you think people continue to have negative feelings toward recent immigrants, despite past, successful adaptations of earlier immigrant groups? What could we do to help people feel more comfortable with and accepting of new immigrants?

Some people in the United States think that compared to earlier immigrants, today's immigrants do not try hard enough to assimilate and learn English. Ivonne Figueroa, an immigrant herself, the editor of a monthly cultural and bilingual publication, and a student of business management and history, points out that this is not entirely true. She describes how patterns of immigrant assimilation (and anti-immigrant attitudes) have not changed all that much in the past 200 years. For example, she explains that the idea that earlier, non-Hispanic immigrants in the U. S. learned English quickly and easily adapted to their new country is really a myth. She says that, according to historical accounts, they mostly spoke their native language at home and even encouraged their children to do the same and to not assimilate too easily to the American culture. They also received some financial assistance from the U. S.

government (similar to today's welfare) to facilitate their settling in to their new country. Similar to today's immigrants, their children did learn English. By the third generation, the grandchildren of the original immigrants spoke only English.

Ms. Figueroa also describes how anti-immigrant attitudes were alive and well then, just like today. In fact, at the turn of the 20th century (about 100 years ago), immigration from Southern and Eastern Europe was restricted, and immigration from Asia was totally prohibited due to the Oriental Exclusion Act of 1882. She also notes that even as recently as the mid-20th century, strong anti-Catholic attitudes were common. And throughout American history, immigrant groups have been blamed for various national problems. Italians were blamed for the 1916 polio epidemic in New York City, and Jewish immigrants were accused of "diluting the nation's pioneer stock."

She concludes that, overall, recent immigrants have many things in common with earlier immigrants: most are here legally, most were poor in their country and struggle to survive here economically, most try to hold onto their cultural traditions, and most are feared by those who harbor anti-immigrant sentiments.

FROM: Figueroa, I. (n.d.). Immigrants. El Boricua: A monthly bilingual, cultural publication for Puerto Ricans, http://www. elboricua.com/index.html. Retrieved February 17, 2011 from http://www.elboricua.com/immigrants.html.

For diasporic groups, whether relocated within their own country or in a foreign country, the culture shock and disorientation can be complicated and even extended due to their strong desire to return home and feeling of rootlessness. Alisse Waterston (2005) recounts the story of her Jewish father's struggles: as a young boy in the 1920s, he narrowly escaped being killed in the horrific massacre of Jews in the small town of Jedwabne, Poland; he resettled in Cuba, then fled again to the United States after the Cuban revolution in the 1960s. Although he achieved economic and professional success, his daughter observes that he never got over:

...the feelings of isolation and loneliness that come from being cast out, from forced absence. I can barely stand all the tears...so often describes himself and his family in the process of running, suffering and barely surviving. My father hasn't ever stopped running, remains confused and still lost.... having traveled through the twentieth century, my father remains burdened by the defining events of the century. (p. 56)

One thing that can ease culture shock and make cultural adaptation easier is having a social support network. This can come from organizations like an international student office or a tourist bureau that can assist with housing, transportation, and so forth. Close relationships with other travelers or host-country acquaintances can also provide support in the form of a sympathetic ear; through these relationships sojourners can relieve stress, discuss, problem-solve, acquire new knowledge, or just have fun (Kashima & Loh, 2006; Lin, 2006).

The role of social support is even more crucial for long-term travelers, such as immigrants. Diasporic individuals often maintain strong relationships with other members of their group, providing for each this much needed social support, sometimes through cyber communities or in face-to-face interaction (Bernal, 2005; Pendery, 2008). If there is little social support or the receiving environment is hostile, immigrants may choose to separate from the majority or host culture, or they may be forced into separation (Berry, 2005).

Another option for immigrants is to adapt in some ways to the new culture, which means accepting some aspects, such as dress and outward behavior, while retaining aspects of the old culture. For many recent immigrants to the United States, this has been a preferred option and seems to lead to less stress. For example, Asian Indians constitute one of the largest immigrant groups in the United States. Many have successfully adapted to U.S. life both professionally and socially. Still many retain viable aspects of their Indian culture in their personal and family lives—continuing to celebrate ethnic or religious holidays and adhering to traditional values and beliefs (Hegde, 2000). However, this integration of two cultures is not always easy, as we'll see in the next section. Families can be divided on the issues of how much to adapt, with children often wanting to be more "American" and parents wanting to hold on to their native language and cultural practices (Ward, 2008).

Border Dwellers Through Socialization

The second group of border dwellers is composed of people who grow up living on the borders between cultural groups. Examples include ethnic groups, such as Latinos, Asian Americans, and African Americans, who live in the predominantly White United States, as well as people who grow up negotiating *multiple* sexual orientations or religions. In addition to those who must negotiate the two cultures they live within, the United States has increasing numbers of multiracial people who often grow up negotiating multiple cultural realities. The 2000 Census form was the first that allowed people to designate more than two races—and since then, the group of people who choose to categorize themselves as multiracial has grown faster than any other (Yen, 2011).

Probably the best known multiracial U.S. American today is President Barack Obama—his father was an exchange student from Kenya and his mother a U.S. American student. Other famous multiracial U.S. Americans include Vin Diesel, who is Black and Italian American; Dwayne Johnson (also known as the "Rock"), who is Black and Samoan; and Tiger Woods, who is African American, European American, and Thai. Genetic experts point out that many of these multiracial individuals could only have been born in the twentieth century. Their complex web of ancestors, originating from distant world regions, could have encountered each other in the United States only within the past 100 years (Wells, 2002).

Typically, cultural minorities are socialized to the norms and values of both the dominant culture and their own; nonetheless, they often prefer to enact those of their own. They may be pressured to assimilate to the dominant culture and embrace its values, yet those in the dominant culture may still be reluctant to accept them as they try to do so (Berry, 2005). For example, a German woman whose family came from Turkey encountered teachers in Germany who perceived her to be part of a Turkish minority and thus had low expectations for her performance (Ewing, 2004). And members of minority groups sometimes find themselves in a kind of cultural limbo—not "gay" enough for gay friends, not "straight" enough for the majority; not Black enough or White enough.

All of the multiracial U.S. Americans we discuss above have had to respond, at some point, to criticism that they did not sufficiently align themselves with one or another of their racial groups. During the 2008 presidential campaign, President Obama was criticized for being "too white." Vin Diesel has been criticized

Border dwellers through socialization include many multiracial individuals and families. How might the concept of border dwellers change as these many children grow up?

for refusing to discuss his Black racial heritage while Dwayne Johnson originally was condemned for not recognizing his Black heritage but later was praised for attending the Black Entertainment Television awards.

Border Dwellers Through Relationships

Finally, many people live on cultural borders because they have intimate partners whose cultural background differs from their own. Within the United States increasing numbers of people cross borders of nationality, race, and ethnicity in this way, creating a "quiet revolution" (Root, 2001). Overall, partners in interethnic and interracial romantic relationships have faced greater challenges than those establishing relationships across religions, nationalities, and class groups.

Did you know that until June 12, 1967, it was illegal in Virginia (and 13 other states) for Whites and Blacks to marry? This ban against miscegenation (interracial sexual relationships) was challenged in Virginia by Mildred and Richard Loving, who had been married in 1958 in Washington, D.C. (where interracial marriages were permitted). In 1967, the Supreme Court declared Virginia's anti-miscegenation ban unconstitutional, thereby ending all race-based legal restrictions on marriage in the United States. Attitudes toward intercultural relationships have changed significantly in the ensuing decades, particularly attitudes toward interracial relations (Taylor, Funk, & Craighill, 2006). For example, in recent surveys, 77 percent of respondents said it's all right for Blacks and Whites to date each other—up from 48 percent who felt this way in 1987. The young are the most accepting; 91 percent of respondents born after 1976 said that interracial dating is acceptable—compared with 50 percent of the oldest generation (Kreager, 2008; Levin, Taylor, & Caudle, 2007).

However, such relationships are not without their challenges. The most common challenges involve negotiating how to live on the border between two religions, ethnicities, races, languages, and, sometimes, value systems. A recent study of intercultural marriages, some based on religious and some on racial and ethnic differences, found that communication played an important role in the success of these relationships. That is, open communication about the differences helped promote relationship growth. If partners were able to understand, appreciate, and integrate each other's similarities and differences, they would be able to use these in an enriching manner (Reiter & Gee, 2009).

The balancing act between cultures can be especially challenging when friends, family, and society disapprove (Fiebert, Nugent, Hershberger, & Kasdan, 2004). A Jewish professor who married a Muslim woman reflects on how people would react if he decided to convert to Islam:

> What a scandalous action! My family would be outraged and my friends startled. What would they say? How would I be treated? What would colleagues at the university do if I brought a prayer rug to the office and, say, during a committee meeting, or at a reception for a visiting scholar, insisted on taking a break to do my ritual prayers? (Rosenstone, 2005, p. 235)

These challenges can be even more pronounced for women, since parents often play an important role in whom they date and marry. A recent study found that women were much more likely than men to mention pressure from family members as a reason that interethnic dating would be difficult (Clark-Ibanez & Felmlee, 2004).

Negotiating Cultural Tensions on the Borders

How do people negotiate the tensions between often-contradictory systems of values, language, and nonverbal behavior of two or more cultures? The answer depends on many factors, such as one's reason for being on the border, length of stay or involvement, receptivity of the dominant culture, and personality characteristics of the individuals (Kim, 2005).

Americans have become much more accepting of Black-White marriages and dating relationships over the past few decades.

In most cases, people in such situations can feel caught between two systems; this experience has been described as feeling as if one were swinging on a trapeze, a metaphor that captures the immigrant's experience of vacillating between the cultural patterns of the homeland and the new country (Hegde, 1998). Writer Gloria Anzaldúa (1999), who is Chicana, gay, and female, stresses that living successfully on the border requires significant flexibility and an active approach to negotiating multiple cultural backgrounds. She struggles to balance her Indian and Spanish heritage, as well as her patriarchal Catholic upbringing, with her spiritual and sexual identity. The result, she says, is the *mestiza*—a person who has actively confronted and managed the negative aspects of living on the border.

Similarly, communication scholar Lisa Flores (1996) shows how Chicana feminist writers and artists acknowledge negative stereotypes of Mexican and Mexican American women—illiterate Spanglish-speaking laborers, passive sex objects, servants of men and children—and transform them into images of strength. In their descriptions and images, Chicana artists are strong, clever bilinguals, reveling in their dual Anglo-Mexican heritage. In so doing, they create a kind of positive identity "home" where they are the center. In addition, they gain strength by reaching out to other women (women of color and immigrant women), and together strive to achieve more justice and recognition for women who live "in the middle" between cultural worlds.

Managing these tensions while living on the border and being multicultural can be both rewarding and challenging. Based on data from interviews she conducted, Janet Bennett (1998) described two types of border dwellers, or, as she labeled them, "marginal individuals": *encapsulated marginal people* and *constructive marginal people*.

Encapsulated marginal people feel disintegrated by having to shift cultures. They have difficulty making decisions and feel extreme pressure from both groups. They try to assimilate but never feel comfortable or at home.

In contrast, **constructive marginal people** thrive in their "border" life and, at the same time, recognize its tremendous challenges, as Gloria Anzaldúa described. They see themselves as choice makers. They recognize the significance of being "in between," and they continuously negotiate and explore this identity.

To summarize, people can find themselves living on cultural borders for many reasons: travel, socialization, or involvement in an intercultural relationship. While border dwelling can be challenging and frustrating, it also can lead to cultural insights and agility in navigating intercultural encounters.

TEST YOUR KNOWLEDGE

- How do individuals come to live on cultural borders?
- What are some benefits and challenges to border dwelling?

The Influence of Cultural Values on Communication

In Chapters 5 and 6, we described how culture influences verbal and nonverbal communication. You might think that these differences would be key to understanding intercultural communication. Just as important is understanding **cultural values**, which are the beliefs that are so central to a cultural group that they are never questioned. Cultural values prescribe what *should* be. Understanding cultural values is essential because they so powerfully influence people's behavior, including their communication. Intercultural interaction often involves confronting and responding to an entirely different set of **cultural values**. Let's see how this works.

About fifty years ago, anthropologists Florence Kluckhohn and Fred Strodtbeck (1961) conducted a study that identified the contrasting values of three cultural groups in the United States: Latinos, Anglos, and American Indians. Later, social psychologist Geert Hofstede (1997, 1998, 2001) and his colleagues extended this analysis in a massive study, collecting 116,000 surveys about people's value preferences in

encapsulated marginal people
people who feel disintegrated by having to shift cultures

constructive marginal people
people who thrive in a border-dweller life, while recognizing its tremendous challenges

cultural values
beliefs that are so central to a cultural group that they are never questioned

individualist orientation
a value orientation that respects the autonomy and independence of individuals

collectivistic orientation
a value orientation that stresses the needs of the group

approximately eighty countries around the world. Psychologist Michael Bond and his colleagues conducted a similar, though smaller, study in Asia ("Chinese Culture Connection," 1987). Together, these studies identified cultural values preferred by people in a number of countries. While these value preferences may apply most directly to national cultural groups, they can also apply to ethnic/racial groups, socioeconomic class groups, and gender groups.

As you read about these cultural value orientations, please keep three points in mind. These guidelines reflect a common dilemma for intercultural communication scholars—the desire to describe and understand communication and behavior patterns within a cultural group and the fear of making rigid categories that can lead to stereotyping:

1. The following discussion describes the *predominant* values preferred by various cultural groups, not the values held by *every person* in the cultural group. Think of cultural values as occurring on a bell curve: Most people may be in the middle, holding a particular value orientation, but many people can be found on each end of the curve; these are the people who *do not go along* with the majority.

2. The following discussion refers to values on the cultural level, not on the individual level. Thus, if you read that most Chinese tend to prefer an indirect way of speaking, you cannot assume that every Chinese person you meet will speak in an indirect way in every situation.

3. The only way to understand what a particular individual believes is to get to know the person. You can't predict how any one person will communicate. The real challenge is to understand the full range of cultural values and then learn to communicate effectively with others who hold differing value orientations, regardless of their cultural background.

Now that you understand the basic ground rules, let's look at six key aspects of cultural values.

Individualism and Collectivism

One of the most central value orientations identified in this research addresses whether a culture emphasizes the rights and needs of the individual or that of the group. For example, many North American and northern European cultural groups, particularly U.S. Whites, value individualism and independence, believing that one's primary responsibility is to one's self (Bellah, Madsen, Sullivan, Swidler, & Tipton, 1996; Hofstede, 2001; Kikoski & Kikoski, 1999). In relationships, as Kaori discovered in our opening vignette, those with this **individualist orientation** respect autonomy and independence, and they do not meddle in another's problems unless invited. For example, in cultures where individualism prevails, many children are raised to be autonomous and to live on their own by late adolescence (although they may return home for short periods after this). Their parents are expected to take care of themselves and not "be a burden" on their children when they age (Triandis, 1995).

In individualistic cultures, children are raised to be autonomous and to live on their own by late adolescence, while parents are expected to not "be a burden" on their children when they age.

In contrast, many cultures in South America and Asia hold a more **collectivistic orientation** that stresses the needs of the group (Hofstede, 2001; Triandis, 1995), as do some Hispanic and Asian Americans in the United States (Ho, 1987). Some argue that working-class people tend to be more collectivistic than those in the middle or upper class (Dunbar, 1997). For collectivists, the primary responsibility is to relationships with others; interdependence in family, work, and personal relationships is viewed positively. Collectivists value working toward relationship

In individualistic cultures, children are raised to be autonomous and to live on their own by late adolescence, while parents are expected to not "be a burden" on their children when they age.

As you were growing up, in what ways were you reared to be individualistic? Collectivistic? Which orientation was the predominant cultural value of your family?

and group harmony over remaining independent and self-sufficient. For example, giving money to a needy cousin, uncle, or aunt might be preferable to spending it on oneself. In many collectivist cultures, too, children often defer to parents when making important decisions (McGoldrick, Giordano, & Pearce, 1996). A U.S. American software consultant who has done extensive employment interviewing with software professionals in India has observed that the cultural tradition of respecting one's parents is very prevalent in India. He is particularly struck by how often adult professionals consult with their parents before deciding whether to accept a job (Budelman, 2006).

As noted earlier, however, not all Japanese or all Indians are collectivistic. In fact, generational differences may exist within countries where collectivism is strong. For example, some Japanese college students show a strong preference for individualism while their parents hold a more collectivistic orientation—which sometimes leads to intercultural conflict (Matsumoto, 2002). Young people in many Asian countries (Korea, Vietnam) are increasingly influenced by Western capitalism and individualism and are now making their own decisions regarding marriage and career, rather than following their family's wishes—a practice unheard of fifty years ago (Shim, Kim, & Martin, 2008). In addition, not all cultures are as individualistic as U.S. culture or as collectivistic as Japanese culture. Rather, cultures can be arranged along an individualism–collectivism continuum (Gudykunst & Lee, 2002) based on their specific orientations to the needs of the individual and the group.

Preferred Personality

In addition to differing on the individualism–collectivism spectrum, cultural groups may differ over the idea of the **preferred personality**, or whether it is more important to "do" or to "be" (Kluckhohn & Strodtbeck, 1961). In the United States, researchers have found that *doing* is the preferred value for many people (Stewart & Bennett, 1991), including European Americans, Asian Americans, and African Americans (Ting-Toomey, 1999). In general, the "doing mode" means working hard to achieve material gain, even if it means sacrificing time with family and friends (Kohls, 2001). Other cultural groups, for example, many Latinos, prefer the *being* mode—which emphasizes the importance of experiencing life and the people around them fully and "working to live" rather than "living to work" (Hecht, Sedano, & Ribeau, 1993).

Some scholars suggest that many African Americans express both a doing mode (fighting actively against racism through social activity for the good of the community) and a being mode (valuing a sense of vitality and open expression of feeling) (Hecht, Jackson, & Ribeau, 2002). Cultural differences in this value orientation can lead to communication challenges. For example, many Latinos believe that Anglos place too much emphasis on accomplishing tasks and earning money and not enough emphasis on spending time with friends and family or enjoying the moment (Kikoski & Kikoski, 1999).

A third value difference concerns the **view of human nature**—in particular, whether humans are considered fundamentally good, evil, or a mixture. The United States, for example, was founded by the Puritans who believed that human nature was fundamentally evil (Hulse, 1996). In the years since the founding of the country, a shift occurred in this view, as evidenced in the U.S. legal and justice systems. It emphasizes rehabilitation, suggesting a view of humans as potentially good. In addition, the fact that the U.S. justice system assumes people are innocent until proven guilty indicates that people are viewed as basically good (Kohls, 2001).

preferred personality
a value orientation that expresses whether it is more important for a person to "do" or to "be"

view of human nature
a value orientation that expresses whether humans are fundamentally good, evil, or a mixture

In many collectivist cultures, adult children often defer to parents when making important decisions.

What kinds of communication problems might occur when members of a diverse work team hold different value orientations toward being and doing? How might someone who usually uses a being mode view someone with a doing mode, and vice versa?

In contrast, cultural groups that view humans as essentially evil, such as some fundamentalist religions, emphasize punishment over rehabilitation. Some evidence indicates that U.S. Americans in general are moving again toward this view of human nature. For example, recent laws such as the "three strikes rule" emphasize punishment over rehabilitation by automatically sending to prison anyone who is convicted three times. Also, incarceration rates in the United States have increased by more than 500 percent since the early 1970s, and among developed countries, the United States now has the highest percentage of incarcerated individuals (Shelden, 2004). As you might imagine, people who differ on the question of human nature can have serious disagreements on public policies concerning crime and justice.

Human–Nature Value

A fourth value that varies from culture to culture is the perceived relationship between humans and nature, or the **human–nature value orientation**. At one end of this value continuum is the view that humans are intended to rule nature. At the other extreme, nature is seen as ruling humans. In a third option, the two exist in harmony. Unsurprisingly, the predominant value in the United States has been one of humans ruling over nature, as evidenced in the proliferation of controlled environments. Phoenix, Arizona, for example, which is in a desert, has more than 200 golf courses—reflecting the fact that Arizonans have changed the natural environment to suit their living and leisure interests. In other parts of the United States, people make snow for skiing, seed clouds when rain is needed, dam and reroute rivers, and use fertilizer to enhance agricultural production. Such interventions generally reflect a belief in human control over nature (Trompenaars & Hampden-Turner, 1997).

In contrast, many in the Middle East view nature as having predominance over humans. This belief that one's fate is held by nature is reflected in the common Arabic saying *"Enchallah"* ("Allah willing"), suggesting that nature will (and should) determine, for example, how crops will grow. A comparable Christian saying is "God willing," reflecting perhaps a similar fatalistic tendency in Christianity. Interestingly, many Spanish-speaking Christians express the same sentiment with the word *"Ojalá,"* which is rooted in *"Enchallah"* and originates from the centuries when southern Spain was a Muslim province.

Many American Indians and Asians value harmony with nature. People who hold this cultural orientation believe that humans and nature are one and that nature enriches human life. For many traditional American Indians, certain animals such as buffalo and eagles are important presences in human activity (Porter, 2002). For example, a yearly "Good Buffalo Festival" is held in Kyle, South Dakota, to educate young Indians about the importance of the buffalo in Lakota culture (Melmer, 2004). Many native cultures believe eagles carry messages to the Creator, and they use eagle feathers in many solemn, sacred ceremonies. The use of feathers can be an important part of the sundance, a religious ceremony practiced by many different American Indian groups. In this ceremony the eagle is viewed as the link between humans and creator. When people see an eagle in the sky during a ceremony, they are especially thankful, since the eagle flies highest of all birds and the moment it disappears into the skies, people's prayers are heard. These traditions show high regard and utmost respect for these animals and reflect a belief in the close and important relationship between humans and nature ("Zuni eagle aviary is a beautiful sign," 2002).

In the United States, differences arise between real estate developers, who believe that humans take precedence over nature, and environmentalists and many Native American groups, who believe that nature is as important as humans. This conflict has surfaced in many disagreements; for example, in controversies over

human–nature value orientation
the perceived relationship between humans and nature

water rights in Oregon (Hemmingsen, 2002) and over the proposed eight-million-acre habitat for the endangered spotted owl in the southwestern United States (McKinnon, 2004).

Power Distance

Power distance, the fifth value orientation, refers to the extent to which less powerful members of institutions and organizations within a culture expect and accept an unequal distribution of power (Hofstede, 2001). In Denmark, Israel, and New Zealand many people value small power distances. Thus, most people in those countries believe that inequality, while inevitable, should be minimized, and that the best leaders emphasize equality and informality in interactions with subordinates. In many situations, subordinates are expected to speak up and contribute.

Reverence for nature plays an important role in many American Indian ceremonies.

Societies that value large power distance—for example, Mexico, the Philippines, and India—are structured more around a hierarchy in which each person has a rightful place, and interactions between supervisors and subordinates are more formal (Hofstede, 2001). Seniority, age, rank, and titles are emphasized more in these societies than in small power distance societies.

People who are used to large power distances may be uncomfortable in settings where hierarchy is unclear or ambiguous. For example, international students who come from countries where a large power distance value predominates may initially be very uncomfortable in U.S. college classrooms, where relations between students and teachers are informal and characterized by equality, a situation you will read about in *It Happened to Me: Nagesh.*

In contrast, U.S. Americans abroad often offend locals when they treat subordinates at work or home too informally—calling them by first name, treating them as if they were friends. For example, when former President Bush visited Europe, he referred to the Belgian Prime Minister by

It Happened to Me: Nagesh

I was amazed when I first saw American classrooms. The students seemed very disrespectful toward the teacher. They had their feet on the desks and interrupted the teacher while he was talking if they didn't understand something. In my country (India), students would never behave this way toward a teacher. I found it difficult to speak up in this kind of classroom situation.

his first name, Guy, which surprised and amused many Belgians—who are accustomed to more formality.

Note that value orientations often represent a cultural ideal rather than a reality. While many Americans say they desire small power distance, the truth is that rigid social and economic hierarchies exist in the United States. Most Americans are born into and live within the same socioeconomic class for their whole lives (Herbert, 2005).

Long-Term Versus Short-Term Orientation

The research identifying the five values we've described has been criticized for its predominately western European bias. In response to this criticism, a group of Chinese researchers developed and administered a similar, but more Asian-oriented, questionnaire to people in twenty-two countries around the world ("Chinese Culture Connection," 1987). They then compared their findings to previous research on value orientations and found considerable overlap, especially on the dimensions of individualism versus collectivism and power distance. These researchers did identify one additional value dimension that earlier researchers hadn't seen—**long-term versus short-term orientation.**

This dimension reflects a society's attitude toward virtue or truth. A **short-term orientation** characterizes cultures in which people are concerned with possessing one fundamental truth, as reflected in the **monotheistic** (belief in one god) religions of Judaism,

power distance
a value orientation that refers to the extent to which less powerful members of institutions and organizations within a culture expect and accept an unequal distribution of power

long-term versus short-term orientation
the dimension of a society's value orientation that reflects its attitude toward virtue or truth

short-term orientation
a value orientation that stresses the importance of possessing one fundamental truth

monotheistic
belief in one god

long-term orientation
a value orientation in which people stress the importance of virtue

polytheistic
belief in more than one god

dialectic approach
recognizes that things need not be perceived as either/or, but may be seen as both/and

dichotomous thinking
thinking in which things are perceived as "either/or"—for example, "good or bad," "big or small," "right or wrong"

Christianity, and Islam. Other qualities identified in the research and associated with a short-term orientation include an emphasis on quick results, individualism, and personal security and safety (Hofstede, 1997).

In contrast, a **long-term orientation** tends to respect the demands of virtue, reflected in Eastern religions such as Confucianism, Hinduism, Buddhism, and Shintoism, which are all **polytheistic** religions (belief in more than one god). Other qualities associated with a long-term orientation include thrift, perseverance and tenacity in whatever one attempts, and a willingness to subordinate oneself for a purpose (Bond, 1991, 1996).

While knowing about these value differences can help you identify and understand problems that arise in intercultural interactions, you might be concerned that this approach to the study of intercultural communication leads to generalizing and stereotyping. The next section presents an approach that helps counteract this tendency to think in simplistic terms about intercultural communication.

A Dialectic Approach

Dialectics has long existed as a concept in philosophical thought and logic. In this book we introduce it as a way to emphasize simultaneous contradictory truths. Thus, a **dialectic approach** helps people respond to the complexities of intercultural communication and to override any tendencies to stereotype people based on cultural patterns. This concept may be difficult to understand because it is contrary to most formal education in the United States, which often emphasizes **dichotomous thinking**, in which things are "either/or"—good or bad, big or small, right or wrong. However, a dialectic approach recognizes that things may be "both/and." For example, a palm tree may be weak and strong. Its branches look fragile and weak, and yet in a hurricane it remains strong because the "weak" fronds can bend without breaking. Similar dialectics exist in intercultural communication; for example, Didier may be a Frenchman who shares many cultural characteristics of other French people, but he also is an individual who possesses characteristics that make him unique. So, he is both similar to and different from other French people. A dialectic approach emphasizes the fluid, complex, and contradictory nature of intercultural interactions. Dialectics exist in other communication contexts such as relationships. Six dialectics that can assist you in communicating more effectively in intercultural interactions are discussed next.

Cultural–Individual

This dialectic emphasizes that some behaviors, such as ways of relating to others, are determined by our culture, while others are simply idiosyncratic, or particular to us as individuals. For example, Robin twists her hair while she talks. This idiosyncratic personal preference should not be mistaken for a cultural norm. She doesn't do it because she is female, or young, or Protestant, or African American. Although it isn't always easy to tell whether a behavior is culturally or individually based, taking a dialectic approach means that one does not immediately assume that someone's behavior is culturally based.

Personal–Contextual

This dialectic focuses on the importance of context or situation in intercultural communication. In any intercultural encounter, both the individual and the situation are simultaneously important. Let's take the example of a French and an American student striking up a conversation in a bar. The immediate situation has an important impact on their communication, so their conversation would probably differ dramatically if it occurred at a synagogue, mosque, or church. The larger situation, including political and historical forces, also plays a role. In the build-up to the Iraq War of 2003, for example, some French students encountered anti-French sentiment in the United States. At the same time, the characteristics of the specific individuals also affect the exchange. Some students would ignore the immediate or larger situation and reject the anti-French sentiment—especially if they were opposed to the war themselves. Others would attach great importance to the larger context and view the French students negatively. The point is that reducing an interaction to a mere meeting of two individuals means viewing intercultural communication too simplistically.

Differences–Similarities

Real, important differences exist between cultural groups; we've identified some of these in this chapter. However, important commonalities exist as well. One of our students summed up this point nicely in *It Happened to Me: Angelina*.

Static–Dynamic

While some cultural patterns remain relatively stable and static for years, they also can undergo dynamic change. For example, many people form impressions about Indians from popular films like *Smoke Signals*—or even children's movies like *Pocahontas* or *The Indian in the Cupboard*, which portray Indians living the rural life they lived

It Happened to Me: *Angelina*

In my first year of college, I had the most memorable friendship with a person from the Middle East. Through this friendship I learned a lot about the way people from the Middle East communicate with friends, family, and authority. My new friend and I differed in many ways—in religion, culture, nationality, race, and language. However, we were both female college students, the same age, and we shared many interests. She dressed like I did and styled her hair similarly, and we shared many ideas about the future and concerns about the world.

centuries ago—even though the majority of Indians in the U.S. today live in urban areas (Alexie, 2003). A static–dynamic dialectic requires that you recognize both traditional and contemporary realities of a culture.

History/Past–Present/Future

An additional dialectic in intercultural communication focuses on the present and the past. For example, one cannot fully understand contemporary relations between Arabs and Jews, Muslims and Christians, or Catholics and Protestants without knowing something of their history. At the same time, people cannot ignore current events. For example, the conflict over where Yasser Arafat was to be buried in the autumn of 2004 flowed from a complex of historical and contemporary relations. His family had resided for generations in Jerusalem and wanted him laid to rest there. Israel, having current control of Jerusalem and viewing Arafat as a terrorist leader of attacks against Israel, refused.

Privilege–Disadvantage

In intercultural interactions, people can be simultaneously privileged and disadvantaged (Johnson, 2006). This can become quite clear when one travels to developing countries. While U.S. Americans may be privileged in having more money and the luxury of travel, they can also feel vulnerable in foreign countries if they are ignorant of the local languages and customs. Poor Whites in the United States can be simultaneously privileged because they are White and disadvantaged due to their economic plight. As a student, you may feel privileged (compared to others) in that you are acquiring a high level of education, but you may also feel economically disadvantaged because of the high cost of education.

While being White involves cultural advantages, being poor involves disadvantages.

This dialectic approach helps us resist making quick, stereotypical judgments about others and their communication behavior. A single person can have individualistic and collectivistic tendencies, can be both culturally similar and different from us, and can be culturally privileged in some situations and culturally disadvantaged in others. All these elements affect communication in both business and personal relationships.

TEST YOUR KNOWLEDGE
- Identify six common core values that differentiate various cultural groups.
- How might these values influence intercultural communication?
- How does adopting a dialectical perspective help us avoid stereotyping and prejudice?

THE INDIVIDUAL, INTERCULTURAL COMMUNICATION, AND SOCIETY

As you have probably gathered by now, intercultural communication never occurs in a vacuum but must be understood in the context of larger societal forces. In this section we first focus on social, political, and historical forces; second, we turn our attention to the role of power in intercultural communication.

Political and Historical Forces

That societal forces can affect intercultural encounters is exemplified by the varying reactions toward some immigrant groups after the attacks of September 11, 2001. Scholar Sunil Bhatia (2008) found, through interviews with Asian Indian-Americans, that these immigrants experienced reactions from others that caused them to question their "American" identity. Before 9/11, they considered themselves well-adapted to American culture. However, after 9/11, people treated them differently. Their neighbors, who knew them well, were much friendlier and sympathetic. However, some strangers were more hostile to them (sometimes mistaking them for Muslims). Thus, they were reminded that they were different; they were not completely accepted as Americans by the American majority.

Historical forces also can influence contemporary intercultural interaction, as we noted earlier in our discussion of dialectics. For example, while slavery is long gone in the United States, one could not understand contemporary Black–White relations in this country without acknowledging its effect. Author James Loewen (1995) describes the twin legacies of slavery that are still with us: (1) social and economic inferiority for Blacks brought on by specific economic and political policies from 1885 to 1965 that led to inferior educational institutions and exclusion from labor unions, voting rights, and the advantage of government mortgages; (2) cultural racism instilled in Whites. The election of Barack Obama as the first African American U.S. president demonstrates significant progress in interracial relations and has presented new opportunities for cross-racial dialogue (Chisholm, 2008; Dyson, 2009). However, the intense political and social conversations that have occurred since the election, often centering around race, might also demonstrate that the historical legacies of racism impact interracial encounters even today (Martin, Trego, & Nakayama, 2010; Simpson, 2008).

As a society, which institutions or contexts now promote the best opportunities for interracial contact? Neighborhoods? Educational institutions? Churches, synagogues, and other places of worship? The workplace? Neighborhoods and workplaces do not seem to provide opportunities for the *type* of contact (intimate, friendly, equal-status interaction) that facilitates intercultural relationships (Johnson & Jacobson, 2005). On the other hand, it appears that *integrated* religious institutions and educational institutions provide the best opportunities for intercultural friendships and the best environment to improve interracial attitudes (Johnson & Jacobson, 2005). For example, a study of six California State University campuses found that the students on these campuses interacted equally, in interracial and intraracial encounters (Cowan, 2005). These campuses are very diverse; no single ethnic or racial group is a majority. However, a more recent study cautions that sometimes students in multicultural campus assume that they have intercultural relationships just by virtue of being surrounded by cultural diversity and may not make the effort to actually pursue intercultural friendships (Halualani, 2008).

Intercultural Communication and Power

As we noted in Chapter 5, the more powerful groups in society establish the rules for communication, and others usually follow these rules or violate them at their peril (Orbe, 1998). A number of factors influence who is considered powerful in a culture. For example, being White in the United States has more privilege attached to it than being Latino (Bahk & Jandt, 2004). While most Whites do not notice this privilege and dominance, most minority group members do (Bahk & Jandt, 2004). Being male also has historically been more valued than being female (Johnson, 2006), and being wealthy is more valued than being poor. Further, being able-bodied is traditionally more valued than being physically disabled (Allen, 2003; Johnson, 2006). Every society, regardless of power distance values, has these kinds of traditional hierarchies of power. While the hierarchy is never entirely fixed, it does constrain and influence communication among cultural groups.

How do power differences affect intercultural interaction? They do so primarily by determining whose cultural values will be respected and followed. For example, faculty, staff, and students in most U.S. universities adhere to the values and communication norms set by the White, male-dominant groups. These values and communication norms emphasize individualism (Kikoski & Kikoski, 1999). Thus, while group work is common in many courses, professors usually try to figure out how to give individual grades for it, and most students are encouraged to be responsible for their own work. Moreover, the university is run on monochronic time (see Chapter 6), with great emphasis placed on keeping schedules and meeting deadlines—and these deadlines sometimes take precedence over family and other personal responsibilities (Blair, Brown, & Baxter, 1994). The communication style most valued in this culture also is very individual-oriented, direct and to the point, and extremely task-oriented, as is the case in many organizations in the United States (Kikoski & Kikoski, 1999).

What is the impact for those who come from other cultural backgrounds and do not fit into this mold—say, for those who have collectivistic backgrounds and value personal relationships over tasks and homework assignments? Or for those whose preferred communication style is more indirect? They may experience culture shock; they also may be sanctioned or marginalized—for example, with bad grades for not participating more in class, for not completing tasks on time, or for getting too much help from others on assignments.

To more fully consider these problems we need to introduce the concept of the **cocultural group**, meaning significant minority groups within a dominant majority that do not share dominant group values or communication patterns. Examples include some Native American, Mexican American, and Asian American individuals who choose not to assimilate to the dominant, White U.S. culture. Researcher Mark Orbe (1998) suggests that cocultural group members have several choices as to how they can relate to the dominant culture: They can assimilate, they can accommodate, or they can remain separate. He cautions that each strategy has benefits and limitations. For example, when women try to assimilate and "act like men" in a male-oriented organization, they may score points for being professional, but they also may be criticized for being too masculine. When African Americans try to accommodate in a largely White management, they may satisfy White colleagues and bosses, but earn the label "oreo" from other African Americans. In contrast, resisting assimilation or remaining apart may result in isolation, marginalization, and exclusion from the discussions where important decisions are made.

cocultural group
a significant minority group within a dominant majority that does not share dominant group values or communication patterns

ETHICS AND INTERCULTURAL COMMUNICATION

How can you communicate more ethically across cultures? Unfortunately, no easy answers exist, but a few guidelines may be helpful.

First, remember that everyone, including you, is enmeshed in a culture and thus communicating through a cultural lens. Recognizing your own cultural attitudes, values, and beliefs will make you more sensitive to others' cultures and less likely to impose your own cultural attitudes on their communication patterns. While you may feel most comfortable living in your own culture and following its communication patterns, you should not conclude that your culture and communication style are best or should be the standard for all other cultures. Such a position is called ethnocentrism, which you learned about in Chapter 4. Of course, appreciating and respecting other cultures does not mean you don't still appreciate and respect your own.

Second, as you learn about other cultural groups, be aware of their humanity and avoid the temptation to view them as an exotic "other." Communication scholar Bradford Hall (1997) has cautioned about this tendency, which is called the "zoo approach."

When using such an approach, we view the study of culture as if we were walking through a zoo admiring, gasping, and chuckling at the various exotic animals we observe. One may discover amazing, interesting, and valuable information by using such a perspective and even develop a real fondness of these exotic people, but miss the point that we are as culturally "caged" as others and that they are culturally as "free" as we are (Hall, 1997, p. 14). From an ethical perspective, the "zoo approach" denies the humanity of other cultural groups. For example, the view of African cultures as primitive and incapable led Whites to justify colonizing Africa and exploiting its rich resources in the nineteenth century.

Third, you will be more ethical in your intercultural interactions if you are open to other ways of viewing the world. The ways that you were taught about the world and history may not be the same as what others were taught. People cannot engage in meaningful communication if they are unwilling to suspend or reexamine their assumptions about the world. For example, some Europeans believe that the United States became involved in the Middle East so it could control its oil interests, while many U.S. Americans believe that concern over weapons of mass destruction and human rights was the motivation. If neither group will consider the opinion of the other, they will be unlikely to sustain a mutually satisfying conversation.

TEST YOUR KNOWLEDGE

■ What three strategies can you use to help you respond ethically during intercultural interactions?

IMPROVING YOUR INTERCULTURAL COMMUNICATION SKILLS

How can you communicate more effectively across cultures? As with ethics, no magic formula exists, but here are several suggestions.

Increase Motivation

Perhaps the most important component is *motivation*. Without the motivation to be an effective communicator, no other skills will be relevant. Part of the problem in long-standing interethnic or interreligious conflicts—for example, between the Israelis and the Palestinians—is the lack of interest, on both sides, in communicating more effectively. Some parties on both sides may even have an interest in prolonging conflict. Therefore, a strong desire to improve one's skills is necessary.

Increase Your Knowledge of Self and Others

In addition to being motivated, you become a more effective intercultural communicator if you educate yourself about intercultural communication. Having some knowledge about the history, background, and values of people from other cultures can help you communicate better. When you demonstrate this type of knowledge to people from other cultures, you communicate that you're interested in them and you affirm their sense of identity. Obviously, no one can know everything about all cultures; nonetheless, some general information can be helpful, as can an awareness of the importance of context and a dialectical perspective.

Self-knowledge also is very important. If you were socialized to be very individualistic you may initially have a hard time understanding collectivistic tendencies. Once you become aware of these differences, however, you can more easily communicate with someone who holds a different perspective. Growing up in a middle-class family may also influence your perceptions. Many middle-class people assume that anyone can become middle class through hard work. But this view overlooks the discrimination faced by people of color and gays and lesbians. How can you increase your cultural self-awareness? Perhaps the best way is to cultivate intercultural encounters and relationships.

Developing facility in intercultural communication occurs through a cyclical process. The more one interacts across cultures, the more one learns about oneself, and then the more prepared one is to interact interculturally, and so on. However, increased exposure and understanding do not happen automatically. Being aware of the influence of culture on oneself and others is essential to increasing one's intercultural experience and competence (Ting-Toomey, 1999).

Where should you start? You can begin by examining your current friendships and reach out from there. Research shows that individuals generally become friends with people with whom they live, work, and worship. So your opportunities for intercultural interaction and self-awareness are largely determined by the type of people and contexts you encounter in your daily routine.

Avoid Stereotypes

Cultural differences may lead to stereotyping and prejudices. As we discussed in Chapter 4, normal cognitive patterns of generalizing make our world more manageable. However, when these generalizations become rigid, they lead to stereotyping and prejudices. Furthermore, stereotyping can become self-fulfilling (Snyder, 2001). That is, if you stereotype people and treat them in a prejudiced or negative manner, they may react in ways that reinforce your stereotype.

On the other hand, we must note, overreacting by being very "sweet" can be equally off-putting. African Americans sometimes complain about being "niced" to death by White people (Yamato, 2001). The guideline here is to be mindful that you might be stereotyping. For example, if you are White, do you only notice bad behavior when exhibited by a person of color? Communicating effectively across cultural boundaries is a challenge—but one we hope you will take up.

Wahoo, the Cleveland Indians mascot, is a controversial figure. To some, Wahoo represents an offensive stereotype; to others, an expression of pride in the team. How might we respond to a similar caricature of African Americans or White Americans?

TEST YOUR KNOWLEDGE

- What are three suggestions for communicating more effectively across cultures?
- Which do you think is the most important? Why?

SUMMARY

Four reasons for learning about intercultural communication are increased opportunity, increased business effectiveness, improved intergroup relations, and enhanced self-awareness. Intercultural communication is defined as communication between people from different cultural backgrounds, and culture is defined as learned patterns of perceptions, values, and behaviors shared by a group of people. Culture is dynamic and heterogeneous, and it operates largely out of our awareness within power structures. Increasing numbers of individuals today live on cultural borders—through travel, socialization, or relationships. Being a "border dweller" involves both benefits and challenges.

Six core cultural values differentiate various cultural groups, and these value differences have implications for intercultural communication. A dialectical approach to intercultural communication can help individuals avoid quick generalizations and stereotyping. There are at least six intercultural communication dialectics: cultural–individual, personal–contextual, differences–similarities, static–dynamic, history/past–present/future, and privilege–disadvantage.

Society plays an important role in intercultural communication because intercultural encounters never occur in a vacuum. Societal forces, including political and historical structures, always influence communication. Power is often an important element in that those who hold more powerful positions in society set the rules and norms for communication. Those individuals who do not conform to the rules because of differing cultural backgrounds and preferences may be marginalized. To ensure that you are communicating ethically during intercultural interactions, attend to the following: avoid ethnocentric thinking, recognize the humanity of others, and remain open to other ways of understanding the world. Finally, you can become a more effective intercultural communicator in at least three ways: by increasing your motivation, acquiring knowledge about self and others, and avoiding stereotyping.

HUMAN COMMUNICATION IN SOCIETY ONLINE

To review this chapter, use the MyCommunicationLab Web site to test your understanding of the following key terms, record your answers to the chapter review questions, and complete the suggested activities. Expand your learning and understanding of chapter concepts by completing additional exercises and activities online. Access code required. Go to www.mycommunicationlab.com for more information or to purchase standalone access.

KEY TERMS

diaspora 152
mediation 154
intercultural communication 155
culture 156
heterogeneous 156
border dwellers 156
voluntary short-term travelers 156
voluntary long-term travelers 156
involuntary short-term travelers 156
involuntary long-term travelers 157
culture shock 157

reverse culture shock/reentry shock 157
encapsulated marginal people 161
constructive marginal people 161
cultural values 161
individualist orientation 162
collectivistic orientation 162
preferred personality 163
view of human nature 163
human–nature value orientation 164
power distance 165

long-term versus short-term orientation 165
short-term orientation 165
monotheistic 165
long-term orientation 166
polytheistic 166
dialectic approach 166
dichotomous thinking 166
cocultural group 169

APPLY WHAT YOU KNOW

1. **Cultural Profile**

   List all the cultural groups you belong to. Which groups are most important to you when you're at college? When you're at home? Which groups would be easiest to leave? Why?

2. **Intercultural Conflict Analysis**

   Identify a current intercultural conflict in the media. It can be conflict between nations, ethnic groups, or gender. Read at least three sources that give background and information about the conflict. Conduct an analysis of this conflict, answering the following questions:

   - What do you think are the sources of the conflict?

   - Are there value differences?

   - Power differences?

   - What role do you think various contexts (historical, social, political) play in the conflict?

3. **Intercultural Relationship Exercise**

   Make a list of people you consider to be your close friends. For each, identify ways that they are culturally similar and different from you. Then form groups of four to six students and answer the following questions. Select a recorder for your discussion so you can share your answers with the rest of the class.

   - Do people generally have more friends who are culturally similar or different from themselves?

   - What are some of the benefits of forming intercultural friendships?

   - In what ways are intercultural friendships different or similar to friendship with people from the same cultures?

   - What are some reasons people might have for not forming intercultural friendships?

Practicing Effective Interpersonal Communication

chapter outline

ACKNOWLEDGING THE "REALITY" OF RELATIONSHIPS

Because interpersonal relationships are so important to us—whether within our families, friendships, intimate partnerships, or workplaces—many of us spend our lives searching for information that will help us create the "perfect" relationship. Go into any bookstore and you will find entire sections dedicated to books that will help us attract the perfect partner, develop lifelong friendships, or deal with a nasty boss. Television sitcoms show us "life" in an enormous variety of "normal" or "dysfunctional" relationships, depending on your point of view. One of the most recent phenomena to hit television is the so-called reality show where seemingly random strangers are stuck together in one situation or another and must "survive" the season. Have you ever noticed, though, that the purpose of the show is never to have the strangers develop positive, healthy interpersonal relationships? Such shows find every way possible to create competition, jealousy, conflict, and dissatisfaction among the participants. And if the survival of strangers together isn't bad enough, you can now potentially find and marry the man or woman of your dreams—all on television. Is the ultimate goal of these shows to find true love and long-lasting happiness in a committed partnership? Most of us don't believe so—especially when the title of the show is something like *How to Marry a Millionaire.*

Yet despite reality shows dominating in the media, healthy and long-lasting interpersonal relationships in a variety of contexts are possible. In order to develop and maintain these healthy relationships, however, we must understand how to balance a number of interpersonal dialectics, which is the focus of this chapter.

UNDERSTANDING INTERPERSONAL COMMUNICATION DIALECTICS

If it is to survive, each relationship must work out many **dialectics**—tension or opposition between interacting forces or elements. Every relationship must contend with several issues, or dialectics, in the negotiation of communication between the parties.

Complementary and Symmetrical Relationships

The first issue is whether the relationship will be complementary or symmetrical in nature. **Complementary relationships** are those that are based on difference; each person brings characteristics that balance or complement those of the other. For example, you may be very logical and systematic in how you study for tests or complete assignments. You create a schedule or a checklist and mark off each task as you complete it. You begin several days before the assignment is due. Your best friend, roommate, or relational partner, however, may like to spend considerable time thinking about how to best understand the material. She may work on many assignments or tasks at the same time. At the last minute, she pulls it all together and finishes the assignment. The relationship is complementary because each of you balances out the strengths and weaknesses of the other as you interact, live, or work together.

Symmetrical relationships are based on similarity; the individuals share traits, interests, and approaches to communication that are essentially alike. Perhaps you and your best friend share the same idea of what constitutes a "real" vacation: throw some clothes together, jump in the car, and drive until you get to someplace interesting. Or perhaps you both like to sit down and thoroughly plan where you'll go and what you'll see.

Dialectics
Tension or opposition between interacting forces or elements

Complementary relationships
Relationships based on difference; each person brings characteristics that balance the characteristics of a relational partner

Symmetrical relationships
Relationships based on similarity; both individuals share traits, interests, and approaches to communication

Your success in college depends on your willingness to use confirming responses to others.

Independent, Dependent, and Interdependent Relationships

A second issue is the nature of independence, dependence, or interdependence the parties will have. In **independent relationships**, partners live separate and disconnected lives. In other words, they have different hobbies or interests and they may take separate vacations. Should the relationship terminate, the partners would not be dramatically impacted by the loss. In **dependent relationships**, partners rely so much on each other that their identities are enmeshed. One of the partners may not be able to make any decision without consulting the other. Should the relationship terminate, the partners would lose essential support and face an identity crisis. Parties in **interdependent relationships** rely on each other and possess mutual influence and importance, but they are not so dependent on the other that they cannot make independent decisions when warranted. Should an interdependent relationship terminate, the partners would feel the loss keenly but have sufficient personal identity to rebuild.

Confirming, Disconfirming, and Rejection Messages

A third key issue or dialectic involves the routine types of relational messages that constitute the ongoing relationships between the parties. The individuals may communicate through disconfirming, confirming, or rejection messages. **Disconfirming messages** deny a relational partner's value by refusing to acknowledge the partner's presence and the importance of the partner's communication. Messages can be disconfirming in many ways. One person might simply ignore the other or change the subject in the middle of a conversation.

Confirming messages, by contrast, value the partner's presence and contributions. We send confirming messages when we look directly at another, nod in response to a message, ask for additional information, or share a similar experience. **Rejection messages** acknowledge but do not fully accept the partner's presence and communication, such as when one person calls another's contribution "stupid" or "nonsense."

Messages possess two important characteristics: *effectiveness* and *appropriateness* (Spitzberg & Cupach 1984). Effective messages accomplish the communication's intended goal, while appropriate messages demonstrate responsiveness to the message's relational and contextual aspects. While some messages lack one or the other of these characteristics, rhetorically sensitive messages communicate both effectively and appropriately.

Defensive and Supportive Communication Climates

Related to effectiveness versus responsiveness is a fourth dialectic concerning the type of atmosphere that is maintained between the parties and that is important to the dyad. The atmosphere may be defensive or supportive. A **defensive climate** is an atmosphere in which at least one of the partners feels threatened and seeks to protect him or herself from attack. Defensiveness usually develops if a relational partner behaves in an evaluative, controlling, manipulative, uninvolved, superior, or dogmatic manner. One of the most common examples of defensiveness in a relational atmosphere occurs when one or both partners show extreme jealousy. Extremely jealous partners may question their partner's fidelity every time they interact with another person, or they may attempt to control or block their interactions with anyone outside the relationship.

Independent relationships
Relationships in which the partners live separate and disconnected lives

Dependent relationships
Relationships in which the partners rely so much on one another that their identities are enmeshed with one another

Interdependent relationships
Relationships in which the partners rely on one another but are not so dependent that they cannot make independent decisions when warranted

Disconfirming messages
Messages that deny the value of a relational partner by refusing to acknowledge his or her presence and communication

Confirming messages
Messages that value the partner's presence and contributions

Rejection messages
Messages that acknowledge the partner's presence and communication, but do not fully accept or agree with the partner

Defensive climate
A climate in which partners feel threatened and seek to protect themselves from attack

A **supportive climate** is an atmosphere in which partners feel comfortable and secure. Understanding, honesty, empathy, equality, and flexibility characterize this climate. Equality and flexibility are the most critical of these qualities. Equality in the relationship means that each partner's experience, knowledge, and relational expectations will be considered when important decisions must be made. Flexibility means that both partners show a willingness to change or modify interests, plans, and expectations when circumstances change.

Author Jack Gibbs (1961) suggests that we can enhance the positive climate in relationships, particularly in group interaction, with a number of important communication strategies. We should describe a specific communication interaction instead of evaluating or judging it. We should focus on solving a problem in the communication—not attempt to control the other's interactions. We should attempt to communicate in a spontaneous fashion instead of entering the communication with a strategy of controlling the communication. We should use the values of empathy and equality when interacting with another. And, finally, Gibbs suggests that we entertain the idea that all solutions be seen as "provisional." In essence, nothing is "carved in stone" and we can reevaluate the appropriateness of a solution if new evidence or information appears.

Assertiveness, Nonassertiveness, and Aggressiveness

A fifth dialectic concerns the need for partners to negotiate the degree of **nonassertiveness, assertiveness,** or **aggressiveness** that each individual will communicate in the relationship. *Nonassertive* partners feel powerless and keep their feelings and thoughts to themselves; they are often unable to express honest feelings comfortably. *Assertive* partners know and communicate their feelings and thoughts straightforwardly and honestly with others; they do not let others speak for them or tell them how they should feel, even though they remain concerned about others' perspectives. *Aggressive* partners assert themselves to an extreme without concern for others' concerns or needs; they stand up for themselves even at another's expense. They have the tendency to force others to believe as they do and engage in verbal attack marked by strong disconfirming messages. We identify effective assertive messages and specific assertive strategies that you can incorporate into your communication later in this chapter.

Rigidity and Flexibility

Rigid partners lack the ability to adapt and cope with changes that occur in a relationship; they possess neither the motivation nor the inclination to learn new ways of interacting. **Flexible partners,** by contrast, adapt and alter their behaviors to accommodate the changes that occur in relationships because all relationships change.

Interaction, Domination, and Passivity

Interactive conversation remains an important aspect of relational initiation and development. Turn-taking that allows each partner an opportunity to engage the conversation promotes interaction. However, when people **dominate** the conversation and do not permit their partners to speak or when one of the partners is passive, and therefore reticent or unwilling to enter the interaction, effective communication becomes virtually impossible.

Within each of these dialectics, what style is most comfortable to you? It is important to remember that the individuals in the dyad—not outsiders to the relationship—decide what will constitute the basic communication between each other. Does your style change within these dialectics in different types of relationships? Are you more passive with your romantic partner than you are with your best friend? The key to successful and competent interpersonal communication is how the individuals in the dyad negotiate the various dialectics we have discussed. The ways in

---

Supportive climate
A climate in which partners feel comfortable and secure

Nonassertiveness
Feeling of powerlessness and inability to express feelings honestly and comfortably

Assertiveness
Ability to communicate feelings honestly and in a straightforward manner

Aggressiveness
Asserting oneself to an extreme without concern for others

Rigidity
Inability to adapt and cope with changes that occur in a relationship

Flexibility
Ability to adapt and alter one's behaviors to accommodate changes in a relationship

Interaction
Turn-taking that allows each partner to engage in a conversation

Dominate
When one partner does not allow the other to speak

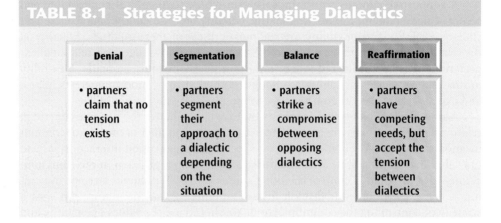

TABLE 8.1 Strategies for Managing Dialectics			
Denial	**Segmentation**	**Balance**	**Reaffirmation**
• partners claim that no tension exists	• partners segment their approach to a dialectic depending on the situation	• partners strike a compromise between opposing dialectics	• partners have competing needs, but accept the tension between dialectics

which the parties negotiate and agree with each other's behavior within each dialectic will assist in maintaining and expanding the relationship over a number of years—or may contribute to the relationship's eventual dissolution.

Strategies for Managing Dialects in Your Relationships

Negotiating and managing dialectics in your relationships reduces the tensions that block relationship development and enhance the possibilities for success. Leslie Baxter (1990) has identified four ways to deal with the dialectical tensions that we may potentially encounter in relationships: denial, segmentation, balance, and reaffirmation (see Table 8.1).

The use of denial simply means the relational partners claim that a particular tension doesn't exist. If a couple thinks they are "inseparable," their individual autonomy may be denied, for example. The use of segmentation as a strategy means that certain spheres of the relationship are treated differently. Individuals in a dyad may be autonomous at work, for example, but connected in social situations. Balance involves a compromise between two dialectics, which might mean the couple strategically identifies the nature of their autonomy and connectedness. Connectedness might mean, then, that they engage in hobbies together but do not smother one another. And, finally, reaffirmation means that the couple has competing needs for both autonomy and connection and that the tension that occurs between them is acceptable in the relationship. In this way, the couple continues to "reaffirm" both their autonomy and their connection within the relationship.

APPLYING INTERPERSONAL DIALECTICS TO FAMILIES

There are two types of families: those we are born into and those we create. The families we are born into become the fundamental building blocks of who we are at any given time. The patterns of interaction within our families are the models for the families we create. Think about the type of relationship your parents or primary caregivers modeled for you. Where did these individuals fall on the complementary/symmetrical dimension? How dependent/independent/interdependent was their relationship? What was the nature of the confirming or disconfirming communication within your family unit? Would you characterize the climate in your family as mostly supportive or mostly defensive? What degree of assertiveness did your parents or caregivers communicate to you, to each other, to others outside the immediate family? Were the rules in your family somewhat rigid or more flexible and changeable over time? Overall, was there a sense of a dominant hierarchy within your family or a feeling of more equal participation among all members?

It is important to remember that no single family dynamic is necessarily better than another. The key to successful and healthy family relationships is the agreement and cooperation among its members about these important dialectics. Healthy family communication is characterized by emotional and physical support between the members—this is a "functional" family. In a "dysfunctional" family, communication is closed, and members are not allowed to express their feelings, needs, hopes, fears, and dreams to each other.

The model your "first" family communicated to you impacts your "second," or created, family. How you approach your romantic relationships and future long-term partnerships will, to some extent, be adapted from this first model. Make a list of your basic expectations for your romantic relationships. Does your list consist primarily of what you want your romantic partner to do and be for you? Does your list include what you want your partner to allow you to do and be for him or her? It is important to remember that men and women may not always have the same expectations for the relationship, particularly in terms of "the talk" that is used to negotiate healthy and long-term support of each other. Men are more likely to suppress feelings and to not talk about relationships, and this is not always healthy.

Much of our family dynamic occurs in the context of family meals. For some families, the ritual of mealtime is the most important time of the day to connect and share the happenings of the day. For some families, the most important ritual is the Sunday dinner, which may be a multigenerational activity. For other families, meals are a scattered affair where family members grab-and-go, whether they 'go' to the television, to after-school activities, or to their separate rooms. What values do children learn through what constitutes "mealtime"? When your family gathers for meals, is the value of equality operating? Are all members of the family encouraged to share equally about their day or week? Or does one member dominate the conversation and take up all of the verbal "space"? Does humility operate at family meals? How do family members show self-discipline in eating? Are members able to open up and talk about their day freely, or is conversation restricted during mealtime?

Anyone who suppresses feelings may jeopardize his or her physical health and, ultimately, a relationship. Yet disclosing feelings also has risks. Self-disclosure must be appropriate to the relationship and the immediate situation. Honestly expressing your feelings can potentially add multiple benefits to the relationship. You confirm both yourself and the other through your honesty; you set an example for the climate in the relationship with supportive and honest self-disclosure; you can become more aware of your own strengths and weaknesses in communication and of your own feelings through self-disclosure; and you can be proactive in managing conflict within the relationship.

For some families, meals are an important time to reconnect and build family ties.

APPLYING INTERPERSONAL DIALECTICS TO FRIENDSHIPS

We meet any number of other people on any given day. How is it that some of these people become our friends? What differentiates an "acquaintance" and a "friend"? We run into acquaintances and have a chat. We seek out friends because we like to

Gunnysacking
Repressing feelings to the point that an individual cannot avoid "dumping" his or her feelings onto the relational partner

be with them. We communicate, for the most part, only superficially with acquaintances; we self-disclose more deeply to our friends. The degree of trust that operates in a true friendship impacts how we accept each other, support each other, and even criticize each other. A strong, trusting friendship allows us to criticize each other when needed because we know the friendship can survive honest critical assessment. As the friendship moves from acquaintanceship into true friendship, we must work out important relational dialectics. Must we think alike on all things, or can we complement each other with our unique habits, quirks, and personalities? Do we have to see each other every day? Week? Year? In what ways do we need our true friends to communicate confirmation? How do we show our support to one another? Will this friendship be characterized by one person being more dominant and the other more passive? How do we negotiate each of these characteristics of the relationship?

The most effective and healthy friendships are characterized by understanding about these dialectics. Notice that we did not say "talking about" these dialectics. Some friendships seem to just naturally move into a level of comfort with the way the dialectics emerge, without the need to speak about them directly. In others, however, the friends may freely talk about expectations and comfort about some aspect of a dialectic. In both of these types of friendships, one of the most important skills for both parties in developing the health of the relationship is assertiveness. Remember that assertiveness is the ability to express rights or views without judging the rights or views of another. When you are assertive, you do not become overly sensitive to the other's point of view, and you don't take disagreements personally. You do not make *your* assertions personal or judgmental about the other. When both parties in a friendship are assertive, they can remain friends even through times of disagreement about a topic, issue, or situation.

Healthy friendships also are characterized by honest and open communication between friends. As we discuss previously, suppressing feelings and thoughts in relationships, particularly in friendships, can cause resentment that may build to the breaking point. Think about your suppression of feelings through the following metaphor, called **gunnysacking**. Each time you hold back on a thought or feeling, you put it into a gunnysack you carry on your back. Each of us carries a sack associated with each of our relationships. Think about the sacks you carry around on your back. When one is empty, it doesn't weigh anything, but every time we avoid a confrontation, swallow a criticism, or ignore a problem in that relationship, we add it to our sack. Every time we do this, the sack gets heavier. Gunnysacks can be big or small, but inevitably they fill up at some point if an individual continues to suppress his or her feelings. So what happens when the sack spills open? It may go something like this:

> Two roommates who are good friends have been living together for several months. One of the roommates likes to think of herself as neat and tidy, and she likes her living space to be free of clutter—with dishes washed and put away, laundry done in a timely manner, and a generally tidy living space. The second, however, pays very little attention to the "look" of the apartment. Clothes fall wherever they are removed, dishes pile up in the sink, and the toothpaste tube lies on the sink without the cap (you get the picture). One day, after roommate number 1 has had her fill, she explodes about the slob she lives with, focusing particularly on the toothpaste tube! Communication experts call this gunnysacking because that burlap bag has just become way too full, and the contents come spilling out in an order that defies logic. The only thing that matters to roommate number 1 is that she is fed up and unable to keep her feelings suppressed any longer.

Has this or a similar experience ever happened to you? So who is "at fault" here? What are the "rules" that have been developing between these friends over time? Is roommate number 2 completely at fault for being a slob? The answer is *no*, because

COMMUNICATION COUNTS IN YOUR CAREER
Five Ways to Say "I"

Conflict is inevitable in any relationship, but how you respond verbally is within your control. Using "I" messages rather than "you" messages will help the other person hear what you have to say without feeling attacked or demeaned. Here are five ways that David Ellis, author of *Becoming a Master Student*, suggests that college students respond to conflict by using "I" messages:

1. *Observation:* describes what you can see, hear, touch, and experience and focuses on facts. Instead of saying, "You are eating like a pig," you can say, "We spent 20 dollars again this shopping trip on junk food like chips and cookies."

2. *Feelings:* describes your own feelings. Rather than saying, "You make me feel stupid," say "I feel foolish when you remember more than I do from our chemistry lecture."

3. *Wants:* describes what you want or need instead of hoping that others will guess what you want them to do or what you need from them. Avoid using the word *need*, if possible. Change your comment from, "You are so lazy around here," to "I would like you to help me with the dishes and the laundry before we go to the movies."

4. *Thoughts:* describes your thinking. Beware of "I" messages that are really judgments, such as "I think you are insensitive," or "I know that you hate my cooking." Try messages like, "I feel secure when you tell me you love me more often," or "I like it when you tell me whether or not you enjoyed the meal I cooked."

5. *Intention:* describes what you plan to do. Rather than depend on the other, state your intentions. Instead of saying, "We have a lot of chores this weekend," say, "I intend to wash the car and vacuum the carpet before studying this weekend. What would you like to do?"

the rules of the relationship have developed through the initial silence of roommate number 1 about what she expects of roommate number 2. When we suppress our thoughts and feelings, we implicitly consent to another's behavior. The box "Communication Counts in Your Career: Five Ways to Say 'I'" provides some examples of ways that you can communicate more effectively in all types of relationships. You may find these skills valuable as you negotiate problems with your roommate or juggle the multiple demands of being a student, spouse, and parent because these and other issues can create conflict.

APPLYING INTERPERSONAL DIALECTICS TO COLLEGE

Whether you are entering college right after high school or returning after several years, there is a good chance that you will develop friendships and even romantic relationships during this time. These interpersonal relationships in the college context are unique in that you are exposed to a much more rich and varied group of individuals. Because many campuses are composed of persons from a wide variety of cultural, ethnic, and geographical origins, it may be more challenging to develop friendships and/or romantic relationships.

Expectations for appropriateness in interpersonal relationships are strongly influenced by culture. As we have discussed earlier in this text, culture is a pattern of perceptions, values, and behaviors shared by a group of people. In other words, culture is the unique way in which we engage in the everyday behaviors—such as eating, socializing, and creating and maintaining relationships—as American, Chinese, or French; male or female; white or Hispanic; and so on. Yet cultures are not homogeneous; they are dynamic and heterogeneous. This means that every individual in a cultural group also is unique. Race, gender, class, and sexual orientation provide

Culture Counts

Individualistic cultures
Cultures that place more importance on the individual within certain types of relationships; value direct, open communication

Collectivist cultures
Cultures that emphasize the importance of the group; value less direct communication and tend to avoid conflict situations

additional layers of culture that impact the ways each of us negotiate the world we live in.

Cultural characteristics impact the interpersonal dialectics we have discussed. Martin and Nakayama (2001) argue that the values of a cultural group represent a worldview—a particular way of looking at the world. They distinguish between individualistic and collectivist cultural worldviews. **Individualist cultures** place more importance on the individual within certain types of relationships. These cultures value direct, open forms of communication. **Collectivist cultures** value less direct communication and tend to avoid conflict. These cultures emphasize the importance of the group (i.e., family, work, or social) and value the group's success over that of any individual in that group. Later in this text, we discuss several cultural influences on group communication.

Dutch social psychologist Geert Hofstede (1980) has identified a number of distinctions between cultural groups. One of them refers to the long- or short-term orientation to life. Some individualistic cultures are more likely to value a "short-term orientation" to life. These cultures emphasize the importance of quick results and of finding an immediate solution. Some Americans, for example, are more likely to want to establish relationships quickly by "telling all" about themselves in the first few interactions. In contrast, collectivist cultures are more likely to value a long-term orientation to life. They emphasize slowly developing relationships over time, tenaciously working toward long-term goals, and practicing the virtue of thrift. What do you think it means to be "thrifty" in developing and maintaining interpersonal relationships?

Another unique communication context operating in college concerns the relationships among faculty, staff, and students. As we will discuss later in this text, the college or campus is a unique organization with a hierarchy of power relationships. At a very basic level, instructors have the power to assign you a grade for the value of your work in their classes. Do you think it is appropriate to develop a friendship with an instructor? What should be the boundaries for appropriate interpersonal relationships? Some faculty like to have students call them by their first names and are willing to tell students about their background and experience and even to disclose some information about their life history; other faculty are not. Which style are you most comfortable with? Is it appropriate for you to socialize with a faculty member outside the classroom?

Your campus may assign you to an advisor within your major's department, and this person will assist you in identifying classes that meet your major's requirements. What other expectations do you have for your advisor? Is it important for this person to know something about you personally to more effectively provide counsel on your career or life goals? Is it important for you to know something about your advisor's experience and credibility to accurately assess his or her advice? Like most communication situations on your campus, the faculty–student communication context will be varied and heterogeneous. In other words, some faculty may be more willing than others to know and understand you and to disclose information about themselves. The box "Communication Counts in Your College Experience: Working with Your Academic Advisor" offers some additional insights about advising and advisors. (You may also access information on advising at the National Academic Advising Association [NACADA] Clearinghouse of Advising Resources website at www.nacada.ksu.edu/Clearinghouse/AdvisingIssues/Core-Values.htm).

APPLYING INTERPERSONAL DIALECTICS TO COMMUNITIES

Many colleges today are attempting to incorporate a variety of service learning or problem-based learning initiatives into the life of the campus and surrounding community. Many of these initiatives have been sponsored by the American Association

COMMUNICATION COUNTS IN YOUR COLLEGE EXPERIENCE
Working with Your Academic Advisor

Your relationship with your academic advisor is potentially one of the most important in your college career. How do you develop this relationship effectively? Consider the following when working with your academic advisor.

First, advisors hold core values, as explained by the National Academic Advising Association. One of these values is particularly important for you to consider:

Advisors are responsible to the individuals they advise

Academic advisors work to strengthen the importance, dignity, potential, and unique nature of each individual within the academic setting. Advisors' work is guided by their beliefs that students

- have diverse backgrounds that can include different ethnic, racial, domestic, and international communities; sexual orientations; ages; gender and gender identities; physical, emotional, and psychological abilities; political, religious, and educational beliefs;

- hold their own beliefs and opinions;

- are responsible for their own behaviors and the outcomes of those behaviors;

- can be successful based on their individual goals and efforts;

- have a desire to learn;

- have learning needs that vary based on individual skills, goals, responsibilities, and experiences;

- use a variety of techniques and technologies to navigate their world.

In support of these beliefs, the cooperative efforts of all who advise include, but are not limited to, providing accurate and timely information, communicating in useful and efficient ways, maintaining regular office hours, and offering varied contact modes.

Advising, as part of the educational process, involves helping students develop a realistic self-perception and successfully transition to the postsecondary institution. Advisors encourage, respect, and assist students in establishing their goals and objectives. Advisors seek to gain the trust of their students and strive to honor students' expectations of academic advising and its importance in their lives.

George D. Kuh, author of *Student Success in College*, states,

Academic advisors can play an integral role in promoting student success by assisting students in ways that encourage them to engage in the right kinds of activities, inside and outside the classroom. Advisors are especially important because they are among the first people new students encounter and should see regularly during their first year. (2006)

He adds that there are four important common themes regarding advising that arise from his Documenting Effective Educational Practices (DEEP) study of 20 schools, which you may wish to consider in choosing and working with your advisor:

1. **Advisors know their students well.** Subscribing to a talent development perspective on education, advisors believe their primary task is to help change students for the better by making certain they take full advantage of the institution's resources for learning. To do this, many advisors go to unusual lengths to learn as much as they can about their students—where they are from, their aspirations and talents, and when and where they need help.

2. **Advisors strive for meaningful interactions with students.** Another way advisors contribute to the quality of student learning and campus life is by helping to develop, support, and participate in mentoring programs. Mentee–mentor relationships help create close connections with one or more key persons, relationships that are especially important for students in underrepresented groups on campus. Also, because connecting *early* with advisees is essential, advisors at DEEP schools are involved in planning and delivering first-year orientation programs and experiences.

3. **Advisors help students identify pathways to academic and social success.** In addition to assisting students with choosing the right courses, advisors encourage students to take advantage of the learning and personal opportunities their school makes available. They make a point of asking students to apply what they are learning in their classes to real-life issues, thereby enhancing student learning in ways that many academic courses alone may not be able to accomplish. Among the high-quality cocurricular experiences that have powerful positive effects on students and their success are service learning, study abroad, civic engagement, internships, and

COMMUNICATION COUNTS IN YOUR COLLEGE EXPERIENCE

(continued)

experiential learning activities. Another key to navigating college effectively is for students to learn the campus culture—the traditions, rituals, and practices that communicate how and why things are done at their school.

4. **Advising and student success is considered a tag team activity.** At high-performing schools, the educational and personal development goals of advising are shared across multiple partners, not just the person "assigned" this task. Faculty, student affairs staff, and mentors along with professional academic advisors make up the multiple early alert and safety net systems for students in place at DEEP schools—particularly for students who institutional research studies indicate may be at risk of dropping out. Such team approaches go a long way toward keeping students from falling through the cracks and getting students the information they need when they need it.

Your responsibility as an advisee, then, is to make yourself available to your advisor, get to know him or her, and use your skills in assertiveness to capitalize on your advisor's values and skill. Advisors can be instrumental in helping you negotiate the political landscape that is your college campus. This individual can also be instrumental in letting you get to know his or her network of professionals, which may enhance your possibilities in landing that perfect job. And, finally, an advisor can be the most important person to write a letter of recommendation when you begin to interview for that job. The key to taking advantage of his or her expertise is your commitment to establishing a positive, assertive, and effective relationship with this important person in your college life.

Source: From "Thinking DEEPly about academic advising and student engagement," by George D. Kuh from *Academic Advising Today*, June 2006, 29, 1, 3. Reprinted by permission of the National Academic Advising Association (NACADA) and the author.

of Colleges and Universities (AAC&U). The AAC&U's policy is that every student deserves to receive a "liberal education," which it defines as

> one that prepares us to live responsible, productive, and creative lives in a dramatically changing world. It is an education that fosters a well-grounded intellectual resilience, a disposition toward lifelong learning, and an acceptance of responsibility for the ethical consequences of our ideas and actions. Liberal education requires that we understand the foundations of knowledge and inquiry about nature, culture, and society; that we master core skills of perception, analysis, and expression; that we cultivate a respect for truth; that we recognize the importance of historical and cultural context; and that we explore connections among formal learning, citizenship, and service to our communities. (From the Statement on Liberal Learning. Adopted by the Board of Directors of the Association of American Colleges and Universities, October 1998. Copyright © 1998 Association of American Colleges and Universities. Reprinted with permission.)

Liberal education is a student-learning and problem-centered approach to preparing students for life beyond the campus, preparing them for the issues of society and the workplace: "Quality liberal education prepares students for active participation in the private and public sectors, in a diverse democracy, and in an even more diverse community. It has the strongest impact when studies reach beyond the classroom to the larger community, asking students to apply their developing analytical skills and ethical judgment to concrete problems in the world around them, and to connect theory with the insights gained in practice" (*Greater Expectations* 2002, 26). The liberal education approach eliminates the artificial distinctions between studies deemed "liberal" (i.e., unrelated to job training) and "practical" (assumed to be related to a job). "A liberal education is practical because it develops just those capacities needed by every thinking adult: analytical skills, effective communication, practical intelligence, ethical judgment, and social responsibility" (26). To clarify, the concept of a liberal education should not be confused with a liberal arts college. Any two-year community college, four-year private college, four-year public university, research-intensive university offering advanced degrees, or any other can offer students a liberal education.

Practically speaking, this means that student work moves beyond the classroom (either using problem-based cases in classrooms or through service-learning projects in the community) to engage in the life of the community in which the campus resides. Whether your campus has this type of initiative or not, you will in your lifetime become a member of some collective community. You may be a parent negotiating with teachers and administrators in your child's school. You may purchase a house and find yourself confronted by a reassessment of property values. You may be a member of a church that has undertaken a project to assist a less-privileged group within the community. Your ability to be sensitive to the interpersonal dialectics operating within this communication context will be regularly tested.

MANAGING CONFLICT IN INTERPERSONAL RELATIONSHIPS

The dialectics discussed earlier in this chapter can result in conflict between the relational partners. Conflict, though, is inevitable in any relationship. Partners vary in their responses to conflict, so managing conflict is essential to establishing true intimacy and in managing the various dialectics we have discussed. Understanding the value of conflict and ways to manage conflict will help you build more effective interpersonal relationships.

Intimacy and Conflict

Issues arise that lead to conflict, and partners vary in their responses to it. Some partners avoid conflict and refuse to deal with issues; they are more likely to surrender. Other partners go on the attack and seek to shift the blame or defeat the other partner; they want to win at all costs. Still other partners confront the issue to solve the problem rather than sidestep it or adopt an "I win, you lose" strategy. In order to make sure your relationships run as smoothly as possible, you must first understand the inevitability of conflict. If you try to avoid conflict, your relationships will suffer. Successful conflict management can ensure the relationship survives and grows more satisfying over time. The existence of conflict does not mean the partners in a relationship are having trouble; conflict exists because we are linked to each other, involved with each other, and connected with each other.

By definition, **conflict** is the perception of incompatible goals and the belief that for one partner to reach his or her goal, the goals of the other partner cannot be met (see Hocker & Wilmot 1997). Sometimes conflict is out in the open, but sometimes it is hidden. When we confront someone directly about a perceived conflict, the conflict is said to be **overt**. When conflict is hidden, or **covert,** we sometimes act in passive-aggressive ways that send mixed messages. For example, you may be angry at a roommate for not pulling his share of the responsibility for keeping the apartment clean or upset with your spouse or children who know you have to study yet don't take the initiative to start supper or throw in a load of laundry. You may say nothing in these situations but act coolly toward the person or people with whom you are upset. When you respond to conflict in these passive-aggressive ways, the conflict remains unresolved, and the relationship suffers.

The way an individual responds to conflict reflects past experiences, which are often a product of family history. Think about the ways your family resolves conflict.

Conflict
The perception of incompatible goals

Overt conflict
Confronting someone directly in a conflict

Covert conflict
Where a partner hides their anger or hostility

Effectively dealing with conflict is an important aspect of any relationship.

Do family members ignore the problem and hope it goes away? Is there competition to see who can "win"? Does your family encourage constructive engagement and discussion of conflict? How you manage conflict will be reflected in your words and actions. While conflict is inevitable, it is also manageable. When you approach conflict as a problem to be solved, and not a challenge for you to win at all costs, you can develop and expand your relationships with others and increase your confidence and self-esteem. A key to becoming more effective at managing conflict is the ability to be adaptable. This is easier said than done. While you may be able to control your feelings and actions during conflict, you cannot control someone else's. In the face of anger, tears, shouting, or accusation, however, we often find it difficult to remain calm. Conflict can spiral out of control if neither party in the relationship is willing to listen and adapt to the needs of the conflict situation. Perhaps even a time-out to cool down and collect your thoughts can help keep a heated conflict from becoming even more destructive. The old practice of counting to ten before you speak is still valuable.

One of the basic values that is essential in important relationships is honesty. We expect honesty in the relationship no matter what the situation. When we deceive people we care about, we lose trust in them and in the relationship. Trust is a critical building block in any interpersonal relationship. When we are trying to manage conflict, it takes courage to remain honest and to trust another. You must describe your feelings honestly and ask the other person to do the same. You must also avoid lashing out with hurtful, aggressive comments, despite how you might feel at the moment. Focus on the positive side of the relationship and its potential for better understanding of yourself and the other. When we are calm and in control of our emotions, we know this is possible. Yet, it is easy to fall back on deception when emotions run high or when we don't want to admit we've made a mistake. Obviously, there are numerous reasons why conflict can emerge in relationships. Therefore, conflict is inevitable but manageable and even potentially beneficial.

To summarize, thus far we have described several issues that reflect the complex nature of interpersonal relationships. Successful negotiation of each of the dialectics will create an atmosphere where conflict can be managed successfully and relationship development and growth can be assured. But before we leave this discussion of how to successfully negotiate these issues, there is one more issue we must explore.

The Value of Conflict

We cannot, nor should we, try to avoid all conflict. Avoiding conflict will not make problems go away. Let us look at the definition of *conflict*. First, conflict is an *expressed struggle*. This means that both parties in a conflict must recognize the conflict and communicate to the other about the conflict. Next, the conflict occurs between *interconnected* individuals. It can hardly be a conflict if the communication occurs between complete strangers who will never see each other again after their brief interaction. The parties' interconnectedness implies that these individuals mean something to each other. The relationship could be between parent and child, life partners, best friends, boss and subordinate, coworkers, teacher and student, or any configuration where the relationship matters to the parties. Finally, conflict exists because the parties see incompatibility between one person's success and another's: If I reach my goal in this situation, you cannot reach yours. You see my success as interfering with your success. We perceive that any win by one of us will be at the expense of the other. At the heart of the conflict is the critical role of *perception*. We may be able to find a solution that meets both parties' needs, but our perceptions prevent us from seeing that as a possibility.

From the outset, we must understand that conflict has the potential to enhance the health and growth of our interpersonal relationships. If managed effectively, our relationships grow and prosper, becoming healthy, long-term, and satisfying. The absence of conflict is not healthy for any relationship.

Pseudoconflict, Destructive Conflict, and Constructive Conflict

Conflict is inevitable but not inevitably destructive. Some conflicts are actually only perceptual misunderstandings. **Pseudoconflict** occurs when the parties are actually in agreement, but perceptions and misunderstandings prevent them from seeing the areas of agreement and compatibility. One or more parties mistakenly believe that goal attainment is impossible for all. Pseudoconflict is easy to resolve if the parties are rhetorically sensitive to the misunderstanding. If the parties are not willing to listen to each other, however, the conflict intensifies.

Destructive conflict occurs when we allow the communication to escalate and spiral out of control. Wilmot and Hocker (2001) characterize destructive conflict as that which escalates; encourages each party to retaliate against the others; causes one or more individuals to dominate and compete with others; and increases the potential for defensiveness, inflexibility, and cross-complaints. The aim becomes to hurt another. Destructive conflict is both unethical and incompetent communication.

Obviously, there are numerous reasons why conflict can emerge in relationships. Smith and Walter (1995) identify several roadblocks that can impede the academic success of adult learners, many of which can also induce conflict:

- Family resentment because of frequent absence from home
- Resentment from coworkers because of absences and trying to improve one's self or one's skill
- Resistance from a spouse who doesn't support a career change, the costs of money or time invested in attending college, or the potential for developing new friends or life directions

Acknowledging that conflict exists is one of the first steps in preventing the escalation of destructive conflict. This expression of the conflict is important. Developing skills that help prevent conflict from escalating into a "win at all costs" war of words are essential to healthy relationships. Conflict management skills are valuable as you negotiate problems with your roommate or juggle the multiple demands of being a student, spouse, and parent. Managing **constructive conflict** begins with recognizing the conflict and being willing to own one's feelings. Turning the tide of destructive conflict means you must recognize when you are being selfish and stupid and admitting this to the other. Managing constructive conflict begins with recognizing the basic importance of the relationship and valuing the relationship more than the conflict. While the parties still may disagree with each other during the conflict, the goal is one of problem solving, not hurting the other. Each participant in the conflict must be flexible and strive to find the best solution for the relationship.

Conflict Management Styles

Thomas and Kilmann (1977), drawing on the work of Blake and Mouton (1964), has identified five possible styles of managing conflict. They base these five styles on the possible combinations of two important elements: concern for self and concern for people. Figure 8.1 shows the possible combinations.

Pseudoconflict
Situation in which the parties are actually in agreement, but perceptions and misunderstanding prevent them from seeing the areas of agreement and compatibility

Destructive conflict
Conflict in which communication escalates, and hurting one another becomes the goal

Constructive conflict
Conflict in which the goal is problem solving, not hurting one another

FIGURE 8.1: Five Styles of Conflict Management.
Source: From K. Thomas, "Conflict and Conflict Management," *Handbook of Industrial and Organizational Psychology,* Marvin Dunnette, editor, 1976. Adapted by permission of Leaetta Hough.

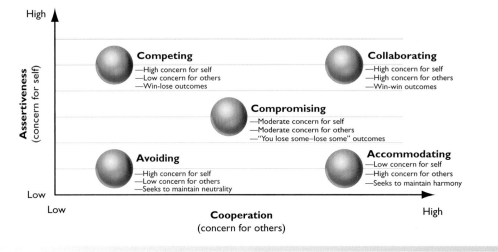

Collaboration

A **collaborating style** is characterized by high concern for self and high concern for people. *Collaboration* means to work together. Both parties share concern for solving a problem in a cooperative manner and consider the ultimate goal to be for both parties to win. Although both parties may initially identify different solutions to the problem, they work together to ultimately develop a solution that meets the needs of all individuals involved. The collaborating style takes work, time, and energy. Collaboration is characterized by assertiveness, perceptions of equality among the participants, belief that all parties and their opinions have value, and motivation to see the conflict through to a satisfying end. This conflict-management style is usually the most effective. However, it may not be appropriate in times of emergency, when an immediate decision must be made.

Competition

A **competing style** is characterized by high concern for self and low concern for other people. Generally, individuals who use a competing style engage in a win-lose approach to the conflict. They must win, and others must lose. These individuals dominate others involved in the conflict and insist that their own opinions and solutions are more valuable than those of others. The dominating individual's communication is aggressive and depends on threats, sarcasm, overt hostility, and disconfirming statements to others. Engaging in a competing style increases the likelihood of destructive conflict.

However, under emergency situations, when an immediate decision must be made, this style might be useful. When individuals in the relationship recognize that emergencies are a part of life and have agreed that under certain circumstances one party may make a decision without communication with the other, this style may be effective. It is critical, though, to understand that this must be agreed on in advance. Here is an example. Perhaps you and your life partner have agreed that neither of you will make a major purchase, say of over $100, without discussing it with the other. But one day when you're traveling on a trip away from home, your car breaks down, and you've got to get repairs so you can meet your client and return home. The repairs, as you'd expect, are considerably more than $100. In this type of circumstance, discussing the options with your partner isn't a consideration.

Collaborating style
Characterized by high concern for self and high concern for people.

Competing style
Characterized by high concern for self and low concern for people.

Accommodation

An **accommodating style** is characterized by high concern for people and low concern for self. Individuals who accommodate other people, yield to their wishes, needs, desires, or solutions. Accommodation is associated with a nonassertive communication approach. It is effective if you really do not care about the outcome of a particular circumstance or situation as much as your partner might. For example, if you want to see a movie this weekend and there's something that your partner really wants to see but you're not interested in it, you might agree to go because you don't really care all that much. The downside of too much accommodation is the tendency to become a pushover for everyone else's ideas but never stand up for your own. The accommodating style is more likely to be used by individuals from collectivist cultures than individualistic cultures. Remember, collectivist cultures attach more value to the group than to individuals, so they are more likely to yield to the group's will.

Avoidance

An **avoiding style** is characterized by low concern for self and low concern for other people. The most common behavior associated with avoidance is withdrawal—either physically or mentally. Individuals who employ this style avoid conflict by withdrawing physically or emotionally. They ignore phone calls or e-mails or simply refuse to respond to requests. Or they change the subject when an uncomfortable situation arises. Avoidance is all too common in many relationships because the parties fear that any type of confrontation will damage the relationship. Avoidance is very common in the initial stages of a relationship when one party doesn't want to be the first one to cause an argument. Unfortunately, avoidance only intensifies the possibility of a more intense conflict.

As we discussed earlier, avoidance causes us to *gunnysack* our problems and concerns. Eventually the gunnysack fills up, and the result is not pretty. In the early stages of a relationship, you may consider such behaviors to be "quirks" in your partner's personality—nothing major. One day, though, you're amazed to find that you've been really angry for the six months you've been picking up after him or her, and you're sick of doing it. You're tired of wiping up toothpaste from the sink, and you don't have time to fill the car up with gas (because he or she always leaves it empty). Today because you're in a hurry and late for a meeting. You explode.

Compromise

The **compromising style** is characterized by moderate concern for self and moderate concern for people. When we compromise, we give up something to gain something. Compromise may be the most often used conflict management style. However, it can be very dangerous. The most critical difference between collaborating and compromising styles is the parties' degree of satisfaction with the outcome. In collaboration, we modify our decision, but we are satisfied by both the process and the outcome of the decision. In a compromise, we give something up, but we may not be particularly happy about it. We do it to expedite the situation, perhaps to avoid a drawn-out conversation or meeting. One of the most common reasons for compromise is that we are too lazy to put the energy and time into the process of collaboration. Compromise as a long-term strategy to conflict management may have the same results as accommodation. Yet compromise can be effective under some circumstances. If the parties see compromise as a short-term approach to a problem, or when the situation is not critical to either party, compromise can work. But it needs to be used only rarely and only until a more comprehensive solution can be found.

CREATING MORE ASSERTIVE RELATIONSHIPS

Assertiveness is one of the most important characteristics of healthy relationships and positive communication climates. Assertiveness is never aggressive, never

Accommodating style
Characterized by low concern for self and high concern for people

Avoiding style
Characterized by low concern for self and low concern for people

Compromising style
Characterized by moderate concern for self and moderate concern for people

TABLE 8.2 Becoming an Assertive Communicator

Tips for Becoming an Assertive Communicator:

Develop a value and belief system that allows you to assert yourself. Give yourself permission to be angry, to say "no," to ask for help, and to make mistakes. Avoid using tag questions ("It's really hot today, isn't it?"), disclaimers ("I may be wrong, but . . ."), and question statements ("Won't you close the door?"), which lessen the perceived assertiveness of speech.

Resist giving into interruptions until you have completed your thoughts. (Instead say, "Just a moment, I haven't finished.")

Stop self-limiting behaviors, such as smiling too much, nodding too much, tilting your head, or dropping your eyes in response to another person's gaze.

When saying "no," be decisive. Explain why you are refusing, but don't be overly apologetic.

Use "I want" or "I feel" statements. Acknowledge the other person's situation or feelings and follow with a statement in which you stand up for your rights (e.g., "I know you're X, but I feel . . .").

Use "I" language (this is especially useful for expressing negative feelings.) "I" language helps you focus your anger constructively and to be clear about your own feelings.

For example:

- ◼ Maintain direct eye contact, keep your posture open and relaxed, be sure your facial expression agrees with the message, and keep a level, well-modulated tone of voice.

- ◼ Listen and let people know you have heard what they said. Ask questions for clarification.

- ◼ Practice! Enlist the aid of friends and family and ask for feedback. Tackle less anxiety-evoking situations first. Build up your assertiveness muscle.

Source: From "Assertive Communication: How to Be Effectively Assertive" from the brochure *Assertive Communication* by Dr. Vivian D. Barnette created from the following works: Alberti, Robert E., and Emmons, Michael. Your Perfect Right. Revised edition. San Luis Obispo, CA: IMPACT, 1990. Bower, Sharon, and Bower, Gordon. *Asserting Yourself*. Reading, Massachusetts: Addison-Wesley, 1976. Bramson, Robert M. Coping with Difficult People. New York: Anchor/Doubleday, 1981. Butler, Pamela. *Self-Assertion for Women*. San Francisco, CA: Harper & Row, 1981 .Smith, Manual J. *When I Say No, I Feel Guilty*. New York: The Dial Press, 1975. Reprinted by permission of Dr. Vivian D. Barnette.

powerless, never an attempt to dominate another. Assertiveness can be thought of as a "caring firmness" in our interactions with another. Assertive communicators act confidently but always see the other person as an equal partner in the communication interaction. When we are assertive we are positive, firm, confident, and involved in the conversation. But we do not talk over another or insist on our own agenda exclusively in the interaction. Table 8.2 shows suggestions for becoming an assertive communicator.

BUILDING COMPETENT AND ETHICAL RELATIONSHIPS IN COLLEGE, CAREER, AND LIFE

Being able to adapt your communication to the unique requirements of a particular communication context is one of the most critical skills of the competent communicator. **Rhetorical sensitivity** is the ability to adapt a message to the people, place, and timing of the communication. We are not implying that you so dramatically change your message that you compromise your ethical standards. Rhetorically sensitive communicators understand the unique elements of each communication situation and audience and adapt their messages accordingly. Morreale, Spitzberg, and Barge (2001) put it this way: "Communication is the process of making community. This means that the choices we make about how to communicate influence what we create and the kinds of personal lives, relationships, and communities we build" (22–23). Yet even when we act in the most communicatively competent manner possible, we cannot control someone else's communication behavior. As we discussed in the previous chapter, conflict is inevitable, so it is essential to have the tools to manage it effectively.

Rhetorical sensitivity
The ability to adapt a message to the people, place, and timing of the communication

The cultural lenses through which we see the world impact the ways we manage conflict as well. In situations when directness is valued, an individual may be more likely to stake out a position in the conflict and defend it. In situations when indirectness is valued, an individual may be more likely to downplay the conflict in an attempt to "save face" (Ting-Toomey & Oetzel 2002).

Today's college classroom learning environment may be characterized by more active student involvement through small group activities and problem solving. Small groups often present unique difficulties, including interpersonal conflict as a result of personality clashes or differences of opinion. Inter-role conflicts often occur because members share some of the same responsibilities without a clear understanding of how to divide the tasks involved or because they simultaneously compete for the same functions.

Your success in college depends upon your willingness to use *confirming* responses to others both in and out of class. Your success also depends on the degree of assertiveness you can develop. *Assertiveness* means being able to ask for what you want and not giving in to others who try to make you do something you don't want to do. It means saying no when you mean no and standing up for yourself without denying other people their rights. So if you're at a party and someone shoves a beer at you and you don't want it, say so. If you've come home from a long day of work and classes and the house is a mess, tell your family that you need their help cleaning it up. If someone tries to pressure you into sexual activity and you're not ready, tell him or her how you feel. Assertiveness also means that once you explain how you feel, you are not required to repeatedly justify your feelings. Once explained, your feelings should be respected. Assertive people act responsibly and accept responsibility for what they will and will not do. It means you're not afraid to speak up, ask questions, or seek information, and you make your own decisions.

Interpersonal relationships are established in dyads and within groups. How group members resolve dialectical tensions will significantly impact the type of climate developed in the group. How may group members respond to conflict? In some cases, groups ignore, prevent, squelch, or, as a last resort, use a leader's status or power to suspend conflict. In most cases, collaboration, which strives for a negotiated settlement between the conflicting parties, proves most beneficial to all concerned. Members focus on solving the problem rather than defending or attacking one another.

Another potential interpersonal conflict involves the nonparticipating member of a group. Groups often have members who, through disinterest, shyness, fear, selfishness, or defensiveness do not actively or verbally participate in discussion, decision making, and problem solving. Typically, such a member shows up to group meetings but says nothing and waits for others to discuss and decide issues to which they readily consent.

The flip side to this potential conflict is the overachieving member. Some group members, whether unconsciously or purposefully, seek to dominate groups with their ideas, opinions, or talk. Motivations for this behavior can range from a desire to be helpful to a desire to be the center of attention or create conflict. In any case, these people tend to bring the free exchange of ideas to a standstill and hinder the group's creativity and task functions. Some strategies for addressing both nonparticipating and over-participating members include the following:

- Assign the problem member a specific task or responsibility—especially one well suited to his or her skills or interests (e.g., "Marcie, would you please prepare a report that provides and explains the demographic of our student body so we can structure our membership drive more carefully?")

- Attend to nonverbal cues so that you sense when a member is about to speak and can respond accordingly to encourage participation or silence (e.g., "Noriko, I noticed that you frowned a bit at what Susan just said. Did you have something to add?")

- Arrange the group's seating to provide encouragement or control to members by sitting them near the leader (e.g., "Jenda, would you please sit next to me for this meeting? I may need to consult with you during the meeting, and it would be helpful to have you physically near.")

- Invite more quiet members to share their insights, thereby encouraging them to speak while helping to monitor those who may speak too much (e.g., "Jan, what do you think about using tickets to control the number of people who attend our open house?")

- Redirect the talk in the group to encourage more quiet members to share (e.g., "That's very interesting, Laughton. Thank you. Nate, what's your opinion on providing additional funds for undergraduate research projects?")

- Talk privately with the problem member (e.g., "Sally, I usually don't hear you speak up in our group on a regular basis. Is there something wrong? I would really like to hear from you." Or, "Patrick, have you noticed that it seems like some of our members are reluctant to speak up during the meeting? I was wondering if you would be willing to help me get the others members to add their thoughts by asking the quieter members questions or inviting them to speak?")

- Directly request change or voluntary self-removal of the problem member (e.g., "Mike, may I ask you to help me out? While what you share in our group is always worthwhile, would you be offended if I asked you to let others talk as well?" Or, "Joe, you really seem to have a problem relating to our group. I wonder if you would feel more comfortable working on another project or with another group. How do you feel about that?")

Ultimately, conflict is inevitable in any relationship, but how you respond verbally is within your control. Using "I" messages rather than "you" messages will help the other person hear what you have to say without feeling attacked or demeaned.

SUMMARY

In this chapter, we have discussed the importance of applying your understanding of the dialectics of interpersonal communication in a variety of communication contexts. We have identified concepts important to your understanding of effective interpersonal communication:

- The ability of the parties to negotiate a variety of dialectics will significantly impact each partner's willingness to grow together, including complementary versus symmetrical relationships, the degree of independence of each party, what constitutes appropriate and effective messages within the relationship, and the degree of flexibility required to keep the relationship functioning.

- Individualistic cultures place more importance on the individual within certain types of relationships. Individualistic cultures value direct, open forms of communication.

- Collectivist cultures value less direct communication and tend to avoid conflict situations. Collectivist cultures emphasize the importance of the group (i.e., family, work, or social group) and value the group's success rather than any individual in that group.

- Conflict is inevitable in relationships, but it can be managed successfully.
- Pseudoconflict is when the parties actually are in agreement but perceptions and misunderstanding prevent them from seeing the areas of agreement and compatibility.
- Destructive conflict is that which escalates; encourages each party to retaliate against the other; causes one or more individuals to dominate and compete with others; and increases the potential for defensiveness, inflexibility, and cross-complaints.
- Constructive conflict begins with recognition and starts the process of managing the conflict by one individual's willingness to own his or her feelings.
- A collaborating style of conflict management is characterized by high concern for self and high concern for the other. *Collaboration* means to work together.
- A competing style of conflict management is characterized by high concern for self and low concern for the other. Generally, individuals who use a competing style engage in a win-lose approach to the conflict.
- An accommodating style of conflict management is characterized by high concern for the other and low concern for self. When we accommodate another, we yield to his or her wishes, needs, desires, or solutions.
- An avoiding style of conflict management is characterized by low concern for self and low concern for the other. The most common behavior associated with avoidance is withdrawal, either physically or mentally.
- Avoidance causes us to gunnysack our problems and concerns. Eventually our gunnysack overflows with increased destructive conflict.
- A compromising style of conflict management is characterized by moderate concern for self and moderate concern for the other. When we compromise, we give something up to gain something.
- Assertive communicators are firm, confident, and empathetic in interacting with others.
- Rhetorical sensitivity is this ability to adapt a message to the people, place, and timing of the communication.

QUESTIONS FOR DISCUSSION

1. What is the most critical issue that can cause misunderstanding within cross-cultural friendships?

2. If you are a member of the dominant cultural group in your campus, organization, or community, do you believe it is ever possible to truly understand what it feels like to live in a minority or ethnic culture?

3. Look around your campus and examine the "integration" of your institution. Are individuals of different racial, ethnic, or religious groups interacting with each other outside of classes? Why or why not?

4. Practice with "I" messages. Imagine that you are talking with someone who has really irritated you. First, write out your messages as a "you" statement. Then convert them to "I" messages, keeping in mind Ellis's "five ways to say 'I'" ideas. Be sure to state what you observe, how you feel, and what you want in your message.

EXERCISES

1. Draw a diagram of your childhood family home and designate where and when it was acceptable to eat. What rooms were off-limits? Was mealtime a family affair conducted in a dining room, or did family members scatter to various rooms? What did you learn about the importance of family from the rituals surrounding mealtime in your home?

2. Summarize a recent conflict you had with a friend or romantic partner. Using the grid summarized in Figure 8.1, identify the strategy you used within this conflict. What other strategy might you have used to manage the conflict more successfully?

3. You have been seeing an individual who is of a different race, ethnicity, or religion. You believe that this relationship has the potential to become a deeper, long-term partnership. You have not told your parents because you believe they would be very upset. What steps might you take to continue nurturing this new relationship without causing harm to your relationship with your parents?

4. Contact your local UnitedWay and identify a not-for-profit or social service agency in your community in need of volunteers. What communication skills are most critical to assisting you in your volunteer work for this agency?

KEY TERMS

Complementary relationships 175
Dialectics 175
Symmetrical relationships 175
Confirming messages 176
Defensive climate 176
Dependent relationships 176
Disconfirming messages 176
Independent relationships 176
Interdependent relationships 176
Rejection messages 176
Aggressiveness 177

Assertiveness 177
Dominate 177
Flexibility 177
Interaction 177
Nonassertiveness 177
Rigidity 177
Supportive climate 177
Gunnysacking 180
Collectivist cultures 182
Individualistic cultures 182
Conflict 185

Covert conflict 185
Overt conflict 185
Constructive conflict 187
Destructive conflict 187
Pseudoconflict 187
Collaborating style 188
Competing style 188
Accommodating style 189
Avoiding style 189
Compromising style 189
Rhetorical sensitivity 190

REFERENCES

Association of American Colleges and Universities. 2002. *Greater expectations: A new vision for learning as a nation goes to college*. Washington, DC: Association of American Colleges and Universities.

Baxter, L.A., (1990). Dialectical contradictions in relationship development. *Journal of Social and Personal Relationships* 7: 69–88,

Blake, R., and Mouton, J. 1964. *The managerial grid*. Houston: Gulf Publishing.

Gibbs, J. (1961). Supportive and defensive climates. *The Journal of Communication, 11(3)*, 141–148.

Hocker, J. L., and Wilmot, W. W. 1997. *Interpersonal conflict*. 5th ed. New York: McGraw-Hill.

Hofstede, G. 1980. Culture's consequences: International differences in work-related values. Newbury Park, CA: Sage.

Kilmann, R. H., and K. W. Thomas "Developing a Forced-Choice Measure of Conflict-Handling Behavior: The MODE Instrument," *Educational and Psychological Measurement*, Vol. 37, No. 2 (1977), 309–325.

Kuh, G. 2006. Thinking DEEPly about academic advising and student engagement. *Academic Advising Today* 29:1, 3. Retrieved June 15, 2006, from www.nacada.ksu.edu/AAT/NW29_2.pdf.

Martin, J. N., and Nakayama, T. K. 2001. *Experiencing intercultural communication: An introduction*. Mountain View, CA: Mayfield.

Morreale, S. P., Spitzberg, B. H., and Barge, J. K. 2001. *Human communication: Motivation, knowledge, & skills*. Belmont, CA: Wadsworth.

NACADA. 2004. NACADA statement of core values of academic advising. Retrieved June 15, 2006, from the

NACADA Clearinghouse of Academic Advising Resources website, www.nacada.ksu.edu/Clearinghouse/AdvisingIssues/Core-Values.htm.

Smith, L. N., and Walter, T. L. 1995. *The adult learner's guide to college success*. Belmont, CA: Wadsworth.

Ting-Toomey, S., and Oetzel, J. G. 2002. Cross-cultural face concerns and conflict styles. In *Handbook of international and intercultural communication*. 2nd ed., eds. W. B. Gudykunst and B. Moody, 143–164. Thousand Oaks, CA: Sage.

Wilmot, W. W., and Hocker, J. L. 2001. *Interpersonal conflict*. New York: Random House.

Small Group Communication

chapter outline

THE IMPORTANCE OF SMALL GROUP COMMUNICATION
Reasons to Study Small Group Communication
Advantages and Disadvantages of Group Work

WHAT IS SMALL GROUP COMMUNICATION?
A Small Number of People
A Common Purpose
A Connection with Each Other
An Influence on Each Other

SMALL GROUP COMMUNICATION AND THE INDIVIDUAL
Types of Communication Roles
Leadership in Small Groups

Effective Small Group Communication
Groupthink
Technology and Group Communication

THE INDIVIDUAL, SMALL GROUP COMMUNICATION, AND SOCIETY
Power and Group Communication
Cultural Diversity and Small Group Communication

ETHICS AND SMALL GROUP COMMUNICATION

IMPROVING YOUR SMALL GROUP COMMUNICATION SKILLS

My most interesting group experience happened last year in my Business Communication class. One of our assignments involved working in teams with students from another campus. Each team had six students (half from our campus and half from the other campus). As a group, we were assigned to select one team on a TV show (either reality or staged—for example, judges on *American Idol*, teams on *Amazing Race*, family salespeople on *American Chopper* or *Pawn Stars*). Using concepts we learned in class, we evaluated the effectiveness of the group communication on the chosen show. We had to show our analysis in a PowerPoint presentation to be posted on a course Facebook page.

It was fun because we could select a show that most of us were interested in and use creativity in our analysis and presentation. Of course, it was a challenge to work virtually without meeting face to face. But most of us worked well together; we "met" often on Facebook or on the course discussion forum, and many of us actually became friends. We completed our tasks on time, helped each other, and always knew what the other members were doing. However, there was one member who never emailed his work on time, rarely communicated with others, and in general didn't do a good, thoughtful job. He never knew what was going on because he never communicated with us. That part was frustrating even though we tried to work around him.

The group experience described by our student Sophia illustrates many of the issues we will discuss in this chapter. As she describes, group work can be productive and fun when group members are motivated and get along. However, it can be frustrating if one or more group members communicate poorly or, as in Sophia's case, fail to participate altogether. It is easy to imagine that Sophia's group presentation would have been better if the entire group had worked together as assigned.

In this chapter, we begin by discussing reasons for studying small group communication; we explain what a small group is and define small group communication. We then identify the benefits and challenges of small group work, some of which are illustrated by Sophia's experience, and discuss the various communication roles and behaviors that help make groups effective and satisfying for group members. Next, we turn to a discussion of group leadership and describe decision-making processes in a common type of group: problem-solving groups. Finally, we discuss the impact of society on small group communication, addressing the issues of power, cultural diversity, and technology in small group communication. We conclude the chapter with suggestions for how you can communicate more effectively and ethically in small groups.

Once you have read this chapter, you will be able to:

- Identify four reasons for learning about small group communication.
- Define *small group communication*.
- Identify and give an example of task, relational, and individual small group roles.
- Define group leadership and identify two reasons why small group leadership is important.
- Describe five theories of group leadership.
- Identify four characteristics of effective small group communication.
- Describe the five steps in the problem-solving agenda.
- Describe the characteristics of communication that occur during the four phases of small group decision making.
- Discuss how diversity influences small group processes.
- Give three guidelines for communicating more ethically in your small group communication.
- Discuss ways to improve your own small group communication skills.

THE IMPORTANCE OF SMALL GROUP COMMUNICATION

Small groups seem to be an integral part of life. You probably belong to a number of groups—social groups, course project groups, work teams at your job, or perhaps support or interest groups in your community. However, you might be surprised to discover that learning how to communicate better in groups can actually enhance your academic and professional achievements. Let's see why this is so.

Reasons to Study Small Group Communication

There are at least four reasons to study small group communication: small groups are a fact of life, they enhance college performance, they enhance your career success, and they can enhance your personal life.

A Fact of Life

If you have mixed feelings about working in small groups, you are not alone. In fact, a term exists, **grouphate**, which describes the distaste and aversion that some people feel toward working in groups (Keyton, Harmon & Frey, 1996). As one of our students told us, "I would rather just do the whole group project myself than try to get together with a group of students I don't know and might not trust to do a good job." A recent study found that students (in a small group communication course) who reported an active dislike for working in groups (grouphate) also reported experiencing less group cohesion, consensus, and relational satisfaction in their group work (Myers & Goodboy, 2005). Thus, it is possible that by actively disliking group work, students are negatively influencing how they experience working with a group.

Regardless of how you feel about working in groups, groups are everywhere. Most of the groups we belong to are either primary or secondary groups (Poole, 1999). **Primary groups** are those that provide us with a sense of belonging and affection, the most common being family and social groups. Social groups fill an important function for many at different phases of life, and there are as many groups as there are interests: social groups for teenage skateboard enthusiasts, young adults who love salsa dancing, older people who play bridge. The purpose of these groups is simply to socialize and enjoy each other's company.

grouphate
the distaste and aversion that people feel toward working in groups

primary groups
groups that provide members with a sense of belonging and affection

Although primary groups fulfill an essential social function in our lives, this chapter's focus is on **secondary groups**: those that meet principally to solve problems or achieve goals, such as support groups or work groups. Secondary groups can involve long-term commitments, as in the case of support groups that meet regularly for months or even years. Support groups, particularly those related to health and wellness issues, have become increasingly popular in the United States in recent years. These groups often "meet" online, instead of or as a supplement to face-to-face meetings (Eysenbach, Powell, Englesakis, Rizo, & Stern, 2004). Their purpose is to bring together people who have a problem in common so that they can provide and receive empathy and sympathy. As one support group expert says, "You're in a good support group when you feel comfortable and safe. You will feel welcome. The group leader will have materials available. It should be structured, but not so structured that you're on a time clock during discussions" ("Support Groups," n.d.). Long-term secondary groups also include standing committees in business and civic organizations. However, probably most common secondary groups are short-term project groups; these include the work groups that students belong to in various classes, as well as work groups in business organizations. Increasingly, most of these groups accomplish their work through technologies such as email, electronic bulletin boards, and chat rooms, which we'll discuss later in the chapter.

secondary groups
groups that meet principally to solve problems

Enhanced College Performance
Considerable research indicates that college students who study in small groups perform at higher intellectual levels, learn better, and have better attitudes toward subject matter than those who study alone (Allen & Plax, 2002). This is probably because studying with others allows you to encounter different interpretations and ideas. As we'll see in the next section, group work can also lead to higher quality thinking and decision making. Thus, learning how to interact more effectively in groups and seeking out learning groups to participate in can lead to enhanced college performance.

Enhanced Career Success
According to a recent *Wall Street Journal* survey, when corporate recruiters rate the most important attributes of job candidates for business jobs, "Topping the list are communication, interpersonal skills and the ability to work well in teams" (Alsop, 2003, p. 11). Whether you are in business or another profession, organizations tend to hire those who have proven they can work well with others (Hansen & Hansen, 2003; Hughes, 2003). Thus your career advancement prospects could very well depend on your success in a collaborative work environment.

Enhanced Personal Life
Most people also participate in at least some small groups outside work. For one thing, most people communicate with family and friends on a regular basis. In addition, many people serve on committees in religious or political organizations, as well as in many other kinds of nonprofit and community organizations. Increasing numbers of people join support groups in order to deal with crises, life transitions, or chronic health conditions. So learning how to communicate better in small group settings can serve you personally, academically, and professionally. Despite its prevalence and importance, group work has both advantages and disadvantages, as we will discuss in the next section.

Advantages and Disadvantages of Group Work
Working in small groups brings many advantages in addition to those already described. Research shows that groups often make higher quality decisions than do individuals. This occurs for at least two reasons. First, a group can produce more

social facilitation
the tendency for people to work harder and do better when others are around

innovative ideas than can an individual working alone. The small group discussion itself actually stimulates creativity. In fact, a research team at Northwestern University analyzed almost 20 million papers published in the past fifty years and confirmed that the most frequently cited research is published by teams, rather than single authors (Brown, 2007; Moore, 2000). This creativity may be due to the **social facilitation** aspect of group work, meaning that "the mere presence of people is arousing and enhances the performance of dominant responses" (Kent, 1994, p. 81). Scholars speculate that the social facilitation response may be innate because, ultimately, we depend on others to survive; or it may result from awareness that others can reward or punish us. In any case, research shows that people often tend to work harder and do better when others are around, particularly if others may be evaluating their performance (Gagné & Zuckerman, 1999).

Second, some evidence indicates that small group work can promote critical thinking, leading to better decisions. A group of people offers more collective information, experience, and expertise than any single person can. For example, if a group member offers an opinion or makes a claim, collectively, other group members may offer evidence that supports or refutes it; they may also contribute alternative opinions or suggestions (Propp, 1999). Because group members have to justify their opinions and judgments to other group members, each opinion is subject to careful scrutiny, which can lead members to recognize the flaws in their own and others' arguments and encourage the group to think more critically (Gokhale, 1995). However, some experts caution that critical thinking and cognitively complex ideas are not automatic consequences of small group discussion. Rather, it may take some leadership to elicit diverse ideas and to then facilitate the type of discussion described above that promotes critical analysis, interpretation, and critiquing (Bensimon & Neumann, 1994).

Of course, group work also has disadvantages. Education scholars Bensimon and Neumann (1994) identify three:

1. Group work can be time consuming. As we will show later in the chapter, effective teams need to establish trust and credibility among members and this takes time. Groups also take more time to make decisions than do individuals.

2. Groups can fall into the trap of too much closeness and too much agreement and then get distracted from the task at hand or jump to premature conclusions and make unwise decisions.

3. Groups can also silence divergent opinions, particularly those of minority group members. Sometimes group members hold to a "mythology of teamwork," believing that the very meaning of team equals consensus of thought and opinion. They then fail to use the critical thinking processes that are so important in effective decision making.

We add a fourth disadvantage: group discussion can be less than satisfying when some group members dominate or withdraw, as happened with Sophia's group in our opening vignette. Such communication behaviors can cause frustration and conflict, preventing members from working productively (Adams & Galanes, 2003) and cohesively. Given these disadvantages, one can admit that teamwork has limits.

Given that most of us need to work in small groups from time to time and that learning how to communicate better in small groups can enhance critical thinking as well as lead to academic and professional success, what do you need to know to be a successful group member? In order to answer this question we first must clarify what we mean by *small group communication*.

"To improve our legal team teamwork, only three of the parachutes will open."

TEST YOUR KNOWLEDGE

- List four reasons for studying small group communication.
- What are some major advantages and disadvantages of group work?

small group communication
communication among a small number of people who share a common purpose or goal, who feel connected to each other, and who coordinate their behavior

WHAT IS SMALL GROUP COMMUNICATION?

To acquire a clear idea of what we'll be discussing in this chapter, let's consider two types of groups: (1) a group of people waiting in line for a movie, and (2) a group of students working on a semester-long research project. The first type of group is not the focus of this chapter, while the second is. We will explain why as we articulate our definition of small group communication. We define **small group communication** as "communication among a small number of people who share a common purpose or goal, who feel connected to each other, and coordinate their behavior" (Arrow, McGrath, & Berdahl, 2000, p. 34). Let's look more closely at who the small group in this definition is.

A Small Number of People

Most experts agree that three is the fewest number of people that can constitute a small group and that five to seven people is the optimum upper limit for working groups. This general guideline may vary depending on whether the small group is working face to face or in virtual teams. In general, small groups of three (whether working in direct contact or virtually) experience better communication in terms of openness and accuracy than do larger groups of six. As group size increases, people may feel more anonymous, and discussions can become unwieldy and unfocused as members tend to break into smaller groups. However, a recent study found that although group size does decrease the quality of communication in face-to-face groups, it has less impact on groups that are working virtually (Lowry, Roberts, Romano, Cheney, & Hightower, 2006). Under this portion of our definition, people waiting in line for a movie would not likely be considered a small group since any number of people can wait for a movie.

We define small group communication as "communication among a small number of people who share a common purpose or goal, who feel connected to each other, and who coordinate their behavior."

A Common Purpose

While a group of people waiting for a movie fulfills the second requirement of our definition—they share a purpose—that purpose is rather limited. Here we focus on communication in small groups that are working toward a common purpose. Sometimes the purpose may be assigned by an instructor or employer—a semester-long course project, completing a marketing research study for a client, or working together to recommend a candidate for a job. Sometimes groups from many organizations meet to solve a specific problem, such as when a task force is assembled to study the state's disaster preparedness. Having a clear purpose or goal is important and is directly (positively) related to group productivity and increased team performance (Crown, 2007).

A Connection with Each Other

People waiting for the movie don't generally feel any sense of group connection, nor do they need to. In contrast, people in work groups need to experience a group identity and recognize their interdependence because—as we saw in Sophia's experience—when members do not feel a sense of connection, the group won't function as it should. The challenge for the small group is to find ways to create a sense of

Think about all the groups you belong to. Which could help you be more successful personally? Academically? Professionally?

group identity for all members, and communication is often the key to making this happen.

An Influence on Each Other

Members of small groups need to coordinate their behavior, and, in doing so, they may exert influence on each other. People waiting for a movie do not need to exert influence on each other, but members of a work group do. This influence can be positive or negative, and each group member contributes to the success or failure of the whole group. Most groups aren't successful without the positive contribution of all members. In Sophia's experience, the negative influence of one member detracted from the success of all.

In sum, a collection of people waiting in line for a movie rarely constitutes a "small group" because they typically don't influence one another, they don't feel connected to each other or develop a shared identity, and they share a common purpose only in the most limited way. We should note that "team" is sometimes used interchangeably with "group," but experts distinguish the two in that a work team is a special type of group: a self-managed group that works on specific tasks or projects within an organization (Engleberg & Wynn, 2010, pp. 11–12) and shares responsibility for specific outcomes for the organization (Landy & Conte, 2010, p. 587). With these features of small groups in mind, in the next section we will look at individual communication in small groups.

TEST YOUR KNOWLEDGE

■ What is a definition of small group communication?
■ How does a small group, as defined in this chapter, differ from a group of individuals waiting in line at a bank?
■ What is the difference between primary groups and secondary groups?

SMALL GROUP COMMUNICATION AND THE INDIVIDUAL

The quality of a group depends on the contributions of individual members—so much so that one reason for ineffective groups is the poor communication skills of individual members (Li, 2007; Oetzel, 2005). Lack of communication among group members can even be disastrous. Poor communication has been cited as the primary cause of several deadly airplane crashes, as Malcolm Gladwell explains in his popular book *Outliers*: "The kinds of errors that cause plane crashes are invariably errors of teamwork and communication. One pilot knows something important and somehow doesn't tell the other pilot . . . a tricky situation needs to be resolved through a complex series of steps and somehow the pilots fail to coordinate and miss one of them" (2008, p. 184). Fortunately, poor teamwork doesn't usually have such disastrous consequences; nevertheless, communication scholar Lawrence Frey (1994) points out that "communication *is* the lifeblood that flows through the veins of groups" (p. X).

To better understand communication processes in small groups, it is helpful to think of its two primary dimensions: task communication and relational communication. Task communication is the more obvious of the two. It focuses on getting the job done and solving the problem at hand; for example, requesting information or asking for clarification. Relational communication focuses on group maintenance and interpersonal relationships, such as offering encouragement or mediating disagreement. These two types of communication are thoroughly mixed during group interaction; in fact, one statement can fill both functions. When a group is getting bogged down in discussion, one member might encourage the group *and* focus on the task by saying something like, "All of these ideas show how creative we are. Which do you think would be the most useful in helping us solve our problem?"

Socializing in a group is not the same as relational communication. While effective relational communication usually facilitates task accomplishment, too much social talk can have a negative impact as it may not only reduce the time that should be used to complete the task, but also distract from the task focus that is critical for group effectiveness (Li, 2007). Effective relational communication (e.g., "It's great to hear about the awesome trips everyone took over spring break, but we should probably get back to our task if we want to finish by the end of the class period") could be key in managing excessive social talk.

To help you understand how individuals can contribute to (or detract from) the performance of task and relationship communication, we next explore the various communication roles that members of small groups perform. We then explore another important ingredient of small groups—leadership; and in so doing, we present several important theories of leadership. Finally, we'll look at principles and processes that can make small groups effective.

Types of Communication Roles

Every group member plays a variety of roles within a group. **Group roles** describe the shared expectations group members have regarding each individual's communication behavior in the group. These roles can involve task communication or relational communication, or both. When you join an established group, you learn these expectations through communication with current members. If all members are new to the group, they rely on their perceptions and beliefs, as well as their group skills and previous group experience, as they work out various role behaviors (Riddle et al., 2000).

For example, our friend Mitchell works for a software company. Although the employees of this company are scattered across the country and primarily work at home, they must work together to design software that meets a client's specific needs. Because Mitchell is the expert at writing software programs, he assumes that role. He is careful not to overstep his role, even if he feels that Giuliana, the designer, is not putting the "buttons" where he would put them or the frames where he thinks they would look best. Similarly, Mitchell and Giuliana make sure to follow the advice of Bob, the market researcher who has studied the client's market needs. In this case, each group member knows his or her roles; they have developed this understanding based on their individual and collective experiences in groups. The owner of Mitchell's company flies everyone out to Los Angeles periodically so they can work together and build relationships. Mitchell flies in from Providence, Rhode Island, while others travel from Minneapolis, Atlanta, Miami, Seattle, Phoenix, and Milwaukee. Others simply drive in from nearby Orange County, Santa Barbara, or San Diego. These face-to-face meetings build work relationships and a sense of cohesion.

Although group roles often evolve as the team works together, sometimes roles are assigned as part of a job description. For example, LaKresha, the chair of her community's Animal Welfare League, always leads the group's discussions, because this is one of her responsibilities as chair. Kristie, as secretary of the organization, always takes notes because that is her role. Effective group members contribute by filling roles that are of interest to them and compatible with their skills, but they also fill roles that the group needs at a particular time. Thus, successful small group work depends on task and relational communication, which in turn depends on individuals' effective performance of task and relational roles (Benne & Sheats, 1948). In addition, small group members may perform a third, less productive type of role, referred to as an individual role. Let's look at these three types of roles and how they contribute to, or detract from, effective group communication.

group roles
the shared expectations group members have regarding each individual's communication behavior in the group

TABLE 9.1   Small Group Task Roles

Task Role	Description	Example
Initiator–contributor	Proposes new ideas or approaches to group problem solving	"How about if we look at campus safety as issues of personal security *and* protection of private property?"
Information seeker	Asks for information or clarification	"How many instances of theft occur on our campus each year?"
Opinion seeker	Asks for opinions from others	"How do you feel about charging students a fee that would pay for extra police protection?"
Information giver	Provides facts, examples, and other relevant evidence	"My research showed that other campuses have solved similar problems by increasing numbers of campus police and improving lighting."
Opinion giver	Offers beliefs or opinions	"I'm often concerned about my personal safety when I walk to certain campus parking lots at night."
Elaborator	Explains ideas, offers examples to clarify ideas	"If the university had increased security patrols, my bike might not have been stolen last month."
Coordinator	Shows relationships among ideas presented	"Installing new light fixtures might improve personal safety and reduce thefts on campus."
Orienter	Summarizes what has been discussed and keeps group focused	"We've now discussed several aspects of personal safety; maybe it's time to turn our attention to issues of protection of private property."
Evaluator–critic	Judges evidence and conclusions of group	"I think we may be overestimating the problem of theft."
Energizer	Motivates group members to greater productivity	"Wow! We've gotten a lot accomplished this evening, and we have only have a few more points to discuss."
Procedural technician	Performs logistical tasks—distributing paper, arranging seating, etc.	"If all four of us sit on the same side of the table, we'll be able to read the diagrams without having to pass them around."
Recorder	Keeps a record of group activities and progress	"We have 10 more minutes; let's see if we can get through our agenda in time to review any questions."

SOURCE: Benne, K. D. & Sheats, P. (1948). Functional roles of group members. *Journal of Social Issues, 4*, 41–49.

Task Roles

Task roles are directly related to the accomplishment of group goals; they include behaviors such as leading the discussion and taking notes. These communication roles often involve seeking, processing, and evaluating information. A list of task roles is provided in Table 9.1.

Let's explore how task roles function within a group using a case study. Lenore and Jaime were part of a campus task force working to improve campus safety. Their small group of seven members met twice a month for several months and discussed the problem and possible solutions. During the discussions, group members filled the various task roles, depending on their particular strengths and interests and the needs of the group, changing roles as needed.

For example, Karin tended to serve as initiator-contributor, proposing new ideas and suggesting that the group look at several dimensions of the problem, such as personal security and the protection of private property. Information seekers, in particular John and Ralph, often asked for clarification of facts or information. Opinion seekers, such as Eliza and Wen Shu, asked how other group members felt about various proposals—say, the potential expense that would be incurred by implementing suggested solutions. In addition, opinion givers responded by sharing how they felt about the expense.

task roles
roles that are directly related to the accomplishment of group goals

As information givers, several members provided statistics about the security problem so that the group could know the extent of the problem. They also provided information on how other campuses had solved similar problems—by increasing numbers of campus police, installing better lighting, and having volunteer "security teams" patrol campus. Serving as elaborator, Lenore told about having her bike stolen and suggested that having an increased number of campus police might have prevented the theft. Jaime often served as coordinator and orienter, showing how various ideas related to each other, while other members filled the role of evaluator-critic, carefully evaluating various ideas. The procedural technician made sure that everyone had paper and pens, and a designated recorder took notes so that at the end of each meeting, members knew what they had covered. One member often served as the energizer, infusing interest into the group when attention and focus lagged.

Not every group has members who can fill each of these roles, and certainly not with the same level of skill. But the more effectively these roles are filled, the better the group will function and the more likely it is that goals will be met.

Relational Roles

In contrast with task roles, **relational roles** help establish a group's social atmosphere (see Table 9.2). Members who encourage others to talk or mediate disagreements are filling relational roles. Group members can fill both task and relational roles, depending on the needs of the group. For example, in Lenore and Jaime's group, one member sent out emails to get the group organized (task role), and he also sent congratulatory emails after the group did a presentation to the student governing council (relational role).

During their discussion of campus safety, some members served as encouragers (praising and accepting others' ideas). Others served as harmonizers (mediating disagreement) or compromisers (attempting to find solutions to disagreements). As communication majors, Lenore and Jaime paid close attention to how the discussion was going and, when necessary, served as gatekeepers, encouraging participation

relational roles
roles that help establish a group's social atmosphere

TABLE 9.2   Small Group Relational Roles

Role	Description	Example
Encourager	Offers praise and acceptance of others' ideas	"That's a great idea; tell us more about it."
Harmonizer	Mediates disagreement among group members	"I think you and Ron are seeing two sides of the same coin."
Compromiser	Attempts to resolve conflicts by trying to find an acceptable solution to disagreements	"I think both of you have great ideas. Let's see how we can combine them."
Gatekeeper	Encourages less talkative group members to participate	"Maria, you haven't said much about this idea. How do you feel about it?"
Expediter	Tries to limit lengthy contributions of other group members	"Martin, you've told us what you think about most of the ideas. Why don't we hear from some of the other members?"
Standard setter	Helps to set standards and goals for the group	"I think our goal should be to submit a comprehensive plan for campus safety to the dean by the end of this semester."
Group observer	Keeps records of the group's process and uses the information that is gathered to evaluate the group's procedures	"We completed a similar report last semester. Let's refer to it before we spend time working on this new one."
Follower	Goes along with the suggestions and ideas of group members; serves as an audience in group discussion and decision making	"I like that idea. That's a really good point."

SOURCE: Benne, K. D. & Sheets, P. (1948). Functional roles of group members. *Journal of Social Issues, 4,* 41–49.

individual roles
roles that focus more on individuals' own interests and needs than on those of the group

from less talkative members, or as expediters, gently limiting the contributions of more talkative members. One group member served as standard setter, periodically reminding his colleagues of the group's standards, while others served as observers, gathering information that could be used to evaluate group performance. In this group, most members served as followers from time to time, simply listening to others' contributions. Overall, the group met its goal of addressing the problems of campus security partly because members effectively filled both task and relational roles as needed.

How can you apply this information to improve your own skills as a group member? First, try to keep these roles in mind during your own group work, noting who is playing which roles and whether some essential role is missing. Once you've made this assessment you can try to fill in the missing role behaviors. For example, if a group seems "stuck" and keeps rehashing the same ideas, you might try the role of initiator-contributor or information giver. Or if one person in the group is dominating the discussion and talking constantly, you might assume the expeditor or gatekeeper role and try to balance out the contributions of the various members. Or if one group member is providing complex information that seems to confuse other group members, you might try the elaborator or coordinator roles to help synthesize and clarify the information.

Individual Roles

The **individual role** tends to be dysfunctional to the group process (See Table 9.3). Group members serving in individual roles focus more on their own interests and needs than on those of the group. Thus they tend to be uninvolved, negative, aggressive, or constantly joking. A group member who consistently assumes one or more negative individual roles can undermine the group's commitment to goals and its sense of cohesion—ultimately resulting in decreased group performance and pro-

TABLE 9.3 Small Group Individual Roles

Role	Description	Example
Aggressor	Attacks other group members, tries to take credit for someone else's contribution	"That's a stupid idea. It would never work."
Blocker	Is generally negative and stubborn for no apparent reason	"This whole task is pointless. I don't see why we have to do it."
Recognition seeker	Calls excessive attention to his/her personal achievements	"This is how we dealt with campus security when I was at Harvard."
Self-confessor	Uses the group as an audience to report non-group-related personal feelings	"I'm so upset at my boyfriend. We had a big fight last night."
Joker	Lacks involvement in the group's process, distracts others by telling stories and jokes	"Hey did you hear the one about . . .?"
Dominator	Asserts control by manipulating group members or tries to take over group; may use flattery or assertive behavior to dominate the conversation	"I know my plan will work because I was a police officer."
Help seeker	Tries to gain unwarranted sympathy from group; often expresses insecurity or feelings of low self-worth	"You probably won't like this idea either, but I think we should consider contracting out our campus security."
Special-interest pleader	Works to serve an individual need, rather than focusing on group interests	"Since I only have daycare on ednesdays, Wcan we meet on Wednesday afternoons?"

SOURCE: Benne, K. D. & Sheats, P. (1948). Functional roles of group members. *Journal of Social Issues, 4,* 41–49.

ductivity. This is why it is so important for other group members to be aware of effective task and relational behaviors and to demonstrate them (Wellen & Neale, 2006).

A common individual role that hinders effectiveness in student projects is the dominator, who insists on doing things his or her way. Another individual role is the blocker, a member who is negative for no apparent reason, as was the case for one of our students (see *It Happened to Me: Tiacko*).

It Happened to Me: Tiacko

In one of my classes, we had to complete a group project. One of our members dominated the discussion and was always very critical. No matter what contributions we made to the project, he always found a way to criticize them. Nothing was good enough for him. Fortunately, we also had some very skilled communicators in our group and they limited his impact on the group by always countering his negative remarks with more positive comments.

As illustrated by Tiacko's experience, group members can deal with critical group members by assuming a relational communication role, complimenting other group members for their ideas (i.e., encourager role), and counteracting criticism with positive feedback, such as "I have to say I thought Tanya's idea was really intriguing. Let's look at how we might implement it in our project." A single member's criticism has less force when several members note the high quality of a contribution. A gatekeeper can also deal with negativity, saying, for example, "it sounds like Denise doesn't think this is a good idea; what do the rest of you think?" Another strategy could be to assume a task role—for example, acting as an opinion seeker—to solicit other supportive opinions, contradicting the negativity of the "blocker" group member.

Another common individual role is the joker. When another member contributes, the joker always has to "one up" the comment with a joke or a story, assuming that others will be interested. This member constantly moves the group off-task. Here, a member filling the orienter role can help the group refocus on the task at hand. You may also be familiar with the self-confessor, who uses the group as his or her own personal audience; the help seeker, who seeks sympathy and expresses insecurity or feelings of low self-worth; and the special-interest pleader, who places his or her individual need or biases above the group goal or focus. These individual roles take up a lot of air time in unproductive conversation.

How can you deal with these types of roles? Perhaps the best strategies come from those relational roles that help the group refocus on the task: the gatekeeper and expeditor roles. Several task roles may also prove helpful—for example, the initiator-contributor, who may start a new line of conversation, or the orienter, who helps the group see where they are in accomplishing their task.

Any group member may serve in any of these roles at any time. In a successful group, like Jaime and Lenore's task force, members play various roles as needed, with minimal indulgence in the individual roles. Some group members play only to their strengths and consistently serve in one or two particular roles. This is fine as long as all the needed roles are being filled.

Think about group experiences you've had. Which task communication roles do you tend to fill? Which relational communication roles? Which communication roles would you like to fill? How flexible have you been in your ability to fill various task and relational roles?

Leadership in Small Groups

As a group member in community, religious, school, or social groups, you have probably noticed that most groups and organizations function better with effective leadership. In fact, a group or organization's success is often directly related to the presence of good leadership. For example, one study showed that the most important influence on worker satisfaction and productivity in organizations is the actions of the immediate supervisor (Bock, 2006). In this section, we explore why leadership is important in small groups and describe exactly what we mean by leadership.

Importance of Good Leadership

Leadership should be a concern for all of us because it is not just a quality for those with formal subordinates. Rather, leadership occurs in many forms and contexts; as one expert says, leadership can take place "during a sales call, a customer service response, a family decision or a meeting with friends" (Gollent, 2007). As we'll see later, there is often little difference between leaders and followers. We can be both leaders and followers at different times in the same group or organization; in fact, we all share in the responsibility for contributing to smooth and effective functioning of the groups we belong to (Komives, Lucas, & McMahon, 1998).

For the most part, leaders are made, not born. Good-quality leadership doesn't just happen, it involves skills that can be learned and that require practice. As we describe leadership characteristics and theories, think about the ways in which you may play leadership roles in the various groups and organizations in which you a member.

Definition of Leadership. What exactly do we mean by "leadership"? Organizational behavior scholar Richard Daft defines it as "an influence relationship among leaders and followers who intend changes and outcomes that reflect their shared purposes" (Daft, 2010, p. 4). Perhaps the most important element in this definition is the idea of an influence relationship. Influence does not just reside in one person, but rather is a process that involves relationships between leaders and followers. In fact, good leaders not only know how to set an example for others, they also know how to follow other people's good examples (Daft, 2010; Northouse, 2010; Rost, 2008).

The second element in Daft's definition of leadership also involves the intention to change; this distinguishes it from the concept of management, which is more about order and stability. In addition, Daft refers to outcomes that reflect the shared purposes of leaders and followers. An important aspect of leadership, then, is to influence others to come together around a common vision. For example, Martin Luther King, Jr., built a shared vision of a society in which people would be judged by their character, not their color; he mobilized his followers to act via nonviolent protest in realizing this vision. Similarly, today's ordinary citizens and students can rally others around a strongly held idea of change.

Effective Leadership in Small Groups

Most small groups have a leader. Some leaders are designated or appointed, whereas some emerge during group interaction. In either case, a good leader can be the key to successful communication in a small group. We will first examine the importance of communication in leadership and then identify the characteristics of a good leader.

It would be easy to assume that leaders are naturally good communicators, but communication researchers have not confirmed this (Pavitt, 1999). As one leadership expert says, "just because leaders are smart doesn't mean they communicate well. Just because a leader sounds good and has an impressive looking presentation, doesn't mean he or she communicates well. In the end, it's not what you say but what your audience hears—and, we argue, what your audience *does*—that counts" (Matha & Boehm, 2008, p. 8).

Most experts agree that communication is key to being an effective leader, regardless of the particular leadership style or the context in which one provides leadership—whether it's providing guidance on a small group project in a communication course, heading up a fund-raising project for your sorority, or leading a support group for cancer patients. According to Matha and Boehm (2008), "communication is the face of leadership" (p. 20). However, it is easy to take communication for granted and focus on other challenges in the group—a reason that many leaders fail at communication. As one leadership communication consultant puts it, "Communication requires discipline, thought, perseverance and the willingness to do it again and again" (Baldoni, 2004, p. 24).

The role of communication in leadership is not a matter of declaring a vision, giving orders, and ensuring that the vision is implemented. Instead, it depends on building trust and commitment to the vision through communication; it is ultimately about bringing people together for a common cause—in short, building relationships (Uhl-Bien, 2006). Leadership experts Robert and Janet Denhardt (2004) describe the essence of leadership as the capacity to "energize" potential followers by *connecting* with people at a personal, sometimes emotional, level so that they become engaged and active. Think about the communication that occurs in many small groups brought together to solve a problem or complete a task:

> The conversation will swirl around inconclusively for a while (sometimes a long time) until one person makes a suggestion that others pick up on and begin to act upon. People's reactions may be based on the substance of what was said or on the way in which it was presented, or most likely, some combination of both. But, in any case, we would say that where people react with energy and enthusiasm, leadership has been exercised. (Denhardt & Denhardt, 2004, p. 20)

Connecting with potential followers can also be part of a larger strategic communication plan. What is **strategic communication**? According to leadership experts Bob Matha and Macy Boehm (2008), it is communication that is *purpose directed*—it directs everyone's attention toward the leader's vision, values, and desired outcomes and motivates people to take

It Happened to Me: Martha

I've worked at several different organizations in different sectors, but I have found that the most important thing that leaders, bosses, or supervisors can do is give their subordinates a sense of empowerment. When you're given a task by your boss, you want her to trust that you'll do a good job—you want her to believe in your abilities and give you the space to succeed. I couldn't work for someone who questioned everything I did or watched my every move.

action to help achieve the vision. This means that a leader must first understand what motivates people and appeal to that, giving them the information they need to do their job, listening to them, and then getting out of their way, as exemplified by the story our student tells about her boss in *It Happened to Me: Martha*.

Effective leaders are committed to communicating willingly and consistently. Because followers are individuals with their own differences, and each leadership situation is unique, there is no one "right" way of communicating. The test of successful leadership communication is whether leaders are able to form meaningful relationships, energize their potential followers, and achieve desired results (Baldoni, 2004). As we will see, there is no one way of leading, and just as there is no one "right" way of communicating, there is no one "right" type of leadership. However, researchers have identified five theories that explain effective leaders: trait theory, functional theory, style theory, transformational leadership theory, and servant leadership theory. Let's examine them one by one.

Trait Theory

Probably the oldest theory concerning leadership in the communication field is trait theory (Stogdill, 1974). **Trait theory** suggests that leaders are born. Some of the traits associated with effective leadership are physical and include being male, tall, and good looking. For example, not since 1896 have U.S. citizens elected a president whose height was below average, and even today, people associate height with leadership ability (Judge & Cable, 2004).

Other studies have examined the relationship of leadership to personality traits. For example, leaders seem to be more extroverted, open to experience, agreeable, and conscientious than nonleaders (Judge, Bono, Ilies, & Gerhardt, 2002; Stogdill,

strategic communication
communication that is purpose directed

trait theory
leadership theory that suggests that leaders are born

1974). Moreover, they seem to be smarter than other people as measured by standard IQ tests (Judge, Colbert, & Ilies, 2004).

Despite the correlation between leaders and particular traits, one cannot ignore the role of society in forming our judgments about who we think makes a good leader. For example, early business writings suggested that the function of the business leader was to "fit in" with others in the workplace. Requirements for fitting in were shared "education, experience, age, sex, race, nationality, faith, politics, and such very specific personal traits as manners, speech, personal appearance" (Barnard, 1938, p. 224). Of course, in 1938, fitting in was only possible for White males of a certain background and education. In addition, the trait approach may reinforce the notion that only people born with certain qualities can achieve leadership, ignoring the fact that only those who have the most status and power in the society also possess these qualities.

Many examples challenge the trait approach to leadership. In recent years a number of people have developed leadership qualities out of a tragedy or a deep motivation to make the world a better place. Candy Lightner, who founded MADD (Mothers Against Drunk Driving) when her own child was killed by a drunk driver, is one of these. Judy Shepard, whose son Matthew was attacked, tortured, and left to die because he was gay, became an outspoken leader and advocate for tolerance and justice (Groutage, 1999). Neither woman was a "born leader," but both took on leadership roles when the situation demanded it.

Perhaps you know of college students who have been motivated to take on similar leadership roles. For instance, undergraduate Sindhura Citineni felt determined to make a difference when confronted by the appalling statistics of world hunger she found while researching on the Internet. Citineni negotiated with her university to sell several simple food items in the cafeteria where part of the revenue went to hunger-relief work—called Hunger Lunch. She then led a group of students who expanded that project into Nourish International, now a nonprofit organization that connects college students from universities around the United States to development projects abroad (http://nourishinternational.org). As you see, while there are some personality characteristics associated with good leadership, most experts now reject the trait theory notion that leaders are born, not made. The four following theories provide more plausible definitions and explanations of effective leadership.

Functional Theory

A second approach to analyzing leadership, the **functional (situational) theory**, stands in direct contrast to the trait approach. Unlike trait theory, which assumes leadership is innate, this theory assumes that leadership behaviors can be learned, even by group members who are not "leadership types." Functional theory assumes that whatever the group needs at a particular time can be supplied by a set of behaviors any group member can contribute (Barnlund & Haiman, 1960; Benne & Sheats, 1948; Pavitt, 1999). Thus this theory argues that the leader can change from time to time, depending on the changing needs of the group.

According to functional theory, a group does not need a designated leader; rather, any group member can serve as leader at any particular time by filling the required role. For example, the leader can fill task roles when the group needs direction, then step into relational roles when group members understand the task but need encouragement. Occasionally, no leadership is needed, such as when the short- and long-term purpose is clear and group members are working well independently.

As we noted earlier, group success does not depend on the number of task behaviors or relational behaviors that group members engage in, but rather on whether they exhibit the required role behavior when needed. For example, too much emphasis on task behaviors can be counterproductive if the task is already clearly defined and understood by all group members. Too much relational leadership is distracting if members view it as getting in the way of completing the group task (Rauch & Behling, 1984). Thus, if a group has almost completed its task and

As an undergraduate, Sindhura Citineni started a campus project to combat world hunger and later led a group of students to form Nourish International, a worldwide nonprofit organization.

functional (situational) theory
a theory that assumes leadership behaviors can be learned

discussion is going smoothly, constant encourager behavior may be distracting and unnecessary.

A related notion is **shared leadership**, also called *collaborative* or *distributed leadership*. Here the functional leadership approach is extended to an organizational level where team relationships become more of a partnership in an organization (MacNeil & McClanahan, 2005). The requirements for this kind of leadership are a balance of power where:

- all members are equal partners;
- all share a common purpose or goal;
- all share responsibility for the work of the group (take an active role and are accountable for completing their individual contribution); all have respect for the person—and skills and ideas that each brings to the team; and
- all work together in complex, real-world situations.

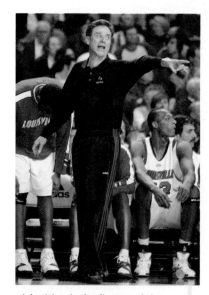

Rick Pitino is the first coach in NCAA history to lead three different basketball teams to the Final Four (Providence, Kentucky, and Louisville). As a leader, he has to make split-second decisions during basketball games.

Style Theory

A third approach to analyzing leadership asserts that a leader's manner or **style** of leading a group determines her or his success. Further, this theory describes three common styles of leadership: authoritarian, democratic, and laissez-faire.

An **authoritarian leader** takes charge and has a high level of intellect and expertise (Lewin, Lippit, & White, 1939). The authoritarian leader makes all the decisions and dictates strategies and work tasks. This type of leadership is appropriate in military, sports, or crisis situations. For example, military organizations have a highly authoritarian structure, and the chain of command must be rigorously followed. In battle, there is no time for discussion and little room for trial and error. This is also true of sports-team leadership. For example, when twenty-five seconds are left in a basketball game and the score is tied, only one person—the coach—can tell the team members how to execute the next play.

Authoritarian leadership is also appropriate in crises. Medical teams in an emergency room generally follow authoritarian leadership—one person, the doctor, directs the others in what needs to be done. This style of leadership may also be followed when time for discussion is short or when the stakes are very high (Meade, 1985).

Democratic leadership is the style we are most familiar with, and the one that seems to work best in many group situations. A **democratic leader's** style is characterized by a great deal of input from group members; the qualities of this leader are best summarized by Lao-tse (550 B.C.E.): "A good leader is one who talks little; when his work is done, his aim fulfilled, they will all say 'We did this ourselves'" (cited in Foels, Driskell, Mullen, & Salas, 2000, p. 677).

In this style, group discussion determines all policies, strategies, and division of labor. Members are free to assume a variety of roles, to contribute when appropriate, and to share leadership. Further, research supports the idea that most groups are more satisfied with a democratic leader than an authoritarian one (Foels et al., 2000; Gastil, 1994).

In contrast, some small group situations call for a **laissez-faire** style. This style is characterized by complete freedom for the group in making decisions. The leader participates minimally and may supply materials and information when asked, but she makes no attempt to evaluate or influence the discussion. The laissez-faire style may work well when little is at stake, as in some social groups like book clubs or gourmet clubs (Barge, 1989). As we can see, these three styles each have their strengths, and different situations call for different leadership styles.

Transformational Leadership Theory

A relatively new theory, **transformational leadership** theory, emphasizes the importance of relationships in leadership. The role of the transformational leader is to em-

shared (collaborative or distributed) leadership
a type of leadership style where functional leadership is extended to an organizational level; all members are equal partners and share responsibility for the work of the group

style theory
theory that asserts that a leader's manner or style determines his or her success

authoritarian leader
leader who takes charge, makes all the decisions, and dictates strategies and work tasks

democratic leader
leader whose style is characterized by considerable input from group members

laissez-faire
a leadership style characterized by complete freedom for the group in making decisions

transformational leadership
a leadership style that empowers group members to work independently from the leader by encouraging group cohesion

charismatic leadership
a leadership style in which extremely self-confident leaders inspire unusual dedication to themselves by relying upon their strong personalities and charm

power group members to work independently from the leader by encouraging collaboration between members and group cohesion. Research identifies at least four general characteristics shared by transformational leaders. First, they have high moral and ethical standards that engender high regard and loyalty from followers. Second, they have a strong vision for the future, which stimulates enthusiasm and builds confidence among followers. Third, they challenge the status quo and encourage innovation in an organization; and last, they recognize unique strengths and capabilities of followers and coach and consult with them to help them develop their full potential (Bono & Judge, 2004). While researchers have attempted to identify very specific personality traits, like agreeableness, conscientiousness, or openness, as characteristics of transformational leaders, only one quality seems to be consistent—extraversion—which includes the ability to convey positive emotions and project optimism and enthusiasm (Bono & Judge, 2004).

Transformational leaders are especially effective when they can motivate followers to perform beyond standard expectations, often by inspiring them to put the collective needs of the group above their own individual needs. When this occurs, groups are empowered, cohesive, and effective (Jung & Sosik, 2002).

A recent study of workers in European health-care facilities compared several different types of leadership (authoritarian, laissez-faire, transformational) to discover which, if any, could lead to better employee involvement and better teamwork, all of which have been shown to reduce stress levels in an often stressful work environment, such as a hospital. The study found that transformational leadership was the most effective in inspiring individual employee involvement (Savič & Pagon, 2008).

Transformational leadership is sometimes confused with **charismatic leadership**, a style proposed by scholars in political science and religious studies. Like transformational leaders, charismatic leaders have a strong belief in their vision. They are also extremely self-confident and able to inspire great dedication and loyalty in their followers. Followers of charismatic (and transformational) leaders are often willing to set high (sometimes unrealistic) objectives and often make tremendous sacrifices, ultimately achieving more than was expected or deemed possible (Rowold & Heinitz, 2007).

As you might imagine, strong communication skills are central to both charismatic and transformational leadership. In fact, a recent study confirms this, finding that both verbal and nonverbal competencies are considered essential (Levine, Muenchen & Brooks, 2010). Public speaking skills—ease and comfort when speaking, pleasant and positive vocal style, and the ability to persuade and motivate a group—were mentioned as very important. But such leaders don't succeed only by speaking; listening was also identified as an important communication skill in these leadership styles.

However, as shown in Table 9.4, there are important differences between charismatic and transformational leaders. Specifically, charismatic leaders rely upon their strong personalities and charm to create loyalty to themselves, while transformational leaders build relationships and strive to create loyalty to the group or organi-

TABLE 9.4 Transformational and Charismatic Leaders

Transformational	Charismatic
Strong Vision	Strong Vision
High Expectations for Followers	High Expectations for Followers
Builds Relationships	Relies on Strong Personality
Creates Loyalty to Organization	Creates Loyalty to Self
Enduring Inspiration	Leadership May Be Short-Lived

zation, not to the individual leader. Thus, when a transformational leader exits the group, the organization is more likely to thrive, since member commitment is to the group. When charismatic leaders leave, the group may falter because the individuals' commitment is to the leader, not to one another. And unlike transformational leaders who manage to inspire their followers for a long time, charismatic leadership may be relatively short-lived, since they may also be autocratic and self-serving, and followers may become disillusioned (Daft, 2010; Pavitt, 1999). In fact, charismatic leadership can have disastrous results: Hitler and Mussolini, for example, were charismatic leaders. While such leaders inspire trust, faith, and belief in themselves, there is no guarantee that their vision or mission will be correct, ethical, or successful.

Servant Leadership Theory

The idea of **servant leadership** was introduced to organizations through Robert Greenleaf's 1970 essay, "The Servant as Leader." The concept was further popularized by writers such as Stephen Covey, whose 1989 bestseller *The Seven Habits of Highly Effective People* made a major impact in the business world.

According to Greenleaf, a servant-leader must excel at ten characteristics. As you can see, the first ones are very specific communication skills and the rest broaden to include more general relational skills:

- awareness
- listening
- empathizing
- persuasion
- conceptualization
- foresight
- stewardship
- healing
- commitment to the growth of others
- building community

You will notice that most of these ten characteristics are communication skills. Servant leadership emphasizes collaboration, trust, and the ethical use of power. The theory proposes that at heart, the individual is a servant first and makes a conscious decision to lead in order to better serve others, not to increase his or her own power. The objective is to enhance the growth of individuals in the organization and to increase teamwork and personal involvement (Greenleaf, 1991, 2002).

Effective Small Group Communication

Now that we have described the important role of communication in effective leadership, and various theories of group leadership, we are ready to ask the question: What communication behaviors are necessary for effective small group interaction? The answer seems to be that effective groups maintain a balance of task and relational communication, and the sequence of each appears to be more important than the relative amount of each. For example, after an intense period of task talk, group members might defuse their tension with positive social, or relational, talk and then return to task talk (Pavitt, 1999).

What types of communication lead to effective sequencing of task and relational communication? And how can members best use these skills when the primary goal of a small group is to solve a particular problem? Experts find that the following four communication processes lead to task effectiveness and member satisfaction (relational effectiveness) in small groups in many situations—whether a team project

servant leadership
a leadership style that seeks to ensure that other people's highest priority needs are being served in order to increase teamwork and personal involvement

Consider the definition of leadership provided in this chapter. In which of your relationships and everyday activities do you provide leadership? In which contexts (school, home, extracurricular activities) are you most likely to provide leadership?

in a *Fortune* 500 company, a fundraising committee for a charity organization, or a small group assignment in a communication course (Oetzel, 1998, 2001, 2005).

1. *Equal participation*: All group members contribute at relatively equal levels, taking approximately the same number of turns talking. You might think that it's not important that everyone talks during a group discussion; or perhaps you yourself tend to be quiet and reserved in group meetings. However, the fact is that if everyone participates, the group can consider a wider variety of ideas, attend to more aspects of the topic, and thus make better decisions. Furthermore, group members who do not contribute feel less commitment to the group outcomes and implementation, and may ultimately sabotage the group effort (Lewis, Isbell, & Koschmann, 2010). What can you, as a group member, do to ensure that everyone participates equally? You can monitor the participation of all members, playing the expeditor role to prevent talkative or domineering members from talking too much and the gatekeeper role in drawing out those nonparticipating members. In addition, if you, as a group member, tend to be silent, consider the importance of expressing your views, even if they are primarily expressions of support and agreement.

2. *A consensus decision-making style*: Members participate in and agree with the decisions made by the group. While it is not always possible to have every group member agree with every decision, nonparticipating members and members who disagree with group decisions can have very negative impacts on group outcomes—as described above. Therefore, it is in the best interests of the group to get buy-in from as many members as possible. As a group member, you can facilitate agreement by encouraging participation of all members (described above), by showing how ideas are related (coordinator role), and by encouraging a cooperative conflict style (described below).

3. *A cooperative conflict style*: The group manages conflict by integrating all parties' interests. As we will see later, some conflict is an inevitable part of small group discussion, and when handled well, it can be productive in sharpening issues and getting out various positions. For now, let's just say that effective groups approach conflict in a cooperative rather than a competitive, divisive manner. This means that the goal in a cooperative approach is to try to turn the conflict into a mutual problem that all members can work on to their mutual benefit. A little later in the chapter, we will provide more specific strategies for dealing with group conflict in a cooperative manner.

4. *A respectful communication style*: Group members demonstrate that other members are valued and important. How is this accomplished? Most often, members show respect by communicating a sense of mutual support and acceptance. This means using the verbal and nonverbal strategies that strengthen interpersonal relationships—described in other chapters in this book. For members of a problem-solving group, it includes being specific and softening messages of criticism; and when promoting a position, it means providing evidence focused primarily on the ideas and tasks and separating the ideas from the person who puts them forward.

How can members best use these skills when the primary goal of a small group is to solve a particular problem? One of the great communication challenges for groups is to pinpoint the problem and all its possible solutions. In this section, we'll first describe a five-step agenda that problem-solving groups have found useful. Second, we'll examine how decision making occurs in small groups including a negative group process—*groupthink*. Finally, we'll describe the characteristics of discussions in small groups whose members are separated geographically and, in particular, the role technology can play in them.

Problem-Solving Agenda

A danger in problem-solving groups is jumping immediately to a solution. One useful tool for avoiding a premature and incomplete solution is to develop and follow a sequence or agenda. In fact, early research surveying hundreds of small group participants identified lack of strong procedural guidelines as one of the primary barriers to effective problem solving (Broome & Fulbright, 1995). While many agendas exist, perhaps the best known are variations of educator John Dewey's five-step procedure (Cragan & Wright, 1999, p. 97). Two points are central to using an agenda effectively, and at first they may sound contradictory. First, researchers have found that most problem-solving groups have less conflict and a more consistent focus when they follow formal procedures (Klocke, 2007). Second, successful groups do not necessarily solve all problems in strict sequential order; they may take a variety of paths (Schultz, 1999). In general, then, groups benefit from keeping the agenda in mind, but members should realize that they may have to cycle back and forth between phases before reaching a solution.

Earlier in the chapter, we discussed the example of a campus task force working to improve campus safety. Let's return to that example and see how that group might follow the five-step problem-solving agenda and the recommendations for effective communication at each step.

STEP 1. *Define and Delineate the Problem.* The first step in solving a problem is to make sure that everyone in the group understands it in the same way. After all, the problem can't be solved unless group members know what it is (and is not). On the campus security task force case study, the group members were successful in part because they agreed on the definition of the problem. They decided their problem was twofold: (1) the personal security of students in dorms and while walking on campus and (2) the protection of students' personal property. They decided that they would not address the security of classroom and office equipment because they were primarily a student group. This helped them narrow the focus and set limits for the discussion of solutions.

STEP 2. *Analyze the Problem.* In some ways, this is the most important phase of the agenda because it determines the direction of potential solutions (Hirokawa & Salazar, 1999). Group members must look at all sides of the problem. To do so, they answer questions like *Who is affected by the problem? How widespread is it?* In the case of the campus security team, the group had to gather data on the exact nature of security problems—the frequency of burglaries, rapes, assaults, and robberies on campus; where and when these incidents were occurring; and what consequences the incidents had. However, a word of caution is in order. In some cases, too much analysis can result in **analysis paralysis** and prevent a group from moving toward a solution. (Rothwell, 1995). Our campus security group, for example, could continue to gather statistics, interview people about the problem, and discuss the problem—and never move on to possible solutions.

STEP 3. *Identify Alternative Solutions.* One challenge at this stage is to avoid rushing to premature solutions; instead, the group should consider several possible solutions. One way to make sure that many solutions are considered is to **brainstorm**, generating as many ideas as possible without critiquing them. By brainstorming, the campus security group put forth a wide range of possible solutions, including putting up more lighting, increasing the number of campus police, and helping students to register their private property (bikes, computers, stereo equipment, and so on) so that stolen property could be traced. Some solutions were more unusual, including suggestions to eliminate foliage where assailants could hide, to sell wristband tracking devices to students, to place guard dogs in dormitories, and to have 24/7 volunteer security details in the dorms.

analysis paralysis
potential pitfall in small group interaction; occurs when excessive analysis prevents a group from moving toward a solution

brainstorm
to generate as many ideas as possible without critiquing them

primary tension
the uncertainty commonly felt in the beginning phase of decision making

STEP 4. *Evaluate Proposed Solutions.* Evaluating proposed solutions involves establishing evaluation criteria. The campus security task force, for example, identified three criteria for its solutions: They had to be economically feasible, logistically feasible, and likely to solve the problem of campus security. With these criteria in mind, the task force had a basis for evaluating each solution. This stage is critical, but it can be difficult. If members are tired or frustrated by all the work they've already done, they may jump to conclusions. However, if they keep to the agenda and carefully consider each alternative, they will quickly reject some solutions and find others attractive. According to one study, a strong positive relationship exists between a group's decision-making performance and members' satisfaction with alternatives chosen (Hirokawa & Salazar, 1999).

STEP 5. *Choose the Best Solution.* While this step may seem redundant, choosing the best solution(s) is not the same as evaluating all proposed solutions. Here it is especially important that everyone participates and buys into the solution, and decision-making procedures are most critical.

The problem-solving agenda is a specific format or set of guidelines that task groups can follow to ensure high-quality solutions. As groups progress through the stages, however, they will need to make multiple decisions. For example, during stage four, the evaluation stage, the group will need to decide what the appropriate criteria are for evaluating proposed solutions, whether they will evaluate all or just some of the proposed solutions, and how they will manage differences of opinion regarding the value of proposed solutions. To help you understand the decision-making process that occurs throughout the problem-solving agenda, in the next section we explore the *process* of decision making.

Decision-Making Phases

How do small groups arrive at good decisions? Are there specific communication processes that can lead to good decisions? What are some warning signs of unproductive decision-making? Is conflict a necessary part of the group decision-making process, or should it be avoided? These are questions we'll tackle in this section. As you can imagine, there is no one recipe for effective decision making. However, there are several phases that seem to represent the communication that occurs in effective problem-solving groups: orientation, conflict, emergence, and reinforcement (Bormann, 1975; Fisher, 1980; Fisher & Ellis, 1993; Wheelan, Davidson, & Tilin, 2003).

Before describing these phases, we should note that most groups do not proceed through them in an orderly, linear fashion. Rather, they may cycle through the first phase twice before moving to the next phase, or they may revert back to the conflict phase after reaching the final, emergence phase (Poole, 1983). With these thoughts in mind, let's look at the four phases individually.

PHASE 1. *Orientation.* During this phase of decision making, group members usually orient themselves to the problem and to each other (if they have just met). Uncertainty at this stage is common and is referred to as **primary tension**. For example, as a group member, you might wonder how the group is going to function. You may have questions about the rela-

It Happened to Me: Kirstin

Being the only communication major in our group, I immediately noticed some problems. The nonverbal cues from two members contradicted their verbal messages. They rolled their eyes or turned their bodies away from the group when they were asked to do a task. When someone asked what was wrong, those two replied "nothing." I knew this did not bode well for the group, so I shared some of my communication skills and knowledge. I encouraged the two nonparticipating members to contribute and asked them if anything was wrong. They told us they were worried because they'd had a bad experience in an earlier group project. We talked about how we all needed to pull together. I was kind of a cheerleader for the group. So we got through this, and the group arrived at a decision and completed the task without any major conflict.

tional aspect of the group processes: Are you going to like the other members? Will you all get along, or will you clash? In *It Happened to Me: Kirstin*, one of our students describes a relational problem that emerged at the beginning of her group project and that contributed to the tension the group felt as they began their talk. As you can see, she played an important relational role as a gatekeeper in encouraging the nonparticipating members to communicate and as a harmonizer in helping the group members work through a situation that seemed well on its way to becoming a conflict situation.

During Phase 1, you may also experience uncertainty about the task you are to undertake: Will everyone contribute equally? Will the work get done efficiently and on time?

Communication at this phase is generally polite, tentative, and focused on reducing uncertainty and ambiguity through clarification and agreement. The importance of the orientation phase is that many relational and task norms are set for the future. Fortunately for Kirstin's group, she realized the importance of group communication and got the group off to a good start.

Regardless of norms that they establish, groups often experience recurring primary tension if they meet over an extended period. For example, at the beginning of each meeting, group members may need to spend time reconnecting and reviewing their views on the task. In response, then, a group member filling the orienter role might summarize what has been accomplished at the most recent meetings, and the recorder could read back minutes or notes from the last meeting.

PHASE 2. *Conflict.* The conflict phase in decision making is characterized by **secondary (recurring) tension**. This phase usually occurs after group members become acquainted, after some norms and expectations are set, and when decision alternatives are to be addressed.

As members become more relaxed, this phase of their communication becomes more animated and honest. Members may interrupt each other, talk loudly, and try on group roles. Some may try to dominate, push their own agendas, and form coalitions in an effort to increase their influence; others may engage in side conversations as they lose their focus on the decision at hand. It is especially important at this time to follow the suggestions for effective group communication mentioned earlier: equal participation, consensus decision making, and respectful communication.

Equal participation is especially important in this phase, and the type of information contributed by members is also important. For example, recent research shows that *unique* information is more useful than *shared* information (information known by all members) in reaching high-quality decisions. That is, when group members repeat what they and every other group member knows and fail to share new information with others, they neglect to take advantage of the diverse valuable group resources (Bonito, DeCamp, & Ruppel, 2008). In order to ensure that unique information is shared, experts suggest assigning members explicit roles like "decision-maker advisor," someone who monitors and encourages information-giving (van Swol, 2009).

Of course, all groups experience some conflict, and a certain amount of conflict can be both healthy and functional because it can increase member involvement (Klocke, 2007). One productive way to handle group conflict is through using a cooperative conflict style that integrates all members' interests (Oetzl, 2005; Poole & Garner, 2006).

PHASE 3. *Emergence.* In the **emergence phase**, the group has worked through the primary and secondary tensions, and members express a cooperative attitude. In successful groups, coalitions dissipate, and group members are less tenacious about holding their positions. Comments become more favorable as members compromise to reach consensus, discuss their problem at length, consider possible alternatives, and eventually generate a group decision (Fisher, 1970, cited in Littlejohn, 2002).

secondary (recurring) tension
conflict or tension found in the second or conflict phase of the decision-making process

emergence phase
the third phase of the decision-making process; occurs when group members express a cooperative attitude

---

Did You Know?
Procedures That Help Groups Agree

List some advantages and disadvantages to each of these procedures. Do some of them promote deeper agreement than others? How so?

- *Voting:* simultaneous (raised hands, vocal), sequential (round robin), or secret (written)
- *Decision rule:* predetermined level of support needed to reach agreement (for example, two-thirds majority, simple majority, or unanimity)
- *Straw poll:* nonbinding voting method that allows the group to get a sense of members' preferences while still allowing them to change preferences
- *Concession:* agreement to eventually agree, in spite of individual preferences
- *Problem-centered leadership:* procedure in which the leader acts as facilitator, guiding group toward agreement
- *Negotiating:* reaching agreement through series of trade-offs

ADAPTED FROM: Sunwolf & Seibold, D. R. (1999). The impact of formal procedure on group processes, members, and task outcomes. In L. R. Frey, D. S. Gouran, & M. S. Poole (Eds.), *Handbook of group communication theory and research* (p. 401). Thousand Oaks, CA: Sage.

This is the longest phase. For various procedures that can help groups reach agreement, see *Did You Know? Procedures That Help Groups Agree.*

Recurring and sustained bouts of secondary tension or conflict can be problematic. In response, members can fill relational roles that promote trust (assuring members that they can rely on each other to put forward their best effort) and cohesion (expressing a desire to remain in the group). Members can also reduce tension by articulating a positive attitude or feeling about their group, the task, or other members and by emphasizing group identity and pride in the group's effort. In short, strong relational bonds within a group promote high-quality decisions and problem solving (Keyton, 1999, 2000), and groups with high trust have fewer relationship conflicts (Peterson & Behfar, 2003).

PHASE 4. *Reinforcement.* During the **reinforcement phase**, members reach consensus, the decision solidifies, and members feel a sense of accomplishment and satisfaction. If a small majority makes the decision, they spend phase four convincing other members of its value. In successful groups, members unify and stand behind the solution. Comments are almost uniformly positive.

Groupthink
Coming to a decision easily with lots of group cohesion may seem like the ideal situation, but it may actually reflect a negative group process—**groupthink**. Groupthink occurs when members arrive at a consensus before all alternatives have been realistically assessed. This occurs when group members feel a pressure to conform; they reject new information and may react negatively to individuals outside the group who volunteer information that contradicts the group decisions. In addition, the group members have an illusion of invulnerability and unanimity. These symptoms produce pressure on group members to go along with the favored group position, assuming not only that the group preferences will be successful but also just and right (Henningsen & Henningsen, 2006). This phenomenon can have disastrous consequences. The term was coined in an analysis of several foreign policy fiascoes, such as the Bay of Pigs Invasion in 1961 and the U.S. decision to invade Iraq in 2003.

reinforcement phase
the final phase of the decision-making process when group members reach consensus, and members feel a sense of accomplishment

groupthink
a negative, and potentially disastrous, group process characterized by "excessive concurrence thinking"

Another example of the disastrous consequences of groupthink was the *Challenger* space shuttle explosion seventy-three seconds into its launch on January 28, 1986. Within days, President Reagan appointed a commission of experts who discovered that the primary cause of the accident was a mechanical failure in one of the joints of the right solid rocket booster. The commission concluded that the contributing cause was a flawed decision-making process at NASA. Several NASA personnel had warned of potential problems with the launch, and numerous opportunities arose to postpone it. However, on each occasion, one or more of the following influences surfaced and reduced the chances for preventing the disaster:

- the unwillingness of individuals to step outside their roles and question those in authority;
- questionable patterns of reasoning by key managers;
- ambiguous and misleading language that minimized the perception of risk;
- failure to ask important questions relevant to the final decision.

In this case, poor communication skills and an unwillingness to explore possible problems and to risk disagreement led to an event that ultimately undermined the respect for prior achievements of the space agency (Gouran, Hirokawa, & Martz, 1986).

What causes people to engage in groupthink? One reason may be a high level of cohesiveness. Although group cohesion is usually viewed as a positive thing, too much of it can lead to premature agreement. Other reasons may be insulation—very tight boundaries that prevent a group from being open to relevant new information (Putnam & Stohl, 1996). Leadership can also promote groupthink: either very strong leadership, where one dominating person promotes only one idea; or the opposite—a lack of leadership, leaving the group without direction. Groupthink can also result from a failure to set norms for decision making or from a failure to follow a problem-solving agenda. Finally, extreme homogeneity in the backgrounds of group members may also lead to rushed solutions rather than careful examination of alternatives (Henningsen & Henningsen, 2006).

Groupthink can be prevented in several ways. For example, following an established procedure and making sure adequate time is spent in discussion before reaching a decision are both helpful. Perhaps even more important, group members should be aware of the causes and consequences of groupthink and encourage critical evaluation (at the appropriate time) of ideas to prevent premature decisions.

Technology and Group Communication

Technology is playing an increased role in group work. Some researchers assert that technology enhances positive outcomes in a diverse workforce, as communication technologies reduce the cues that often lead to stereotypes and prejudice. For example, in virtual teams, members cannot see the gender, skin color, or age of their colleagues, which may equalize contributions and facilitate discussion (Scott, 1999).

For example, Marek, one of our students, works for an international pharmaceutical company and often collaborates on projects with group members whom he has never met. Members of his team are scattered around the globe in multiple time zones. Thus he may be online with Luc in Montreal, Caroline in London, Liana in Buenos Aires, Ahmed in Riyadh, Setsuko in Osaka, and Giles in Melbourne. Although he may not have met his group members face to face, their tasks are well defined, and this enables the group to complete their

In deciding to protest a tuition increase, might groupthink lead the group to neglect to consider how the increased revenue might actually benefit students?

GSS software ensures that every group member has an equal chance to participate since anyone can submit a comment at any time.

When people work together in virtual teams, periodic face-to-face meetings are important to build trust and cohesion.

projects with few problems. Moreover, their diverse cultural backgrounds enhance the group's ideas and produce a stronger product.

Teams like these that are separated by time or distance rely on a variety of technologies. Some are immediate and synchronous, like audio and teleconferencing technologies that allow members to see and hear each other from remote locations. Another technology is Group Support Software (GSS), a computer-aided program that supports real-time discussion between members regardless of physical location; with GSS, each participant sits at a computer terminal and the discussion is facilitated by the software program. The best known of these programs is Group Decision Support Software (GDSS) (Broome & Chen, 1992).

An additional trend involves combining several technologies such as live videoconferences, text-based document sharing, audio connections, and shared whiteboards on which participants in one location can write, allowing participants in other locations to see their notes. An increasing number of people are working in virtual (or distributed) work teams; in fact, nearly two-thirds of U.S. employees have participated in virtual work (Connaughton & Shuffler, 2007). A virtual work team is a group of people identified as a team by their organization. The members are responsible for making decisions important to their organization; moreover, it may be culturally diverse, geographically dispersed, and have members who communicate electronically substantially more than they do face to face.

Virtual teams face a number of challenges, including distance, geography, and available technology (Poole & Garner, 2006). Some experts say that the communication problems between virtual team members are related to the number of time zones that separate them (Smith, 2001). If only a few time zones away, members can come to work earlier or later and still have overlapping workdays. If members are separated by many time zones, it becomes a much bigger challenge, particularly on Fridays and Mondays. However, other experts say that distance is not necessarily a big problem, and that teams find a way to work with the geographical distance and time differences (Connaughton & Shuffler, 2007). For example, one company with team members in the United States and Australia (a fifteen–time zone difference) has a policy that members from each country take turns getting up at 2 a.m. once a month for videoconferencing with members from the other country. The rest of the time, they rely on voicemail and email.

How can virtual teams work together most effectively? There seem to be two guidelines. One is to engage in frequent communication, which seems to reduce conflict and build trust, and the second is to choose the most appropriate communication technology for the task at hand (Maznevski & Chudoba, 2000; Schiller & Mandviwalla, 2007). Each technology works best in its niche. Telephone and videoconferences provide high-quality communication in real time, but when dealing with large time differences, email is probably better. Some experts suggest that face-to-face communication, particularly at the beginning of a group project, enhances the effectiveness of virtual teams (Connaughton & Shuffler, 2007).

A recent study compared the effectiveness of face-to-face and virtual student groups all working on the same task—a final class project in which students were presented with a survival scenario and required to work together to decide what they would need to survive after a plane crash in northern Canada (Li, 2007). After the task was completed, the researchers asked the students to assess their group's performance in terms of task and relational procedures (e.g., cohesion, process satisfaction, satisfaction with outcomes) as well as the quality of their communication. How satisfied were they with group cohesion? How satisfied were they with the group's processes? With its outcomes? Who do you think performed better, the virtual groups or the students who were working face to face? Not surprisingly, each type of team was effective in some ways. The virtual teams demonstrated somewhat higher quality task behaviors, but also took more time than did the face-to-face groups to complete the tasks. The face-to-face groups were better at performing relational role behaviors and completed the task more quickly, but—contrary to the researchers' expectations—did not have significantly better group outcomes. Perhaps this is because some of their relational role behaviors (e.g., too much social talk) did not actually facilitate high-quality task completion.

In sum, it seems that virtual teams—whether in business, academic, or social contexts—may be most useful for tasks that do not require quick decisions, but their work can be enhanced by frequent communication and even face-to-face meetings when possible.

TEST YOUR KNOWLEDGE

- What is the difference between task and relational role behaviors in small group communication? How are they related to each other?
- What is the definition of group leadership, and why is leadership important in small group communication?
- What are the four elements of effective small group communication?
- What are the five steps in the problem-solving agenda?
- What is groupthink? What are its causes, and what are some strategies for avoiding it?
- What is a virtual team, and in what circumstances are virtual teams most effective?

THE INDIVIDUAL, SMALL GROUP COMMUNICATION, AND SOCIETY

Small group communication, like all communication, is influenced by societal forces. The world outside influences this form of communication in two important respects: (1) the way power is used inside and outside groups, and (2) the role cultural diversity plays.

Power and Group Communication

Small groups function within the influences of the societal forces we have discussed throughout this book: political, economic, and historical. People communicating in small groups bring with them their identities and the hierarchical meanings associated with those identities (see Chapter 3). Those group members who hold the values and follow the communication rules of the dominant group in society may more easily contribute to the group and dominate it, which may cause resentment among those who feel marginalized in society generally (Oetzel, 2005).

Groups also establish a power structure. For example, a group member may be elected or appointed to lead a group, which allows that person to wield *legitimate* power (French & Raven, 1959). Much of an individual's power is derived from her

society/social status and standing. For example, when an individual is appointed to lead a group, this usually occurs because of her position within the social hierarchy of the organization.

These power arrangements come with benefits and drawbacks. On the one hand, pro-

It Happened to Me: Sarah

We had one girl in our group who was headstrong, but very nice. She wanted to do the project "her way." She insisted that we follow her suggestions. If we didn't, she refused to participate and made comments that undermined the group work. If we did listen to her, then she was sweet and cooperative, and everything went fine. Some members wanted to try to please her; others resented her manipulation, and this situation caused a lot of conflict in the group.

ductive uses of power can facilitate group processes (Sell, Lovaglia, Mannix, Samuelson, & Wilson, 2004). On the other hand, leaders or group members may turn legitimate power into *coercive* power, or threats, to get others to do what they want. For example, they may threaten to withdraw or undermine the process if group members don't do what they want, as experienced by one of our students in *It Happened to Me: Sarah*. In dealing with this dominating member, Sarah's group might have tried some relational roles such as expediter and/or harmonizer to prevent the dominator from derailing the group discussions.

The use of coercive power is usually unproductive because, as you can see in Sarah's experience, group members resent the threats and may reciprocate by using coercive power when they get the chance. Thus, too much power or a struggle for power can lead to resentment and poor decision making (Broome & Fulbright, 1995). In contrast, researchers find that groups whose members share power equally exhibit higher quality communication. When everyone participates and contributes to the discussion equally, power will more likely be distributed equally. In contrast, the unequal power of social hierarchies often occurs in the small group situation because members bring their identities and experiences to the group. Thus members' cultural identities, which fall along a power hierarchy, can impact small group work. Let's examine how this happens.

Cultural Diversity and Small Group Communication

Given the changing demographics in the United States and abroad, small groups will increasingly include members whose backgrounds differ. As we discussed in Chapter 7, cultural backgrounds influence communication patterns, and small group communication is no exception (Broome & Fulbright, 1995; Poole & Garner, 2006). For example, people from countries where a collectivistic orientation dominates may be most concerned with maintaining harmony in the group, whereas members with an individualistic orientation may be more assertive and competitive in groups (Oetzel, 1998). These differences can lead to challenges in accomplishing group goals (Crown, 2007).

How does cultural diversity affect small group processes? Does it result in poor communication, more conflict, lower productivity, and less satisfaction? Or can diverse groups, with their various viewpoints, make better, more effective, and more creative decisions?

Research indicates that even though interactions might be more complex, especially in the early stages of group work, diversity can lead to positive and productive outcomes. Let's look at how diversity influences four aspects of group communication: innovation, efficacy, group processes, and group enjoyment.

Innovation

Several researchers have found that groups with a diverse membership are more innovative than homogeneous groups (King & Anderson, 1990). In one study, ethnically diverse groups produced higher quality ideas in brainstorming tasks (McLeod, Lobel, & Cox, 1996). In a study of *Fortune* 500 teams, racially diverse groups came up with a greater number of innovative ideas than did homogeneous groups (Cady & Valentine, 1999).

This makes sense, because having different perspectives means also having a variety of information sources to apply to a problem or issue (Salazar, 1997). This variety of information broadens people's views and their ability to evaluate. So, ultimately, a diverse workforce operating in a rapidly changing world is better able to monitor, identify, and respond quickly and innovatively to external problems than a homogeneous one (Haslett & Ruebush, 1999). What are the implications for you, as a potential group/team member in professional, academic, or social settings? If the group is a diverse one, know that the potential is there for innovative work.

But also remember that for maximum innovation and effectiveness, you and other team members need to encourage equal participation.

Performance (Efficacy)

Some research studies report that diverse groups work more effectively (Bowers, Pharmer, & Salas, 2000), while other studies report the opposite (van Knippenberg, De Dreu, & Homan, 2004). This isn't surprising, given the many types of diversity and the fact that each group develops communication and processes that may help or hinder performance. Communication in diverse groups may be more challenging at the onset, so that cultural differences in attitudes and communication styles may lead to early conflict (Poole & Garner, 2006). However, if group members handle these differences well, the outcome may be as good as or better than in homogeneous groups (Larson, 2007; Oetzel, 2005; Poole & Garner, 2006).

There are several ways to accomplish this. One is by focusing the group's attention on the goal of the group, something shared by all, rather than on individual cultural differences (Crown, 2007; Poole & Garner, 2006). A second strategy is to explore commonalities among group members—for example, shared interests, activities, or experiences. In a college course, group members may discover that they are enrolled in other courses together as well or that they participate in the same extracurricular sport or social activity. In a business setting, the team members may find that they have shared professional experiences or hobbies. Some discussion of these commonalities helps solidify relationships, leading to enhanced group cohesion.

It seems that building early group cohesion in diverse groups smoothes the way to managing differences in later discussions (Bantz, 1993; Oetzel, 2005; Polzer, Milton, & Swann, 2002). As a group member, you can help a diverse group perform more productively by facilitating cohesion early on in the team effort.

Group Processes

As we discussed in Chapter 7, one way that individuals differ across cultures is in their preference for individualism or collectivism, and these preferences have an impact on **group processes**. To understand these preferences, one group of researchers used a method quite similar to the study we described above. They randomly assigned students to task groups so that each group had varying degrees of age, gender, and ethnic diversity. Their group task was a course assignment in which they analyzed conversations using various theories presented in class. The students then filled out a questionnaire measuring their communication processes in the group (e.g., participation rate, listening, respect, and conflict management), their own individualistic–collectivist tendencies, and their satisfaction with the group work (Oetzel, 1998).

Interestingly, ethnic, gender, and age diversity in this study had very little effect on the communication process, but those who preferred more interdependent or collectivistic interaction participated more and cooperated more in the group, thus having a more positive impact on group processes. Group members who convey respect and participate in a cooperative manner are also likely to put forth substantial effort toward completing a task and to encourage the contributions of others. Why? Effective communication by some may reduce isolation and encourage effort of all group members. Not surprisingly, those members who participated more were more satisfied with the group outcome.

Like the other studies, this research suggests that groups that are diverse in terms of race, ethnicity, and gender don't necessarily experience more difficult processes. Moreover, because people are diverse and different in so many ways, one can't make assumptions about any collection of individuals based on physical attributes like age, race, or gender.

Another implication is that team leaders can implement team-building exercises to increase interdependence, promote an open communication climate, and help es-

group processes
the methods, including communication, by which a group accomplishes a task

tablish group cohesion (Oetzel, 2001). This kind of leadership, as well as effective group member communication, can enhance cooperation, participation, satisfaction, and effort.

Group Enjoyment

While diverse groups may be more innovative and effective, are they more enjoyable? To explore this question, another study examined the experience of college students who worked in groups that were composed of either (1) mostly Whites or (2) mostly ethnic minorities (Asians, Asian Americans, African Americans, Hispanics, and others of mixed ethnicity). The researchers found that minorities and White students all preferred minority-dominated teams to White-dominated teams. How can one explain these findings? The researchers suggest that some level of collectivism may have been working in the minority-oriented groups, and whether or not it was, members of these groups were more attentive to relational harmony (Paletz, Peng, Erez, & Maslach, 2004).

What are the implications to be drawn from all these studies that have examined the effect of diversity on group work? First, it seems there are two types of diversity: demographic diversity (age, gender, ethnicity, and race) and deeper cultural differences in attitudes and values (individualism and collectivism preferences) that also play an important role (Crown, 2007). Some research shows that demographic differences may influence group processes early in a group's history, while value differences may have more of an impact later on (Ilgen, Hollenbeck, Johnson, & Jundt, 2005).

Second, culturally diverse groups *may* produce more innovative ideas, *may* be more enjoyable, and *can* be as productive as homogeneous groups. However, enjoyment and productivity do not occur automatically in these groups; they depend largely on the communication skills of the group members, which do not always come naturally. "Many people believe that good communication skills are 'common sense.' Contrary to expectations, the problem with common sense is that it is not all that common" (Oetzel, 2005, p. 366). Thus, leaders of culturally diverse groups need to focus on helping all team members, including reticent ones, learn to participate fully and to communicate respectfully in a way that promotes collaboration, group cohesion, and consensus building.

These findings suggest that organizations need to develop policies and programs allowing for and valuing the unique characteristics of each group (Cady & Valentine, 1999). Further, with proper education and development, diverse teams have the potential to experience higher levels of satisfaction and lower turnover (Cox, 1994, cited in Cady & Valentine, 1999). Supporting this idea is the finding that groups with high diversity but without proper education in group process are associated with high turnover and more conflict (Poole & Garner, 2006; Sargent & Sue-Chan, 2001).

To summarize, communicating in groups occurs within societal structures—whether the groups are teams working in a small business, task forces in a nonprofit organization, or small problem-solving groups in a college course. These social structures establish power relations and status hierarchies that in turn come into play in group interaction. The cultural backgrounds of group members also influence group communication, and if handled well, cultural diversity can enhance group innovation, performance, communication processes, and enjoyment. However, the bottom line is that effective group work flows from effective and ethical communication skills, the topics we turn to next.

Think about a small group experience you've had recently. What did other group members say that made you (and others) feel a part of the group? What was said that made you (and others) feel excluded from the group?

TEST YOUR KNOWLEDGE

■ What is the difference between legitimate and coercive power in small groups?

- What are some different types of cultural diversity that can be found in groups?
- Under what conditions are diverse groups more productive, innovative, and enjoyable than homogeneous groups?

ETHICS AND SMALL GROUP COMMUNICATION

Ethical communication in small groups is especially important because the success of the group and the task depend on it. One might argue that being in a group carries additional ethical responsibilities because one's individual actions can affect how people think about and react to other members of the group and their ideas. In short, in groups, you are no longer responsible only for yourself but for other members as well. Consider three types of ethical guidelines: (1) those aimed at strengthening group relationships, (2) those dealing with specific communication practices, and (3) those related to group decisions.

Relational ethics involve demonstrating commitment to the group. For example, an ethical small group member attends group meetings and participates. As we've discussed, equal participation, buy-in, and establishing trust are all important aspects of group success that cannot be achieved when members are absent from or silent in group discussions. Another relational ethic involves doing your fair share of the group work, as equal participation extends to sharing equally in the responsibilities for completing the tasks. A third ethical guideline to strengthen small group relationships is to maintain open channels of communication (maintaining contact with other group members, contacting others when needed, and responding to others in a timely manner).

In considering ethical communication practices in small groups, it might be helpful to think about the ethical guidelines discussed in Chapter 1 and consider how they might apply to a small group context. First, being truthful in your communication is particularly important, as you are making contributions that affect larger collective decisions (Hargrove, 1998). Truthfulness also includes being accurate and avoiding exaggeration. For example, if you were reporting facts about crime on campus, you would offer statistics, not just say "I found out that crime is really a huge problem." Although you should strive for accuracy and honesty in your language, there may be times when you should not say everything you know—for example, when you should respect the confidentiality of others, including group members. If your friend has been raped and you know this information might be helpful to your group discussion about campus security, you should ask for your friend's permission before divulging this information. Similarly, group members may disclose personal information in the group discussion that they may not wish repeated outside the group.

Secondly, ethical group members also work toward communicating authentically, as discussed in Chapter 1. Why is authentic communication essential? As we noted earlier, group cohesion and trust are important to the performance and success of groups. Authentic communication that is open and free from pretense and language that is inclusive and not hurtful to others go a long way in promoting the kind of group cohesion necessary for group effectiveness. Finally, as a receiver, you must listen with an open mind while also evaluating others' contributions. Doing so will enhance the quality of discussions and help prevent groupthink, in which groups jump to premature conclusions and decisions.

A third area of small group ethics concerns the collective actions of the group members. How to make ethical decisions as a group? How to act ethically as a group? For example, what if you find a project paper on the Internet that closely resembles the project you've been working on? Your group is running out of time at the end of the semester and it would be easy to copy portions of the paper, making only a few minor changes. What ethical guidelines apply here? Perhaps the ethics of fairness and taking responsibility for one's own actions apply. Submitting someone else's work instead of your own is not fair to other students in the course who did their own work, and taking responsibility for poor time management as a group is a more ethical action than using someone else's work.

TEST YOUR KNOWLEDGE

- What are three areas of ethical guidelines for small group work?
- Which guidelines do you think are most important, and why?

✖IMPROVING YOUR SMALL GROUP COMMUNICATION SKILLS

While no strategies will work in every group communication situation, two strategies can help you be more effective in many of them.

First, cultivate an interdependent or collectivist attitude, a "we" orientation instead of a "me" orientation, and work toward collaborative communication (Lewis, Isbell, & Koschmann, 2010). This means that you must sacrifice some of your personal ambition, needs, and wants in favor of the group's needs and work to ensure buy-in from all group members. People who are extremely individualistic may find this difficult. Yet those with a more collectivist attitude can influence group processes toward more effective communication, more participation, and more satisfaction of all members (Oetzel, 2005).

In addition to cultivating an interdependent attitude, striving for cohesion also is very important in successful small group relationships and task accomplishment. Cohesion occurs when team members trust each other. Further, group success depends on the participation of each member, but members are unlikely to give their best to the group if they can't trust other members to do the same. Trust is particularly important in virtual teams, where members have less face-to-face interaction that might otherwise provide important cues to the intent or attitude of fellow group members. Several strategies build trust and cohesion:

- Focus on the strengths of all group members, and recognize their contributions to group goals. Be sure to acknowledge all group achievements.
- Remind the group of common interests and background experiences. Doing this can help build cohesion, prevent unnecessary conflict, and strengthen group identity.
- Be observant and notice when a member might be feeling unappreciated or uninvolved in the group. Encourage that person to participate. People gain trust and become more trusting as they participate, especially if their participation is encouraged. Fortunately, more trust leads to more cohesion and stronger group identity, which in turn leads to better communication, more satisfaction, and more cohesion.

In sum, the effectiveness of a small group depends in large part on the communication and the relationships established among the members. As a group member, you can promote (or inhibit) the productive communication needed. We believe that using the tools discussed in this chapter will not only make your small group work more effectively but will also make it more enjoyable.

TEST YOUR KNOWLEDGE

- What are two general strategies for improving your small group communication?
- Why is cohesion so important in small group communication?
- What is a collectivist perspective, and how does it enhance small group work?

SUMMARY

Small group communication is a fact of life, and learning to be a better small group communicator can enhance your academic performance, your career achievement, and your personal success.

Small group members share a common purpose, are interdependent, and exert influence on each other. The primary benefit of small groups is that they are more productive and creative than individuals working alone. The disadvantages are that decisions take longer; groups can silence minority opinions, get distracted, and make poor decisions; and relational problems and conflicts can make the experience less than satisfying.

Communication is the "lifeblood that flows through the veins of the small group." Thirteen task and eight relational roles are required for effective group work. In effective groups, individuals fill these roles as needed at any given time during group work. Eight individual roles also exist that group members may fill; these roles, however, tend to be dysfunctional and unproductive. A group's or organization's success is often directly related to the presence of good leadership. Leadership is defined as an influence relationship among leaders and followers who intend changes and outcomes that reflect their shared purposes. Finally, five theories of leadership—trait, style, functional, transformational, and servant—explain leadership effectiveness.

The most common type of small group is the problem-solving group, which often follows a five-stage agenda: (1) defining the problem, (2) analyzing the problem, (3) identifying alternative solutions, (4) evaluating the proposed solutions, and (5) choosing the best solution. Related to the five-stage agenda are the four phases of decision making that most groups complete in every stage of the problem-solving agenda: orientation and primary tension, conflict and secondary tension, emergence, and reinforcement.

Although group cohesion is generally beneficial, too much of it can lead to groupthink.

Technology plays an increasing role in small group work, as we touched on here.

Societal forces impact small group processes via the role of power in small group work and through cultural diversity. While cultural diversity can present challenges for group processes, it can also produce innovative, efficient, and enjoyable group experiences if handled appropriately. Building cohesion and trust in early stages of group work is particularly important in diverse groups.

There are three types of ethical guidelines that should guide small group work: (1) those aimed at strengthening group relationships, (2) those dealing with specific communication practice, and (3) those related to group decisions.

Skills for achieving effective group communication include cultivating an interdependent attitude and striving for trust and cohesion.

HUMAN COMMUNICATION IN SOCIETY ONLINE

To review this chapter, use the MyCommunicationLab Web site to test your understanding of the following key terms, record your answers to the chapter review questions, and complete the suggested activities. Expand your learning and understanding of chapter concepts by completing additional activities and exercises online. Access code required. Go to www.mycommunicationlab.com for more information or to purchase standalone access.

KEY TERMS

grouphate 198
primary groups 198
secondary groups 199
social facilitation 200
small group communication 200
group roles 203
task roles 204
relational roles 205
individual roles 206
strategic communication 209

trait theory 209
functional (situational) theory 210
shared (collaborative or distributed)
    leadership 211
style theory 211
authoritarian leader 211
democratic leader 211
laissez-faire 211
transformational leadership 211
charismatic leadership 212

servant leadership 213
analysis paralysis 215
brainstorm 215
primary tension 216
secondary (recurring) tension 217
emergence phase 217
reinforcement phase 218
groupthink 218
group processes 223

APPLY WHAT YOU KNOW

1. **Group Roles Activity**
   Think of a recent group experience you've had. Look at the lists of task, relational, and individual role behaviors in Tables 9.1 through 9.3. Record all behaviors and roles that you filled. Which behaviors (if any) were missing in your group? Which other roles might you have filled?

2. **Group Problem-Solving Activity**
   This activity can be assigned either as an individual or small group exercise. Identify a problem you have encountered recently on your campus. Come up with a viable solution to this problem by following the problem-solving agenda. Which steps of the agenda were relatively easy? Which were more difficult? Why?

3. **Groupthink Exercise**
   Consider experiences you've had in group work. Answer the following questions concerning groupthink. After answering the questions, meet with several classmates and compare answers. Then, as a group, come up with suggestions for ensuring against groupthink.

- Have you ever felt so secure about a group decision that you ignored all the warning signs that the decision was wrong? Why?

- Have you ever applied undue pressure to members who disagreed in order to get them to agree with the will of the group?

- Have you ever participated in a "we-versus-they" feeling—that is, depicting those in the group who are opposed to you in simplistic, stereotyped ways?

- Have you ever served as a "mind guard"—that is, have you ever attempted to preserve your group's cohesiveness by preventing disturbing outside ideas or opinions from becoming known to other group members?

- Have you ever assumed that the silence of the other group members implied agreement?

Adapted From: Meade, L. (2003). Small group home page. *The message: A communication website.* Retrieved June 19, 2006, from http://lynn_meade.tripod.com/id62.htm

Communicating in Organizations

10

Lauro's first assignment in his organizational communication class was to list all the organizations he interacted with for one day. As he went through his day, buying a cup of coffee at Starbucks, interviewing for a job, listening to class lectures, ordering lunch at Burger King, and tutoring at a community center, he had a realization. Almost every interaction he had that day either occurred with representatives of organizations or within organizations.

We live in a society of organizations. You may not realize it, but organizations shape your life in many ways. For example, legislative bodies and law enforcement agencies implement formal codes—like traffic laws—that constrain your daily behavior. Educational institutions shape what counts as knowledge, such as when schools determine whether evolutionary theory, intelligent design, or both will be taught in science classes. In addition, religious groups influence popular moral beliefs about issues such as gay marriage or abortion rights.

Business corporations also are major players in shaping our society. Some argue that because they control vast economic resources, huge transnational corporations have become even more powerful than governments, and thus heavily influence government personnel and policy, educational content and practices, and international relations (Deetz, 1992). Corporations also affect our lifestyle desires and choices. For instance, why do consumers want and purchase new, "improved" cell phones, iPads, and computers when their current ones work perfectly well (Deetz, 1992)?

Even though organizations cast a strong influence on individuals, individuals also affect organizations—as consumers, as supporters and participants in religious and civic institutions, and as individuals who work for, or against, specific organizations. Although living in an organizational society generally means you can't escape the influence of organizations, you can have a profound effect on them, just as they do on you. Your ability to have this effect depends on your understanding of organizations and your skills communicating with and within them.

In this chapter we explain what we mean by *organizational communication* and explore the types of communication that commonly occur within organizations. First we look at how individuals communicate within organizations. Then we broaden the discussion to examine the ways society impacts the interactions between individuals and organizations as well as how organizations influence society and individuals. We wrap up this chapter with a discussion of ethical issues associated with communication in and by organizations and offer ways to improve your ability to manage conflict more effectively within organizations.

✕ Once you have read this chapter, you will be able to:

- Define organizations and explain their structures and communication functions.
- Discuss three types of communication that are integral to organizations.
- Understand the types of communication that occur among coworkers and explain their functions.
- Discuss the current social influences on organizations and organizational communication.
- Clarify the role of power in organizations and organizational communication.
- Distinguish between individual and communal perspectives on organizational ethics.
- Identify four steps involved in a strategic approach to conflict management.

THE IMPORTANCE OF ORGANIZATIONAL COMMUNICATION

Because you participate in organizations regularly, you will benefit from understanding how to communicate more effectively with and within them. Doing so will enhance your professional success, allow you to ask more informed questions about everyday organizational practices, and help you decide what organizations you wish to frequent and support.

Much of your success within organizations is connected to your communication abilities. For example, if you want an organization to hire you, you must first display good interviewing skills. If you want a promotion, it may be essential to understand your boss's goals and beliefs (Eisenberg, Monge, & Farace, 1984). And if you seek public or civic office, you must have strong public-speaking and social-influence skills to gain support from your political party and endorsements from influential organizations.

In addition to enhancing your professional success, understanding organizational communication will help you ask more informed questions about everyday organizational practices, such as how the corporation you work for determines pay raises, how a nonprofit charity you support can become a United Way organization, or how you can influence legislation in your community. Knowing what questions to ask and how to ask them will improve your ability to accomplish your goals. Finally, given that a wide variety of religious, corporate, and community organizations exist, there is a limit to how many you can support. Understanding how to question organizations and how to interpret their responses and policies can help you make informed choices regarding which ones to embrace. For example, you might decide not to purchase products or services from for-profit organizations that force their employees to work mandatory overtime at the expense of their home lives. Or you might decide that you are better off working for an organization whose goals and beliefs you support strongly, since your agreement with those goals likely will influence your career success.

In sum, organizational communication is central to a person's ability to navigate successfully the myriad legal, educational, religious, corporate, and civic organizations one confronts across a lifetime.

TEST YOUR KNOWLEDGE

- What are the benefits of studying organizational communication?

DEFINING ORGANIZATIONAL COMMUNICATION

Next, we define what we mean when we say *organization*, and we explain the role communication plays in it. As part of this definition, we focus on two aspects common to all organizing efforts: communication functions and structures. We then conclude this section by examining the role of communication in establishing organizational cultures.

Organizations from a Communication Perspective

Scholars from a variety of fields including sociology, economics, psychology, and business management are interested in understanding organizational life. However, communication scholars bring a particular focus to the study of organizations. From their perspective, communication is not just another variable of organizational life. Thus, it is not merely the oil that lubricates other parts of the machine or the glue that binds parts together. Put bluntly, without communication, they argue, there are no "parts"; there is no "machine."

Consider the organization of a college classroom, for instance. Communication scholars argue that it is in the *process of interacting* as student and teacher—giving and listening to lectures, taking and grading exams—that the meaning of these abstract roles becomes real. In this view, then, communication is the process that calls organizations into being. Thus communication scholars argue that *communication constitutes organizations*. It enables or creates them.

From this perspective, then, **organizations** are defined as the set of interactions that members of groups use to accomplish their individual and common goals (Taylor & Van Every, 1993). Two parts of this definition are important: That organizations are composed of group members' interactions, and that organizational members pursue goals.

A dyad (a pair of individuals) creates and maintains a relationship through communication; this same process occurs within organizations. As individuals in organizations maintain, or alter, their communication practices, they influence the organization itself. For example, if a new store manager is hired who encourages employees to be more courteous in their interactions with each other as well as with customers, the nature of the organization is likely to change. Employee turnover may be reduced, employees may feel more positively about their jobs and therefore work harder, and the more positive interactions with clients could increase sales. Thus, just changing an organization's communication interactions can significantly affect the organization and its members.

Individuals join organizations such as Habitat for Humanity because they can accomplish their goals more effectively if they work with others.

In addition to being composed of communication interactions, our definition indicates that organizations are purposeful. Organizations are not random groupings of people; organizational members come together to accomplish individual and collective goals. For example, organizations such as Greenpeace, Doctors without Borders, and Habitat for Humanity exist because their individual members want to make positive changes in the world, and they can do so more effectively if they work together.

Communication Function and Structure

Organizational communication is interaction that organizes purposeful groups, and it generally exhibits several properties—two of which are especially relevant here. The first we will call **function**, by which we mean the goals and effects of communication. Traditionally, scholars recognized three major functions of organizational communication (Daniels, Spiker, & Papa, 1996). **Production** refers to communication

organizations
the set of interactions that members of groups use to accomplish their individual and common goals

function
the goals and effects of communication

production
a function of organizational communication in which activity is coordinated toward accomplishing tasks

that coordinates individuals' activities so they can accomplish tasks. For example, when a manager creates a set of store opening and closing procedures, informs employees of monthly sales goals, or develops a standardized process for assembling products, she allows employees to accomplish various tasks. The **maintenance** function of organizational communication serves to maintain existing aspects of the organization. Consider, for example, awarding an employee-of-the-month plaque, conducting a performance review, and clarifying a vague set of workflow procedures—all of which enforce the status quo and keep the system running smoothly. A third function is **innovation**, which involves communication that encourages change in the organization. Examples might include suggestion boxes, restructuring and retraining, policy revisions, and the like.

You may have noticed that in the most of these examples the three traditional functions overlap considerably. Let's take performance reviews as an illustration. As a manager, you may hope to reinforce the status quo (maintenance) by providing an employee with positive feedback, but you may also hope to instigate change (innovation) in that employee's behavior by offering suggestions for improvement. Also, most performance reviews involve other goals not adequately captured by the three-function model, such as negotiating trust, flexing egos, and so forth. With closer examination, you may see that at least some of these performance-review goals are at odds with one another. In fact, most organizational communication serves multiple, even competing, functions.

The second major property of organizational communication is **structure**. Traditionally, communication structure referred to lines of communication, or a system of pathways through which messages flow. Such a conduit model of communication emphasizes *direction*: **downward communication** (with subordinates), **upward communication** (with superiors), and **horizontal communication** (with peers) (Putnam, Phillips, & Chapman, 1996). Note that direction-based metaphors presume **hierarchy**, a kind of power structure in which some members exercise authority over others. A more contemporary way to define structure is as *recurring patterns of interaction among members*. Rather than treating messages as literal objects moving through conduits, this newer definition points to communication networks that emerge among members. It recognizes that such networks may be hierarchical, though other possibilities exist.

Another important distinction exists between **formal structure** and **informal structure**. Formal structure refers to the officially designated channels of communication, whereas informal structure refers to unspoken but understood channels (Blau & Meyer, 1987; Roy, 1995). As an analogy, think of sidewalks on your campus as the official walkway (formal structure), while footprints worn in the grass represent the shortcuts and detours people take from the path they are given (informal structure). Thus, formal structures are explicit or desired patterns of interaction (that is, what the organization suggests we do). Informal structures are patterns of interaction that develop spontaneously. Most organizational members use both formal and informal structures, for example, following corporate procedures for requesting a leave of absence (formal) and asking a friend in a position of power to recommend their leave request to the boss (informal).

Of the many features of organizational communication we might choose to discuss, we highlight function and structure because they have surfaced continually in scholarly visions of organizational communication.

Organizational Culture

In addition to structure and function, each organization also develops a distinct organizational culture. **Organizational culture** refers to a pattern of shared beliefs, values, and behaviors, or "the system of meanings and behaviors that construct the reality of a social community" (Cheney, Christensen, Zorn, & Ganesh, 2004, p. 76). More informally, organizational culture can be thought of as the "personality"

maintenance
a function of organizational communication in which the stability of existing systems is preserved

innovation
a function of organizational communication by means of which systems are changed

structure
recurring patterns of interaction among organizational members

downward communication
in a traditional conduit model of communication, communication with subordinates

upward communication
in a traditional conduit model of communication, communication with superiors

horizontal communication
in a traditional conduit model of communication, communication with peers

hierarchy
a power structure in which some members exercise authority over others

formal structure
officially designated channels of communication, reflecting explicit or desired patterns of interaction

informal structure
unspoken but understood channels of communication, reflecting patterns that develop spontaneously

organizational culture
a pattern of shared beliefs, values, and behaviors

Did You Know?

Comparing Corporate Cultures

What type of organizational culture do you think you would find most compatible? Are you aware of any current organizations whose culture sounds appealing to you? How influential do you think an organization's culture is on employees' job satisfaction?

Two organizations whose culture is discussed widely in business and popular cultural media are Groupon's and Google's. Both are known for being relaxed, innovative, and creative. However, when Google attempted to buy Groupon in 2010, many experts believed the two organizations would not be a good fit for one another because of differences in their organizational cultures. Here one author describes what he sees as the differences in the cultures of Groupon and Google.

"In Groupon's bustling 1,000-person Chicago headquarters, heroes include comedy writers, improv actors, and buzzing rooms of salespeople. There is an office elaborately decorated as a bedroom for an imaginary, deranged tenant. It's hilarious, but also the kind of thing that the brains at Google probably wouldn't find funny, or support.

Why? Because Groupon is primarily a sales and writing organization, built on people-power and smiles. Google, meanwhile, is the master algorithm. Yes, there are lots of people at Google, too, including many sales and support staff. But Google's culture is dominated by engineers—the sort of high-GPA geniuses who can answer all of the brain-teaser Google interview questions—and by the image of being clean and non-evil."

FROM: Frommer, D. (2010, November 24). Here's the problem with Google buying Groupon: A clash of corporate cultures. *Business Insider Online*. Retrieved July 10, 2011, from http://www.businessinsider.com/google-groupon-culture-clash-2010-11#ixzz1RpxNlsJ9

of an organization (McNamara, 2008). As these definitions suggest, organizational cultures are created as people act and interact with one another.

Organizational cultures are composed of the languages, habits, rituals, ceremonies, stories, beliefs, attitudes, and artifacts performed by members of that group. For example, universities and colleges usually have specific names for their student unions, nicknames for buildings, rituals that occur around graduation and/or sporting events, and beliefs about what constitutes a good education. As newcomers, students, faculty, and staff become familiar with and integrated into the organization, they learn the specific languages, attitudes, stories, and so on enacted by that organization.

Organizational cultures develop as a result of organizations' attempts to integrate, or assimilate, new members and as they respond to internal and external feedback. Thus, organizational culture is not static but changes over time. The television shows *Mad Men* and *Pan Am*, for example, are engaging, in part, for their depictions of specific organizational cultures that no longer exist—an ad agency and an airline in the 1960s. As these shows reveal through their depictions of male/female work relationships and employee drinking and smoking practices, organizational culture reflects larger cultural values as well as the beliefs, attitudes, and practices of the specific organizations, which can and do change over time.

Edgar Schein (2002), a management professor, argues that to understand an organization's core values or culture, one must examine three aspects (or layers) of the organization: its artifacts, stated beliefs, and underlying assumptions. He suggests that one first examine the organization's artifacts, such as the furniture, the pictures hanging on the walls, and employees' attire as well as the organization's communication style, rituals, and stories. He points out that artifacts can be ambiguous or misleading but do portray the image or culture the organization wishes to display, which tells us something about that culture.

Secondly, he recommends that one identify the values and beliefs espoused by organizational leaders. That is, what do the leaders claim the organization stands for? These beliefs, however, may not be consistent with what the organization truly values. For example, Kenneth Lay and other executives at Enron publicly extolled their company for its strong ethical stance, though it was later proven that many executives had engaged in highly unethical behavior.

The third and final aspect one should analyze to understand an organization's culture is the underlying assumptions or beliefs that influence organizational members' behavior. One way to do this is to evaluate the values and behaviors the organization actually rewards rather than what it claims to value.

For example, a company may say it is "family friendly" and offer work–life policies designed to enhance employees' lives, but at the same time fail to promote people who refuse to work on weekends or who actually use work–life policies on maternity or paternity leave (Kirby & Krone, 2002).

Each organization develops its own culture, though some organizations may share similar cultural characteristics. One cultural characteristic that is common to a variety of organizations is gender. That is, organizational cultures often are classified as masculine or feminine based on the values they embrace. For instance, fire stations, law enforcement groups, and the military all share a "masculine culture" that values risk taking, courage, and bodily strength (Highgate & Upton, 2005; Prokokos & Padavik, 2002; Thurnell & Parker, 2008). On the other hand, "feminine cultures" such as Mary Kay Cosmetics and nursing are described as sharing a value of family-friendly policies, open communication, and participative and egalitarian decision making (Everbach, 2007).

Nonetheless, organizations can be of a similar type or serve a similar function but still have aspects of their culture that differ considerably. Thus, although they are all restaurants, the organizational cultures of McDonald's, Applebee's, and Hooters differ. If you were to assess their cultural differences as Schein suggests, you might think about who the employees are, the type of clothing employees wear, how they interact with patrons and each other, and what type of qualities are rewarded and valued. Even a brief visit to these establishments quickly reveals cultural differences.

In addition to the corporate culture, groups within organizations develop their own subcultures (Martin, 2002). In law firms, for example, support staff, law clerks, and the firm's law team likely each develop their own unique subculture. The lawyers may even develop separate subcultures—for example, one for partners and one for associates. Each group may have its own style of dress, its own values and stories, and its own practices for celebrating birthdays, promotions, or weddings. This illustration also suggests that the subcultures within such an organization likely differ in their power and interests (Howard-Grenville, 2006). Thus, they likely impact the corporate culture to varying degrees, with the more powerful groups having a stronger overall influence.

Now that you have been introduced to the basic features of organizations, in the following section we discuss how individuals become members of organizations and the important role communication serves in supervisor–subordinate and coworker relationships.

TEST YOUR KNOWLEDGE

- What is the contemporary definition for organizational structure? How does it differ from the previous description of organizational structure?
- What three aspects of the organization does Edward Schein recommend we analyze in order to understand an organization's culture?

ORGANIZATIONAL COMMUNICATION AND THE INDIVIDUAL

If you wish to influence the organizations you interact with, you need to understand some of the basic types of communication that help create organizations and organizational life. It is important to be familiar with guidelines for how you might perform these types of communication most successfully. Although all the communication skills and abilities we examine in this book will definitely make you a better communicator in organizational contexts, here we focus on three types of communication that are integral to organizations: assimilation, supervisor–subordinate communication, and coworker communication. We also explore three types of organizational dilemmas or tensions that employees must manage.

Assimilation

In the organizational context, **assimilation** refers to the communicative, behavioral, and cognitive processes that influence individuals to join, identify with, become integrated into, and (occasionally) exit an organization (Jablin & Krone, 1987). When you join an organization, you usually don't become an accepted member of the group automatically, nor do you immediately identify with the organization and its members. Instead, over time you go through a process in which you and others begin to see you as an integral and accepted part of the organization. The pledge process for sororities and fraternities is one highly ritualized form of assimilation.

Assimilation is a common experience for individuals who join any type of organization, whether it is a business, a religious group, or a social group. However, you probably most often think of assimilation as occurring when you begin a new job. Assimilation is similar to the process of cultural adaptation experienced when individuals enter a new cure, as we discussed in Chapter 7.

Organizational identification is a stage of assimilation that occurs when an employee's values overlap with the organization's values (Bullis & Tompkins, 1989). For example, Arizona Public Service (a utility company) values community involvement, encourages its employees to volunteer, and even provides time off for workers to do so. Some new hires, however, may not inherently value volunteerism, and others may even resist the corporation's attempt to influence their behavior outside work. However, over time, some of these new hires will begin to identify more strongly with the organization and its values, and their attitudes will change. Those who had not given much thought to volunteering may now see it as a corporate responsibility, and those who were opposed may come to see time off for community service as a benefit.

Of course, not every new employee experiences organizational identification. Some employees never come to accept their organization's values. For instance, if an employee values an environment in which coworkers become friends and socialize frequently, he or she likely will never identify with a highly competitive sales organization in which employees work independently and socialize only rarely. Such employees often leave their jobs, or if they remain, they never come to see themselves as part of the organization.

Over time, most people do identify with the organizations they join, and they become increasingly integrated. If they leave such organizations, they go through a process of decoupling their identities from the organization and move from being seen as insiders to once again being viewed as outsiders. This leaving

assimilation
the communicative, behavioral, and cognitive processes that influence individuals to join, identify with, become integrated into, and (occasionally) exit an organization

organizational identification
the stage of assimilation that occurs when an employee's values overlap with the organization's values

When these soldiers joined the U.S. Army, they were not immediately integrated. As they learned about the organizational culture and its rules, they became assimilated.

process can be difficult, especially if one does not have a new identity and organizational affiliation. For example, people who retire often feel sad and disconnected because they have lost an important identity.

The communication process most central to assimilation is information seeking, a reciprocal process in which individuals seek out information that helps them adapt to the organization and the organization attempts to convey information that will assist in this process. Two organizational communication scholars, Vernon Miller and Fred Jablin (1991), developed a typology of the information-seeking tactics that newcomers use to ascertain organizational roles, rules, and norms. These strategies take the same forms as other types of uncertainty-reduction techniques and include active, passive, and interactive strategies (Berger, 1979).

The passive strategies new members use include observation and surveillance. These strategies involve watching others' communication and behavior or interpreting stories about past communication and behavior so that one can infer the rules and norms of the organization. For example, if you wonder what time employees typically arrive for work, you could go to work quite early one day and observe who arrives at what time, or you might attend to stories about people who arrived consistently late to work and what happened to them.

Active strategies include overt questioning, indirect questioning, disguising conversations, and questioning third parties. In these instances, the employee tries to discern organizational expectations by acquiring information from others. For example, a new employee might directly ask a more experienced coworker, "Are we expected to stay after 5 p.m.?" or she might pose the question more indirectly by saying, "How often do most employees stay past 5 p.m.?" Or she could engage in a disguising conversation by complaining about how late she had to stay in her previous job, to see how her colleague responds. In addition, she might ask a third party (a secretary) rather than a primary source (her supervisor) whether employees at her level are expected to stay past five o'clock.

Finally, new employees seek information through the interactive strategy of "testing limits." A newcomer tests limits by seeing how far he or she can push specific boundaries. For instance, an employee might determine whether leaving at 5 p.m. is acceptable by leaving consistently at that time and then noting how people respond. (To see a different perspective on organizational assimilation, see *Alternative View: What Is a "Real Job"?*).

The communication strategies that employees use to assimilate to their workplaces often set the tone for how they will interact with the organization. Another type of communication that influences how employees' interact act at work is supervisor–subordinate communication.

Supervisor–Subordinate Communication

Supervisor–subordinate communication occurs when one person has the formal authority to regulate the behavior of another. In hierarchical organizations, virtually all employees engage in supervisor–subordinate communication, even CEOs—who must report upward to boards of directors (their supervisors) and downward to other organizational members (their subordinates).

When organizational hierarchies exist, subordinates frequently attempt to please their supervisors to keep their jobs, receive raises and promotions, or perhaps even to become supervisors themselves someday. By the same token, successful supervisors must motivate and manage their subordinates. These sets of needs and goals impact how supervisors and subordinates communicate. At times, a supervisor and subordinate's needs can be such that they communicate in ways that create misunderstandings and problems. An example of this is called semantic-information difference.

Alternative VIEW
What Is a "Real Job"?

How would you define what a "real job" is? What types of jobs do you think of as not being "real jobs"? Where have you heard the term "real job," and who taught you its meaning?

In Robin Clair's work *The Political Nature of a Colloquialism, "A Real Job": Implications for Organizational Assimilation* (1996), she critiques current models of organizational assimilation, such as Miller and Jablin's, for assuming that any work that occurs prior to or aside from working for an organization is not "real" work. To help us understand how individuals become socialized outside the context of organizations and to understand what constitutes work, she studied the popular expression "real job" by asking undergraduate students to write an essay about a time they encountered the term. She did so in order to examine what students mean by the term "real job" as well as to understand who was socializing them into a belief about what a real job looks like.

In their essays, Clair's respondents identified five dominant characteristics of a "real job":

- The money (i.e., one is well paid)
- Utilizes one's education
- Is enjoyable
- Requires 40 hours of work per week/8 hours per day
- Advancement is possible

Specific jobs that were identified as *not* being "real jobs" included serving in volunteer organizations such as the Peace Corps, working in a fast-food restaurant, working for one's family, or not making enough money to provide for a family. Overall, the respondents suggested that people with a college degree do not belong in unskilled labor positions, which for them did not constitute "real jobs."

A number of respondents did acknowledge that the concept of a "real job" was a social construction and some even rejected it. But even those who embraced jobs that others might consider not a "real job" continued to compare their own work to the societal standard and felt the need to justify their choices.

When asked who shaped their perceptions of what constitutes a real job, respondents pointed to family members (particularly fathers), friends, and coworkers. As Clair also points out, however, socialization is not a linear process in which society socializes young people into a particular belief about what constitutes a real job. Instead, she argues, those who are being socialized also serve to socialize themselves and others by the ways they talk about their own and others' employment plans and desires.

SOURCE: Clair, R. (1996). The political nature of a colloquialism, "A real job": Implications for organizational assimilation. *Communication Monographs*, 63, 249–267.

Semantic-information distance describes the gap in information and understanding between supervisors and subordinates on specific issues (Dansereau & Markham, 1987). What causes this gap? Behaviors of both subordinates and supervisors contribute, but we'll look at the subordinate side first. See *It Happened to Me: Yoshi* for an employee's view on this communication gap.

When subordinates are hesitant to communicate negative news and present information in a more positive light than is warranted, they engage in a behavior called **upward distortion** (Dansereau & Markham, 1987). Why do subordinates do this? Employees naturally edit the information they send upward because not everything is relevant to their bosses and because they can manage many issues without the supervisor's intervention. However, when workers withhold or alter important information, supervisors may be making decisions based on distorted and inadequate information. This can impair their ability to perform their own jobs successfully. For example, if an employee knows that an important production deadline is looming, he or she may be reluctant to tell the supervisor that the deadline can't be

semantic-information distance describes the gap in information and understanding between supervisors and subordinates on specific issues

upward distortion occurs when subordinates are hesitant to communicate negative news and present information to superiors in a more positive light than is warranted

met for fear of reprisals or blame. Fear of negative repercussions is probably the most important reason that employees distort information as they communicate with their supervisors.

Supervisors, too, may communicate a more positive image than they actually perceive. Why? They do so in part because they need to motivate employees and to create and maintain employee satisfaction with the organization. Employee satisfaction is central to the supervisor–subordinate relationship and, ultimately, to the supervisor's ability to influence subordinates and impact their performance. For example, employee satisfaction has been linked to decreased absenteeism and decreased turnover as well as increased productivity (Richmond, McCroskey, & Davis, 1986).

It Happened to Me: Yoshi

Upward distortion creates difficulties and makes it impossible to fix a lot of organizational problems. I usually have a conversation with my coworker about problems in our department on a weekly basis. When we talk, he blows off steam and tells me exactly what the problem is and how it can be fixed; however, when he talks to our manager, he tends to simplify the problem and makes it seem like it is due to his own shortcomings instead of the operation's. This in turn makes it almost impossible to really get the problem fixed. I think that one big cause of this upward distortion is the fact that most managers have the attitude that they don't want excuses, they just want results. How can we address a problem with our manager if he doesn't want to hear anything negative?

Although the reasons for it make intuitive sense, semantic-information distance can cause problems in supervisor–subordinate relationships. Supervisors need accurate, honest information to perform successfully. Therefore, when they become aware that employees have been distorting information, they are unlikely to trust or reward those employees. Of course, supervisors also need to communicate clearly so subordinates have the information they need to perform their jobs competently.

What can supervisors do to minimize semantic-information distance as well as increase employees' (as well as their own) satisfaction and success? As you might imagine, we suggest that they engage in effective communication. Although many communication strategies contribute to supervisor success, we highlight four: openness, supportiveness, motivation, and empowerment.

Openness occurs when communicators are willing to share their ideas and listen to others in a way that avoids conveying negative or disconfirming feedback (Cheney, 1995; Jablin, 1979). When supervisors are open, they create an environment of trust that decreases the likelihood that upward communication will be distorted.

Even though openness is a desirable characteristic, one can engage in *too much* openness. For example, if an employee is on leave to undergo rehabilitation for addiction, a supervisor typically should not share that information directly, or even indirectly, with others, as doing so would be inappropriate. In addition, sometimes supervisors need to shield their employees from information. For example, informing subordinates of a possible layoff before the decision is final could cause unnecessary stress and panic.

Supportive supervisors provide their subordinates with access to information and resources. Thus, supportive supervisors explain roles, responsibilities, and tasks to those they manage; they also take the time to answer employees' questions. Further, managers are supportive when they give their subordinates the tools, skills, education, and time they need to be successful. Overall, supervisors who help their employees solve problems, listen actively, provide feedback, and offer encouragement are not only supportive, they are successful (Whetton & Cameron, 2002).

Productive and successful supervisors are able to motivate their subordinates. Workers experience **motivation** when they feel personally invested in accomplishing a specific activity or goal (Kreps, 1991). Many U.S. American supervisors and organizations focus on creating extrinsic or external motivators, such as pay raises,

openness
a state in which communicators are willing to share their ideas as well as listen to others in a way that avoids conveying negative or disconfirming feedback

supportiveness
refers to supervisors who provide their subordinates with access to information and resources

motivation
feeling personally invested in accomplishing a specific activity or goal

bonuses, promotions, titles, and benefits. However, supervisors who can instill intrinsic motivation in their subordinates are more successful. Intrinsic motivation occurs when people experience satisfaction in performing their jobs well, find their jobs to be enriching, and are, therefore, dedicated to their organizations or professions (Cheney et al., 2004).

Supervisors can create intrinsic motivation by setting clear and specific goals that are challenging but attainable and by engaging workers in the creation of those goals. In addition, they need to provide frequent and specific feedback, including praise, recognition, and corrections. Positive feedback is especially important because it encourages job satisfaction, organizational identification, and commitment (Larson, 1989). Finally, intrinsic motivation thrives in a positive work environment that stresses camaraderie or social relationships.

Positive communication between supervisors and their subordinates is characterized by openness and the empowerment of subordinates.

Empowerment, the fourth characteristic that improves communication, relates to the supervisor's ability to increase employees' feelings of self-efficacy. He or she does this by instilling the feeling that the subordinate is capable of performing the job and has the authority to decide how to perform it well (Chiles & Zorn, 1995). In general, supervisors who empower their subordinates function more like coaches than traditional managers. They encourage employees to be involved in decision making, to take responsibility for their tasks, and to provide suggestions for improving their own and the organization's performance. Employees who feel empowered are more likely to develop intrinsic motivation and to communicate openly with their supervisors.

Communication is also central to subordinates' success on the job. Subordinates who get along with their supervisors are much more likely to be satisfied and successful. Consequently, subordinates use a variety of means to manage and maintain the quality of their relationships with their supervisors. Studies of subordinate communication tactics determined that employees who use three specific upward communication tactics—ingratiation, assertiveness, and rationality—were most likely to positively affect their manager's perceptions of them (Dockery & Steiner, 1990; Wayne & Ferris, 1990).

Ingratiation refers to behavior and communication designed to increase liking. It includes friendliness and making one's boss feel important. Of course, one can be too ingratiating and come off as being insincere, but genuine respect and rapport can be effective. **Assertive** subordinates who can express their opinions forcefully without offending or challenging their bosses also tend to engender liking and approval. In addition, subordinates who can argue **rationally**—meaning that they communicate with their bosses through reasoning, bargaining, coalition building, and assertiveness—are often adept at managing their supervisors. Finally, employees who understand their bosses' professional and personal goals as well as their strengths and weaknesses, and who can adapt to their preferred communication styles, can create positive working relationships.

empowerment
employees' feelings of self-efficacy

ingratiation
behavior and communication designed to increase liking

assertiveness
expressing one's opinions forcefully without offending others

rationality
the ability to communicate through reasoning, bargaining, coalition building, and assertiveness

Communicating Coworkers

Along with assimilation and supervisor–subordinate communication, communication with coworkers is fundamental to organizations and their employees. Sometimes the communication that occurs among coworkers or peers is described as *horizontal*, because it is directed neither upward (to superiors) nor downward (to subordinates). No matter how they are described, workplace relationships are distinctive interpersonal relationships that influence both the individuals within them and the organization as a whole (Sias, 2005).

Employees become friends with their colleagues for many of the same reasons they develop other types of interpersonal relationships—proximity, attraction, and similarity. Some people, especially those who live alone, may spend more time with their colleagues than they do with anyone else. Even people who live with others may spend as much—or more—time with coworkers as they do with their families or housemates. However, unlike other interpersonal relationships, friendship development at work is affected by an additional dimension—how supervisors treat individual employees. If supervisors are perceived to treat some employees more favorably and this treatment is perceived as undeserved, coworkers may dislike and distrust favored employees. On the other hand, if a manager is seen as treating a subordinate more negatively than others and the treatment is perceived as unwarranted, it can increase employee interaction and cohesiveness (Graen & Graen, 2006; Sias & Jablin, 1995).

Coworkers in organizations engage in both formal–professional and informal–personal interactions. The formal–professional category includes communication about tasks, solving problems, making plans, and influencing one another's beliefs and decisions (Kram & Isabella, 1985). In addition, coworkers engage in considerable informal, or personal, interaction. In fact, adults draw many of their friends from the pool of people at work, and approximately 50 percent of employees state that they have engaged in a romance at work (Vault, 2003). Coworkers also can serve as an important source of emotional and social support (Rawlins, 1994).

The professional and the personal aspects of coworker communication and relationships are not distinct. Rather, professional interactions influence coworkers' personal relationships, and vice versa. Sias and Cahill (1998) found that more talk about more topics among coworkers not only resulted from increased closeness in their relationships but also contributed to it. Thus, coworkers who also are friends tend to communicate more intimately and about more topics, both professionally and personally, than those who are not (Sias, Smith, & Avdeyeva, 2003). They also tend to be both less careful and more open in their communication with each other (Sias & Jablin, 1995). Therefore, they are likely to provide increased and more useful task-related information to each other.

As you might expect, being isolated from employee networks can result in isolation from quality work-related information (in addition to loneliness) and cause one to be at an information disadvantage relative to one's colleagues (Sias, 2005). Research indicates that this information disadvantage has important consequences. Poor coworker communication and lack of access to information have been found to predict lower job satisfaction and commitment.

The presence of friendly relationships among coworkers has positive consequences for individuals and organizations. When employees feel connected to their colleagues, they provide each other with support and assistance that can increase their success. Such relationships also intensify workers' loyalty to the company and increase job satisfaction and organizational identification, which can help minimize job turnover (Kram & Isabella, 1985).

Despite the ease, attractiveness, and advantages of forming close relationships at work, such relationships can require careful navigation. Friendship, by its nature, is egalitarian, but power differences often occur among coworkers. Even employees at the same level in the organization may have different levels of informal power, and the situation can become increasingly problematic if one of them receives a promotion and thereby acquires greater formal power in the organization. In addition, coworkers may find themselves torn between their loyalty to the organization and their loyalty to a friend. For example, how should one respond if a friend engages in unethical behavior at work, decides to become a whistleblower, or quits in protest over a denied promotion? It can be difficult for individuals to decide how to respond in a way that protects their own as well as their friends' interests. Finally, it can be more difficult to be objective with a friend, to withhold confidential information, and to provide honest feedback.

In addition, other employees can develop negative perceptions and interpretations of the friendships and courtship relationships of their colleagues. Coworkers may question the motives of the partners, may believe that the individuals involved are conspiring to affect corporate policy, or may perceive that the relationship partners treat others unfairly in comparison. For instance, if two salespeople become close, their coworkers may perceive that they are sharing information or client lists that permit them to be more successful than those outside the relationship. In addition, because of the potential for trouble and bad feelings, some organizations have explicit policies that discourage "affectional" relationships, which may include friendships but most certainly include romance. For suggestions on how supervisors can encourage good coworker communication, see *Did You Know? Encouraging Effective Coworker Communication*.

Did You Know?
Encouraging Effective Coworker Communication

How do you communicate with your coworkers? How effective are you when you communicate with them? Which of the following strategies would help you be more effective?

- **Communicate your vision.** If you're the team leader, your job is really about communicating clearly. By choosing words that connect with different learning styles and personality types, you can paint a picture of the end goal everyone can get excited about.

- **Make sure your expectations are clear.** Team members won't be able to be successful if they don't know what's expected of them. Make sure that everyone knows what they need to do to be successful—this creates a collaborative environment that is more open and trusting and ultimately more supportive and productive.

- **Be definitive about a time frame.** Let others know specifically when you need what you're requesting of them. If the time frame spans a long period, establish checkpoints (one week, two weeks) where you can check in to find out how things are going. This keeps a big project from going horribly wrong when the writers have been holed up in an office for three weeks playing video games and suffering from writers' block.

- **Invite feedback and questions.** The "open door" policy may be a myth in some offices, but listening nondefensively—to questions, concerns, and criticism—is a huge part of building honest communication with others. This shows that everyone has a voice in the success of the project and helps create the openness for creativity and trust to emerge.

- **Encourage and support good communication.** To show others that improving teamwork is important, you might host a series of lunches, invite a speaker in to give an afternoon seminar on communications skills, or hire a consultant to help with team relations. The most important way to encourage good communication is to model it yourself—to make mistakes, to honestly explain what happened, and to try again, all in the name of moving toward better communication with your peers.

FROM: Murray K. (2005, February). Improve staff communications. Retrieved September 5, 2005, from www.revisionsplus.com/February article.doc. Reprinted by permission of the author.

Organizational Dilemmas

Although organizations can provide many benefits to an individual, including status, money, a sense of belonging, and even a significant part of one's identity, they also can create physical and psychological distress. Thus in addition to being proficient at the three key types of organizational communication, members of organizations may have to communicatively manage and respond to three types of organizational dilemmas: emotion labor, stress and burnout, and work–life conflict.

Emotion Labor

As we discussed earlier, employees learn a variety of norms for organizational behavior during assimilation. Some of these norms pertain to emotion display rules (Scott & Myers, 2005). Emotion display rules are the explicit or implicit rules that organizations have for what emotions can be appropriately displayed and how those emotions should be communicated. For example, firefighters learn early in the assimilation process that they should not express strong negative emotions such as fear, disgust, and panic (Scott & Myers, 2005). Instead, they learn to speak in calm tones, to offer verbal assurances, and to suppress any comments that might distress the public. Similarly, the employees at the local grocery store have learned to show cheerfulness and helpfulness toward customers, even if they actually feel irritation, anger, or frustration. Consequently, no matter how their day is going, they greet customers with a friendly hello, offer assistance, and wish customers a good day as they leave the store.

It Happened to Me: Sonya

For a year, I worked on a cruise line as an assistant cruise director. My job was to organize activities and help entertain the passengers. I helped with bingo games, organized costume contests, and participated in various games with the passengers. In addition, I was expected to dance with the passengers in the evening at the nightclub. Unfortunately, I often had to deal with passengers who had had a few drinks and wanted to "get friendly" or invite me back to their rooms. No matter how the passenger behaved, I was expected to be polite, pleasant, and friendly without, of course, ever actually becoming involved with one! It was really difficult sometimes. I would be so angry, upset, or embarrassed at how a passenger behaved, but I could never show it. This is one of the major reasons I did not sign up again after my first year on the ship.

When the organization expects or requires workers to display particular feelings, employees are engaging in emotion labor (Hochschild, 1983). Typically, organizations ask employees to alter their emotional behavior in three ways. First, they may ask employees to heighten or increase their expressions of joy (i.e., cruise ship and other tourism employees), to appear mean or indifferent (debt collectors and law officers, on occasion), or to convey "a vaguely pleasant professional demeanor" (nurses and receptionists) (Cheney et al., 2004, p. 68). (For one student's experience with emotion labor, see *It Happened to Me: Sonya*.)

Some scholars believe that performing emotion labor benefits employees. They argue that when workers perform emotions they do not actually feel, they can better cope with stress (Conrad & Witte, 1994), and they are more able to interact in emotionally satisfying ways with their clients (Shuler & Sypher, 2000). These scholars suggest that social workers, emergency medical personnel, and other employees in the social services find their work easier and more meaningful when they perform emotion labor.

Others believe it can be harmful (Tracy, 2000; Waldron, 1994), especially when it is required and when it benefits the organization but not the employee. For example, Sarah Tracy (2005), an organizational communication scholar, studied correctional officers' emotion labor and its consequences. She found that the officers often were expected to manage contradictory emotional displays—for example, showing respect for inmates but not trusting them, or nurturing them while also being tough.

She discovered that performing these contradictory emotions led some of the officers to experience withdrawal, paranoia, stress, and burnout. Thus, consistently having to perform emotion labor, especially when the requirements are ambiguous and contradictory, may cause psychological and physical harm to some workers.

Stress and Burnout

As you just read, correctional officers often experience stress and burnout. But they are not the only employees who suffer in this way; stress and burnout have become widespread in the American workplace, and the terms have become common in everyday speech. However, burnout includes a very specific set of characteristics, including exhaustion, cynicism, and ineffectiveness (Maslach & Leiter, 1997; Maslach, 2003). It is a chronic condition that results from the accumulation of daily stress, where stress is defined as a common response to important and consequential demands, constraints, or opportunities to which one feels unable to respond (McGrath, 1976).

Exhaustion, which is a core characteristic of burnout, can include physical, emotional, or mental exhaustion. It expresses itself as physical fatigue, loss of affect (or emotion), and an aversion to one's job. Employees who are emotionally exhausted may try to reduce the emotional stress of working with others by detaching from them, a behavior called depersonalization, which is related to the second characteristic of burnout—cynicism. Cynicism is manifested as an indifferent attitude toward others. A person with a cynical attitude may view others as objects or numbers and may also express hostility and harsh criticism toward them. Employees might feel ineffective, the third characteristic of burnout, which occurs when workers negatively evaluate their own performance. Ineffectiveness may result in absenteeism, decreased effort, and withdrawal (Richardsen & Martinussen, 2004).

Burnout arises due to a combination of personality factors (for example, how well one manages ambiguity and stress) and organizational stressors. Organizational stressors are aspects of one's job that create strain. Some of the more significant organizational stressors include work overload; confusion, conflict, and ambiguity related to job roles; being undermined by a supervisor (Westman & Etzion, 2005); and low levels of social support (Koniarek & Dudek, 1996).

Workload refers to the amount of work an individual is expected to perform. Work overload occurs when employees feel they have more work than they can accomplish, and this is a major contributor to feelings of exhaustion. Despite expectations that technology, and especially computer technology, would lessen the burden for workers in the United States, people today are working longer hours and dealing with heavier workloads than before the advent of these technologies. In addition, workers frequently find that now they are never "away" from the job, since they are instantly and constantly available through cell phones, BlackBerries, and pagers. The resulting work pressures are having an increasingly negative effect on individuals, families, and organizations (Glisson & Durick, 1988).

Work overload also is related to our second major organizational stressor—role confusion, conflict, and ambiguity. Role ambiguity occurs when employees do not understand what is expected of them. This is most likely to occur when one begins a new job, but it also occurs when organizations undergo change (Chambers, Moore, & Bachtel, 1998). Because today's workers are faced with continual change due to budget cuts, reorganizations, and new technologies, they frequently experience role ambiguity (Chambers et al., 1998).

Job stress tends to be high for health care workers because of the highly consequential demands inherent in the job and the fact that, in some cases, even the most highly skilled professionals are unable to save a patient's life.

burnout
a chronic condition that results from the accumulation of daily stress, which manifests itself in a very specific set of characteristics, including exhaustion, cynicism, and ineffectiveness

To give some perspective on the role ambiguity and confusion play as work stressors, consider this. As recently as twenty years ago, newly hired engineers primarily needed to communicate with other engineers, most of whom were born in the United States and were native speakers of English. Since that time, however, U.S. companies have hired more engineers from other countries and have expanded their operations around the world. Consequently, many engineers now need to communicate with and supervise others who do not share their native culture and background. They have been required to develop intercultural communication skills they never expected would be necessary and to become conversant with cultures outside the United States. Some long-term employees are unsure of their ability to respond appropriately. Employees in many industries face similar challenges as organizations respond to changing market conditions, globalization, and new technology. Unfortunately, uncertainty about one's job duties and one's ability to perform those duties creates considerable stress for workers.

Role conflict arises when employees find it difficult to meet conflicting or incompatible job demands (Igbaria & Guimaraes, 1993). For example, the correctional officers we mentioned in our discussion of emotion labor experienced considerable role conflict. On the one hand, they were expected to act like social workers whose job it was to treat prisoners with respect, to nurture them, and to facilitate their well-being and rehabilitation; on the other hand, they were expected to function as paramilitary agents whose job it was to maintain order and safety, to mistrust the prisoners, and to be tough. Similarly, when managers are told to treat their employees fairly and humanely but also to meet tight production deadlines, they suffer from role conflict. Research indicates that being asked to perform such incompatible tasks on the job gives rise to considerable stress and ill effects (Rizzo, House, & Lirtzman, 1970). For example, role conflict and ambiguity can cycle into burnout, leading workers to experience feelings of ineffectiveness in their jobs.

To complete our discussion of organizational stressors and burnout, we focus squarely on communication issues. When employees feel undermined by their supervisors, whether through having information withheld, being denied the resources they need to do their jobs, or being treated unfairly, they are more likely to experience cynicism and a lack of efficacy (Maslach & Leiter, 1997). They may feel they cannot accomplish their work because they lack the resources to do so, and they may believe that even if they do perform well, they will not be rewarded.

Communication with coworkers can contribute to burnout when one's colleagues are unable to provide the social support one needs to cope with organizational stressors. Feelings of burnout then may spread from one employee to his or her colleagues. This fact, combined with the faster pace of most organizations, can lead to a breakdown of community within the organization and disconnect coworkers from one another (Maslach & Leiter, 1997).

Interestingly, research has established that communication itself can be an important moderator of employee burnout. Findings show that supervisor communication that includes active listening, effective feedback, participative decision making, and supportiveness can decrease the severity of subordinate burnout (Casey, 1998; Golembiewski, Boudreau, Sun, & Luo, 1998). Similarly, communication with coworkers that conveys warmth and support and reaffirms the meaning of one's work can help employees cope with burnout (Casey, 1998).

If you would like to see if you are experiencing burnout, go to www.mindtools .com/pages/article/newTCS_08.htm and take the Burnout Self-Test

Work–Life Conflict

A third type of organizational dilemma that workers face is work–life conflict, defined by the difficulties individuals and families face as they try to balance job and home responsibilities. Since the 1990s, work–family balance has become an issue of concern and another type of role conflict, especially for dual-career couples (Kirby & Krone, 2002). As more women have entered the workforce and more families have become reliant on two incomes, people are finding it difficult to manage their competing demands. The pervasiveness of communication technologies such as email, cell phones, instant messaging, and pagers has made it difficult for some workers to ever get away from work and focus on the other aspects of their lives.

In response to these concerns, organizations began to develop family-friendly policies, such as flextime, family leave, and dependent-care benefits (Morgan & Milliken, 1992). However, studies have shown that many employees do not take advantage of these benefits (Kirby & Krone, 2002; Rapoport & Bailyn, 1996). The reality is researchers have found that some employees are discouraged from taking advantage of these benefits or are not informed about their existence. For example, managers may indirectly communicate that employees should not use the available benefits because it causes problems for them, their departments, and the organization (Rapoport & Bailyn, 1996).

A study of Corning, Xerox, and Tandem Computers determined that employees who used such benefits experienced negative career consequences (Rapoport & Bailyn, 1996). Once employees discovered that their coworkers suffered when they used the company's family leave or flextime benefits, they simply stopped requesting them. Kirby and Krone (2002) conducted another study whose title aptly describes this organizational policy: "The Policy Exists, But You Can't Really Use It." The irony is that some organizations receive credit for being family friendly while not having to actually implement their policies (Jenner, 1994; Solomon, 1994). However, when workers are not able to balance the many demands in their lives, they, their families, and society at large suffer the consequences.

Although both men and women must manage work–life issues, much of the research on work–life conflict has focused on the difficulties working women face as they try to manage paid and unpaid labor. Men are perceived to work as hard or harder at paid work than women, but research indicates that women contribute at least twice as much unpaid labor to their families, resulting in high levels of work–life conflict (Alberts, Tracy, & Trethewey, 2011). To read another perspective on how the experience of work–life conflict differs between women and men, see *Alternative View: Men Now Have More Work–Life Conflict than Women*.

To summarize, communication is central to an individual's life within an organization, and individuals face many communication-related issues as they navigate organizations. Such challenges involve assimilation as well as communication with supervisors, subordinates, and coworkers. Inevitably, conflicts arise, as do a variety of potential organizational dilemmas, including emotion labor, stress and burnout, and work–life conflict. Thus, successful individuals are those who are able to communicate effectively as they negotiate the challenges, conflicts, and dilemmas of organizational life. However, as you've seen throughout this book, if you only consider individual forces or factors, you can't understand the whole picture. Individuals and organizations both are subject to numerous societal forces, the topic we turn to next.

TEST YOUR KNOWLEDGE

- What is organizational identification? How is it related to the process of assimilation?
- What four communication strategies contribute to supervisors' success?
- How are (1) emotion labor, (2) stress and burnout, and (3) work–life conflict related to one another? How do they differ?

Alternative VIEW
Men Now Have More Work–Life Conflict than Women

Who do you think is more like to experience conflict when trying to manage paid and unpaid work, men or women? Why? If you believe women experience more conflict, why do think that more men than women in this study reported it?

Though it may come as a surprise to stressed-out working moms, a new report says American men now experience more work–life conflict than women. The Families and Work Institute tries to explain why in a study, *The New Male Mystique*, that takes its cue from Betty Friedan.

Much like the conflict women felt when they first entered the workforce in large numbers, the institute says men today feel "the pressure to do it all in order to have it all." That is, be the breadwinner, spend more time with the kids, and wash the dishes after dinner, thank you very much. The report finds a host of factors contributing to this pressure, including "flat earnings, long hours, increasing job demands, blurred boundaries between work and home life, and declining job security."

Perhaps not surprisingly, work–life conflict is most acute for men in demanding jobs, those who work longer hours, and those in dual-earner households. Based on the results of a 2008 national survey of 1,298 men, the institute reports that 60 percent of men in dual-earner couples reported work–family conflicts, up from 35 percent in 1977. Among women, the percentages rose much less, to 47 percent from 41 percent.

But here's a tidbit that would make Friedan worry: fathers actually work 3 hours more per week on average than men the same age without young children at home. Spouses, good luck bringing that up at the dinner table.

What can mitigate male work–life conflict? The study suggests supportive supervisors and a flexible work schedule. That way, men will know they're not alone with their struggle that, at least, now has a name.

SOURCE: Ludden, J. (2011, June 30). Men now have more "work-life conflict" than women, study says. *National Public Radio*. Retrieved July 14, 2011, from http://www.gpb.org/news/2011/06/30/men-now-have-more-work-life-conflict-than-women-study-says

THE INDIVIDUAL, ORGANIZATIONAL COMMUNICATION, AND SOCIETY

In this section, we explore how organizations and the societies in which they are located exert influence upon each other and the individuals within them. First we examine two of the most significant societal forces that impact organizational communication—history and globalization. Next, we discuss four of the important recent organizational practices that influence individuals and society, including the development of a new social contract between organizations and employees, the increase in organizations' use of contingent workers, the rise of urgent organizations, and the blurring of boundaries between home and work. Finally, we examine power relations within organizations and their impact on employees. We address these topics to explicate how each has influenced beliefs about organizational communication and its performance.

Societal Influences on Organizations

Organizations are shaped in part by the societies in which they are located. As societies change over time, so do the organizations within them. In addition, as organizations spread their operations into new cultures, they must change and adapt to those cultures to be successful. In the next section, we focus on these two societal influences on organizations: (1) social change and its impact on organizations and the communication within them, and (2) globalization and its effects on organizations and organizational communication.

Historical Forces

Prevailing beliefs about work, individuals, and knowledge creation have influenced what people expect of organizations as well as how they are expected to act within them. For example, until the early 1900s, popular talk about organizational techniques took a moral tone. Journalists, novelists, clergy, and other prominent figures often described business owners as men of superior character, which they were obligated to model for the betterment of the lower, working class (Barley & Kunda, 1992). During this time, managers' and owners' opinions and communication were considered important while those of the working classes were not.

By the 1930s, a major change in thinking about organization and communication occurred. Due to cultural changes as well as researchers such as Mary Parker Follett (1942), people began to question the absolute right of managers to command and control employees and began to focus, instead, on the human relations function of organizations. That is, management began to be seen as needing to educate (through teaching and persuading), to interact with employees (by seeking input), and to integrate everyone's input. Thus, for the first time, organizational theorists and managers came to believe that workers needed to have a voice in the organization.

A variety of developments around the 1960s prompted another shift in thinking about organizations and communication (Barley & Kunda, 1992) toward what we might call a *systems mentality*. Military operations research began to find a home in industry, and the rise of computers fostered interest in organizational communication processes. Across many academic disciplines, researchers began a quest for general, even universal, theoretical principles. Biologist Ludwig von Bertalanffy (1968), for instance, developed a highly influential **general systems theory** that, he believed, applied as well to the social sciences as it did to the life and physical sciences. Many organization scholars agreed. They saw organizations as systems not only composed of many subsystems but also embedded in larger systems. Hence, they sought to develop strategies for communication that occur within the units or subsystems of the organization as well for communication that occurs between the organization and its environment.

Today, one of the most important societal factors to impact organizations, and the individuals who work within them, is globalization. **Globalization** refers to the increasing connectedness of the world in economic, political, and cultural realms (Cheney et al., 2004). Although we typically think of globalization in economic terms, it also describes the ways in which political and cultural events affect people around the world. For example, terrorist attacks in Europe and the Middle East influence tourists' travel plans as well as governments' political alliances. From an economic perspective, conflict in the Middle East leads both to fears that oil production will suffer and to higher energy costs in the United States and other countries reliant on this source of oil. Because of globalization, people in the United States are connected intimately to other parts of the world; as a result, decisions and events in far-removed places can affect them.

Although many scholars and experts agree on what globalization is, considerable disagreement exists concerning whether globalization, specifically economic globalization, is a positive or negative force in individuals' lives. Proponents believe that globalization leads to decreased trade barriers that result in increased prosperity and economic development across societies (Krugman, 2002). Critics, however, argue that globalization leads to a growing gap between the rich and the poor since transnational organizations can operate without oversight by national and international institutions that protect the interests of individuals (Ganesh, Zoller, & Cheney, 2005). More specifically, these critics maintain that this lack of oversight leads to companies attempting to profit by ignoring worker safety, not providing fair compensation, and exploiting the environment.

What are the communication implications of globalization? First, it means that more people and businesses have intercultural contact and that they need to learn

general systems theory theory that organizations are a system composed of many subsystems and embedded in larger systems, and that organizations should develop communication strategies that serve both

globalization the increasing connectedness of the world in economic, political, and cultural realms

how to communicate more effectively across cultures, as we noted in Chapter 9. Many categories of individuals need to interact with support personnel around the world, even in their nonwork lives, and increasingly workers in multinational organizations must communicate and work with people from diverse cultures. Second, global forces such as market deregulation may have leveling or homogenizing effects on organizational practices all over the world.

Influence of Organizations on Individuals and Society

Not only are organizations influenced by society and cultures, they influence them and the individuals who comprise them. In this section, we explore four trends in contemporary organizations and the ways in which they impact society and individuals' lives. These trends include the new social contract, contingent workforces, urgent organizations, and blurred boundaries between work and life.

The New Social Contract

Over the past twenty-five years, a fundamental change has occurred in the relationship between individuals and their employers (Chilton & Weidenbaum, 1994; Jablin & Sias, 2001). Until recently, employees expected to spend years, if not their entire working lives, with a single company and to be rewarded for their service and loyalty with job security and good retirement benefits (Eisenberg, Goodall, & Trethewey, 2010). This is no longer the case. Along with globalization, an increase in organizations' willingness to lay off workers during economic downturns and corporate restructuring have led to a **new social contract** between employers and employees. Under this "new social contract," loyalty is not expected by workers or organizations and job security rarely exists (Eisenberg et al., 2010). This means that if it is deemed profitable, companies are quick to sell or merge with other corporations, and employees are willing to jump ship if the right opportunity arises.

A number of individuals have argued that the current financial crisis in the United States and across the world has led to a greater imbalance in the social contract between companies and employees. They argue that organizations have used the crisis as an excuse to engage in hiring practices that benefit organizations at great cost to employees. Although not everyone agrees, it is true that during the "Great Recession" approximately 7 million people have lost their jobs (Zuckerman, 2011) and the number of Americans working part-time because full-time work is not available has doubled in the past five years to 9.2 million people (Coy, Conlin & Herbst, 2010).

This change in the employee–employer relationship has resulted in job holders more fearful of or unable to change jobs, so the unemployed now are willing to settle for low wages and/or no benefits. It also has led to an increase in job and career shifting as well as to an increase in the employment of contingent workers—workers who do not have a long-term commitment to their organizations nor their employers to them.

Contingent Workers

Contingent employees work in temporary positions, part-time or as subcontractors (Belous, 1989; Jablin & Sias, 2001). Based on this definition, experts estimate that as many as one-third of U.S. employees are contingent workers (U.S. General Accounting Office, 2000).

Proponents of the trend toward the increased use of contingent workers argue that this practice is a productive response to the forces of a global marketplace. They point out that contingent work offers flexibility both to management and to workers. Firms can use contingent arrangements to maximize workforce flexibility in the face of seasonal and cyclical forces and the demands of just-in-time production. This same flexibility, they say, helps some workers balance the demands of

new social contract
assumes that loyalty is not expected by workers or organizations and that job security is unlikely

contingent employees
individuals who work in temporary positions, part-time or as subcontractors

family and work (U.S. Department of Labor, 2008). In addition, working in different organizations is believed to help contingent workers develop a wide set of skills that can lead to innovation (Jablin & Sias, 2001). Some commentators claim that these changes have led to the lowest unemployment rate in the United States and have allowed people to obtain better jobs than in the past.

On the other hand, detractors argue that companies often hire contingent workers simply to reduce employee wages, even though these employees perform the same amount and value of work (Conrad & Poole, 2005). They also point out that current tax, labor, and employment laws increase the likelihood of this practice by giving employers incentives to create contingent employment positions merely to sidestep their legal financial obligations to employees and to society. For certain types of contingent workers such as contractors, for example, employers do not have to make contributions to Social Security, unemployment insurance, workers' compensation, and health insurance; they also can save the administrative expense of withholding, and they are relieved of responsibility to the worker under labor and employment laws. At least one study has confirmed that such practices are fairly widespread; a 1989 General Accounting Office (GAO) study found that 38 percent of the employers the GAO examined had misclassified employees as independent contractors (U.S. Department of Labor, 2008).

Although some employees voluntarily choose contingent work to evade their own tax obligations, to provide flexibility, or to supplement retirement income, a large percentage of workers who hold part-time or temporary positions do so involuntarily. Many have been forced into temporary or part-time work due to organizational mergers, layoffs, restructuring, and downsizing (Lipson, 2011) or because they have limited choices. A significant portion of contingent workers is drawn from the most vulnerable sectors of the workforce—the young, female, and/or Hispanic. To read about one employee's experience as a contingent worker, see *Communication in Society: The Disposable Worker*.

Overall, contingent employees are more likely than traditional full-time workers to have low family incomes and are less likely to receive health insurance and pension benefits through their employers. The expansion of contingent work has contributed to the increasing gap between high- and low-wage workers and to the increasing sense of insecurity among workers (U.S. Department of Labor, 2008). The rise in the number of contingent workers has raised concerns that the United States is moving toward a two-tiered system in which more highly educated and trained employees are supported by lower paid part-time and temporary workers (Jablin & Sias, 2001). Experts worry that this division of workers may result in a caste system whereby permanent employees look down on and denigrate temporary or part-time workers.

Miller (2009) argues that a "disposable workforce" may not be good for organizations, either. Contingent employees are aware of the organizations' lack of commitment to them—especially during economic downturns, when they are the first to be let go; this decreases their loyalty to the organization and their commitment to its goals. Also, because organizations are less likely to invest time and money in socializing contingent workers and providing them with the support needed to be successful (Jablin & Sias, 2001), such employees are likely to feel disconnected from the organization and less likely to buy into its organizational culture. In turn, employees' lack of identification with the organization likely decreases job satisfaction and increases job turnover.

In addition, working alongside a contingent workforce can encourage traditional employees to question the value of organizational commitment and loyalty (Gossett, 2001; Miller, 2009). These traditional employees also may be less likely to form relationships and support networks with employees they see as transitory, which can negatively impact all employees' performance and the organization's productivity.

How do you feel about your job prospects once you leave college? Why? What can you do to make your career opportunities the strongest?

COMMUNICATION IN SOCIETY
The Disposable Worker

How do you think the shift from permanent jobs to contingent jobs has affected employee communication and relationships? How do you believe it affects families? In what ways can organizations maintain interpersonal contact with their contingent workers who work outside of the office?

On a recent Tuesday morning, single mom Tammy DePew Smith woke up in her tidy Florida townhouse in time to shuttle her oldest daughter, a high school freshman, to the 6:11 a.m. bus. At 6:40 she was at the desk in her bedroom, starting her first shift of the day with LiveOps, a Santa Clara (Calif.) provider of call-center workers for everyone from Eastman Kodak (EK) and Pizza Hut (YUM) to infomercial behemoth Tristar Products. She's paid by the minute—25 cents—but only for the time she's actually on the phone with customers.

By 7:40, Smith had grossed $15. But there wasn't much time to reflect on her early morning productivity; the next child had to be roused from bed, fed, and put onto the school bus. Somehow she managed to squeeze three more shifts into her day, pausing only to home-school her 7-year-old son, make dinner, and do the bedtime routine. "I tell my kids, unless somebody is bleeding or dying, don't mess with me."

As an independent agent, Smith has no health insurance, no retirement benefits, no sick days, no vacation, no severance, and no access to unemployment insurance. But in recession-ravaged Ormond Beach, she's considered lucky. She has had more or less steady work since she signed on with LiveOps in October 2006. "LiveOps was a lifesaver for me," she says.

You know American workers are in bad shape when a low-paying, no-benefits job is considered a sweet deal. Their situation isn't likely to improve soon; some economists predict it will be years, not months, before employees regain any semblance of bargaining power. That's because this recession's unusual ferocity has accelerated trends—including offshoring, automation, the decline of labor unions' influence, new management techniques, and regulatory changes—that already had been eroding workers' economic standing.

The forecast for the next five to 10 years: more of the same, with paltry pay gains, worsening working conditions, and little job security. Right on up to the C-suite, more jobs will be freelance and temporary, and even seemingly permanent positions will be at greater risk. "When I hear people talk about temp vs. permanent jobs, I laugh," says Barry Asin, chief analyst at the Los Altos (Calif.) labor-analysis firm Staffing Industry Analysts. "The idea that any job is permanent has been well proven not to be true." As Kelly Services (KELYA) CEO Carl Camden puts it: "We're all temps now."

FROM: Coy, P., Conlin, M., & Herbst, M. (2010, January 7). The disposable worker. *Bloomberg Business Week*. Retrieved September 17, 2011 from http://www.businessweek.com/magazine/content/10_03/b4163032935448.htm. http://www.businessweek.com/magazine/content/10_03/b4163032935448_page_4.htm

However, the increased use of a contingent workforce is, in part, a response to the competitive demands that U.S. companies face, the topic we take up next.

Competitiveness and Urgent Organizations

Another significant change is the rise of **urgent organizations**. Urgent organizations are companies that attempt to "shorten the time in which they develop new products and respond to customer demands" (Eisenberg, Goodall, & Trethewey, 2010, p. 17). Urgent organizations occur because of the intense time pressures related to global competition and the subsequent consumer demand for innovation and immediate fulfillment of wants and needs. Apple and other technology companies manifest many of the behaviors typical of urgent organizations. For example, the first iPhone was sold to the public in June 2007, and then just ten weeks later its price was dropped $200 in response to customer demand (though doing so infuriated those "early adopters" who bought the phone in June and July). In July 2008, just one year later, the iPhone 3G was released, with the price once again reduced, this time by half. Similarly, Walmart attempts to compete globally by requiring all of its

urgent organizations
companies that try to shorten the time it takes to develop new products and respond to customer demands

suppliers to abide by a policy that requires every vendor to either lower the price or increase the quality of each product every year (Fishman, 2006).

Urgent companies evolve and thrive because they are successful. Speed and quick response time provide them with an edge; companies that release products first tend to attract the most media and consumer attention, and clients and consumers are more likely to patronize companies that respond quickly to their requests for services and products.

Of course, when organizations increase the speed of innovation and delivery of services, it means that the employees of those organizations also are under time pressures to increase productivity and response time. This development has led to the issue we discuss next, the blurring of boundaries between work and home.

Blurred Boundaries Between Home and Work

The time pressures associated with urgent organizations have led to a blurring of the boundaries between individuals' work and nonwork lives. These pressures in conjunction with the advent of new communication technologies have increased organizations' ability to intrude into what has traditionally been one's nonwork life. The widespread use of email, cell phones, text messaging, and instant messaging has made it possible, and in some instances mandatory, that employees respond to organizations' demands at almost any hour of the day or night, during weekends as well as weekdays, and even when on vacation. Interestingly, just as the use of contingent workers has had a more profound impact on low-wage earners, the blurring of boundaries has had a stronger effect on high-wage earners, leading to positions that are now described as "extreme jobs" (Hewlitt, 2007; Schor, 1992).

Extreme jobs are those held by well-paid employees who are required to work more than sixty hours per week (often many more) as well as being subjected to unpredictable workflow, tight deadlines, responsibilities that amount to more than one job, expectations of work performance outside regular work hours, client availability twenty-four/seven, extensive travel, many direct reports, and/or physical presence at the workplace ten or more hours per day. Jobs with such extreme requirements often negatively affect employees' personal and family lives as well as their ability to contribute to their communities.

Organizations, Communication, and Power

Organizations in the United States historically have been hierarchical, meaning that power, decision-making authority, and control have been held by a relatively small percentage of people within the organization, including managers, vice presidents, presidents, and chief executive officers (CEOs). To a great extent this is still true today. Although a hierarchical structure seems natural and normal to most of us, it can lead to power differences and to communication behavior that negatively affects those workers who hold little or no power. In the discussion that follows, we examine three of the communication problems that can result from power differences.

The widespread use of technology in many jobs has caused a blurring of the boundaries between work and time off.

Bullying

Organizational **bullying** refers to repeated, hostile behaviors that occur in the workplace over an extended period and that are intended, or are perceived as intended, to harm one or more parties who are unable to defend themselves (Lutgen-Sandvik, Tracy, & Alberts, 2005). Although interpersonal conflict is common in organizations, and perhaps necessary, bullying is not necessary. Bullying differs from conflict in that conflict can be constructive and positive. In addition, intent to harm may not be present in

bullying
repeated hostile behaviors that are or are perceived to be intended to harm parties who are unable to defend themselves

quid pro quo
requests for sexual favors as a condition of getting or keeping a job or benefit; one of two types of sexual harassment recognized by federal law

hostile work environment
an intimidating, hostile, or offensive workplace atmosphere created by unwelcome and inappropriate sexually based behavior; one of two types of sexual harassment recognized by federal law

typical interpersonal conflict, and the parties in an interpersonal conflict often are relatively equal in power. However, in bullying, the intent to harm is a defining element, and power differences are key. Bully targets lack the ability to defend themselves and have limited strategies with which to respond. During interpersonal conflict, participants both act and are acted upon. In contrast, in bullying interactions, one party (or group) is the actor or perpetrator and one (or more) person(s) is the target.

You may wonder why we bring up the issue of bullying, since it may not seem like a prevalent problem. However, it probably is more common than you think. One study found that 30 percent of more than 400 respondents claimed that they had been bullied at some point in their careers (Lutgen-Sandvik et al., 2005). Eleven percent revealed that they had been bullied in just the past year. These statistics are similar to reports from workers in Great Britain, though somewhat higher than those reported in Scandinavia. In addition, bullying is important because, fundamentally, it is a communication issue (Alberts, Lutgen-Sandvik, & Tracy, 2005). Of the twenty-two behaviors used to enact bullying, seventeen of them involved verbal interaction, such as ridicule, rumors, false allegations, insults, and threats of violence (Alberts et al., 2005).

Because bullying does occur regularly and is related to one's power in the organization, scholars have sought to determine strategies that can help targets respond. However, because targets typically have low power in the organization, their options are limited. For example, a problem-solving approach involves discussing the issue and seeking resolution. It requires that all parties be able to participate openly. This is rarely true for the target of bullying. Similarly, compromising can occur only if one has leverage within the organization, meaning that each party must be able to offer something in return for a change in the other's behavior, which a low-power person may not possess. Obliging, or accommodating to the bully's demands, may be the only strategy if one wishes to remain in the organization. Withdrawing may be an option if one is willing to leave, and targets report that leaving the organization was the most effective, and often only, solution to the problem. Competing typically is not a useful strategy; it only intensifies the bully's abusive behavior. For a student's account of organizational bullying, see *It Happened to Me: Bob.*

It Happened to Me: Bob

I still can't believe it happened to me. About a year ago I was transferred to a new branch of my credit union. Within a few months, my supervisor began to criticize everything I did and make sarcastic and mean comments about me in front of other people. I tried to talk to her about it, but she just told me I was too thin-skinned. I don't know if it is because I am one of only a few males in the office or what. Finally, it got so bad that I asked for a meeting with my supervisor and her supervisor. During our meeting, I became so upset that I started having chest pains. I thought I was having a heart attack and had to go to the hospital by ambulance. It turns out it was a panic attack. When I got back to work a few days later, my supervisor started ridiculing me for having a panic attack. I have asked for a transfer, but I am also looking for another job.

Sexual Harassment

Sexual harassment describes unwanted sexual attention that interferes with an individual's ability to do his or her job and/or behavior that ties sexual favors to continued employment or success within the organi-zation (Equal Employment Opportunity Commission, 1980). Federal law recognizes two types of sexual harassment, quid pro quo and hostile work environment (Roberts & Mann, 2000). **Quid pro quo** is the request for sexual favors as a condition of getting or keeping a job or benefit. ("You do what I ask, and I'll help you advance in the organization.") A **hostile work** environment results when a coworker or supervisor engages in unwelcome and inappropriate sexually based behavior and creates an intimidating, hostile, or offensive atmosphere. Indulging in inappropriate verbal and nonverbal behaviors; repeatedly asking someone for a date; calling coworkers or subordinates by affectionate names (e.g., honey, sweetie); touching, patting, and stroking; and displaying posters and objects of a sexual nature can all constitute acts of sexual harassment.

Even with this list of criteria, however, people could differ over what constitutes a hostile work environment. As a guideline, the U.S. Court of Appeals (Aeberhard-Hodges, 1996) ruled that sexual harassment should be examined from the perspective of what a "reasonable woman," not a "reasonable person," would find offensive. This led some to this central question: If a reasonable woman standard prevailed, would men, even "reasonable men," ever be sure how to behave? The court's ruling, however, rests on the understanding that women are the most frequent targets of sexual harassment and that their experiences in the workplace and around issues of sexuality often differ markedly from men's.

At this point, you might be wondering how bullying differs from sexual harassment. We see sexual harassment as a specific type of bullying behavior because it contains many of the same elements: It is rooted in power differences, the target typically is unable to defend himself or herself, and the target perceives it as hostile and intentional.

As you can see, sexual harassment primarily is a communicative behavior. Because of this, researchers have typically explored how targets can use communication to respond effectively. The typical strategies recommended include confronting the harasser and stating that the behavior must stop, complaining to one's boss or the human relations department, suing, or leaving the organization (Sigal, Braden-Maguire, Patt, Goodrich, & Perrino, 2003).

However, the majority of female targets of sexual harassment (in fact 95 percent or more) do not respond assertively by confronting the harasser or reporting the harasser to a supervisor or the organization (Gruber & Smith, 1995; Rudman, Borgida, & Robertson, 1995). Why not? Sexual harassment typically occurs between people of unequal power, so confronting the harasser may not be an option. Targets risk losing their jobs, seeing the harassment intensify, or losing out on promotions and raises.

Complaining to a third party does sometimes work, particularly in organizations that have a clearly articulated sexual harassment policy and in which the human resources department has been empowered to handle sexual harassment cases effectively. However, some organizations do not wish to deal with these issues, or do not see them as important, so complaining to a third party does not always result in a benefit. Of course, suing the harasser and the organization that allows harassment is possible, but not every case is settled to the target's satisfaction, and the process can be long, painful, and ultimately unrewarding.

Finally, although leaving the organization does tend to resolve some aspects of the problem, some employees lack the option of leaving or find that leaving takes considerable time and effort. In addition, leaving one's job may resolve the physical/behavioral aspect of the harassment, but it does not help targets manage the long-term physical or psychological effects of harassment, does not address the impact of the harassment on the target's career, and does not result in changes in the perpetrator or the organization.

None of this means that targets should tolerate inappropriate behavior, but it does mean that they should carefully consider their options before committing to a response strategy. Targets should consider what response will be most effective in their specific situations. To do so, targets of sexual harassment (or bullying) might consider the following options. First, a target should consider responding assertively the first time the harassment occurs. This strategy is most likely to be successful when the perpetrator and target have equal power or a relationship of trust. If direct confrontation does not seem to be an option or has not been successful, then the target should consider approaching his or her supervisor, human resources department, or an organizational ombudsperson. Many organizations want to and will respond to such complaints, recognizing that the organization as a whole is harmed by such behavior.

If confrontation and appealing to authorities have not succeeded, targets must assess their needs and options carefully. They might consider seeking social support from family and friends, seeking assistance from a counselor or therapist to help them manage the emotional distress, developing strategies to avoid the perpetrator (if possible), and/or requesting a transfer or another job.

Unfortunately, the most common strategy targets select is to do nothing. This is not a response that, in the long run, benefits the individual or the organization. Moreover, doing nothing is especially problematic if the target has not even determined what other options exist. Too often, targets assume their efforts will be unsuccessful before they even make an attempt. If you do become a target, we encourage you not to make this assumption.

Employee Privacy and Monitoring

Monitoring employees electronically and in other ways is a growing part of the way American companies do business (American Management Association, 2005). According to the American Management Association's survey, 76 percent of employers monitor workers' Web connections, while 50 percent store and monitor employees' computer files. Workers are exposed to many other types of privacy-invasive monitoring as well. These include drug testing, closed-circuit video monitoring, email monitoring, instant message monitoring, phone monitoring, location monitoring, personality and psychological testing, and keystroke logging.

Although employers do have an interest in monitoring employees in order to address security risks, sexual harassment, and acceptable performance of work duties, these activities may diminish employee morale and dignity as well as increase worker stress (DiTecco, Cwitco, Arsenault, & Andre, 1992). To better understand the complexities of this issue, read *It Happened to Me: Nichole*. In addition, monitoring may interfere with employee productivity. A study of 134 corporate employees examined the effects of monitoring and found that productivity

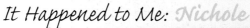

It Happened to Me: Nichole

The chapter on organizational communication helped me better understand a problem I encountered with Residential Life at my college. It wasn't about drinking or drugs, or letting in strangers, or any of the usual problems that students have with the dorm; it was about my Resident Assistant, who now is my boyfriend.

Just to clarify, there were no rules stated that I could not date my RA, and he was never told he couldn't date his residents. Plus, there is actual love involved, not just random friends-with-benefits hookups and we really feel as though we have met the right person. But, Residential Life has a huge problem with our relationship, and they called us into a meeting. We both felt as though it was a violation of our privacy. We had the meeting, he quit his job, and we are still dating, ten months strong!

Now, though, when I look at the relationship through the eyes of the school, I can see their problems with it. What would have happened if an employee of the college got me pregnant? Also, he lived in my hall and his duty was to keep us in line, but there was huge preferential treatment going on. I mean, would my boyfriend really write me up for anything? So now I see that they had a point. But I don't understand why nothing was ever said about this practice being against the rules.

diminished when people believed they were being monitored for quality (Stanton & Julian, 2002). Nonetheless, employers and employees can develop policies that meet the needs of both parties. Both sides must have a voice in developing the policies, and the process itself must be transparent (Trethewey & Corman, 2001).

In conclusion, organizations experience significant impact from the society and historical time period in which they exist. Two societal factors currently influencing corporations in the United States are globalization and changing power relations in the workplace. Globalization has meant that many jobs have been transferred from the United States to other countries, and both consumers and employees now must increase their contact with workers around the world. This change has been accompanied by an increased focus on power relationships at work and their impact on employees. This tendency to critique organizational uses of power has also led to more discussion of organizational ethics, which we examine next.

TEST YOUR KNOWLEDGE

- What is globalization? What are the communication implications of globalization?
- How has the "social contract" between individuals and organizations changed over the past twenty-five years?
- In what ways can organizations exert power over individuals?

ETHICS AND ORGANIZATIONAL COMMUNICATION

Due to organizational behavior such as providing bonuses to CEOs who lead failing financial companies and phone hacking by members of the Rupert Murdoch-owned News Corporation, U.S. Americans are paying more attention to business ethics than perhaps ever before (MSNBC.com News Service, 2011) However, observers don't agree on where responsibility for ethical behavior and communication rests within the organization. For example, who should be held accountable for the phone hacking conducted by reporters of News Corp.? Should only the reporters themselves be prosecuted? Should the manager of the newspaper also be accountable? How about Rupert Murdoch himself? Is he responsible for the ethical standards within his company? When attempting to determine the ethical choices and decisions organizations should make, people usually view the process either from the *individual perspective* or the *communal perspective* (Brown, 1989).

Many U.S. Americans take an individualistic perspective, viewing ethical failures as resting on the shoulders of specific individuals within the organization. From this outlook, each person in the corporation is responsible for his or her own behavior. In the case of News Corp., then, only the reporters themselves as well as others who knew about their behavior but did not "blow the whistle" are accountable. In the communal view, however, individuals are considered to be members of community and are all partially responsible for the behavior of its members. The assumption here is that the ethical standards within an organization are created by and should be monitored and reinforced by all of its members. From this perspective, everyone within the News Corp. organization, especially the managers and owners, is responsible, because they had a duty to create and maintain high ethical standards within the company.

When ethics is discussed in organizational contexts, the focus typically is on the rights of the individual—such as the rights to free speech or privacy—and policies and behaviors that infringe on these rights are seen as unethical. However, a communal approach focuses on the "common good," or what is in the best interests of the entire community. Thus, the morality of an action is assessed based on its consequences for the group. In an individualistic approach, the responsibility for phone hacking at *News of the World* lies with the reporters who directly engaged in it. From a communal approach, the reporters' phone hacking is harmful to the organization as well as society, and the people responsible for that harm are the members of the organization collectively, that is, the organization itself.

Problems exist with both approaches. When we view individuals alone as responsible, they alone are punished while the organization is left essentially unchanged. Yet, when we view corporations in a completely communal way and hold them responsible for their unethical practices, no individual may be held accountable or liable. Consequently, those responsible for the decision to engage in unethical and often illegal practices may not suffer any consequences—and may be free to continue these practices.

How should we balance these two approaches? Most likely, we need to hold both the organization and the individuals who lead them responsible for their practices—just as political leaders are tried in war courts for crimes against humanity, even though their subordinates performed the atrocities. At the same time, corporate leaders need to consider the impacts of their decisions on both individuals and society.

How is communication a factor in organizational ethics? Communication figures in organizational ethics in two ways (Cheney et al., 2004). First, many of the ethical issues in organizations revolve around communication. For example, organizations have to decide when to tell employees of impending layoffs, they develop advertising campaigns that communicate the identity of their corporation and its products to consumers, and they must decide how to communicate information regarding their profits and losses to shareholders and Wall Street. Second, the ways in which an organization defines, communicates about, and responds to ethical and unethical behavior shape how individuals within the organization behave. If corporate policy and organizational leaders are vague on the issue of ethics, or worse yet, fail to address it, employees may believe that ethics is not a central concern of the organization and may behave accordingly. For example, in 2005, *Esquire* magazine published an article about the alleged ethical violations of military recruiters. The military personnel interviewed for the article claimed that despite written policies that encouraged ethical behavior, their communication with their superiors revolved only around their success or failure at meeting their recruitment goals and never about *how* they met those goals.

Thus, they concluded that recruiting ethically was a secondary, or perhaps even an unnecessary, consideration.

TEST YOUR KNOWLEDGE
- How do the individual and communal approaches to organizational ethics differ?
- What role does communication play in organizational ethics?

IMPROVING YOUR ORGANIZATIONAL COMMUNICATION SKILLS

Much of the time, if not most, people are only willing to engage in conflict when they are angry and/or emotional. How often have you been involved with, or observed others engaging in, highly emotional conflict at work? As you probably have noted, this style of conflict engagement typically doesn't resolve anything and may cause long-lasting damage to one's relationships with others.

A better way to manage conflict with co-workers is to use a strategic approach to conflict management. People who use a strategic approach prepare for their conflicts and engage in **strategy control** (Canary & Lakey, 2012). When behaving strategically, one assesses the available information and options, which increases one's understanding of the conflict and the other party. In turn, these behaviors help people choose conflict behaviors that are responsive to the partner's as well as their own needs and increase the possibility for cooperation, collaboration, and compromise.

When using a strategic approach, before you even initiate a discussion over an issue in conflict, you should know what you want to occur as a result of the interaction. If you wish to confront your coworker about not doing his fair share of a joint project, you should first decide what your goal is. Do you want your colleague to apologize? To stay late until the report is finished? To complete the project by himself? To take the lead on the next joint project? Or do you desire some combination of these outcomes? You will be far more successful and satisfied with your conflict interactions if you go into them knowing what you want.

Second, decide if the issue is worth confronting—or worth confronting now. You may know what you want, but do you have a reasonable chance of accomplish-

strategy control
assessing the available information and options in order to increases one's understanding of the conflict and the other party before engaging in conflict communication

ing your goals? That is, how likely is your coworker to apologize or to successfully take the lead on your next joint project? If the answer truly is "highly unlikely," you may choose not to engage in the conflict or to seek other solutions. For example, you might decide to ask your supervisor to assign someone else to work with you. Alternatively, you may decide you do want to have the conversation, but perhaps not right now, because both of you are hungry and tired.

If you decide that the conflict is worth confronting, you next want to try to understand the other party's goals, that is, what he or she wants. What, for example, do you think your coworker's goal is? Does he want to receive credit for the work without having to do it? Does he want assistance with parts of the project he doesn't feel competent to complete? Is he busy with other projects and wants more time to finish the project? Depending on your understanding of his goals and interests, you will likely suggest different solutions. Please remember, however, the tendency for each of us to attribute negative motivations to others' behavior. If you are upset, you will be particularly like to believe your colleague's goal is to avoid work but receive the rewards of it. Recognize that your attributions may be incorrect and that you probably will need to talk with your coworker in order to determine what his motivations really are.

You have one more step to complete before you are ready to talk with your colleague; you need to plan the interaction. More specifically, you should think about when and where the conversation should take place and what tactics you believe will be most effective. Typically, you will want to choose a time when neither you nor your coworker is angry, rushed, or stressed. In addition, you should probably have the conversation in private. If others are around, one or both of you may behave more competitively or avoid the interaction entirely because you are embarrassed to be observed by others. Finally, you should think through how you will explain your dissatisfaction with the current state of affairs neutrally and how you will frame your suggested solutions. Once you have done all of this, you are ready to talk with your colleague and discuss calmly what the two of you can do to reduce your feeling that you alone are working on the project.

TEST YOUR KNOWLEDGE

- What is mean by "a strategic approach" to managing conflict?
- What are the four steps to the "strategic approach" to conflict management?

SUMMARY

Organizations have a powerful influence on individuals' lives; consequently, it is important to learn how to communicate effectively in organizational contexts. Doing so can enhance professional success, allow one to ask more informed questions about everyday organizational practices, and help individuals decide which organizations they wish to frequent and support.

Organizations are composed of interactions that members use to accomplish their individual and common goals. The two fundamental properties of organizations are function, or the goals and effects of communication, and structure, or the lines of communication through which messages flow.

Some of the basic types of communication that occur and that affect employee success within the organization include assimilation, supervisor–subordinate communication, and coworker communication. In addition, employees can face three types of organizational dilemmas during their careers: emotion labor, stress and burnout, and work–life conflict.

Three of the most significant societal forces that impact organizational communication are history, globalization, and power; each influences beliefs about organizational communication and its performance. Power differences in organizations can result in three specific communication problems for workers—bullying, sexual harassment, and employee monitoring.

Ethical issues in organizational communication are key for twenty-first-century workers, as is becoming a more effective communicator. When assessing the ethical choices and decisions organizations should make, people usually approach the process from the individual perspective or the communal perspective. Each approach has consequences for the organization, and the most ethical approach combines the two perspectives. Finally, conflict management skills are among the most important organizational communication skills one can develop, and a strategic approach to conflict management can help you significantly improve your ability to manage conflict with your colleagues.

HUMAN COMMUNICATION IN SOCIETY ONLINE

To review this chapter, use the MyCommunicationLab Web site to test your understanding of the following key terms, record your answers to the chapter review questions, and complete the suggested activities. Expand your learning and understanding of chapter concepts by completing additional activities and exercises online. Access code required. Go to www.mycommunicationlab.com for more information or to purchase standalone access.

KEY TERMS

organizations 233
function 233
production 233
maintenance 234
innovation 234
structure 234
downward communication 234
upward communication 234
horizontal communication 234
hierarchy 234
formal structure 234
informal structure 234

organizational culture 234
assimilation 237
organizational identification 237
semantic-information distance 239
upward distortion 239
openness 240
supportiveness 240
motivation 240
empowerment 241
ingratiation 241
assertiveness 241
rationality 241

burnout 245
general systems theory 249
globalization 249
new social contract 250
contingent employees 250
urgent organizations 252
bullying 253
quid pro quo 254
hostile work environment 254
strategy control 258

APPLY WHAT YOU KNOW

1. **Understanding Emotion Labor**
   Think of five jobs that require employees to engage in emotion labor and delineate the emotions that these employees are "expected" to display. What emotions are they expected to suppress? What contradictory emotions and behaviors are they expected to perform? Which of the five jobs that you listed appears to have the heaviest emotion labor load?

2. **Understanding Relationships at Work**
   Form a group with one or more of your classmates. Assume that you are a work group that has been charged with developing a fraternization policy for your job. Develop a policy about the types of relationships that are appropriate in your workplace and how people who have these relationships should communicate and behave while at work.

3. **Improving Your Job Interview Skills**
   Go to Job.Interview.net's "Mock Interviews" site at www.job-interview.net/sample/Demosamp.htm and review the information about communicating effectively during job interviews. Engage in one of the mock interviews provided, and then write a brief analysis of your performance. Explain what you did well and what you could have done better.

EXPLORE

1. Go to the *Psychology Today* website and locate the page on workplace Self Tests. Select two self-tests (such as the Entrepreneurial Personality Profile or the Leadership Style test) and complete them. After completing the tests, analyze your score. Does the score you received reflect your understanding of yourself and your work life? Which of you answers surprised you? How can this information help you in your future career?

2. Go to a job interviewing website such as the U.S. Labor's Job Interview Tips or About.com's Job Interview Tips and read the suggestions offered for how to interview for a job effectively. Afterward, develop a short checklist of helpful hints for interviewing that you can keep on hand for future job interview.

3. Locate a website devoted to exploring work-life issues, such as the Center for Work-Life Policy site or the Canadian Center for Occupational Health and Safety's Work/Life page, and read at least one essay on work-life issues. After reading the essay, write a brief summary of it that you could share with your classmates.

11

Mass Media and Communication

chapter outline

I always record my favorite soap opera so I can watch it when I have time. Sometimes I watch it later the same day, but sometimes I wait until the end of the week and "veg out" on hours of it. My best friend in college got me hooked on this soap opera, and now it's a part of my everyday life.

This student's experience with television is not unique; many television viewers are devoted to a favorite show and don't want to miss a single episode. When you think about this behavior on the individual level, you probably view it as a matter of choice or taste. When communication scholars analyze television viewing on the social level, however, they examine the influence media have on individuals and how media messages exert influence. For example, in August 2001, when the soap opera *The Bold and the Beautiful* ran a segment about HIV, researchers noted that telephone calls to the National STD and AIDS Hotline rose dramatically (Kennedy, O'Leary, Beck, Pollard, & Simpson, 2004). More recently, in 2010, *Law & Order SVU* ran an episode that highlighted the backlog of untested rape kit samples (Rubin, 2010). Rape kits store the evidence collected after a reported rape to help convict suspected rapists. Actress Mariska Hargitay, who plays a detective on that show, testified before a House committee about this issue (Dwyer & Jones, 2010). Although her television character is fictional, Hargitay uses her image to be an advocate. Soap operas and other television programs, like other types of mass media from radio to film, can influence people's lives in important ways.

In this chapter, we first look at the importance of media in everyday life. We then briefly examine the major forms of mass media. Next, we investigate how individuals use media and the influence that media messages have on individuals. Then we consider media usage within the context of the societal framework and explore the influence media have on society overall. Finally, we discuss media activism as a means for individuals to express media ethics, and we introduce guidelines for becoming more effective consumers of media. Although the Internet is also a type of media, we address that topic where we will focus on the role of digitally mediated communication.

Once you have read this chapter, you will be able to:

- Be able to identify the main forms of mass media.
- Describe various models of media.
- Understand five issues in media studies: social identities, understanding the world, media events, media violence, and media economics.
- Identify five ethical issues with mass media.
- Describe three ways to be a more effective consumer of media messages.

THE IMPORTANCE OF MASS MEDIA

Media hold a very important place in our society. As an indication of their importance to you, consider these questions. If you met someone who did not watch television shows, see or rent movies, or listen to the radio, would you be surprised? What if the same person never heard of Lady Gaga, Stephen Colbert, Oprah Winfrey, A-Rod, or J-Lo? Would knowing this change your interaction with that person? What topics could you and couldn't you discuss? If you concluded that many topics would be off limits, you can see that media messages serve important social functions. For example, they help people bond with others who like or dislike the same shows, movies, advertisements, singers, or actors. Media messages and images also help shape how people view the world and what they understand—and perhaps misunderstand —about events around the globe. Because people are so deeply immersed in this media environment, however, they rarely think about their participation in it. Nevertheless, it is indeed an interaction, as individuals participate in the communication process by selecting certain programs and agreeing or disagreeing with what they hear or see.

Why is media studies important? To begin with, U.S. Americans watch an enormous amount of television, although the exact number of hours is difficult to pin down. In 2005, Nielsen Media Research reported that the average U.S. household watched 8 hours and 11 minutes of television per day, which is the highest level recorded since Nielsen began measuring television viewing in the 1950s. The Washington State Department of Health (n.d.) notes that, on average, African Americans watch about 2 hours per day more than other U.S. Americans. Of all U.S. Americans, children watch the most television and are the center of most concern about television viewing.

People turn to communication media both for information and entertainment. For example, in the aftermath of the Japanese earthquake and tsunami in March 2011, 83 percent of Japanese said they got their news about the natural disaster primarily from television (comScore, 2011). While the Internet has become increasingly important in seeking out information, including information about the Japanese earthquake and tsunami, it is important to recognize that television remains the primary information source. Of course, not all people turned to television. People at work may not have had access to television, but could check frequently for news on the Internet while working at their computers. People traveling by car relied on radio for their information.

Media scholars today recognize that they work during an era of rapid media change and development. For example, communication scholars Jennings Bryant and Dorina Miron (2004) identified six kinds of changes that are currently affecting and being affected by mass communication:

1. new form, content, and substance in mass communication;
2. new kinds of interactive media, such as the Internet;
3. new media ownership patterns in a global economy;
4. new viewing patterns and habits of audiences;
5. new patterns in family life; and
6. new patterns of interactive media use by youth.

Because of the rapid pace of these changes, measuring and studying their influence can be a challenge.

While it is difficult to measure the precise power of media messages, these messages surround and influence people every day. The importance of media in our everyday lives and in our society has been rapidly increasing. The rise of the Internet, cell phones, and other "new media" has led to a distinction being made between "mass media" and "new media." In this chapter, we will focus on mass media. To help you understand the term *mass media*, we discuss this topic next.

WHAT ARE MASS MEDIA?

Mediated communication refers to communication that is transmitted through a channel, such as television, film, radio, and print. We often refer to these channels of communication more simply as media.

The word **media** is the plural form of *medium*. Television is one communication medium; others include film, radio, magazines, advertisements, and newspapers. When you pick up the telephone to speak to someone, you are using yet another communication medium. When you write a letter, your communication is mediated by the form of letter writing. Even the voice and the body can be considered media of communication.

For all the complexity and variety of media studies, its focus typically falls on **mass media**, or mediated communication intended for a large audience. Mass-mediated messages are usually produced and distributed by large organizations or industries in the business of mass communication. Mass media businesses are also known as **culture industries** because they produce television shows, made-for-television movies, video games, and other cultural products as an industry. The creation of these cultural products is not driven by individual artists, but by large groups of workers in for-profit (and some nonprofit) organizations.

The study of media is often a moving target, as changes in media continually occur. Part of understanding the influence of media on our everyday lives entails understanding the changes that have occurred and what media were available in other time periods. Historically, communication has been framed by the media available during a given time. Let's now look at some of these industries and the media texts they produce.

One of the first media addressing a large public were newspapers. During the nineteenth century, many newspapers grew in distribution and readership as the cost of mass printing declined. As expansion westward continued in the United States, the newspaper played a critical role in community building. Newspapers flourished during this period in staggering numbers. For example, "Before the end of 1867, at least four newspapers had been published in Cheyenne, a town that still had a population well under 800, in the Wyoming Territory" (Boorstin, 1965, p. 131). These numbers are all the more impressive in view of today's decline in newspaper readership. As you can see, different eras embraced different communication media.

Today, when most people think of newspapers, they first think of large-circulation papers in large metropolitan areas, such as the *New York Times, Washington Post,* and *Los Angeles Times*. They might also think about smaller, local papers, including the *Corvallis Gazette-Times*, the *Nome Nugget*, and the *Knoxville News Sentinel*. Because large-circulation newspapers serve different needs from local papers, many readers subscribe to both. Other newspapers target specific demographic groups, such as immigrant communities, ethnic and racial communities, gay and lesbian communities, or retirees. Some are bilingual. Others are referred to as the "alternative" press. These alternative-press newspapers attempt to present perspectives and voices that may not be heard in the mainstream press. Examples of alternative papers include the *Seattle Stranger*, the *San Francisco Bay Guardian*, and New York City's *Village Voice*.

Another development that followed the lowered cost of mass printing was the development of the magazine. Magazines are produced weekly, monthly, bimonthly, or quarterly. Some, such as *Newsweek, Harper's, Reader's Digest*, and *Smithsonian*, target broad, general audiences. Other magazines focus on more limited audiences— *Ebony, Latina, Men's Health*, and *Woman's World*, for example—and still others on very specific topics, as shown by the titles *Gourmet Magazine, Hot Rod Magazine*, and *Rhode Island Magazine*. Like newspapers, magazines offer important forums

media
the plural form of *medium*, a channel of communication

mass media
mediated communication intended for large audiences

culture industries
large organizations in the business of mass communication that produce, distribute, or show various media texts (cultural products) as an industry

Some magazines offer important forums for political discussions. Others address distinct interests, such as sports, travel, gardening, and more.

Should consumer-created media such as blogs, Twitter, and video sites like YouTube and Vimeo be considered mass media? Why or why not? In what ways are their functions similar to, or different from, those of mass media created by larger organizations?

mass-market paperbacks
popular books addressed to a large audience and widely distributed

e-books
electronic books read on a computer screen instead of a printed page

for political discussions, but they also address distinct interests, such as crafts, hobbies, or travel.

Popular books are another medium addressed to a large audience. Sometimes called **mass-market paperbacks**, these books include romance novels, self-help books, and comic books, as well as other genres that are produced in very large numbers and distributed widely. **E-books** (electronic books) constitute a recent development in mass media. E-books are books read on a computer screen instead of a printed page. Currently, it is not clear how important a form of media this will become. Though e-reader devices are becoming increasingly user-friendly, many readers still say they prefer the printed page.

Motion pictures, first shown commercially in the 1890s, flourished throughout the twentieth century. Although today people can make movies relatively cheaply with digital video, high-quality productions that draw large audiences cost millions of dollars to produce, distribute, and advertise. Therefore, movie studios with adequate resources dominate the motion picture industry. While some documentary movies do become popular, such as *March of the Penguins*, *Fahrenheit 9/11*, and *Supersize Me*, most best-selling movies are purely entertainment-oriented, such as the *Harry Potter* movies, *The Dark Knight*, *The Chronicles of Narnia*, and *Captain America*. Typically, large-budget films receive the widest distribution and the most publicity, but small-budget films can also reach audiences and sometimes offer alternative views of important social issues.

Like movies, radio technology emerged in the late nineteenth century. At first, it had important applications at sea, but in the 1920s stations sprang up all over the United States. As journalism professor Jane Chapman notes, "Radio's take-off was swift, and public enthusiasm for it peaked during the 'golden age' of the 1930s and 1940s" (2005, p. 147). Radio programming included not only news and commentary but also quiz shows, dramas, and situation comedies. With the rise of television, the Internet, and other competing media, radio broadcasting has become much more specialized, with radio stations serving specific audiences by broadcasting classical music, jazz, country music, news, sports, or other focused content. Audiences for these specialized programs are often targeted based on identities, such as age, socioeconomic class, race and ethnicity, or language. Today, radio is also broadcast over the Internet, via satellite, and through podcasts. And while commercial enterprises dominate radio in the United States, nonprofit radio, such as National Public Radio and Pacifica, also exists.

Popular music, another form of mass media, existed long before radio, and people listened to it live in public and private venues and, later, on gramophones and record players. Popular music now also plays on television and via other communication media, such as CDs, DVDs, and MP3 players. As different trends grew in popularity, a large number of commercial enterprises arose to glean the profits. In turn, many smaller companies have gone out of business or been bought out, so that fewer, but larger, music corporations select, produce, and distribute the music we hear today.

Television is among the most familiar forms of communication media. Early in its development, in the mid-twentieth century, networks such as ABC, CBS, and NBC dominated, since they were the only providers of content. The rise of cable television, with its multiple specialized channels, has taken significant market share away from the networks, yet they remain important and continue to draw large audiences. Since its inception, cable television has expanded to include pay channels such as HBO, Showtime, and Cinemax. In addition, satellite television is challenging cable television. Because television programming is expensive, the medium is dominated by commercial enterprises; however, the United States also has nonprofit television stations, many of which belong to the Public Broadcasting network or to the satellite network Deep Dish TV. In addition, cable TV stations are required to provide public, educational, and government access channels.

All told, these many forms of mass media saturate our world and penetrate deeply into our individual consciousness, yet we still have some choices regarding which messages to accept. Let's see how this works.

active agents
seekers of various media messages and resisters of others

TEST YOUR KNOWLEDGE

■ What are some of the most common forms of mass media?

THE INDIVIDUAL AND MASS MEDIA

Media scholars are interested in the impact media messages have on individuals, but they are also interested in how individuals decide which media messages to consume or avoid. Marketers and media producers especially want to know how they might predict and characterize individuals' choices so that they can more effectively influence consumer choice. In this section we'll explore both aspects of individual media consumption—how media messages influence us and how we become **active agents**, or active seekers, of various media messages and resisters of others. With the term *active agent*, we stress that even though people inhabit a densely media-rich environment, they need not be passively bombarded by media messages.

How Media Messages Affect the Individual

One approach to studying the influence of media messages relies on the linear model. Recall that in Chapter 1 we described how early models conceived of communication as a linear process involving the transfer of information without feedback from one person to another. Similarly, when it comes to media, there is a traditional linear model that portrays communication as a process that occurs in a linear fashion—for example, on a path from the television to the viewer. In this traditional approach, scholars focus on the sender, the medium, the audience, and the effect of the message. This model views media communication as a process that moves from one source to many receivers. While researchers who use this approach recognize that people are not passive viewers or consumers of media messages, they are interested only in measuring the influence of media messages on the individual, not vice versa.

By understanding the effects of media messages, communication scholars in the linear tradition hope to assist public policy debates about media regulation. For example, their research findings might be used in debates about the effects on viewers of violence or sexuality in the media. So, on a societal level, research based on the linear model often influences public policy decision making. On an individual level, this kind of research may help you select the types of television shows you watch or the movies you allow your children to see.

As an analytic tool, the linear model of media analysis has its limits. For example, critics argue that its simplicity cannot account for the multiple ways people respond to media messages (Sproule, 1989). Viewers are not merely passive receivers of messages, these critics say, nor do they necessarily believe or imitate everything they watch or read. Those who watched *Modern Family*, for example, did not necessarily model their family behaviors on the

STARBUCKS GETS A RADIO STATION

mass media effects
the influence that media have on
people's everyday lives

show's characters. Nor did everyone who watched the trial of Casey Anthony, accused of murdering her daughter, Caylee, agree with the jury's verdict (Hightower &
Sedensky, 2011).

On the other hand, the linear model does highlight the power and influence of
media messages. Some people did try to imitate the antics of Johnny Knoxville on
the MTV television show *Jackass*, resulting in very serious injuries despite televised
warnings against trying to imitate the stunts. And in a classic example, a mass panic
was set off when thousands of listeners to Orson Welles' 1938 Halloween radio
broadcast, *War of the Worlds*, believed that Martians were landing in New Jersey.

Scholars who study media influence work in an area called **mass media effects**.
The study of mass media effects has undergone significant changes over the years, as
researchers have disagreed about how much effect a particular media message has
on people's everyday lives (McQuail, 1987). In the 1930s, Paul Lazarsfeld and his
colleagues studied radio's effect on listeners and, in particular, its effect on voting behavior. This study, titled *The People's Choice* (Lazarsfeld, Berelson, & Gaudet,
1948), argued that media had limited effects, as they found that radio tended to reinforce preexisting beliefs rather than shape new ones.

Today, the focus on effects remains important in media research. For example,
contemporary researchers have examined media images of beautiful bodies and
how those images influence people's perceptions of their own bodies and their re-
sultant behavior in response to those images, including dieting, working out, taking
diet pills, and undergoing cosmetic surgery. An early influential book, *The Beauty
Myth* by Naomi Wolf, argued that these images of beauty are unattainable and are
used against women. Originally published in 1991, it has remained a best seller; a
new edition was released in 2002. In their study of the effects of entertainment television and sports media, Kimberly Bissell and Peiqin Zhou (2004) found a high
correlation between images of thin women's bodies that appear repeatedly in entertainment television and eating disorders among college-age women who watched
those shows.

Another area of inquiry among media-effects scholars involves media images of
violence. In their study of media usage among middle-school children in ten regions
in the United States, Michael Slater and his colleagues found that aggressive young
people seek out violent media and that exposure to media violence can predict aggression (Slater, Henry, Swaim, & Anderson, 2003). Thus, they see media violence
and aggression as mutually reinforcing and call their model a *downward spiral model*
to describe the powerful, negative influence the interaction has on youth. Those
youth who are prone to violent behaviors seek out violent media that reinforce more
violent behavior. More recently, Bushman and Gibson (2011) have also found that
aggression continues long after engaging with violent video games.

Promoting health through media messages is another significant area of inquiry
among scholars seeking to understand media effects. In a recent study on antidrug
advertisements for adolescents, Hunyi Cho and Franklin J. Boster (2008) compared
antidrug messages framed around the costs of using drugs (loss) versus the benefits of
avoiding them (gain). The study found that framing loss rather than gain was more
effective among adolescents who had friends who used drugs. There was no difference among adolescents whose friends did not use drugs. In order to engage the most
effective communication messages to promote public health, media effects scholars
are also trying to better understand how media messages can be more effective.

How Individuals Choose Media Messages

Advertisers, political campaign strategists, and communication scholars all want to
understand which groups of people consume which media texts. They want to know
who watches *Grey's Anatomy*, who reads the *New York Times*, and who reads
People magazine. As you might guess, this type of information enables advertisers to

target their messages more accurately toward certain consumers. It also enables campaign strategists to focus their message to attract more votes. But why would media scholars be interested in this information?

Media scholars need this information so that they can correctly target their research. For example, if scholars want to study the effect of a particular **media text**—for example, a television show, advertisement, or movie—they need to know which audience group to study. If they want to know how people interpret a particular media text, they need to know the audience of that text. Or if scholars want to know about the economic influence of particular media texts, they need to know which audience groups advertisers target with these messages.

As an individual, you are constantly faced with media choices, and your choices have increased considerably in the past decade due to the increased predominance of online news and blogging as well as instant downloads of movies and TV episodes. Researchers are interested in not only *what* we choose but how we choose. See how one of our students considers this in *It Happened to Me: Josh*.

Although Josh doesn't mention it explicitly, both what people choose and how they choose are related to their identities. And, as we noted in Chapter 3, identities are not fixed; they are dynamic across time and situations. With them, media choices change as well. For example, as a child, Josh may have been a fan of Saturday morning cartoons or *Sesame Street*, but as a young adult, perhaps he preferred

Monday Night Football or MTV's *Real World*. Josh's age and the ages of his friends likely influence the movies he selects. But age is only one aspect of identity—and perhaps one of the simplest factors that influence media choices. Other aspects, such as regional identity, might also have an effect, but they are more difficult to correlate with media tastes.

media text
a television show, advertisement, movie, or other media event

selective exposure
the idea that people seek media messages and/or interpret media texts in ways that confirm their beliefs and, conversely, resist or avoid messages that challenge their beliefs

It Happened to Me: Josh

I love comedies, but I seem to be the only person who doesn't like Will Ferrell movies. We saw *Stepbrothers* with some friends and I just wasn't impressed. Some of the scenes were verbally and physically exaggerated and every time I looked around and saw others laughing, I wondered why I didn't find it funny. I'd say Ferrell's last funny movie was *Old School*, and I think I like it because Vince Vaughn is more my style of humor. To me, Will Ferrell's type of humor is more slapstick, and I like a more "dry" humor. I always give every movie a chance, but I know that I have my favorite actors.

Selective Exposure

Selective exposure theories help us understand how identity plays a role in media tastes and preferences. These theories are based on the idea that people seek media messages and interpret media texts in ways that confirm their beliefs—and, conversely, that they resist or avoid messages that challenge their beliefs. Depending upon their personal and political beliefs, some people enjoyed watching the royal wedding of Prince William and Kate Middleton. Others chose not to watch the wedding.

One television show that was studied heavily in terms of selective exposure is *The Cosby Show*, a prime-time situation comedy that ran from 1984 to 1992. According to selective exposure theory, if someone believes racism no longer exists, then she or he is likely to interpret media messages as confirming or reinforcing this perception. In a study of *The Cosby Show*, Sut Jhally and Justin Lewis (1992) set up focus groups. Twenty-six of these focus groups were composed of White viewers of the show, and twenty-three were composed of African American viewers. In analyzing the White focus group responses, Jhally and Lewis found that Whites were more likely to think that *The Cosby Show* proved Black people can succeed; therefore, they said, African Americans who did not succeed were to blame for their own failure. In other words, as the White focus groups saw it, personal failings rather than discrimination or racism were what blocked success. In contrast, Black respondents saw *The Cosby Show* as a "cultural breakthrough" in terms of positive portrayals of Black culture (p. 121). Thus, they expressed far more concern about the pervasive

Alternative VIEW
Hostile Media Effect

In what ways do you selectively expose yourself to media messages? Do you generally listen to the same news commentators rather than seeking alternative voices? Do you watch the same shows your friends watch, or do you look for something different?

Selective exposure theories tell us that people tend to consume media that reinforce or support their own views. Yet, some media researchers counter this idea. Why? Researchers have found that people on both sides of an issue can be exposed to the same media coverage, and when asked what they thought of the coverage, both groups say that it was biased against their views. If both sides find the same coverage biased, it may undermine the idea that people only seek messages that confirm their views. Thus, the researchers concluded that while bias in media news stories surely does occur, another kind of bias rests with the viewer—a phenomenon called the "hostile media effect" because it reflects a general hostility toward media.

In their study, Albert C. Gunther and Kathleen Schmitt (2004) used the controversy over genetically modified foods to understand the hostile media effect. In part, their study found that regardless of respondents' position on genetically modified foods, they viewed news media stories as biased against them. However, when respondents saw the same information in a student essay format, the hostility tended to be absent or at least minimal. The researchers conclude, then, that the hostile media effect is created by the perception that a media message has the potential to influence large numbers of people for or against a particular viewpoint.

If the selective exposure theory is correct, and people tend to select media messages that support their own views, then why would they interpret these messages to be biased against them? There is no easy answer, but perhaps questions of bias and media selection need to be thought about in more complicated ways. When charges of bias arise against a media source, how often do we consider that the bias may be our own?

SOURCE: Gunther, A. C., & Schmitt, K. (2004). Mapping boundaries of the hostile media effect. *Journal of Communication, 54,* 55–70.

negative images of African Americans in media and the influences of those images on viewers. As you can see, while both racial groups were watching the same television show, their interpretations were very different.

Selective exposure theories point to the ways that both groups interpret the show to confirm their own beliefs and views. Those who subscribe to selective exposure theory argue that people rarely inhabit a media environment that challenges their social identities, including their religious and political beliefs, notions about gender, or ideas about race. Not all scholars subscribe to this theory, however: see *Alternative View: Hostile Media Effect.*

Another line of media research, called **uses and gratifications** studies and explores how people use media messages and what types of gratifications they find in some media texts rather than others. Working within this approach, researchers might want to know why viewers watch *The Bachelor* instead of *Dancing with the Stars, Rookie Blue* instead of *Law and Order,* or *Wipeout* instead of *Big Brother.* For example, a researcher might note that a certain type of entertainment is popular—say, violent movies, romance novels, or wrestling—and wish to explore why so many people seek out those kinds of texts and what needs they satisfy. Denis McQuail and his colleagues (1972) suggested four general uses and gratifications that audiences have for media texts:

- information
- personal identity
- integration and social interaction
- entertainment

uses and gratifications
the idea that people use media messages and find various types of gratifications in some media texts rather than in others

The first motivation, information seeking, is straightforward: audiences want to learn from some media presentations, as in the case of a news event. The second motivation, personal identity, refers to the idea that viewers may use media messages to affirm some aspect of their personal identity—for example, as mothers, consumers, or political conservatives. The third motivation, integration and social interaction, underscores the role that media can play in helping people connect with others, as they do when discussing sports or the events on a soap opera. Finally, the entertainment motivation refers to the use of media for pleasure, or the desire simply to be entertained. Of course, these motivations can overlap, so that we can watch a program for information, while at the same time using it as a topic for conversation with others, which would fit within McQuail's third motivation.

Cultural Values in Media Consumption

Understanding why some groups choose one program over another highlights the cultural values at work in the consumption of media. In his study of television preferences among Israeli adults, Jonathan Cohen (2002) examined viewing habits and choice. He found that factors influencing media selection included loyalty to particular channels, preferences for certain types of shows, and even the language of the programs, as programming in Israel is available in Hebrew, English, and other languages. His conclusion was that "Most Israeli viewers seem to prefer native programming, whether due to language problems or to cultural resonance" (p. 218). Cohen suggests that Israeli audiences use television not only for entertainment but also to affirm their Israeli identities and as a context for social interaction with other Israelis.

According to selective exposure theories, people seek out media that confirm what they already believe. What beliefs might viewers of Fox News and MSNBC disagree on?

Determining why people seek specific media texts and not other texts is very important from an economic perspective. After all, a media corporation does not want to spend a lot of money on a television show or magazine if it is going to fail. However, it is notoriously difficult to predict which media texts will become popular and which will not. *Desperate Housewives*, for example, was described as "the surprise hit of the television season" (Glaister, 2005). In spite of major investments in market research, there is no completely foolproof way to predict audience response.

Of course, the inability to accurately predict audience response does not mean that media producers have no information on trends. In certain eras, viewers are more interested in Westerns or police dramas, reality shows or evening soap operas than they are during other periods. Today, reality shows are quite popular. Furthermore, advertisers know that some groups prefer to consume certain kinds of media. For example, the advertising that appears during televised football games reveals what advertisers have learned about that audience through careful market research and analysis.

How Individuals Resist Media Messages

While media messages bombard people every day, individuals do not necessarily, or even easily, accept all that they receive. In addition, people actively resist certain media texts. For example, some people sought out and watched *Kill Bill* films, *Restrepo, 127 Hours*, and similar graphic movies. Others actively avoided them. Why? We resist media texts every day for many reasons, including something as hard to quantify as individual taste and something as personal as what we see as negative portrayals of our political, moral, or religious views; our interests, age, or level of education; or our gender, sexuality, and racial and ethnic identities. Other far less political reasons can create consumer resistance as well, as our student reveals in *It Happened to Me: Jessica*.

Resisting media messages entails much more than simply whether we go to a particular movie or watch a particular video. It is also about how we resist the power of media to shape our identities. For example, in one study, Meenakshi Gigi Durham (2004) interviewed South Asian immigrant teenage girls living in the United States. She explored the question of how these girls dealt with traditional Indian notions of female gender expectations in the context of available media. She found that the only mainstream U.S. show they liked to watch was *Friends*, which they found to be funny, while they disliked *Dawson's Creek*, which they thought was unrealistic. In general, they distanced themselves from mainstream U.S. media. In contrast, they consumed large amounts of media (films, popular music) from India, which they rented from Indian grocery stores and restaurants, borrowed from others, and watched or downloaded from the Internet. They particularly identified with the narratives in *Mississippi Masala, Bend It Like Beckham,* and *American Desi,* three Indian films with narratives involving "taboo relationships between Indian girls and men of different racial/cultural backgrounds" (p. 154). Durham concludes that these adolescent girls use media to create new identities, and that these identities do not conform to stereotypes of either Asian Indian women or U.S. American women.

It Happened to Me: Jessica

My boyfriend really wanted me to go see *127 Hours*. Although I do like James Franco, I just couldn't imagine sitting through a long movie watching someone suffering and cutting his arm off. So, I said no anyway, even though he mentioned it four or five times. He was unhappy that I wouldn't go to this movie, but I just didn't want to sit through that kind of emotional drama.

A television show produced by Radio Canada from 2004 to 2006, *Les Bougon,* highlighted the interrelatedness of social identities and media consumption and the complexities of consumption and resistance. *Les Bougon* was described in the *New York Times* as "a politically incorrect version of *Father Knows Best*, with twists so wicked and crude that even fans of *The Simpsons* might blush" (Krauss, 2004). The Canadian magazine *Macleans* described the Bougon family as "rough, truculent, beer-soaked urban trash. In their commitment to not working, though, they come out as likeable, funny anarchists" (Aubin, 2004). This representation of a poor family created a controversy in Canada, as well as high ratings. This television show was popular across social class identities in Québec, even if the classes interpreted it differently. For example, poor people may have liked the show because they interpreted it as empowering to their identities, and they saw this family as heroes for using the system to their advantage. In contrast, well-to-do viewers may have appreciated the program as a satire. Others, in any social class, may simply have seen a tight-knit family loving and protecting each other to survive (Cernetig, 2004).

As you have seen through our discussion, communication researchers are interested in all aspects of the relationship between individuals and the media messages that surround them. First, they wonder what effect media messages have on individuals; and second, they explore how individuals choose, resist, and interpret these messages. Research has revealed that the answers to both questions involve complex processes related to individual identity, individual needs, and individual taste. Audiences respond to and interpret texts based on both their individual and social identities, and therefore, different social groups can consume the same text while being affected by it differently and interpreting it differently. However, all individual responses and choices occur in a larger social context. Thus, to provide a more complete picture, we now shift our attention to the role of media at the societal level.

TEST YOUR KNOWLEDGE

- What strategies do media consumers use to select and reject media texts?
- Why might audiences prefer to watch media texts that affirm the values and beliefs they already hold?

THE INDIVIDUAL, MASS MEDIA, AND SOCIETY

content analysis
approach to understanding media that focuses on specific aspect of the content of a text or group of texts

Why do media play such an important role in society? One reason is that they often serve as the voice of the community. In this way, media offer people a means of thinking about themselves, their places in the world, and the societal forces around them. As individuals, we can only choose from among the media choices available. Societal forces, including the government, economics, media organizations, and advertisers, largely determine which media options are available. In the following section we'll look at three important roles that media play in society: confirming social identities, helping people understand the world, and helping individuals understand important public events. And finally, because no discussion of media and society would be complete without a discussion of media violence and media economics, we will conclude with these topics.

Confirming Social Identities

As we've noted, media representations influence our understanding of social identities, such as gender or age identity as well as the identities of others. This is one of the functions of media usage we examined as we discussed uses and gratifications. For example, images we see on television and in films, magazines, and newspapers shape our sense of what it is to be a man or woman. These views often create or enforce a hierarchy of identities, often portraying men as more powerful than women. Thus, media messages not only shape the way we understand social identities; they also show us which social identities are valued. For example, as Associated Press reviewer Christy Lemire (2005) noted in her review of the film *Deuce Bigalow: European Gigolo*, "Making fun of homosexuality seems to be the one area of humor that has yet to be ruled off-limits by political correctness; such jokes also appeared in the far superior *Wedding Crashers* earlier this summer." If Lemire's analysis is correct, this "permission" to joke about one particular social identity can reinforce a hierarchy in which heterosexuality is valued over homosexuality.

One approach to understanding how and what media communicate about various social identities is content analysis. **Content analysis** focuses on some specific aspect of a text's content. Bernard Berelson (1952/1971), a behavioral scientist, explains that content analysis took off during the late 1930s, with the work of Harold Laswell and his colleagues (see Chapter 2), who were concerned with "propaganda and public opinion and the emergence of radio as a great mass medium of communication."

How does content analysis work? To begin, a researcher might want to know how many non-White characters appear on the television show *Monk*, which is set in San Francisco, a very multiethnic and multicultural city, or on *NCIS: Los Angeles*, a show set in a city where Whites are a minority population. The researcher would thus watch a number of episodes, count the number of non-White characters, note the kinds of roles they play and which characters are central, and finally, draw conclusions based on these data. Recently, actress Geena Davis became quite concerned about the imbalance between males and females in media representations. In two large studies on television programs and films, males outnumbered females by 70 percent to 30 percent (Belkin, 2010). In order to try to understand these content differences and their impact on children, she founded the Geena Davis Institute on Gender and Media (http://www.thegeenadavisinstitute.org/). Further, researcher Caroline Aoyagi (2004) conducted a content analysis of TV shows set in the state of Hawaii and concluded the following:

> No one can blame the big television networks for their love affair with the beautiful islands of Hawaii, but as several new shows are set to launch or are already on air, the lack of Asian Pacific Americans in the shows' casts have many wondering: what Hawaii is this?
>
> In a state where Asian Pacific Islander Americans [APIA] make up more than 80 percent of the population and whites are considered the minority, a look at

the new line-up of shows for FOX, the WB network, and NBC show no APIA lead actors and only one or two APIAs in supporting roles (p. 1).

Images of male beauty are socially constructed.

A content analysis of television shows, thus, can provide data on racial representation in media. Content analysis also can reveal the kinds of topics that arise most often, the way episodes and conflicts are resolved most frequently, the number and types of conflicts that occur, and many other issues. In their study of television news in Los Angeles and Orange County, California, Travis Dixon and Daniel Linz (2002) employed content analysis to determine whether correlations existed between pretrial publicity and race. Using the American Bar Association's definition of potentially prejudicial information, they found that "Blacks and Latinos are twice as likely as Whites to have prejudicial information aired about them, and Latinos are three times more likely than Whites to have prejudicial information aired when they victimize Whites" (p. 133). Through content analysis, then, these two scholars were able to show a strong correlation between the race of the accused and the reporting of prejudicial information in the news. Moreover, they found that reporting of prejudicial information dramatically increased when the crime victim was White. Here you can see how media confirm social identities.

Similarly, Cheryl Law and Magdala Peixoto Labre (2002) conducted a content analysis of images of male bodies in thirty years of popular magazines, specifically *GQ, Rolling Stone*, and *Sports Illustrated*. They found that "the images of men in popular magazines became more lean and muscular from 1967 to 1997, and that the V-shaped male figure also became more prevalent over time" (p. 705). As the researchers report, "this content analysis suggests that the new ideal seen in the mass media does not represent the body type most men have" (p. 706), and they speculate on the effect these images have on men's behavior, for example, their use of steroids, diets, and workouts. Because this was a content analysis and not a media-effects study, the researchers did not survey male readers of these magazines to find out whether they actually went on diets, used steroids, and so on. Instead, the point of the study is to highlight what media messages communicate to men (and women) about the ideal male image and male social identity.

Content analysis by itself does not reveal why viewers choose to watch particular television shows or consume other kinds of media messages. Collecting demographic information about an audience's racial, ethnic, or age composition may give some insight as to which groups are drawn to what kind of content, but, again, this is not the primary purpose of content analysis. For example, the study we mentioned earlier by Dixon and Linz did not try to explain whether or why southern Californians preferred pretrial television news coverage with prejudicial information about minorities, or why the television news industry produces this kind of news. What their data do confirm, however, is that Blacks and Latinos are represented more negatively in news programs.

Some studies use a more detailed analysis of media messages than content analysis does, and this approach can help us better understand which social identities are being confirmed and elevated. Such studies, which rely on textual analysis, typically focus on fewer media texts than content analyses do. Researchers who conduct textual analyses of media messages take an approach similar to literary critics when they explore meanings in a literary work. However, in textual analysis, any kind of media image can be considered a text. For example, in her study of the news coverage of Freaknik, a spring break event that used to draw African American college students to Atlanta, Marian Meyers (2004) looked closely at the news reports of sexual violence against African American women perpetrated by African American men. "In essence," she wrote, "the news criminalized Black men primarily with respect to property damage while decriminalizing them concerning their abuse of women. The safety of Black women appears of less consequence than that of property" (p. 113). Thus, these news reports confirmed an identity of Black men as criminals while undermining the identity of Black women as crime victims.

In her study of masculinity, Helene Shugart (2008) focused on the media construction of the "metrosexual" in the context of commercialism. Metrosexuals are men who are meticulous about their appearance—not only their physiques, but also their clothing, hair styles, and so forth. In her textual analysis of the metrosexual, Shugart found that metrosexuality "bore all the hallmarks of a fad or a trend" (p. 295), but metrosexuality also "served a vital and strategic rhetoric function as part of a much larger and ongoing cultural discourse about masculinity(ies)" (p. 295). Because commercialism has threatened traditional masculinity by insisting on enhancing masculinity through the purchase of various products, metrosexuality helped to reconcile the contradiction between the commercial masculinity and a more traditional or normative masculinity.

Thus, what people see, hear, and read in the media can confirm identities, but so can their media choices. Although our social identities are not absolute predictors of media choices, trends do emerge if we look at the correlations between media consumption and various social identities. Nielsen Media Research has studied the most popular television shows among all U.S. Americans and among African Americans as a subgroup, revealing that their choices are similar in some respects and different in others, and thus, that racial identities do somewhat correlate with media consumption, as noted in *Did You Know? Nielsen Media Research*.

In addition, people often choose media images that not only confirm their identities but also help them deal with the various issues involved in any identity. For example, some women are drawn to the USA Network shows *Covert Affairs* and *In Plain Sight*, which feature strong women characters—one working as a CIA agent and the other as a U.S. marshal—who work in male-dominated environments. These characters help women envision how they can operate successfully in masculine environments and retain their gender identity.

How does media coverage favor some identities over others? The amount of coverage, as revealed by content analysis, is sometimes the controlling factor. For example, in their study of the Salt Lake City Olympics in 2002, Billings and Eastman (2003) found that NBC devoted more time to reporting on male athletes and White athletes than on other groups. The potential effect of this imbalance is that the identities of particular viewers are reinforced, while the identities of other viewers are undermined. Remember, however, that more extensive coverage can also have the opposite effect. For example, if an identity is portrayed with great frequency in a negative way, that identity can be undermined, as Dixon and Linz found in their analysis of pretrial coverage in southern California (2002).

As you learned in Chapter 3, social identities help shape individuals' outlook on the world; at the same time, individuals interpret media texts from their identity positions. Media critics have been instrumental in bringing to the public's attention these issues of identity confirmation and media bias in portraying identities. As a result, many with identities that media portray less positively have come to recognize their exclusion. The effect can be anger or disengagement when few, if any, images exist of one's own social group acting in positive ways.

Did You Know?

Nielsen Media Research

What kinds of shows or movies do you like to watch, and which aspects of your social identities might guide these media choices? How might these choices sustain or challenge your social identities?

Nielsen ratings are widely used in the television industry to determine audience viewing, and they are used to set advertising rates. Note their findings on the top-rated television shows for African Americans and for the U.S. population at large, shown in the tables included here. How might social identities play a role in the popularity of some television shows?

The following were the highest-rated prime-time television programs in African American households for one week in June 2011:

Rank	Program	Network	Household Rating %
1	*The Voice*	NBC	6.2
2	*So You Think You Can Dance-Thu*	FOX	6.0
3	*America's Got Talent*	NBC	5.8
4	*Law and Order: L.A.*	NBC	5.7
5	*So You Think You Can Dance-Wed*	FOX	5.6
6	*America's Got Talent-Wed*	NBC	5.5
7	*America's Got Talent-Tue*	NBC	5.4
7	*NCIS: Los Angeles*	CBS	5.4
9	*The Voice: Results Show*	NBC	5.3
10	*Wipeout-Thurs*	ABC	4.8
10	*Criminal Minds*	CBS	4.8
10	*CSI: NY*	CBS	4.8

The following were the highest-rated prime-time television programs in all U.S. households (including African American homes) for one week in June 2011.

Rank	Program	Network	Household Rating %
1	*America's Got Talent-Wed*	NBC	7.5
2	*America's Got Talent-Tue*	NBC	7.1
3	*The Voice*	NBC	6.8
4	*NCIS*	CBS	6.2
5	*America's Got Talent (6/22)*	NBC	6.1
6	*The Voice: Results Show*	NBC	6.0
7	*NCIS: Los Angeles*	CBS	5.9
8	*The Mentalist*	CBS	5.2
9	*The Bachelorette*	ABC	5.1
9	*CSI*	CBS	5.1

SOURCE: Nielsen Media Research. (n.d.). Top primetime programs—African American homes. Retrieved July 12, 2011, from Nielsen Media Research. (n.d.). Television—Week of June 20, 2011. Retrieved July 12, 2011, from http://www.nielsen.com/us/en/insights/top10s/television.html

Understanding the World

Media play a key role in helping people understand the world. Most people will never travel to the Ukraine, North Korea, Iraq, Palestine, Rwanda, Indonesia, Somalia, or Brazil, but they can learn something about these places through media. They may see these distant regions on the Travel Channel or in *National Geographic* magazine, or they may see news about them on CNN, MSNBC, or other news channels.

However, the texts that media organizations produce can distort the images of faraway places as well as enhance them, especially if viewers have never been to the parts of the world represented. In her study of AP wire photographs of Afghan women—both during and after the Taliban regime—Shahira Fahmy (2004) found that "1 percent of [published] AP photographs portrayed women revealing their face and hair." Thus, even after the fall of the Taliban, Afghan women are depicted wearing their burqas—despite the fact that many photos exist that portray "images of Afghan women removing their burqas as a sign of liberation" (p. 110). In this study, Fahmy brings to light the discrepancy between the pool of available AP photographs and the ones selected for publication in the United States, noting that the ones that editors select shape and sometimes distort our impressions of the subject.

As another example of the media's power to shape knowledge and understanding, prior to the disappearance of Natalee Holloway in the spring of 2005, there had been little U.S. news coverage of the Caribbean island of Aruba. Many U.S. Americans did not know that Aruba was Dutch or that it operated under the Dutch legal system—much less what the technicalities of that system were. In contrast, media provide U.S. audiences with extensive detail on the British royal family. As another example, U.S. media coverage of weather typically stops at our northern and southern borders, as if weather didn't exist in Canada or Mexico. As you can see, by choosing what to cover and how extensively, media shape audience understanding of what is and isn't important in the world.

Agenda-Setting Capacity

This power of media coverage to influence individuals' view of the world is referred to as its **agenda-setting capacity**. Thus, in agenda-setting research, scholars focus on audience perceptions of reality and attempt to discover how or whether media coverage correlates with these audience perceptions. For example, Lowry, Nio, and Leitner (2003) studied correlations between crime rates, news coverage on crime, and public attitudes about crime from 1978 to 1998. Existing data indicated that in March 1992, only 5 percent of the public thought that crime was the most important problem. By August 1994, however, 52 percent felt that way. What accounted for this jump? By correlating the amount of television news coverage with the crime rates, the researchers found that the amount of news coverage was far more influential than actual crime rates in this change in public perception. By focusing so much attention on crime reporting, the theory goes, media set the public agenda for what was important. Agenda-setting studies often look at long time periods, as the crime-coverage study did, in order to correlate media coverage to changes in audience perceptions.

In another study using an agenda-setting perspective, Jochen Peter (2003) focused on the issue of fourteen European nations and their integration into the European Union (EU). Here, however, he did not find a simple correlation between more news coverage of EU integration and public attitudes about the importance of this issue. Instead he found that when political elites agreed about integration, public involvement or interest in the issue declined. Coverage of disagreement among political elites over EU integration did correlate, though, with public involvement in the issue. Thus, content and the degree of exposure play parts in setting the public's agenda.

agenda-setting capacity
the power of media coverage to influence individuals' view of the world

Cultivation theory has been used to emphasize the role of news coverage of crime in the perceptions of crime rates.

Cultivation Theory

Media messages also play a critical role in acculturating individuals. **Cultivation theory** proposes that long-term immersion in a media environment leads to "cultivation," or enculturation, into shared beliefs about the world. Unlike other approaches that focus on specific media messages, television programs, movies, or other kinds of text, "Cultivation analysis is concerned with the more general and pervasive consequences of cumulative exposure to cultural media" (Morgan & Signorielli, 1990, p. 16). Initiated by George Gerbner (2002) and his colleagues, cultivation analysis seeks to uncover how television, in particular, influences those who are heavy viewers. Those who watch television news, the theory goes, will share certain beliefs or distortions about the world. Moreover, this theory argues that media coverage shapes attitudes about one's own society and the issues it faces. For example, although crime rates have gone down overall in recent years, many U.S. Americans feel more insecure than ever. In their study on fear of crime, Daniel Romer, Kathleen Hall Jamieson, and Sean Aday (2003) surveyed 2,300 Philadelphia residents. Within that population group, they found a relationship between the widespread belief that crime is a significant problem and the amount of local television news coverage of crimes. The point of the study is that Philadelphia media coverage cultivates attitudes and beliefs that shape everyday life in Philadelphia, with a key element of daily life being an exaggerated fear of crime.

In a recent cultivation study, Jeff Niederdeppe and his colleagues (2010) studied the ways that local television news covers cancer prevention because the "sheer volume of news coverage about cancer causes and prevention has led to broad speculation about its role in promoting fatalistic beliefs" (p. 231), Niederdeppe and colleagues developed three hypotheses comparing local television news coverage with local newspaper coverage of various cancer issues and their fourth hypothesis focused on the relationship between local TV news viewing and fatalistic beliefs about cancer prevention They found that there is "a tendency for local TV news to focus on aspects of cancer that are likely to cultivate the beliefs that everything causes cancer or that there are too many recommendations about cancer prevention" (p. 246). In both these studies, then, immersion in the television environment shaped, or cultivated, a particular view of the world.

Media Hegemony

A different way of explaining how media influence how we understand the world is through **hegemony**. Hegemony refers to the process by which people consent to particular understandings as reflected in media representations. For instance, we come to understand what "mother" means through often idealized images of mothers on television programs, films, and other media. While there are no laws that regulate what a "mother" must do, we consent to these images of motherhood and we expect mothers to engage in certain behaviors, such as throwing birthday parties for their children. In contrast, our hegemonic understanding of "fathers" does not include that kind of activity. Fathers can, of course, throw birthday parties for their children, but it is not part of the hegemonic construction of fatherhood.

Masculinity, as represented in media content, has been a rich site for investigating how hegemony functions. For example, in his work on hegemony, communication scholar Nick Trujillo (1991) studied the media representations of Nolan Ryan, a base-

cultivation theory
idea that long-term immersion in a media environment leads to "cultivation," or enculturation, into shared beliefs about the world

hegemony
the process by which we consent to social constructions, rather than having them imposed on us

ball pitcher, to show how masculinity is constructed. He found five features of how Ryan was portrayed: (1) male athletic power, (2) ideal image of the capitalist worker, (3) family patriarch, (4) White rural cowboy, and (5) symbol of male (hetero)sexuality. Trujillo asks that we consider the negative consequences of this construction of masculinity. Additionally, in his study of the television show *thirtysomething*, Hanke (1990) analyzes the way that hegemonic masculinity shifts slightly to focus on men "who are more open to domestic concerns and interpersonal relationships" (p. 245). His analysis focuses on hegemony as a process in which masculinity shifts to respond to changing social needs. Hegemony is a process by which we all participate in the social construction of ourselves and others. If we violate these hegemonic notions, we risk alienation. This approach to the study of media content helps us better understand the contours and limits of how we might present ourselves and interpret others, as hegemony outlines what is acceptable, normal, or even ideal.

Interpreting Media Events

The term **media event** applies to those occasions or catastrophes that interrupt regular programming. Like rhetorical events, in media events create vast numbers of media messages. Examples include the funeral of John F. Kennedy, the Olympics, or the attacks of September 11, 2001. Media scholars are interested in the coverage of such events because such coverage can shape viewers' understanding of what has occurred and create powerful responses. For example, Daniel Dayan and Elihu Katz (1992) found that media events bring society closer together. As a new form of "high holidays of mass communication" (p. 1), these events both reinforce and celebrate national identity.

Some media events are staged by public relations officers to garner media attention on a particular issue. When the president of the United States calls a press conference, for example, he is creating a media event. Then, of course, the representatives of various news media are present to report what he says. In these cases, the president and his public relations staff carefully control many aspects of the conference—where it will be staged, what kinds of issues will be raised, who will be present, what video images will be shown, and so on. Other politicians, movie stars, and lawyers in high-profile cases also commonly create media events to bring attention to themselves and/or their causes.

Not everyone, however, can attract this kind of media attention. People seeking media attention who lack notoriety or celebrity must use other measures. For example, during the World Trade Organization meetings in Seattle in 1999, protestors used the Internet and alternative newspapers to plan a large march in downtown Seattle. The violence that erupted between police and some protesters drew considerable media attention and was broadcast widely (DeLuca & Peeples, 2002). More recently, when the Duke and Duchess of Cambridge visited Canada in June 2011, they aroused the anger of anti-monarchy activists; moreover, animal rights advocates were upset by their participation in a rodeo in Calgary. In various places during the tour, Canadian protestors created media events by staging large public protests.

Media events often focus on important rituals while promoting a variety of less obvious messages, or subtexts. Examples of rituals include royal marriages, state funerals, and presidential inaugurations. These events, media observers say, go well beyond the occasion to promote important cultural values through media coverage. For example, in their analysis of the British queen's Golden Jubilee, Claire Wardle and Emily West (2004) concluded that the British press framed the event not simply as an anniversary celebration for the queen, but as a sign of British national strength, thus converting it to a nationalistic celebration.

Media events are filled with messages that shape one's view of the world and invite one to view the world in a particular way. The funerals of Yasser Arafat and Ronald Reagan, the inaugurations of George W. Bush and Barack Obama, and

media event
occasions or catastrophes that interrupt regular programming

many other media events are worthy of examination for the underlying assumptions and meanings they communicate beyond reporting the facts. For example, in addition to explaining what occurred, such events can stimulate nationalistic feelings, celebrate a nation's history or values, or reinforce specific political beliefs and positions. Another example of a powerful media event was the 2010 earthquake in Haiti and the 2011 earthquake and tsunami in Japan. Media played a key role in bringing attention to these human tragedies, which in turn prompted huge numbers of people to make donations to relief organizations.

Monitoring Media Violence

Representations of violent acts in media are common and are an increasingly important area of research, as well as a concern among parents and other groups. As you might surmise, our society is ambivalent about **media violence**, as indicated by the range of responses to it. On the one hand, a large number of people must be entertained by it, or why would there be so many violent books, movies, and video games? On the other, media producers and editors make intentional decisions to keep certain violent images out of the public view (beheadings, coffins, bodies). In addition, we are inventing tools such as parental control devices for television to protect certain members of society from witnessing violence. These conflicting trends reveal tensions between the principles of censorship, freedom of the press, and protection of children.

Parents play an important role in their children's media viewing, as well as the way in which their children interpret the programs they watch.

While no clear-cut definition of violence exists, most people generally consider shootings, stabbings, and other kinds of killings and attempted killings to be violent. Slapping, hitting, and fighting of all types also constitute violence. Most of the concern about media violence focuses on its impact on children. The American Academy of Pediatrics, for example, is particularly concerned about the influence of media violence on children under 8 years of age. Based on current research (2002), they have concluded that media violence has the following effects on children:

- increased aggressiveness and antisocial behavior,
- increased fear of becoming victims,
- less sensitivity to violence and to victims of violence, and
- increased appetite for more violence in entertainment and in real life.

media violence
representations of violent acts in media

V-chip
device that identifies television program ratings by content and can block programming designated by the owner

These concerns are not new. People, especially parents, began to worry about media violence in television almost as soon as broadcasting began in 1946. Also, as we noted earlier, numerous studies have shown that "media violence contributes to a more violent society" (Anderson & Bushman, 2002, p. 2377). Research has also demonstrated that although cartoons are far more violent than prime-time television, an intervention by parents and adults can influence how children respond to those violent images. For example, in her study of 5- to 7- and 10- to 12-year-old children, Amy Nathanson (2004) found that when parents and other adults simply discussed the production techniques of a program, this either had no effect on children or it increased the influence of the violent images. In contrast, when parents underscored the fictional nature of a program's characters, the children were better able to deal with the violence and were less afraid.

In response to concerns about children and television content, in 1998 the Federal Communications Commission (2003) mandated that half of all new televisions 13 inches or larger manufactured after July 1, 1999, and *all* sets 13 inches or larger manufactured after January 1, 2000 must have a **V-chip** installed. A V-chip identifies program ratings by content and can block programming that is designated by the owner, typically the parent(s). For example, a parent who does not want a child to watch programs with TV-14 ratings can block such programs from being shown.

Similar systems have been developed to block access to certain kinds of Web sites on the Internet and other media.

Of course, not all violent images presented in media are fictional. Television news journalists must decide what is and is not too horrifying to broadcast. For example, recent Internet broadcasts of hostages in Iraq being beheaded have not been shown on U.S. network television. Images of people leaping to their deaths from the World Trade Center towers on September 11, 2001, also were considered too troubling to broadcast.

The Federal Communications Commission has oversight of the appropriateness of television programming, but it focuses more on the major network channels than on cable channels. Moreover, the commission can fine broadcasters for presenting inappropriate materials, but these fines are typically for indecency rather than violence. Sometimes broadcasters warn audiences that an upcoming image may not be suitable for all audiences—one approach to dealing with extremely violent images. For example, some television newscasters provided such warnings before showing the numerous bodies of victims of the 2004 Indian Ocean tsunami. Cable broadcasts, particularly pay-per-view, have more leeway in their programming, since the assumption is that viewers have actively sought out and paid for a particular type of programming.

Analyzing Media Economics

Mass communication today is dominated by the large corporations that produce and distribute media messages. Thus, the economics of media production shapes mass communication and gives it a unique and powerful role in our society. No individual can easily compete with a multinational corporation in producing and distributing media messages. Therefore, these huge media corporations determine which messages are available, and this ownership can have consequences for society in important ways. The Walt Disney Company, one of the world's largest media conglomerates, owns several television networks as well as TV and movie production and distribution companies; these, together with its publishing and merchandising divisions and Disney character licensing, give the company enormous influence on the messages that fill the media environment. An equally wide-reaching media conglomerate is News Corporation, headed by Australian-born entrepreneur Rupert Murdoch.

In the area of media studies concerned with economic issues, scholars focus on **political economy**, or the ways in which media institutions produce texts in a capitalist system and the legal and regulatory frameworks that shape their options for doing so. Political economists also examine how these media products are marketed in order to understand what they reveal about our society. This approach is an extension of the work of Karl Marx, the influential nineteenth-century socialist thinker, and it emphasizes the economics of media, rather than its messages or audiences, although all those components are interrelated. An example of this theory's application can be seen in one researcher's analysis of the recent decision by ABC to cease broadcasting the Miss America pageant. After all, the researcher noted, "a little more than a decade ago [this pageant] had copped about 27 million viewers; last month it drew a record-low 9.8 million" (de Moraes, 2004). With a small viewing audience, the demand for and price of advertising during the pageant also dropped. Thus, the theory goes, economic factors largely determine what media content people are exposed to.

Earlier in this chapter, we introduced the term *culture industries* to refer to organizations that produce, distribute, or show various media texts. In the United States, these culture industries most often are media corporations or media industries that operate for profit. In some other countries, however, culture industries are more like U.S. public television—meaning that they are nonprofit media organizations—and this economic structure affects content and programming. Consider for a

How well does the V-chip serve its intended purpose? What measures do you think society should take to limit children's exposure to inappropriate media content?

political economy
the ways in which media institutions produce texts in a capitalist system and the legal and regulatory frameworks that shape their options for doing so

moment how a nonprofit media organization might develop programming as compared with a for-profit organization. What factors might guide their decision making? PBS, for example, needs to please the public and the government, both of which fund it. In contrast, for-profit networks need to please shareholders and advertisers by drawing large audiences.

While television networks have historically been identified with specific nations—for example, CBC with Canada and BBC with Britain—globalization has recently sparked and sustained transnational television networks. Many media corporations with significant financial backing are moving in this direction. Though initial attempts at transnational broadcasting in the early 1980s to mid-1990s faced many difficulties and most did not survive (Chalaby, 2003), today, transnational television networks are growing, and some of these include U.S.-based networks such as CNN International and MTV. Some are European-based, such as BBC World, Euronews, and Skynews. More studies need to be done to determine how this global flow of information and entertainment may be influencing societies.

In China, another kind of change has been occurring in the mass media system, related in part to globalization. As the Chinese economy has moved toward a capitalist or free-enterprise model, the state-owned mass media system has experienced changes, including the "rise of semi-independent newspapers and broadcasting stations, the proliferation of private Internet content providers and unlicensed cable networks, and increasing cross-investment by the media into other commercial enterprises, including joint ventures with international media giants" (Akhavan-Majid, 2004, p. 553). In her study of these new Chinese media, Akhavan-Majid argues that "non-state actors (e.g., citizens, journalists, entrepreneurs)" (2004, p. 554) have used loopholes in official Chinese policies to creatively open new media opportunities. As you can see, changes in political and economic structures can be intimately intertwined with changes in mass media.

Political economists also analyze the mergers and acquisitions that occur in the media industry as a way of understanding changes in programming. For example, when NBC acquired the Bravo channel (2001), it added performing arts and arts films to its roster as well as some riskier programs, including *Boy Meets Boy* (2003) and *Queer Eye for the Straight Guy* (2003–2007) (and *Girl* (2008)). In a news release related to this sale, Bob Wright, Vice Chairman of General Electric and Chairman and CEO of NBC, noted that "Bravo, with its desirable demographic, is a perfect strategic addition to our portfolio, providing a particularly good fit with NBC's network and cable viewers" (Cablevision, 2000). In analyzing these developments, a political economist might focus on the economic reasons behind this acquisition and the potential future revenues to be generated by appealing to this desirable demographic group. (*Desirable* typically refers to an audience with the size and demographic profile to bring in high advertising revenues.) As Bravo continues to search for desirable audiences, the network has moved to new television programming, including *Top Chef, Flipping Out, Million Dollar Decorators, Millionaire Matchmaker,* and *The Real Housewives of New Jersey.*

Of course, political economists cannot predict the kinds of media texts that will emerge from any specific merger. They know that television stations seek viewers who are more affluent so they can attract more advertisers, but political economists do not know (nor does anyone) what kinds of shows will attract affluent viewers. While television production companies try to create—and television networks try to buy—television programs that will draw large audiences, they do not always succeed. Political economists cannot and do not predict such successes, either. Instead, they focus on the ways that corporate media influence the information we get, the consequences of capitalist media corporations on society, and the demands that this political and economic structure places on journalists, broadcasters, and other media workers.

In the context of the 2003 Federation Communications Commission's decision to relax restrictions on ownership of media, understanding and unraveling the complex relationships among media economics, media ownership, and media content can be crucial. For example, because news is sold for profit, the profit motive shapes what readers consider "news." This commercial pressure influences the work of journalists as well as the way media organizations are run. One leading scholar in this area, Robert McChesney (1998), raised this alarm more than a decade ago:

> The American media system is spinning out of control in a hyper-commercialized frenzy. Fewer than ten transnational media conglomerates dominate much of our media; fewer than two dozen account for the overwhelming majority of our newspapers, magazines, films, television, radio, and books. With every aspect of our media culture now fair game for commercial exploitation, we can look forward to the full-scale commercialization of sports, arts, and education, the disappearance of notions of public service from public discourse, and the degeneration of journalism, political coverage, and children's programming under commercial pressure. (p. 4)

By focusing on the political and economic structures in which media industries operate, political economists offer a unique perspective on the influence of media in our lives. Their analysis of areas that many people ignore reveals the potential consequences of the business of media on all of us.

Societal issues very much influence individuals' interactions with media. Moreover, both personal and social identities are key to one's interactions with media and how one interprets media violence. Given the profits to be made, media economics ensures that media violence will remain pervasive as long as people continue to purchase products with violent content.

TEST YOUR KNOWLEDGE

- How do media events reaffirm values and social identities?
- What role does the media play in how we understand the world?
- How do media events invite particular ways of viewing the world?
- What are common concerns about media violence, and how are these concerns being addressed?
- How are media influenced by the political and economic systems that they operate within?

☒ ETHICS AND MASS MEDIA

Because media messages are so powerful, they can generate powerful responses. One potential response is **media activism,** or the practice of organizing to communicate displeasure with certain media images and messages, as well as to advocate for change in future media texts. The issues that media activists address are important because they highlight many significant ethical questions surrounding mediated communication. Media activism, of course, is not limited to the United States. Media activist groups have mobilized around the world to express ethical concerns about media coverage on a range of issues.

Voicing ethical concerns through media activism is not a recent phenomenon. People have been concerned about media content and images for centuries. The notions of freedom of speech and freedom of the press articulated in the U.S. Constitution reflect one response to media control. In the early twentieth century, as silent movies became popular entertainment, concerns about their racy content and the transition to talking movies led to calls for government regulation of media. In an

media activism
the practice of organizing to communicate displeasure with certain media images and messages, as well as to force change in future media texts

Did You Know?

The Hays Code

What kinds of restrictions do you believe are appropriate in mass media? Which of the Hays Code rules seem valid today? Should the media industry and/or government regulate the kinds of media messages that are available? Explain the reasons behind your answers.

All of the following regulations are taken from the Hays Code.

- Dances which emphasize indecent movements are to be regarded as obscene.
- Complete nudity is never permitted. This includes nudity in fact or in silhouette or licentious notice thereof by other characters in the picture.
- The use of the flag shall be consistently respectful.
- No film or episode may throw ridicule on any religious faith.
- Adultery and Illicit Sex, sometimes necessary plot material, must not be explicitly treated, or justified, or presented attractively.
- Illegal drug traffic, and drug addiction, must never be presented.
- White slavery shall not be treated.

EXCERPTED FROM: Motion Picture Association of America, Inc. (1930–1955). *A Code to Govern the Making of Motion Pictures.*

attempt to avoid government regulation, Hollywood established the Hays Office to create its own system of regulation. The **Hays Code**, which was published in 1930, established strict rules for media content with the goal of wholesome entertainment (*see Did You Know? The Hays Code*). Some of the Hays regulations still apply today, such as the ban on exposing children's sex organs. Other regulations, however, have become outdated, such as the ban against portraying sexual relationships between interracial couples or using vulgar expressions or profanity, which the code specified as including the words "God, Lord, Jesus, Christ (unless used reverently); cripes; fairy (in a vulgar sense)."

The Hays code came about because of media activism in the 1920s, and it continued to set industry standards until the late 1960s, when the **MPAA** (Motion Picture Association of America) devised its rating codes. These codes have changed slightly since then, but most people are familiar with the G, PG, PG-13, R, and NC-17 ratings. Today, media activism has concentrated largely on the ethics of four areas: children's programming, representations of cultural groups, news reporting, and alternative programming. Let's look at each of these in turn.

Complaints about content in television shows and its influence on children led to the creation of the **TV Parental Guidelines** (by the TV Parental Guidelines Monitoring Board), which are a self-regulating system of the television industry. These guidelines rate programs in terms of appropriateness for particular age groups. You have probably noticed the rating codes in the upper-left corner of the television screen. (An explanation of the ratings is available at www.tvguidelines.org/ratings .htm.) This kind of rating system is voluntary, so unless an adult activates the V-chip or an adult is present to change the channel or turn off the television, the rating system may not work as it was intended.

The second ethical focus of media activists has been distortions perpetrated or reinforced by media. The concern here is that such portrayals create stereotypes and misunderstandings. Minority groups, in particular, have had such concerns, as we can see in the number of media activist groups focused on media representations of racial and sexual minorities.

These activists argue that when people have limited contact with minority groups, they are likely to gain false impressions from media misrepresentations. In

Hays Code
self-imposed rules for Hollywood media content instituted in 1930 with the goal of creating "wholesome entertainment"

MPAA
Motion Picture Association of America

TV Parental Guidelines
a self-regulating system of the television industry that rates programs in terms of appropriateness for particular age groups

turn, these distorted images may lead to hate crimes or discriminatory government policies, such as racial profiling. Media activist groups that monitor media producers and challenge them to create responsible and accurate images include MANAA (Media Action Network for Asian Americans) and GLAAD (Gay and Lesbian Alliance Against Defamation) as well as organizations that have broader goals but that include a media activist focus, such as the National Organization for Women (NOW) and the League of United Latin American Citizens (LULAC).

A third category of activist groups has focused on structural issues in media industries and the consequences for consumers. For example, organizations like FAIR (Fairness and Accuracy in Reporting, www.fair .org), the Annenberg Public Policy Center's factcheck.org, the Arthur W. Page Center for Integrity in Public Communication (thepagecenter .comm.psu.edu) and the National Public Radio program On the Media (www.onthemedia.org) are some of the organizations that focus on the news media and their accuracy and fairness in reporting various issues and the inclusion of diverse viewpoints.

The fourth ethical focus of media activists has been to find and provide media texts that offer alternatives to mainstream sources. For example, Clean Flicks was created by and for those who are concerned that movies have too much violence and sex. Clean Flicks offered alternatives that were free of profanity, graphic violence, nudity, and sexual content until they lost a court battle in 2006 and were prohibited from editing films. Many newspapers, radio programs, and Internet sites are available for those who want alternatives to mainstream news media coverage so that they can hear a diversity of voices and opinions. Earlier we discussed the alternative press, but there is also alternative radio programming, such as the Progressive Radio Network, and other alternative media outlets, such as Amy Goodman and Juan Gonzalez's daily television program *Democracy Now!* Other alternative views are expressed as humor in print, online in *The Onion*, and on television on *The Daily Show* and *The Colbert Report*.

Finally, some activists use media to communicate specific ethical concerns and messages to a wide audience. Thus, despite the fact that they lack the backing of huge media conglomerates, activists have used media to educate or influence audiences regarding cruelty to animals; the situations in Palestine, Guantánamo, and Afghanistan; violence against women; anti-Semitism; genocide; racism; and more. To get their messages out, these groups set up Web sites and Web casts, solicit funds to run advertisements on television or in mainstream newspapers or magazines, and sometimes organize demonstrations at strategic times and places.

As new media outlets develop (for example via the Internet, cable TV, and satellite radio) and the world continues to confront new challenges, new ethical issues and new ways of communicating will continue to emerge. We cannot forecast the future, but we do know that the ongoing process of change in the media environment shows no signs of abating. Media activists will continue to try to shape the media messages we receive, while at the same time, media producers will continue to try to sell what people are interested in purchasing. And so, bombarded as you are by media and the messages of a range of media activists, how can you become a responsible media consumer? Let's explore this topic next.

The GLAAD Media Awards is an annual event that honors responsible and accurate media images of lesbians, gays, transgendered individuals, and bisexuals.

BECOMING A MORE EFFECTIVE MEDIA CONSUMER

As a potential consumer of practically nonstop messages coming from radio, television, newspapers, magazines, advertisements, movies, and so on, you need strategies for dealing with this complex media environment. The solution cannot be boiled

As an active media consumer, you can talk back to your television as well as discuss media messages with family and friends.

down to a set of simple guidelines, of course, but here are some ideas to consider when interacting with media. To become more effective in your media consumption, be an active agent in your media choices, be mindful of the media choices you make, and speak out if you find media content offensive.

Be an Active Agent

How can you become an active consumer of media? First, don't just watch or read whatever is available. Make deliberate choices about media you expose yourself to so that you can better control the effect that media messages have on you. As you become more selective, you express a set of media-related values, which in turn indicates to media providers what type of media programming they should be providing.

As an active agent, then, seek out those media that meet your needs and avoid or resist others. In order to be a truly active agent, however, you have to think about the basis for your media choices. Are you avoiding some media messages simply because they challenge your beliefs? If so, this probably is not the best way to navigate through the media environment. Sometimes, you can benefit from being open-minded about the views and perspectives of others.

Broaden Your Media Horizons

People often live within the confines of a particular media environment and, like a fish in water, can't see the limits. With the vast possibilities now available via the Internet, in libraries, and through other media outlets, you have access to practically the whole world. Even if your only language is English, you have many media options available to you.

As you work to broaden your horizons, obtain a range of views on world events. Try to understand why other people view the world the way they do, no matter how different their views are from your own. Try to understand the rising anti-Americanism coming from around the world. You may disagree with what you hear, or even find it offensive, but by seeing the complexity of issues involved you can gain a better understanding of the world we live in.

Overall, being a responsible and effective consumer of media is not easy. It certainly extends far beyond lounging around watching whatever is on television. Becoming an active partner in this complex communication process is a challenge, one we hope you will take up.

Talk Back

You can benefit from talking back or challenging the messages you receive via news commentators, politicians, reporters, or even characters in television programs. In other words, if you hear something you disagree with or that sounds wrong, point this out, even if only to yourself. For example, suppose you hear a reporter covering a natural disaster refer to "innocent victims." What, you might ask yourself, is a "guilty victim" in the context of an earthquake, or in any context for that matter? Questioning and noticing these kinds of empty phrases makes you a more active consumer of media. As you watch or listen, you might also consider why one news story is given more time than another one, or why a particular story is reported at all, and what that prioritizing and selection communicates about what is and isn't valued.

Talking back also includes being attentive to the ethical implications of media to which you are exposed, particularly if it promotes some social identities at the expense of others. More specifically, be aware of the ways that, for example, women and racial minorities, sexual minorities, and religious minorities are portrayed and what influences these images may have on the groups depicted. If you watch movies that mock particular cultural or religious groups, that denigrate women, or that misrepresent the experiences of certain individuals, consider the implications. You not only ratify this depiction by your attendance, but you also encourage the production of more of this type of media with your dollars.

Talking back, however, can involve much more than talking to the images that come to you in media or making choices about which images to support or resist. If you find something particularly objectionable, you can contact the television station, magazine, or newspaper that has offended you. For example, if you believe that specific programs manipulate or attempt to unfairly influence children, use the "contact us" information on the station's Web site to let the producers of those programs, and the companies that advertise in that medium, know exactly how you feel. Or you can complain to the Federal Communications Commission, the federal agency that regulates radio, television, wire, cable, and satellite. On the other hand, if you believe specific media have a positive influence and should be more widely produced or distributed, let advertisers and media companies know that as well. Certainly, praising a job well done is as important a form of talking back as raising objections.

In general, few consumers are sufficiently deliberate about the media messages they select. But because media messages have such a powerful impact on consumers, and because you can have some influence on the availability of specific types of media, you benefit society when you become an active and critical media consumer.

TEST YOUR KNOWLEDGE

- How do media activists respond to media messages they find objectionable?
- What are some concerns that contemporary media activists have raised?

SUMMARY

Media, in all their variety, play a powerful role in our lives. The entertainment and information they provide influence how we see ourselves and the world around us. We refer to the messages that come to us via media as *mediated communication* because they are mediated, or transmitted, through a channel, such as television, film, radio, or print. Mass media communication refers to communication that is directed at a mass audience. Individuals choose what types of media texts to watch, read, listen to, purchase, or avoid.

Media scholars are interested in how we make these decisions, and marketers and media producers also want to know how they might predict and characterize our choices: how we choose what to consume and how we resist the rest. Complicating our individual choices, however, are social forces that shape the media options that are available.

Media play a number of important roles in our lives as individuals as well as in our society: confirming our social identities, helping us understand the world, and helping us understand important public events. In addition, media shape the images of real and imagined violence and wield enormous economic influence.

Media activism—the practice of organizing to communicate displeasure with certain media images and messages—is one way that people express their ethical views and respond to objectionable media messages and powerful media corporations. Today, media activism has concentrated largely in four areas: children's programming, representations of cultural groups, news reporting, and alternative programming.

Finally, consumers of media can and should become more aware of their own media consumption habits. Guidelines for improving media consumption skills include being active in making media choices, broadening media horizons, and speaking out when media content is offensive.

HUMAN COMMUNICATION IN SOCIETY ONLINE

To review this chapter, use the MyCommunicationLab Web site to test your understanding of the following key terms, record your answers to the chapter review questions, and complete the suggested activities. Expand your learning and understanding of chapter concepts by completing additional activities and exercises online. Access code required. Go to www.mycommunicationlab.com for more information or to purchase standalone access.

KEY TERMS

media 265
mass media 265
culture industries 265
mass-market paperbacks 266
e-books 266
active agents 267
mass media effects 268
media text 269

selective exposure 269
uses and gratifications 270
content analysis 273
agenda-setting capacity 277
cultivation theory 278
hegemony 278
media event 279

media violence 280
V-chip 280
political economy 281
media activism 283
Hays Code 284
MPAA 284
TV Parental Guidelines 284

APPLY WHAT YOU KNOW

1. Research a popular media text—for example, a magazine, television show, or newspaper—that targets an identity group different from your own. What elements do you find in this text that differ from a text targeted at one of your identity groups?

2. Select and study a media event such as the Super Bowl, Miss America Pageant, or a famous murder trial, and identify the rituals that surround this event. How does the media event affirm U.S. cultural values?

3. Select a media activist group to study. Go to their Web page and identify their concerns about media. What strategies do they use to promote their messages? Who is their audience? How do they plan to change media in the ways that concern them?

4. Pick a major media event (whether a ritual event or a natural disaster) and compare how it was covered by several different media outlets. Look at news coverage overseas as well to help you compare the differences and similarities.

12
Developing Your Presentation

Jacob Lawrence, The Library, 1960. Tempera on fiberboard, 24 × 29 7/8 in. (60.9 × 75.8 cm). Smithsonian American Art Museum, Washington, DC. Photo credit: Smithsonian American Art Museum, Washington, DC/Art Resource, NY. © 2007 The Jacob and Gwendolyn Lawrence Foundation, Seattle/Artists Rights Society (ARS), New York.

> "Freedom of speech is of no use to a man who has nothing to say."
>
> Franklin D. Roosevelt

A good friend of ours who has lived in Hong Kong for several years recently remarked that she found traveling back to the United States exhausting. Her reason? Not so much the long plane trip or the 13-hour time difference, but, as she explained, "When I begin to hear airport public announcements in English instead of Cantonese, I suddenly feel compelled to pay attention to every word. All that listening wears me out!"

Few of us can take for granted that others will listen to us merely because we are speaking their native language. However, when we study the presentational speaking process and learn its component skills and principles, we certainly increase the likelihood that others will listen to us out of genuine, compelling interest.

Far from being a rare talent possessed only by an inspired few, public speaking, or presentational speaking, is a teachable, learnable process—a process of developing, supporting, organizing, and presenting ideas orally. It is a process that has much in common with expository writing. Yet preparing an oral presentation and writing a paper are not exactly the same. For one thing, the language you use when you speak is less formal and more conversational than the language you use when you write. You are more likely to use shorter words, more first- and second-person pronouns (I and you), and shorter sentences when you speak than when you write. Second, while a writer can rely on parenthetical citations and Works Cited pages to document his or her sources, a speaker must document sources orally, within the text of the speech itself. And third, perhaps the most important way in which presentational speaking and writing differ is that speaking is more redundant than writing. What might seem unnecessary repetition in a paper is essential in a presentation.

Chapter Objectives

After studying this chapter, you should be able to

- Explain the practical value of presentational speaking skills.
- List the nine components of the audience-centered public speaking model.
- Define speaker anxiety, explain what causes it, and offer at least three suggestions for managing it.
- Suggest three questions and three strategies that can help a speaker discover a topic.
- List the three general purposes for presentations.
- Explain how to write an audience-centered specific-purpose statement.
- List and explain four criteria for a central idea.
- Explain how to generate main ideas from a central idea.
- Describe three sources and five types of supporting material for a presentation, and offer guidelines for using each type effectively.
- List six types of library resources.

The 5th Wave   By Rich Tennant

Welllll—everyone seems to be in a good mood.

A person listening to a presentation does not have the luxury of rereading something he or she missed or did not understand the first time. Neither can the listener rely on paragraphing to indicate when a speaker is moving on to another point or idea. Instead, the listener must depend on the speaker to repeat important ideas and to provide oral organizational cues, such as transitions, previews, and summaries. Certainly you can apply to presentational speaking some of the skills and strategies you have learned as a writer. But you will also learn new and sometimes slightly different ones. As with the writing process, the more you practice, the easier and more "natural" the presentational speaking process will become.

Still not convinced that you want or need to learn presentational speaking? Perhaps you will feel more motivated if you consider that the skills you will develop as you study presentational speaking will be of practical use in the future. They will give you an edge in other college courses that require oral presentations. They may help you convince some current or future boss that you deserve a raise. And they may even land you a job. Ethernet inventor Bob Metcalf recently told a group of MIT students (who expected, no doubt, to hear technology-related advice) that "Communication is key" to their success.[1] Young entrepreneurs in technical fields need presentation skills, Metcalf pointed out, to "secure funding, win customers, recruit talented employees, and talk with the media."

The communication skills that Metcalf was talking about are grounded in the five communication principles for a lifetime and can be learned and practiced in the various stages of the presentational speaking process. Let's begin our discussion of presentational speaking with an overview of that process. Then—because even if you are fully convinced of the value of learning to speak in public, you may still feel nervous about delivering a presentation—we will explore why you feel that way and offer suggestions for managing your anxiety and developing confidence. In the final pages of this chapter, we will focus more closely on the first five stages of the public speaking process, which involve generating, exploring, and developing ideas for presentations.

AN OVERVIEW OF THE PRESENTATIONAL SPEAKING PROCESS

Chances are that you didn't complete a driver-education course before you got behind the wheel of a car for the first time. Similarly, you don't have to read an entire book on public speaking before you give your first presentation. An overview of the presentational speaking process can help you with your early assignments, even if you have to speak before you have a chance to read Chapters 12 through 16.

Figure 12.1 illustrates the presentational speaking process. Viewing the model as a clock, you find "Select and narrow topic" at 12 o'clock. From this stage, the process proceeds clockwise, in the direction of the arrows, to "Deliver presentation." Each stage is one of the tasks of the public speaker:

1. Select and narrow topic.
2. Identify purpose.

FIGURE 12.1:   An Audience-Centered Model of the Presentational Speaking Process

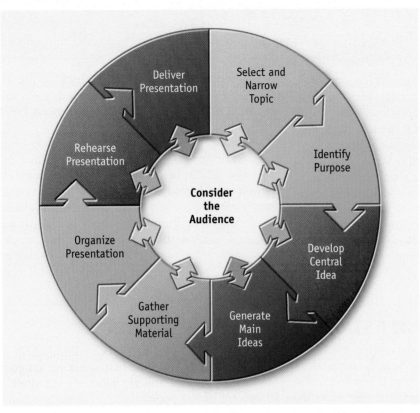

3. Develop central idea.

4. Generate main ideas.

5. Gather supporting material.

6. Organize presentation.

7. Rehearse presentation.

8. Deliver presentation.

Note that a ninth component, "Consider the audience," appears at the center of the model. Double-headed arrows connect this center with every other stage, illustrating that at any point you may revise your ideas or strategies as you learn more about your audience. Your audience influences every decision you make.

Audience-centered presentational speakers consider and adapt to the audience at every stage of the speaking process. They are inherently sensitive to the diversity of their audiences. While guarding against generalizations that might be offensive, they acknowledge that cultural, ethnic, and other traditions affect the way people process messages. They apply the fundamental principle of appropriately adapting their messages to others. How? They might choose to use pictures to help them communicate. They might select topics and use illustrations with universal themes such as family and friendship. They might adjust the formality of their delivery and even their dress to whatever is expected by the majority of the audience members. The fundamental communication principle of adapting to the audience is the key to the success of any presentation.

Adapt

Developing Your Presentation STEP BY STEP
Consider Your Audience

A well-known Chinese proverb says that a journey of a thousand miles begins with a single step. Developing and delivering a presentation may seem like a daunting journey. But we believe that if you take it one step at a time and keep your focus on your audience, you'll be rewarded with a well-crafted and well-delivered message.

To help you see how the audience-centered presentation process unfolds step by step, we will explore each step of that process by showing how one student prepared and delivered a presentation. Ben Johnson, a student at the University of Nevada, Reno, participated in the 132nd annual contest of the Interstate Oratorical

Association. His presentation, "Coricidin: No Prescription Needed," is outlined in Chapter 13.2 In the pages ahead, we will walk you through the process Ben used to develop his award-winning presentation.

Ben thought about his audience even before selecting his topic. Realizing that his listeners would include both students and faculty, he decided to look for a topic that was relevant to both groups. And he knew that he could discuss complex issues, using a fairly advanced vocabulary. The Developing Your Presentation Step by Step feature will provide a window through which you can watch Ben at work on each step of the presentational speaking process.

UNDERSTANDING SPEAKER ANXIETY

The above overview of the stages of the public speaking process should help to increase your understanding of how to prepare for your first speaking assignment. However, if you still feel nervous at the prospect, you are definitely not alone. One study found that more than 80 percent of the population feel anxious when they speak to an audience.[3] Another survey discovered that people are more afraid of public speaking than of death![4]

Also known as stage fright or communication apprehension, **speaker anxiety is anxiety about speaking in public that is manifested in physiological symptoms such as rapid heartbeat, butterflies in the stomach, shaking knees and hands, quivering voice, and increased perspiration.** You might be surprised at the names of some of the people who have admitted to experiencing speaker anxiety. John F. Kennedy and Winston Churchill, among the greatest orators of the twentieth century, were anxious about speaking in public. Contemporary public figures who have talked about their speaker anxiety include Katie Couric, Conan O'Brien, Jay Leno, and Oprah Winfrey.[5] In fact, almost everyone feels at least some anxiety about speaking or performing in public. Why?

To answer this question and to manage your own anxiety, you need both accurate information and practical advice. Even if the prospect of giving a presentation makes you feel a sense of heightened excitement rather than fear, you can use these suggestions to make your excitement help you, rather than distract you.

It is important to understand that speaker anxiety results from your brain signaling your body to help with a challenging task. The body responds by increasing its breathing rate and blood flow and by pumping more adrenaline, which in turn results in the all-too-familiar symptoms of a rapid heartbeat, butterflies in the stomach, shaking knees and hands, quivering voice, and increased perspiration.

Although these physical symptoms may annoy and worry you, remember that they indicate that your body is trying to help you with the task at hand. The same increased oxygen, blood flow, and adrenaline that cause the uncomfortable symptoms can actually be helpful. You may find that you speak with heightened enthusiasm. Your brain thinks faster and more clearly than you would have believed possible. Your state of increased physical readiness can help you speak better.

Keep in mind, too, that most speakers feel more nervous than they look. Although the antiperspirant advertising slogan "Never let 'em see you sweat" suggests that our increased perspiration, along with our shaking hands and knocking knees, is likely to be visible to our audience, rarely is this true. Communication **researchers call the mistaken belief that the physical manifestations of a speaker's nervousness are apparent to an audience the illusion of transparency** and have found that simply informing speakers that their nervousness is not as apparent as they think can improve the quality of their speeches.[6]

Speaker anxiety is a normal physiological reaction. It can actually help us in our speaking tasks. Its physical symptoms are seldom apparent to anyone else; rarely does it become so severe that it is actually debilitating. Still, it can be uncomfortable. Some practical tips can help you manage that discomfort and further build your confidence in your speaking ability.

MANAGING SPEAKER ANXIETY

Perhaps you've read books or magazine articles that address the topic of speaker anxiety with such advice as "Look over the audience's heads, rather than at them" and "Imagine that your audience members are naked." Interesting though they may be, these techniques are not particularly helpful in reducing speaker anxiety. (After all, wouldn't you be pretty anxious if you had to talk to a group of naked people?) In addition, these strategies create new problems. Gazing at the back wall robs you of eye contact with your audience, an important source of information about how they are responding to your speech. And your audience can tell if you are looking over their heads instead of at them. Rather than pay attention to your speech, they may begin to glance surreptitiously over their shoulders to find out what in the world you're staring at.

If these techniques won't help, what will? Fortunately, several proven strategies exist for managing anxiety.

Know How to Develop a Presentation

Communication researchers have found that public speaking instruction decreases students' perception of their own speaker anxiety.[7] If you have read the first part of this chapter, then you have already taken this first step toward managing anxiety—learning about the public speaking process. Just knowing what you need to do to develop a presentation can boost your confidence in being able to do it.

Be Prepared

Being well prepared will also mean less anxiety. Being prepared includes selecting an appropriate topic, researching that topic thoroughly, and organizing your ideas logically. But perhaps most important, it also includes rehearsing your presentation. Research suggests that people who experience high speaker anxiety typically spend less time rehearsing than do those who report lower speaker anxiety.[8]

When you rehearse your presentation, imagine that you are giving it to the audience you will actually address. Stand up. If you cannot rehearse in the room where you will deliver the presentation, at least imagine that room. Practice rising from your seat, walking to the front of the room, and beginning your presentation. Speak aloud, rather than rehearsing silently. Thorough preparation that includes realistic rehearsal will increase your confidence when the time comes to deliver your presentation.

Even performers like Barbra Streisand suffer from communication anxiety; we all need to take positive steps to control anxiety before a performance.

Adapt

Focus on Your Audience

The fundamental communication principle of being audience-centered is key to reducing speaker anxiety. As you are preparing your presentation, consider the needs, goals, and interests of your audience members. As you rehearse your presentation, visualize your audience and imagine how they may respond; practice adapting your presentation to the responses you imagine. The more you know about your audience and how they are likely to respond to your message, the more comfortable you will feel about delivering that message. And as you finally deliver your presentation, focus on connecting to your listeners. The more you concentrate on your audience, the less you can attend to your own nervousness.

Verbal

Focus on Your Message

Focusing on your message can also be a constructive anxiety-reducing strategy. Like focusing on your audience, it keeps you from thinking too much about how nervous you are. In the few minutes before you begin your presentation, think about what you are going to say. Mentally review your main ideas. Silently practice your opening lines and your conclusion. Once you are speaking, maintain your focus on your message and your audience, rather than on your fears. Communication researchers have found that most public speakers become progressively more comfortable as they speak, a phenomenon they term **habituation**.[9]

Aware

Give Yourself a Mental Pep Talk

Even if you focus primarily on your audience and your message, you are bound to have some lingering thoughts about your performance. Rather than allowing yourself to dwell on how worried or afraid you are, make a conscious effort to think positively. Remind yourself that you have chosen a topic you know something about. Give yourself a mental pep talk before getting up to speak: "I know I can give this presentation. I have prepared and practiced, and I'm going to do a great job." This kind of positive thinking can help you manage your anxiety.

Use Deep-Breathing Techniques

Two of the physical symptoms of nervousness are shallow breathing and rapid heart rate. To counter these symptoms, take a few slow, deep breaths before you get up to speak. As you slowly inhale and exhale, try to relax your entire body. These simple strategies will increase your oxygen intake and slow your heart rate, making you feel calmer and more in control.

Take Advantage of Opportunities to Speak

As you gain public speaking experience, you will feel more in control of your nervousness. Past successes build confidence. This course will provide opportunities for frequent practice, which will increase your skill and confidence.

Seek Professional Help

For a few people, the above strategies may not be enough help. These people may still experience a level of speaker anxiety that they consider debilitating. If you feel that you may be such a person, ask your communication instructor where you might turn for additional help. Some college or university departments of communication maintain communication labs that teach students various additional strategies to help manage counter-productive anxiety.

One such strategy is **systematic desensitization, which helps you learn to manage anxiety through a combination of general relaxation techniques and visualization of successful and calm preparation and delivery of a presentation.**

Another proven strategy is **performance visualization: viewing a videotape of a successful effective speaker, becoming familiar enough with the videotaped presentation that you can imagine it, and eventually visualizing yourself as the speaker.**[10] This process may offer one of the best long-term strategies for managing speaker anxiety. Studies suggest that student speakers who practice performance visualization view themselves as more positive, vivid, and in-control speakers both immediately after performance visualization and up to several months later.[11]

Additional services may be available through university counseling or other student support services. If you think that you might benefit from professional help, find out what is available and use it.

SELECTING AND NARROWING YOUR TOPIC

Sometimes a speaker is invited or assigned to speak on a certain topic and doesn't have to think about selecting one. At other times, however, a speaker is given some guidelines—such as time limits and perhaps the general purpose for the presentation—but otherwise allowed freedom to choose a topic. When this happens to you—as it almost certainly will in your communication class—you may find your task made easier by exploring three questions: Who is the audience? What is the occasion? What are my interests and experiences?

Who Is the Audience?

As we have noted several times throughout this book, the principle of appropriately adapting messages to others is central to the communication process. In presentational speaking, that adaptation begins with topic selection. Who are the members of your audience? What interests and needs do they have in common? Why did they ask you to speak?

One professional speaker calls the answers to such questions "actionable intelligence"—information that you can use as you select your topic.[12] Your college classmates are likely to be interested in such topics as college loans and the job market. Older adults might be more interested in hearing a speaker address such topics as the cost of prescription drugs and investment tax credits. Thinking about your audience can often yield an appropriate topic.

Adapt

What Is the Occasion?

You might also consider the occasion for which you are being asked to speak. A Veteran's Day address calls for such topics as patriotism and service to one's country. A university centennial address will focus on the successes of the institution's past and a vision for its future.

What Are My Interests and Experiences?

Self-awareness, another communication principle you already know, can also help you discover a topic. Exploring your own interests, attitudes, and experiences may suggest topics about which you know a great deal and feel passionately, and result in a presentation that you can deliver with energy and genuine enthusiasm. One speaker thinking about her own interests and experiences quickly produced the following list of possible topics:

San Diego, California: city of cultural diversity

Are world climates really changing?

The reconstructed Globe Theatre

Working at Six Flags

What a sociologist does

Even after considering audience, occasion, and personal interests and experiences, you may still find yourself facing a speaking assignment for which you just cannot come up with a satisfactory topic. When that happens, you might try silent brainstorming, scanning Web directories and Web pages, or listening and reading for topic ideas.

Silent Brainstorming

Silent brainstorming, a technique used by small groups to generate creative ideas, is a useful strategy for generating topics for presentations. A silent brainstorming session of about 3 minutes yielded the following list of 11 potential topics:

Gargoyles

Gothic architecture

Notre Dame

French food

Disney's *The Hunchback of Notre Dame*

Collecting Disney movie celluloids

Grammy Award winning movie themes

Academy Award winning movies of the 1940s

The Motion Picture Academy's Lifetime Achievement Award

John Wayne

The California Gold Rush

On the Web

The Internet can be a useful source to help you search for an interesting speech topic. Remember, the best topic is one that relates to your audience, the occasion, and your own interests and background. Consider using a Web directory such as Yahoo! to help you find a topic that meets the three criteria we've noted. Here's the address:

www. yahoo. com

Another interesting source of speech ideas is current headlines. Here's a source that has links to many media outlets, including most major news networks: www. totalnews. com

Having generated a list of topics, you can now go back to it and eliminate topics that don't have much promise or that you know you would never use. For example, you may not have any real interest in or reason for discussing the California Gold Rush. However, perhaps your film course has given you good background for discussing Academy Award winning movies of the 1940s or some other decade. Keep the topics you like in your class notebook. You can reconsider them for future assignments.

Scanning Web Directories and Web Pages

You know how addicting it can be to surf the Web—to follow various categories and links out of interest and curiosity. What may seem an idle pastime can actually be a good way to discover potential speech topics. For example, a recent random search on Yahoo! starting with the general category of Health yielded the following subcategories and possible topics, arranged from broad to narrow:

> Diseases and conditions
>
> Depression
>
> Prevention of depression
>
> Benefits of fish

An additional advantage of this strategy is that you now have both a broad topic and one or more potential sources for your presentation. An article found in the final subcategory discusses the role of omega-3 fats, found in fish, as a critical component of nerve cells.

Listening and Reading for Topic Ideas

It is not unusual to see on television or read in a newspaper something that triggers an idea for a presentation. For example, the following list of quite varied topics was suggested by the headlines in a recent daily newspaper:

Corporate accounting scandals

Forest fires in the southwestern United States

Diagnosing breast cancer

U.S. government aid to foreign nationals

Political turmoil in South America

Listen and Respond

The nightly news is not the only media source of potential topics. You might also get topic ideas from television talk shows or from general interest or news magazines. Or you might get an idea from a book. Perhaps you have just read Daniel Goleman's *Working with Emotional Intelligence*. You might decide to give a speech on what emotional intelligence is and why it is important in the workplace.

You might also find a topic in material you have studied for a class. Perhaps you recently had an interesting discussion of minimum mandatory sentencing in your criminology class. It might make a good topic for a presentation. And your instructor would probably be happy to suggest additional resources.

Even a topic that comes up in casual conversation with friends may make a good speech topic. Perhaps everyone in your dorm seems to be sniffling and coughing all at once. "It's sick-building syndrome," gasps one. Sick-building syndrome might be an interesting topic for a presentation.

The point is to keep your eyes and ears open. You never know when you might see or hear a potential topic. If you do, write it down. Nothing is so frustrating as to know you had a good idea for a topic but not to be able to remember what it was!

If you discover potential topics through brainstorming, surfing the Web, or listening or reading, you should still consider the communication principles of adapting to your audience and being aware of your own interests and experiences before you make your final topic selection. And you will also need to consider the time limits of the speaking assignment. Many good topics need to be narrowed before they are appropriate for a given assignment. Be realistic. Although many beginning speakers worry about how they will ever fill 3 minutes, in reality more speakers run over their time limits than under.

One strategy for narrowing topics is to construct the kinds of categories and subcategories created by Web directories. Write your general topic at the top of a list, making each succeeding word or phrase more specific and narrow. For example, in order to narrow the topic "animals," write it down and then write an increasingly specific list of topics under it:

Aware Adapt

Animals

Pets

Developing Your Presentation STEP BY STEP
Select and Narrow Your Topic

While lazily scanning the newspaper headlines one Sunday afternoon, Ben happens on one that catches his eye. He settles down to read the article, which discusses a relatively new form of drug abuse—the abuse of common over-the-counter cold medications. Ben is surprised. He had no idea that such med-

ications could produce the kind of side effects that would lead to their abuse. As he finishes the article, another thought goes through his mind: Maybe the abuse of over-the-counter cold medicines would make a good topic for his upcoming persuasive presentation.

Reptiles

Bearded dragons

Caring for a bearded dragon

If you have 10 minutes for your presentation, you might decide that the last topic is too narrow. If so, just go back one step. In 10 minutes, you may be able to discuss characteristics and habits of bearded dragons, as well as how to care for them.

IDENTIFYING YOUR PURPOSE

Now that you have a topic in mind, you need to clarify your purpose for your presentation. If you are unclear about exactly what you hope to accomplish, you probably won't accomplish anything, except to ramble about your topic in some sort of vague way. A clear purpose, on the other hand, can help you select main ideas, an organizational strategy, and supporting material, and can even influence the way in which you deliver the presentation. You should determine both your general purpose and your specific purpose for every presentation that you give.

General Purpose

Your general purpose is the broad reason for giving your presentation: to inform, to persuade, or to entertain. When you inform, you teach. You define, describe, or explain a thing, person, place, concept, or process. You may use some humor in your presentation; you may encourage your audience to seek out further information about your topic. But your primary purpose for speaking is to give information.

If you are using information to try to change or reinforce your audience's ideas or convictions or to urge your audience to do something, your general purpose is persuasive. The insurance representative who tries to get you to buy life insurance, the candidate for state representative who asks for your vote, and the coordinator of Habitat for Humanity who urges your fraternity to get involved in building homes all have persuasive general purposes. They may offer information about life expectancy, the voting record of an incumbent opponent, or the number of people in your community who cannot afford decent housing, but they use this information to convince you or to get you to do something. Their primary purpose is persuasive.

The speaker whose purpose is to entertain tries to get the members of his or her audience to smile, laugh, and generally enjoy themselves. For the audience members, learning something or being persuaded about something is secondary to having a good time. Most after-dinner speakers speak to entertain. So do most stand-up comedians and storytellers.

In your speech class, the general purpose for each assignment will probably be set by your instructor. Because the general purpose influences the way you develop and organize your presentation, as well as the way you deliver it, it is important that you be aware of your general purpose throughout the process of developing and delivering your presentation.

Aware

Specific Purpose

Knowing whether you want to inform, persuade, or entertain clarifies your general purpose for speaking. You also need to determine your specific purpose. **A specific purpose is a concise statement of what your listeners should be able to do by the time you finish your presentation.** In other words, a specific purpose is an audience-centered behavioral goal for your presentation. You can begin a specific-purpose statement for any presentation with these words:

Verbal

> At the end of my presentation, the audience will . . .

And then specify a behavior. For example, if you are giving an informative presentation on eating disorders, you might state,

> At the end of my presentation, the audience will be able to explain the causes and most successful treatments for anorexia and bulimia.

If your topic is Zen meditation and your general purpose is to persuade, you might say,

> At the end of my presentation, the audience will try Zen meditation.

Wording your specific purpose like the examples above will help you keep your audience foremost in your mind during the entire presentation preparation process.

Recap

Identify Your Purpose

General Purpose

- To inform—to define, describe, or explain a thing, person, place, concept, or process
- To persuade—to change or reinforce audience members' ideas or convictions, or to urge them to do something
- To entertain—to amuse an audience

Specific Purpose

- Specifies what you want audience members to be able to do by the end of your presentation
- Uses the words "At the end of my presentation, the audience will . . ."

Examples of General Purposes	Examples of Specific Purposes
To inform	At the end of my presentation, the audience will be able to list two benefits for adults of learning to play a musical instrument.
To persuade	At the end of my presentation, the audience will enroll in a music appreciation course.
To entertain	At the end of my presentation, the audience will be laughing at my misadventures as an adult cello student.

Every subsequent decision you make while preparing and delivering your presentation should be guided by your specific purpose. As soon as you have formulated it, write it on a note card and keep it with you while you are working on your presentation. Think of it as a compass pointing true north—toward your audience. Refer to it often.

DEVELOPING YOUR CENTRAL IDEA

While your specific purpose indicates what you want your audience to know or do by the end of your presentation, **your central idea makes a definitive point about your topic.** It focuses on the content of the speech.

Professional speech coach Judith Humphrey explains the importance of a central idea:

Ask yourself before writing a speech . . . "What's my point?" Be able to state that message in a single clear sentence. Everything else you say will support that single argument.[13]

Sometimes, as in the following example, wording the central idea can be as simple as copying the part of the specific purpose statement that specifies what the audience should be able to do.

TOPIC: Foreign-language education

SPECIFIC PURPOSE: At the end of my presentation, the audience will be able to explain two reasons foreign-language education should begin in the elementary grades.

CENTRAL IDEA: Foreign-language education should begin in the elementary grades.

Even though they may seem similar, the specific purpose and central idea are used quite differently. The specific purpose guides you as you prepare your presen-

Developing Your Presentation STEP BY STEP
Determine Your Purpose

Ben's assignment is to prepare and deliver a persuasive presentation, so he knows that his general purpose is to persuade. He will have to try to change or reinforce his audience's attitudes and beliefs about the abuse of common over-the-counter cold medications and perhaps also get his listeners to take some sort of action.

Ben also knows that his specific purpose should begin with the phrase "At the end of my presentation, the audience will . . . ." So he jots down,

At the end of my presentation, the audience will know about the cold medication Coricidin.

As Ben thinks further about this draft specific purpose, he sees some problems with it. How can he determine what his audience "knows" at the end of his presentation? And just what is it the audience should know about Coricidin? He edits his purpose statement to read,

At the end of my presentation, the audience will be able to discuss the current epidemic of abuse of the common cold medication Coricidin.

This version is more specific, but perhaps more appropriate for an informative speech than a persuasive one. What does he want his audience to do about the problem? Maybe a better statement would be

At the end of my presentation, the audience will take steps to end the abuse of the cold medication Coricidin.

Ben is pleased with this third version. It is a concise statement of what he wants his audience to do at the end of his speech. He is ready to move to the next step of the process.

tation; the central idea will guide the audience as they listen to the presentation. Although the specific purpose is never actually stated in the presentation itself, the central idea is, usually at or near the end of the speaker's introduction. It provides the focus for the body of the presentation.

Adapt

The most successful central ideas meet the following criteria: They are audience-centered; they reflect a single topic; they are complete declarative sentences; and they use direct, specific language. Let's consider each of these criteria in turn.

Audience-Centered

If your specific purpose is audience-centered, your central idea probably will be, too. It should reflect a topic in which the audience has a reason to be interested and should provide some knowledge they do not already have or make some claim about the topic that they may not have previously considered. The second of the following central ideas is more appropriate to an audience of college students than the first.

Effective speakers state their central idea during their introductory remarks to help their audience focus on the main points covered in the body of the speech.

INAPPROPRIATE: Taking Advanced Placement classes in high school can help fulfill your general education requirements. *(Inappropriate because taking Advanced Placement classes is something college students either did or did not do in the past. They cannot make any decisions about them at this point.)*

APPROPRIATE: Taking Web-based classes can help fulfill your general studies requirements. *(Appropriate because students are probably looking for various options for completing required courses. They can choose to take courses on the Web.)*

A Single Topic

A central idea should reflect a single topic. Trying to cover more than one topic, even if multiple topics are related, only muddles your presentation and confuses the audience.

MULTIPLE TOPICS: Clubbing and running in marathons are two activities that appeal to many college students.

SINGLE TOPIC: Clubbing appeals to many college students.

A Complete Declarative Sentence

Your central idea should be more than just the word or phrase that is your topic—it should make a claim about your topic. Questions may help you come up with a cen-

Developing Your Presentation STEP BY STEP
Develop Your Central Idea

Ben knows from reading Chapter 12 that his central idea should be a complete declarative sentence that states a single audience-centered idea. He knows too that sometimes you can develop your central idea by copying the part of your specific purpose statement that specifies what the audience should do. So he writes,

We should take steps to end the abuse of the cold medication Coricidin.

tral idea, but questions themselves are not good central ideas, because they don't make any kind of claim. A central idea should be a **declarative sentence—a complete sentence that makes a statement, as opposed to asking a question.**

Verbal

TOPIC:	Study abroad
QUESTION:	Should students consider opportunities to study abroad?
CENTRAL IDEA:	Study abroad provides significant advantages for students in most fields of study.

Direct, Specific Language

A good central idea should use direct, specific language, rather than qualifiers and vague generalities.

VAGUE:	Crop circles are not what they seem to be.
SPECIFIC:	Although they have been variously attributed to alien forces and unknown fungi, crop circles are really just a clever hoax.

GENERATING MAIN IDEAS

If the central idea of a presentation is like the thesis statement of a paper, **the main ideas of a presentation correspond to the paragraph topics of a paper. They support or subdivide the central idea and provide more detailed points of focus for developing the presentation.**

Getting from the central idea to related but more specific main ideas can seem a challenging task, but actually you can use the central idea to generate main ideas. Here's how.

Write the central idea at the top of a sheet of paper or a word-processing document. Then ask yourself three questions:

1. Does the central idea have *logical divisions?*
2. Can I think of several reasons the central idea is true?
3. Can I support the central idea with a series of *steps or a chronological sequence?*

You should be able to answer yes to one of these questions and to write down the corresponding divisions, reasons, or steps. Let's apply this strategy to several examples.

Does the Central Idea Have *Logical Divisions*?

Suppose that your central idea is "Most accomplished guitarists play three types of guitars." The phrase "three types" is a flag that indicates that this central idea does indeed have logical divisions—those being, in this case, the three types of guitars. You list the three that come to mind:

1. Acoustic
2. Classical
3. Electric

You don't need to use Roman numerals or to worry particularly about the order in which you have listed the types of guitars. Right now you are simply trying to generate main ideas. They aren't set in concrete, either. You may revise them—and your central idea—several times before you actually deliver the presentation. For example, you may decide that you need to include steel guitars in your list. So you revise your central idea to read "four types of guitars" and add "steel" to your list.

Developing Your Presentation STEP BY STEP
Determine Your Main Ideas

With his central idea in hand, Ben knows that he next needs to generate main ideas for his presentation. He asks three questions:

- Does the central idea have logical divisions?
- Can I think of several reasons the central idea is true?
- Can I support my central idea with a series of steps or a chronological sequence?

Ben's central idea does not seem to have logical divisions, but he can certainly provide reasons it is true. He jots down his central idea and writes *because* at the end of it:

We should take steps to end the abuse of the cold medication Coricidin <u>because</u>

And then he adds,

1. Coricidin abuse is rapidly becoming a significant problem.
2. Coricidin is widely available to teenagers.
3. Parents and teachers have only compounded the problem.

Ben thinks at first that these might make three good main ideas for his speech. Then he realizes that ideas 2 and 3 are really subdivisions of the same point—why Coricidin abuse is a growing trend. Additionally, glancing back at his purpose statement reminds him that he wants his audience to take steps to end Coricidin abuse. So he revises his original list of main ideas to read,

1. Coricidin abuse is rapidly becoming a significant problem.
2. Coricidin poses a problem because it is widely available to teenagers and because parents and teachers remain largely unaware of its abuse potential.
3. In addition to government and retailer regulation, personal action is needed to solve the problem of Coricidin abuse.

Now Ben has main ideas that both support his central idea and fulfill his specific purpose.

Can You Think of Several *Reasons* the Central Idea Is True?

If your central idea is "Everyone should study a martial art," you may not be able to find readily apparent logical divisions. Simply discussing judo, karate, and taekwando would not necessarily support the argument that everyone should study one of them. However, the second question is more productive: You can think of a number of *reasons* everyone should study a martial art. You quickly generate this list:

1. Martial arts teach responsibility.
2. Martial arts teach self-control.
3. Martial arts teach a means of self-defense.

Unlike the list of types of guitars, this list is written in brief complete sentences. Whether words, phrases, or sentences, the purpose of your first list of main ideas is just to get the ideas in written form. You can and will revise them later.

Can You Support the Central Idea with a Series of *Steps* or a *Chronological Sequence*?

"The events of September 11, 2001, were the climax of a decade of deadly terrorist attacks against the United States." It seemed like a pretty good central idea when you came up with it. But now what do you do? It doesn't have any logical divisions.

You couldn't really develop reasons that it is true. However, you could probably support this central idea with a chronological sequence or a history of the problem. You jot down the following list:

1. 1993—Bomb explodes in the underground parking garage of the World Trade Center, killing six people.
2. 1995—Car bomb in Riyadh, Saudi Arabia, kills seven people, five of them American military and civilian National Guard advisers.
3. 1996—Bomb aboard a fuel truck explodes outside a U.S. Air Force installation in Dhahran, Saudi Arabia, killing 19 U.S. military personnel.
4. 1998—Bombs destroy the U.S. embassies in Nairobi, Kenya, and Dar es Salaam, Tanzania. Three hundred and one people are killed, including 13 Americans.
5. 2000—Bomb damages the USS Cole in the port of Aden, Yemen, killing 17 American sailors.
6. 2001—Hijacked airliners crash into the World Trade Center in New York, the Pentagon in Washington, D.C., and a field in Pennsylvania, killing more than 3000.[14]

These six fatal terrorist attacks, arranged in chronological order, could become the main ideas of your speech.

How many main ideas should you have? Your topic and time limit will help you decide. A short presentation (3 to 5 minutes) might have only two main ideas. A longer one (8 to 10 minutes) might have four or five. If you find that you have more potential main ideas than you can use, decide which main ideas are likely to be most interesting, relevant, and perhaps persuasive to your audience. Or combine two or more closely related ideas.

GATHERING SUPPORTING MATERIAL

By the time you have decided on your main ideas, you have a skeleton presentation. Your next task is to flesh out that skeleton with **supporting material,** both verbal and visual. **Verbal supporting material includes illustrations, explanations, descriptions, definitions, analogies, statistics, and opinions—material that will clarify, amplify, and provide evidence to support your main ideas and your thesis. Visual supporting material includes objects, charts, graphs, posters, maps, models, and computer-generated graphics. You can also support your speech with audio aids such as music or sounds from a CD-ROM or DVD.** The speaker who seeks out strong verbal and visual supporting material is adhering to the fundamental communication principles of effectively using verbal and nonverbal messages.

Sources of Supporting Material

Like a chef who needs to know where to buy high-quality fresh fruits and vegetables for gourmet recipes, you need to know where to turn for supporting material that will effectively develop your presentation and achieve your specific purpose. We will discuss three potential sources of supporting material: you and people you know, the Internet, and the library.

You and People You Know

You needn't look far for at least some of the supporting material for your presentation. If you were self-aware as you selected your topic, you may be your own source. You may have chosen a topic about your hobby—collecting CDs, raising cockatiels, or cooking. You may have chosen a topic with which you have had some personal experience, such as undergoing plastic surgery or negotiating a favorable apartment lease. Or you may have discovered your topic through listening to others. Your roommate may have confided in you about her mother's treatment for melanoma. Your political science professor may have delivered a fascinating lecture on the changes in Hong Kong after its 1998 return to China.

The point is that you don't necessarily need to consult the Internet or run to the library for every piece of supporting material for every topic on which you speak. For the presentations mentioned above, it would be logical to begin by considering your own personal experience in having plastic surgery or negotiating a favorable apartment lease or by interviewing your roommate or your political science professor. It is true that most well-researched presentations will include some objective material gathered from the Internet or from library resources. But don't overlook your own expertise and experience or that of people you know. As an audience-centered speaker, realize, too, that personal knowledge or experience has the added advantage of heightening your credibility in the minds of your listeners. They will respect your authority if they realize that you have firsthand knowledge of the topic on which you are speaking.

The Internet

Only a few short years ago, the **Internet (a vast collection of hundreds of thousands of computers accessible to millions of people all over the world)** was more of a research curiosity than a serious source of supporting material. Now it is the first place many of us turn when faced with a research task.

The most popular Internet information-delivery system is the World Wide Web. You have probably accessed material on the Web through a **directory (an Internet site that offers the user ever-more-specific categories through which to search the Web) or through a search engine.**

You can use directories and search engines in two ways: by clicking on subject categories that are in turn broken down into ever-more-specific subcategories or by entering keywords or phrases into a designated space and clicking on a "Find" command. In either case, you will then have to sort through **the hits—the listed Web sites (locations on the Web that include a number of related Web pages) and Web pages (individual files or screens that may be part of a larger Web site) dealing with the topic you entered.**

The Web sites and Web pages you discover may include personal pages, books, periodicals, newspapers and wire services, reference material, and government documents. In addition, you may discover indexes and catalogs for accessing these various kinds of resources. You can even find sites designed to help you prepare and deliver your presentations. Although the sheer volume of material may be overwhelming for even the most experienced researchers, two strategies can help.

First, explore the advanced or Boolean search capabilities of your directory or search engine. **A Boolean search is a Web search in which words are tied together so that a search engine can hunt for the resulting phrase.** Most offer directions on how to limit your search to those sites that are most relevant to what you are looking for. For a Boolean search, you enclose phrases in quotation marks or parentheses so that the search yields only those sites on which all the words of the phrase appear together, rather than sites that contain any one of the words. You can also insert the word or between two parenthetical phrases, directing your search to include documents in which either phrase appears. Or you can insert the word *and* between parenthetical phrases to indicate that you wish to see results that contain both phrases. These relatively simple strategies can help you narrow a list of hits from, in some cases, millions to a more workable number.

A second strategy for sorting through information you discover on the World Wide Web has to do with the principle of appropriately interpreting verbal and nonverbal messages. Specifically, you need to evaluate the sites you discover, according to a consistent standard. The following six criteria can serve as such a standard:[17]

1. *Accountability.*   Find out what organization or individual is responsible for the Web site. A good place to start is to examine the domain, indicated by the last three letters of the site's URL. The following domains are used by the types of organizations indicated:[18]

.com or *.net*	commercial sites
.org	nonprofit groups
.edu	educational institutions
.gov	government agencies
.mil	military groups

   You can also try entering the name of the organization, enclosed in quotation marks, in a search engine. If you cannot identify or verify the author or sponsor of a Web site, be extremely wary of the site. If no one is willing to be accountable for the information, you cannot be accountable to your audience for using it. Search elsewhere.

2. *Accuracy.*   Sources of facts should be documented on a Web site just as they are in a print source. An additional advantage of the Web is that it can provide a hyperlink to any original source. **Hyperlinks are usually colored and underlined words or images in the text. Clicking with your mouse on a hyperlink will take you directly to the linked site.**

   Web sites should also be relatively free of errors in grammatical usage and mechanics. If a site contains such errors, it might also contain errors in content.

3. *Objectivity.*   As noted above, you need to know who has posted the site. Consider the philosophies and possible biases of the organization or individual responsible for the site. Are those beliefs, interests, and biases likely to slant the information? The more objective the author, the more credible the facts and information.

4. *Date.*   Many sites include information about when the site was posted and when it was last updated. In most cases, when you are concerned with factual data, the more recent, the better.

5. *Usability.*   If you have spent much time exploring the Internet, you have probably at one time or another called up a site that contained such complex graphics that it took a long time to load or even caused your computer to crash. Frames, graphics, and multimedia resources can enhance a site, or they can simply complicate it. Consider the practical efficiency of the sites you explore.

6. *Sensitivity to diversity.*   A diversity-sensitive Web site will be free of bias against either gender, against any ethnic, racial, or sexual-preference subgroup, and against people with disabilities.[19]

   Federal agencies are required by law to make their Web sites accessible to people with disabilities. For example, federal Web sites must be accessible in a mode that allows people with low vision to view them without relying on audio input.[20] Other requirements include making sure hyperlinks can be detected by color-blind users and providing audio and video clips with written captions for people with hearing disabilities.[21]

The Library

Despite the explosion of World Wide Web resources in recent years, the library remains a rich source of supporting material. Most libraries, from the largest research university library to the smallest village public library, house the following kinds of resources:

Books

Periodicals

Full-text databases

Newspapers

Reference resources

Government documents

Special services

Books   The word *library* is almost synonymous with the word *book*. In spite of the predictions of some that electronic resources will someday make books obsolete, for now books remain central to the holdings of most libraries.

A library's books are housed in the stacks, often several floors of shelves of books. Books are organized in the stacks according to **call number, a reference number assigned to each book,** which encodes the subject or topic, as well as the author. **Most libraries use the Library of Congress classification system of call numbers.**

A library's central catalog of all its books is called the card catalog. Today, most card catalogs are electronic ones. Banks of computer monitors in a central location in the library provide directions for looking up the books you need. Many college and university card catalogs these days are also accessible from remote locations, meaning that you can search them online and build preliminary bibliographies of books and call numbers before ever coming to the library building itself.

You may be able to print out the card catalog records for the books you want. If you have to copy them from the screen, be sure to include the author's name, title of the book, publisher and date of publication, and the library's call number. Use a consistent format so that later you can easily interpret the information.

Books will be important sources as you prepare your presentations. They can provide in-depth coverage of topics, which is not possible in shorter publications. However, because most books are written 2 or 3 years before they are published, they are inherently outdated. If your presentation addresses a current topic or if you want to use current examples, you will probably not find the information you need in books. You will turn instead to periodicals and newspapers, available both online and in hard copy.

Periodicals

The term periodicals refers both to magazines, such as *Time, People, and Sports Illustrated,* **and to professional journals,** such as *College English and the Quarterly Journal of Economics.* Both types of periodicals can be useful for presentations.

Periodical indexes are the equivalent of card catalogs in helping you locate information you need; **they contain a listing of bibliographical data for articles published in a group of magazines or journals during a given time period.** A number of such indexes cover many topics and most of the thousands of periodicals published. Many periodical indexes are available on CD-ROM, and many can be accessed either from the library or from remote locations. In most periodical indexes, entries are indexed alphabetically according to both subject and author. Most people use them by searching for subjects or keywords, much as they would conduct a World Wide Web search. Some periodical indexes are **full-text databases, meaning that you can access not only bibliographical information but also the texts of the articles themselves.**

Following are some frequently used periodical indexes and full-text databases:

- *The Reader's Guide to Periodical Literature* is the oldest periodical index and the one that many researchers first learn to use. It indexes popular magazines and a few trade and professional journals. Libraries can subscribe to the *Reader's Guide* either in hard copy or as an electronic database.

Developing Your Presentation STEP BY STEP
Gather Supporting Material

With a draft of his specific purpose, central idea, and main ideas in hand, Ben begins to research Coricidin abuse. Fortunately, he had kept the newspaper article that gave him the idea for the topic, so he has one source already. Because this first source is a newspaper, Ben decides to check out other newspapers.

He goes online to his university library's Web site. There he accesses the database Newspaper Source, where he discovers another article entitled "Latest Trend in Drug Abuse: Youths Risk Death for Cough-Remedy High," in the December 29, 2003, issue of USA Today. Newspaper Source provides the full text of that article.

While Ben is online, he uses Google to search for additional information on his topic and discovers a site called TheAntiDrug.com. The National Youth Anti-Drug Media Campaign, an initiative of the White House Office of National Drug Control Policy, maintains the site. Ben decides it is another credible source.

Ben records in MLA format on note cards the essential bibliographical information for these and other sources he discovers. Then he begins to read carefully and take notes. As he does so, he copies verbatim material accurately and puts quotation marks around it.

- *Info Trac* is a collection of indexes available through a single source. *Info Trac* includes the *Expanded Academic Index* and the *Business Index Backfile.*

- *The Public Affairs Information Service (P.A.I.S.) Bulletin,* available in both hard copy and electronic formats, indexes both periodicals and books in such fields as sociology, political science, and economics.

- *LEXIS/NEXIS* is an extensive full-text subscription database of periodicals, newspapers, and government documents. It is an excellent source of very current information.

- *Academic Search Premier* is billed as the world's largest multidisciplinary academic database. Updated daily, it provides full text of more than 4700 scholarly publications in virtually every academic field.

Newspapers

You can find information that is only hours old by reading the latest edition of a daily newspaper. Newspapers also offer the most detailed coverage available of current events.

Newspapers today exist in three formats. The first is the traditional newsprint format. However, libraries usually keep only the most recent newspapers (probably less than a week old) in their racks because they take up so much storage space. Back issues are kept on microfilm, the second format. And in recent years, many newspapers, from major national newspapers to local and college newspapers, have also become available online.

As with books and periodicals, you need a subject index to help you find newspaper articles of potential value to your research. **Newspaper indexes, listing bibliographic data for articles published in a newspaper or group of newspapers during a given time period,** are published by a number of medium-to-large newspapers. Your library may subscribe to several of these. In addition, electronic indexes such as the *National Newspaper Index* reference multiple newspapers. *Newspaper Source* also provides full texts of selected articles from some 30 national and international newspapers and more than 200 regional U.S. newspapers. Keep in mind, too, that if you need information about a specific event and you know the day on which it occurred, you can locate a newspaper from that or the following day and probably find a relevant news story about the event.

Reference Resources

A library's reference resources include encyclopedias, dictionaries, directories, atlases, almanacs, yearbooks, books of quotations, and biographical dictionaries. As a speaker, you may at one time or another use most of these types of materials. Like periodicals, newspapers, and microfilm, reference resources are usually available only for in-house research and cannot be checked out.

Government Documents

Government agencies at all levels publish information on almost every conceivable subject, as well as keeping records of most official proceedings. **Once a dauntingly complex collection of pamphlets, special reports, and texts of speeches and debates, government documents today are much more readily accessible through the World Wide Web.**

The most important index of government documents has long been the *Monthly Catalog of U.S. Government Publications,* available online in recent years. At present, several government agencies are in the final stages of developing a more comprehensive online *National Bibliography of U.S. Government Publications.*[22]

Special Services

Interlibrary loan and reciprocal borrowing privileges are among the special services that can help you find resources not otherwise available through your own library or online. Say you are reading an article and discover a reference to a book you would like to see. Your library does not own the book. **You might be able to use interlibrary loan to locate the book at another library and have it sent to your library within a few days.** Or, if your library has **reciprocal borrowing privileges with another library, you may be able to go to that library yourself and locate the book.**

Types of Supporting Material

If you have explored your own knowledge and insights and those of people you know, discovered material on the Internet, and examined a variety of library resources, you probably have a wealth of potential supporting material. Now you will need to decide what to use in your presentation. Keeping in mind your audience's knowledge, interests, and expectations will help you to determine where an illustration might stir their emotions, where an explanation might help them to understand a point, and where statistics might convince them of the significance of a problem. Let's discuss these and other types of supporting material and consider suggestions for using them effectively.

Illustrations

Illustrations offer an example of or tell a story about an idea, issue, or problem a speaker is discussing. They can be as short as a word or phrase or as long as a well-developed paragraph. Sometimes speakers will offer a series of brief illustrations, as Illinois State Senator Barack Obama did in his address to the Democratic National Convention in July 2004:

Verbal

> . . . we have more work to do. More to do for the workers I met in Galesburg, Illinois, who are losing their union jobs at the Maytag plant that's moving to Mexico, and now are having to compete with their own children for jobs that pay seven bucks an hour. More to do for the father I met who was losing his job and choking back tears, wondering how he would pay $4,500 a month for the drugs his son needs without the health benefits he counted on. More to do for the young woman in East St. Louis, and thousands more like her, who has the grades, has the drive, has the will, but doesn't have the money to go to college.[23]

Other speakers may offer longer and more detailed illustrations:

> Toby Lee, six years old, was sitting in the bleachers at the Hutchinson Ice Arena, just outside Minneapolis, Minnesota. He got up and walked toward his mother

to get money for the concession stand. To the horror of his parents, Toby slipped and fell through the 13-inch space between the seat and the footboard, dropped 8 feet and landed headfirst on the concrete floor. Still conscious, he was rushed to the hospital, where he later died of severe head injuries.[24]

Obama's illustrations and the story of Toby Lee are true examples. However, sometimes a speaker will use instead a **hypothetical illustration—one that has not actually occurred.** If you decide to use a hypothetical illustration, it is important to make clear to your audience that the scene you describe never really happened. Note how Matthew uses the word *imagine* to make clear to his audience that his illustration is hypothetical:

Imagine an evening outing: You and your two children decide to have a fun night out. You look up to your rearview mirror to see a car slam into the back of your car—WHAM—killing your children. You survive the crash and so does the individual who rear-ended you.[25]

Whether you choose to use brief or extended illustrations, true or hypothetical ones, remember this principle: Everybody likes to hear a story. An illustration almost always ensures audience interest. In addition, communication researchers have found that listeners are less likely to generate counterarguments to a persuasive message supported by examples and personal narratives.[26]

The following suggestions should help you use illustrations effectively in your presentations.

Verbal

- Be sure that your illustrations are directly relevant to the idea or point they are supposed to support.
- Choose illustrations that are typical, not exceptions.
- Make your illustrations vivid and specific.
- Use illustrations with which your listeners can identify.
- Remember that the most effective illustrations are often personal ones.

Descriptions and Explanations

Probably the most commonly used forms of supporting material are descriptions and explanations. To describe is to provide detailed images that allow an audience to see, hear, smell, touch, or taste whatever you are describing. **Descriptions—word pictures—**can make people and scenes come alive for an audience, as does this description of an all-too-common encounter:

You're walking down the main street when a loud thumping bass sound approaches you. To your annoyance, it is one of those hot rod drivers with all his car windows down, and from his tiny capsule, irritating, distorted sound waves of "Did It for the Nookie" hit your ears at 90 decibels.[27]

An explanation of how something works or why a situation exists can help an audience understand conditions, events, or processes. In her presentation on "superbugs," Amanda explains how disease-resistant strains of bacteria develop:

Bacteria are able to mutate when they are continually exposed to an antibiotic, rendering the antibiotic virtually useless against it. And the frequency with which antibiotics are prescribed today makes our pharmacies virtual classrooms for infections.[28]

Verbal

Although descriptions and explanations are part of most presentations, they lack the inherent interest factor that illustrations have. The following suggestions may help you to keep audiences from yawning through your descriptions and explanations:

- Avoid too many descriptions and explanations.
- Keep your descriptions and explanations brief.
- Describe and explain in specific and concrete language.

This speaker effectively uses an electronic presentation aid to complement his use of descriptions and explanations.

Definitions

For each technical or little-known term in their presentations, speakers should offer a **definition, or statement of what the term means.** However, they do not need to define terms with which most or all audience members are likely to be familiar. If you determine that you should define a word or phrase for your audience, consider whether you can best define it by **classification, the format of a standard dictionary definition,** or by an **operational definition, explaining how the word or phrase works or what it does.** Joni uses both kinds of definition in this excerpt from her speech on the dangers of oral polio vaccination:

Verbal

> Polio is a virus which attacks the tissue in the spinal cord and brain, causing inflammation. The effects of this inflammation range from fever and vomiting to bodily paralysis and damage to the nerve cells which control breathing and circulation.[29]

The first sentence defines *polio* by placing it in the general category in which it belongs (viruses) and then differentiating it from other viruses. This is a definition by classification. The second sentence describes what polio does. This is an operational definition.

To use definitions effectively, consider the following suggestions:

- Use definitions only when necessary.
- Be certain that your definitions are understandable.
- Be sure that any definition you provide accurately reflects your use of the word or phrase throughout the presentation.

Analogies

An analogy demonstrates how unfamiliar ideas, things, and situations are similar to something the audience already understands. Speakers can use two types of analogies in their presentations. The first is a **literal analogy, or comparison of two similar things.** Kyle uses a literal analogy to compare the African slave trade to other historical travesties:

Verbal

The trans-Atlantic slave trade was one of the greatest tragedies in human history, rivaled by such horrible events as the Jewish Holocaust and the Spanish invasion of the Americas.[30]

The second type of analogy is **a figurative analogy, a comparison of two seemingly dissimilar things that in fact share a significant common feature.** In a recent speech to an environmental group, former Colorado Governor Richard Lamm drew on a figurative analogy that compared humanity's continuing long-term challenges to the flow of a river:

> . . . River issues were the long-term flowing issues, which went on over generations if not centuries. The full sweep of history reveals some issues like the fight for religious freedom, the gradual, if glacial, emancipation of women, the search for freedom for self-government, the fight against authoritarian governance, etc. These issues can be observed in some form over the sweep of history.[31]

Two suggestions can help you use analogies more effectively in your presentations:

- Be certain that the two things you compare in a literal analogy are very similar.
- Make the similarity between the two things compared in a figurative analogy apparent to the audience.

Statistics

Verbal

Statistics, or numerical data, can represent hundreds or thousands of illustrations, helping a speaker express the significance or magnitude of a situation. Statistics can also help a speaker express the relationship of a part to the whole. In this brief excerpt from a presentation on bogus airline parts, Jon uses both types of statistics:

> . . . 26 million parts are installed on airplanes every year in the U.S., and the FAA estimates that at least 2% of these parts are counterfeits.[32]

Skilled speakers learn how to use statistics to their greatest advantage. For example, they try to make huge numbers more readily understandable and more dramatic to their audiences. Nicole emphasizes the vast amount of computer waste with a memorable image:

> . . . outdated computer waste in America alone could fill the area of a football field piled one mile high.[33]

Or a speaker might present statistics about the world's growing population in these terms:

> In an average minute, 245 people are born and 107 die, for a net gain by the minute of 138 . . . 8300 an hour, 200,000 per day, 6 million per month, and 72 million a year.[34]

In addition to simplifying and dramatizing your statistics, you can use statistics more effectively if you utilize the following three suggestions:

- Round off large numbers.
- Use visual aids to present your statistics.
- Cite the sources of your statistics.

Opinions

Verbal

The opinions of others can add authority, drama, and style to a presentation. A speaker can use three types of opinions: expert testimony, lay testimony, and literary quotations.

Expert testimony (the opinion of someone who is an acknowledged expert in the field under discussion) is perhaps the type of opinion most frequently employed by speakers. If you lack authority on your topic, cite someone who can offer such expertise. In her speech on the college credit card crisis, Jeni realized that her audience might not believe that the misuse of credit cards by college students is a widespread problem. So Jeni quoted an expert:

> Ruth Suswein, executive director of the Bankcard Holders of America, told the . . . *Pittsburgh Post Gazette,* "I defy you to go on any college campus and find any student who doesn't know some other student who has messed up using credit cards."[35]

In the days and weeks that followed the September 11, 2001, terrorist attacks, countless eyewitnesses and people affected in various ways by the tragedy told their personal stories to reporters and news anchors. Audiences already aware of the magnitude of the tragedy—the number of lives lost and the damage inflicted—were perhaps even more moved by the stories of such individuals as Lisa Jefferson. Jefferson was the GTE customer care representative who stayed on the line for 15 minutes with Todd Beamer, a passenger on United Flight 93 that eventually crashed in Pennsylvania. Of course, few speakers will have eyewitnesses at hand when they speak. But they can use **lay testimony by quoting firsthand witnesses of dramatic or traumatic events.** Such lay testimony can stir an audience's emotions and provide the most memorable moments of a presentation.

Finally, speakers may wish to include **literary quotations (citations from a work of fiction or nonfiction, a poem, or another speech)** in their presentations. Newspaper publisher Mike Curtin quoted science fiction writer H. G. Wells in his speech on the importance of language education:

> H. G. Wells, the English writer who achieved fame with his publication of *The Time Machine* and *The War of the Worlds,* . . . wrote, "Civilization is a race between education and catastrophe."[36]

Whether you use expert testimony, lay testimony, or literary quotations, consider the following suggestions for using opinions effectively in your presentations:

- Be certain that any authority you cite is actually an expert on the subject you are discussing.
- Identify your sources.
- Cite unbiased authorities.
- Cite opinions that are representative of prevailing opinion. If you cite a dissenting viewpoint, identify it as such.
- Quote or paraphrase your sources accurately and note the context in which the remarks were originally made.
- Use literary quotations sparingly.

Acknowledgment of Supporting Material

Once you have supporting material in hand, you must decide whether it must be credited to a source. Some information is so widely known that you may not need to acknowledge a source. For example, you need not credit a source if you say that former FBI official Mark Felt has been identified as the long-anonymous Watergate informant "Deep Throat." This fact is general knowledge and is widely available in a variety of sources. However, if you decide to use any of the following, then you must give credit:

- Direct quotations, even if they are only brief phrases
- Opinions, assertions, or ideas of others, even if you paraphrase them rather than quote them verbatim

DIVERSITY AND COMMUNICATION
Adapting to Diverse Audiences

One of the principles we've stressed throughout this book is the importance of adapting your message to others. Many, if not most, of the presentations you give will be to audiences that represent a mix of cultures and backgrounds rather than a single cultural tradition. Although you may not have immediate plans to deliver a presentation in Singapore, Moscow, Tokyo, or Warsaw, it will not be unusual for you to face audience members who come from one of these cities when you speak on campus or in your hometown.

People from the predominant culture in North America usually prefer a structured presentation that follows an outlined pattern; they also prefer an introduction that previews the ideas you'll present and a conclusion that crisply summarizes the essential points you've made. But a Russian or Eastern European audience would expect a less tightly structured presentation. When you're in doubt about listener preferences, we recommend being structured and organized. But realize that not all audience members may expect information to be presented as *you* prefer. One study found that members of some cultures prefer a more formal oratorical style of delivery than the conversational, extemporaneous style that is usually taught in American presentational speaking classes.[37] For example, Japanese speakers addressing a predominantly Japanese audience begin a presentation by making respectful references to their audience.

You may still be wondering, "So, what should I do when I speak to people who have a cultural background different from my own?" Here are some ideas

that may help you.[38] First, consider using a variety of different types of supporting materials. A mix of stories, examples, statistics, and other supporting illustrations can appeal to a wide range of audience backgrounds. Also consider the power of images over words. Use visual aids to illustrate your talk. Pictures and images can communicate universal messages—especially emotional ones. Telling a good story to illustrate your ideas is another effective strategy to appeal to a wide range of audience preferences. Most audiences value a good story with a point or moral that is relevant to the point you want to make. Our overarching suggestion: Be aware of who will be in your audience. If you're unsure of your listeners' speaking-style preferences, ask for tips and strategies from audience members or people you trust before you design or deliver your presentation.

- Statistics
- Any nonoriginal visual materials, including graphs, tables, and pictures

Integrating an **oral citation (an oral recounting of information about a source, such as the author, title, and publication date)** into your presentation is not difficult. For example, you might say,

> According to an article entitled "Wider Student Use Is Urged for New Meningitis Vaccine," published in the May 27, 2005, edition of *The New York Times,* the U.S. Centers for Disease Control and Prevention are now recommending "wider use of a new meningitis vaccine for adolescents and college freshmen," including routine vaccination for 11- and 12-year olds.[39]

Aware
Verbal
Nonverbal
Listen and Respond
Adapt

As you select your illustrations, descriptions, explanations, definitions, analogies, statistics, and opinions, be guided not only by the suggestions provided in this chapter for each type of supporting material but also by the five communication principles for a lifetime. The best supporting material reflects self-awareness, taking advantage of your own knowledge and experience. Effective verbal supporting material is appropriately worded, concrete, and vivid enough that your audience can visualize what you are talking about. Effective visual supporting material enhances, rather than detracts from, your verbal message. Sensitivity to your audience will help you choose the verbal and visual supporting material that is most appropriately adapted to them. If a presentation is boring, it is probably because the speaker has not used the fundamental principles of communication as criteria for selecting supporting material.

SUMMARY

Public speaking is a teachable, learnable process of developing, supporting, organizing, and presenting ideas. Presentational speaking skills can help you in other college courses and in the workplace.

The stages of the public speaking process center around consideration of the audience, who influence every decision a speaker makes. A speaker's tasks include selecting and narrowing a topic, identifying a general and specific purpose for speaking, developing the central idea of the presentation, generating main ideas, gathering supporting material, organizing the presentation, and finally, rehearsing and delivering the presentation.

Nearly everyone feels some anxiety about speaking in public. Speaker anxiety triggers physiological responses that may be worrisome but are actually your body's attempt to help you. Focusing on your audience and message and giving yourself mental pep talks can help you manage speaker anxiety, as can knowing how to develop a presentation, being well prepared, and seeking out opportunities to speak. Professional help is available for those few who continue to suffer debilitating speaker anxiety.

As you begin to prepare your presentation, you will first have to select and narrow your topic, keeping in mind the audience, the occasion, and your own interests and experiences. You may find helpful such strategies as silent brainstorming, scanning Web directories and Web pages, and listening and reading for topic ideas. Once you have a topic, you need to identify both your general and your specific purpose. General purposes include to inform, to persuade, and to entertain. Specific purposes are determined by the general purpose, the topic, and the audience. You will also need to decide on the central idea for the presentation. You can use that central idea to help you generate your main ideas, which are usually logical divisions of the central idea, reasons the central idea is true, or a series of steps or a chronological sequence that develops the central idea.

Next, you will need to discover support for your main ideas. As a presentational speaker, you have at least three potential sources of supporting material: yourself and people you know, the Internet, and the library. Personal knowledge and experience increase the likelihood that the audience will find you a credible speaker. To supplement your own knowledge and experience, you might turn to the vast resources available on the Internet. And most likely, you will still use library resources—books, periodicals, newspapers, reference resources, government documents, and various special services—as sources of supporting material.

The types of supporting material you can use in a presentation include illustrations, descriptions, explanations, definitions, analogies, statistics, and opinions. Simple guidelines can help you use each of these types of supporting material effectively and cite your sources correctly.

DISCUSSION AND REVIEW

1. Explain how presentational speaking skills can be of practical use, both while you are in college and afterward.

2. Sketch and label the stages of the audience-centered public speaking model.

3. Explain what causes the symptoms of speaker anxiety.

4. Offer at least three suggestions for managing speaker anxiety.

5. Suggest both criteria and strategies for discovering a good presentation topic.

6. What are the three general purposes for presentations?

7. With what phrase should an audience-centered, specific-purpose statement begin?

8. In what ways does a central idea differ from a specific purpose?

9. What are the characteristics of a good central idea?

10. List the three questions that you can apply to generate main ideas from a central idea.

11. Where might you find supporting material for a presentation?

12. List and explain the six criteria for evaluating Web sites.

13. What resources are available in most libraries?

14. What types of supporting material might you use in your presentations?

PUTTING PRINCIPLES INTO PRACTICE

1. Interview someone who regularly speaks in public as part of his or her job. Ask that person how he or she deals with speaker anxiety and what stages or steps he or she goes through in developing a speech.

2. Brainstorm a list of at least ten possible topics for an informative classroom presentation.

3. Write a specific-purpose statement for an informative presentation and a persuasive presentation on each of the following topics:

    Rap music

    Graduate school

    Primary elections

    Athletes as role models

    Credit cards

4. Generate at least three main ideas from each of the following central ideas. Apply the questions suggested in this chapter: Does the central idea have logical divisions? Can you think of several reasons the central idea is true? Can you support the central idea with a series of steps or a chronological sequence?

    Students who commute have at least three advantages over students who live on campus.

    Diplomatic relations between the United States and China have been strained over the last decade.

    Sleep deprivation is dangerous.

    Three specific strategies can help you deal with unsolicited telemarketers.

    Women should have annual mammograms.

5. Use a World Wide Web search engine to answer the following questions.[40] They're not as obvious as you think!

    a. How long did the Hundred Years War last?

    b. Which country makes Panama hats?

    c. From what animal do we get catgut?

    d. What is a camel's hair brush made of?

    e. The Canary Islands in the Pacific are named after what animal?

    f. What was King George VI's first name?

    g. What color is a purple finch?

    h. Where are Chinese gooseberries from?

6. Read a story in a newspaper or national news magazine. See how many different types of supporting material you can identify in the story.

7. The following passage comes from a book entitled *Abraham Lincoln, Public Speaker,* by Waldo W. Braden:

The Second Inaugural Address, sometimes called Lincoln's Sermon on the Mount, was a concise, tightly constructed composition that did not waste words on ceremonial niceties or superficial sentiment. The shortest Presidential inaugural address up to that time, it was only 700 words long, compared to 3700 words for the First, and required from 5 to 7 minutes to deliver.[41]

Now determine which of the following statements should be credited to Braden if you were to use them in a presentation:

- Lincoln's Second Inaugural is "sometimes called Lincoln's Sermon on the Mount."
- Because he was elected and sworn in for two terms as President, Abraham Lincoln prepared and delivered two inaugural addresses.
- Lincoln's Second Inaugural was 700 words and 5 to 7 minutes long.

13
Organizing and Outlining Your Presentation

chapter outline

ORGANIZING YOUR MAIN IDEAS

ORGANIZING YOUR SUPPORTING MATERIAL

ORGANIZING YOUR PRESENTATION FOR THE EARS OF OTHERS

INTRODUCING AND CONCLUDING YOUR PRESENTATION

OUTLINING YOUR PRESENTATION

SUMMARY

Jim Macbeth, Mostly Round & Flat, © Jim Macbeth/Super-Stock, Inc.

"Don't agonize. Organize."

Florynce R. Kennedy

Developing a presentation is like building a house. Just as a building contractor frames out a house early in the building process, a speaker frames out a presentation by completing the first four stages of the speech preparation process—selecting and narrowing a topic, identifying a general and a specific purpose, determining a central idea, and generating main ideas. Framing completed, the contractor assembles all the materials needed for the house: windows, doors, cabinets, hardware, and flooring; the speaker finds and adds supporting material to the presentation "frame," the fifth stage of the process. Once the house is framed out and the building materials are ready, the contractor must organize the work of the electricians, plumbers, carpenters, and carpet layers. Similarly, the speaker must organize ideas and supporting material.

In this chapter, we will discuss strategies for organizing and outlining your presentation, and we will explore ways to introduce and conclude your presentation effectively. Grounded in the five communication principles for a lifetime with which you are now familiar, these suggestions and strategies will result in an essentially complete "house"—a presentation that is ready to be rehearsed and delivered.

Chapter Objectives

After studying this chapter, you should be able to

- Explain the practical value of presentational speaking skills.
- List and explain five strategies for organizing main ideas in a presentation.
- Define the principles of primacy, recency, and complexity and explain how each can be applied to organizing main ideas.
- List and explain five strategies for organizing supporting material in a presentation.
- Explain three ways to organize a presentation for the ears of others.

- List and explain the five functions of a presentation introduction.
- Suggest at least five strategies for getting an audience's attention in a presentation introduction.
- List and explain the four functions of a presentation conclusion.
- Define a preparation outline and explain how a speaker would use one.
- Outline a presentation according to standard outline format.
- Define a delivery outline and explain how a speaker would use one.

ORGANIZING YOUR MAIN IDEAS

You have already completed the first five stages of audience-centered presentation preparation:

- Select and narrow a topic.
- Determine your purpose.
- Develop your central idea.
- Generate main ideas.
- Gather supporting material.

Now it is time to put your presentation together, organizing the ideas and information you have generated and discovered.

Verbal

Logical organization is one way you can communicate your verbal message effectively. A logically organized presentation has three major divisions—an introduction, a body, and a conclusion. The introduction catches the audience's attention and previews the body. The body presents the main content of the presentation. The conclusion summarizes the main ideas and provides memorable closure to the presentation.

Professional speaker Larry Tracy suggests a strategy he calls "3–1–2" for drafting the organization of a presentation.[1] It works like this:

1. Take a stack of 3 × 5 cards. Label one card "3" and write on it your "bottom line" message. This is the core of your conclusion.

2. Label another card "1" and write on it where the presentation will go—your preview.

3. Next, place the supporting points that flow from "1" to "3" on a series of cards marked "2a," "2b," "2c," etc. These will become the main ideas of the body of your presentation.

The advantage of the "3–1–2" strategy, says Tracy, is that it clarifies from the start of the drafting process where the presentation is going, ensuring more logical structure. He adds, "Just remember: You draft 3–1–2, but . . . you deliver 1–2–3."

Regardless of whether you use Tracy's drafting process, one recommended by your public speaking instructor, or one of your own devising, you will need to consider early on how best to organize your main ideas. Then you will organize your supporting material for maximum impact, and devise signposts to lead your audience through your presentation. Finally, you will need to develop an effective introduction and conclusion. Once you have made the necessary decisions about these component parts, you will be ready to outline the entire presentation.

Organizing Ideas Chronologically

If you determine that you can best develop your central idea through a series of steps, you will probably organize those steps—your main ideas—chronologically. **Chronological organization is based on sequential order, according to when each step or event occurred or should occur.** If you are explaining a process, you will want to organize the steps of that process from first to last. If you are providing a historical overview of an event, movement, or policy, you might begin with the end result and trace its history backward in time. Examples of topics that might lend themselves to chronological organization include the process for stripping and refinishing a piece of furniture, the four hurricanes that hit Florida in 2004, and the history of higher education for women.

If you intend to describe a series of different types of procedures in your presentation, you may find that it works well to organize your main ideas topically.

Organizing Ideas Topically

If your main ideas are natural divisions of your central idea, you will probably arrange them according to topical organization. **Topical organization may be simply an arbitrary arrangement of main ideas that are fairly equal in importance.** For example, if you are giving an informative presentation on the various instrument families of the modern symphony orchestra, your main ideas will probably be strings, woodwinds, brass, and percussion. The order in which you discuss these instrument groups may not really matter.

At other times, topical organization is less arbitrary. **The principle of recency suggests that audiences remember best what they hear last.** If you want to emphasize the string section of an orchestra, you will purposefully place that family last in your presentation.

Another principle that can help guide your topical organization is **the principle of primacy, which suggests that you discuss your most convincing or least controversial idea first.** To adapt to an audience who may be skeptical of some of your ideas, discuss first those points on which you all agree. If you are speaking to an anti–gun-control audience about ways to protect children from violence in schools, don't begin by advocating gun control. Instead, begin by affirming family values and education in the home, perhaps move on to the importance of small classes and adequate counseling in schools, and only then discuss gun control as a possible preventive measure.

One other type of topical organization is **organization according to complexity, moving from simple ideas and processes to more complex ones.** Many skills you have learned in life have been taught by order of complexity. In first grade, you learned to read easy words first, then moved on to more difficult ones. In third grade, you learned single-digit multiplication tables before moving on to more complex double- and triple-digit multiplication problems. In junior high school, you learned to use the library's catalog before you began a research project. And in high school, you learned to drive by practicing simple maneuvers in the parking lot before going out on the highway. Similarly, if you are giving a presentation on how to trace your family's genealogy, you might discuss readily available, user-friendly Internet sources before explaining how to access old courthouse records or parish registries of births, deaths, and baptisms.

Organizing Ideas Spatially

"Go down the hill two blocks and turn left by the florist. Then go three blocks to the next stoplight and turn right. The place you're looking for is about a block farther, on your right." When you offer someone directions, you organize your ideas spatially. **Spatial organization means arranging items according to their location, position, or direction.**

Presentations that rely on description are good candidates for spatial organization. For example, discussions of the route taken by Sir Edmund Hillary and Tenzing Norgay when climbing Mt. Everest in 1953 and the molecular structure of DNA would lend themselves to spatial organization. Or, rather than organizing your presentation on Florida's 2004 hurricanes chronologically, you might choose to organize it spatially, according to where each hurricane made landfall.

Organizing Ideas to Show Cause and Effect

Cause-and-effect organization actually refers to two related patterns: identifying a situation and then discussing the resulting effects (cause–effect) and presenting a situation and then exploring its causes (effect–cause).

A speaker discussing the consequences of teenage pregnancy might use a cause–effect pattern, establishing first that teenage pregnancy is a significant social issue and then discussing various consequences or effects. On the other hand, a speaker who speaks on the same topic but who chooses to explore the reasons for the high rate of teen pregnancy will probably use an effect–cause pattern, discussing teenage pregnancy first as an effect and then exploring its various causes. As the recency principle would suggest, a cause–effect pattern emphasizes effects; an effect–cause pattern emphasizes causes.

Organizing Ideas by Problem and Solution

If, instead of exploring causes or consequences of a problem or issue, **you want either to explore how best to solve the problem or to advocate a particular solution, you will probably choose problem-and-solution organization.** For example, if you were speaking on how listeners can protect themselves from mountain lion attacks in the American West, you might first establish that a significant problem exists, then talk about solutions to that problem. Or if you were talking about ending discrimination against overweight people, you could first establish that such discrimination exists and is harmful, then talk about the solutions. Although you can use problem-and-solution organization for either informative or persuasive presentations, you are more likely to use it when your general purpose is to persuade—to urge your audience to support or adopt one or more of the solutions you discuss.

Note that the topics in both of the above examples also lend themselves to organization by cause and effect. You could, for example, discuss mountain lion attacks as an effect and explore why the frequency of such attacks has increased in recent years (causes). Or you could talk about discrimination against the overweight as a cause and discuss the harmful effects of such discrimination. How do you decide which organizational pattern to use? Return to your specific purpose. If it is for your audience to be able to explain how best to guard against mountain lion attacks, select the problem-and-solution organizational strategy. If it is for your audience to be able to explain the harmful effects of discrimination against those who are overweight, use the cause-and-effect strategy of organization. Let both your general and your specific purpose continue to guide your presentation as you organize your main ideas.

Recap
Organizing Your Main Ideas

Strategy	Description
Chronological	Organization by time or sequence
Topical	Arbitrary arrangement of topics or organization according to recency, primacy, or complexity
Spatial	Organization according to location or position
Cause-and-effect	Organization by discussing a situation and its causes or a situation and its effects
Problem-and-solution	Organization by discussing a problem and then various solutions

ORGANIZING YOUR SUPPORTING MATERIAL

Once you have organized your main ideas, you are ready to organize the supporting material for each idea. Suppose that you find that you have two brief illustrations, a statistic, and an opinion in support of your first main idea. How should you organize these materials to communicate your verbal message most effectively?

The same organizational patterns you considered as you organized your main ideas can also help you organize your supporting material. For example, you might arrange a group of brief illustrations chronologically. At other times, you might find it more useful to organize supporting material according to the principle of recency, primacy, or complexity. You would employ the principle of recency if you saved your most convincing statistic for last. You would use primacy if you decided to present first the opinion with which you were certain your audience would agree. And you might arrange two explanations according to the principle of complexity, presenting the simplest one first and working up to the more complex one. Two additional principles that may help you organize supporting material are specificity and arrangement from "soft" to "hard" evidence.

Sometimes your supporting material includes both very specific illustrations and a more general explanation. **The principle of specificity suggests that you offer your specific information and follow it by your general explanation or make your general explanation first and then support it with your specific illustrations.** In his speech on wearing ribbons to show support for a cause, Tony offers a series of brief illustrations first, followed by a more general explanation:

> Battling AIDS, surviving breast cancer, putting your life back together after 9/11, just being brave while your country is at war; all of these are situations that cause people to seek out support and comfort in others. We start looking for ways to connect with people around us, even total strangers. A simple way proven effective in the past and possible for the future is simply cutting off a ribbon and pinning it to your clothes.[2]

Another principle that can help you organize your supporting material is moving from "soft" evidence to "hard" evidence. **Hypothetical illustrations, descriptions, explanations, definitions, analogies, and opinions are usually considered soft evidence. Hard evidence includes factual examples and statistics.** Allie moves from soft evidence to a hard statistic as she discusses the widespread prescribing of selective serotonin reuptake inhibitors, or SSRIs:

> The *PR Newswire* of April 14, 2003, explains that when people suffer from depression or an anxiety disorder, there could be a problem with their serotonin

Developing Your Presentation STEP BY STEP
Organize Your Speech

As he begins to integrate his supporting material in his speech on Coricidin abuse, Ben finds that he has four items to help him explain the ingredient in Coricidin that is the catalyst for abuse. He decides to arrange these four items in order of complexity—from stating where DXM can be found, to explaining its physical side effects:

1. DXM is found in over 100 cold medications, including those with "DM" or "Tuss" in their names.

2. Coricidin is the drug of choice because it's easier than swallowing several bottles of Robitussin.
3. As the National Institute on Drug Abuse indicates on TheAntiDrug.com Web site, last updated April 11, 2004, DXM closely resembles PCP and, when taken in excess, causes hallucinations.
4. According to *USA Today* of December 29, 2003, when abused, Coricidin can cause depressed breathing, an irregular heartbeat, seizures, coma, and even death.

Recap
Organizing Your Supporting Material

Strategy	Description
Chronology	Organization by time or sequence
Recency	Most important material last
Primacy	Most convincing or least controversial material first
Complexity	From simple to more complex material
Specificity	From specific information to general overview or from general overview to specific information
"Soft" to "hard" evidence	From hypothetical illustrations and opinions to facts and statistics

balance. Thus, it is unsurprising that SSRIs are frequently prescribed for a variety of mood disorders. *ABC News* of June 21, 2003, reports that one out of every eight Americans has been prescribed at least one SSRI.[5]

ORGANIZING YOUR PRESENTATION FOR THE EARS OF OTHERS

Adapt

You now have a fairly complete, logically organized plan for your presentation. But if you tried to deliver it at this point, your audience would probably become confused. What are your main ideas? How is one main idea related to the next? What supporting material develops which main idea? To adapt your logically organized message to your audience, you need to provide **signposts, or organizational cues for their ears.** You do this by adding previews, transitions, and summaries that allow you to move smoothly from one idea to the next throughout the presentation.

Previews

A preview "tells them what you're going to tell them"—it is a statement of what is to come. Previews help your audience members anticipate and remember the main ideas of your presentation. They also help you move smoothly from the introduction

ETHICS AND COMMUNICATION
The Ethics of Primacy and Recency

Jessica knows that, according to the principle of recency, she should discuss last what she wants her audience to remember best. However, in her presentation on the risk of counterfeit prescription drugs, Jessica thinks that it may be more ethical to reveal immediately to her audience how costly the problem is in terms of both dollars and human lives. Is it ethical for Jessica to save that important statistic for last?

to the body of your presentation and from one main idea to the next. **The initial preview is usually presented in conjunction with, and sometimes as part of, the central idea.** Note how Yarmela states her central idea and then previews her three main ideas near the end of the introduction to her presentation on genetic testing:

> Genetic testing is seen as the wave of the future, but too many Americans are putting their faith in these tests that simply are not adequate. In order to understand this problem, we will first examine the problems that are occurring with genetic testing, then look at the causes, and finally discuss the solutions that must occur in order to stop more tragedies from taking place.[6]

In addition to offering an initial preview, a speaker may also offer **internal previews at various points throughout a presentation. These previews introduce and outline ideas that will be developed as the presentation progresses.** Meleena provides an internal preview just before the final main idea of her presentation on sexual harassment in schools:

> Now . . . we can look at some things that we can all do, as parents, teachers, and students, to stop sexual harassment in our schools. There are two ways to prevent these causes from recurring. The first is education and the second is immediate action.[7]

When Meleena delivers this preview, her listeners know that she is going to talk about two possible solutions to the problem she has been discussing. Their anticipation increases the likelihood that they will hear and later remember these solutions.

Verbal and Nonverbal Transitions

A **transition** signals to an audience that a speaker is moving from one idea to the next. Effective **verbal transitions are words or phrases that show relationships between ideas in your presentation.** They include simple enumeration (*first, second,*

Verbal
Nonverbal

Canadian Prime Minister Jean Charest uses a nonverbal signpost to help listeners follow his transitions.

third); synonyms or pronouns that refer to earlier key words or ideas (the word *they* at the beginning of this sentence refers to the phrase "verbal transitions" in the previous sentence); and words and phrases that show relationships between ideas *(in addition, not only . . . but also, in other words, in summary, therefore, however).* As you begin to rehearse your presentation, you might need to experiment with various verbal transitions to achieve a coherence that seems natural and logical to you. If none of the verbal alternatives seems quite right, consider a nonverbal transition.

Nonverbal transitions are sometimes used alone and sometimes in combination with verbal transitions. An effective **nonverbal transition might take the form of a facial expression, a pause, a change in vocal pitch or speaking rate, or movement.** Most good speakers will use a combination of verbal and nonverbal transitions to help them move from one idea to the next throughout their presentations.

Summaries

Like previews, **a summary—a recap of what has been said**—provides an additional opportunity for the audience to grasp a speaker's most important ideas. Most speakers use two types of summaries: internal summaries and a final summary.

Internal summaries, like internal previews, **occur within and throughout a presentation and recap what has been said so far in the presentation.** You might want to use an internal summary after you have discussed two or three main ideas, to ensure that the audience keeps them firmly in mind as you move into another main idea. You can combine an internal summary with an internal preview. Rebecca clarifies what she has just discussed, as well as what she will discuss next, in this combined internal summary/preview from her presentation on Rohypnol, the so-called date-rape drug:

> Having examined the problem of Rohypnol and why it has become such a danger in today's society [summary], we can now explore solutions at the commercial and personal levels to purge this drug from our system [preview].[8]

You may also want to provide your audience with **a final opportunity to hear and remember your main ideas, in the form of a final summary in your conclusion.** While your initial preview gave your audience their first exposure to your main ideas, your final summary will give them their last exposure to those ideas. Near the end of Stephanie's presentation on cruise ship violence, she provides this final summary of her three main ideas:

> Today we outlined violence on cruise ships and the need for recourse; we then discussed the nature of these criminal environments and lack of laws; and finally, we explored solutions for handling or avoiding these crimes even if the authorities are not supportive.[9]

Adding previews, transitions, and summaries to your well-organized presentation applies the fundamental principles of using both verbal and nonverbal messages effectively and of adapting your message to others, increasing the likelihood that your audience will grasp your main ideas and the logic of your organizational strategy.

Verbal
Nonverbal
Adapt

INTRODUCING AND CONCLUDING YOUR PRESENTATION

At this point, you have pretty well developed the ideas and content of the body of your presentation, and you have strategies for organizing that material. But you have not yet given much thought to how you are going to begin and end the presentation. That's okay. Even though you will deliver it first, you usually plan

Adapt

your introduction last. You need to know first what you're introducing—especially your central idea and main ideas. Once you do, it is time to plan how you are going to introduce and conclude your presentation. While they make up a relatively small percentage of the total presentation, your introduction and conclusion provide your audience with first and final impressions of you and your presentation. They are important considerations in adapting your message to others.

Introductions

Your introduction should convince your audience to listen to you. More specifically, it must perform five functions: get the audience's attention, introduce the topic, give the audience a reason to listen, establish your credibility, and preview your main ideas. Let's briefly consider each of these five functions.

Get the Audience's Attention

If an introduction does not capture the audience's attention, the rest of the presentation may be wasted on them. You have to use verbal messages effectively to wake up your listeners and make them want to hear more.

There are several good ways to gain an audience's attention. One commonly used and quite effective one is to open with an illustration. Tony opens his speech on forgiveness with a moving personal illustration:

> For my fifteenth birthday, my mother promised that we would spend the whole day together, and she would take me anywhere I wanted to go and buy me anything I wanted. You see, my mother was a single mom, and the true gift to me was just spending time with her; she was always at work. Well, I was so excited that the night before my birthday I couldn't sleep, and I woke up at dawn on my birthday, and I waited. And I waited, and I waited, and I waited. Well, 1:00 PM came around, and my mother was still sleeping. You see, I knew that she'd been up drinking all night the night before, and that she'd probably wake up angry at me if I was to wake her up. So I waited. And then 5:00 PM came around, and I gathered up the courage to wake her up. And when I did, she slapped me; she threw $60 at me and said, "Get out of my face."[10]

Other strategies are to ask a rhetorical question, relate a startling fact or statistic, quote an expert or a literary text, tell a humorous story, or refer to historical or recent events. Federal Reserve Chairman Alan Greenspan used humor to capture the attention of the 2005 graduating class of the Wharton School of the University of Pennsylvania:

> I have more in common with you graduates than people might think. After all, before long, after my term at the Federal Reserve comes to an end, I too will be looking for a job.[11]

Eileen uses a historical reference to open her presentation on mental health privacy:

> A bright political future loomed ahead of Thomas Eagleton in 1972. George McGovern had chosen him as his vice presidential running mate for the '72 elections, and his popularity was high among Americans. But then the press found out that Eagleton had received shock treatment for depression when he was younger. Eagleton was immediately dropped from the ticket and shunned from the political world.[12]

The 5th Wave   By Rich Tennant

SAFETY SEMINAR

© The 5th Wave, www. the5thwave. com.

Still other speakers might get their audience's attention by referring to a personal experience, referring to the occasion, or referring to something said by a preceding speaker. While not all of these strategies will work for all presentations, at least one of them should be an option for any presentation you make. And with a little practice, you may find yourself being able to choose from several good possibilities for a single presentation.

Introduce the Topic

Within the first few seconds of listening to you, your audience should have a pretty good idea of what your topic is. The best way to achieve this objective is to include a statement of your central idea in your introduction.

Give the Audience a Reason to Listen

Verbal

Not only do you have to get your audience's attention and introduce your topic—you have to motivate your listeners to continue to listen. Show the audience how your topic affects them and those they care about. Catherine uses rhetorical questions to drive home to her audience the relevance and importance of her speech on a healthy diet:

> What if I told you that, by decreasing one food item in your and your loved ones' diet, you could significantly lessen the chance for metabolic syndrome (or obesity); heart disease; coronary artery disease; osteoporosis due to calcium depletion; high blood pressure; colon, kidney, breast, prostate, and liver cancer? Would you change the menu at your and your loved ones' next meal?[13]

By the end of your introduction, your audience should be thinking, "This concerns me!"

Establish Your Credibility

A credible speaker is one whom the audience judges to be believable, competent, and trustworthy. Be aware of the skills, talents, and experiences you have had that are related to your topic. You can increase your credibility by telling your audience about your expertise. For example, in your introduction to a persuasive presentation on studying abroad, you might say:

> I know first-hand how studying abroad can broaden your worldview, increase your understanding of another culture, and enrich your academic studies. Last fall, I studied at the Sorbonne in Paris.

Preview Your Main Ideas

As we discussed above, you should provide an initial preview of your main ideas at or near the end of your introduction, to allow your listeners to anticipate the main ideas of your presentation.

Conclusions

While your introduction creates a critically important first impression, **your conclusion leaves an equally important final impression.** Long after you finish speaking, your audience will hear the echo of effective final words. An effective conclusion serves four functions: to summarize the presentation, to reemphasize the main idea in a memorable way, to motivate the audience to respond, and to provide closure. Let's consider each of these functions.

Summarize the Presentation

The conclusion offers a speaker a last chance to repeat his or her main ideas. Most speakers summarize their main ideas between the body of the presentation and its conclusion or in the first part of the conclusion.

Reemphasize the Central Idea in a Memorable Way

The conclusions of many famous speeches contain many of the lines we remember best:

> . . . that government of the people, by the people, for the people, shall not perish from the earth. *(Abraham Lincoln)*[14]

> Old soldiers never die; they just fade away. *(General Douglas MacArthur)*[15]

> Free at last! Free at last! Thank God almighty, we are free at last! *(Martin Luther King Jr.)*[16]

Use your final verbal message effectively. Word your thoughts so that your audience cannot help but remember them.

Verbal

Motivate the Audience to Respond

Think back to your specific purpose. What do you want your audience to be able to do by the end of your presentation? If your purpose is to inform, you may want your audience to think about your topic or to seek more information about it. If your purpose is to persuade, you may want your audience to take some sort of action—to write a letter, make a phone call, or volunteer for a cause. Your conclusion is where you can motivate your audience to respond. Travis closes his presentation on sleep deprivation with this admonition:

> Before we are all, literally, dead on our feet, let's take the easiest solution step of all. Tonight, turn off your alarm, turn down your covers, and turn in for a good night's sleep.[17]

Provide Closure

You may have experienced listening to a presentation and not being certain when it was over. That speaker did not achieve the last purpose of an effective conclusion: providing **closure, or a sense that the presentation is finished.**

One good way to provide closure is to refer to your introduction by finishing a story, answering a rhetorical question, or reminding your audience of your introduction. Kyle had opened his presentation by quoting President Theodore Roosevelt, who declared in 1907 that depletion of America's natural resources would diminish

Recap

The Purposes of Introductions and Conclusions

Verbal
Nonverbal

Your introduction should . . .	■ Get your audience's attention.
	■ Introduce your topic.
	■ Give your audience a reason to listen.
	■ Establish your credibility.
	■ Preview your main ideas.
Your conclusion should . . .	■ Summarize your presentation.
	■ Reemphasize your central idea in a memorable way.
	■ Motivate your audience to respond.
	■ Provide closure.

the future prosperity of the country. Kyle provides closure to his presentation by referring again to Roosevelt's warning:

> If President Theodore Roosevelt were alive today, he'd certainly be concerned at the state and the future of our national forests. Therefore, it's so important that we heed his advice and we do everything that we can to protect our national forests—for our physical well-being, our financial well-being, and for the prosperity of future generations.[18]

You can also achieve closure by using verbal and nonverbal signposts. For example, you might use such transitions as "finally" and "in conclusion" as you move into your conclusion. You might pause before you begin the conclusion, slow your speaking rate as you deliver your final sentence, or signal by falling vocal inflection that you are making your final statement. Experiment with these strategies until you are certain that your presentation "sounds finished."

OUTLINING YOUR PRESENTATION

With your introduction and conclusion planned, you are almost ready to begin rehearsing your presentation. By this point, you should have your preparation outline nearly complete. **A preparation outline is a fairly detailed outline of central idea, main ideas, and supporting material and may also include the specific purpose, introduction, and conclusion.** A second outline, which you will prepare shortly, is a delivery outline, the notes from which you will eventually deliver your presentation.

Preparation Outline

Although few presentations are written in manuscript form, most speakers develop a fairly detailed preparation outline that helps them to ensure that their main ideas are clearly related to their central idea and are logically and adequately supported. A speaker who creates a preparation outline is applying the first fundamental principle of communication: becoming increasingly aware of his or her communication. In addition to helping the speaker judge the unity and coherence of the presentation, the preparation outline also serves as an early rehearsal outline and is usually the outline handed in as part of a class requirement.

Instructors who require students to turn in a preparation outline will probably have their own specific requirements. For example, some instructors ask you to include your introduction and conclusion as part of your outline, while others ask you to outline only the body of the presentation. Some ask that you incorporate signposts into the outline or write your specific purpose at the top of the outline. Be certain that you listen to and follow your instructor's specific requirements regarding which elements to include.

Almost certainly, your instructor will require that you use standard outline format. **Standard outline format, which uses numbered and lettered headings and subheadings, lets you become more aware of the exact relationships among various main ideas, subpoints, and supporting material in your presentation.** Even if you haven't had much experience with formal outlines, the following guidelines can help you produce a correct outline.

Aware

Use Standard Numbering

Outlines are numbered by using Roman and Arabic numerals and uppercase and lowercase letters followed by periods, as follows:

I. First main idea
   A. First subdivision of I
   B. Second subdivision of I
      1. First subdivision of B
      2. Second subdivision of B
         a. First subdivision of 2
         b. Second subdivision of 2
II. Second main idea

You will probably not need to subdivide beyond the level of lowercase letters in most presentation outlines.

Use at Least Two Subdivisions, If Any, for Each Point

You cannot divide anything into fewer than two parts. On an outline, every I should have a II, every A should have a B, and so on. If you have only one subdivision, fold it into the level above it.

Line Up Your Outline Correctly

Main ideas, indicated by Roman numerals, are written closest to the left margin. The *periods* following these Roman numerals line up, so that the first letters of the first words also line up:

I. First main idea
II. Second main idea
III. Third main idea

Letters or numbers of subdivisions begin directly underneath the first letter of the first *word* of the point above:

I. First main idea
   A. First subdivision of I
   B. Second subdivision of I

If a main idea or subdivision takes up more than one line, the second line begins under the first letter of the first word of the preceding line:

I. First main idea
   A. A rather lengthy subdivision that runs more than one line
   B. Second subdivision

Within Each Level, Make the Headings Grammatically Parallel

Regardless of whether you write your preparation outline in complete sentences or in phrases, be consistent within each level. In other words, if I is a complete sentence, II should also be a complete sentence. If A is an infinitive phrase (one that begins with to plus a verb, such as "to guarantee greater security"), B should also be an infinitive phrase.

Following is a sample preparation outline for the presentation we've been watching Ben Johnson prepare in the Developing Your Presentation Step by Step feature.[19] Your instructor may give additional or alternative requirements for what your preparation outline should include or how it should be formatted.

Sample Preparation Outline

Writing the purpose statement at the top of the outline helps the speaker keep it in mind. But always follow your instructor's specific requirements for how to format your preparation outline.

Ben catches his reader's attention by opening his presentation with an illustration. Other strategies for effectively getting audience attention were discussed earlier in the chapter.

Ben writes out and labels his central idea and preview. Again, follow your instructor's requirements.

The first main idea of the presentation is indicated by the Roman numeral I. This main idea has two subpoints, indicated by A and B.

Subpoints 1, 2, 3, and 4 provide supporting material for A.

Ben's oral citation for this Web site is sufficient; he should also have the Web address available for his instructor or any other audience member who might want it.

Purpose

At the end of my presentation, the audience will take steps to end the abuse of the cold medication Coricidin.

Introduction

Three days before Christmas, Jill and Jim Darling went to check on their daughter to make sure she was getting ready for school. When they opened the door to the bathroom, they found their daughter Jennifer unconscious on the floor. Jill frantically called 911, and then they waited helplessly for the paramedics. Only moments after the ambulance arrived, the high school senior was pronounced dead. The cause of Jennifer's death remained a mystery until investigators discovered a small plastic bag in her room containing 32 red pills. According to the January 27, 2003, issue of *University Wire,* the pills were an over-the-counter cold medication known as Coricidin. When used by adults, these pills are an effective method for decreasing the symptoms of the common cold, but in the hands of a child they become a dangerous hallucinogenic drug. These seemingly harmless pills are part of a new national epidemic of substance abuse by teenagers and children as young as 6.

Central Idea

We should take steps to end the abuse of the cold medication Coricidin.

Preview

For this reason we must first educate ourselves about the danger of Coricidin and the threat it poses for teens, and next uncover the cause for this growing trend, so that finally we may pose some viable solutions to safeguard our children's health.

Body Outline

I. Coricidin abuse is rapidly becoming a significant problem.

    A. Coricidin contains the cough suppressant Dextromethorphan, or DXM.

        1. DXM is found in over 100 cold medications, including those with "DM" or "Tuss" in their names.

        2. Coricidin is the drug of choice because it's easier than swallowing several bottles of Robitussin.

        3. As the National Institute on Drug Abuse indicates on *TheAntiDrug.com* Web site, last updated April 11, 2004, the drug closely resembles PCP, and when taken in excess, causes hallucinations.

        4. According to *USA Today* of December 29, 2003, when abused, Coricidin can cause depressed breathing, an irregular heartbeat, seizures, coma, and even death.

    B. Coricidin abuse is widespread.

        1. The American Association of Poison Control Centers told the *Boston Globe* of January 11, 2004, that there were over 14,000 calls to poison control centers last year to report the intentional overdose of cold medication.

        2. According to the January 29, 2004, Scripps Howard News Service, there were more than 3000 cases of Coricidin abuse in 2003 alone.

        3. A report by *CNN* on December 30, 2003, explains that overdoses tend to occur in clusters. A 13-year-old girl brought 80 Coricidin tablets to her

middle school in Naples, Florida, and gave some to six of her friends. Each friend took at least five pills. The recommended dose for an adult is no more than one pill every six hours. The school was in chaos as three students lost consciousness and had to be rushed to the hospital. The girl who distributed the pills thought it would be "fun to feel messed up and act. . . drunk."

Signpost: So if the drug poses such a threat, why has nothing been done to stop it? There are two main reasons that Coricidin has become such a problem. First, the pills and information on how to use them are widely available to teenagers. Second, there is a lack of awareness from parents and teachers.

This signpost summarizes Ben's first main idea—that Coricidin abuse is significant—and previews his second main idea— why the problem has occurred.

II. Coricidin abuse has become a problem for two reasons.

    A. Coricidin is widely available to teenagers.

        1. *CBS News* reports on December 29, 2003, that some stores have begun keeping Coricidin behind the counter, but for the most part the pills are easily obtainable by teens.

        2. A box of 16 pills only costs about $5, and because the drug is safe when taken correctly, the Food and Drug Administration has made no move to regulate it. Jeff Hegelson, a 19-year-old abuser, told ABC's *20/20* on January 9, 2004, "As far as drugs go, you don't need to know a dealer. If you can find a Walgreen's or a grocery store, you're set."

        3. The Internet has contributed to the problem.

            a. The *Milwaukee Journal Sentinel* of October 24, 2003, explains that full-strength DXM can be purchased online. Two Wisconsin teens were arrested after purchasing a 50-gram bottle of DXM over the Internet and then reselling the pills.

            b. A simple Web search returns hundreds of sites giving detailed instructions on how many pills to take to get high.

            c. There are even recipes explaining how to extract DXM from Coricidin in order to achieve a more potent drug.

        4. In an interview with the previously cited *Boston Globe,* Dr. Michael Shannon, Chief of Emergency Medicine at Children's Hospital in Boston, says, "It's rampant. Look at who's taking it. These are kids who are unable to buy alcohol, unable to buy cigarettes. . . and now you've got something that you know is in many households. It's cheap, it's legal, and it's easy to obtain and nobody questions you if you have it in your backpack."

    B. The attitudes of parents and teachers also complicate the problem.

        1. Donna Oldham suspected that her son was abusing drugs, but she was shocked when she learned that he was getting his fix legally at the local pharmacy. Donna told the *Chicago Daily Herald* of September 8, 2003, "Most parents would have no idea their kids were doing this. It's not like pot or cocaine. It's this legal drug that a lot of people probably have in their own medicine cabinets. Unless you know what to look for, you're going to miss it."

        2. The February 19, 2004, *Modesto Bee* explains that approximately 2/3 of teen drug abuse is from drugs found in the home or ones that you can get at the drugstore. Traditionally, parents and school officials watch out for illegal substances and alcohol. If a student were caught with a bottle of alcohol or marijuana, he or she would be suspended. But when a box of Coricidin is found in that student's backpack, school officials don't give it a second thought.

Having established the problem and discussed its causes, Ben turns to solutions.

Signpost: After exploring the problem and cause of this drug abuse, it's clear that Coricidin poses a threat, and something must be done to stop it.

III. Solutions at both the national and personal levels can ensure that no more harm is done.

    A. On a national level, the use of Coricidin by minors needs to be regulated more carefully.

        1. According to the *San Antonio Express News* of January 11, 2003, a bill was introduced in New Mexico making it illegal to sell products with DXM to minors and requiring stores to keep the pills behind the counter or in areas that require assistance. Other state governments need to follow suit.

        2. Retailers can also help solve the problem. The previously cited *Chicago Daily Herald* reports that last year Wal-Mart started requiring customers to be at least 18 if they wanted to buy Coricidin, and they weren't allowed to purchase more than three boxes at a time.

A final signpost makes clear that Ben will talk about what individual audience members can do about Coricidin abuse.

Signpost: However, restrictions alone are not enough to stop this problem; action must be taken at the personal level as well.

    B. We must begin to create awareness about the danger of Coricidin.

Aware that many of his listeners are not parents, Ben suggests appropriate actions for both groups.

        1. Parents should watch for boxes of the drug in their child's room or backpack and ask questions if they notice cold pills being used frequently.

        2. Those people without children can log on to Drugfreeamerica.org or *TheAntiDrug.com* to learn more about drug prevention as well as additional ways to join the fight against this abuse.

           a. Donate time or money.

           b. Inform your friends and family about the dangers of Coricidin.

Conclusion

In his conclusion, Ben returns to the illustration with which he began the presentation.

It's been a year since Jim and Jill Darling watched helplessly as their daughter died on the bathroom floor, but the drugs that took her life still pose a tremendous danger to children and teens across the country. Today we gained an understanding of the dangers of Coricidin, next uncovered the cause for this trend, and finally posed some viable solutions to safeguard our youth. Jim Darling said he "hopes his daughter's death has served as a wake-up call for law enforcement, teachers and parents." No parents should ever have to watch their child die, but as long as Coricidin remains easily available, the lives of our children will be at risk.

Delivery Outline

As you rehearse your presentation, you will find yourself needing to look at your preparation outline less and less. You have both the structure and the content of your presentation pretty well in mind. At this point, you are ready to develop a shorter delivery outline.

Your delivery outline should provide all the notes you will need to make your presentation as you have planned, without being so detailed that you will be tempted to read it rather than speak to your audience. Here are a few suggestions for developing a delivery outline:

- *Use single words or short phrases whenever possible.*
- *Include your introduction and conclusion in abbreviated form.* Even if your instructor does not require you to include your introduction and conclusion on your preparation outline, include an abbreviated version of them on your delivery

outline. You might even feel more comfortable delivering the presentation if you have your first and last sentences written out in front of you.

- *Include supporting material and signposts.*   Write out in full any statistics and direct quotations and their sources. Write your key signposts—your initial preview, for example—to ensure that you will not have to grope awkwardly as you move from one idea to another.

- *Do not include your purpose statement.*   Because you will not actually say your purpose statement during your presentation, do not put it on your delivery outline.

- *Use standard outline form.*   Standard outline form will help you find your exact place when you glance down at your speaking notes. You will know, for example, that your second main idea is indicated by II.

It might have been easier for this student to deliver an effective message if she had prepared a concise delivery outline on note cards.

Here is a delivery outline for Ben Johnson's presentation on the abuse of Coricidin.

Although you may write the first version of your delivery outline on paper, eventually you will probably want to transfer it to note cards. They don't rustle as paper does, and they are small enough to hold in one hand. Two or three note cards will probably give you enough space for your delivery outline. Type or print neatly on one side only, making sure that the letters and words are large enough to read easily. Plan your note cards according to logical blocks of material, using one note card for your introduction, one or two for the body of your presentation, and one for your conclusion. Number your note cards to prevent getting them out of order while you are speaking.

A final addition to your note cards as you rehearse your presentation will be **delivery cues such as "Louder," "Pause," or "Walk two steps left." These will remind you to communicate the nonverbal messages you have planned.** Write your delivery cues in a different color ink so that you don't confuse them with your verbal content.

SUMMARY

Once you have found supporting material, you are ready to organize your ideas and information. Depending on your topic, purpose, and audience, you can organize the main ideas of your presentation chronologically, topically, spatially, by cause and effect, or by problem and solution. You can sometimes organize supporting material according to one of these same patterns, or you can organize it according to the principles of recency, primacy, complexity, or specificity or from soft to hard evidence.

With your presentation organized, you will want to add signposts—previews, transitions, and summaries—to make your organization clearly apparent to your audience. A carefully planned introduction will get your audience's attention, introduce your topic, give the audience a reason to listen, establish your credibility, and preview your main ideas. In an equally carefully planned conclusion, you can summarize your presentation, reemphasize the central idea in a memorable way, motivate your audience to respond, and provide closure.

A final step before beginning to rehearse your presentation is to prepare a detailed preparation outline and a delivery outline that eventually becomes your speaking notes.

DISCUSSION AND REVIEW

1. List and explain five strategies for organizing the main ideas in a presentation.

2. List and explain five strategies for organizing supporting material in a presentation.

3. List and define three types of verbal signposts.

4. How can you make a nonverbal transition?

5. List and explain five functions of a presentation introduction.

6. How can you get your audience's attention in your introduction?

7. List and explain four functions of a presentation conclusion.

8. What is included on most preparation outlines? What are such outlines used for?

9. What is included on most delivery outlines? What are such outlines used for?

PUTTING PRINCIPLES INTO PRACTICE

1. Take notes as you listen to a presentation, either live or on audiotape or videotape. Then organize your notes into an outline that you think reflects both the speaker's organization and the intended relationship among ideas and supporting material.

2. Read one of the speeches in Appendix E. Answer the following questions:

   a. How are the main ideas organized?

   b. Look closely at the supporting materials. If two or more are used to support any one main idea, what strategy do you think the speaker used to organize them?

   c. Is there an initial preview statement? If so, what is it?

   d. Is there a final summary? If so, what is it?

   e. Find at least one example of each of the following:

   A transition word or phrase

   An internal preview

   An internal summary

3. Draft an introduction for a presentation on one of the following topics:

   Strategies for surviving a tornado

   Private-school vouchers

   Mars up close

   Celebrities and the press

   In addition to introducing the topic and previewing your main ideas, be sure to plan strategies for getting your audience's attention and giving them a reason to listen. Also devise a way to establish your own credibility as a speaker on that topic.

4. Miguel, who plays guitar in a mariachi band, plans to give an informative presentation on mariachi music. He wants to talk a little about the history of mariachi bands, the kind of music they play, and their role in Mexican and Mexican-American culture. In addition, he plans to introduce the instruments most commonly used in mariachi music: trumpet, guitar, and such percussion instruments as tambourines and maracas.

   Miguel asks you to help him develop a good introduction for the presentation. How do you think he might best introduce his presentation to achieve all five functions of a presentation introduction?

14
Delivering Your Presentation

Jacob Lawrence, The Life of Harriet Tubman, #21: Every antislavery convention held within 500 miles of Harriet Tubman found her at the meeting. She spoke in words that brought tears to the eyes and sorrow to the hearts of all who heard her speak of the suffering of her people. 1940. Casein tempera on hardboard, 17 7/8 × 120. Hampton University Museum. Photo credit: The Jacob and Gwendolyn Lawrence Foundation/Art Resource, NY. © 2007 The Jacob and Gwendolyn Lawrence Foundation, Seattle/Artists Rights Society (ARS), New York.

> *"O the orator's joys! To inflate the chest, to roll the thunder of the voice out from the ribs and throat, to make the people rage, weep, hate, desire . . ."*
>
> *Walt Whitman*

Which is more important: the content of a presentation or the way it is delivered? Speakers and speech teachers have argued about the answer to this question for thousands of years. In the fourth century BC, the Greek rhetorician Aristotle declared delivery "superfluous." On the other hand, when his contemporary and fellow Athenian Demosthenes was asked to name the three most important elements for a speaker to master, he is reported to have replied, "Delivery, delivery, delivery."

The debate continues. Which is more important: content or delivery? It is clear that the way you deliver a speech influences the way listeners respond to you and to your message. In a now-classic study, Alan H. Monroe found that audience members equate effective presentational speaking with such nonverbal factors as direct eye contact, alertness, enthusiasm, a pleasant voice, and animated gestures.[1] Another researcher concluded that delivery was almost twice as important as content when students gave self-introduction presentations, and three times as important when students gave persuasive presentations.[2] Other scholars have found that delivery provides important information about a speaker's feelings and emotions and will in turn affect listeners' emotional responses to the speaker.[3] Most speech teachers today believe that both content and delivery contribute to the effectiveness of a presentation. As a modern speechwriter and communication coach suggests,

Nonverbal

> In the real world—the world where you and I do business—content and delivery are always related. And woe be to the communicator who forgets this.[4]

In this chapter, we will discuss how you can apply the five communication principles for a lifetime to delivery. We will talk about both verbal and nonverbal delivery skills. We will consider how important it is to be aware of the words you use and of such nonverbal cues as gestures, eye contact, and facial expression. We will discuss how to determine what presentation aids might be effective for your audience, and we'll offer guidelines for both the preparation and the use of various types of presentation aids.

Aware
Verbal
Nonverbal
Listen and Respond
Adapt

Chapter Objectives

After studying this chapter, you should be able to

- List and describe the four methods of delivery and provide suggestions for effectively using each one.

- List and explain five criteria for using words well.

- List and define three types of figurative language that can be used to make a presentation memorable.

- Explain ways to create verbal drama and cadence in a presentation.

- Identify and illustrate characteristics of effective delivery.

- List 11 types of visual aids from which a speaker might select, and provide suggestions for using each type effectively.

- Offer four general guidelines for preparing and using effective presentation aids.

METHODS OF DELIVERY

Audiences today generally expect speakers to use clear, concise, everyday language and conversational delivery style, as opposed to the flowery language and dramatic, choreographed gestures used by speakers a century ago. However, different audiences expect and prefer variations of this delivery style. For example, if you are using a microphone to speak to an audience of 1000 people, your listeners may expect a relatively formal delivery style. On the other hand, your communication class would probably find it odd if you delivered a formal oration to your 25 classmates.

People from different cultures also have different expectations of speakers' delivery. Listeners from Japan and China, for example, prefer subdued gestures to a more flamboyant delivery style. British listeners expect a speaker to stay behind a lectern and use relatively few gestures.

Speakers should consider and adapt to their audience's expectations, their topic, and the speaking situation as they select from four basic methods of delivery: manuscript speaking, memorized speaking, impromptu speaking, and extemporaneous speaking. Each is more appropriate to some speaking contexts and audiences than to others, and each requires a speaker to use a slightly different delivery style. Let's consider each of these four delivery methods in more detail.

Adapt

Manuscript Speaking

Perhaps you remember the first presentation you ever had to give—maybe as long ago as elementary school. Chances are that you wrote your speech out and read it to your audience.

Unfortunately, **manuscript speaking, or reading a presentation from written text,** is rarely done well enough to be interesting. Most speakers who rely on a manuscript read it in either a monotone or a pattern of vocal inflection that makes the presentation sound as if it were being read. They are so afraid of losing their place that they keep their eyes glued to the manuscript and seldom look at the audience. These challenges are significant enough that most speakers should avoid reading from a manuscript most of the time.

Verbal

However, there are some exceptions. Sometimes effective verbal messages depend on careful and exact phrasing. For example, because an awkward statement made by the U.S. Secretary of State could cause an international crisis, he or she usually has remarks on critical issues carefully scripted. A company manager or administrator presenting a new, potentially controversial company policy to employees or customers might also deliver that announcement from a manuscript.

If you ever have to speak on a sensitive, critical, or controversial issue, you too might need to deliver a manuscript presentation. If so, consider the following suggestions:[5]

Nonverbal

- Type your manuscript in short, easy-to-scan phrases on the upper two-thirds of the paper so that you do not have to look too far down into your notes.
- Use appropriate nonverbal messages. Try to take in an entire sentence at a time so that you can maintain eye contact throughout each sentence.
- Do not read the manuscript too quickly. Use a slash mark (/) or some other symbol to remind you to pause in strategic places.
- Vary the rhythm, inflection, and pace of your delivery so that the presentation does not sound like it is being read.
- Use gestures and movement to add further nonverbal interest and emphasis to your message.

Memorized Speaking

After that first speech you read in elementary school, you probably became a more savvy speaker, and the next time you had to give a speech, you decided to write it out and memorize it. You thought that no one would be able to tell you had written it out first. What you didn't know then, but probably do now, is that **delivering a presentation word for word from memory without using notes, called memorized speaking,** sounds stiff and recited. In addition, you run the risk of forgetting parts of your speech and having to search awkwardly for words in front of your audience. And you forfeit the ability to adapt to your audience while you are speaking.

However, speaking from memory is occasionally justifiable. Memorized speaking might be appropriate in the same instances as manuscript speaking, when exact wording is critical to the success of the message, and when the speaker has time to commit the speech to memory. If you must deliver a short presentation within narrowly proscribed time limits, memorizing and rehearsing it will allow you to time it more accurately. Three guidelines can help you use nonverbal messages effectively when you deliver a presentation from memory:

- Do not deliver your memorized speech too rapidly.

- Avoid patterns of vocal inflection that make the speech sound recited. Focus on what you are saying, and let your voice rise and fall to emphasize key words and phrases and to reflect the structures of your sentences. Consider recording your presentation and listening to it to ensure that your vocal delivery sounds like a conversation rather than a recitation.

Nonverbal

- Use gestures and movement to add interest and emphasis to your message.

Impromptu Speaking

In September 1993, then-President Bill Clinton stood before a joint session of Congress to deliver an important speech about health-care reform. What happened during the first 9 minutes of that presentation has become what political advisor and commentator Paul Begala calls "part of the Clinton legend":

> The teleprompter screens are whizzing forward and backwards with last year's speech, trying to find it, and finally, they killed it all together and reloaded it. Nine minutes the guy went without a note, and no one could tell.[6]

Although you can usually plan your presentations, there are times—as illustrated by Clinton's experience—when the best plans go awry. In other, more likely instances, you may be asked to answer a question or respond to an argument without advance warning or time to prepare a presentation. At such times, you will have to call on your skills in **impromptu speaking, or speaking "off the cuff" with no advance preparation.** Five guidelines can help you avoid fumbling for words or rambling:

Adapt

- Consider your audience. A quick mental check of who your audience members are and what their interests, expectations, and knowledge are can help ensure that your impromptu remarks are audience-centered.

- Be brief. As one leadership consultant points out,

You're not the star—not this time, anyway. If you were the luminary, they would not have asked you to speak without warning. You're merely expected to hit a theme, say a few nice words, and then depart.[7]

One to three minutes is probably a realistic time frame for most impromptu presentations.

- Organize. Think quickly about an introduction, body, and conclusion. If you want to make more than one point, use a simple organizational strategy such as chronological order—past, present, and future. Or construct an alphabetical list, in which your main ideas begin with the letters A, B, and C.[8]

Aware
Nonverbal

- Draw on your personal experience and knowledge. Audiences almost always respond favorably to personal illustrations, so use any appropriate and relevant ones.

- Use gestures and movement that arise naturally from what you are saying.
- Be aware of the potential impact of your communication. If your subject is at all sensitive or your information is classified, be noncommittal in what you say.

Extemporaneous Speaking

We have saved for last the method of speaking that is the most appropriate choice for most circumstances: **extemporaneous speaking. This is the speaking style taught today in most public speaking classes and preferred by most audiences. When you speak extemporaneously, you develop your presentation according to the various stages of the audience-centered public speaking model, stopping short of writing it out.** Instead, you speak from an outline and rehearse the presentation until you can deliver it fluently. Your audience will know that you have prepared, but will also have the sense that the presentation is being created as they listen to it—and to some extent, it is. In short, the extemporaneous presentation is a well-developed and well-organized message delivered in an interesting and vivid manner. It reflects your understanding of how to use both verbal and nonverbal messages effectively and your ability to adapt these messages to your audience.

**Aware
Verbal
Nonverbal
Adapt**

Although the presentational speaking chapters in this book offer numerous guidelines for extemporaneous speaking, consider these four when you reach the rehearsal and delivery stages:

- Use a full-content preparation outline when you begin to rehearse your extemporaneous presentation. Be aware of your growing confidence in delivering it, and continue to decrease your reliance on your notes.
- Prepare an abbreviated delivery outline and speaking notes. Continue to rehearse, using this new outline.
- Even as you become increasingly familiar with your message, do not try to memorize it word for word. Continue to vary the ways in which you express your ideas and information.
- As you deliver your presentation, adapt it to your audience. Use gestures and movement that arise naturally from what you are saying.

EFFECTIVE VERBAL DELIVERY

While you will not write out most presentations word for word, you will want to think about and rehearse words, phrases, and sentences that accurately and effectively communicate your ideas. At the same time, you will want to give your message a distinctive and memorable style. Let's examine some guidelines for effectively using and understanding words and word structures in a presentation.

Using Words Well

The most effective words are specific and concrete, unbiased, vivid, simple, and correct.

Specific, Concrete Words

A specific word refers to an individual member of a general class—for example, *ammonite* as opposed to the more general term *fossil*, or *sodium* as opposed to *chemical*. Specific words are often concrete words, appealing to one of the five senses and clearly communicating an image. For example, which of the following pairs of words creates a more specific mental picture: *dog* or *poodle*, *utensil* or *spatula*, *toy* or *Lego*? In each case, the second word is more specific and concrete than the first and better communicates the image the speaker intends. For maximum clarity in your communication, use more specific, concrete words than general, abstract ones in your presentations.

Verbal

Unbiased Words

Unbiased words are those that do not offend, either intentionally or unintentionally, any sexual, racial, cultural, or religious group—or any audience member who may belong to one of these groups. Although a speaker can fairly easily avoid overtly offensive language, it is more difficult to avoid language that more subtly stereotypes or discriminates. The once-acceptable usage of a masculine noun (*man, mankind*) to refer generically to all people may now be offensive to many audience members. Other words that reflect gender bias include *chairman, waiter,* and *congressman.* Even if you yourself do not consider these terms offensive, a member of your audience might. When possible, you should adapt to your audience by choosing instead such unbiased gender-neutral alternatives as *chairperson* or *chair, server,* and *member of Congress.*

Vivid Words

Vivid words add color and interest to your language. Like concrete words, they help you communicate mental images more accurately and interestingly. Most speakers who try to make their language more vivid think first of adding adjectives to nouns—for example, *distressed oak table* instead of *table*, or *scruffy tabby cat* instead of *cat*. And certainly the first phrase of each example is more vivid. However, speakers less frequently consider the potential power of substituting vivid verbs for "blah" verbs—for example, *sprout* instead of *grow,* or *devour* instead of *eat.* When searching for a vivid word, you might want to consult a thesaurus, or collection of synonyms. But do not feel that the most obscure or unusual synonym you find will necessarily be the most vivid. Sometimes a simple word can evoke a vivid image for your audience.

Simple Words

Simple words are generally an asset to a speaker. They will be immediately understandable to an audience. In his essay "Politics and the English Language," George Orwell includes this prescription for simplicity:

> Never use a long word where a short one will do. If it is possible to cut a word out, always cut it out. Never use a foreign phrase, a scientific word, or a jargon word if you can think of an everyday English equivalent.9

Selected thoughtfully, simple words can communicate with both accuracy and power.

Correct Words

Finally, and perhaps most obviously, you should use correct words when you speak. A correct word means what the speaker intends and is grammatically correct in the phrase or sentence in which it appears. Grammatical and usage errors communicate

Aware

a lack of preparation and can lower your credibility with your audience. Be aware of any errors you make habitually. If you are uncertain of how to use a word, look it up in a dictionary or ask someone who knows. If you are stumped by whether to say "Neither the people nor the president *knows* how to solve the problem" or "Neither the people nor the president *know* how to solve the problem," seek assistance from a good English handbook. (By the way, the first sentence is correct!)

Verbal

Crafting Memorable Word Structures

We have discussed the importance of using words that are concrete, unbiased, vivid, simple, and correct. Now we will turn our attention to word structures—phrases and sentences that create the figurative language, drama, and cadences needed to make a presentation memorable.

Figurative Language

One way to make your presentation memorable is to use **figurative language, or figures of speech,** including **metaphors (implied comparisons), similes (overt comparisons using *like* or *as*), and personification (the attribution of human qualities to nonhuman things or ideas). Such language is memorable because it is used in a way that is a little different from ordinary, expected usage.** Nineteenth-century Missouri Senator George Graham Vest used all three types of figurative language to good advantage in his short but memorable "Tribute to the Dog" (delivered in Warrensburg, Missouri, in 1870, and nominated by columnist William Safire as one of the greatest speeches of the Second Millennium).[10] Vest makes the abstract concept of malice more concrete with the metaphor "the stone of malice." He uses a simile to compare the dog's master to a prince: "He guards the sleep of his pauper master as if he were a prince." And he personifies death, which "takes [the dog's] master in its embrace." Vest's speech is memorable at least in part because of the figurative language he employs.

Drama

Another way in which you can make your word structures more memorable is to use language to create **drama** in your presentation by **phrasing something in an unexpected way.** Three specific devices that can help you achieve verbal drama are omission, inversion, and suspension.

When you strip a phrase or sentence of nonessential words that the audience expects or with which they are so familiar that they will mentally fill them in, you are using omission. A captain of a World War II Navy destroyer used omission to inform headquarters of his successful efforts at finding and sinking an enemy submarine. He cabled back to headquarters:

Sighted sub—sank same.

Inversion—reversing the normal order of words in a phrase or sentence—can also create drama in a presentation. John F. Kennedy inverted the usual subject–verb–object sentence pattern to object–subject–verb to make this brief declaration memorable:

This much we pledge. . . . [11]

A third way to create drama through sentence structures is to employ verbal **suspension, saving a key word or phrase for the end of a sentence, rather than placing it at the beginning.** Speaking to the Democratic National Convention in July 2004, former U.S. President Jimmy Carter used suspension to dramatize the importance of America's global role:

At stake is nothing less than our nation's soul.[12]

Advertisers use this technique frequently. Instead of saying "Coke goes better with everything," one copywriter some years ago decided to make the slogan more memorable by suspending the product name until the end of the sentence. He wrote,

Things go better with Coke.

Cadence

A final way to create memorable word structures is to create **cadence, or language rhythm.** A speaker does this not by speaking in a singsong pattern, but by using such stylistic devices as parallelism, antithesis, repetition, and alliteration.

Parallelism occurs when two or more clauses or sentences have the same grammatical pattern. After the bitterly contested U.S. presidential election of 2000, George W. Bush used simple parallel structures to emphasize the importance of finding common ground and building consensus:

Our future demands it, and our history proves it.[13]

Antithesis is similar to parallelism, except that the two structures contrast in meaning. Nobel Laureate Elie Wiesel used antithesis in his 1999 Millennium Lecture on "The Perils of Indifference":

Indifference . . . is not only a sin, it is a punishment.[14]

Repetition of a key word or phrase can add emphasis to an important idea and memorability to your message. Note the repetition of the key phrase "It is a violation of human rights" in this excerpt from a speech by Hillary Rodham Clinton:

It is a violation of human rights when babies are denied food, or drowned, or suffocated, or their spines broken, simply because they are born girls.

It is a violation of human rights when women and girls are sold into the slavery of prostitution.

It is a violation of human rights when women are doused with gasoline, set on fire, and burned to death because their marriage dowries are deemed too small.[15]

Maya Angelou mesmerizes her audiences with her extraordinary skill in the effective use of language.

A final strategy for creating cadence is to use **alliteration, the repetition of an initial consonant sound several times in a phrase, clause, or sentence.** Kicking off the "space race" in 1962, John F. Kennedy coined this alliterative phrase:

hour of change and challenge[16]

The repetition of the *ch* sound added cadence—and memorability—to the passage.

EFFECTIVE NONVERBAL DELIVERY

At this point, you know how important it is to deliver your presentation effectively and what delivery style most audiences today prefer. You are familiar with the four methods of delivery and know how to maximize the use of each one. And you have some ideas about how to use effective and memorable language. But you may still be wondering, "What do I do with my hands?" "Is it all right to move around while I speak?" "How can I make my voice sound interesting?" To help answer these and other similar questions, and to help you use nonverbal messages more effectively, we will examine five major categories of nonverbal delivery: eye contact, physical delivery, facial expression, vocal delivery, and personal appearance.

Eye Contact

Of all the nonverbal delivery variables discussed in this chapter, the most important one in a presentational speaking situation for North Americans is **eye contact. Looking at your audience during your presentation** lets them know that you are interested in them and ready to talk to them. It also permits you to determine whether they are responding to you. And most listeners will think that you are more capable and trustworthy if you look them in the eye. Several studies document a relationship between eye contact and speaker credibility, as well as between eye contact and listener learning.[17]

How much eye contact do you need to sustain? One study found that speakers with less than 50% eye contact are considered unfriendly, uninformed, inexperienced, and even dishonest by their listeners.[18] Is there such a thing as too much eye contact? Probably not, for North American audiences. Be aware, though, that not all people from all cultures prefer as much eye contact as North Americans do. Asians, for example, generally prefer less.

Adapt

By walking up close to her audience, this speaker establishes a connection with her listeners.

The following suggestions can help you use eye contact effectively when you speak in public:

- Establish eye contact with your audience before you say anything. Eye contact sends the message, "I am interested in you. I have something I want to say to you. Tune me in."
- Maintain eye contact with your audience as you deliver your opening sentence without looking at your notes.
- Try to establish eye contact with people throughout your audience, not just with the front row or only one or two people. Briefly look into the eyes of an individual, then transfer your eye contact to someone else. Do not look over your listeners' heads! They will notice if you do so and may even turn around to try to find out what you are looking at.

Physical Delivery

Gestures, movement, and posture are the three key elements of physical delivery. A good speaker knows how to use effective gestures, make meaningful movements, and maintain appropriate posture while speaking to an audience.

Gestures

The hand and arm movements you use while speaking are called gestures. Nearly all people from all cultures use some gestures when they speak. In fact, research suggests that gesturing is instinctive and that it is intrinsic to speaking and thinking.[19] Yet even if you gesture easily and appropriately in the course of everyday conversation, you may feel awkward about what to do with your hands when you are in front of an audience. To minimize this challenge, consider the following guidelines:

- Focus on the message you want to communicate. As in ordinary conversation, when you speak in public, your hands should help to emphasize or reinforce your verbal message. Your gestures should coincide with what you are saying.
- Again, as in conversation, let your gestures flow with your message. They should appear natural, not tense or rigid.
- Be definite. If you want to gesture, go ahead and gesture. Avoid minor hand movements that will be masked by the lectern or that may appear to your audience as accidental brief jerks.
- Vary your gestures. Try not to use the same hand or one all-purpose gesture all the time. Think of the different gestures you can use, depending on whether you want to enumerate, point, describe, or emphasize ideas.
- Don't overdo your gestures. You want your audience to focus not on your gestures, but on your message.
- Make your gestures appropriate to your audience and situation. When you are speaking to a large audience in a relatively formal setting, use bolder, more sweeping, and more dramatic gestures than when you are speaking to a small audience in an informal setting. Consider, too, the culture-based expectations of your audience. Americans in general tend to use more gestures than do speakers from other cultures. If you are speaking to a culturally diverse audience, you might want to tone down your gestures.

Nonverbal

"Hang him, you idiots! Hang him! ... 'String him up' is a figure of speech!"

Nonverbal

Adapt

Nonverbal

Adapt

Nonverbal

Adapt

Movement

Another element of physical delivery is **movement, or a change of location during a presentation.** You may have wondered, "Should I walk around during my presentation, or should I stay in one place?" "Should I stay behind the lectern, or could I stand beside or in front of it?" "Can I move around among the audience?" The following criteria may help you to determine the answers to these questions:

- Like gestures, any movement should be purposeful. It should be consistent with the verbal content of your message; otherwise it will appear to be aimless wandering. You might signal the beginning of a new idea or major point in your speech with movement. Or you might move to signal a transition from a serious idea to a more humorous one. The bottom line is that your use of movement should make sense to your listeners. No movement at all is better than random, distracting movement.

- If such physical barriers as a lectern, a row of chairs, or an overhead projector make you feel cut off from your audience, move closer to them. Studies suggest that physical proximity enhances learning.[20]

- Adapt to the cultural expectations of your audience. British listeners, for example, have commented to your authors that American lecturers tend to stand too close to an audience when speaking. If you think that movement will make your audience uncomfortable, stay in one carefully chosen spot to deliver your presentation.

Posture

Posture (your stance) is the third element of physical delivery you should consider when delivering a presentation. One study suggests that your posture may reflect on your credibility as a speaker.[21] Another study suggests that "fear contagion," the spread of fear throughout a crowd, is largely a response to posture cues.[22] Certainly, slouching lazily across a lectern does not communicate enthusiasm for or interest in your audience or your topic. On the other hand, you should adapt your posture to your topic, your audience, and the formality or informality of the speaking occasion. For example, it may be perfectly appropriate, as well as comfortable and natural, to sit on the edge of a desk during a very informal presentation. In spite of the fact that few speech teachers or texts attempt to advocate specific speaking postures, speakers should observe some basic commonsense guidelines about their posture:

- Avoid slouching, shifting from one foot to the other, or drooping your head.

- Unless you are disabled, do not sit while delivering a presentation. The exception might be perching on the edge of a desk or stool (which would still elevate you slightly above your audience) during a very informal presentation.

Like your gestures and movement, your posture should not call attention to itself. It should reflect your interest in and attention to your audience and your presentation.

Facial Expression

Your facial expression plays a key role in expressing your thoughts, emotions, and attitudes.[23] Your audience sees your face before they hear what you are going to say, giving you the opportunity to set the tone for your message even before you begin speaking.

Social psychologist Paul Ekman has found that facial expressions of primary emotions are virtually universal, so even a culturally diverse audience will be able to read your facial expressions clearly.[24]

Throughout your presentation, your facial expression, like your body language and eye contact, should be appropriate to your message. Present somber news

DIVERSITY AND COMMUNICATION
The Academic Quarter

When speaking at a Polish university a few years ago, one of your authors expected to begin promptly at 11:00 am, as announced in the program and on posters. By 11:10 it was clear that the speech would not begin on time, and your author began to despair of having any audience at all.

In Poland, it turns out, both students and professors expect to adhere to the "academic quarter." This means that most lectures begin at least 15 minutes, or a quarter of an hour, after the announced starting time.

If your author had asked a Polish professor about the audience's expectations, he would have known about this custom in advance. One way to avoid such misunderstandings is to talk with people you know who are familiar with the cultural expectations. Try to observe other speakers presenting to similar audiences. And ask specific questions, including the following:

1. Where does the audience expect me to stand while speaking?
2. Do listeners expect direct eye contact?
3. When will the audience expect me to start and stop my talk?
4. Will listeners find movement and gestures distracting or welcome?
5. Do listeners expect presentation aids?

Keep cultural differences in mind as you rehearse and deliver presentations to diverse audiences.

wearing a serious expression. Relate a humorous story with a smile. To communicate interest in your listeners, keep your expression alert and friendly. Consultants criticized both George W. Bush and John Kerry for their inappropriate facial expressions during the 2004 U.S. presidential debates, noting specifically that Bush needed to control his grimaces and smirks and Kerry needed to develop a more natural, authentic smile.[25]

To help ensure that you are maximizing your use of this important nonverbal delivery cue, rehearse your presentation in front of a mirror; or better yet, videotape yourself rehearsing your presentation. Consider as objectively as possible whether your face is reflecting the emotional tone of your ideas.

Vocal Delivery

We have already discussed the importance of selecting words and word phrases that will most effectively communicate your ideas, information, and images. We referred to this element of delivery as verbal delivery. **Vocal delivery,** on the other hand, **involves nonverbal vocal cues—not the words you say, but the way you say them.** Effective vocal delivery requires that you speak so that your audience can understand you and will remain interested in what you are saying. Nonverbal vocal elements include volume, pitch, rate, and articulation.

Nonverbal

Volume

Volume is the softness or loudness of your voice. It is the most fundamental determinant of audience understanding. If you do not speak loudly enough, even the most brilliant presentation will be ineffective, because the audience simply will not hear you. In addition, volume can signal important ideas in your presentation; you can deliver a key idea either more loudly or more softly than the level at which you have been speaking. Consider these guidelines to help you appropriately adapt the volume of your voice to your audience's needs:

Adapt

- Speak loudly enough that the members of your audience farthest from you can hear you without straining. This will ensure that everyone else in the room can hear you, too.

- Vary the volume of your voice in a purposeful way. Indicate important ideas by turning your volume up or down.
- Be aware of whether you need a microphone to amplify your volume. If you do and one is available, use it.

There are three kinds of microphones, only one of which demands much technique. The *lavaliere microphone* is the clip-on type often used by news reporters and interviewees. Worn on the front of a shirt or a jacket lapel, it requires no particular care other than not thumping it or accidentally knocking it off.

The *boom microphone* is used by makers of movies and TV shows. It hangs over the heads of the speakers and is remote controlled, so the speakers need not be particularly concerned with it.

The third kind of microphone, and the most common, is the *stationary microphone*. This is the type that is most often attached to a lectern, sitting on a desk, or standing on the floor. Generally, the stationary microphones used today are multidirectional. You do not have to remain frozen behind a stationary mike while speaking. However, you will have to keep your mouth about the same distance from the mike at all times to avoid distracting fluctuations in the volume of sound. You can turn your head from side to side and use gestures, but you will have to limit other movements.

Under ideal circumstances, you will be able to practice before you speak with the type of microphone you will use. If you have the chance, figure out where to stand for the best sound quality and how sensitive the mike is to extraneous noise. Practice will accustom you to any voice distortion or echo that might occur so that these sound qualities do not surprise you during your presentation.[26]

Pitch

While volume is the loudness or softness of your voice, **pitch refers to how high or low your voice is.** To some extent, pitch is determined by physiology. The faster the folds in your vocal cords vibrate, the higher the habitual pitch of your voice. In general, female vocal folds vibrate much faster than do those of males. However, you can raise or lower your habitual pitch within a certain range. **Variation in pitch, called inflection,** is a key factor in communicating the meaning of your words. You know that a startled "Oh!" in response to something someone has told you communicates something quite different than a lower-pitched, questioning "Oh?" Your vocal inflection indicates your emotional response to what you have heard. Vocal inflection also

Developing Your Presentation STEP BY STEP
Rehearse Your Presentation

Ben begins to rehearse his presentation. From the beginning, he stands and speaks aloud, practicing gestures and movement that seem appropriate to his message.

At first, Ben uses his preparation outline (pp. 62–65). These early rehearsals go pretty well, but the speech runs a little long. Ben needs to edit it.

He wonders whether he can cut any of his plentiful supporting material. Examining his preparation outline again, he notes that he has two statistics to support the widespread abuse of Coricidin, one from the American Association of Poison Control Centers and another from the Scripps Howard News Service. The statistic from the American Association of Poison Control Centers seems more credible. He decides to cut the other statistic before he prepares his speaking notes and continues with his rehearsals.

helps to keep an audience interested in your presentation. If your pitch is a monotone, the audience will probably become bored quickly. To help you monitor and practice your pitch and inflection as you prepare to speak, record and play back your presentation at least once as you rehearse. Listen carefully to your pitch and inflection. If you think you are speaking in too much of a monotone, practice the presentation again with exaggerated variations in pitch.

Rate

Another vocal variable is **rate, or speed**. How fast do you talk? Most speakers average between 120 and 180 words per minute but vary their rate to add interest to their delivery and to emphasize key ideas. To determine whether your speaking rate is appropriate and purposeful, become consciously aware of your speaking rate. Record your presentation during rehearsal and listen critically to your speech speed. If it seems too fast, make a conscious effort to slow down. Use more **pauses (a few seconds of silence during a presentation)** after questions and before important ideas. If you are speaking too slowly, make a conscious effort to speed up.

Articulation

Articulation is the enunciation of speech sounds. As a speaker, you want to articulate distinctly to ensure that your audience can determine what words you are using. Sometimes we fall into the habits of mumbling or slurring—saying *wanna* instead of *want to,* or *chesterdrawers* instead of *chest of drawers.* Some nonstandard articulation may be part of a speaker's **dialect, a speech style common to an ethnic group or a geographic region.** One dialect with which most of us are probably familiar is the dialect of the southern United States, characterized by a distinctive drawl. Although most native speakers of English can understand English dialects, studies have shown that North American listeners assign more favorable ratings to, and can recall more information presented by, speakers with dialects similar to their own.[27] If your dialect is significantly different from that of your listeners or if you suspect that it could be potentially distracting, you may want to work to improve or standardize your articulation. To do so, be aware of key words or phrases that you have a tendency to drawl, slur, or chop. Once you have identified them, practice saying them distinctly and correctly.

Appearance

What would you wear to deliver a presentation to your class? To address your city council? The fact that you probably would wear something different for these two occasions suggests that you are already aware of the importance of a speaker's **appearance, both dress and grooming.** There is considerable evidence that your personal appearance affects how your audience will respond to you and your message. If you violate your audience's expectations, you will be less successful in achieving your purpose. The following guidelines might help make your wardrobe selection a bit easier the next time you are called on to speak:

- Never wear anything that would be potentially distracting—for example, a T-shirt with writing on it. You want your audience to listen to you, not read you.

- Consider wearing appropriate clothing as a presentation aid. For example, if you are a nurse or emergency technician, wear your uniform when you speak about your profession. (We will discuss presentation aids in more detail shortly.)

- Take cues from your audience. If you know that they will be dressed in business attire, dress similarly. If anything, you want to be a bit more dressed up than members of your audience.

- When in doubt about what to wear, select something conservative.

Aware

Nonverbal

Adapt

EFFECTIVE PRESENTATION AIDS

We have already discussed two elements of delivery: verbal delivery and nonverbal delivery. A third element used with increasing frequency in this era of sophisticated computer presentation software is the presentation aid. The term **presentation aid refers to anything your audience can listen to or look at to help them understand your ideas.** Charts, photographs, posters, drawings, graphs, videos, and CDs are some of the types of presentation aids frequently used by speakers.

Presentation aids can be invaluable to a speaker. They help you gain and maintain your audience's attention.[29] They communicate your organization of ideas. They illustrate sequences of events or procedures. And they help your audience understand and remember your message. In addition, chances are that, for at least one of the assignments in your communication class, you will be required to use a presentation aid. Because presentation aids are valuable supplements to your speeches and because students of communication are so often required to use them, let's discuss first the types of presentation aids that are available to you, including computer-generated ones. Then we will discuss guidelines for preparing presentation aids, and finally provide some general suggestions for using your presentation aids effectively.

Types of Presentation Aids

If you are required to use a presentation aid for an assignment or if you think a presentation aid might enhance your message, you have a number of options from which to select. You might decide to use an object or a model; a person; such two-dimensional presentation aids as drawings, photographs, maps, charts, or graphs; or a videotape, CD-ROM, DVD, audiotape, or audio CD.

Objects

The first type of presentation aid you ever used—perhaps as long ago as preschool "show and tell"—was probably an object. You took to school your favorite teddy bear or the new remote-control car you got for your birthday. Remember how the kids crowded around to see what you had brought? Objects add interest to a talk because they are real. Whether the members of your audience are in preschool or college, they like tangible, real things. If you use an object as a presentation aid, consider these guidelines:

- Make certain the object can be handled easily. If it is too large, it may be unwieldy; if it is too small, your audience won't be able to see it.
- Don't use dangerous or illegal objects as presentation aids. They may make your audience members uneasy or actually put them at risk.

Models

If it is impossible to bring an object to class, you may be able to substitute a model. You cannot bring a 1965 Ford Thunderbird into a classroom, but you may be able to construct and bring a model. You could probably not acquire a dog's heart to bring to class, but you might be able to find a model to use for your explanation of how heartworms damage that vital organ. If you use a model as a presentation aid, be sure that the model is large enough to be seen by all members of your audience.

People

You might not think of people as potential presentation aids, but they can be. President George W. Bush has used ordinary people as visual aids for some of his most important speeches, "asking them to stand and then telling stories of their sacrifices or heroism . . . a way of coming down from the stage, as it were, and mingling with the crowd."[30] In other instances, people can model costumes, play a sport with you, or demonstrate a dance. Consider the following guidelines if you are going to ask someone to assist you by acting as a presentation aid for a speech:

- Rehearse with the person who will be helping you.
- Don't have the person stand beside you doing nothing. Wait until you need your presentation aid to have him or her come to the front.
- Don't let your presentation aid steal the show. Make his or her role specific and fairly brief. As the speaker, you should remain the "person of the hour."

Drawings

You can use simple drawings to help illustrate or explain ideas that you are talking about. For example, you could sketch the tunnels of a fire ant mound to show your audience why it is so difficult to eradicate an entire colony. You could sketch the plants and animals crucial to the life cycle of the Florida Everglades. If you use a drawing as a visual aid, consider these suggestions:

- Keep your drawings large and simple. Line drawings are often more effective than more detailed ones.
- Consider drawing or photocopying your drawing onto a sheet of overhead transparency film and using an overhead projector to show the drawing to your audience.
- Your drawing does not have to be original artwork. If you need help, you could ask a friend to help you prepare a drawing or you could utilize computer software to generate a simple image. Just be sure to credit your source if you use someone else's sketch.

Photographs

If you are giving a speech on urban forestry, you might want to show your audience good color pictures of trees appropriate for urban sites in your area. In this case, photographs would show color and detail that would be nearly impossible to achieve with drawings. The biggest challenge to using photographs as presentation aids is size; most photos are simply too small to be seen clearly from a distance. If you want to use a photograph, you will usually have to enlarge it. Consider the following options for making photographs into viable presentation aids:

- Many copy centers or photo shops can produce poster-size color photocopies.
- Transfer your photograph to a slide and project it onto a screen.
- Store digital photos on a computer disk. Then, when you want the photos, you can bring them up on your computer screen and use a video projection system to enlarge them for your audience.

Maps

Like photographs, most maps are too small to be useful as presentation aids; you must enlarge them in some way. Consider these suggestions for using maps effectively in a presentation:

- Enlarge your map by photocopying it or by transferring it to a slide. An outline map with few details can be copied or drawn on overhead transparency film.
- Highlight on your map the areas or routes you are going to talk about in your presentation.

Charts

Charts can summarize and organize a great deal of information in a small space. Consider using a chart any time you need to present information that could be organized under several headings or in several columns. The chart in Figure 14.1 displays 2000 United States census statistics on population age groups.[31] You can prepare charts quite easily by using the Table feature in your word-processing program. Keep in mind these guidelines:

- Whether you use a large flip chart, transfer your chart to an overhead transparency, or use a computer presentation program, be certain your chart is big enough to be seen easily.

- Keep your chart simple. Do not try to put too much information on one chart. Eliminate any unnecessary words.

- Print or type any lettering on a chart, instead of writing in script.

Graphs

Graphs are effective ways to present statistical relationships to your audience. They help to make data more concrete. You are probably already familiar with the three main types of graphs. **A bar graph consists of bars of various lengths representing percentages or numbers. It is useful for making comparisons. A round pie graph shows how data are divided proportionately. And a line graph can show both trends over a period of time and relationships among variables.** Figure 14.2 illustrates all three types of graphs, displaying the statistics from the chart in Figure 14.1. All three graphs were generated by Microsoft Excel. The following guidelines will help you use graphs more effectively in your presentations:

- Make your graphs big, by drawing them on a large piece of paper, by drawing or copying them on an overhead transparency, or by putting them on a computer disk for projection.

FIGURE 14.1: Chart

Population of the United States, by Age (Source: 2000 Census)	
Age	**Number**
0 to 9 years	40,000,000
10 to 19 years	41,000,000
20 to 34 years	59,000,000
35 to 54 years	83,000,000
55 to 64 years	24,000,000
over 64 years	35,000,000

FIGURE 14.2:   Three Types of Graphs: Bar Graph, Line Graph, and Pie Graph

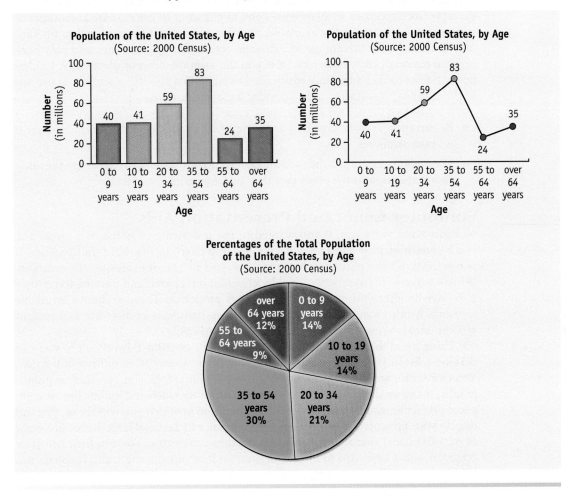

- Keep your graphs simple and uncluttered.
- Remember that many computer programs will generate graphs from statistics. You don't usually need to draw your own.

CD-ROMs and DVDs

CD-ROMs and DVDs allow a speaker to retrieve audio and visual information easily and quickly. One CD-ROM can contain hundreds of words, pictures, or sounds. If you were talking about President Franklin Roosevelt's New Deal, you could click your mouse to let your audience hear Roosevelt speak. If you wanted to show various images of Monet's garden, you could retrieve and project those pictures with ease. Both CD-ROMs and DVDs can be used in combination with a large-screen video projector or a liquid crystal display (LCD) panel connected to an overhead projector. If you plan to use a CD-ROM or DVD, remember these guidelines:

- Be certain that the equipment you will need will be available in the room in which you are going to speak.
- Have the equipment set up and ready to go before you speak.

Audiotapes and Audio CDs

If you want to supplement your speech with audio presentation aids—say, music or excerpts from speeches or interviews—you might want to use cassette audiotapes or audio CDs. Both are readily available, and their sound can be amplified to fill various size rooms. The advantage of a cassette tape is that you can tape and play back original material, such as an interview you did with the dean of students. A CD has better fidelity and can be more easily cued to begin in a specific place. If you use one of these audio presentation aids, consider these suggestions:

- Be certain that your tape or CD is amplified so that your audience can hear it without straining.
- Use audio presentation aids sparingly. You do not want them to engage the audience's attention to the point that they interfere with the speech.

Computer-Generated Presentation Aids

Not too many years ago, if you wanted to use a drawing or graph as a visual aid, you had to draw it by hand on a blackboard, flip chart, or overhead transparency. If you wanted to use a photograph or map, you had to have it professionally enlarged. While speakers still use overheads, blackboards, flip charts, and posters, today they also have another option: computer graphics programs. These programs, available for both Windows and Macintosh operating systems, can both create and present professional-looking visual aids inexpensively and easily.

Using a graphics program such as Microsoft's popular PowerPoint™, you can develop a list of your main points that audience members can refer to as you speak. You can create graphs and charts. You can use clip art, or you can scan in photographs, maps, or drawings. You can even incorporate video and audio clips. If computer-projection equipment is available in the room in which you will speak, you can display your presentation by connecting a computer to a special large-screen projector or an LCD panel that fits on top of an overhead projector. You can then run your program with a keyboard or mouse, or even set it to run automatically. If you do not have access to such equipment, you can transfer the images you have created to slides, overhead transparencies, or paper.

Among the advantages of learning to use computer graphics programs such as PowerPoint for classroom presentations is that they are an important way to adapt your message to audiences who increasingly expect sophisticated technical support. You will undoubtedly encounter and be expected to use these programs again in the business world. Gaining experience with them now can give you an edge in seeking employment and in making your earliest business presentation more effective.

However, such programs also have inherent risks. As one consultant points out,

> When you darken the room and give the audience a preprogrammed, oh-so-beautiful, PowerPoint presentation, the audience will say, "I'm not part of this experience. That guy up there has done it all." The result: Your colleagues will mentally go on vacation. . . .[32]

The solution? As with other presentation aids we have discussed, don't let your PowerPoint slides become your presentation—use them to supplement it. Don't use too many slides. Make certain that the ones you do use contain significant information in a simple, uncluttered style. Don't overuse bulleted text. Instead, take advantage of the ease with which you can create and show such visual elements as graphs, charts, and photos on PowerPoint slides. Finally, practice with your PowerPoint slides so that you can time them to coincide with your oral presentation.

Guidelines for Preparing Presentation Aids

In addition to the specific guidelines for preparing and using various specific types of presentation aids that we have just discussed, four general guidelines can help you prepare all types of presentation aids more effectively.

Select the Right Presentation Aids

As is evident from the above discussion, you have a number of options for presentation aids. If you are trying to decide which to use, consider these suggestions:

1. Adapt to your audience. Let their interests, experiences, and knowledge guide your selection of presentation aids. For example, an audience of accountants would readily understand arbitrage charts that might be incomprehensible to a more general audience. If you will be speaking to a large audience, be certain that everyone will be able to see or hear your presentation aid.
2. Be constantly aware of your specific purpose. Be certain that your presentation aid contributes to its achievement.
3. Consider your own skill and experience. Use equipment with which you have had experience, or allow yourself ample time to practice. It may be better to make an overhead transparency of your Power-Point image if the alternative is to fumble with an unfamiliar computer and LCD projector.
4. Take into account the room in which you will speak. If it has large windows and no shades, for example, do not plan to use a visual presentation aid that will require a darkened room. If you plan to run a PowerPoint presentation, be sure that both hardware and software are available and in good working order.

Make Your Presentation Aids Easy to See

You have probably experienced the frustration of squinting and straining to read a speaker's too-small presentation aid. If you are going to remember only one thing about using a presentation aid, remember this: Make it big!

Keep Your Presentation Aids Simple

Don't cram too much information on any single presentation aid. Limit text to key words or phrases. Leave plenty of white space.

Polish Your Presentation Aids

Especially in this day of readily available, professional-looking computer graphics, audiences have high expectations for the appearance of presentation aids. A sloppy, hand-drawn visual will detract from even the best verbal message. Prepare your presentation aids well in advance of your speaking date and make them as attractive and professional as possible. Even if you can't run a PowerPoint presentation in the room in which you are speaking, consider using such a program to produce your presentation aids.

Steve Jobs, chief executive officer of Apple Computer, uses a large-screen projector to make sure his audience can see his PowerPoint presentation and the product he used to create it.

Guidelines for Using Presentation Aids

Once you have prepared potentially effective presentation aids, you will want to utilize them effectively as well. In addition to the guidelines offered earlier in this chapter for using specific types of presentation aids, the following general suggestions will help you more effectively adapt various types of presentation aids to your audience.

Adapt

Adapt

Rehearse with Your Presentation Aids

The day of your speech should not be the first time you deliver your presentation while holding up your chart, turning on your projector, or cueing your CD. Practice setting up and using your presentation aids until you feel at ease with them. Consider during rehearsal what you would do at various stages of the speech if you had to carry on without your presentation aid. Electricity fails, equipment fails to show up, and bulbs burn out. Have contingency plans.

Maintain Eye Contact with Your Audience, Not with Your Presentation Aids

You can glance at your presentation aids during your talk, but do not talk to them. Keep looking at your audience.

Explain Your Presentation Aids

Always talk about and explain your presentation aids. Do not assume that the audience will understand their relevance and how to interpret them.

Time the Display of Your Presentation Aids to Coincide with Your Discussion of Them

Don't put a presentation aid in front of your audience until you are ready to use it. Likewise, remove your presentation aid after you are finished with it. Keeping presentation aids in front of an audience before or after you use them will only serve to distract from your message.

Do Not Pass Objects, Pictures, or Other Small Items among Your Audience

Passing things around distracts audience members. Either people are focused on whatever they are looking at or they are counting the number of people who will handle the object before it reaches them. If the item is too small for everyone to see it when you hold it up, it is not a good presentation aid.

Use Handouts Effectively

Handing out papers during your presentation can also distract audience members. If possible, wait to distribute handouts until after you have spoken. If your audience needs to refer to the material while you're talking about it, go ahead and pass out the handouts; then, at various points in your presentation, tell audience members where in the handout they should focus.

Use Small Children and Animals with Caution

Small children and even the best-trained animals are unpredictable. In a strange environment, in front of an audience, they may not behave in their usual way. The risk of having a child or animal detract from your presentation may be too great to justify their use as presentation aids.

ETHICS AND COMMUNICATION
Profanity in an Audio Presentation Aid

Matt wants to talk to his college classmates about the use of profanity in rap music. He plans to play sound clips of several profane lyrics from current hits to illustrate his point. Should Matt play these songs, even though doing so might offend several members of his audience?

Use Technology Thoughtfully

Computer-generated graphics, LCDs, and DVDs have become increasingly common components of presentations as more and more classrooms and seminar rooms are equipped for them. However, resist the temptation to use them just because they are glitzy. One speechwriter and presentation coach warns against this bleak but all-too-common scenario:

> The presenter says, "And now, I'd like to talk about quality." And lo and behold . . . the word *quality* flashes on a screen. Now, folks, does this slide offer any new information? Does it clarify a complex point? Does it strengthen the bond between presenter and audience? You know the answer: a resounding "no."[33]

Be sure that the technology you use helps you communicate your message. And be sure that you know how to operate the hardware and that you rehearse with it.

SOME FINAL TIPS FOR REHEARSING AND DELIVERING YOUR PRESENTATION

Throughout this chapter, we have described and offered suggestions for effective verbal and nonverbal delivery and use of presentation aids. In addition to the tips offered throughout the chapter, the following suggestions will help you make the most of your rehearsal time and ultimately deliver your presentation successfully.

- Finish your preparation outline several days before you must deliver the presentation. Begin to rehearse from the preparation outline. Revise the presentation as necessary so that you can deliver it within your given time limits. Prepare your delivery outline and speaking notes. Continue to rehearse and to modify your speaking notes as necessary.

- Practice, practice, practice. Rehearse aloud as often as possible. Only by rehearsing will you gain confidence in both the content of the presentation and your delivery.

- Practice good delivery skills while rehearsing. Rehearse your presentation standing up. Pay attention to your gestures, posture, eye contact, facial expression, and vocal delivery, as well as the verbal message. Rehearse with your presentation aids.

- If possible, practice your presentation for someone. Seek and consider feedback from someone about both the content and your delivery.

- Tape record or videotape your presentation. Becoming more aware of your delivery can help you make necessary adjustments.

Listen and Respond

Aware

- Re-create the speaking situation in your final rehearsals. Try to rehearse in a room similar to the one in which you will deliver the presentation. Use the speaking notes you will use the day you deliver the presentation. Give the presentation without stopping. The more realistic the rehearsal, the more confidence you will gain.

- Get plenty of rest the night before you speak. Being well rested is more valuable than frantic, last-minute rehearsal.

- Arrive early. If you don't know for certain where your room is, give yourself plenty of time to find it. Rearrange any furniture or equipment and check and set up your presentation aids.

- Review and apply the suggestions offered in Chapter 12 for becoming a more confident speaker. As the moment for delivering your presentation nears, remind yourself of the effort you have spent preparing it. Visualize yourself delivering the presentation effectively. Silently practice your opening lines. Think about your audience. Breathe deeply, and consciously relax.

- After you have delivered your presentation, seek feedback from members of your audience. Use the information you gain to improve your next presentation.

Developing Your Presentation STEP BY STEP

Deliver Your Presentation

The long-awaited day of Ben's presentation has arrived at last. He got a full night's sleep last night and ate a light breakfast before setting out for class. As he waits to speak, Ben visualizes himself delivering his speech calmly and confidently. When his name is called, he rises, walks to the front of the room, and establishes eye contact with his audience before he begins to speak.

During his speech, Ben focuses on adapting his message to his listeners. He looks at individual members of his audience, uses purposeful and well-timed gestures, and speaks loudly and clearly.

Even before he hears his classmates' applause, Ben knows that his presentation has gone well.

SUMMARY

Once you have developed, supported, and organized your presentation, you are ready to begin to rehearse aloud in preparation for delivering it. The way in which you deliver your presentation will in large part determine your success as a speaker.

As you begin to consider how you will deliver your presentation, you will select from four methods of delivery: manuscript speaking, memorized speaking, impromptu speaking, or extemporaneous speaking. Extemporaneous speaking is the style taught today in most presentational speaking classes and preferred by most audiences.

Once you know what method of delivery you will use, you should begin to think about and rehearse words, phrases, and sentences that will best communicate your intended message and give it a distinct and memorable style. The most effective language is concrete, unbiased, vivid, simple, and correct. You can also make your presentation memorable by using figurative language and language that creates drama and cadence.

Nonverbal variables are also critical to effective delivery. Physical delivery includes a speaker's gestures, movement, and posture. Eye contact is perhaps the most important delivery variable, determining to a large extent your credibility with your audience. Facial expression plays a key role in expressing thoughts, emotions, and attitudes. Vocal delivery includes such elements as volume, pitch, rate, and articulation. And finally, your personal appearance can also affect how your audience responds to you and your message.

Presentation aids may not always be necessary, but they are used with increasing frequency. Presentation aids may include objects or models, people, drawings, photographs, maps, charts, graphs, videotapes, CD-ROMs, DVDs, audiotapes, and audio CDs. Today, many presentation aids can be created and displayed by computer graphics programs such as PowerPoint. Guidelines for using any type of presentation aid include selecting the right one for the audience, occasion, and room and making the presentation aid simple, easy to see or hear, and polished. As you prepare to use any presentation aid, be sure that you rehearse with it, maintain eye contact with your audience, explain your presentation aid, time your use of your presentation aid, refrain from passing things around or using handouts indiscriminately, remember that small children and animals are unpredictable presentation aids, and use technology thoughtfully.

Final suggestions for rehearsing your presentation include allowing ample time for and conducting realistic rehearsals, audiotaping or videotaping your presentation, and practicing your presentation for someone who will offer feedback. Final tips for delivering your presentation include getting plenty of rest the night before you speak, arriving early, and applying the suggestions offered in Chapter 12 for becoming a more confident speaker.

DISCUSSION AND REVIEW

1. In what way(s) does delivery contribute to the success of a presentation?

2. What delivery method is most commonly taught and used today?

3. Give an example of how culture can influence audience expectations for speaker delivery.

4. Under what circumstances might a speaker want to deliver a manuscript or memorized speech?

5. How does an extemporaneous presentation differ from an impromptu presentation?

6. List and explain five criteria for effectiveness of words in a presentation.

7. List and define three types of figurative language that can be used to make a presentation memorable.

8. How might you create verbal drama in a presentation?

9. What is cadence? Describe briefly four strategies for achieving it in a presentation.

10. List and define the three key elements of physical delivery and provide suggestions for effectively using each one.

11. What is the most important nonverbal delivery variable for most North American audiences?

12. What can facial expression communicate during a presentation?

13. List and define four nonverbal elements of vocal delivery, and provide suggestions for using each one effectively.

14. How should you dress when you are going to deliver a presentation?

15. List 11 types of presentation aids from which a speaker might select, and provide suggestions for effectively using each type.

16. Offer four general guidelines for preparing effective presentation aids.

17. Provide eight general guidelines for using presentation aids effectively in a presentation.

18. Offer nine general guidelines for rehearsing and delivering a presentation.

PUTTING PRINCIPLES INTO PRACTICE

1. Consult either a print thesaurus or the electronic thesaurus that is part of your word-processing program and find a more concrete or specific word to express each of the following:

go	happy
say	green
big	cat
dark	street
good	car

2. Listen to a political campaign speech in person or on television. Pay particular attention to the politician's delivery. Critique his or her use of gestures, movement, posture, eye contact, facial expression, vocal delivery, and appearance. What advice would you give this politician?

3. Videotape one of your presentations, during either rehearsal or delivery to your class. Analyze your strengths and weaknesses based on the principles and suggestions offered in this chapter.

4. You are a speech consultant to the superintendent of your local school district. She is about to begin working on her annual "State of the District" address, which she gives to an audience of about 250 teachers, parents, and community members. This year, she wants to enliven her presentation of enrollment statistics, student achievement facts, and the state of the physical plant with some presentation aids. Write an advisory memo to the superintendent in which you suggest types of presentation aids she might employ and ways of using each one effectively.

5. You will need the following materials to complete this assignment:

One or two pieces of paper or poster board measuring at least 15 by 20 inches

Felt-tipped markers or a set of marking pens in at least two different colors

A ruler or straightedge

A pencil with an eraser

Three speech topics are listed below, each with a brief description and information that could be communicated with the help of a presentation aid. Design one or more presentation aids for one of the three speeches.

a. A speech about various kinds of organizing tools that college students could use to help them keep track of assignments and projects. These tools include paper wall calendars, paper daytimers, personal information-management software, handheld electronic organizers, and Internet-based calendars.[34]

b. A speech about the spread of AIDS. The number of new cases of HIV infection in 2004 on various continents are listed below.[35]

North America: 44,000

Caribbean: 53,000

Latin America: 240,000

Europe and Central Asia: 231,000

North Africa and Middle East: 92,000

Sub-Saharan Africa: 3.1 million

East Asia: 290,000

South and Southeast Asia: 890,000

Oceania: 5,000

c. A speech that discusses Web sites offering useful information about nutrition and diet. Sites might include the following:

■ www. mypyramid. gov/ tips_resources/ index. html provides tips and resources from the USDA to help you choose healthful food and physical activity.

■ www. dietsite. com allows users to enter recipes to obtain a calorie count.

■ www. mealsforyou. com offers thousands of healthful recipes.

15
Speaking to Inform

Diana Ong, The Defense.
© Diana Ong/SuperStock, Inc.

If you think knowledge is expensive, try ignorance."

Derek Bok

This is the information age. With the help of today's technology, we are immersed in facts, data, and words. The Internet is an overflowing fount of information on every conceivable topic. Information is a good thing: It is necessary to help us live our lives. But the volume of information may create a problem. There is often too much of a good thing. Trying to use and interpret all the information we encounter can be like trying to take a drink from a fire hose; the volume of information makes this nearly an overwhelming task.

Countless times each day, you are called on to share information with others. Whether it's directions to your house, the answer to a question from a teacher, or an update on a project at work, your competence as a communicator is often based on how clearly you can present information to others. One survey of both speech teachers and students who had taken a communication course found that the single most important skill taught in a presentational speaking class is how to give an informative presentation.[1] This is not surprising, given the importance of sending and receiving information in our lives.

The purpose of a message to **inform is to share information with others to enhance their knowledge or understanding of the information, concepts, and ideas you present.** When you inform someone, you assume the role of a teacher by defining, illustrating, clarifying, or elaborating on a topic.

Speaking to inform others can be a challenging task. The information you communicate to someone else is rarely, if ever, understood exactly as you intend it. As we have noted, we're each different from one another. We literally experience the world in different ways. As a student, you have firsthand experience that just because a teacher presents information, you don't always soak up knowledge like a sponge. Informing or teaching others is a challenge because of a simple fact: *Presenting information does not mean that communication has occurred.* Communication happens when listeners make sense of the information.

Chapter Objectives

After studying this chapter, you should be able to

- Explain the purpose of speaking to inform.
- Describe and illustrate five types of informative presentations.
- Identify and use appropriate strategies for organizing informative presentations.

- Identify and use strategies for making informative presentations clear.
- Identify and use strategies for making informative presentations interesting.
- Identify and use strategies for making informative presentations memorable.

Aware
Verbal
Nonverbal
Listen and Respond
Adapt

Another challenge of speaking to inform is to keep your informative message from becoming a persuasive one. It cannot be denied that informing and persuading are interrelated. Information alone may persuade someone to think or do something in a different way. However, if you intentionally try to change or reinforce your listeners' feelings, ideas, or behavior, your speech may become more persuasive than informative.

In this chapter, we will suggest ways to build on your experience and enhance your skill in informing others. We will examine different types of informative tasks and identify specific strategies to help you organize your messages and make them clear, interesting, and memorable. Throughout our discussion we will remind you of the five communication principles for a lifetime.

TYPES OF INFORMATIVE PRESENTATIONS

When preparing an informative presentation, your first task, after considering the needs and backgrounds of your audience, is to select a topic. Although you may be assigned a topic based on your job, experience, or expertise, there are times (such as in a communication class) when you are given a free hand in determining what you will talk about. Identifying the type of informative presentation you will deliver can help you select and narrow your topic, organize your message, and select appropriate supporting material.

Presentations about Objects

A speech about an object might be about anything tangible—anything you can see or touch. You may or may not show the actual object to your audience while you are talking about it. Objects that could form the basis of an interesting presentation might include these:

Objects from your own collection (antiques, compact discs, baseball cards)
The Eiffel Tower
Cellos
Digital cameras
The Roosevelt Memorial
Toys

The time limit for your speech will determine the amount of detail you can share with your listeners. Even in a 30- to 45-minute presentation, you cannot talk about every aspect of any of the objects listed. So you will need to focus on a specific purpose.

Presentations about Procedures

A presentation about a procedure discusses how something works (for example, how blood travels through the human circulatory system), or describes a process that produces a particular outcome (such as how grapes become wine). At the close of such a presentation, your audience should be able to describe, understand, or perform the procedure you have described. Here are some examples of procedures that could be the topics of effective informative presentations:

How to surf the Internet
How state laws are made
How to refinish furniture
How to select a personal digital assistant (PDA)

How to plant an organic garden

How to select and purchase a stock

Notice that all of these examples start with the word *how.* A presentation about a procedure usually focuses on how a process is completed or how something can be accomplished. Presentations about procedures are often presented in workshops or other training situations in which people learn skills. One good way to teach people a skill is to follow the acronym T-E-A-C-H, which stands for Tell-Example-Apply-Coach-Help.[2]

- *Tell.*　Describe what you want your listeners to know.
- *Example.*　Show them an example of how to perform the skill.
- *Apply.*　Give them an opportunity to apply the knowledge by performing the skill.
- *Coach.*　Provide positive coaching to encourage them.
- *Help.*　Help them learn by correcting mistakes.

Many presentations about procedures include visual aids. Whether you are teaching people how to install a computer modem or how to give a presentation, showing them how to do something is almost always more effective than just telling them how to do it.

Presentations about People

A biographical presentation could be about someone famous or about someone you know personally. Most of us enjoy hearing about the lives of real people, whether famous or not, living or dead, who have some special quality. The key to making an effective biographical presentation is to be selective. Don't try to cover every detail of your subject's life. Relate the key elements in the person's career, personality, or other significant life features so that you build to a particular point, rather than just recite facts about an individual. Perhaps your grandfather was known for his generosity, for example. Mention some notable examples of his philanthropy. If you are talking about a well-known personality, pick information or a period that is not widely known, such as the person's private hobby or childhood. One speaker gave a memorable presentation about his friend:

> To enter Charlie's home was to enter a world of order and efficiency. His den reflected his many years as an Air Force officer; it was orderly and neat. He always knew exactly where everything was. When he finished reading the morning paper, he folded it so neatly by his favorite chair that you would hardly know that it had been read. Yet for all of his efficiency, you knew the minute you walked into his home that he cared for others, that he cared for you. His jokes, his stories, his skill in listening to others drew people to him. He never met a stranger. He looked for opportunities to help others.

Note how these details capture Charlie's personality and charm. Presentations about people should give your listeners the feeling that the person is a unique, authentic individual.

One specific type of presentation about a person is an introduction of another speaker and his or her topic. There are two cardinal rules for introducing another speaker: Be brief, and be accurate. Remember that the audience has come to hear the main speaker, not to listen to you. And be certain that you know how to pronounce the speaker's name and that you have accurate information about him or her.

Presentations about Events

Where were you on September 11, 2001, the day terrorists attacked the World Trade Center and the Pentagon? Chances are that you clearly remember where you were and what you were doing on that and other similarly fateful days. Major events punctuate our lives and mark the passage of time.

A major event can form the basis of a fascinating informative presentation. You can choose to talk about an event that you have either witnessed or researched. Your goal is to describe the event in concrete, tangible terms and to bring the experience to life for your audience. Have you experienced a major disaster such as a hurricane or a tornado? Have you witnessed the inauguration of a president, governor, or senator? Or you may want to re-create an event that your parents or grandparents lived through. What was it like to be at Pearl Harbor on December 7, 1941? How did people react when Neil Armstrong took his first steps on the moon on July 20, 1969?

You may have heard a recording of the famous radio broadcast of the explosion and crash of the dirigible *Hindenburg*. The announcer's ability to describe both the scene and the incredible emotion of the moment has made that broadcast a classic. As that broadcaster was able to do, your purpose as an informative speaker describing an event is to make that event come alive for your listeners and to help them visualize the scene.

Presentations about Ideas

Presentations about ideas are by nature more abstract than the other types of presentations. The following principles, concepts, and theories might be topics of idea presentations:

Principles of time management

Freedom of speech

Evolution

Theories of communication

Buddhism

Animal rights

As you look at this list, you may think, "Those topics sure look boring." The key to gaining and maintaining interest in your presentation about an idea lies in your selection of supporting material. A good speaker selects illustrations, examples, and anecdotes that make an otherwise abstract idea seem both exciting and relevant to the audience.

Verbal

STRATEGIES FOR ORGANIZING YOUR INFORMATIVE PRESENTATION

As with any presentation, your audience will more readily understand your informative presentation if you organize your ideas logically. Regardless of the length or complexity of your message, you must follow a logical pattern in order to be understood.

Organizing Presentations about Objects

Presentations about objects may be organized topically; a topical pattern is structured around the logical divisions of the object you're describing. Here's a sample topical outline for a speech about an object—a nuclear power plant:

I. The reactor core
   A. The nuclear fuel in the core
   B. The placement of the fuel in the core
II. The reactor vessel
   A. The walls of a reactor vessel
   B. The function of the coolant in the reactor vessel
III. The reactor control rods
   A. The description of the control rods
   B. The function of the control rods

Presentations about objects may also be organized chronologically. A speaker might, for example, focus on the history and development of nuclear power plants; such a presentation would probably be organized chronologically. Or, depending on the speaker's specific purpose, the presentation could be organized spatially, describing the physical layout of a nuclear power plant.

Organizing Presentations about Procedures

Speeches about procedures are usually organized chronologically, according to the steps involved in the process. Anita organized chronologically her explanation of how to develop a new training curriculum in teamwork skills:

I. Conduct a needs assessment of your department.
   A. Identify the method of assessing department needs.
   B. Implement the needs assessment.

II. Identify the topics that should be presented in the training.
   A. Specify topics that all members of the department need.
   B. Specify topics that only some members of the department need.

III. Write training objectives.
   A. Write objectives that are measurable.
   B. Write objectives that are specific.
   C. Write objectives that are attainable.

IV. Develop lesson plans for the training.
   A. Identify the training methods you will use.
   B. Identify the materials you will need.

Note that Anita grouped the tasks into steps. Her audience will remember the four general steps much more easily than they could have hoped to recall the curriculum development process if each individual task were listed as a separate step.

Organizing Presentations about People

One way to talk about a person's life is in chronological order—birth, school, career, family, professional achievements, death. However, if you are interested in presenting a specific theme, such as "Winston Churchill, master of English prose," you may decide instead to organize Churchill's experiences topically. You could first discuss Churchill's achievements as a brilliant orator whose words defied the German military machine in 1940, and then trace the origins of his skill to his work as a cub reporter in South Africa during the Boer War of 1899 to 1902.

When speaking about Native American rock art in Texas, this speaker may find it helpful to organize her speech either topically, spatially, or chronologically.

Organizing Presentations about Events

Most speeches about an event follow a chronological arrangement. But a presentation about an event might also describe the complex issues or causes behind the event and be organized topically. For example, if you were to talk about the Civil War, you might choose to focus on the three causes of the war:

I. Political
II. Economic
III. Social

Adapt

Although these main points are topical, specific subpoints may be organized chronologically. However you choose to organize your speech about an event, your goal should be to ensure that your audience is enthralled by your vivid description.

Organizing Presentations about Ideas

Most presentations about ideas are organized topically (by logical subdivisions of the central idea) or according to complexity (from simple ideas to more complex ones). The following example illustrates how Thompson organized a presentation about philosophy into an informative speech:

I. Definition of philosophy
   A. Philosophy as viewed in ancient times
   B. Philosophy as viewed today

II. Three branches of the study of philosophy
   A. Metaphysics
     1. The study of ontology
     2. The study of cosmology
   B. Epistemology
     1. Knowledge derived from thinking
     2. Knowledge derived from experiencing
   C. Logic
     1. Types of reasoning
     2. Types of proof

Thompson decided that the most logical way to give an introductory talk about philosophy was first to define it and then to describe three branches of philosophy. Because of time limits, he chose only to describe three branches or types of philosophy. He used a topical organizational pattern to organize his message.

STRATEGIES FOR MAKING YOUR INFORMATIVE PRESENTATION CLEAR

Think of the best teacher you ever had. He or she was probably a great lecturer with a special talent for making information clear, interesting, and memorable. Like teachers, some speakers are better than others at presenting information clearly. In this section, we will review some of the principles that can help you become the kind of speaker whose presentations are memorable.[3]

A message is clear when the listener understands it in the way the speaker intended. Phrased in baseball terminology, a message is clear when what I threw is what you caught. How do you make your messages clear to others? First, be aware (mindful) of what you intend to communicate. Is the message clear to you? Say to yourself, "If I heard this message for the first time, would it make sense to me?"

If the message makes sense to you, select appropriate words that are reinforced with appropriate nonverbal cues to express your ideas. If you detect that your listeners are puzzled by what you say, stop and try another way to express your ideas.

Aware
Verbal
Nonverbal
Listen and Respond
Adapt

Adapt your message to your audience. Be audience centered. Keep your listeners in mind as you select and narrow a topic, fine-tune your purpose, and complete each preparation and presentation task. Here are several additional specific strategies to make your message clear.

Simplify Ideas

Your job as a presentational speaker is to get your ideas over to your audience, not to see how much information you can cram into your speech. The simpler your ideas and phrases, the greater the chance that your audience will remember them.

Let's say you decide to talk about state-of-the-art personal computer hardware. Fine—but just don't try to make your audience as sophisticated as you are about computers in a 5-minute presentation. Discuss only major features and name one or two leaders in the field. Don't load your presentation with details. Edit ruthlessly.

Verbal

Pace Your Information Flow

Arrange your supporting material so that you present an even flow of information, rather than bunch up a number of significant details around one point. If you present too much new information too quickly, you may overwhelm your audience. Their ability to understand may falter.

You should be especially sensitive to the flow of information if your topic is new or unfamiliar to your listeners. Make sure that your audience has time to process any new information you present. Use supporting material to regulate the pace of your presentation.

Again, do not try to see how much detail and content you can cram into a presentation. Your job is to present information so that the audience can grasp it, not to show off how much you know.

Verbal
Adapt

Relate New Information to Old

Most of us learn by building on what we already know. We try to make sense out of our world by associating the new with the old. When you meet someone for the first time, you may be reminded of someone you already know. Your understanding of calculus is based on your knowledge of algebra.

When presenting new information to a group, help your audience associate your new idea with something that is familiar to them. Use an analogy. Tell bewildered college freshmen how their new academic life will be similar to high school and how it will be different. Describe how your raising cattle over the summer was similar to taking care of any animal; they all need food, water, and shelter. By building on the familiar, you help your listeners understand how your new concept or information relates to their experience.

Verbal

STRATEGIES FOR MAKING YOUR INFORMATIVE PRESENTATION INTERESTING

He had them. Every audience member's eyes were riveted on the speaker. It was as quiet as midnight in a funeral home. Audience members were also leaning forward, ever so slightly, not wanting to miss a single idea or brilliant illustration. No one moved. They hung on every word. How can you create such interest when you speak? Here are several strategies that can help you keep your audiences listening for more.

Relate to Your Listeners' Interests

Your listeners may be interested in your topic for a variety of reasons. It may affect them directly; it may add to their knowledge; it may satisfy their curiosity; or it may

Adapt

entertain them. These reasons are not mutually exclusive. For example, if you were talking to a group of businesspeople about the latest changes in local tax policies, you would be discussing something that would affect them directly, add to their knowledge, and satisfy their curiosity. But your listeners' primary interest would be in how the taxes would affect them. By contrast, if you were giving a lecture on 15th-century Benin sculpture to a middle-class audience at a public library, your listeners would be interested because your talk would add to their knowledge, satisfy their curiosity, and entertain them. Such a talk can also affect your listeners directly by making them more interesting to others. If your audience feels that they will benefit from your presentation in some way, your presentation will interest them.

Throughout this book, we have encouraged you to adapt to your communication partners—to develop an audience-centered approach to presentational speaking. Being an audience-centered informative speaker means that you are aware of information that your audience can use. Specifically, what factors help maintain audience interest? Consider the following strategies.[4]

- *Activity and movement.* We are more likely to listen to a story that is action-packed than to one that listlessly lingers on an idea too long.
- *Issues and events close to an audience.* To capture your listeners' attention, relate your information to what is happening in your school, community, or state. Not surprisingly, most people are interested in themselves. Therefore, one of the secrets to making a presentation interesting is to use examples to which your audience can relate. Make it personal. When appropriate, mention specific audience members' names.
- *Conflict.* Clashes of ideas; stories that pit one side against another; or opposing forces in government, religion, or interpersonal relationships grab attention. The Greeks learned long ago that the essential ingredient of any play, be it comedy or tragedy, is conflict.

DIVERSITY AND COMMUNICATION
Using an Interpreter

It is quite possible that you may at some time be asked to speak to an audience that does not understand English. In such a situation, you will need an interpreter to translate your message so that your audience can understand you. When using an interpreter, consider the following tips:

1. Realize that a presentation that may take you 30 minutes to deliver without an interpreter will take at least an hour to present with an interpreter. Edit your message to make sure it fits within the time limit.
2. Even with an experienced interpreter, you'll need to slow your speaking rate a bit. Also, be sure to pause after every two or three sentences to give the interpreter time to translate your message.
3. Don't assume that your audience doesn't understand you just because you are using an interpreter. Don't say anything that you don't want your audience to hear.
4. If you have many facts, figures, or other detailed data, write this information down before you speak, and give it to your interpreter.
5. Humor often doesn't translate well. Be cautious of using a joke that was a real knee-slapper when you told it to your colleagues in your office; it may not have the same effect on people with a different cultural background and different language. Also, even a very skilled interpreter may have difficulty communicating the intended meaning of your humor.
6. Avoid using slang, jargon, or any terms that will be unfamiliar to your listeners or interpreter.
7. When possible, talk with your interpreter before you deliver your presentation. Tell him or her the general points you will present. If possible, give the interpreter an outline or a transcript if you are using a manuscript.

Another way you can make your message interesting is to think about why you are interested in the topic. Once you are aware of your own interests and background, you can often find ways to establish common bonds with your audience.

Use Attention-Catching Supporting Material

Supporting material is effective if it both clarifies your ideas and keeps your listeners' attention. One classic type of supporting material often used in informative speaking is definition. But if you are trying to tell your listeners about a complex or abstract process, you will need more than definitions to explain what you mean. When describing abstract ideas or processes, it's usually more difficult to hold listeners' attention. Research suggests that you can demystify a complex process and increase audience interest if you first provide a simple overview of the process with an analogy, model, picture, or vivid description.[5]

Before going into great detail, first give listeners the "big picture" or convey the gist of the process. Analogies (comparisons) are often a good way to do this. For example, if you are describing how a personal computer works, you could say that it stores information the way a filing cabinet does or that computer software works like a piano roll on an old-fashioned player piano. In addition to using an analogy, consider using a model or other visual aid to show relationships among the steps of a complex process.

You can also describe the process, providing more detail than you do when you just define something. Descriptions answer questions about the *who*, *what*, *where*, *why*, and *when* of the process. Who is involved in the process? What is the process, idea, or event that you want to describe? Where and when does the process take place? Why does it occur, or why is it important to the audience? (Of course, not all of these questions apply to every description.)

Establish a Motive for Your Audience to Listen to You

Most audiences will probably not be waiting breathlessly for you to talk to them. You will need to motivate them to listen to you.

Some situations have built-in motivations for listeners. A teacher can say, "There will be a test covering my lecture tomorrow. It will count as 50% of your semester grade." Such threatening methods may not make the teacher popular, but they certainly will motivate the class to listen. Similarly, a boss might say, "Your ability to use these sales principles will determine whether you keep your job." Your boss's statement will probably motivate you to learn the company's sales principles. However, unlike a teacher or a boss, you will rarely have the power to motivate your listeners with such strong-arm tactics, and you will therefore need to find more creative ways to get your audience to listen to you.

One way to arouse the interest of your listeners is to ask them a question. Speaking on the high cost of tuition, you might ask, "How many of you are interested in saving tuition dollars this year?" You'll probably have their attention. Then proceed to tell them that you will talk about several approaches to seeking

On the Web

The Internet is a vast resource of material for informative speeches. In addition to using search engines to perform keyword searches, you may want to take advantage of such resources as Web-based encyclopedias, almanacs, and statistical databases. Take a look at the following:

www. infoplease. com provides access to a number of informative resources, including *The Columbia Electronic Encyclopedia, 6th ed., and the Information Please Almanac*.

factfinder. census. gov is a user-friendly site that offers population, housing, economic, and geographic data from the U.S. Census Bureau.

www. fedstats. gov offers official statistical information from more than 100 federal government agencies.

Colin Powell's use of memorable word pictures helps his audience visualize the images he talks about.

Verbal

low-cost loans and grants. "Who would like to save money on their income taxes?" "How many of you would like to have a happier home life?" "How many of you would like to learn an effective way of preparing your next speech?" These are other examples of questions that could stimulate your listeners' interest and motivate them to give you their attention. Besides using rhetorical questions, you can begin with an anecdote, a startling statistic, or some other attention-grabbing device.

Don't assume that your listeners will be automatically interested in what you have to say. Pique their interest with a question. Capture their attention. Motivate them to listen to you. Tell them how the information you present will be of value to them. As the British writer G. K. Chesterton once said, "There is no such thing as an uninteresting topic; there are only uninterested people."

Use Word Pictures

Words have the power to create powerful images that can gain and hold an audience's attention. Consider using a word picture to make your message vivid and interesting. **Word pictures are lively descriptions that help your listeners form a mental image by appealing to their senses of sight, taste, smell, sound, and touch.** The following suggestions will help you construct effective word pictures:

- Form a clear mental image of the person, place, or object before you try to describe it.

- Describe the appearance of the person, place, or object. What would your listeners see if they were looking at it? Use lively language to describe the flaws and foibles, bumps and beauties of the people, places, and things you want your audience to see. Make your description an invitation to the imagination—a stately pleasure dome into which your listeners can enter and view its treasures with you.

- Describe what your listeners would hear. Use colorful, onomatopoetic words, such as *buzz, snort, hum, crackle,* or *hiss.* These words are much more descriptive than the more general term *noise.* Imitate the sound you want your listeners to hear with their "mental ear." For example, instead of saying "When I walked in the woods, I heard the sound of twigs breaking beneath my feet and wind moving the leaves above me in the trees," you might say, "As I walked in the woods, I heard the *crackle* of twigs underfoot and the *rustle* of leaves overhead."

- Describe smells, if appropriate. What fragrance or aroma do you want your audience to recall? Such diverse subjects as Thanksgiving, nighttime in the tropics, and the first day of school all lend themselves to olfactory imagery. No Thanksgiving would be complete without the rich aroma of roast turkey and the pungent, tangy odor of cranberries. A warm, humid evening in Miami smells of salt air and gardenia blossoms. And the first day of school evokes for many the scents of new shoe leather, unused crayons, and freshly painted classrooms. In each case, the associated smells greatly enhance the overall word picture.

- Describe how an object feels when touched. Use words that are as clear and vivid as possible. Rather than saying that something is rough or smooth, use a simile, such as "the rock was rough as sandpaper" or "the pebble was as smooth as a baby's skin." These descriptions appeal to both the visual and tactile senses.

- Describe taste, one of the most powerful of the senses, if appropriate. Thinking about your grandmother may evoke for you memories of her rich, homemade noodles; her sweet, fudgy, nut brownies; and her light, flaky, buttery pie crust. Descriptions of these taste sensations would be welcome to almost any audience, particularly your fellow college students subsisting mainly on dormitory food or their own cooking! More important, such description can help you paint an accurate, vivid image of your grandmother.

- Describe the emotion that a listener might feel if he or she were to experience the situation you relate. If you experienced the situation, describe your own emotions. Use specific adjectives rather than general terms such as *happy* or *sad*. One speaker, talking about receiving her first speech assignment, described her reaction with these words: "My heart stopped. Panic began to rise up inside. Me? . . . For the next five days I lived in dreaded anticipation of the forthcoming event."[6]

Note how effectively such words and phrases as "my heart stopped," "panic," and "dreaded anticipation" describe the above-mentioned speaker's terror at the prospect of giving a speech—much more so than if she had said simply, "I was scared." The more vividly and accurately you can describe emotion, the more intimately involved in your description the audience will become. One final word of caution: Don't describe horrific events too explicitly. You will risk alienating your audience, rather than engaging them.

Create Interesting Presentation Aids

Research about learning styles suggests that many of your listeners are more likely to remember your ideas if you can reinforce them with presentation aids. Pictures, graphs, posters, and computer-generated graphics can help you gain and maintain audience members' attention, as well as increase their retention of the information you present. Today's audiences are exposed daily to a barrage of messages conveyed through highly visual electronic media—CD-ROM, DVD, the World Wide Web, and video. They have grown to depend on more than words alone to help them remember ideas and information. When you present summaries of data, a well-crafted line graph or colorful pie chart can quickly and memorably reinforce the words and numbers you cite.

Nonverbal

Use Humor

"Humor is the spice of speeches," says comedian Michael Klepper. "Too little and your message may be bland or lifeless, too much and it can burn the mouth."[7] The challenge is to use just the right kind of humor in the right amounts. Use humor wisely by considering the following ideas:[8]

- *Use humor to make a point.* Don't just tell jokes for the sake of getting a laugh. Make sure your story or punch line relates to your message. Here's an example of how a brief joke was used to make a point about the value of teamwork:

    I read recently about a veterinarian and a taxidermist who decided to share a shop in a small town in Ohio. The sign in the front window read: "Either way, you get your dog back."

    There is an important lesson there. We need to work together to solve our problems. People from marketing need to work with operations people. Designers need to work with engineers. Then, when we find a problem that one part of the organization can't solve, someone else may suggest a solution. It doesn't matter who comes up with the solution. The important thing is to "get your dog back."[9]

- *Make yourself the butt of the joke.* Audiences love it when you tell a funny or embarrassing story about yourself. And if the joke's on you, you don't have to worry about whether you will offend someone else.

- *Use humorous quotations.* You don't have to be a comedy writer to be funny. Quote humorous lines of proverbs, poetry, or sayings from others. But remember, what may be funny to you may not be funny to your audience. Some people love the humor of George Carlin; some don't. Try out your quotes and jokes on others before you present them from behind the lectern. Also, don't try to pass off a quotation from someone else as one of your own; always give credit for quotations you use.

- *Use cartoons.* Using an overhead projector to display a cartoon or scanning a cartoon into your computer presentation may be just the right way to make your point. Make sure your cartoon is large enough to be seen by everyone in the audience. As with any humor, don't overdo your use of cartoons.

STRATEGIES FOR MAKING YOUR INFORMATIVE PRESENTATION MEMORABLE

Adapt

If you've made your message clear and interesting, you're well on your way to ensuring that your audience members remember what you say. The goal is for your ideas to stick in your listeners' minds as if they were made of Velcro, rather than slide off as if they were made of Teflon. When you inform or teach, your job is to ensure as much retention of what you have conveyed as possible, by presenting the information as effectively as you can. People remember what is important to them. So one of the keys to making a message memorable is, again, to adapt your message to your listeners. Presenting a well-organized message will also go a long way toward helping your listeners remember what you say. Here are several strategies for making your presentation memorable.

Build In Redundancy

It is seldom necessary for writers to repeat themselves. If readers don't quite understand a passage, they can go back and read it again. When you speak, however, it is useful to repeat key points. As we have noted before, audience members generally cannot stop you if a point in your presentation is unclear or if their minds wander; you need to build in redundancy to make sure that the information you want to communicate will get across. Most speech teachers advise their students to structure their presentations as follows:

Verbal

1. *Tell them what you're going to tell them.* In the introduction of your presentation, provide a broad overview of the purpose of your message. Identify the major points you will present.
2. *Tell them.* In the body of your presentation, develop each of the main points mentioned during your introduction.
3. *Tell them what you've told them.* Finally, in your conclusion, summarize the key ideas discussed in the body.

Use Adult Learning Principles

If your audience consists of adult listeners, you will need to ensure that you deliver your message in the way that adults learn best. **Adult learners prefer the following:**[10]

- **To be given information they can use immediately**
- **To be involved actively in the learning process**
- **To connect their life experiences with the new information they learn**
- **To know how the new information is relevant to their busy lives**
- **To receive information that is relevant to their needs**

Adapt

Most people who have office jobs have in-baskets (or simply "in-piles") on their desks, where they place work that needs to be done. Similarly, adult learners tend to have "mental in-baskets"; as audience members, they have mental agendas of what they want or need to gain from listening to a presentation. Remember the characteristics of adult learners, and don't forget about the important principle of adapting your message to others. You will make your message memorable and also have more success in informing your audience if you tailor your information to address *their* agenda.

Reinforce Key Ideas Verbally

You can reinforce an idea by using such phrases as "This is the most important point" or "Be sure to remember this next point; it's the most compelling one." Suppose you have four suggestions for helping your listeners chair a meeting, and your last suggestion is the most important. How can you make sure your audience knows that? Just tell them: "Of all the suggestions I've given you, this last tip is the most important one. Here it is: Never fail to distribute an agenda before you chair any meeting." Be careful not to overuse this technique. If you claim that every other point is a key point, soon your audience will not believe you.

Verbal

Reinforce Key Ideas Nonverbally

You can also signal the importance of a point with nonverbal emphasis. Gestures serve the purpose of accenting or emphasizing key phrases, as italics do in written communication.

A well-placed pause can provide emphasis and reinforcement for a point. Pausing just before or just after you make an important point will focus attention on your thought. Raising or lowering your voice can also reinforce a key idea.

Verbal

Movement can help emphasize major ideas. Moving from behind the lectern to tell a personal anecdote can signal that something special and more intimate is about to be said. Remember that your movement and gestures should be meaningful and natural, rather than seeming arbitrary or forced. Your need to emphasize an idea can provide the motivation to make a meaningful movement.

Sample Informative Presentation

Alton Tisino
Texas State University–San Marcos

The Power of Music[11]

When I woke up this morning, one thing on my mind was music. I'm sure everyone wakes up with a certain tune or a favorite song in their head. Music is a treasured art form that we all share. Sometimes we can hear a song, and it will take us back to a significant time in our lives; or other times, a song can give us inspiration or motivate us to continue whatever it is we are doing. Whether it is in a car or at home, or at a restaurant or even in an elevator, music plays a big part in our daily lives and can bring us together like no other art form.

So why is music so powerful? What are the elements that make music so special? Some people say they like the beat of a song, some people say they like the melody in a song, while others simply enjoy the lyrics in a song. Well, according to world-famous composer Duke Ellington, there are three major elements in music: rhythm, melody, and harmony. In order for us to discover what makes music so special, we must first understand these terms, and then see how music itself is beneficial to us in our daily lives.

The *Dictionary of Music* defines *rhythm* as "the division of impulses, sound, and accents or movement in musical time." There are many theories on how rhythm was transformed into music. But, I'd like to cite poet Langston Hughes and his explanation on how rhythm was transformed into music:

> The rhythm of the heart is the first and most important rhythm in human life. Thousands of years ago men transformed the rhythm of the heartbeat into a drumbeat. And the rhythm of music began. They made a slow steady drumbeat to walk to or march to, a faster beat to sing to, and a changing beat to dance to. Rhythm is something we share in common. You and I, with all the plants and animals and people in

Alton establishes a motive for his audience to listen by referring to music experiences common to all people.

Alton further arouses the interest of his listeners by asking two rhetorical questions.

Alton previews the two main ideas of his presentation.

Alton uses both a definition and an explanation to clarify the role of rhythm in music.

the world and with all the stars and moon and sun and all the vast universe beyond this wonderful earth which is our home.[12]

Now that we have found our rhythm, we must look further into the foundation of music and discover melody.

Melody is defined as "an arrangement of single tones in a meaningful sequence." A melody gives life to a song and is the root for every tune you will ever hear. We have now found our melody and now we're only missing one piece to the puzzle of music.

Harmony is defined as "the sound resulting from the simultaneous sounding of two or more tones consonant with each other." Rhythm and melody would not be complete without harmony.

Now that we discovered the foundations of music, let me now explain to you how music is beneficial to us.

Many health experts believe music is good for the digestive system. According to researchers at the *Continuous Music Network,* slow music is better for your digestive system than no music at all. Clinical studies show that people take on average three mouthfuls when there's soothing music in the background, versus four mouthfuls when no tunes are played at all.

While music can help us relax at the dinner table, it can also help us go that extra mile when exercising. The music network Galaxie program director Mike Guinta stated that "Studies show men increase their workout time by 30 percent and women by 25 percent. . . ." Scientific studies have shown that music keeps your mind off the physical discomfort of a straining activity. I can personally recall a time I felt I could no longer go on with the strenuous activity of a workout. But somehow by listening to music on my headphones, it gave me an extra boost of energy.

Studies also have shown that unborn babies who listen to classical music in the mother's womb become smarter. Many therapists and psychiatrists have their patients listen to music to help them relax and deal with stress and depression. These are just a few of the many benefits that music has for us.

We have discovered the three major elements in music: rhythm, melody, and harmony. Whether it be the hard-hitting drums of rock, the melodic tunes of our favorite pop songs, or the harmonic, complex style of jazz, music is the universal language of the world because it can generate the feelings of human emotions—joy, sorrow, love, and pain—thus making it beneficial in our daily lives.

The fact of the matter is we make our own music all the time. Now let me explain to you how we do this. Just by being alive, our heartbeat makes its own rhythm. We make melody by arranging our thoughts in a meaningful sequence. And we make the final stage of music, harmony, simply by interacting with each other. We all have rhythm, and we all have music, and with music we have good times.

Alton provides a signpost to summarize his first subpoint and preview the next one.

This signpost signals Alton's move from his first main idea to his second main idea.

Having offered statistical evidence that music is beneficial to exercise, Alton relates a brief personal anecdote.

As part of the necessary built-in redundancy of informative presentations, Alton briefly summarizes his main ideas.

By explaining how the elements of music apply to everyone's life, Alton draws on the principles that adult learners prefer to connect their life experiences with the new information they have learned and that they prefer relevant information.

Alton closes his presentation with a reference to George Gershwin's famous song "I Got Rhythm."

Principles For a Lifetime: Enhancing Your Skills

Principle One: Be aware of your communication with yourself and others.
- Be conscious of the type of informative message you are developing (presentation about an object, a procedure, a person, an event, or an idea), to help you determine how best to organize your message.
- Be consciously aware of using strategies that will make your informative messages clear, interesting, and memorable.

Principle Two: Effectively use and interpret verbal messages.

- Use supporting material such as stories, examples, and illustrations to gain and maintain attention.
- Use word pictures to make images and stories interesting and memorable.
- Pace the flow of the information you present to enhance message clarity.
- Relate new information to old information to increase clarity and retention.
- Verbally reinforce ideas to help make your message memorable.
- Use simple ideas rather than complex ideas to make your message clear.
- Build in message redundancy to enhance message retention.

Principle Three: Effectively use and interpret nonverbal messages.

- Use presentation aids to make messages clear, interesting, and memorable.
- Observe the nonverbal behavior of your audience to help you determine whether your message has been communicated clearly.
- Nonverbally reinforce ideas to make your message memorable.

Principle Four: Listen and respond thoughtfully to others.

- Before you deliver you presentation to an audience, talk and listen to audience members to help you customize your message for them.

Principle Five: Appropriately adapt messages to others.

- Adapt the structure and flow of your presentation to your listeners to enhance message clarity.
- Adapt your examples and illustrations to your listeners to help gain and maintain interest and attention.
- Develop a motivation for your audience to listen to you.

SUMMARY

To inform is to teach someone something you know. In this chapter, you have studied the goals, principles, and strategies that presentational speakers use to inform others.

There are five basic types of informative presentations. Messages about ideas are often abstract and generally discuss principles, concepts, or theories. Messages about objects discuss tangible things. Messages about procedures explain a process or describe how something works. Messages about people can be about either the famous or the little known. Messages about events describe major occurrences or personal experiences.

Strategies for organizing your informative presentation will vary according to the type of informative presentation and your specific purpose. A presentation about an object may be organized topically, chronologically, or spatially. A presentation about a procedure will usually be organized chronologically. Presentations about either people or events are also usually organized chronologically but can be organized topically. And a presentation about an idea will probably be organized topically.

To make your message clear, use simple rather than complex ideas, pace the flow of your information, and relate new information to old ideas. In order to increase interest in your presentation, relate information to your listeners, find and use attention-catching supporting material, establish a motive for your audience to listen to you, use vivid word pictures, use humor appropriately, and create intriguing and clear presentation aids. Finally, to make messages memorable, build in some redundancy (tell them what you're going to tell them; tell them; tell them what you've told them), use principles of adult learning, and reinforce key ideas both verbally and nonverbally.

DISCUSSION AND REVIEW

1. What is informative speaking?
2. What is the purpose of speaking to inform?
3. Describe the five types of informative speaking.
4. Explain how to organize each type of informative presentation.
5. What are three strategies to make your informative message clear?
6. Identify six strategies that can enhance interest in your informative talk.
7. What are four strategies that can make your presentation memorable?

PUTTING PRINCIPLES INTO PRACTICE

1. From the following list of suggested topics for an informative presentation, select five and develop a specific-purpose sentence for each. For one of those topics, identify two to four major ideas. Organize them topically, chronologically, or according to some other logical pattern of organization.

   How to get a better grade in your communication class

   The spread of terrorism in the world

   How the U.S. Constitution was written

   A historical person I wish I could meet

   What makes a good teacher

   The best way to lose weight

   How to buy a digital camera

   Surrogate parenthood

   Safe-driving principles

   How the stock market works

   Social Security

2. Replace each of the following words with a livelier one:

   cat   work
   airplane   light
   house   eat
   walk   study

3. Look up the origin of the following words in a comprehensive dictionary, such as the *Oxford English Dictionary* or the *Etymological Dictionary of Modern English*.

   logic   teacher
   pillow   dance
   love   amateur
   communication disciple

4. Write a word picture—a vivid, colorful description that appeals to the senses—of one of the following scenes:

   Your first day learning how to drive

   Visiting your father or mother at work

   A holiday when you were six

   A visit to your grandparents' house

   Your first day at college

   Your most frightening experience

   Your most memorable birthday celebration

16

Speaking to Persuade

Edouard Pignon, The Meeting. 1936. Oil on canvas. 130 × 95 cm. Inv.D.97-8-1; AM1997-142. Photo: R. G. Ojeda. Musee des Beaux-Arts, Lille, France. Photo credit: Reunion des Musées Nationaux/Art Resource, NY. © 2007 Artists Rights Society (ARS), New York/ADAGP, Paris.

> ❝ *Give me the right word and the right accent and I will move the world.*"
>
> *Joseph Conrad*

From ancient times to the present, the skill of persuasion has been highly valued. Consider:

- In ancient Greece, citizens accused of crimes would spend a tidy sum to hire skilled orators to argue their cases before a judge in hopes of gaining their freedom; today, skilled trial lawyers are still well paid, both for their knowledge of the law and for their persuasive skill.
- During the Super Bowl, advertisers spend thousands of dollars per second on TV commercials to persuade you to buy their products.
- It is estimated that, during the 2004 U.S. presidential election, George W. Bush spent more than $345 million to persuade the citizens of the United States to vote for him.

But you don't have to be an attorney, an advertiser, or a politician to draw on the highly valued skill of persuasion. Whether you're asking your roommate to help you clean the kitchen, seeking an extension on your term paper, or trying to convince the school board not to raise taxes, you too will need to wield the power to persuade.

In 333 BC, Aristotle was among the first to write a comprehensive guide to persuasion. His work, *The Rhetoric*, was used by other Greek and Roman writers who sought to summarize principles and strategies of persuasion. The chapter you

Chapter Objectives

After studying this chapter, you should be able to

- Define persuasion and describe four strategies for motivating listeners.
- Define attitudes, beliefs, and values and explain why a speaker should know which one he or she is targeting in a persuasive message.
- Define and provide examples of propositions of fact, value, and policy.
- Define credibility; analyze its three factors; and describe how to enhance initial, derived, and terminal credibility.

- Define and provide an example of inductive, deductive, and causal reasoning and reasoning by analogy.
- List and explain eight logical fallacies.
- Explain three ways to make emotional appeals in a persuasive presentation.
- List and explain four ways to organize a persuasive message.
- List and explain the five steps of the motivated sequence.
- Provide specific suggestions for adapting to receptive audiences, neutral audiences, and unreceptive audiences.

are reading draws on some of that more-than-2000-year-old classic advice and updates it with contemporary research. We first define persuasion, noting how it is similar to and different from informing others, and then describe how persuasion works by explaining how to motivate an audience. We'll also offer suggestions for developing a persuasive speech; present ideas to help you organize your persuasive message; and provide methods to help you move an audience with your credibility, use of logic, and use of emotional appeals. Finally, although we hope that all of the audiences you face are receptive to your persuasive speeches, we'll help you adapt your message not only to receptive audiences but also to those who are neutral or unreceptive.

PERSUASION DEFINED

Persuasion is the process of attempting to change or reinforce attitudes, beliefs, values, or behavior. When we persuade, we are inviting someone to modify or maintain the way he or she thinks, feels, or behaves.

In the previous chapter, we described strategies for informing others—presenting new information so that others will understand and remember what is communicated. Because informative speaking and persuasive speaking are related, we will build on the suggestions we offered for informing others. Like an informative presentation, a persuasive presentation needs to be well organized; to have a clear beginning, middle, and end; to use interesting supporting material; to have smooth transitions; and to be skillfully delivered. As a persuasive speaker, you will need to develop arguments supported with evidence. But in a persuasive presentation, the speaker invites the listener to make an explicit choice, rather than just offering information about the options. Also, when you persuade, you will do more than teach; you will ask your audience to respond thoughtfully to the information you present. Persuasive speakers intentionally try to change or reinforce their listeners' feelings, ideas, or behavior.

Coercive communication, unlike persuasive communication, takes away an individual's free choice. In the opening pages of this book we suggested that an effective communicator not only is understood and achieves his or her goal, but also is ethical. **Using force to achieve your goal is coercion,** not persuasion. **Using weapons, threats, and other unethical strategies may momentarily achieve what you want, but it certainly is not appropriate or ethical to use such means.** Efforts to persuade should be grounded in giving people options rather than forcing them to respond in a certain way. To be ethical, the persuader has an obligation to be honest and forthright in crafting messages.

Now that you have an understanding of what persuasion is and isn't, you undoubtedly have questions about how to begin to develop a persuasive message. You start your preparation for a persuasive presentation as you begin preparing for any

ETHICS AND COMMUNICATION
Hidden Agendas

David is trying to get business people to invest in the new Internet company he works for. He told a group of people at a Chamber of Commerce meeting that he wanted to inform them about some of the new and exciting ideas his company was developing. His real purpose, however, was to get people to invest in his company. Was it ethical of David not to tell his listeners that he really wanted them to become investors?

speech, by considering the needs, interests, and background of your audience. Ethically adapting to listeners is important in any communication situation, but is especially important when persuading others.

The audience-centered model of public speaking, introduced in Chapter 12 and shown again in Figure 16.1, can help you design and deliver a persuasive presentation just as it can an informative one. Audience analysis is at the heart of the speechmaking process; it affects every choice you make as a speaker. Before we talk about the nuts and bolts of developing a persuasive presentation, we'll describe the psychology of persuasion—what motivates an audience to respond to your persuasive appeal. Understanding how an audience is likely to respond to your message not only can help you to develop your presentation but also can help you be a smarter consumer of persuasive messages that come your way.

MOTIVATING YOUR AUDIENCE: THE PSYCHOLOGY OF PERSUASION

How does persuasion work? What makes you dial the phone to have a piping hot cheese-and-pepperoni pizza delivered to your door after watching a television commercial for pizza? What motivates people to do things that they wouldn't do unless they were persuaded to do so? Let's look at four explanations of why people respond to efforts to persuade.

FIGURE 16.1: An Audience-Centered Model of the Presentational Speaking Process

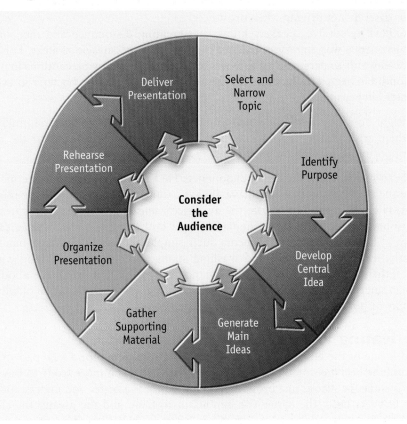

What can you do to motivate your audience to act in a certain way? You might try to create cognitive dissonance, appeal to their needs or fears, or promise a positive result if they follow your advice.

Motivating with Dissonance

When you are presented with information that is inconsistent with your current thinking or feelings, you experience a kind of mental discomfort called cognitive dissonance. For example, if you frequently drive while you are drowsy and then you learn that drowsy driving is a major contributor to traffic accidents, dissonance theory predicts that you will experience cognitive dissonance. The incompatibility between your behavior and your new knowledge will make you feel uncomfortable. And your discomfort may prompt you to change your thoughts, likes or dislikes, feelings, or behavior so that you can restore your comfort level or sense of balance—in this case, by not driving when drowsy.

Skilled persuasive speakers know that creating dissonance and then offering their listeners a way to restore balance is an effective persuasive strategy. For example, Sean wants to persuade his listeners to take greater safety precautions in preparing food. He begins by focusing on the health threat posed by bacteria in even the cleanest kitchens:

Verbal

> Right now, as you sit and listen to me speak about kitchen bacteria, millions of them are probably reproducing in your kitchen, simply waiting for the perfect opportunity to join you for lunch.[1]

Sean is deliberately creating dissonance. He knows that his audience members value their health and that they have always assumed their kitchens to be relatively clean. His next task is to restore the audience's sense of balance. He assures them that solutions exist and that "they are simple and you can start them as early as today."[2] If the audience implements such simple actions as washing hands frequently, using paper towels, and washing sponges and dishcloths along with the dishes, then they can resolve their dissonance and once again feel secure about their kitchen safety. The need to resolve dissonance provides one explanation of why people may respond to a speaker's attempts to persuade.

Motivating with Needs

Need is one of the best motivators. When you go shopping for a new pair of shoes because the heel has come off your old pair, you are much more likely to buy shoes than is someone who is just browsing. As a speaker, the better you understand what your listeners need, the better you can adapt to them and the greater the chances that you can persuade them to change an attitude, belief, or value or get them to take some action.

Adapt

The classic theory that outlines our basic needs was developed by Abraham Maslow.[3] If you've taken a psychology course, you have undoubtedly encountered this theory, which has important applications for persuasion. Maslow suggested that **a hierarchy of needs motivates the behavior of all people. Basic physiological needs (such as needs for food, water, and air) have to be satisfied before we attend to any other concern.** Once our physiological needs are met, we think next about safety needs. We need to feel safe and to be able to protect those we love. Comfortable and secure, we attend next to social needs, including the needs to be loved and to belong to a group. The next level of need is the need for self-esteem, or to think well of ourselves. Finally, if these first four levels of need have been satisfied, we may attend to the need for self-actualization, or achieving our highest potential. Figure 16.2 illustrates Maslow's classic five levels of needs, with the most basic at the bottom.

As a persuasive speaker, understanding and applying the hierarchy of needs helps you to adapt to your audience. One practical application is to do everything in your power to ensure that your audience's physiological needs are met. For example, if your listeners are sweating and fanning themselves, they are unlikely to be very interested in whether Bigfoot exists or whether the city should re-open River Park. If you can turn on the air-conditioning or fans, you will stand a greater chance to persuade them.

Another way in which you can apply the need hierarchy is to appeal to an audience's basic needs. For example, Mike knows that most of his audience members have young friends or family members who routinely ride school buses. As he begins to talk about the problem of safety hazards on school buses, he appeals to the audience's need to protect those they love. Similarly, at one time the U.S. Army used the recruiting slogan "Be all that you can be" to tap into the need for self-actualization, or achievement of one's highest potential.

FIGURE 16.2: Maslow's Hierarchy of Needs

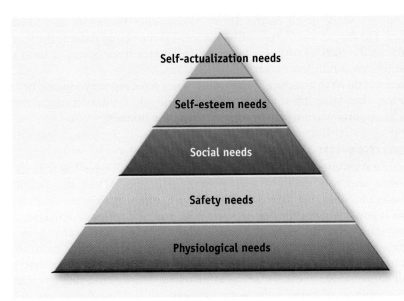

Motivating with Fear Appeals

Verbal

One of the oldest ways to convince people to change their minds or their behavior is by scaring them into compliance. Fear works. The appeal to fear takes the form of a verbal message—an "if-then" statement. *If* you don't do X, *then* awful things will happen to you. "If you don't get a flu shot, then you will probably catch the flu." "If you don't wear a seatbelt, then you are more likely to die in an automobile accident." "If you don't vote for me, then my opponent in this election will ruin the country." These are examples of fear appeals. A variety of research studies support the following strategies for effectively using fear as a motivator.[4]

- *A strong threat to a family member or someone whom members of the audience care about will often be more successful than a fear appeal directed at the audience members themselves.* Here's an example: "If your parents don't have a smoke alarm in their house, they are ten times more likely to die in a house fire."

- *The more respected the speaker, the greater the likelihood that the appeal to fear will work.* If you're trying to motivate your audience with fear, you may not have the credibility to convince them that the threat will harm them, but you could use the opinion of someone who is highly believable, competent, and trustworthy. Quoting a doctor if you're talking about a health issue, or an award-winning teacher if you're talking about an education issue, will probably be more effective than just stating your own opinion when trying to motivate with fear.

- *Fear appeals are more successful if you convince your audience that the threat is real and will affect them unless they take action.* In trying to convince her audience to eat less fat and exercise more, Doreen said, "An overly fatty diet coupled with lack of exercise is the primary cause of heart disease in the United States. Eat less fat and get more exercise, or you may die prematurely."

- *Increasing the intensity of a fear appeal increases the likelihood that the fear appeal will be effective; this is especially true if the listener can take the action the persuader is suggesting.*[5] Research findings suggest that the more fear and anxiety produced by a message, the more likely it is that the listener will respond. Strong, credible fear appeals seem to work better than mild fear appeals if evidence exists to support the claim.

Fear appeals work based on the theory of cognitive dissonance and Maslow's need theory. The fear aroused creates dissonance. Taking action reduces the fear and can meet a need—such as to live a long life, to be safe from harm, to have good friends, or to have a fulfilling career.

Of course, you have an ethical responsibility not to overstate your case or fabricate evidence when using a fear appeal. The persuader always has an ethical responsibility to be truthful when trying to arouse fear in the listener.

Motivating with Positive Appeals

Verbal

From a political candidate's TV ad: "Vote for me and you'll have lower taxes and higher wages, and your children will be better educated." Does this politician's promise have a familiar ring to it? It sounds like what most politicians offer—better days ahead if you'll vote for the person you see on your TV screen. Politicians, salespeople, and most other successful persuaders know that one way to change or reinforce your attitudes, beliefs, values, or behavior is to use a positive motivational appeal. Positive motivational appeals are verbal messages promising that good things will happen if the speaker's advice is followed. The key to using positive motivational appeals is to know what your listeners value. Most Americans value a comfortable, prosperous life; stimulating, exciting activity; a sense of accomplishment; world, community, and personal peace; and overall happiness and content-ment. In a persuasive presentation, you can motivate your listeners to respond to your message by describing what good, positive things will happen to them if they follow your advice.

SELECTING AND NARROWING YOUR PERSUASIVE TOPIC

With a basic understanding of how persuasion works, we're ready to focus on the specifics of developing a persuasive talk. As with any presentation, after you've thought about your audience, the next step is to select and narrow your topic. In a communication class, you may be given some latitude in selecting your topic. The best persuasive topic is one about which you feel strongly. If your listeners sense that you are committed to and excited about your topic, the chances are greater that they will be interested and involved as well. In most nonclassroom persuasive-speaking situations, you probably won't be asked to pick a persuasive topic; your topic will stem from your personal convictions. When you have the flexibility of selecting your own topic, the principle of appropriately adapting messages to others can guide your choice. Know the local, state, national, and international issues that interest and affect your listeners. Should the city build a new power plant? Should convicted child molesters be permitted to live in any neighborhood they like? Should the United States drop economic sanctions against Cuba? These and other controversial issues make excellent persuasive speech topics. Avoid frivolous topics, such as "why you should make your own potholders," when so many important issues challenge the world and your listeners.

Aware
Adapt

Pay particular attention to print and electronic media so that you remain in-formed about important issues of the day. Daily newspapers and national weekly news magazines such as *Time, Newsweek,* and *U.S. News & World Report* can sug-gest potential persuasive topics. Another interesting source of controversial issues is talk radio; both local and national programs can provide ideas for persuasive topics. Chat rooms on the Internet and home pages of print and broadcast media can also provide ideas for persuasive presentations.

After you have chosen a topic for your persuasive message, keeping up with the media can give you additional ideas for narrowing your topic and for finding inter-esting and appropriate supporting material for your presentation.

Verbal

IDENTIFYING YOUR PERSUASIVE PURPOSE

Once you have a topic for your persuasive presentation, your next step is to identify both a general and a specific purpose. The general purpose is easy—to persuade. The specific purpose requires more thought. The way you word your specific pur-pose will help you focus your message. When your general purpose is to persuade, your specific purpose will target your audience's attitudes, beliefs, values, or behav-ior. You can, as you recall from our definition of persuasion, try to *reinforce* atti-tudes, beliefs, values, and behavior the audience already holds; or you can try to *change* their attitudes, beliefs, values, or behavior. Reinforcing what an audience al-ready knows or thinks is relatively easy, but it is more of a challenge to change their minds. To increase your chances for success, it is important to be aware of the differ-ences among attitudes, beliefs, and values and to know which one you are targeting in your specific purpose statement. Let's examine the terms *attitude, belief,* and *value* in more detail.

Aware

An attitude is a learned predisposition to respond favorably or unfavorably to something. In other words, attitudes represent likes and dislikes. Because many attitudes are formed quickly and often with little evidence, they are relatively suscepti-ble to change if the person who holds them is exposed to additional evidence or gains more experience. For example, we may like a song we hear on the radio, then decide after we buy the single that we don't really like it so well after all. We may think that we don't like spinach, then discover that a friend's Florentine dip is deli-cious. As a persuasive speaker, you would probably have a good chance to succeed if your specific purpose targeted audience attitudes about the following issues:

- At the end of my presentation, the audience will favor making downtown streets one way to regulate traffic flow.
- At the end of my presentation, the audience will agree that the community needs a new elementary school.

A belief is the way in which we structure our perception of reality—our sense of what is true or false. Perhaps you believe that the earth is round, that God exists, and that your local bank is a financially sound institution. We base our beliefs on our own past experiences and on the experiences of other people. Beliefs are more difficult to alter than attitudes. If your audience were skeptical, you would need a great deal of evidence to succeed with these specific purpose statements:

- At the end of my presentation, the audience will testify that ghosts exist.
- At the end of my presentation, the audience will acknowledge that the increase in highway traffic deaths is related to the increase in the speed limit for large trucks.

A value is an enduring conception of right or wrong, good or bad. If you value something, you classify it as good or desirable and its opposite or its absence as bad or wrong. If you do not value something, you are indifferent to it. Values determine your behavior and goals. For example, because you value honesty, you refuse to cheat on a test. Because you value freedom, you support asylum for political refugees. Values are stable and deeply ingrained. Although it is not impossible to change the values of an audience, it is much more difficult than trying to change at-titudes or beliefs. Political and religious points of view are especially difficult to modify. If you were speaking to a right-wing conservative Republican audience, you would find it difficult to achieve these specific purposes:

- At the end of my presentation, the audience will campaign for the Democratic ticket in the upcoming election.
- At the end of my presentation, the audience will support the right of art muse-ums to show whatever kinds of art the museum directors deem appropriate.

Figure 16.3 illustrates that attitudes lie fairly close to the surface of our convic-tions, with values the most deeply ingrained in the center of the model. Be aware of whether your specific purpose aims to change or reinforce an attitude, a belief, a value, or a behavior, and be realistic in assessing what you will need to do in your presentation to effect change.

DEVELOPING YOUR CENTRAL IDEA AS A PERSUASIVE PROPOSITION

Verbal

After clarifying their specific purpose, most persuasive speakers find it useful to cast their central idea as **a proposition, or statement with which they want their audience to agree.** A well-worded proposition is a verbal message that can help you further fine-tune your persuasive objective and develop strategies for convincing your audi-ence that your proposition is true. There are three categories of propositions: propo-

FIGURE 16.3: Comparing Attitudes, Beliefs, and Values

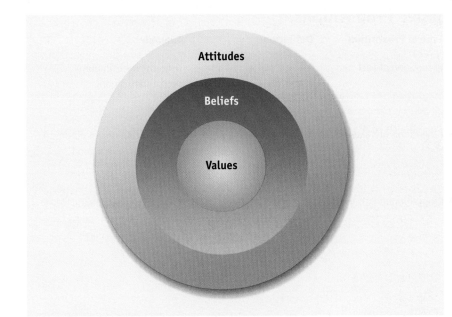

Attitudes—our likes and dislikes—are more likely to change than are our beliefs or values. Our sense of what is right and wrong—our values—are least likely to change.

sitions of fact, propositions of value, and propositions of policy. Let's examine each of these types in more detail.

Propositions of Fact

Propositions of fact are claims that something is or is not the case or that something did or did not happen. A speaker who used a proposition of fact as the central idea of a persuasive presentation would focus on changing or reinforcing an audience's beliefs—what they think is true. Propositions of fact can become central ideas for persuasive speeches. Here are some examples:

U.S. foreign embassies and consulates are vulnerable to terrorist attacks.

Nuclear power plants are safe and efficient.

People who were abused by their parents are more likely to abuse their own children.

A speech based on one of these propositions would need to include credible evidence to support the accuracy of the conclusion.

Propositions of Value

As the word *value* suggests, **propositions of value call for the listener to judge the worth or importance of something.** A simple example would be "Tattoos are beautiful." Other value propositions compare two ideas, things, or actions and suggest that one is better than the other. Here are two examples:

Small high schools are better than large high schools.

Rock music is better than classical music.

Recap
Persuasive Propositions:

Type of Proposition	Definition	Example
Proposition of Fact	A claim that something is or is not the case or that it did or did not happen	Asbestos exists in our elementary school.
Proposition of Value	A claim that calls for the listener to judge the worth or importance of something	Using calculators for elementary math is a good idea.
Proposition of Policy	A claim advocating a specific action to change a policy, procedure, or behavior	Casino gambling should be legalized in all states.

Propositions of Policy

The third type of proposition, **the proposition of policy, advocates a specific action—changing a regulation, procedure, or behavior.** Propositions of policy include the word *should*. Here are some examples:

All first-year college students should have their own laptop computers.

The Honors Program should have a full-time faculty coordinator.

The city should build a new public library.

The speaker who develops a proposition of policy is often likely to go one step beyond influencing an audience's attitudes, beliefs, and values, and urge them to take action.

With your specific purpose and central idea in hand, you are ready to move to the next stages in the presentational speaking process. In most cases, you can draw your main ideas from several *reasons* the persuasive proposition is true. Then you will be ready to begin gathering supporting material.

SUPPORTING YOUR PRESENTATION WITH CREDIBILITY, LOGIC, AND EMOTION

Aristotle defined *rhetoric* as the process of "discovering the available means of persuasion."[6] What are those "available means"? They are the various strategies you can use to support your message. Aristotle suggested three: (1) **emphasizing the credibility or ethical character of a speaker (ethos); (2) using logical arguments (logos); and (3) using emotional appeals to move an audience (pathos).**

Ethos: Establishing Your Credibility

If you were going to buy a new computer, to whom would you turn for advice? Perhaps you would consult your brother, the computer geek, or your roommate, the computer science major. Or you might seek advice from *Consumer Reports*, the monthly publication of studies of various consumer products. In other words, you would turn to a source that you consider knowledgeable, competent, and trustworthy—a source you think is credible.

Credibility is an audience's perception of a speaker's competence, trustworthiness, and dynamism. It is not something a speaker inherently possesses or lacks; rather, it is based on the listeners' attitude toward the speaker. Your listeners, not you, determine whether you have credibility.

Teachers and researchers have for centuries sought to understand the factors audiences consider in deciding whether a speaker is credible. Aristotle thought that a public speaker should be ethical, possess good character, display common sense, and be concerned for the well-being of his audience. Quintilian, a Roman teacher of public speaking, advised that a speaker should be "a good man speaking well." These ancient speculations about the elements that enhance a speaker's credibility have been generally supported by modern research.

One clear factor in credibility is **competence. A speaker should be informed, skilled, or knowledgeable about the subject he or she is discussing.** You will be more persuasive if you can convince your listeners that you know something about your topic. How? You can use verbal messages effectively by talking about relevant personal experience with the topic. If you have taken and enjoyed a cruise, you can tell your audience about the highlights of your trip. You can also cite evidence to support your ideas. Even if you have not taken a cruise yourself, you can be prepared with information about what a good value a cruise is—how much it costs and what is included, versus how much the same tour would cost if one were to travel by air and stay and eat in hotels.

A second factor in credibility is **trustworthiness. While delivering a speech, you need to convey honesty and sincerity to your audience.** You can't do this simply by saying, "Trust me." You have to earn trust. You can do so by demonstrating that you are interested in and experienced with your topic. Again, speaking from personal experience makes you seem a more trustworthy speaker. Conversely, having something to gain by persuading your audience may make you suspect in their eyes. That's why salespeople and politicians often lack credibility. If you do what they say, they will clearly benefit by earning sales commissions or being elected to public office.

A third factor in credibility is a speaker's **dynamism, or energy.** Dynamism is often projected through delivery. Applying the communication principle of effectively using and understanding nonverbal messages, a speaker who maintains eye

Bono uses his charismatic speaking style to help persuade his audience to support his cause.

contact, has enthusiastic vocal inflection, and moves and gestures purposefully is likely to be seen as dynamic. **Charisma is a form of dynamism. A charismatic speaker possesses charm, talent, magnetism, and other qualities that make the person attractive and energetic.** President Franklin Roosevelt and Diana, Princess of Wales, were considered charismatic speakers by many people.

A speaker has opportunities throughout a presentation to enhance his or her credibility. The first such opportunity results in **initial credibility. This is the impression of your credibility listeners have even before you begin speaking.** They grant you initial credibility based on such factors as your appearance and your credentials. Dressing appropriately and having a brief summary of your qualifications and accomplishments ready for the person who will introduce you are two strategies for enhancing your initial credibility.

The second credibility-building opportunity yields **derived credibility. This is the perception your audience forms as you deliver your presentation.** If you appropriately adapt your message to your audience, you will enhance your derived credibility. Specific strategies include establishing common ground with your audience, supporting your arguments with evidence, and presenting a well-organized message.

The last form of credibility, called **terminal credibility, is the perception of your credibility your listeners have when you finish your presentation.** A thoughtfully prepared and well-delivered conclusion can enhance your terminal credibility, as can maintaining eye contact through and even after your closing sentence. Also, apply the communication principle of listening and responding thoughtfully to others. Be prepared to answer questions after your presentation, regardless of whether a question-and-answer period is planned.

Nonverbal

Adapt

Logos: Using Evidence and Reasoning

In addition to being considered a credible speaker, you will gain influence with your audience if you can effectively use logically structured arguments supported with evidence. As we noted earlier, Aristotle called logical arguments *logos*, which, translated from Greek, means "the word." Using words effectively to communicate your arguments to your listeners is vital to persuading thoughtful and informed listeners. The goal is to provide logical proof for your arguments. **Proof consists of both evidence and reasoning. Evidence is another word for the illustrations, definitions,**

Recap
Enhancing Your Credibility

Enhancing Your Initial Credibility: Before You Speak
- Dress appropriately.
- Have a brief summary of your qualifications and accomplishments ready for the person who will introduce you.

Enhancing Your Derived Credibility: As You Speak
- Establish common ground with your audience.
- Support your arguments with evidence.
- Present a well-organized message.

Enhancing Your Terminal Credibility: After You Speak
- Prepare your conclusion, and deliver it well.
- Maintain eye contact through and even after your closing sentence.
- Be prepared to answer questions after your presentation.

statistics, and opinions that are your supporting material. **Reasoning is the process of drawing conclusions from your evidence.** There are three major ways to draw logical conclusions: inductively, deductively, and causally.

Inductive Reasoning

Reasoning that arrives at a general conclusion from specific instances or examples is known as inductive reasoning. You reason inductively when you claim that a conclusion is probably true because of specific evidence. For example, if you were giving a speech attempting to convince your audience that Hondas are reliable cars, you might use inductive reasoning to make your point. You have a 1994 Honda Civic that has 140,000 miles on it and has required little repair other than routine maintenance. Your brother has a Honda Accord and has driven it twice as long as any other car he has ever owned. Your mom just returned from a 3000-mile road trip in her Honda Odyssey minivan, which performed beautifully. Based on these specific examples, bolstered by statistics from many other Honda owners, you ask your audience to agree that your general conclusion is probable: Hondas are reliable cars.

Reasoning by analogy is a special type of inductive reasoning. An analogy demonstrates how an unfamiliar idea, thing, or situation is similar to something the audience already understands. If you develop an original analogy, rather than quote one you find in a printed source, you are reasoning inductively. Here's an example of reasoning by analogy: The new mandatory rear seatbelt laws that were enacted in Missouri saved lives; Kansas should also develop mandatory rear seatbelt laws. The key to arguing by analogy is to claim that the two things you are comparing (such as driving habits in Missouri and Kansas) are similar, so that your argument is a sound one. Here's another example: England has a relaxed policy toward violence being shown on television and has experienced no major rise in violent crimes; the United States should therefore relax its policy on showing violence on TV.

Verbal

Holocaust survivor, author, and human rights activist Elie Wiesel uses the rhetorical devices of evidence and reasoning to appeal to his audiences.

Deductive Reasoning

Reasoning from a general statement or principle to reach a specific conclusion is called deductive reasoning. Deductive reasoning can be structured as **a syllogism, a three-part argument that consists of a major premise, a minor premise, and a conclusion.** In a message in which you are attempting to convince your audience to vote for an upcoming school bond issue, your syllogism might look like this:

MAJOR PREMISE: Keeping schools in good repair extends the number of years that the buildings can be used.

MINOR PREMISE: The proposed school bond issue provides money for school repairs.

CONCLUSION: The proposed school bond issue will extend the number of years that we can use our current buildings.

Contemporary logicians note that when you reason deductively, your conclusion is certain rather than probable. The certainty of the conclusion rests primarily on the validity of the major premise and secondarily on the truth of the minor premise. If you can prove that keeping schools in good repair extends the useful life of the buildings and if it is true that the proposed bond issue provides money for school repairs, then your conclusion will be certain.

Causal Reasoning

You use causal reasoning when you relate two or more events in such a way as to conclude that one or more of the events probably caused the others. For example, you might argue that public inoculation programs during the twentieth century eradicated smallpox.

As we noted when we discussed cause-and-effect as a persuasive organizational strategy, there are two ways to structure a causal argument. One is by reasoning from cause to effect, or predicting a result from a known fact. You know that you have had an inch of rain over the last few days, so you predict that the aquifer level will rise. The inch of rain is the cause; the rising aquifer is the effect. The other way to structure a causal argument is by reasoning from a known effect to the cause. National Transportation Safety Board accident investigators reason from effect to cause when they reconstruct airplane wreckage to find clues to the cause of an air disaster.

The key to developing any causal argument is to be certain that a causal relationship actually exists between the two factors you are investigating. A few summers ago, a young science student was involved in a project involving counting chimney swifts in a given area just before sunset. He counted the most swifts on the Fourth of July. However, it would not have been valid to argue that fireworks (or watermelon or hot dogs or anything else connected with the Fourth of July) caused an increase in the number of chimney swifts seen in the area. The Fourth of July holiday and the bird count were not related by cause and effect.

Recap

Inductive, Deductive, and Causal Reasoning

Type of Reasoning	Reasoning begins with . . .	Reasoning ends with . . .	Conclusion is . . .	Example
Inductive	specific examples	a general conclusion	probable or not probable	Dell, Gateway, and IBM computers are all reliable. Therefore, PCs are reliable.
Deductive	a general statement	a specific conclusion	certain or not certain	All professors at this college have advanced degrees. Tom Bryson is a professor at this college. Therefore, Tom Bryson has an advanced degree.
Causal	something known	a speculation about causes or effects of what is known	likely or not likely	The number of people with under-graduate degrees has risen steadily since 1960. This increasing number has caused a glut in the job market for people with degrees.

Trying to establish a causal link where none exists is one type of **logical fallacy—false reasoning that occurs when someone attempts to persuade without adequate evidence or with arguments that are irrelevant or inappropriate.** To be a better-informed consumer, as well as a more ethical persuasive speaker, you should be aware of some of the following common logical fallacies.

Aware

Causal Fallacy

Making a faulty cause-and-effect connection between two things or events, such as trying to link the Fourth of July with the chimney swift count, is **a causal fallacy,** or, to use its Latin name, *post hoc, ergo propter hoc* ("after this; therefore, because of this"). Simply because one event follows another does not mean that the two are related.

Bandwagon Fallacy

"Jumping on the bandwagon" is a colloquial expression for thinking or doing something just because everybody else is. **Someone who argues that "everybody thinks that, so you should too" is using the bandwagon fallacy.** Speakers using the bandwagon fallacy often use the word *everybody:*

Everybody knows that taxes are too high.

Everybody agrees that the government should support a strong military.

Either-Or Fallacy

"Either we support the bond issue or we end up busing our students to another school district!" shouts Lupe in a moment of heated debate among the members of the school board. **This either-or fallacy oversimplifies the issue by offering only two choices and ignores the fact that there may be other solutions** to the district's problem of dilapidated buildings (for example, purchasing portable classroom buildings or drawing new attendance zones within the district).

Hasty Generalization

A person who tries to draw a conclusion from too little evidence or nonexistent evidence is making a hasty generalization. For example, one person's failing a math test does not necessarily mean that the test was too difficult or unfair.

Personal Attack

Making a personal attack on someone connected with an idea, rather than addressing the idea itself, is a logical fallacy. This approach is also known as an *ad hominem* argument, a Latin phrase that means "to the man." "The HMO bill is a bad idea because it was proposed by that crazy senator" is an example of a personal attack. Don't dismiss an idea solely because you have something against the person who presents it.

Red Herring

Someone who argues against an issue by bringing up irrelevant facts or arguments to distract others from the issue is using a red herring. This fallacy takes its name from the old trick of dragging a red herring across a trail to distract dogs who are following a scent. Speakers use a red herring when they want to distract an audience from certain issues. For example, a congressional representative who has been indicted for misuse of federal funds calls a press conference and spends most of the time talking about a colleague's sexual indiscretions.

Appeal to Misplaced Authority

When advertisers trot out baseball players to endorse breakfast cereal and movie stars to pitch credit cards, they are guilty of an **appeal to misplaced authority—using** someone without the appropriate credentials or expertise to endorse an idea or product. Although baseball players may know a great deal about the game of baseball, they are no more expert than most of us about cereal. Movie stars may be experts at acting but probably not in the field of personal finance.

Non Sequitur

If you argue that students should give blood because it is nearly time for final exams, you are guilty of **a non sequitur** (Latin for "it does not follow")—**your idea or conclusion does not logically follow from the previous idea or conclusion.**

Persuasive speakers who provide logical proof (evidence and reasoning) for their arguments and who avoid logical fallacies heighten their chances for success with their audience. But good speakers know that evidence and reasoning are not their only tools. Emotion is another powerful strategy for moving an audience to support a persuasive proposition.

Pathos: Using Emotion

People often make decisions based not on logic but on emotion. Advertisers know this. Think of the soft-drink commercials you see on television. There is little rational reason that people should spend any part of their food budget on soft drinks. They are "empty calories." So soft-drink advertisers turn instead to emotional appeals, striving to connect feelings of pleasure with their product. Smiling people, upbeat music, and good times are usually part of the formula for selling soft drinks.

One way to make an emotional appeal is with emotion-arousing verbal messages. Words such as *mother, flag, freedom,* and *slavery* trigger emotional responses in listeners. Patriotic slogans, such as "Remember the Alamo" and "Give me liberty, or give me death," are examples of phrases that have successfully aroused emotions in their listeners.

Verbal

Another way to appeal to emotions is by using concrete illustrations and descriptions. Although illustrations and descriptions are themselves types of evidence or supporting material, their impact is often emotional, as in the following example:

> Michelle Hutchinson carefully placed her three-year-old daughter into her child safety seat. She was certain that Dana was secure. Within minutes Michelle was involved in a minor accident, and the seat belt that was never designed to hold a child safety seat allowed the seat to lunge forward, crushing the three-year-old's skull on the dash. Dana died three days later. . . . [7]

Effective use of nonverbal messages can also appeal to an audience's emotions. Visual aids—pictures, slides, or video—can provide emotion-arousing images. A photograph of a dirty, ragged child alone in a big city can evoke sadness and pain. A video clip of an airplane crash can arouse fear and horror. A picture of a smiling baby makes most of us smile, too. As a speaker, you can use visual aids to evoke both positive and negative emotions.

When you use emotional appeals, you do have an obligation to be ethical and forthright. Making false claims, misusing evidence or images, or relying exclusively on emotion without any evidence or reasoning violates standards of ethical presentational speaking.

ORGANIZING YOUR PERSUASIVE MESSAGE

You already know that how you organize a presentation can have an impact on your listeners' response to your message. Some speakers gather stories, examples, facts, and statistics to achieve their persuasive goal and then develop an organizational structure for these materials. Other speakers organize the presentation first and then collect supporting material. In reality, the organization of your presentation usually emerges after you have done at least some initial research and thinking about both your message and your audience. An audience-centered speaker adapts the organizational structure of the presentation based on the needs, attitudes, beliefs, behaviors, and background of the audience. Most persuasive presentations are organized according to one of four strategies: problem and solution, cause and effect, refutation, or the motivated sequence—a special variation of the problem-and-solution format.

Adapt

Problem and Solution

Problem-and-solution organization is the most basic organizational pattern for a persuasive presentation. The problem-and-solution strategy works best when a problem can be clearly documented and a solution or solutions proposed to deal with the evils of the problem.

When you use problem-and-solution organization, apply the principle of appropriately adapting messages to others. If you are speaking to an apathetic audience or one that is not even aware that a problem exists, you can emphasize the problem portion of the message. If your audience is already aware of the problem, you can emphasize the solution or solutions. In either case, your challenge will be to provide ample evidence that your perception of the problem is accurate and reasonable. You'll also need to convince your listeners that the solution or solutions you advocate are the most appropriate ones to solve the problem.

Adapt

Note how Nicholas organizes his presentation, "The Death of Reading," in a problem-and-solution pattern:[8]

I. PROBLEM: Reading is a dying activity.
   A. Each year more than 500 courts hear arguments to ban books.
   B. Since 1990, more than 2000 libraries across America have closed.
   C. Leisure reading has decreased more than 50% since 1975.

II. SOLUTIONS:
   A. Teach children that reading as an activity has worth and beauty.
   B. Teach children that books in and of themselves only express ideas and should not be banned.
   C. Support programs such as "One City, One Book" that encourage community involvement and literary discussion.
   D. Give books as gifts.
   E. Allow others to see you read.

The persuasive presentation at the end of this chapter offers an example of a message organized by first stating the problem and then presenting some specific solutions.

Cause and Effect

A speaker who employs cause-and-effect organization can either identify a situation and then discuss the resulting effects (cause–effect) or present a situation and then explore its causes (effect–cause).

Regardless of which variation you choose, you should apply the fundamental principle of being aware of your communication with yourself and others. Specifically, you must analyze and then convince your listeners of the critical causal link. An effect may have more than one cause. For example, standardized test scores may be low in your state both because of low per-pupil expenditures and because of a lack of parental involvement in the schools. To argue that only one of the two factors causes the low test scores would not be accurate. It is also possible for two situations to coexist but not be causally related. Perhaps standardized test scores are indeed low in your state, and your state has a lottery. Both situations exist, but one does not cause the other. However, if two or more situations are causally related, a cause-and-effect strategy can work well for a persuasive presentation. Here is an example of a persuasive outline organized from cause to effect:[9]

Aware

I. CAUSE: The foster care system is in crisis.
   A. Since 1987, there has been a 90% increase in the number of children placed in foster care nationally.
   B. During that same time, there has been a 3% decrease in the number of licensed foster homes.

II. EFFECT: Children in foster care are at risk.
   A. Children in the foster care system are five times more likely to die as a result of abuse than children in the general population.
   B. 80% of federal prisoners spent time in the nation's foster care system as children.

Refutation

A third way to organize your efforts to persuade an audience is especially useful when you are facing an unreceptive audience—one that does not agree with your point of view or your specific proposition. **Refutation is an organizational strategy by which you identify objections to your proposition and then refute those objections with arguments and evidence.** You will be most likely to organize your persuasive message by refutation if you know your listeners' chief objections to your proposition. In fact, if you do not acknowledge such objections, the audience will probably think about them during your presentation anyway. Credible facts and statistics will generally be more effective than emotional arguments in supporting your points of refutation.

Suppose, for example, that you plan to speak to a group of junior high school teachers, advocating a school reconfiguration that would eliminate the junior high and send the teachers either to middle school or to high school. They would undoubtedly have some concerns about their own welfare and that of their students, as well as issues of loyalty to their present administrators. You could organize your presentation to this group according to those three issues. Your major points could be as follows:

I. The school reconfiguration will not jeopardize any of your jobs or programs.
II. The school reconfiguration will actually benefit students by requiring fewer changes in schools during their critical pre-adolescent years.
III. Principals and lead teachers will be reassigned at their same levels in the schools to which they will move.

Adapt

Utilizing refutation as your organizational strategy is one way to adapt your message to your audience.

The Motivated Sequence

The motivated sequence, devised by Alan Monroe, is a five-step organizational plan that integrates the problem-and-solution organizational method with principles that have been confirmed by research and practical experience.[10] The five steps involved are attention, need, satisfaction, visualization, and action.

Attention

Adapt

Your first task in applying the motivated sequence, and the first stage in appropriately adapting your message to others, is to get your listeners' attention. You already know attention-getting strategies for introductions: rhetorical questions, illustrations, startling facts or statistics, quotations, humorous stories, and references to historical or recent events. The attention step is, in essence, your application of one of these strategies.

Sherry begins her presentation about reforming sex offender registries with this attention-catching illustration:

> Maureen Kanka felt her neighborhood was like any other. She never knew danger lurked across the street from her house until her 7-year-old daughter, Megan, disappeared. Megan's body was later found dumped in a nearby park. A puppy had been used to lure Megan into a neighbor's house where she was raped, strangled, and suffocated.[11]

Need

After getting your audience's attention, establish why your topic, problem, or issue should concern your listeners. Tell your audience about the problem. Adapt your message to them by convincing them that the problem affects them directly. Argue that there is a need for change. During the need step (which corresponds to the problem step in a problem-and-solution strategy), you should develop logical arguments backed by evidence. It's during the need step that you create dissonance or use a credible fear appeal to motivate listeners to respond to your solution. Sherry develops her need step as follows:

> State and local authorities are dismally failing to keep track of convicted child molesters, meaning that thousands of perpetrators like Megan's killer are unidentified, putting millions of children at risk. Problems in sex offender registries are allowing thousands of sexual predators to roam unchecked.[12]

Satisfaction

After you explain and document a need or problem, identify your plan (or solution) and explain how it will satisfy the need. You need not go into painstaking detail. Present enough information so that your listeners have a general understanding of how the problem may be solved. Sherry suggests two legislative solutions in her satisfaction step:

> At the government level, federal coordination is a must. A truly national registry needs to be created. However, a national registry alone will not fix the problem. Thus, a second piece of legislation should put coded notations onto sex offenders' driver's licenses and require the licenses to be presented for annual routine automobile registration. Furthermore, license bureaus would be required to contact police when offenders change addresses.[13]

Verbal

Visualization

Now you need to give your audience a sense of what it would be like if your solution were adopted or, conversely, if it were not adopted. **Visualization—a word picture of the future**—applies the fundamental principle of effectively using and understanding verbal messages. An appropriate presentation aid can also help your audience visualize the implications of your persuasive message. **With a positive visualization approach, you paint a rosy picture of how wonderful the future will be if your satisfaction step is implemented. With a negative visualization approach, you paint a bleak picture of how terrible the future will be if nothing is done; you use a fear appeal to motivate your listeners to do what you suggest to avoid further problems.** Or you might combine both approaches: The problem will be solved if your solution is adopted, but things will get increasingly worse if it is not. An ethical speaker takes care to ensure that the positive or negative visualization message is accurate and not overstated. Sherry offers negative visualization to drive home the urgency of her message:

In the final step of Monroe's motivated sequence, the speaker calls for the audience to take action.

It is too late to save Megan Kanka. Her parents will never again be met by the joy of her smile and the contributions she could have made to our society will never be fulfilled.[14]

Action

The final step of the motivated sequence requires that you adapt your solution to your audience. Offer them some specific action they can take to solve the problem you have discussed. Identify exactly what you want them to do. Give them simple, clear, easy-to-follow steps. Provide a phone number to call for more information, an address to which they can write a letter of support, or a petition to sign at the end of your presentation. Sherry suggests a specific action step her listeners can take to solve the problem she has identified:

Adapt

> On a personal level, we can help police follow up on offenders missing from the registry by being on guard and watching for signs of abuse among children in our families and neighborhoods.[15]

The action step is your conclusion. You remind your audience of the problem (need step), give them the solution (satisfaction step), and remind them what great things will happen if they follow your advice (positive visualization) or what bad things will happen if they don't do what you say (negative visualization). Finally, unless they are unreceptive to your ideas, tell them what they need to do next (action step).

Adapt

You can adapt the motivated sequence to your topic and the needs of your audience. For example, if you are speaking to a knowledgeable, receptive audience, you do not need to spend a great deal of time on the need step. Your listeners already know that the need is serious. They may, however, feel helpless to do anything about it. Clearly, you would want to emphasize the satisfaction and action steps.

On the other hand, if you are speaking to a neutral or apathetic audience, you will need to spend time getting their attention and proving that a problem exists, that it is significant, and that it affects them personally. You will emphasize the attention, need, and visualization steps. In the final section of this chapter, we will offer additional strategies for persuading receptive, unreceptive, and neutral audiences.

Is there one best way to organize a persuasive message? The answer is no. The organizational strategy you select must depend on your audience, your message, and your desired objective. What is important is that you remember that your decision can have a major effect on your listeners' response to your message.

HOW TO ADAPT IDEAS TO PEOPLE AND PEOPLE TO IDEAS

Donald C. Bryant's definition of rhetoric emphasizes the principle of appropriately adapting a message to an audience: "Rhetoric" he said, "is the process of adjusting ideas to people and people to ideas."[16] And with this thought we've come full circle in the process of developing a persuasive message. As we have emphasized throughout our discussion of presentational speaking, analyzing your audience and adapting to them is at the heart of the speech-making process; it's one of the fundamental communication principles for a lifetime. In a persuasive presentation, that adaptation begins with identifying your specific purpose and understanding whether you are trying to change or reinforce attitudes, beliefs, values, or behavior. It continues with your selection of an organizational strategy. For example, if your audience members are unreceptive toward your ideas, you might choose to organize your speech by refutation, addressing the audience's objections head on. Both research studies and experienced speakers can offer other useful suggestions to help you adapt to your audience. Let's look at some specific strategies for persuading receptive, neutral, and unreceptive audiences.

The Receptive Audience

It is usually a pleasure to address an audience that already supports you and your message. You can explore your ideas in depth and can be fairly certain of a successful appeal to action if your audience is receptive.

Recap

Organizational Patterns for Persuasive Presentations

Organizational Pattern	Definition	Example
Problem and Solution	Organization by discussing a problem and then its various solutions	I. Tooth decay threatens children's dental health. II. Inexpensive, easy to apply sealants make teeth resistant to decay.
Cause and Effect	Organization by discussing a situation and its causes or a situation and its effects	I. Most HMOs refuse to pay for treatment they deem "experimental." II. Patients die who might have been saved by "experimental" treatment.
Refutation	Organization according to objections your listeners may have to your ideas and arguments	I. Although you may think that college football players get too much financial aid, they work hard for it, spending 20 to 30 hours a week in training and on the field. II. Although you may think that college football players don't spend much time on academics, they have 2 hours of enforced study every weeknight.
Motivated Sequence	Alan H. Monroe's five-step plan for organizing a persuasive message; the five steps are attention, need, satisfaction, visualization, and action	I. Attention: "An apple a day keeps the doctor busy." What has happened to the old adage? Why has it changed? II. Need: Pesticides are poisoning our fresh fruits and vegetables. III. Satisfaction: Growers must seek environmentally friendly alternatives to pesticides. IV. Visualization: Remember the apple poisoned by Snow White's wicked stepmother? You may be feeding such apples to your own children. V. Action: Buy fruits and vegetables raised organically.

Adapt

One suggestion that may help you make the most of such a speaking opportunity is to identify with your audience. Emphasize your similarities and common interests. The introduction of your message may be a good place in which to do this.

Another suggestion is to be overt in stating your speaking objective, telling your audience exactly what you want them to do, and asking audience members for an immediate show of support. If your audience is already receptive, you need not worry that being overt will antagonize them. Rather, it will give you more time to rouse them to passionate commitment and action.

A third suggestion for persuading a receptive audience is to use emotional appeals. If your audience already supports your position, you can spend less time providing detailed evidence. Rather, you can focus on moving your receptive audience to action with strong emotional appeals.

The Neutral Audience

Many audiences will fall somewhere between being wildly enthusiastic and being hostile. They will simply be neutral. Their neutrality may take the form of indifference: They know about the topic or issue, but they don't see how it affects them or they can't make up their minds about it. Or their neutrality may take the form of ignorance: They just don't know much about the topic. Regardless of whether your neutral audience is indifferent or ignorant, your challenge is to get them interested in your message.

One way to get a neutral audience interested is to "hook" them with an especially engaging introduction or attention step. Brian provided such an introduction to his persuasive presentation about the number of Americans who live with chronic pain:

"I can't shower because the water feels like molten lava. Every time someone turns on a ceiling fan, it feels like razor blades are cutting through my legs. I'm dying." Meet David Bogan, financial advisor from Deptford, New Jersey; Porsche, boat, and homeowner; and a victim of a debilitating car accident that has not only rendered him two years of chronic leg pain, but a fall from the pinnacle of success. Bogan has nothing now. Life to him, life with searing pain, is a worthless tease of agony and distress.[17]

Another strategy for persuading neutral audiences is to refer to universal beliefs or common concerns. Protecting the environment and having access to good health care might fall in the latter category.

A third strategy for neutral audiences is to show how the topic affects not only them but also people they care about. For example, parents will be interested in issues and policies that affect their children.

Finally, be realistic about what you can accomplish. People who are neutral at the beginning of your presentation are unlikely to change in just a few minutes to having strong opinions. Persuasion is unlikely to occur all at once or after one presentation of arguments and issues.

The Unreceptive Audience

One of your biggest challenges as a speaker is to persuade audience members who are unreceptive toward you or your message. If they are unreceptive toward you personally, your job is to seek ways to enhance your credibility and persuade them to listen to you. If they are unreceptive toward your point of view, several strategies may help.

First, don't immediately announce your persuasive purpose. Immediately and explicitly telling your listeners that you plan to change their minds can make them defensive. Focus instead on areas of agreement. As you would with a

neutral audience, refer to universal beliefs and concerns. Instead of saying to your unreceptive audience, "I'm here this morning to convince you that we should raise city taxes," you might say, "I think we can agree that we have an important common goal: achieving the best quality of life possible here in our small community."

Second, if you think your audience may be unreceptive, advance your strongest arguments first. This strategy is the principle of primacy. If you save your best argument for last (the recency principle), your audience may already have stopped listening.

Third, acknowledge the opposing points of view that members of your audience may hold. Summarize the reasons they may oppose your point of view; then cite evidence and use arguments to refute the opposition and support your conclusion. In speaking to students seeking to hold down tuition costs, a dean might say, "I am aware that many of you struggle to pay for your education. You work nights, take out loans, and live frugally." Then the dean could go on to identify how the university could provide additional financial assistance to students.

Finally, as with a neutral audience, don't expect a major shift in attitude from an unreceptive audience. Set a realistic goal. It may be enough for an 8- to 10-minute presentation just to have your listeners hear you out and at least think about some of your arguments.

Sample Persuasive Presentation

William Stephens
Sheridan College

Cruisin' Out of Control[18]

Each year more than twelve million vacationers pack their bags, head for ocean ports, and embark on cruises. We love the sumptuous banquets, the impeccable service, and especially the pristine scenery. Unfortunately, as the October 2001 *Natural Life* reported, the trips we take are "endangering the very ecosystems [we're] so keen to observe." According to Ross Klein's book *Cruise Ship Blues,* pollution by hundreds of luxury liners sailing the seas is fouling the world's oceans and beaches, destroying vast food supplies on which we depend, threatening endangered species, and spreading deadly diseases.

Today we'll expose the dirty underside of the cruise ship industry, explore reasons these liners continue to pollute our oceans and coastlines, and examine some steps we must take to remedy this shameful situation. Think of a cruise ship—the largest of which carry 5,000 passengers—as a floating city. Each day people shower and flush toilets; crews launder tons of linens; staffs prepare 20,000 meals and dispose of the scraps; photo labs, dry cleaners, and beauty parlors use and toss tanks of toxic chemicals. At the same time, clean-up crews collect countless plastic containers, cardboard boxes, batteries, burned-out fluorescent and mercury vapor light bulbs, and medical wastes. We may assume that this mass of toxic trash is stored in holding bins and processed when the vessels return to port. But according to Oceana, an environmental protection group, we'd be wrong. Why? As the group stated in a February 1, 2003, article, "unlike cities . . . cruise ships are exempt from the . . . Clean Water Act." That means they are virtually free to dump these wastes and pollute at will. And pollute they do! In his book, Klein estimates that each day a large cruise ship produces 500,000 gallons of wastewater and 50,000 gallons of sewage. Ships may discharge gray water from showers, laundry, and dishwashing virtually anywhere. The Environmental Protection Agency discovered that some gray water actually had "higher levels of disease-causing bacteria than raw sewage." The reason? Cruise ships often combine chemical wastes and sewage with the gray water to circumvent regulations about dumping the most harmful products.

William captures the attention of his listeners with a startling statistic about the number of people who go on cruises annually. His use of the first person ("we") helps him establish common ground with his listeners.

William previews his speech.

William's analogy of a cruise ship as "a floating city" helps listeners comprehend the daily waste that such a ship produces.

In May 2002, the Ocean Conservancy reported that because cruise ships use less water per flush, sewage on cruise ships is more concentrated than that from cities. An October 2003 report jointly published by Blue Water Network and Ocean Advocates confirmed that more than 98% of cruise ships discharge effluents that would be illegal on land. The Conservancy reveals that ballast water, used to stabilize the ship and control its buoyancy, poses another problem. Ships can suck up to thirty tanker trucks of ballast, including marine plants and animals, transport this biological soup thousands of miles, and discharge it, releasing non-native plants and animals to compete with and harm local species. Ballast water also carries diseases like cholera into clean areas.

Every day a cruise ship produces seven tons of garbage and solid waste, which workers often dump directly into the ocean. The damages from such practices are legion. First, according to the Smithsonian Institution's *Ocean Planet,* the polluted coastal water destroys shellfish beds and contaminates oysters, clams, and lobsters. Our next seafood platter may be palatable but poisonous. Second, Smithsonian says the sewage-polluted waters carry viral hepatitis, cholera, typhoid fever, and intestinal diseases. In one recent year, 2,400 United States beaches were temporarily closed because of bacteria. Unfortunately, some coastal states do not even monitor the water quality, and no federal laws require notifying the public of the pollution. Third, *Americas* of July/August 2003 explains that the raw sewage promotes massive growth of algae, which rob the water of oxygen and thus kill fish and other marine life. Recently such a huge "dead zone" has developed in the Gulf of Mexico. In addition, Oceana confirms that sewage has destroyed almost 90% of Caribbean coral reefs. Fourth, endangered species are succumbing to cruise ship pollution. For example, the *Anchorage Daily News* of July 22, 2001, reports that such pollutants are killing orcas, or killer whales, in Alaskan waters. In 2000, the orcas monitored were some of the most contaminated marine mammals ever measured. Some contained more than 500 times the level of contaminants considered safe.

William turns next to the harm—the effects—caused by the pollution he has documented.

How has such a devastating situation evolved? A number of factors have come together to create the disaster. First, laws governing the dumping of waste are inadequate. *Americas* of July/August 2003 reports that international laws are largely non-existent. U.S. laws are weak and applicable only to a narrow band of water along the U.S. coasts. For example, cruise ships may legally dump treated sewage 3 miles off the U.S. coast, but the definition of "treated" is so vague that ships often get away with dumping untreated sewage anywhere. Beyond 12 miles, ships can legally discharge raw sewage, which tides return to soil our shores. Second, the July 12, 2001, *Christian Science Monitor* reveals that most cruise lines register their fleets in foreign countries, exempting themselves from most U.S. laws and taxes. Such avoidance means that you and I, not the polluters, pay the bill for coastal clean-up.

Notice the use of a rhetorical question to provide a transition into William's next main idea.

Third, cruise ships openly violate the few laws and voluntary agreements that supposedly regulate them. One of the worst is Royal Caribbean Cruise Lines. Save Our Shores Foundation reports that this giant company's claim to be pro-environment is only a public relations ploy. In reality the line has been fined more than $30 million for illegally discharging oil, garbage, and sewage—and then falsifying its records as a cover-up. Royal Caribbean merely writes off these fines as business expenses and continues to pollute. And because so many regulations are non-binding agreements called Memoranda of Understanding, the October 2003 report *The Cruise Industry and Environmental History and Practice* tells us that the cruise lines feel free to violate them, claiming they are not breaking any laws but merely breaking their word. Rarely are violating ships caught. In fact, companies give financial bonuses to officers who routinely dump their wastes to save disposal and water treatment costs and so return from cruises under budget. Fourth, according to the General Accounting Office, the ships get away with illegal dumping because our Coast Guard, the agency responsible for monitoring compliance and conducting inspections, is so hopelessly over-extended that it can't do an adequate job. It uses less than 1 percent of its resources to monitor cruise ships. In addition, the Guard often schedules its inspections, allowing ships time to conceal illegal activities and falsify logs.

Unfortunately, without extensive reform, the situation will get worse as cruise ships become bigger and more numerous. *The New York Times* of February 1, 2004, reports that the *Queen Mary 2* completed its maiden voyage on January 26. As long as the Empire State Building is high and twenty-three stories tall, the ship is the largest ocean liner yet built. But it won't hold that title for long. *CNN* of January 26, 2004, tells us that Royal Caribbean has ordered an even larger cruise ship scheduled for delivery in two years. *Americas* estimates that in the next 7 years the cruise business will double. Oceana reports that between 2001 and 2005 cruise lines expect to add 36 new ships, increasing the industry's capacity by 45%. What will our coastal waters be like then? Studies published by Bluewater Network and Ocean Advocates in October 2003 reveal that some ship-polluted Alaskan waters already have fecal bacteria levels 100,000 times the allowable standards.

William uses negative visualization of the future as larger and larger cruise ships are launched.

So what can we do to remedy this ever-growing threat? Obviously the government must replace the non-binding Memoranda of Understanding with much stricter regulations about cruise ship discharges, especially raw sewage. The *Congressional Record* of April 2, 2004, tells us that Representative Sam Farr of California has just introduced the "Clean Cruise Ship Act of 2004," which closes some of the loopholes in federal law that have allowed cruise lines to escape prosecution for some discharges of polluted water. If it can survive the expected powerful lobbying from the cruise industry, its impact could be significant. The bill requires cruise ships operating in U.S. waters to install the latest technology for treating emissions. Some devices, now available and reasonably priced, leave water cleaner than the natural ocean. Oceana estimates that companies could equip their ships with these devices for about $1.50 per passenger per day — about the price of a soft drink.

Another rhetorical question serves as a transition to the satisfaction step of the presentation.

In addition, Congress must extend the Coast Guard's authority randomly to inspect the cruise ships and their logs. Of course, this extension means that the Guard must increase its budget and employ more inspectors. By levying stiffer fines for the violations, Congress can fund these additional services. You and I also have a part to play. As most of us will someday take a cruise, we must make sure we support responsible cruise lines, not those that repeatedly violate existing laws. In addition, we should support those few cruise lines actually registered in the United States who pay taxes to finance the monitoring and maintenance of coastal waters. According to a personal correspondence from Ross Klein on February 16, 2004, those are Cruise West, Glacier Bay, and American Safari. On board, we should watch for illegal dumping. We can videotape violations and even earn rewards for reporting violators. The *Juneau Empire* carried the story of an engineer who did just that. He reported a Holland American ship for dumping polluted bilge water in Alaska's Inside Passage and earned a half million dollar reward for his vigilance. As U.S. citizens, who comprise 82% of cruise passengers, we can pressure the cruise lines to clean up their act.

William includes himself and his listeners as potential cruise ship passengers who can and should take action. "This concerns you" is his underlying message.

Today we've exposed the dirty underside of the cruise ship industry, explored some reasons this nasty situation has developed, and finally examined several steps we must take to remedy this dangerous situation. For too long we've allowed the cruise ship industry to make their fortunes at the expense of our environment. It's time we told the cruise lines to shape up or ship out.

Finally, William summarizes his main points as he concludes his presentation.

SUMMARY

Persuasion is the process of attempting to change or reinforce attitudes, beliefs, values, or behaviors. Several theories suggest how persuasion works—how listeners may be motivated to respond to a persuasive message. Cognitive dissonance is a sense of mental disorganization or imbalance that arises when new information conflicts with previously organized thought patterns. Cognitive dissonance may prompt a person to change attitudes, beliefs, values, or behavior. Maslow's classic hierarchy of needs is another approach that attempts to explain why people may be motivated to respond to persuasive appeals to various levels of need. Both fear appeals and positive motivational appeals can also motivate listeners to respond to your persuasive message.

Preparing and presenting a persuasive message require the same general approach as preparing any other kind of presentation. When you have a choice of persuasive topics, select a topic that is of interest to you and your listeners. Your specific purpose will target your audience's attitudes, beliefs, values, or behavior. Attitudes are learned predispositions to respond favorably or unfavorably toward something. A belief is one's sense of what is true or false. Values are enduring conceptions of right or wrong, good or bad. Of the three, attitudes are most susceptible to change; values are least likely to change. After clarifying your specific purpose, you can word your central idea as a proposition of fact, value, or policy.

Ways to organize your persuasive message include problem and solution, cause and effect, refutation, and the motivated sequence. The motivated sequence includes five steps: attention, need, satisfaction, visualization, and action.

A key to persuading others is to establish your credibility as a speaker. Credibility is an audience's perception of a speaker's competence, trustworthiness, and dynamism. Enhancing your initial credibility (what you do before you speak), your derived credibility (what you do during your presentation), and your terminal credibility (what you do after your presentation) will help you improve your overall credibility as a presentational speaker.

Reasoning, the process of drawing a conclusion from evidence, is integral to the persuasive process. The three primary types of reasoning are inductive, deductive, and causal. You can also reason by analogy. You can be an effective and ethical persuader by avoiding reasoning fallacies such as the causal fallacy, the bandwagon fallacy, the either-or fallacy, hasty generalization, personal attack, red herring, appeals to misplaced authority, and non sequiturs.

In addition to persuading others because of who you are (ethos) or how well you structure your logical arguments (logos), you can also move an audience to respond by using emotional appeals (pathos).

Finally, be prepared to adapt your persuasive messages to receptive, neutral, and unreceptive audiences. Throughout the persuasive speaking process, being aware of your messages and others' messages, effectively using verbal and nonverbal messages, listening and responding to your audience, and adapting to your listeners can enhance your skill as a persuasive speaker.

DISCUSSION AND REVIEW

1. Where might you turn if you needed ideas for a topic for a persuasive presentation?

2. Define attitudes, beliefs, and values. Why is it important that a persuasive speaker know which one he or she is targeting in a persuasive presentation?

3. What is a proposition of fact? Give one original example.

4. What is a proposition of value? Give one original example.

5. What is a proposition of policy? Give one original example.

6. List and explain four ways to organize a persuasive presentation.

7. When would you be most likely to organize a presentation by refutation?

8. List and explain the five steps of the motivated sequence.

9. What is credibility?

10. Define initial, derived, and terminal credibility, and explain how to enhance each one.

11. Define and provide an example of inductive reasoning.

12. How is reasoning by analogy different from using an analogy as supporting material?

13. Define and provide an example of deductive reasoning.

14. Define and provide an example of causal reasoning.

15. List and explain eight logical fallacies.

16. How can you appeal to your listeners' emotions in a persuasive presentation?

17. What is cognitive dissonance? How can you apply the theory in a persuasive presentation?

18. List and explain the five levels of Maslow's hierarchy of needs. How can you apply the theory in a persuasive presentation?

19. Provide specific suggestions for adapting to receptive audiences, neutral audiences, and unreceptive audiences.

PUTTING PRINCIPLES INTO PRACTICE

1. Watch a C-SPAN, CNN, or network news broadcast of a politician arguing for or against a particular proposition. Decide whether it is a proposition of fact, value, or policy. Identify the organizational pattern and the persuasive strategies the speaker uses.

2. Identify three nationally or internationally known speakers whom you consider to be credible. Analyze why these speakers are credible, according to the three components of credibility.

3. Identify the logical fallacy in each of the following arguments:

   a. We must raise taxes to finance the construction of new streets. Otherwise, we will have to rely on four-wheel-drive vehicles to get around.

   b. Breaking that mirror this morning was the reason I did so poorly on my history test.

   c. Everybody knows that you can't get a decent summer job around here.

   d. You should be concerned about your grade in that class because your new part-time job pays well.

   e. Jane grew up in a state that spends less money on education than any state in the United States; she could not possibly have any useful ideas about how to improve our children's test scores on standardized tests.

4. Develop a specific purpose statement and central idea for a persuasive message. Describe strategies you would use if you were to give this presentation to a receptive audience. Identify strategies you would use if you were to give this presentation to a neutral audience. Finally, suggest strategies you would use if you were to give this presentation to an unreceptive audience.

17

Presenting with Technology

By Jennifer Kammeyer
Instructor, San Francisco State University
Communication Coach, Technology and Venture Capital Industries
www.jenniferkammeyer.com

chapter outline

Courtesy of BigStock®

Every day in classrooms and conference rooms around the world people communicate with each other using presentation technology. Sometimes the technology improves communication, sometimes it does not. Whether it helps or hinders is not random. Technology helps when it complements the speaker and it hinders when it takes over or distracts the audience. This chapter is designed to help you improve your communication when using presentation technology. It teaches a method of creating and delivering presentations based on research regarding what helps audiences learn the material being presented.

This chapter will explain why visuals enhance communication and what research has demonstrated regarding using PowerPoint in the classroom. To help you improve your speeches using PowerPoint or Keynote, this chapter then gives you general principles and specific suggestions for using presentation technology effectively.

Chapter Objectives

After studying this chapter, you will be able to

- Explain the purpose of speaking to inform.
- Understand the visual nature of communication in our culture.
- Explain the results of research on presentation effectiveness.
- List and define the multimedia learning principles.
- List and define the Five Quick Guides for effective presentations.
- Create a story before creating a presentation.
- Apply basics of design elements and principles to presentations.
- Create an effective multimedia presentation.

COMMUNICATING IN A VISUAL CULTURE

PowerPoint, the most popular presentation aid technology, is used over 1.25 million times per hour across the world (Mahin, 2004). It is used for meetings in industry, for lectures in academia, and it is taught in 79% of basic communication courses in colleges in the U.S. (Morreale, Hugenberg, & Worley, 2006). Yet, the use of PowerPoint, or any computer-generated slides, is a controversial topic with some people because it is often used poorly and ineffectively.

PowerPoint is used often because we live in a time when technology is prevalent and visual information is common. Sixty-two percent of all Americans have used their mobile device for accessing digital data and tools, such as texting, taking pictures, and recording or watching a video (Horrigan, 2008). Plus, in just a few years time, contents of the web have transitioned from primarily text to include many visuals (Madden, 2007). This current technical and visual time period necessitates different communication skills than were required a decade ago. In the area of public speaking, the difference includes audience expectations that visuals are an integral part of speeches (Cyphert, 2007). Just as consumers expect to see their news with a visual component, they expect to see a visual component in public speeches, be that in a business meeting or within the classroom.

Presentation killers   Courtesy of BigStock®

In addition to being a social norm in a visual society, a visual component in public speeches grabs attention and helps audiences remember content. Researchers have found that when a speech does not include a visual aid, the audience recalls 70% of the information three hours after the speech and only 10% of the information three days later; however, when the message is delivered in a speech with visual aids, the recall after three hours is 85% and after three days it is 65% (Griffin, 2006).

RESEARCH ON PRESENTATION EFFECTIVENESS

Psychologists have shown that humans can only learn so much at once (Miller, 1956), that the brain processes information through both visual and verbal channels (Paivio, 1986, 2006), and that learning is greater when information is communicated in a multimodal fashion (Mayer, 1991, 1992, 2005). This is important for slide presentations because the audience listens to a speaker and reads slides simultaneously, using both channels to learn. Over the decades, many scholars have researched the effectiveness of using slide presentations to teach. Three overall themes emerge in the existing research on computer-generated slides.

1. Students prefer the use of PowerPoint in the classroom.
2. The general use of PowerPoint does not hinder, but does not necessarily improve learning outcomes.
3. By manipulating slide design elements, audience satisfaction and learning outcomes can improve.

First, several studies of computer-generated slide use in the classroom show that students prefer it, believe it enhances learning, and that it improves instructor credibility (Atkins-Sayre, et al., 1998; Blokzijil & Naeff, 2004; Smith & Woody, 2000; Szabo & Hastings, 2000). This means that students would rather have a teacher use slides then not use them and that if a teacher uses slides, the students tend to think more highly of that instructor. It also means that students think they learn better when slide presentations are used along with lectures.

Second, much of the research on slides has yet to demonstrate improved learning, even though adding PowerPoint did not harm learning outcomes (Levasseur & Sawyer, 2006). Many studies show that adding computer-generated slides in lectures resulted in students learning just the same as when the instructor lectured or used the white board. The most likely reason for this is that the slides were not designed or delivered effectively.

Third, studies that specifically manipulate slide elements show that both satisfaction and learning can increase (Alley & Neeley, 2005; Alley, et al., 2006; Apperson, et al., 2008; Bartsch & Cobern, 2003; Blokzijl & Naeff, 2004; Bradshaw, 2003; Earnest, 2003; Kammeyer, 2008; Mackiewicz, 2007). That means if slides are designed in a specific way that learning can increase. The common thread in these studies is that simpler slides are better. There are seven pieces of slide presentation advice from these studies.

1. Use a single complete sentence and a supporting visual on each slide (Alley and Neeley 2005; Alley, et al., 2006).
2. Do not add irrelevant pictures (Bartsch and Cobern 2003).
3. Do not add extras that interfere, such as colored backgrounds (Bradshaw 2003).

4. Use modest slide layouts with little added special effects (Blokzijl and Naeff 2004).

5. Use 2D instead of 3D graphs with cool colors (blues, greens) and high contrast with white or black background (Mackiewicz, 2007-1).

6. Use **Gill Sans** and **Souvenir Lt.** fonts. They are comfortable-to-read and are perceived as professional and interesting (Mackiewicz, 2007-2).

7. Create presentation based on a story using slides with pictures, not bullet points, and verbally explain slides to maximize learning (Kammeyer, 2008).

Courtesy of BigStock®

Once we understand how manipulating slide design can increase learning, the next step is to learn how to design and deliver effective slides. To create multimedia presentations that can increase audiences' learning: (1) follow multimedia learning principles, (2) develop a story, (3) design a powerful presentation, and (4) deliver the presentation so that the technology complements you as a speaker. The rest of this chapter focuses on these techniques.

PRINCIPLES FOR CREATING A MULTIMEDIA PRESENTATION

When creating computer-generated slides, combining words and pictures facilitates greater learning because it uses both nonverbal and verbal cognitive processing channels (Mayer, 2005). There are multimedia design principles that can increase learning by decreasing when information presented exceeds the brain's ability to assimilate that information. The goal is to give the audience as much information as they can process, without overloading the brains' ability to learn. In the simplest form, this means giving information both verbally and visually.

Speech Preparation Presumptions

Before jumping into presentation creation techniques, you presumably have researched the audience, understand the purpose of the presentation, and know the topic well. It is also presumed that the presentation is an extemporaneous speech, not an impromptu nor a manuscript speech.

Multimedia Learning Principles

The multimedia learning principles specifically designed to prevent extraneous overload include coherence, signaling, redundancy, and spatial and temporal contiguity (Mayer, 2005). The coherence principle states that learning is improved when multimedia presentations are free from extraneous information. Extraneous information can include tangential stories, unrelated graphics, or irrelevant special effects. The signaling principle states that learning is improved when cues help focus attention on critical aspects of the presentation. Cues can include previews, headlines, summaries, and repeated graphical elements. The redundancy principle states that learning is *reduced* when information presented is redundant and directly competes for the same cognitive resource, such as reading text aloud that is also shown on a slide. When the identical words are presented to both the verbal and the visual channel, extra processing is needed to reconcile the auditory and printed stream of words. The spatial and temporal contiguity principles state that it is better to put information close in time and space. Spatial contiguity is when words are placed near relevant pictures. Temporal contiguity is when narration occurs simultaneously with relevant pictures or text (but not the exact same words because that would create redundancy).

Kammeyer's Five Quick Guides
for effective presentations

1) If in doubt, leave it out.

2) Use a cue, they'll follow you.

3) Show the glory, tell the story.

4) If it's related, keep it integrated.

5) Be seen, use the black screen.

These multimedia learning principles have been tested on computer screens (Mayer, 2005) and projected slides (Kammeyer, 2008) and shown to increase learning. Using these research-based techniques can improve your computer-generated slide presentations.

Five Quick Guides

To get started on improving your presentations, follow Kammeyer's five quick guides that encapsulate Dr. Mayer's multimedia learning principles. The guides are easy to remember and will give you effective presentations.

If in doubt, leave it out. Include only relevant information on slides and leave anything that is not directly relevant off the slides. A funny but unrelated story will only reduce learning. The same goes for sexy graphics with moving parts and thrilling music. Unless it is directly related to the material on the slide it overloads the audience's brain capacity and defeats your purpose as a presenter. If you having any doubt of something's relevance, don't add it.

Use a cue, they'll follow you. Use cues at the beginning, the end, and at every transition during your presentation. A cue is something that signals to the audience where you are in the organization of your material. A cue can be a headline or a visual agenda slide. You see cues in textbooks as chapter outlines, headings, and summaries. Cues remind the audience where you are going and where you have been, setting a framework for them to learn what you are sharing. By giving cues your audience will retain more information.

Show the glory, tell the story. Make your slide presentations primarily pictures with only one complete, declarative sentence on each slide. Use NO BULLET POINTS. Bullet points are often used to help the presenter remember what to say. Put these points in the notes section of your presentation and deliver them orally. Give the audience a few seconds to read the sentence and look at the picture, then tell the story behind that slide.

If it's related, keep it integrated. It is easier for people to remember things if they are close to each other in space and in time. Keep labels for graphs on top of or very close to the actual graph. If you show a picture of a piece of equipment, put the name of the equipment right next to the picture. Only describe a picture or a scenario when the audience can view it—not before or after.

Be seen, use the black screen. A helpful and underused function of most projector remote controls is the black screen button. To bring the audience's attention away from the presentation technology and back to the speaker, simply black out the screen. This permits you to use PowerPoint or Keynote as a support, but not as a crutch. Using the black screen function also allows you to discuss an item in detail or engage the audience in an exercise without the distraction of a slide in the background.

Combined with an understanding of the PowerPoint research, these five quick guides are the basis for creating better computer-generated slide presentations. The rest of this chapter gives the detail needed for you to make and deliver compelling slides.

CREATING A STORY BEFORE THE PRESENTATION

The multimedia presentation creation process begins with developing a story. A story has a deliberate flow with a beginning, middle, and end. Developing a story

Title: Share the title of your presentation, the date, and your name.		
Opener: Grab the audience's attention then give the overarching benefit statement that the audience should remember.		
BEGINNING: Set up the story from the audience's point of view including the characters and the challenge to be resolved.		
Setting *(Where is the audience in time, space, and frame of mind?)*		
Character *(What role does the audience play in this scenario?)*		
Challenge *(What problem or conflict does the audience have?)*		
Call to Action *(What should the audience do to overcome the challenge?)*		
Resolution *(What does the audience want or where to they want to be?)*		
MIDDLE: Develop the action of the story with key points and support for those key points.		
Preview all key points first, and then repeat the first key point and give detail, then repeat the next key point with detail, etc.		
Key Point:	Explanation, Example, Evidence:	Source of Information:
END: Create the story resolution. Repeat to the audience how they solve their challenge by taking your call to action.		

Story outline

before starting to make your slides ensures that what you have to share is solid before a presentation is created.

Communication scholar Walter Fisher's Narrative Paradigm assumes that people are essentially storytellers. Because of this, presentations that tell a story can be more engaging. To tell a story, you must develop characters, define the setting, and create and resolve a conflict (Atkinson, 2008). Consider the analogy of watching a movie: when you watch a movie, in the beginning you learn about the characters and where the movie is taking place; then you learn what challenge the characters are facing; and, eventually, the challenge or conflict is resolved one way or another. Think of organizing the flow of your presentation in this same story fashion.

To create a story it helps to follow an outline that encourages the flow of a story, not a typical paper-writing outline. The story outline format below, adapted from Cliff Atkinson's story template in his book *Beyond Bullet Points*, was specifically created for short speeches that are typically given in the classroom. This outline format can be created in a word processing program by using the table feature.

To complete the story outline, first write the title and the opener, then answer the questions in the BEGINNING section. Who is the audience and what is the setting? (e.g., college students ready for spring break) What problem or challenge does the audience face that you, as the speaker, will address? (e.g., where to go on vacation) What benefit will the audience get from listening to you? (e.g., learn how to choose a location based on cost and popularity). After completing the BEGINNING section, move to the MIDDLE section. Write a sentence that previews all key points and then put the key points of your story in the far left column. For a short speech, there may only be two or three key points. Next, put explanations or examples of the key point in the middle column. Use the right column to cite the sources of your information. To finish the story template, complete the END section by specifically stating how the challenge is resolved, or the benefit the listener gets from the speech.

After you finish the story template, tell the story aloud to a friend or classmate. To tell your story, read the story template in the following order:

1. read the title, introduce yourself, and state the opener;
2. read the BEGINNING section including all the rows;
3. preview your key points in the MIDDLE section;
4. read the first key point and then move to the right and read the explanations for the first key point and cite the sources;
5. go back and read the second key point, followed by its explanations, etc.;
6. read the END section for the conclusion.

The story should make sense and be complete at this point, even without the visuals of a presentation.

By creating a story before creating visuals, the entire presentation will be stronger because the speech can stand on its own and the slides will supplement the verbal communication. Many poor presentations start with the speaker opening PowerPoint or Keynote and starting a linear outline of ideas that does not have the elements of a story. That process can lead to spewing a bunch of information without the structure that fosters audiences learning.

After the story template is complete, the material must be transferred to PowerPoint or Keynote. This step is called the storyboard. Make the Title your first slide and put the Opener in the notes section of that first slide. The second slide will be your BEGINNING section. Write the Call to Action as the headline and put all the other information in the notes section of that second slide. Then, create an agenda slide that previews all of your key points. Lastly, make each key point the headline of a new slide, and make the END section the closing slide. This storyboard step creates a visual flow of the presentation. At this juncture it is beneficial to take pencil to paper or chalk to board and draw basic ideas of visuals to represent your key points. These do not need to be artistic sketches; just rough drawings of what might be useful. You will then want to create or find visuals reflecting your ideals.

Finding Art and Graphics

Each of your key ideas needs a visual representation in the presentation slides. Clip art and pictures are found easily on the Internet, and much of it is free. Although the Internet is a great source for finding art and photos, there are two caveats: (1) respect copyright laws, and (2) avoid over-used art. Don't steal somebody's photo without getting permission. Many photo sites sell photography for a reasonable price, and that is a good way to insure you have permission to use the work. Also, there are certain images that can be found, but are used by so many people that they become ineffective, such as a picture of a light bulb to represent a new idea, so avoid these clichés.

The best alternative to using art and photos found on the Internet is to create your own graphics. Not everyone is a graphic artist, but most people have a digital camera and access to shape art in a presentation software program. Pictures found in everyday life can represent most ideas. A picture of a messy room can represent chaos. A person sitting alone at a bus stop can represent solitude or loneliness. Pictures of somebody doing the steps of a process can represent the process. With just a few clicks of a digital camera uploaded to a computer, story concepts can be graphically represented in an effective way that the audience has never seen before. The same can be said for using shapes to represent an abstract or realistic concept. Most programs allow you to drag and drop different shapes so that even beginning users can create diagrams and basic graphics.

Only use video or moving art when it has a very specific purpose. Video can be used to demonstrate an idea, but it should be very relevant, clear, and short. Assuming that each slide takes one minute to deliver, a video clip on a slide should be no more than 30 seconds long. The same is true for a sound clip. It may be effective, for example, to play a sound clip of a famous person stating a quotation while their picture is on the slide, but that clip should be short. Moving art can be used to demonstrate steps in a process, such as showing the movement of arms for a golf swing demonstration.

After you have created a story outline and found or created supporting visuals, you are ready to start creating a multimedia presentation that tells a story, following Kammeyer's Five Quick Guides that encapsulate principles shown to increase learning.

DESIGNING A POWERFUL PRESENTATION

While following the Five Quick Guides will substantially improve presentations, more guidance is needed to fill in the details. This section outlines basic design principles and makes practical suggestions for creating slides.

Design Elements and Principles

Even people with no formal design training can use basic design elements and principles to improve their presentations. Paying attention to the elements (things you put on a slide) and the principles (how you put things on a slide) can help you create multimedia presentations that better communicate your desired message.

The basic design elements are color, line, shape, texture, and font. To design presentations, the basic elements need to be addressed on every slide.

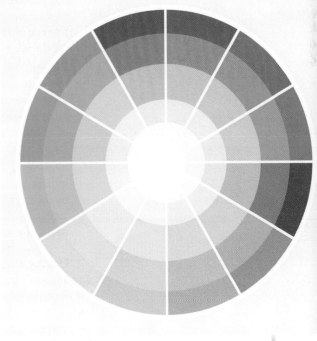

Courtesy of BigStock®

Color Wheel

Color can communicate. For example, using primarily monochromatic elements on a slide and adding one contrasting color brings attention to the differently colored item, indicating its importance. To create a pleasing look, use colors adjoining on the color wheel. To create a bold look, use colors opposite each other on the wheel.

Lines can be solid, dotted, dashed, curved, or straight, and can range from very thin to very thick. Lines can define sections, emphasize items, and represent objects and movement. A line that is under some text and above other text can define the above text as superior or as conceptually broader than the text below. A line down the middle of a slide can split the slide into two content zones.

Shapes are the building blocks for most diagrams. For example, block arrows placed the same direction side-by-side represents movement in the direction of the arrowheads. Circles overlapped can represent the intersection of different items. A square next to a circle can represent a difference of items.

Texture can be applied to lines and shapes to change their meaning. A curving line that is smooth may represent calm water, while one with a rough texture may represent tumultuous water. Items that have more texture can be perceived as more realistic and smoother items more abstract. Visual texture can also be created by stacking visual items on a slide, such as putting a photograph on top of a patterned square or a piece of clip art on top of an actual photograph.

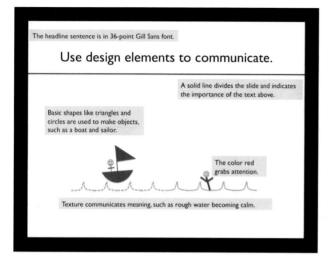

Font is the style of the text used. There are two basic groups of fonts: serif and sans serif. Serif fonts have little lines at the end of letters designed to help move the eye from one letter to the next. They are best for long passages of text, not presentations. Sans serif fonts are simple without little lines so each letter appears more distinct. Sans serif fonts, such as **Gill Sans**, are typically used in design for headlines and short bursts of texts that need to stand out. The font size 36 for headlines and 24 for on-slide text are best for projected presentations.

The basic design principles, or how to put together the design elements, are contrast, alignment, repetition, balance, and space, sometimes put into the acronym of CARBS. Robin Williams defines basic design principles and explains how they can be used in her book *The Non-Designer's Design Book*, while this section gives a very brief overview.

Contrast is used to draw attention by making elements on the slide different from one another. Contrast can be achieved using design elements such as color, shape, and space. A more brightly colored item will pull attention, indicating its importance, as will an item that is larger or has more space around it. Use contrast intentionally to communicate what is important.

Alignment is how elements of a slide line up with each other and the edges of the slide. The simplest way to create alignment when using the multimedia learning principles technique is with a left aligned full-sentence headline and a center aligned supporting graphic.

Repetition, or consistency, helps create cohesiveness in a presentation. Repeating the same color background and font for headlines is an example of design repetition. Another example of repetition is using 2–3 graphics that represent the key ideas on a visual agenda slide and then repeating each individual graphic on the slide for each key point (Remember: *Use a cue, they'll follow you*).

Balance, or proximity, is the intentional use of symmetry in design. If items on the slide are symmetrical, it communicates a sense of order and formality. The use of asymmetry can intentionally communicate chaos or can highlight the importance of one item. When designing slides, deliberately place things in or out of balance to communicate your point.

Space is the unfilled part of the slide, and it is used in design to communicate. If items on a slide are close to one another with very little space in between, that indicates they are related. If items are far apart, then they are unrelated (Remember: *If it's related, keep it integrated*). Something that has more space around it can be perceived as being more important. Pay attention to the empty parts of your slides because space communicates.

Having awareness of design elements and principles will help you produce more appealing slides. Remember, every single thing you put on a slide communicates to the audience: make that communication intentional.

DELIVERING DYNAMIC PRESENTATIONS

Once your multimedia presentation is created, there is a skill set needed to deliver it effectively that is different than delivering a speech without a visual aid or with a physical object as a visual aid. Most importantly, the technology should complement, not compete with, the speaker.

Remember, the idea behind following the multimedia learning principles is that you fill visual and verbal channels without overloading either. Certain presentation delivery tips help achieve that balance.

To deliver dynamic presentations the number one rule to remember is that you, the speaker, are the center of attention. Your job is to engage the audience and make sure they are assimilating the information being shared through your words and the slide presentation (Remember: *Show the glory, tell the story*). While speaking, you are in control. You take and keep control with your body language, your voice, and your use of the technology. Being in control does not mean that the audience cannot participate; it just means that you decide when they participate. Being in control also means that you adjust your speech based on the constant feedback you get from your audience, including the style of your delivery and the pace of your presentation.

Leveraging Your Body and Voice

Face the audience at all times and do not look back at the projection screen. Your body should be front and center and the projection screen should be off to one side. To track the progress of the presentation, position the laptop that is hooked to the projector so that it can be seen by glancing down and then look back up at the audience. Being front and center and keeping your body and eyes facing the audience will keep you in control.

Share the stage with technology

Voice is another essential element for keeping the focus on the speaker. Not only are the words chosen important, but pace, rhythm and volume of your voice determines the audience's engagement. If a speaker is enthusiastic and speaks slowly enough to be understood, he or she is likely to engage the audience. If the tone and volume of the speaker's voice varies, it will be more enjoyable for the audience to listen. So vary your voice and keep up the enthusiasm.

Using Technology to Your Advantage

In addition to remaining the center of attention with both your body and voice, the third element to keeping control is the effective use of technology. As mentioned earlier, where the technology is within the room makes a difference. As much as possible, place the projector in a spot that does not block peoples' view, set the screen off center, and have the presentation laptop on a low table that you can see while presenting. If the set up is not ideal, do the best possible to adjust the technology so you are the center of attention. Also, keep the lights up and NEVER look at the projected screen.

Another way to share the audience's attention between the speaker and technology is to use a remote control and the black screen option (Remember: *Be seen, use the black screen*). A remote control allows you to move about the room and not be stuck at the podium or table that holds the laptop. The black screen button allows you to use the presentation as visual support and the make the screen go black to focus the audience's attention back on you. This is a very powerful tool because as a speaker it allows you to use technology when it is supportive, and instantly turned off when it is not needed. For example, if somebody asks a question, you can use the black screen and answer the question without distracting the audience with a visual that is inconsistent with the verbal message you are delivering.

Twitter and Texting

There are technologies other than computer-generated slide presentations that are in almost every speaking venue today. Those are the mobile devices that allow people to call, text, Google, Twitter, and blog. Cultural norms are still being defined around what is acceptable to use in public venues. Speaking on the phone in a classroom or other venue has been culturally set as taboo and it is not seen very often. On the other hand, texting and using mobile devices for other purposes is still common. In most cases, the use of mobile technology during a speaking engagement is distracting to both the audience and the speaker. Speakers have the right to ask that these devices be put away and not used during the presentation. Speakers can control the use of these devices by actively engaging the audience with questions so that they do not have time or inclination to verify a fact just stated on Google. On the other hand, some speakers are embracing this technology and encouraging it as a form of interaction.

Mobile social networking technology can be used as a specific form of audience interaction and engagement. Some speakers are encouraging the use of these technologies, as a way to get audiences more involved with the material. At an industry conference called "Always On" that is co-hosted by a Stanford/MIT organization called Venture Lab, as the speakers present there is a simultaneous blog projected on a large screen along side the speaker's slides. On the blog, participants in the room and those watching remotely via video webcasts are invited to comment. So, as the speaker is presenting, bloggers can support or disagree with a particular point and the entire audience can read what they think. In another example, speakers invite audience members to use Twitter to send comments or questions directly to the speaker during the presentation. Some speakers find this a less disruptive way to get feedback from the audience than people verbally interrupting. The speaker can weave in answers to the specific questions tweeted or texted without stopping the flow of the presentation. As mobile devices and social networking technologies continue to become more prevalent in our culture, our society will adjust patterns and norms of its use, including how it is used in speaking venues.

MULTIMEDIA PRESENTATION EXAMPLE

Following an example is a good way to start improving your multimedia presentation skills. This example walks you through a speech on the topic of Alzheimer's disease. It includes: 1) story outline, 2) the storyboard, 3) the presentation slides, and 4) the notes section of each slide. The process of developing the presentation is given step-by-step, making it easy for you to follow and emulate.

Story Outline

Filling out a story outline before you start creating a presentation gives you a strong narrative that can then be supported by your slides. Notice how the characters are defined (students who care about the world) in the BEGINNING, the key points are listed in the left column of the MIDDLE, and the END circles back to the call to action (take action to help those suffering) to resolve the conflict. Remember to practice telling your story aloud to your friends before you move on to creating the presentation.

Title: Alzheimer's Disease: You can make a difference	
Opener: Alzheimer's disease is a far-reaching illness with no known cause or cure, but your actions can make a difference.	
BEGINNING: Set up the story from the audience's point of view including the characters and the challenge to be resolved.	
Setting *(Where is the audience in time, space, and mind?)*	In a classroom, listening to fellow students share how they want to change the world.
Character *(What role does the audience play here?)*	Students who care about the world and want to make a difference.
Challenge *(What problem does the audience have?)*	The students don't know about Alzheimer's disease or what they can do to make a difference.
Call to Action *(What should the audience do?)*	The students should take action to help those suffering from Alzheimer's disease.
Resolution *(What does the audience want?)*	Students want to feel like they can have a positive effect on this problem.

MIDDLE: Develop the action of the story with key points and support for those key points.

Preview all key points first, and then repeat the first key point and give detail, then repeat the next key point with detail, etc.

Key Point:	Explanation:	Evidence Source:
Alzheimer's disease has a negative effect on both the people with the disease and their caregivers.	5.4 million Americans are living with Alzheimer's disease. One in eight older Americans have the disease and it is the 6th leading cause of death in the U.S.	The Alzheimer's Association. 2012 Alzheimer's disease facts and figures. *Alzheimer's and Dementia: The Journal of the Alzheimer's Association*. March 2012; 8:131–168.
	Alzheimer's disease impacts memory and mental abilities, leaving patients in need of total care and burdening others.	Personal experience my grandma suffering from Alzheimer's disease; Caregiving Costs retrieved 2/24/12 from http://www.caregiving.org/
The cause of Alzheimer's disease is unknown and there is currently no cure, but there are ways to decrease suffering.	Although genetics can increase chances of getting Alzheimer's disease, the cause is not known and there is currently no cure.	Alzheimer's Disease Fact Sheet. Retrieved 3/25/15 from National Institute on Aging http://www.nia.nih.gov/alzheimers/publication/alzheimers-disease-fact-sheet
	There are interventions that help people cope, such as family education and cognitive, psychosocial, and emotional treatments.	http://www.informedhealthonline.org/dementia-in-alzheimer-s-disease-can-non-drug-interventions-like.557.en.html; http://www.helpguide.org/elder/alzheimers_prevention_slowing_down_treatment.htm Retrieved 5/7/12
You can make a difference by taking action to help those suffering from Alzheimer's disease.	You can make a difference by sharing Alzheimer's information, becoming an Alzstar athlete, making a donation, or signing a petition for a strong national plan.	Ways to Move the Cause Forward retrieved 3/25/12 from http://www.actionalz.org/

END: Create the story resolution. Repeat to the audience how they solve their challenge by taking your call to action.

Alzheimer's disease has a negative effect on people who have the disease and their caregivers. There is currently no known cause or cure, but you can make a difference by taking action to help those suffering from Alzheimer's disease.

Story Outline derived from the Story Template in *Beyond Bullet Points* by Cliff Atkinson

Storyboard

Sketching basic ideas of visuals to support your key points of the presentation is the storyboard step. From the story outline, put the information from the BEGINNING section on the first and second slides. The third slide is a visual agenda that represents the key points. Slide four, five, six, and seven each explain a key point from the MIDDLE section and slide eight summarizes and represents the END section. Remember, at this point the words don't need to be perfect and the sketches are just rough concepts. The storyboard is a connection between the story outline and the multimedia presentation.

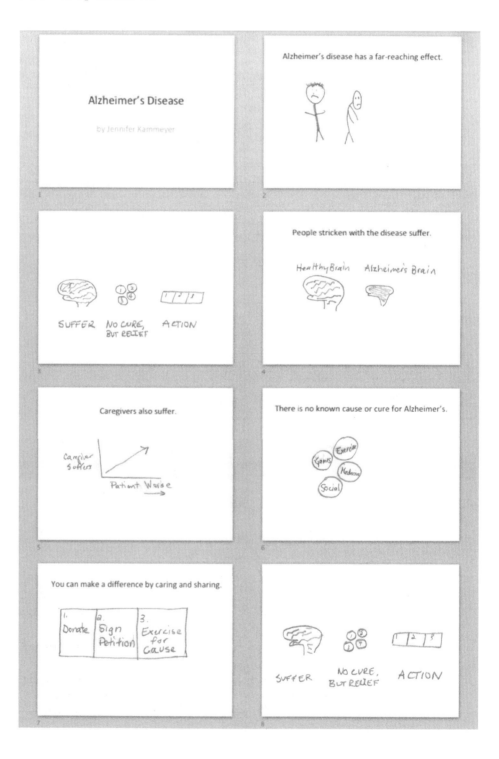

Presentation Slides

After the storyboard, you need to edit headlines and find or create the graphics to support each slide. Remember to use a full declarative sentence for each headline. This effort creates the visuals to support your already strong story. Once you have created the slides, look at them in the slide sorter view to see if you have implemented the Five Quick Guides and the basic design elements and principles.

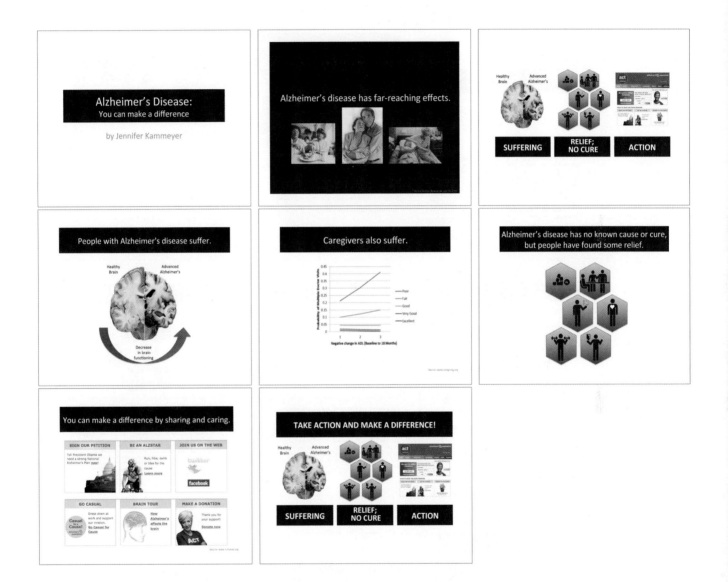

Notice that the pictures on the slides do not exactly match the sketch from the storyboard. That is to be expected, since the storyboard sketches represent rough ideas. In terms of design, in this example you see a contrast of slide headline text and background, alignment of a centered headline and centered pictures. You also see repetition of the visual agenda on slide three and slide eight. On the visual agenda slide, there is symmetrical balance and shared space between the three pictures to show their equal importance. Slide six has pictographs of people created by a graphic artist to represent the ways people find relief from Alzheimer's disease. There are no bullet points on any of the slides.

Notes Section

When your slides do not have bullet points, you need to use the notes section to write what you plan to say during your speech. Your notes should start with a statement that has the same meaning as the headline, but does not repeat it verbatim. Then each of your supportive explanations from the story outline should be written in the notes section, along with any cited source you plan to share aloud.

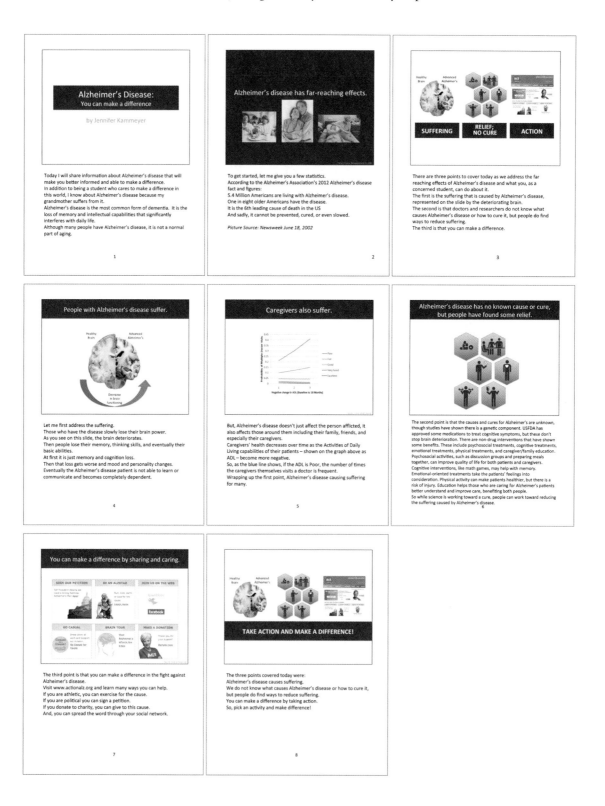

SUMMARY

In today's visual culture, when you give a speech the audience often expects to see a slide presentation. In order to have that presentation improve, and not hinder, your communication, it needs to be designed and delivered in an effective manner. The presentation technique described in this chapter includes: (1) following Kammeyer's Five Quick Guides based on multimedia learning principles, (2) creating a story before you create the slides, (3) paying attention to how design communicates, and (4) delivering the presentation in a dynamic manner in which the slides complement your verbal message. Follow this advice and you will leverage the benefits of multimedia technology and communicate more effectively.

REFERENCES

Apperson, J. M., Laws, E. L., Scepansky, J. A. (2008). An assessment of student preferences for PowerPoint presentation structure in undergraduate courses. *Computers & Education, 50,* 148-153.

Alley, M., Neeley, K. (2005). Rethinking the Design of Presentation Slides: A Case for Sentence Headlines and Visual Evidence. *Technical Communication, 52,* 417–426.

Alley, M., Schreiber, M., Ramsdell, K., & Muffo, J. (2006). How the Design of Headlines in Presentation Slides Affects Audience Retention. *Technical Communication, 53,* 225–234.

Atkins-Sayre, W., Hopkins, S., Mohundro, S., & Sayre, W. (1998, November). *Rewards and Liabilities of Presentation Software as an Ancillary Tool: Prison or Paradise.* Paper presented at the Annual Meeting of the NCA, New York.

Atkinson, C. (2008). *Beyond Bullet Points: Using Microsoft PowerPoint 2007 to Create Presentations that Inform, Motivate, and Inspire.* Redmond, WA: Microsoft Press.

Bartsch, R. A. & Cobern, K. M. (2003). Effectiveness of PowerPoint presentations in lectures. *Computers & Education, 41,* 77–86.

Blokzijl, W., & Naeff, R. (2004). The Instructor as Stagehand; Dutch Student Responses to PowerPoint. *Business Communication Quarterly, 67,* 70–77.

Bradshaw, A. C. (2003). Effects of Presentation Interference in Learning with Visuals. *Journal of Visual Literacy, 23,* 41–68.

Cyphert, D. (2007). Presentation Technology in the Age of Electronic Eloquence: From Visual Aid to Visual Rhetoric. *Communication Education, 56,* 168–192.

Griffin, C. L. (2006). *Visual Aids, Invitation to Public Speaking, p. 290.* Belmont, CA: Thomson Wadsworth. Citing Linkugel, W. & Berg, D. (1970). *A Time to Speak, pp. 68–96.* Belmont, CA: Wadsworth.

Horrigan, J. (2008). Mobile Access to Data and Information. *PEW/INTERNET & AMERICAN LIFE PROJECT.* Retrieved 3/17/08 from http://www.pewinternet.org/pdfs/PIP_Mobile.Data.Access.pdf.

Kammeyer, J. M. (2008). "Applying Cognitive Processing Theory and Multimedia Principles to PowerPoint: Will learning increase?" Masters Thesis Collections. San Francisco State University: San Francisco.

Levasseur, D. G. & Sawyer, J. K. (2006). Pedagogy Meets PowerPoint: A Research Review of the Effects of Computer-Generated Slides in the Classroom. *The Review of Communication, 6,* 101–123.

Mackiewicz, J. (2007-1). Perceptions of Clarity and Attractiveness in PowerPoint Graph Slides. *Technical Communication, 54,* 145–156.

Mackiewicz, J. (2007-2). Audience Perceptions of Fonts in Projected PowerPoint Text Slides. *Technical Communication, 54,* 295–306.

Madden, M. (2007). Online Video. PEW/INTERNET & AMERICAN LIFE PROJECT. Retrieved 8/15/07 from http://www.pewinternet.org/pdfs/PIP_Online_Video_2007.pdf

Mahin, L. (2004). PowerPoint Pedagogy. *Business Communication Quarterly, 67,* 219–222.

Mayer, R. (2005). *The Cambridge Handbook of Multimedia Learning.* New York: Cambridge University Press.

Mayer, R. E. & Anderson, R. B. (1991). Animations need narrations: An experimental test of dual-coding hypothesis. *Journal of Educational Psychology, 83,* 484–490.

Mayer, R. E. & Anderson, R. B. (1992). The instructive animation: Helping students build connections between words and pictures in multimedia learning. *Journal of Educational Psychology, 84,* 444–452.

Miller, G.A. (1956). The Magical Number Seven, Plus or Minus Two: Some Limits on our Capacity for Processing Information. *Psychological Review, 63,* 81–97. Retrieved 10/10/2006 from http://psychclassics.yorku.ca/miller.

Morreale, S., Hugenberg, L., & Worley, D. (2006). The Basic Communication Course at U.S. Colleges and Universities in the 21st Century: Study VII. *Communication Education, 55,* 415–437.

Paivio, A. (1986). Mental Representations. New York: Holt, Rinehart & Winston. Experts retrieved 3/8/08 from http://tip.psychology.org/paivio.html.

Paivio, A. (2006, September). *Dual Coding Theory and Education.* Paper presented at Pathways to Literacy Achievement for High Poverty Children Conference. The University of Michigan School of Education, Ann Arbor, MI.

Smith, S. M. & Woody, P. C. (2000). Interactive Effect of Multimedia Instruction and Learning Styles, *Teaching of Psychology, 27,* 220–223.

Szabo, A., & Hastings, M. (2000). Using IT in the undergraduate classroom: Should we replace the blackboard with PowerPoint? *Computers & Education, 35,* 175–187.

Appendix

Sample Speeches for Discussion and Evaluation

INFORMATIVE SPEECH
Taming Hostile Audiences:
Persuading Those Who Would Rather Jeer than Cheer

Larry Tracy[1]
Delivered to the Washington, D.C., Chapter of the National Speakers Association,
Washington, D.C. January 8, 2005

Thank you, Sylvia, for that fine introduction. As professional speakers, we know how a poor introduction can be deflating. Sylvia, on the other hand, was somewhat inflating in her kind remarks.

I am frequently asked how I got into the field of presentations coaching after being a colonel in the U.S. Army. The first time that question was asked of me, my answer, I'm afraid, was a bit flippant. After reflection, however, I decided it was indeed quite accurate. I said that early in my career, I concluded (as did my superiors, I believe) that I could talk better than I could shoot. From that time on, I seemed to become the duty briefer no matter what my primary assignment. Ultimately, as Sylvia mentioned in her introduction, I was selected to head the Pentagon's top briefing team, responsible for daily intelligence presentations to the Chairman of the Joint Chiefs of Staff and the Secretary of Defense.

My experience with hostile and difficult audiences came later when the Department of State requested the Army to assign me to the Department for the specific task of speaking and debating controversial foreign policy issues throughout the U.S. and abroad. Initially, I found it flattering that State Department officials believed I was qualified to take on this task, but after the first few "confrontations," I realized these officials had decided it was better to place an Army colonel in jeopardy than a promising diplomat.

In all seriousness, however, that assignment was a wonderful life-changing experience. The almost 400 presentations, debates, and panels in which I participated caused me to enter the field of speech training as my post-Army career. I knew that few people in this field had the "real-world" experience I had gained and could now pass on to others.

Let me say something that may offend some of you. Although you are all professional speakers, I submit that you are not a true professional if you are only capable of speaking to groups that agree with you. The true professional speaker can deal with the jeers as well as the cheers. The true professional knows how to persuade the "nonpersuadable," not just preach to the choir.

There is no greater challenge in the field of speaking than the task of bringing around to your position audience members who are initially opposed to what you are advocating. Many people are inclined to take a fatalistic position at the prospect of dealing with such an audience. But that attitude is self-defeating. Bringing such an audience to your side by the lucidity of your reasoning, the coherence of your message, and the excellence of your presentation skills will indeed make you a complete speaker.

As you have no doubt discovered, speakers in today's world must blend substantive mastery, focused structure, and stylistic elegance to a degree not required previously.

In today's contentious business and government climate, adversarial panels, debates, and presentations on controversial issues are more the rule rather than the exception. I want to divide today's presentation into two parts. In Part One, I'll emphasize the importance of mastering the fundamentals of the speaking art. In Part Two, I'll show how to apply these fundamentals to persuading audiences inclined to disagree with you.

Part One: The Fundamentals of the Speaking Art

I know that some of you are thinking "Hold on, we're professional speakers. We don't need any advice on "fundamentals." Just get to the good stuff—how to tame hostile audiences." Well, I disagree with those of you thinking that way. I have given over 3000 presentations, and I always review the fundamentals. Let me use a sports analogy to emphasize this point. By doing so, I am departing from the advice I teach in my workshops—"Men, go easy on the sports metaphors; you run the risk of alienating people in your audience who are not sports nuts." So please indulge me this one time, as the comparison is so apt.

Professional football players are superb athletes, who, in their games, employ complex formations, options, and plays. Yet, when they report to training camp, they initially practice only football fundamentals—blocking, tackling, running, passing, and catching. Only after honing these skills do these athletes move to their complex formations and plays.

Professional speakers should do no less. It is especially important when you are preparing to face a demanding audience. You may get by with a less-than-polished presentation when you are addressing people who agree with you and only wish to have their views reinforced. It is, however, sheer folly to speak to an audience opposed to you without a strict adherence to the fundamentals of the speaking art.

Now, just what am I referring to with the word *fundamentals*? I don't mean just the platform skills of body language, eye contact, gestures, and vocal inflection. They are indeed important tools for the speaker, but I mean something deeper. If your presentation does not take into consideration the objections, questions, and other obstacles to understanding, it is unlikely the audience will accept and act upon your message.

Don't think of a presentation as merely a series of words strung together, any more than a bridge is merely wires and steel haphazardly connected. Just as there are sound engineering principles in bridge construction that take into consideration soil composition, prevailing winds, stress and strain, etc., there are sound principles which must be followed in the construction of a presentation.

Your mission as a speaker, to either a supportive or nonsupportive audience, is to provide maximum information in minimum time in the clearest possible manner. Keep in mind that every presentation is actually four presentations: (1) the one you plan to deliver, (2) the one you actually deliver, (3) the one your audience hears you deliver, and (4) the one you wish you had delivered. I hope my presentation today will help you to deliver as you have planned and practiced, be on the same page as the audience, and have fewer of those "I wish I had said it this way" moments.

A motto of the National Speakers Association of a few years ago very elegantly described professional speakers as enjoying "The privilege of the platform." As a speaker, you have the rare opportunity to "write on the brains" of the people in your audience. Never undertake a presentation without that thought uppermost in your own mind.

To communicate effectively and persuasively with any audience, you need "actionable intelligence" on these people. Note that I do not use the term "audience analysis," which is a favorite phrase of most of my colleagues in the field of presentations training. That phrase reminds me of high school students dissecting a frog.

When addressing an audience, you are dealing with living, breathing human beings with beliefs, attitudes, biases, prejudices, etc. Into that mix you will be adding new information. You must know their "what's in it for me" button, the pushing of which will cause them to listen to your message. You must know what problems these people have, so that your presentation can provide the information to solve these problems. This information must be delivered so it will be received by audience members. You must, in short, open the minds of these audience members.

So just how do you open the minds of an audience so your facts will be heard and accepted? You do so by going back to the teaching of history's greatest speech coach—Aristotle. He considered "Ethos," which we would call "source credibility," the most important part of a speaker's means of persuasion. He wrote in *The Rhetoric,* the seminal work on public speaking, that an audience which knew nothing of the subject being addressed would accept the position being advocated by the speaker if that person was considered to have "Ethos."

Moving that Aristotelian precept to our times, we base our view of whether a speaker has credibility on three elements:

1. Expertise
2. Believability
3. Likability

Your audience members want to know that you bring to the table information that will shorten their learning curve, that you have the credentials to speak on this issue, that you are telling the truth, not merely a glib speaker selling snake oil. Finally, they must like you. We all tend to accept information from people we like, and we reject it from people we do not like. Interpersonal skills are intimately connected to speaking skills.

Credibility is subjective. No one in this room, including me, can say "I have credibility to speak on my specialty." Your audience members will decide if you are credible. If they do so, you are in a position to bring them to your point of view. If they do not, you are wasting your time speaking to them.

With all that in mind, I want to show you a systematic way of following the fundamentals of speaking. It is what I call the S3P3 system, the heart of my executive workshops. It has worked for me, and it works for my clients who, for the most part are not nearly as experienced in speaking as you are. Therefore, I know it will work for you. Let me again ask you to open your mental PowerPoint, this time visualizing a pyramid supported by three pillars. The levels of the pyramid are, from base to apex, Planning, Practicing, and Presenting. The pillars are Substance, Structure, and Style.

Substance is the content of the presentation. Always remember that the purpose of a presentation is to convey information from speaker to audience. Style refers to how you look, how you sound, your choice of words—all those attributes we ascribe to a good public speaker. Substance without style is a dry and boring recitation of data. Style without substance is shallow and meaningless. Structure is the skeletal outline, or scaffolding, of the presentation. That's the word a young British Army lieutenant named Winston Churchill used in the title of a brilliant essay written in 1897, "The Scaffolding of Rhetoric." The future British Prime Minister emphasized that audience members needed a guide to show them where the speaker and they were going on this joint journey. A reading of Churchill's memorable World War Two speeches, [which were said to have] "marched the English language into battle," demonstrates that he followed the advice he developed in his youth.

Such organization is vital for an oral presentation. A written memo can have faulty structure, but can be reread. There is no instant replay of the oral presentation. Some examples of this structure are problem-solution, cause and effect, chronological. The presentation must have a beginning, a middle, and an end. It must also have transitions which send signals to the audience that new elements will be discussed.

Now, let's look at that pyramid, starting with that wide base. In Planning, you must develop a concrete objective, aimed at intersecting with the problems, needs, wants, and concerns of your audience. This is always important, but especially so when facing a demanding audience. Know specifically what you wish to have this audience do with the information you are providing. It is here where you draft your presentation, and this can best be done, in my opinion, by following my 3-1-2 system. While this system is counterintuitive, it virtually guarantees that you will have both focus and theme, vital for an oral presentation.

Take a stack of 3 × 5 cards. Mark one with a "3" and place on it the "bottom line" message you wish to impart to your audience. In front of these words, put "In summary," "In conclusion," or some other phrase signaling the end of your presentation. You now have your conclusion, as well as a mini-presentation, especially beneficial when making a business or sales presentation when time for the presentation is reduced at the last minute. Take another card, mark it with "1" and use it to tell the audience where you are taking them on this oratorical journey. Next, place the supporting points that flow from "1" to "3" on a series of cards marked "2A," "2B," "2C," etc.

Using the 3-1-2 system will enable you to present maximum relevant content within the limited amount of time your audience may have to listen to you. You'll have more focus, because you will know when you start drafting where you are going in the presentation. Most importantly, audience members will see a structure to your presentation, enabling them to follow and, in the best of cases, ultimately agree with your argument. Just remember: you draft 3-1-2, but when you have the allotted time, you deliver 1-2-3.

Now to Practicing, something many of us find rather odious. It is, however, vitally important, especially when preparing to face a difficult audience. Thorough practice will permit you to hone your presentation skills, anticipate questions, and it will certainly build your confidence.

I teach my clients a three-step practice process. First, practice by yourself, with a tape recorder and, if possible, a video camera. You are at your weakest at this stage and do not want anyone criticizing your performance. Listen for your "uh's" and "y'knows." The [fewer] of those abominations you utter, the less you will irritate your audience. Men, listen for a droning monotone. Ladies, listen for a high pitch. Next, ask a colleague to be your "audience." This should be a person who can offer constructive criticism and comments. The third stage is to convene a "Murder Board," a realistic simulation with colleagues role-playing your prospective audience. I'll cover this in more detail in just a few minutes when we focus on communicating with a demanding audience.

Finally, you reach that apex: Presenting. This is when you put voice to thought within a structure that facilitates audience comprehension and agreement with the position you are advocating, done with the style most appropriate to make your presentation memorable and successful. Eye contact, purposeful gestures, pleasant vocal inflection, skillful answering of questions, are all part of the presentation. If you have practiced well, you will present well.

For those of us who deliver similar presentations over and over, the challenge is to keep your material fresh. To do so, take a tip from the theatre. Actors who play the same role night after night refer to this as "creating the illusion of the first time." As speakers, you can add new material, and you can concentrate on getting yourself "pumped." Your obligation is to not be boring to members of your audience who are hearing your words for the first time.

Part Two: Persuading Hostile Audiences

Now let's see how we can apply these fundamentals to communicate with, and perhaps persuade, people who are adamantly opposed to our position.

We live in an increasingly high-tempo, fast-moving, information-laden, real-time age, and the pace is picking up. Audiences are knowledgeable, critical, impatient, and demanding. Public debates and panels on controversial issues are becoming common. Perhaps it has been the institutionalization of presidential and other political debates over the last several years that has led to this state of affairs. Perhaps there is a "Super Bowl" desire deep in our national psyche that craves the clash of ideas, issues, and rivals. A debate or confrontational panel means sharing the platform with a person or persons opposed to you, perhaps with an audience acting as cheerleader for these opponent(s). You will then know how the Christians in the Roman Coliseum felt as they looked at the hungry lions.

To be an effective presenter under such circumstances, a flexible "blueprint" must be developed for transferring information and perceptions from the speaker's mind to the minds of audience members. When facing a skeptical or hostile audience, you must keep in mind that the information you are presenting is probably at variance with the preconceived opinions and biases of audience members. Anticipating how audience members will react and what lines of attack any opponent(s) will follow is an absolute necessity. Knowing your vulnerabilities and developing responses/counterattacks will enable you to snatch victory from the jaws of defeat, if I may use an overdone cliché.

I'll illustrate how failure to develop an effective counterattack had profound consequences for one of our political leaders several years ago. To make this interesting, I'd like to make a wager with you that in a few minutes, as I recount this story, some of you will be able to repeat, almost verbatim, something you saw and heard on television about 16 years ago. Any takers?

I didn't think there would be. Let me tighten the focus. It's a cool October evening in 1988, and two Senators are in the vice-presidential debate. They are Lloyd Bentsen and Dan Quayle.

I'm starting to see some knowing nods. I told you you'd remember.

Quayle had been a controversial choice to be on the Republican ticket, due to his relative youth. To counter this perception, his campaign compared his age, and his time in the Congress, to that of the late President John F. Kennedy. In his memoirs, Quayle says that his "handlers," as he derisively referred to his debate prep team, feared Bentsen would turn the tables and make an unfavorable comparison of Quayle to Kennedy. They advised him to avoid any mention of Kennedy so Bentsen would not have an opportunity to skewer him. This was foolish advice, because in a debate one has no control over the questions. Quayle attempted to avoid the Kennedy comparison, but eventually, in response to a reporter's question, said he was the same age as Kennedy was in 1960, and had served the same number of years in the Congress as had the late president.

Now I see a lot of knowing smiles, and I would venture more than half of you know what happened next. Senator Bentsen said—and repeat after me—"Senator, I knew Jack Kennedy. Jack Kennedy was a friend of mine. Senator, you are no Jack Kennedy." What was Quayle's response? "That was uncalled for."

The remark by Bentsen, and Quayle's stunned reaction, was the most devastating and best-remembered exchange in the history of American political debates. Dan Quayle's image was permanently damaged, even though the Bush–Quayle ticket went on to win the November 1988 election.

The Bentsen–Quayle debate provides an excellent lesson for all presenters. You must seek to anticipate the most daunting objections and questions your audience will raise. Failure to do so could result in public humiliation, the fate suffered by then-Senator Quayle. Despite the fact that Quayle was, by all accounts, an effective Vice President, he never recovered from the Bentsen broadside. His every gaffe of the next four years was exaggerated by the media and TV comedians because it fit the image of the youthful, bumbling, politician established in the debate.

Could Quayle have neutralized Bentsen's broadside? Yes, with an intensive "Murder Board," which I've mentioned in passing and will discuss in a few minutes. Had Quayle and his advisers decided to act on their worst fears, rather than put their heads in the sand and hope for the best, think how effective this response to Bentsen would have been: "Senator, if you want to say who is not a John F. Kennedy, I would suggest you look at your running mate. The only thing Governor Dukakis and JFK have in common is the state of Massachusetts." Such a response would have taken little imagination to devise. A lemon could have been turned into lemonade by luring Bentsen into an "ambush," as a means of guaranteeing the hit on Dukakis. Quayle's risk-averse coaches, however, took the cautious approach, hoping to deny Bentsen the chance to launch the attack they feared. Quayle and the Republican Party were ill-served by such incompetence. If Quayle had delivered such a response, his supporters in the audience would have responded with robust applause, Bentsen's comment would not have captured the headlines, and Quayle would have been credited with a quick-thinking comeback. The exchange would probably have been forgotten, and Quayle, who did well in the rest of the debate, would have possibly been viewed as the winner, or at worst the debate would have been judged a draw. Instead, he was considered the clear loser.

Now let's move away from recent history and back to today. A presenter can connect with even a skeptical audience by showing that he or she shares certain views with members of the audience. You must develop rapport and seek to establish common ground with the audience. If you don't, there is no chance of success in bringing these people to your side. You simply must, at the outset, open the minds of audience members. Let me illustrate once again with a visual image. Imagine a car that is out of gas at point A. This is your prospective audience, which lacks the vital information you will be imparting. You wish to drive this car to point B—acceptance of your information. If the gas cap—the minds of audience members—is closed, any "gas" you pour will wind up on the ground. So how do you get that "gas cap" open? You can do so by getting audience members to like or respect you. You can establish personal contact, perhaps by phone, with key members of the audience well before the presentation. In so doing, you'll not only establish that needed "human connection," you'll also gain additional intelligence on why these people are opposed to you.

Arrive early so you can have conversations with people who are opposed to you. Learn more about their concerns, and why they are opposed to the position you are advocating. Perhaps you will learn who will be the troublemakers. You can speak with them in a nonconfrontational way. These people, in turn, may now see you more as a human being, not a remote corporate figure. During the actual presentation, mention the names of the people with whom you have conferred. Nothing is so sweet to the human ear as the sound of his or her name, especially if it is mentioned positively before others. These people that you mention will probably be less inclined to ask tough questions, as it could appear less than gracious after your kind remarks. Next, find that necessary common ground by emphasizing areas where you and the audience agree, even at a high level of abstraction. This at least puts you and the audience on the same page, even if it is a small page. After establishing that there are points of agreement, you can then move to the arguments supporting your position.

A technique I used in facing audiences initially opposed to the position I was advocating was to acknowledge that we in Washington had done a poor job of articulating our policy, and I could therefore understand why so many people in the audience were opposed to this policy. I would then say I hoped to fill in some of those gaps with my presentation. In this way, I was providing audience members with the opportunity to "save face," perhaps even [become] willing to change their mind as a result of the new information I was about to present. Remember that people don't want to admit they were wrong, and you cannot persuade people to change their mind; they must persuade themselves.

Now, let's look at three tactics for dealing with demanding audiences. First, The Murder Board: The term "Murder Board" comes from military briefings. It is a rigorous practice, a simulation of the actual presentation to be made. It consists of colleagues role-playing the actual audience, asking the type of questions this audience is likely to ask. As its rather macabre name implies, the Murder Board is intended to be more difficult and demanding than the actual presentation. In football terms, it is a full-pads scrimmage. This realistic practice session is the most effective shortcut to speaking excellence. It allows you to make your mistakes when they don't count. It allows you to be exposed to those tough questions, leading to focused research, which enables you to provide succinct, accurate answers in the actual presentation. In sum, the Murder Board increases the odds that you will shine. When faced with the audience inclined more to jeer than cheer, it is essential to have such rigorous preparation—unless you take some perverse joy in public humiliation.

Next, stay within your evidence: During the give-and-take of a presentation with a demanding audience, you may be tempted to go beyond the hard, factual evidence that is the underpinning of your argument. An analogy or metaphor may be stretched beyond its limits, or a conclusion stated that is simply not supported by the facts. This can destroy the credibility you have established up to that point and provide a lucrative target for those strongly opposed to you. Credibility lost is difficult to regain.

Finally, you simply must maintain your composure in the face of hostility: It is quite natural to let your emotions take over if a person in the audience starts to harangue you. Natural, but a recipe for disaster if you lose your temper. Audiences will adopt an "us against the speaker" attitude if you respond in kind to a heckler or a person making obnoxious remarks.

I'll illustrate with an example from my own speaking experience when I was called a liar by an audience member. I was on a panel at a major university, addressing U.S. Latin American policy. The three other members of the panel were professors from the university, all opposed to that policy. The audience was composed primarily of students, who, in the Q&A session, were aggressive but fair. Then a man in his 40s rose, asked a question to which I responded. This was then followed by two more, which were loud personal attacks against my honesty. I felt my Irish temper starting to boil. My instinct was to lash back. Fortunately, for reasons I still don't understand, I did not. Instead, I said, "Look, everybody in this auditorium wants to give me a hard time, and I just can't let you have all the fun." I broke eye contact, but he kept shouting.

At that point, another person shouted at the questioner "Will you sit down and shut up? We want to get at him too." That struck me as funny—perhaps I have a perverted sense of humor—and I laughed. The audience joined in, and even my adversaries on the panel laughed. We then had a fairly civil discussion of policy issues.

What would have happened if I had succumbed to the temptation of responding sharply to this man's accusations? The audience would have sided with him, I would have been booed, and the evening would have been quite unpleasant. The moral of this story? Keep your cool, no matter how provoked you may be. Your audience will respect you and may turn on the heckler who is taking up their time. I fortuitously learned a valuable lesson that day.

Let me make some final observations about our profession. Emotions do indeed play an important role with any audience, but it is still verifiable, factual data that persuades reasonable people to come to your side. Above all, remember that you cannot persuade an audience; audience members must persuade themselves. Never tell them that you are going to persuade, sell, or convince them. Do so and you are dead in the water. Allow audience members to "save face" by providing backing for your position with oral footnotes and with information they did not have prior to listening to you. Remember to maintain your composure, avoid personal attacks, and always keep in mind what you want your audience to do as a result of listening to your argument.

I think a fitting way to conclude may be with one of my favorite quotations about the true purpose of speaking to any group. It comes from the birthplace of speech training and the art of persuasion, ancient Greece. The people of Athens, although admiring the speaker with the stentorian voice, dramatic gesture, and clever turn of phrase, nevertheless realized the purpose of any presentation was to cause audience members to take the action the speaker wished them to take. So it was said, in comparing the greatest speaker of the day with one who had lived many years before: "When Demosthenes speaks, people say 'how well he speaks'. But when Pericles spoke, people said, 'Let us march.'"

Thank you, and good luck in all your speaking ventures, to friend and foe alike.

PERSUASIVE SPEECH

Blinded by the Light

Erica Radcliffe[2]

On June 14, 2003, Bishop Thomas O'Brien was on his way home from celebrating mass. During his routine drive home, he heard a loud noise on the passenger side of his car and noticed his windshield had been damaged by what he thought was a rock. It wasn't until two days later that, according to *CNN.com* March 19, 2004, Bishop O'Brien was arrested by police, not for a cracked windshield, but rather for having struck and killed 43-year-old Jim Reed. In *The Washington Post* of February 10, 2004, Bishop O'Brien contends he never saw Reed in the roadway. The cause of his temporary blindness: the glare from streetlamps and headlights of oncoming traffic.

But this growing epidemic of excessive artificial nighttime lighting, better known as light pollution, isn't confined to this one tragic incident. According to an AAA publication of March 2003, nighttime glare from excessive lighting on roadways and from headlights is responsible for an average of 38,000 traffic accidents each year. But the effects of untamed illumination do more than put us at risk behind the wheel. Since *The New York Times* of August 30, 2003, reports that the United States wastes as much as 2 billion tax dollars every year in bad lighting, and because 99% of Americans live in areas tainted by light pollution, we must first look at the problems it creates, next investigate the causes, before finally figuring out some solutions that will help us flick the switch fueling light pollution.

Although often underestimated, excessive nighttime lighting can produce a plethora of safety, health, and environmental impacts. First, while bright light after dark may seem like a safety precaution, it can actually be a safety hazard. According to *The Santa Fe New Mexican* of July 27, 2003, too much lighting on sidewalks or in alleyways creates shadows, making unsuspecting passersby more susceptible to crime. Here we see a woman walking on what appears to be a well-lit sidewalk. However, in this photo she's gone, but she didn't go far; in fact, she only moved 4 feet to her left—now well hidden by the shadows created from the excessive lighting.

Light pollution also affects our safety on the road. According to *The Vail Daily* of September 25, 2003, after a nighttime fill-up, it takes our eyes 10 minutes to readjust from unnecessary lighting at gas stations once we're back on the road. And a study presented at the 2003 meeting of the National Transportation Research Board confirmed that only 5% of drivers recognized a pedestrian on a road with glare.

Light pollution not only affects our safety, but also has a direct impact on our health. *Discover Magazine* of July 2003 explains that light pollution can "trigger deadly hormonal imbalances." According to *ABC Science Online* of February 18, 2003, the increased and unnatural levels of light we are exposed to after dark is likely raising the risk of cancers. And an August 22, 2003, article by the Harvard Center for Cancer Prevention reports that nighttime light exposure may significantly increase the risk of breast and colon cancer. According to *Life Extension Magazine* of January 2004, light from sources as small as a night-light or television inhibits cancer-fighting melatonin production, compromising our immune systems, making us more susceptible to any number of diseases.

And if your eyesight is not as good as it used to be, recent studies have found that light pollution also affects our vision. *CNN.com,* updated daily and last accessed March 23, 2004, revealed that 55% of children who slept with a light on before the age of 2 were diagnosed with myopia, or nearsightedness, 30% more than those that slept in complete darkness, leading to increased risk of glaucoma, retinal detachment, and macular degeneration in old age. Finally, light pollution is leaving its mark on the environment. *The Norfolk Eastern Daily Press* of September 15, 2003, warns that every 100-watt bulb left on during the hours of darkness all year releases a quarter of a ton of carbon dioxide into the atmosphere, contributing significantly to global warming.

All of us are plagued by the three biggest causes of light pollution: industrialization, commercial competition, and our growing fear of the dark. Due to urban sprawl, the *Audubon Magazine* Web site accessed March 13, 2004, and updated monthly reveals that only 10% of us live in an area where we can see all the stars that should be visible under normal nighttime conditions. According to *The Providence Journal-Bulletin* of August 3, 2003, astronomers at Kitte Peak National Observatory have been complaining about the lights from Phoenix, an area that lies over 120 miles away.

Commercial competition is also responsible. The *Progressivegrocer.com,* updated daily and last accessed March 3, 2004, explains that many small businesses are now forced to expand their hours due to competition from larger chain stores. This rising need for 24-hour service only leads to more unnecessary excess lighting. Advertisements are also a problem. *American Demographic* of December 1, 2003, explains that outdoor advertising is a 6-billion-dollar industry on the rise; over the past 10 years, spending on outdoor ads has risen 97%. According to the February 10, 2004, *Pittsburgh Post-Gazette,* billboards "ruin drivers' night vision" as they use excessive lighting to get consumers' attention quickly on highways or busy city streets.

Finally, it's our own age-old fear of the dark. According to the previously cited *New York Times,* recent studies have found that contrary to popular belief, over-lighting does not reduce crime, but instead, as we saw earlier, merely alleviates our fear of crime, creating a dangerous false sense of security. So maybe it's time we conquered this fear, and we can start by looking at some solutions.

Although the problem seems glaring, it is one of the most easily curable forms of pollution, but must be addressed on a community, industry, and an individual level. The previously cited *Norfolk Eastern Daily Press* explains that the Norfolk city government now requires that white bulbs in street lamps be replaced with low-light-polluting orange bulbs. Road signs and billboards should be replaced with prismatic material, explains *The Pasadena Citizen* of September 16, 2003. This new, highly reflective material eliminates the need for overhead lighting on all road signs because it uses a car's headlights to light up the signs, illuminating them only when needed.

Businesses must also do their part. *The New Haven Register* of September 24, 2003, explains large light-emitting commercial buildings should surround their properties with fences and trees, reducing light pollution from the site. To eliminate unnecessary overnight light pollution, the previously cited *Vail Daily* explains that in that part of Colorado, business lights must be shut off 1 hour after closing. According to the May 17, 2003, *ABC News.com,* by going dark at night, some office buildings and school systems are saving as much as 1 million dollars every year.

But you can start fighting light pollution right now. The AAA Foundation for Traffic Safety offers tips to handle glare for safer driving at night. Please feel free to take one. And as soon as you get home, replace those 200-watt bulbs with 100s and turn out the lights when you leave a room. If you have a nightlight, place it low on a wall facing away from you and keep it as dim as possible. If you tend to fall asleep with the TV on, many sets can now be programmed to shut off after a certain period of time. And according to the Home Depot Web site, last accessed March 23, 2004, you can purchase a Motion Sensor Security Light that only turns on when needed for as little as $12.97.

Today, we have seen the problems, looked at the causes, and finally, viewed some solutions to help us fight light pollution. Bishop Thomas O'Brien served Phoenix's 480,000 Catholics for 21 years. He now owns the title of the first-ever felony conviction for a U.S. Roman Catholic bishop. This is clearly one time Bishop O'Brien would have given anything not to be blinded by the light.

Glossary

absolute pertaining to the belief that there is a single correct moral standard that holds for everyone, everywhere, every time

action-oriented listening style that reflects a preference for error-free and well-organized speaking

active agents seekers of various media messages and resisters of others

adaptors gestures used to manage emotions

age identity a combination of self-perception of age along with what others understand that age to mean

agenda-setting capacity the power of media coverage to influence individuals' view of the world

analysis paralysis potential pitfall in small group interaction; occurs when excessive analysis prevents a group from moving toward a solution

artifacts clothing and other accessories

artistic proofs artistic skills of a rhetor that influence effectiveness

assertiveness expressing one's opinions forcefully without offending others

assimilation the communicative, behavioral, and cognitive processes that influence individuals to join, identify with, become integrated into, and (occasionally) exit an organization

asynchronous communication in which messages are sent and received at different times

attachment an emotional tie, such as the closeness young children develop with their caregivers

attraction theory a theory that explains the primary forces that draw people together

attractiveness the appeal one person has for another, based on physical appearance, personalities, and/or behavior

attribution theory explanation of the processes we use to judge our own and others' behavior

attributional bias the tendency to attribute one's own negative behavior to external causes and one's positive actions to internal states

audience analysis the process of determining what an audience already knows or wants to know about a topic, who they are, what they know or need to know about the speaker, and what their expectations might be for the presentation

authoritarian leader leader who takes charge, makes all the decisions, and dictates strategies and work tasks

avatars digital alter-egos or versions of oneself, used in MMOGs

avoiding stage of romantic relational dissolution in which couples try not to interact with each other

behaviorism the focus on the study of behavior as a science

blogs short for weblogs; online diaries or news commentaries

bonding stage of romantic relational development characterized by public commitment

border dwellers people who live between cultures and often experience contradictory cultural patterns

brainstorm to generate as many ideas as possible without critiquing them

bullying repeated hostile behaviors that are or are perceived to be intended to harm parties who are unable to defend themselves

burnout a chronic condition that results from the accumulation of daily stress, which manifests itself in a very specific set of characteristics, including exhaustion, cynicism, and ineffectiveness

categorization a cognitive process used to organize information by placing it into larger groupings of information

cause–effect pattern one used to create understanding and agreement, and sometimes to argue for a specific action

channel the means through which a message is transmitted

charismatic leadership a leadership style in which extremely self-confident leaders inspire unusual dedication to themselves by relying upon their strong personalities and charm

chronemics the study of the way people use time as a message

chronological pattern one that follows a timeline

circumscribing stage of romantic relational dissolution in which couples discuss safe topics

cocultural group a significant minority group within a dominant majority that does not share dominant group values or communication patterns

cocultural theory explores the role of power in daily interactions

cognitive complexity the degree to which a person's constructs are detailed, involved, or numerous

cognitive representation the ability to form mental models of the world

cohort effect the influence of shared characteristics of a group that was born and reared in the same general period

cohort effect the process by which historical events influence the perceptions of people who grew up in a given generation and time period

collectivistic orientation a value orientation that stresses the needs of the group

communicating information using nonverbal behaviors to help clarify verbal messages and reveal attitudes and moods

communication ethics the standards of right and wrong that one applies to messages that are sent and received

computer-mediated communication (CMC) the exchange of messages carried through an intervening system of digital electronic storage and transmitted between two or more people

conclusion closing material of a speech where the speaker reviews the main points, may challenge the audience to act, and leaves the audience with a positive view of speaker and topic

confirming communication comments that validate positive self-images of others

congruent verbal and nonverbal messages that express the same meaning

connotative meaning the affective or interpretive meanings attached to a word

constructive marginal people people who thrive in a border-dweller life, while recognizing its tremendous challenges

constructs categories people develop to help them organize information

content analysis approach to understanding communication that focuses on specific aspects of the content of a text or group of texts

content analysis approach to understanding media that focuses on a specific aspect of the content of a text or group of texts

content meaning the concrete meaning of the message, and the meanings suggested by or associated with the message and the emotions triggered by it

content-oriented a listening style that reflects an interest in detailed and complex information, simply for the content itself

contingent employees individuals who work in temporary positions, part-time or as subcontractors

contradicting verbal and nonverbal messages that send conflicting messages

critical approach an approach used not only to understand human behavior but ultimately to change society

critical listening listening skills that are useful in a wide variety of situations—particularly those involving persuasive speaking

cultivation theory idea that long-term immersion in a media environment leads to "cultivation," or enculturation, into shared beliefs about the world

cultural capital cultural knowledge and cultural competencies that people need to function effectively in society

cultural values beliefs that are so central to a cultural group that they are never questioned

culture learned patterns of perceptions, values, and behaviors shared by a group of people

culture learned patterns of perceptions, values, and behaviors shared by a group of people

culture industries large organizations in the business of mass communication that produce, distribute, or show various media texts (cultural products) as an industry

culture shock a feeling of disorientation and discomfort due to the lack of familiar environmental cues

cyberbullying the deliberate and repeated misuse of communication technology by an individual or group to threaten or harm others

cyberspace the online world; often used synonymously with the Internet

deception concealment, distortion, or lying in communication

decoding receiving a message and interpreting its meaning

deliberative rhetoric the type of rhetoric used to argue what a society should do in the future

delivery the presentation of a speech before an audience

demand touching a type of touch used to establish dominance and power

demand-withdrawal an interaction pattern in which one partner criticizes or tries to change the other partner, who responds by becoming defensive and then disengaging—either psychologically or physically

democratic leader leader whose style is characterized by considerable input from group members

demographic analysis the portion of an audience analysis that considers the ages, races, sexes, sexual orientations, religions, and social class of the audience

denotative meaning the dictionary, or literal, meaning of a word

dialect a variation of a language distinguished by its vocabulary, grammar, and pronunciation

dialectic approach recognizes that things need not be perceived as "either/or," but may be seen as "both/and"

diaspora group of immigrants, sojourners, slaves, or strangers living in new lands while retaining strong attachments to their homelands

dichotomous thinking thinking in which things are perceived as "either/or"—for example, "good or bad," "big or small," "right or wrong"

differentiating stage of romantic relational dissolution in which couples increase their interpersonal distance

diffusion of innovations theory that suggests that in order for people to accept a new technology like the computer, they have to see it as useful and compatible with their vales and lifestyle

digital information that is transmitted in a numerical format based on only two values (0 and 1)

digital divide inequity of access between the technology "haves" and "have nots"

disability identity identification with physical or mental impairment that substantially impact everyday life

disconfirming communication comments that reject or invalidate a positive or negative self-image of our conversational partners

downward communication in a traditional conduit model of communication, communication with subordinates

e-books electronic books read on a computer screen instead of a printed page

Ebonics a version of English that has its roots in West African, Caribbean, and U.S. slave languages

ego-defensive function the role prejudice plays in protecting individuals' sense of self-worth

elocutionists scholars in the 19th century who promoted the study of the mechanics of public speaking, including proper pronunciation, grammar, and gestures

emblems gestures that stand for a specific verbal meaning

emergence phase the third phase of the decision-making process; occurs when group members express a cooperative attitude

emoticons pictographs used to convey relational information in computer-mediated communication, such as the smiley face :-)

empowerment employees' feelings of self-efficacy

enacting identities performing scripts deemed proper for particular identities

encapsulated marginal people people who feel disintegrated by having to shift cultures

encoding taking ideas and converting them into messages

establishing social control using nonverbal behavior to exercise influence over other people

ethics standards of what is right and wrong, good and bad, moral and immoral

ethnic identity identification with a particular group with which one shares some or all of these characteristics: national or tribal affiliation, religious beliefs, language, and/or cultural and traditional origins and background

ethnocentrism the tendency to view one's own group as the standard against which all other groups are judged

ethnographic relating to studies in which researchers actively engage with participants

ethos the rhetorical construction of character

evaluating assessing your reaction to a message

experimenting stage of romantic relational development in which both people seek to learn about each other

expressing and managing intimacy using nonverbal behaviors to help convey attraction and closeness

eye contact looking directly into the eyes of another

feedback the response to a message

field of availables potential partners and friends, typically much larger via CMC than via face-to-face relationships

field of experience the education, life events, and cultural background that a communicator possesses

filtering removing nonverbal cues

forensic rhetoric rhetoric that addresses events that happened in the past with the goal of setting things right after an injustice has occurred

formal structure officially designated channels of communication, reflecting explicit or desired patterns of interaction

frame a structure that shapes how people interpret their perceptions

friendship touch touch that is more intimate than social touch and usually conveys warmth, closeness, and caring

function the goals and effects of communication

functional (situational) theory a theory that assumes leadership behaviors can be learned

functional touch the least intimate type of touch; used by certain workers such as dentists, hairstylists, and hospice workers, as part of their livelihood; also known as professional touch

fundamental attribution error the tendency to attribute others' negative behavior to internal causes and their positive behaviors to external causes

gender identity how and to what extent one identifies with the social construction of masculinity and femininity

general purpose whichever of three goals—to inform, persuade, or entertain—dominates a speech

general systems theory theory that organizations are a system composed of many subsystems and embedded in larger systems, and that organizations should develop communication strategies that serve both

generalized other the collection of roles, rules, norms, beliefs, and attitudes endorsed by the community in which a person lives

gestures nonverbal communication made with part of the body, including actions such as pointing, waving, or holding up a hand to direct people's attention

globalization the increasing connectedness of the world in economic, political, and cultural realms

grammar the structural rules that govern the generation of meaning in a language

group processes the methods, including communication, by which a group accomplishes a task

group roles the shared expectations group members have regarding each individual's communication behavior in the group

grouphate the distaste and aversion that people feel toward working in groups

groupthink a negative, and potentially disastrous, group process characterized by "excessive concurrence thinking"

haptics the study of the communicative function of touch

hate speech use of verbal communication to attack others based upon some social category

Hays Code self-imposed rules for Hollywood media content instituted in 1930 with the goal of creating "wholesome entertainment"

hegemony the process by which we consent to social constructions, rather than having them imposed on us

heterogeneous diverse

heuristic use of language to acquire knowledge and understanding

hierarchy a power structure in which some members exercise authority over others

homogeneity a high degree of similarity

horizontal communication in a traditional conduit model of communication, communication with peers

hostile work environment an intimidating, hostile, or offensive workplace atmosphere created by unwelcome and inappropriate sexually based behavior; one of two types of sexual harassment recognized by federal law

human communication a process in which people generate meaning through the exchange of verbal and nonverbal messages in specific contexts, influenced by individual and social forces, and embedded in culture

human relations approach to management that holds that the job of management is actually to educate, interact, and integrate

human–nature value orientation the perceived relationship between humans and nature

humanism a system of thought that celebrates human nature and its potential

hurtful messages messages that criticize, tease, reject, or otherwise cause an emotional injury to another

identity who a person is; composed of individual and social categories a person identifies with, as well as the categories that others identify with that person

illustrators signals that accompany speech to clarify or emphasize the verbal messages

imaginative use of language to express oneself artistically or creatively

immediacy how close or involved people appear to be with each other

individual roles roles that focus more on individuals' own interests and needs than on those of the group

individualist orientation a value orientation that respects the autonomy and independence of individuals

informal structure unspoken but understood channels of communication, reflecting patterns that develop spontaneously

informational listening listening skills that are useful in situations requiring attention to content

informative use of language to communicate information or report facts

ingratiation behavior and communication designed to increase liking

initiating stage of romantic relational development in which both people behave so as to appear pleasant and likeable

innovation a function of organizational communication by means of which systems are changed

instrumental use of language to obtain what you need or desire

integrating stage of romantic relational development in which both people portray themselves as a couple

intensifying stage of romantic relational development in which both people seek to increase intimacy and connectedness

interactional use of language to establish and define social relationships

intercultural communication communication that occurs in interactions between people who are culturally different

Internet a system of networks that connects millions of computers around the world

interpersonal violence physical violence against a partner or child

interpretation the act of assigning meaning to sensory information

interpretive approach contemporary term for humanistic (rhetorical) study

intimate distance (0 to 18 inches) the space used when interacting with those with whom one is very close

introduction opening material of a speech from which the audience members gain a first impression of the speech's content and of the speaker

involuntary long-term travelers people who are border dwellers permanently but not by choice, such as those who relocate to escape war

involuntary short-term travelers people who are border dwellers not by choice and only for a limited time, such as refugees forced to move

jargon the specialized terms that develop in many professions

jealousy a complex and often painful emotion that occurs when a person perceives a threat to an existing relationship

kinesics nonverbal communication sent by the body, including gestures, posture, movement, facial expressions, and eye behavior

Knapp's stage model model of relationship development that views relationships as occurring in "stages" and that focuses on how people communicate as relationships develop and decline

label a name assigned to a category based on one's perception of the category

laissez-faire a leadership style characterized by complete freedom for the group in making decisions

lexical choice vocabulary

listening the process of receiving, constructing meaning from, and responding to spoken and/or nonverbal messages

listening style a set of attitudes, beliefs, and predispositions about the how, where, when, who, and what of the information receiving and encoding process

logos rational appeals; the use of rhetoric to help the audience see the rationale for a particular conclusion

long-term orientation a value orientation in which people stress the importance of virtue

long-term versus short-term orientation the dimension of a society's value orientation that reflects its attitude toward virtue or truth

looking-glass self the idea that self-image results from the images others reflect back to an individual

love-intimate touch the touch most often used with one's romantic partners and family

Machiavellian tactics having a third party convey one's unhappiness about a relationship

maintenance a function of organizational communication in which the stability of existing systems is preserved

mass media mediated communication intended for large audiences

mass media effects the influence that media have on people's everyday lives

mass-market paperbacks popular books addressed to a large audience and widely distributed

Massively Multiplayer Online Games (MMOGs) text-based "virtual reality" games in which participants interact with enrichments, objects, and other participants

matching hypothesis the tendency to develop relationships with people who are approximately as attractive as we are

media the plural form of *medium*, a channel of communication

media activism the practice of organizing to communicate displeasure with certain media images and messages, as well as to force change in future media texts

media augmentation approach a theoretical perspective that sees views mediated communication as complementing or augmenting face-to-face communication

media deficit approach a theoretical perspective that sees mediated communication as less useful than face-to-face communication

media event occasions or catastrophes that interrupt regular programming

media richness theory theory that describes the potential information-carrying capacity of a communication medium

media text a television show, advertisement, movie, or other media event

media violence representations of violent acts in media

mediation peaceful third-party intervention

messages the building blocks of communication events

methods the specific ways that scholars collect and analyze data which they then use to prove or disprove their theories

monochronically engaging in one task or behavior at a time

monotheistic belief in one god

motivation feeling personally invested in accomplishing a specific activity or goal

MPAA Motion Picture Association of America

multiracial identity one who self-identifies as having more than one racial identity

mutable subject to change

national identity a person's citizenship

naturalistic relating to everyday, real-life situations, such as a classroom, café, or shopping mall

new media a collection of mediated communication technologies that are digital and converging and tend to be interactive

new social contract assumes that loyalty is not expected by workers or organizations and that job security is unlikely

noise any stimulus that can interfere with, or degrade, the quality of a message

nominalists those who argue that any idea can be expressed in any language and that the structure and vocabulary of the language do not influence the speaker's perception of the world

nonverbal behavior all the nonverbal actions people perform

nonverbal codes distinct, organized means of expression that consists of symbols and rules for their use

nonverbal communication nonverbal behavior that has symbolic meaning

openness a state in which communicators are willing to share their ideas as well as listen to others in a way that avoids conveying negative or disconfirming feedback

orator a public speaker

organization the process by which one recognizes what sensory input represents

organizational culture a pattern of shared beliefs, values, and behaviors

organizational identification the stage of assimilation that occurs when an employee's values overlap with the organization's values

organizations the set of interactions that members of purposeful groups use to accomplish their individual and common goals

paradigm belief system that represents a particular worldview

paralinguistics all aspects of spoken language except the words themselves; includes rate, volume, pitch, stress

participants the people interacting during communication

particular others the important people in an individual's life whose opinions and behavior influence the various aspects of identity

passing away the process by which relationships decline over time

pathos the rhetorical use of emotions to affect audience decision making

people-oriented a listening style that is associated with friendly, open communication and an interest in establishing ties with others

performance of identity the process or means by which we show the world who we think we are

persona the identity one creates through one's public communication efforts

personal distance (18 inches to 4 feet) the space used when interacting with friends and acquaintances

personal language use of language to express individuality and personality

phishing the practice of trying fraudulently to get consumer banking and credit card information

phonology the study of the sounds that compose individual languages and how those sounds communicate meaning

podcast audio file stored digitally

political economy the ways in which media institutions produce texts in a capitalist system and the legal and regulatory frameworks that shape their options for doing so

polychronically engaging in multiple activities simultaneously

polytheistic belief in more than one god

power distance a value orientation that refers to the extent to which less powerful members of institutions and organizations within a culture expect and accept an unequal distribution of power

pragmatics field of study that emphasizes how language is used in specific situations to accomplish goals

predicted outcome theory a theory that attempts to explain how reducing uncertainty can lead to attraction or repulsion

preferred personality a value orientation that expresses whether it is more important for a person to "do" or to "be"

prejudice experiencing aversive or negative feelings toward a group as a whole or toward an individual because she or he belongs to a group

primary groups groups that provide members with a sense of belonging and affection

primary tension the uncertainty commonly felt in the beginning phase of decision making

problem–solution pattern one in which the speaker describes various aspects of a problem and then proposes solutions

production a function of organizational communication in which activity is coordinated toward accomplishing tasks

professional touch type of touch used by certain workers, such as dentists, hairstylists, and hospice workers, as part of their livelihood; also known as functional touch

prototype an idealized schema

proxemics the study of how people use spatial cues, including interpersonal distance, territoriality, and other space relationships, to communicate

proximity how physically close one is to others

pseudoanonymity projecting a false identity

public distance (12 to 25 feet) the distance used for public ceremonies such as lectures and performances

public sphere the arena in which deliberative decision making occurs through the exchange of ideas and arguments

qualitative methods methods in which researchers study naturally occurring communication rather than assembling data and converting it to numbers

quantitative methods methods that convert data to numerical indicators, and then analyze these numbers using statistics to establish relationships among the concepts

quid pro quo requests for sexual favors as a condition of getting or keeping a job or benefit; one of two types of sexual harassment recognized by federal law

racial identity identification with a particular racial group

rationality the ability to communicate through reasoning, bargaining, coalition building, and assertiveness

reflected appraisals the idea that people's self-images arise primarily from the ways that others view them and from the many messages they have received from others about who they are

regulating interaction using nonverbal behaviors to help manage conversational interaction

regulators gestures used to control conversation

regulatory use of language to control or regulate the behaviors of others

reinforcement phase the final phase of the decision-making process when group members reach consensus, and members feel a sense of accomplishment

relational maintenance behaviors that couples perform that help maintain their relationships

relational roles roles that help establish a group's social atmosphere

relational trajectory models relationship development models that view relationship development as more variable than stage models

relationship meaning what a message conveys about the relationship between the parties

relative pertaining to the belief that moral behavior varies among individuals, groups, and cultures and across situations

relativists those who argue that language serves not only as a way for us to voice our ideas but "is itself the shaper of ideas, the guide for the individual's mental activity"

relaxation the degree of tension displayed by one's body

religious identity aspect of identity defined by one's spiritual beliefs

responding showing others how you regard their message

reverse culture shock/reentry shock culture shock experienced by travelers upon returning to their home country

rhetor a person or institution that addresses a large audience; the originator of a communication message but not necessarily the one delivering it

rhetoric communication that is used to influence the attitudes or behaviors of others; the art of persuasion

rhetoric communication that is used to influence the attitudes or behaviors of others; the art of persuasion

rhetorical analysis used by researchers to examine texts or public speeches as they occur in society with the aim of interpreting textual meaning

rhetorical audience those people who can take the appropriate action in response to a message

rhetorical critic an informed consumer of rhetorical discourse who is prepared to analyze rhetorical texts

rhetorical event any event that generates a significant amount of public discourse

rhetoricians scholars who study the art of public speaking and the art of persuasion

role expectations the expectation that one will perform in a particular way because of the social role occupied

Sapir-Whorf hypothesis idea that the language people speak determines the way they see the world (a relativist perspective)

schemas cognitive structures that represent an individual's understanding of a concept or person

script a relatively fixed sequence of events that functions as a guide or template for communication or behavior

secondary (recurring) tension conflict or tension found in the second or conflict phase of the decision-making process

secondary groups groups that meet principally to solve problems

selection the process of choosing which sensory information to focus on

selective attention consciously or unconsciously attending to just a narrow range of the full array of sensory information available

selective exposure the idea that people seek media messages and/or interpret media texts in ways that confirm their beliefs and, conversely, resist or avoid messages that challenge their beliefs

self-concept the understanding of one's unique characteristics as well as the similarities to, and differences from, others

self-esteem part of one's self-concept; arises out of how one perceives and interprets reflected appraisals and social comparisons

self-fulfilling prophecy when an individual expects something to occur, the expectation increases the likelihood that it will

self-respect treating others, and expecting to be treated, with respect and dignity

self-serving bias the tendency to give one's self more credit than is due when good things happen and to accept too little responsibility for those things that go wrong

semantic-information distance describes the gap in information and understanding between supervisors and subordinates on specific issues

semantics the study of meaning

sensing the stage of listening most people refer to as "hearing"; when listeners pick up the sound waves directed toward them

servant leadership a leadership style that seeks to ensure that other people's highest priority needs are being served in order to increase teamwork and personal involvement

service-task functions using nonverbal behavior to signal close involvement between people in impersonal relationships and contexts

setting the physical surroundings of a communication event

sexual coercion physically nonviolent pressure to engage in unwanted sex

sexual identity which of the various categories of sexuality one identifies with

shared (collaborative or distributed) leadership a type of leadership style where functional leadership is extended to an organizational level; all members are equal partners and share responsibility for the work of the group

short-term orientation a value orientation that stresses the importance of possessing one fundamental truth

signposts transitions in a speech that help an audience understand the speaker's organization, making it easier for them to follow

similarity degree to which people share the same values, interests, and background

small group communication communication among a small number of people who share a common purpose or goal, who feel connected to each other, and who coordinate their behavior

social class identity an informal ranking of people in a culture based on their income, occupation, education, dwelling, child-rearing habits, and other factors

social distance (4 to 12 feet) the distance most U.S. Americans use when they interact with unfamiliar others

social facilitation the tendency for people to work harder and do better when others are around

social movement a large, organized body of people who are attempting to create social change

social network theory theory that proposes that the patterns of connections among people affect their social behavior and communication

Social Networking Sites (SNSs) web-based service where people construct their profiles, identify others with whom they share a connection, and interact with others within the system

social penetration theory a theory that proposes relationships develop through increases in self-disclosure

social position place in the social hierarchy, which comes from the way society is structured

social presence degree of psychological closeness or immediacy engendered by various media

social presence theory suggests that face-to-face communication is generally high in this kind of social presence, and that media vary in the amount of social presence they convey

social role the specific position or positions one holds in a society

social science approach contemporary term for the behaviorist approach

social-polite touch touch that is part of daily interaction in the United States; it is more intimate than professional touch but is still impersonal

sophists the first group to teach persuasive speaking skills in the Greek city-states

soundscape the everyday sounds in our environments

spam unwanted commercial messages and advertisements sent through email

spatial pattern one that arranges points by location and can be used to describe something small

special-occasion speeches evocative speeches intended to entertain, inspire, celebrate, commemorate, or build community

specific purpose what a speaker wants to inform or persuade an audience about, or the type of feelings the speaker wants to evoke

speech act theory branch of pragmatics that suggests that when people communicate, they do not just say things, they also do things with their words

spoofing misrepresenting oneself online

stagnating stage of romantic relational dissolution in which couples try to prevent change

stereotype threat process in which reminding individuals of stereotypical expectations regarding important identities can impact their performance

stereotyping creating schemas that overgeneralize attributes of a specific group

strategic communication communication on that is purpose directed

strategy control assessing the available information and options in order to increases one's understanding of the conflict and the other party before engaging in conflict communication

structure recurring patterns of interaction among organizational members

style theory theory that asserts that a leader's manner or style determines his or her success

sudden death the process by which relationships end without prior warning for at least one participant

supporting materials information that supports the speaker's ideas

supportive listening listening skills focused not only on understanding information but also "listening" to others' feelings

supportiveness refers to supervisors who provide their subordinates with access to information and resources

symbol something that represents something else and conveys meaning

synchronous communication in which messages are sent and received at the same time

Synergetic Model of Communication a transactional model based on the roles individual and societal forces, contexts, and culture play in the communication process

syntax the rules that govern word order

task roles roles that are directly related to the accomplishment of group goals

technocapital access to technological skills and resources

terminating stage of romantic relational dissolution in which couples end the relationship

textual analysis similar to rhetorical analysis; used to analyze cultural "products," such as media and public speeches

theory a set of statements that explains a particular phenomenon

thesis statement a statement of the topic of a speech and the speaker's position on it

time-oriented a listening style that prefers brief, concise speech

topical pattern one that has no innate organization except that imposed by the speaker

trait theory leadership theory that suggests that leaders are born

transformational leadership a leadership style that empowers group members to work independently from the leader by encouraging group cohesion

truth bias the tendency to not suspect one's intimates of deception

turning point model a model of relationship development in which couples move both toward and away from commitment over the course of their relationship

TV Parental Guidelines a self-regulating system of the television industry that rates programs in terms of appropriateness for particular age groups

uncertainty reduction theory a theory that argues relationship development is facilitated or derailed by participants' efforts to reduce their uncertainty about each other

understanding interpreting the messages associated with sounds or what the sounds mean

upward communication in a traditional conduit model of communication, communication with superiors

upward distortion occurs when subordinates are hesitant to communicate negative news and present information to superiors in a more positive light than is warranted

urgent organizations companies that try to shorten the time it takes to develop new products and respond to customer demands

uses and gratifications the idea that people use media messages and find various types of gratifications in some media texts rather than in others

V-chip device that identifies television program ratings by content and can block programming designated by the owner

value-expressive function the role played by prejudice in allowing people to view their own values, norms, and cultural practices as appropriate and correct

view of human nature a value orientation that expresses whether humans are fundamentally good, evil, or a mixture

visual aids audiovisual materials that help a speaker reach intended speech goals

vocalizations uttered sounds that do not have the structure of language

voice qualities qualities such as speed, pitch, rhythm, vocal range, and articulation that make up the "music" of the human voice

voluntary long-term travelers people who are border dwellers by choice and for an extended time, such as immigrants

voluntary short-term travelers people who are border dwellers by choice and for a limited time, such as study-abroad students or corporate personnel

withdrawal/avoidance a friendship termination strategy in which friends spend less time together, don't return phone calls, and avoid places where they are likely to see each other

World Wide Web (WWW) a system of interlinked hypertext documents contained on the Internet

References

Chapter 1

Alberts, J. K., Yoshimura, C. G., Rabby, M. K., & Loschiavo, R. (2005). Mapping the topography of couples' daily interaction. *Journal of Social and Personal Relationships, 22,* 299–323.

Andersen, P. A., Lustig, M. W., & Andersen, J. F. (1990). Changes in latitude, changes in attitude: The relationship between climate and interpersonal communication predispositions. *Communication Quarterly, 38,* 291–311.

Barnlund, D. C. (1962). Consistency of emergent leadership in groups with changing tasks and members. *Speech Monographs, 29,* 45–52.

Buller, D. B., & Burgoon, J. K. (1996). Interpersonal deception theory. *Communication Theory, 6,* 203–242.

Buck, R., & VanLear, C. A. (2002). Verbal and nonverbal communication: Distinguishing symbolic, spontaneous and pseudo-spontaneous nonverbal behavior. *Journal of Communication, 52,* 522–541.

Christians, C., & Traber, M. (Eds.). (1997). *Communication ethics and universal values.* Thousand Oaks, CA: Sage.

Dickens, T. E. (2003). General symbol machines: The first stage in the evolution of symbolic communication. *Evolutionary Psychology, 1,* 192–209.

Diener, M. (2002, January). Fair enough: To be a better negotiator, learn to tell the difference between a lie and a *lie. Entrepreneur Magazine.* Retrieved March 16, 2006, from http://www.Entrepreneurmagazine.com

Dixon, M., & Duck, S. W. (1993). Understanding relationship processes: Uncovering the human search for meaning. In S. W. Duck (Ed.), *Understanding relationship processes, Vol. 1: Individuals in relationships* (pp. 175–206). Newbury Park, CA: Sage.

Duck, S. (1994). *Meaningful relationships: Talking, sense and relating.* Newbury Park, CA: Sage.

Eisenberg, E. M., Goodall, H. L., Jr., & Trethewey, A. (2010). *Organizational communication: Balancing creativity and constraints.* New York: St. Martin's.

Emanuel, R. (2007). Humanities: Communication's core discipline. *American Communication Journal, 9*(2). Retrieved March 11, 2009, from http://www.acjournal.org/holdings/vol9/summer/articles/discipline.html

FoxNews.com (2010, November 24). Tom DeLay convicted of money laundering. Retrieved February 17, 2011, from http://www.foxnews.com/politics/2010/11/24/jury-convicts-delay-money-laundering-trial/

Gergen, K. J. (1982). *Toward transformation in social knowledge.* New York: Springer.

Johannesen, R. (1990). *Ethics in human communication.* Prospect Heights, IL: Waveland.

Jones, A., & Koppel, N. (2010, August 7). Ethical lapses felled long list of company executives. WallStreetJournal.com. Retrieved February 17, 2011, from http://online.wsj.com/article/SB1000142405274870330970457541384208937 5632.html

Kant, I. (1949). *Fundamental principles of the metaphysic of morals* (tr. by T. K. Abbott, Trans.). Indianapolis: Bobbs-Merrill. (Original work published 1785)

Laswell, H. D. (1948). The structure and function of communication in society. In L. Bryson Ed.), *The Communication of Ideas.* New York: Harper.

Leventhal, R. (2011, February 16). Victims respond after Madoff points fingers at banks in first interview from prison. FoxNews.com. Retrieved February 17, 2011, from http://www.foxnews.com/us/2011/02/16/victims-respond-madoff-points-fingers-banks-interview/

Martin, J. N., & Nakayama, T. K. (2005). *Experiencing intercultural communication* (2nd ed.). Boston: McGraw-Hill.

McCabe, D. L., & Trevino, L. K. (1996). What we know about cheating in college: Longitudinal trends and recent developments. *Change, 28,* 28–33.

McCord, L. B., Greenhalgh, K., & Magasin, M. (2004). Businesspersons beware: Lying is a crime. *Graziadio Business Report, 7*(23). Pepperdine University. Retrieved December 30, 2009, from http://gbr.pepperdine.edu/043/lying.html

McCornack, S. A., & Parks, M. R. (1986). Deception detection and relationship development: The other side of trust. In M. L. McLaughlin (Ed.), *Communication Yearbook 9* (pp. 377–389). Newbury Park, CA: Sage. Retrieved March 16, 2006, from http://www.natcom.org/policies/External/EthicalComm

Mead, G. H. (1934). *Mind, self, and society.* Chicago: University of Chicago Press.

National Communication Association (2003). What is communication? *Pathways.* Retrieved October 24, 2008, from http://www.natcom.org/nca/Template2.asp?bid=339

Passer, M. W., & Smith, R. E. (2004). *Psychology: The science of mind and behavior* (2nd ed.). New York: McGraw Hill.

Paul, R., & Elder, L. (2008). *The miniature guide to critical thinking concepts and tools.* Dillon Beach, CA: Foundation for Critical Thinking Press.

Robinson-Smith, G. (2004). Verbal indicators of depression in conversations with stroke survivors. *Perspectives in Psychiatric Care, 40,* 61–69.

Rogers, E. M., & Chafee, S. H. (1983). Communication as an academic discipline: A dialogue. *Journal of Communication, 3,* 18–30.

Sartre, J. P. (1973). *Existentialism and humanism* (P. Mairet, Trans.) London: Methuen Ltd. (Original work published 1946)

Schirato, T., & Yell, S. (1996). *Communication & cultural literacy: An introduction.* St. Leonards, Australia: Allen & Unwin.

Shannon, C. E., & Weaver, W. (1949). *A mathematical model of communication.* Urbana, IL: University of Illinois Press.

Tolhuizen, J. H. (1990, November). *Deception in developing dating relationships.* Paper presented at the Speech Communication Association Convention, Chicago, IL.

Warren, S. F. & Yoder, P. J. (1998). Facilitating the transition to intentional communication. In A. Wetherby, S. Warren, & J. Reichle (Eds.). *Transitions in Prelinguistic Communication* (pp. 39–58). Baltimore: Brookes Publishing

Watzlawick, P., Beavin, J., & Jackson, D. D. (1967). *Pragmatics of human communication.* New York: W. W. Norton.

Wokutch, R. E., & Carson, T. L. (1981). The ethics and profitability of bluffing in business. In Lewickis, Saunders, & Minton (Eds.), *Negotiation: Readings, exercises, and cases* (pp. 341–353). Boston: Irwin/McGraw-Hill.

Chapter 2

Alberts, J. K. (1988). An analysis of couples' conversational complaint interactions. *Communication Monographs, 5,* 184–197.

Alcoff, L. (Winter 1991–1992). The problem of speaking for others. *Cultural Critique, 20,* 5–32.

Bartholomew, K. (1990). Avoidance of intimacy: An attachment perspective. *Journal of Social and Personal Relationships, 7,* 147–178.

Becker, J. A. H., Ellevold, B., & Stamp, G. H. (2008). The creation of defensiveness in social interaction II: A model of defensive communication among romantic couples. *Communication Monographs, 75*(1), 86–110.

Bowlby, J. (1982). Attachment and loss: Vol I: Attachment (2nd ed.). New York: Basic Books.

Borda, J. L. (2002). The woman suffrage parades of 1910–1913: Possibilities and limitations of an early feminist rhetorical strategy. *Western Journal of Communication, 66,* 25–52.

Bormann, E. G. (1980). *Communication theory.* New York: Holt, Rinehart and Winston.

Burrell, G., & Morgan, G. (1988). *Sociological paradigms and organizational analysis.* Portsmouth, NH: Heinemann.

Calafell, B. M., & Delgado, F. P. (2004). Reading Latina/o images: Interrogating Americanos. *Critical Studies in Media Communication, 21,* 1–21.

Campbell, K. K. (1994). *Women public speakers in the United States, 1925–1993: A bio-critical sourcebook.* Westport, CT: Greenwood

Carbaugh, D. (1990). Communication rules in Donahue discourse. In D. Carbaugh (Ed.), Cultural communication and intercultural contact (pp. 119–149). Hillsdale, NJ: Lawrence Erlbaum.

Carbaugh, D. (1999). "Just listen": "Listening" and landscape among the Blackfeet. *Western Journal of Communication, 63,* 250–270.

Carbaugh, D., & Berry, M. (2001). Communicating history, Finnish and American discourses: An ethnographic contribution to intercultural communication inquiry. *Communication Theory, 11,* 352–366.

Caughlin, J. P., & Vangelisti, A. L. (1999). Desire for change in one's partner as a predictor of the demand/withdraw pattern of marital communication. *Communication Monographs, 66*(1), 66–89.

Christensen, A. (1987). Detection of conflict patterns in couples. In K. Hahlweg & M. J. Goldstein (Eds.), *Understanding major mental disorder: The contribution of family interaction research* (pp. 250–265). New York: Family Process Press.

Christensen, A. (1988). Dysfunctional interaction patterns in couples. In P. Noller & M. A. Fitzpatrick (Eds.), *Perspectives in marital interaction* (pp. 31–52). Philadelphia: Multilingual Matters Ltg.

Christensen, A., & Heavey, C. L. (1990). Gender and social structure in the demand/withdraw pattern of marital conflict. *Journal of Personality and Social Psychology, 59,* 73–81.

Cloud, D. L. (2010). The irony bribe and reality television: Investment and detachment in The Bachelor. *Critical Studies in Media Communication, 27*(5), 413–437.

Cohen, H. (1994). *The history of speech communication: The emergence of a discipline, 1914–1945.* Annandale, VA: Speech Communication Association.

Craig, R. T. (1999). Communication theory as a field. *Communication Theory, 9,* 119–161.

Denzin, N. K. & Lincoln, Y. S. (Eds.). (2005), *Handbook of qualitative research* (3rd ed). Thousand Oaks, CA: Sage.

Dues, M., & Brown, M. (2004). *Boxing Plato's shadow: An introduction to the study of human communication.* Boston: McGraw-Hill.

Eldridge, K. A., Sevier, M., Jones, J., Atkins, D. C., & Christensen, A. (2007). Demand-withdraw communication in severely distressed, moderately distressed, and nondistressed couples: Rigidity and polarity during relationship and personal problem discussions. *Journal of Family Psychology, 21,* 218–226.

Eldridge, K. A., & Christensen, A. (2002). Demand-withdraw communication during couple conflict: A review and analysis. In P. Noller & J. A. Feeney (Eds.), *Understanding marriage: Developments in the study of couple interaction* (pp. 289–322). Cambridge: Cambridge University Press.

Ellis, C. (2007). Telling secrets, revealing lives: Relational ethics in research with intimate others, *Qualitative Inquiry, 13*(1), 3–29.

Engels, J. (2009). Uncivil speech: Invective and the rhetorics of democracy in the early republic. *Quarterly Journal of Speech, 95*(3), 311–334.

Fowler, C., & Dillow, M. R. (2011). Attachment dimensions and the Four Horsemen of the Apocalypse. *Communication Research Reports, 28*(1), 16–26.

Glaser, B. G., & Strauss, A. (1967). *Discovery of grounded theory: Strategies for qualitative research.* Chicago: Aldine de Gruyter.

González, M. C. (2000). The four seasons of ethnography: A creation centered ontology for ethnography. *International Journal of Intercultural Relations, 24,* 525–539.

Guerrero, L. K., Farinelli, L., & McEwan, B. (2009) Attachment and relational satisfaction: The mediating effect of emotional communication. *Communication Monographs, 76*(4), 487–514.

Hill, L. (2010). Gender and genre: Situating *Desperate Housewives. Journal of Popular Film and Television, 38*(4), 162–169.

Jacobson, N. S. (1989). The politics of intimacy. *Behavior Therapist, 12,* 29–32.

Jacobson, N. S. (1990). Commentary: Contribution from psychology to an understanding of marriage. In F. D. Fincham & T. N. Bradbury (Eds.), *The psychology of marriage.* New York: Guilford Press.

Kraybill, D. B. (2001). *The riddle of Amish culture (revised ed.)* Baltimore: Johns Hopkins University Press.

Kraybill, D. B., Nolt, S. M., & Weaver-Zercher, D. L. (2010). *Amish grace: How forgiveness transcended tragedy.* San Francisco, Ca: John Wiley.

Lazard, L. (2009). V. 'You'll Like This—It's Feminist!' Representations of strong women in horror fiction. *Feminism in Psychology, 19*(11), 132–136.

Lindlof, T. R., & Taylor, B. C. (2002). *Qualitative communication research methods* (2nd ed.). Thousand Oaks: Sage.

Lindsley, S. L. (1999). A layered model of problematic intercultural communication in U.S.-owned *maquiladoras* in Mexico. *Communication Monographs, 66*(2), 145–168.

Litwin, A. H., & Hallstein, L. O. (2007). Shadows and silences: How women's positioning and unspoken friendship rules in organizational settings cultivate difficulties among some women at work. *Women's Studies in Communication, 30*(1), 111–142.

Martin, J. N., & Butler, R. L. W. (2001). Towards an ethic of intercultural communication research. In V. H. Milhouse, M. K. Asante, & P. O. Nwosu (Eds.), *Transcultural realities: Interdisciplinary perspectives on cross-cultural relations* (pp. 283–298). Thousand Oaks, CA: Sage.

Milburn, T. (2010). The relevance of cultural communication: For whom and in what respect? *Communication Monographs, 77*(4), 439–441.

Miller, W. L., & Crabtree, B. F. (2005). Clinical Research. In N. K. Denzin & Y. S. Lincoln (Eds.), *Handbook of qualitative research* (3rd ed., pp. 605–640). Thousand Oaks, CA: Sage.

Mumby, D. (1997). Modernism, postmodernism, and communication studies: A rereading of ongoing debates. *Communication Theory, 7,* 1–28.

Mumby, D. (2005). Theorizing resistance in organization studies: A dialectical approach. *Management Communication Quarterly, 19*(1), 19–44.

Noller, P. (1993). Gender and emotional communication in marriage: Different cultures or differential social power? *Journal of Language and Social Psychology, 12,* 132–152.

Papp, L. M., Kouros, C. D., & Cummings, M. (2009). Demand-withdraw patterns in marital conflict in the home. *Personal Relationships, 16,* 285–300.

Piliavin, I. M., Rodin, J., and Piliavin, J. A. (1969). Good samaritanism: An underground phenomenon? *Journal of Personality and Social Psychology, 13,* 289–299.

Rholes, W. S., Simpson, J. A., Tran, S., Martin III, A. M., & Friedman, M. (2007). Attachment and information seeking in romantic relationships. *Personality and Social Psychology Bulletin, 33,* 422–438.

Shugart, H. (2008). Managing masculinities: The metrosexual moment. *Communication and Critical/Cultural Studies, 5*(3), 280–300.

Sommerson, W. (2004). White men on the edge: Rewriting the borderlands in *Lone Star. Men and Masculinities, 6*(3), 215–239.

Strauss, A., & Corbin, J. (1998). *Basics of qualitative research: Techniques and procedures for developing grounded theory* (2nd ed.). Newbury Park, CA: Sage.

Suter, E. A. (2004). Tradition never goes out of style: The role of tradition in women's naming practices. *Communication Review, 7,* 57–87.

Tanno, D. (1997). *Communication and identity across cultures.* Thousand Oaks, CA: Sage.

Trethewey, A. (1997). Resistance, identity, and empowerment: A postmodern feminist analysis of clients in a human service organization. *Communication Monographs, 64,* 281–301.

Zaeske, S. (2002). Signature of citizenship: The rhetoric of women's antislavery petitions. *Quarterly Journal of Speech, 88,* 147–168.

Chapter 3

Abrams, J., O'Connor, J., & Giles, H. (2002). Identity and intergroup communication. In W. B. Gudykunst & B. Mody (Eds.), *Handbook of international and intercultural communication* (2nd ed., pp. 225–240). Thousand Oaks, CA: Sage.

Allen, B. (2004). *Difference matters: Communicating social identity.* Long Grove, IL: Waveland.

Americans with Disabilities Act of 1990, as amended with Amendments of 2008. Retrieved May 13, 2011, from: http://www.ada.gov/pubs/adastatute08.htm

Arana, M. (2008, November 30). He's not black. *Washington Post,* p. B1. Retrieved December 31, 2008, from www.washingtonpost.com/wp-dyn/content/article/2008/11/28/AR2008112802219.html

Azuri, L. (2006, November 17). Public debate in Saudi Arabia on employment opportunities for women. *Inquiry and Analysis 300.* Retrieved March 16, 2009, from www.memri.org/bin/articles.cgi?Area=ia&ID=IA30006&Page=archives

Baker, C. (2003, November 30). What is middle class? *The Washington Times.* Retrieved January 16, 2005, from www.washtimes.com/specialreport/20031129105855741 2r.htm

Bennett-Haigney, B. (1995, August). Faulkner makes history at the Citadel. *NOW Newsletter.* Retrieved March 1, 2006, from www.now.org/nnt/08-95/citadel.html

Blumer, H. (1969). *Symbolic interactionism: Perspective and method.* Englewood Cliffs, NJ: Prentice Hall.

Bock, G. (1989), Women's history and gender history: Aspects of an international debate. *Gender & History, 1:* 7–30.

Bourdieu, P. (1984). *Distinction: A social critique of the judgment of taste.* (R. Nice, Trans.). London: Routledge & Kegan Paul.

Butler, J. (1990). *Gender trouble: Feminism and the subversion of identity.* New York: Routledge.

Butler, J. (1993). *Bodies that matter: On the discursive limits of "sex."* New York: Routledge.

Candiotti, S., Koppel, A., Zarrella, J., & Bash, D. (2006, October 3). Attorney: Clergyman molested Foley as teen. *CNN.* Retrieved December 31, 2008, from www.cnn.com/2006/POLITICS/10/03/foley.scandal/index.htm

Carbaugh, D. (2007). Cultural discourse analysis: Communication practices and intercultural encounters. *Journal of Intercultural Communication Research, 36,* 167–182.

Cardillo, L. W. (2010). Empowering narratives: Making sense of the experience of growing up with chronic illness or disability. *Western Journal of Communication, 74*(5), 525–546.

Cauchon, D. (2010, September 14). Gender pay gap is smallest on record. *USA Today.* Retrieved on March 22, 2011, from http://www.usatoday.com/money/workplace/2010-09-13-wage-gaps_N.htm

Cohen, A. (2010, September 22). Justice Scalia Mouths Off on Sex Discrimination. *Time.* Retrieved May 12, 2011, from: http://www.time.com/time/nation/article/0,8599,2020667,00 .html

Cooley, C. H. (1902). *Human nature and the social order.* New York: Scribner's.

Corey, F. C. (2004). A letter to Paul. *Text and Performance Quarterly, 24,* 185–190.

Corey, F. C., & Nakayama, T. K. (2004). Introduction. Special issue "Religion and Performance." *Text and Performance Quarterly, 24,* 209–211.

Cornell University. (2004). Fear factor: 44 percent of Americans queried in Cornell national poll favor curtailing some liberties for Muslim Americans. *Cornell News.* Retrieved December 6, 2006, from www.news.cornell.edu/releases/Dec04/Muslim.Poll.bpf.html

Croizet, J., & Claire, T. (1998). Extending the concept of stereotype threat to social class: The intellectual underperformance of students from low socioeconomic backgrounds. *Personality and Social Psychology, 24*(5), 588–594.

Daigle, K. (2011, February 12). India's census counts 'third gender.' Edge Boston. Retrieved March 22, 2011, from: http://www.edgeboston.com/?116206

Davies, R., & Ikeno, O. (Eds.). (2002). *The Japanese mind: Understanding contemporary culture.* Boston: Tuttleman.

Drum Major Institute for Public Policy. (2005). Middle class 2004: How Congress voted. Retrieved June 12, 2006, from www.drummajorinstitute.org/library/report.php?ID=4

Edwards, R. (1990). Sensitivity to feedback and the development of the self. *Communication Quarterly, 38,* 101–111.

El Nasser, H. (2010, March 15). Multiracial no longer boxed in by the Census, *USA Today.* Retrieved May 12, 2011, from: http://www.usatoday.com/news/nation/census/2010-03-02-census-multi-race_N.htm

Erickson, A. L. (1993). *Women and property in early modern England.* London: Routledge.

Fassett, D. L., & Morella, D. L. (2008). Remaking (the) discipline: Marking the performative accomplishment of (dis)ability. *Text and Performance Quarterly, 28*(1–2), 139–156.

Foucault, M. (1988). *History of sexuality* (R. Hurley, Trans.). New York: Vintage Books.

Fussell, P. (1992). *Class: A guide through the American status system.* New York: Touchstone.

Guzman, I. M., & Valdivia, A. N. (2004). Brain, brow, and booty: Latina iconicity in U.S. popular culture. *Communication Review, 7,* 205–221.

Hacker, A. (2003). *Two nations: Black and White, separate, hostile, unequal.* New York: Scribner.

Harwood, J. (2006). Communication as social identity. In G. J. Shepherd, J. St. John, & T. Striphas (Eds.), *Communication as...: Perspectives on theory* (pp. 84–90). Thousand Oaks, CA: Sage.

Hecht, M. L. (1993). 2002—A research odyssey. *Communication Monographs, 60,* 76–82.

Hecht, M. L., Jackson R. L., III, & Ribeau, S. A. (2003). *African American communication: Exploring identity and culture.* (2nd ed). Mahwah, NJ: Lawrence Erlbaum Associates.

Henderson, B., & Ostrander, R. N. (2008). Introduction to special issue on disability studies/performance studies. *Text and Performance Quarterly, 28*(1–2), 1–5.

Hirschman, C. (2003, May). The rise and fall of the concept of race. Paper presented at the Annual Meeting of the Population Association of America, Minneapolis, MN.

Hutcheson, J., Domke, D., Billeaudeaux, A., & Garland, P. (2004). U.S. national identity, political elites, and a patriotic press following September 11. *Political Communication, 21,* 27–50.

Johnson, A. G. (2001). *Privilege, power and difference.* Boston: McGraw-Hill.

Jones, N. A., & Smith, A. S. (2001). The two or more races population. *Census 2000 Brief (U.S. Census Bureau Publication No. C2KBR/01-6).* Washington, DC: U.S. Government Printing Office.

Kimmel, M. S. (2005). *The history of men: Essays in the history of American and British masculinities*. Albany: State University of New York Press.

Koshy, S. (2004). *Sexual naturalization: Asian Americans and miscegenation*. Stanford, CA: Stanford University Press.

Kraybill, D. B. (1989). *The riddle of Amish culture*. Baltimore: Johns Hopkins University Press.

Lagarde, D. (2005, September 22–28). Afghanistan: La loi des tribus. *L'Express International*, 30–37.

Lengel, L., & Warren, J. T. (2005). Introduction: Casting gender. In L. Lengel & J. T. Warren (Eds.), *Casting gender: Women and performance in intercultural contexts* (pp. 1–18). New York: Peter Lang.

Lindemann, K. (2008). "I can't be standing up out there": Communicative performances of (dis)ability in wheelchair rugby. *Text and Performance Quarterly, 28*(1–2), 98–115.

Lerner, M. (2008, November 18). Minnesota disciplines four doctors, two for inappropriate contact. *Star-Tribune*. Retrieved May 3, 2011, from: http://www.startribune.com/lifestyle/34691559.html?page=all&prepage=1&c=y#continue

Loden, M., & Rosener, J. B. (1991). *Workforce America: Managing workforce diversity as a vital resource*. Homewood, IL: Business One Irwin.

Lucas, K. (2011). Socializing messages in blue-collar families: Communication pathways to social mobility and reproduction. *Western Journal of Communication, 75*(1), 95–121.

Manczak, D. W. (1999, July 1). Raising your child's self-esteem. *Clinical Reference Systems*, 1242.

Marshall, G. A. (1993). Racial classification: Popular and Scientific. In S. G. Harding (Ed.), *The "racial" economy of science: Toward a democratic future* (pp. 116–127). Bloomington: Indiana University Press.

Martin, J. N., & Harrell, T. (1996). Reentry training for intercultural sojourners. In D. Landis & R. S. Bhagat (Eds.), *Handbook of intercultural training* (2nd ed., pp. 307–326). Thousand Oaks, CA: Sage.

McGlone, M. S., & Aronson, J. (2006). Stereotype threat, identity salience, and spatial reasoning. *Journal of Applied Development Psychology, 27*(5), 486–493.

Mead, G. H. (1934). *Mind, self, and society*. Chicago: University of Chicago Press.

Mikkelsen, E. G., & Einarsen, S. (2001). Bullying in Danish work-life: Prevalence and health correlates. *European Journal of Work and Organizational Psychology, 10*, 393–413.

Milbank, D. (2007, August 29). A senator's wide stance. "I am not gay." *Washington Post*, p. A2. Retrieved December 31, 2008, from www.washingtonpost.com/wp-dyn/content/article/ 2007/08/28/AR2007082801664.html

Noy, C. (2004). Performing identity: Touristic performances of self-change. *Text and Performance Quarterly, 24*(2), 115–138.

Office for National Statistics. Retrieved July 8, 2009, from www.ons.gov.uk/about-statistics/classifications/archived/ethnic-interim/presenting-data/index.html

Online Glossary. (2005, January). Prentice Hall. Retrieved January 16, 2005, from www.prenhall.com/rm_student/html/glossary/a_gloss.html

Palladino, G. (1996). *Teenagers: An American history*. New York: Basic Books.

Papalia, D. E., Olds, S. W., & Feldman, R. D. (2002). *A child's world: Infancy through adolescence*. New York: McGraw-Hill.

Pew Forum on Religion and Public Life. (2008, November 20). *How the News Media Covered Religion in the General Election*. Retrieved December 31, 2008, from http://pewforum.org/docs/?DocID=372

Phelps, J. L., Belsky, J., & Crnic, K. (1998). Earned security, daily stress, and parenting: A comparison of five alternative models. *Development and Psychology, 10*, 21–38.

Philipsen, G. (1992). *Speaking culturally: Explorations in social communication*. Albany, NY: SUNY Press.

Rawls, J. (1995). Self-respect, excellence, and shame. In R. S. Dillon (Ed.), *Dignity, character, and self-respect* (pp. 125–131). New York: Routledge.

Roland, C. E., & Foxx, R. M. (2003). Self-respect: A neglected concept. *Philosophical Psychology. 16*(2) 247–288.

Rosenblith, J. F. (1992). *In the beginning: Development from conception to age two*. Newbury Park, CA: Sage.

Sanders, W. B. (1994). *Gangbangs and drive-bys: Grounded culture and juvenile gang violence*. New York: Aldine de Gruyter.

Sen. Craig restroom tanking as tourist destination. (2008, December 28). *Washington Post*. Retrieved December 31, 2008, from www.cbsnews.com/stories/2008/12/28/strange/main4688671.shtml

Sheridan, V. (2004, November). *From Vietnamese refugee to Irish citizen: Politics, language, culture and identity*. Paper presented at the International Association of Languages and Intercultural Communication, Dublin City University, Dublin, Ireland.

Shih, M., Pittinsky, T. L., & Ambady, N. (1999). Stereotype susceptibility: Identity salience and shifts in quantitative performance. *Psychological Science. 10*(1), 80–83.

Sloop, J. M. (2004). *Disciplining gender: Rhetoric of sex identity in contemporary U.S. culture*. Amherst: University of Massachusetts Press.

Smith, J. L., & White, P. H. (2002). An examination of implicitly activated, explicitly activated, and nullified stereotypes on mathematical performance: It's not just a women's issue. *Sex Roles, 47*(3–4), 179–191.

Steele, C. M., & Aronson, J. (1995). Stereotype threat and intellectual test performance of African Americans. *Journal of Personality and Social Psychology, 69*(5), 797–811.

Sullivan, H. S. (1953). *The interpersonal theory of psychology*. New York: Norton.

Sullivan, T. A., Warren, E., & Westbrook, J. (2001). *The fragile middle class: Americans in debt*. New Haven: Yale University Press.

Taylor, J. (2005, June 6). *Between two worlds*. How many Americans really attend church each week? Retrieved January 30, 2006, from http://theologica.blogspot.com/2005/06/how-many-americans-really-attend.html

Ting-Toomey, S. (1999). *Communicating across cultures*. New York: Guilford.

Trethewey, A. (2001). Reproducing and resisting the master narrative of decline: Midlife professional women's experiences of aging. *Management Communication Quarterly, 15*, 183–226.

Venkat, V. (2008, Feb. 16–29). Gender issues: From the shadows. *Frontline, India's National Magazine, 25*(4). Retrieved March 3, 2011, from http://www.frontlineonnet.com/Fl2504/Stories/20080229607610000.htm

Vevea, N., "Body Art: Performing Identity Through Tattoos and Piercing," *Paper presented at the annual meeting of the NCA 94th Annual Convention, TBA, San Diego, CA Online*. Retrieved March 11, 2011, from http://www.allacademic.com/meta/p258244_index.html

Waters, M. C. (1990). *Ethnic options: Choosing identities in America*. Berkeley: University of California Press.

Wax, E. (2005, September 26–October 2). Beyond the pull of the tribe: In Kenya, some teens find unity in contemporary culture. *Washington Post*, National Weekly Edition, 22(49), 8.

Zinzer, L. (2010, July 7). South African cleared to compete as a woman. *New York Times*. Retrieved May 13, 2011, from: http://query.nytimes.com/gst/fullpage.html?res=9803E2DE1430F934A35754C0A9669D8B63&ref=castersemenya

Chapter 4

Applegate, J. (1982). The impact of construct system development on communication and impression formation in persuasive contexts. *Communication Monographs, 49*, 277–289.

Bradbury, T. N., & Fincham, F. D. (1988). Individual difference variables in close relationships: A contextual model of marriage as an integrative framework. *Journal of Personality and Social Psychology, 54*, 713–721.

Braithwaite, C. (1990). Communicative silence: A cross-cultural study of Basso's hypothesis. In D. Carbaugh (Ed.), *Cultural communication and intercultural contact* (pp. 321–327). Hillsdale NJ: Lawrence Erlbaum Associates.

Brislin, R. (2000). *Understanding culture's influence on behavior* (2nd ed.). Belmont, CA: Wadsworth.

Bruner, J. (1991). *Acts of meaning*, Cambridge: Harvard University Press.

Bruner, J. S. (1958). Neural mechanisms in perception. *Research Publication of the Association for Research in Nervous and Mental Disease, 36*, 118–143.

Burgoon, J. K., Berger, C. R., & Waldron, V. R. (2000). Mindfulness and interpersonal communication. *Journal of Social Issues, 56*, 105–127.

Burleson, B. R., & Caplan, S. E. (1998). Cognitive complexity. In J. C. McCroskey, J. Daly, & M. M. Martin (Eds.), *Communication and personality: Trait perspectives*. Cresskill, NJ: Hampton.

Chaiken, S. (1986). Physical appearance and social influence. In C. P. Herman, M. P. Zanna, & E. T. Higgins (Eds.), *Physical appearance, stigma, and social behavior: The Ontario Symposium* (Vol. 3, pp. 143–144). Hillsdale, NJ: Erlbaum.

Chapin, J. (2001). It won't happen to me: The role of optimistic bias in African American teens' risky sexual practices. *Howard Journal of Communications, 12*, 49–59.

Classen, C. (1990). Sweet colors, fragrant songs: Sensory models of the Andes and the Amazon. *American Ethnologist, 14*, 722–735.

Deutsch, F. M., Sullivan, L., Sage, C., & Basile, N. (1991). The relations among talking, liking, and similarity between friends. *Personality and Social Psychology Bulletin, 17*, 406–411.

Dijk, T. A., van (1977). *Text and context: Explorations in the semantics and pragmatics of discourse*. London: Longman.

Dillard, J. P., Solomon, D. H., & Samp, J. A. (1996). Framing social reality: The relevance of relational judgments. *Communication Research, 23*, 703–723.

Douglas, W. (1990). Uncertainty, information-seeking, and liking during initial interaction. *Western Journal of Speech Communication, 54*, 66–81.

Douthat, R. (2005, November). Does meritocracy work? *Atlantic*, 120–126.

Ehrenreich, B. (2001). *Nickel and dimed: On (not) getting by in America*. New York: Metropolitan Books.

Estroff, H. (2004, September/October). Cupid's comeuppance. *Psychology Today*. Retrieved March 15, 2006, from www .psychologytoday.com/articles/pto-20040921-000001.html

Fisher, K. (1997). Locating frames in the discursive universe. *Sociological Research Online, 2*(3). Retrieved October 25, 2008, from www.socresonline.org.uk/2/3/4.html

Fiske, S. T., & Taylor, S. E. (1991). *Social cognition* (2nd ed.). New York: McGraw-Hill.

Greenough, W. T., Black, J. E., & Wallace, C. S. (1987). Experience and brain development. *Child Development, 58*, 539–559.

Griffin, E. (1994). *A first look at communication theory*. New York: McGraw-Hill.

Gueguen, N., & De Gail, M. (2003). The effect of smiling on helping behavior: Smiling and good Samaritan behavior. *Communication Reports, 16*(2), 133–140.

Hacker, A. (2003). *Two nations: Black and White, separate, hostile, unequal*. New York: Scribner.

Heider, F. (1958). *The psychology of interpersonal relations*, New York: Wiley.

Heine, S. J., & Lehman, D. R. (2004). Move the body, change the self: Acculturative effects on self-concept. In A. Schaller & C. Crandall (Eds.), *The psychological foundations of culture* (pp. 305–31). Hillsdale, NJ: Erlbaum.

Herz, R. S., & Inzlicht, M. (2002). Sex differences in response to physical and social factors involved in human mate selection: The importance of smell for women. *Evolution and Human Behavior, 23*, 359–364.

Hurley R. W., & Adams, M. C. B. (2008). Sex, gender and pain: An overview of a complex field. *Anesthesia and Analgesia. 107*, 309–17.

Jong, P. F. de, Koomen, W., & Mellenbergh, G. J. (1988). Structure of causes for success and failure: A multidimensional scaling analysis of preference judgments. *Journal of Personality and Social Psychology, 55*, 718–725.

Kanizsa, G. (1979). *Organization in vision.* New York: Praeger.

Kellerman, K. (2004). A goal-direct approach to compliance-gaining: Relating differences among goals to differences in behavior. *Communication Research, 31*, 345–347.

Kelley, H. H. (1973). The processes of causal attribution. *American Psychologist, 28*, 107–128.

Kim, M. S. (2002). *Non-Western perspectives on human communication.* Thousand Oaks, CA: Sage.

Kirouac, G., & Hess, U. (1999). Group membership and the decoding of nonverbal behavior. In R. S. Feldman & P. Philippot (Eds.), *The social context of nonverbal behavior* (pp.182–210). New York: Cambridge University Press.

Krivonos, P. D., & Knapp, M. L. (1975). Initiating communication: What do you say when you say hello? *Central States Speech Journal, 26*, 115–125.

Lakoff, G. (1987). *Women, fire, and dangerous things: What categories reveal about the mind.* Chicago: University of Chicago Press.

Langer, E. J. (1978). Rethinking the role of thought in social interaction. In J. H. Harvey, W. Ickes, & R. F. Kidd (Eds.), *New directions in attribution research* (Vol. 2, pp. 3–58). New York: Wiley.

Levinthal, D., & Gavetti, G. (2000, March). Looking forward and looking backward: Cognition and experiential search. *Administrative Science Quarterly*, 1–9.

Link, B. G., & Phelan, J. C. (August, 2001). Conceptualizing stigma. *Annual Review of Sociology, 27*, 363–385.

Lupfer, M. B., Weeks, M., & Dupuis, S. (2000). How pervasive is the negativity bias in judgments based on character appraisal? *Personality and Social Psychology Bulletin, 26*, 1353–1366.

Manusov, V., & Spitzberg, B. (2008). Attributes of attribution theory: Finding good cause in the search for a theory. In D. O. Braithwaite & L. A. Baxter (Eds.), *Engaging theories in interpersonal* (pp. 37–49). Thousand Oaks, CA: Sage.

Markus, H. R., Mullally, P. R., & Kitayama, S. (1997). Selfways: Diversity in modes of cultural participation. In U. Neisser & D. A. Jopling (Eds.), *The conceptual self in context* (pp. 13–59). Cambridge, UK: Cambridge University Press.

McCoy, N. L., & Pitino, L. (2002). Pheromonal influences on sociosexual behavior in young women. *Physiology and Behavior, 75*, 367–375.

"Middle of the Class" (2005, July 14). Survey: America. *Economist.* Retrieved March 10, 2006, from www.economist .com/displayStory.cfm?Story_id =4148885

Morgan, M. J. (1977). *Molyneux's question : Vision, touch and the philosophy of perception.* Cambridge, NY: Cambridge University Press.

Neale, M. A., & Bazerman, M. H. (1991). *Cognition and rationality in negotiation.* New York: Free Press.

Pearce, W. B. (1994). *Interpersonal communication: Making social worlds.* New York: HarperCollins.

Pew Research Center for People and the Press. (2005, September 8). Huge racial divide over Katrina and its consequences. Retrieved June 1, 2006, from http://people-press.org/reports/pdf/255.pdf

Planalp, S. (1993). Communication, cognition, and emotion. *Communication Monographs, 60*, 3–9.

Putnam, L. L., & Holmer, M. (1992). Framing, reframing and issue development. In L. L. Putnam & M. E. Roloff (Eds.), *Communication and negotiation* (pp. 128–155). Newbury Park, CA: Sage.

Ross, L. (1977). The intuitive psychologist and his shortcomings: Distortions in the attribution process. In L. Berkowitz (Ed.), *Advances in experimental social psychology* (Vol. 10, pp. 173–220). New York: Academic Press.

Rothenberg, P. S. (1992). *Race, class, and gender in the United States.* New York: St. Martin's Press.

Samter, W., & Burleson, B. R. (1984). Cognitive and motivational influences on spontaneous comforting behavior. *Human Communication Research, 11*, 231–260.

Scollon, R., & Wong-Scollon, S. (1990). Athabaskan-English interethnic communication. In D. Carbaugh (Ed.), *Cultural communication and intercultural contact* (pp. 259–287). Hillsdale, NJ: Erlbaum.

Seligman, M. (1998). *Learned optimism.* New York: Simon & Schuster.

Shore, B. (1996). *Culture in mind: Cognition, culture and the problem of meaning.* New York: Oxford University Press.

Sillars, A. L, Roberts, L. J., Leonard, K. E., & Dun, T. (2000). Cognition during marital conflict: The relationship of thought and talk. *Journal of Social and Personal Relationships, 17*, 479–502.

Sillars, A. L, Roberts, L. J., Leonard, K. E., & Dun, T. (2002). Cognition and communication during marital conflicts: How alcohol affects subjective coding of interaction in aggressive and nonaggressive couples. In P. Noller & J. A. Feeney (Eds.), *Understanding marriage: Developments in the study of couples' interaction* (p. 85–112). Cambridge, U.K.: Cambridge University Press.

Singh, D., & Bronstad, P. M. (2001). Female body odour is a potential cue to ovulation. *Proceedings of the Royal Society: Biological Science, 268*, 797–801.

Siu, W. L. W., & Finnegan, J. R. (2004, May). An exploratory study of the interaction of affect and cognition in message evaluation. Paper presented at the International Communication Association Convention, San Francisco, CA.

Smith, S. W., Kopfman, J. E., Lindsey, L., Massi, Y. J., & Morrison, K. (2004). Encouraging family discussion on the decision to donate organs: The role of the willingness to communicate scale. *Health Communication. 16*, 333–346.

Snyder, M. (1998). Self-fulfilling stereotypes. In P. S. Rothenberg (Ed.), *Race, class and gender in the U.S.: An integrated study* (pp. 452–457). New York: St. Martin's Press.

Stephan, C., & Stephan, W. (1992). Reducing intercultural anxiety through intercultural contact. *International Journal of Intercultural Relations, 16*, 89–106.

Ting-Toomey, S. (1999). *Communicating across cultures.* New York: Guilford.

U.S. National Research Council. (1989). *Improving risk communication.* Committee on risk perception and communication. Washington, DC: National Academy Press.

Weick, K. (1995). *Sensemaking in organizations.* Thousand Oaks, CA: Sage.

Wilson, G., & Nias, D. (1999). Beauty can't be beat. In J. A. DeVito & L. Guerrero, (Eds.), *The nonverbal communication reader: Classic and contemporary readings* (2nd ed., pp. 92–132). Prospect Heights, IL: Waveland Press.

Chapter 5

American Civil Liberties Union (1994). Free speech: Hate speech on campus. Retrieved May 31, 2011, from http://www.aclu.org/free-speech/hate-speech-campus

American Heritage Dictionary of the English Language. 4th ed, (2000). Boston: Houghton-Mifflin. Retrieved June 12, 2006, from http://www.bartleby.com/cgibin/texis/webinator/ahdsearch?search_type=enty&query=wise&db=ahd&submit=Search

Aries, E. (1996). *Men and women in interaction: Reconsidering the differences.* New York: Oxford University Press.

Austin, J. L. (1975). *How to do things with words* (2nd ed.). Cambridge, MA: Harvard University Press.

Aylor, B., & Dainton, M. (2004). Biological sex and psychological gender as predictors of routine and strategic relational maintenance. *Sex Roles: A Journal of Research, 50*, 689–697.

Baker, M. (1991). Gender and verbal communication in professional settings: A review of research. *Management Communication Quarterly, 5*, 36–63.

Bippus, A. M., & Young, S. L. (2005). Owning your emotions: Reactions to expressions of self versus other-attributed positive and negative emotions. *Journal of Applied Communication Research, 33*, 26–45.

Bowen, S. P. (2003). Jewish and/or woman: Identity and communicative styles. In A. González, M. Houston, & V. Chen (Eds.), *Our voices: Essays in culture, ethnicity, and communication* (4th ed.). Los Angeles: Roxbury.

Boxer, D. (2002). Nagging: The familial conflict arena. *Journal of Pragmatics, 34*, 49–61.

Burrell, N. A., Donohue, W. A., & Allen, M. (1988). Gender-based perceptual biases in mediation. *Communication Research, 15*, 447–469.

Canary, D. J., & Emmers-Sommer, T. M. (1997). *Sex and gender differences in personal relationships.* New York: Guilford.

Canary, D. J., & Hause, K. S. (1993). Is there any reason to research sex difference in communication? *Communication Quarterly, 41*, 129–144.

Caughlin, J. P. (2002). The demand/withdrdaw pattern of communication as a predictor of marital satisfaction over time: Unresolved issues and future directions. *Human Communication Research, 28*, 49–85.

Chomsky, N. (1957). *Syntactic Structures*, The Hague/Paris: Mouton.

Coltri, L. S. (2004). *Conflict diagnosis and alternative dispute resolution.* Upper Saddle River, NJ: Prentice Hall.

Crystal, D. (2003). *The Cambridge encyclopedia of the English language.* New York: Cambridge University Press.

Dance, F. E. X., & Larson, C. E. (1976). *The functions of human communication.* New York: Holt, Rinehart, & Winston.

Duke, M.P., Fivush, R., Lazarus, A., & Bohanek, J. (2003). Of ketchup and kin: Dinnertime conversations as a major source of family knowledge, family adjustment, and family resilience (Working Paper #26). Retrieved September 6, 2011 from http://www.marial.emory.edu/research/

Edwards, J. V. (2004). Foundations of bilingualism. In T. K. Bhatia & W. C. Ritchie (Eds.), *The handbook of bilingualism* (pp. 7–31). Malden, MA: Blackwell.

Ellis, A., & Beattie, G. (1986). The language channel. *The psychology of language.* New York: Guilford.

Fromkin, V., & Rodman, R. (1983). *An introduction to language.* New York: Holt, Rinehart, and Winston.

Gong, D. (2004). When Mississippi Chinese talk. In A. González, M. Houston, & V. Chen (Eds.), *Our voices: Essays in culture, ethnicity, and communication* (4th ed.). Los Angeles: Roxbury.

Gray, J. (1992). *Men are from Mars, women are from Venus.* New York: HarperCollins.

Hannah, A. & Murachver, T. (2007). Gender preferential responses to speech. *Journal of Language and Social Psychology, 26*(3), 274–290.

Hecht, M. L., Jackson, R. L. II, & Ribeau, S. A. (2003). *African American communication.* Mahwah, NJ: Lawrence Erlbaum Associates.

Hegarty, P., & Buechel, C. (2006). Androcentric reporting of gender differences in APA journals: 1965–2004. *Review of General Psychology, 10*(4), 377–389.

Heilman, M. E. (2001). Description and prescription: How gender stereotypes prevent women's ascent up the organizational ladder. In "Gender, hierarchy and leadership," Ed. L. Carli & A. Eagly. *Journal of Social Issues, 57*(4), 657–674.

Heilman, M. E., Caleo, S., & Halim, M. L. (2010), Just the thought of it! Effects of anticipating computer-mediated communication on gender stereotyping. *Journal of Experimental Social Psychology, 46*(4), 672–675.

Hoijer, H. (1994). The Sapir-Whorf hypothesis. In L. Samovar & R. E. Porter (Eds.), *Intercultural communication: A reader* (pp. 194–200). Belmont, CA: Wadsworth.

Hudson, R. A. (1983). *Sociolinguistics.* London: Cambridge University Press.

Hyde, J. S. (2006). Gender similarities still rule. *American Psychologist, 61*(6), 641–642.

Jacobson, C. (2008). Some notes on gender-neutral language. Retrieved May 23, 2008, from http://www.english.upenn.edu/~cjacobso/gender.html

Kenneally, C. (2008, April 22). When language can hold the answer. *New York Times*, p. F1.

Kikoski, J. F., & Kikoski, C. K. (1999). *Reflexive communication in the culturally diverse workplace*. Westport, CT: Praeger.

Kim, M. S. (2002). *Non-Western perspectives on human communication*. Thousand Oaks, CA: Sage.

Knott, K., & Natalle, E. (1997). Sex differences, organizational level, and superiors evaluations of managerial leadership. *Management Communication Quarterly, 10*(4), 523–540.

Koerner, F. F. K. (2000). Towards a "full pedigree" of the "Sapir-Whorf hypothesis." In M. Putz & M. H. Verspoor (Eds.), *Explorations in linguistic relativity* (pp. 1–23). Amsterdam: John Benjamins.

Kohonen, S. (2004). Turn-taking in conversation: Overlaps and interruptions in intercultural talk. *Cahiers, 10.1*, 15–32.

Krieger, L. (2004, February 26). Like, what dew you mean, tha-yt I hav-yvee an accent? *Detroit Free Press*, p. 16A.

Kubany, E. S., Bauer, G. B., Muraoka, M., Richard, D. C., & Read, P. (1995). Impact of labeled anger and blame in intimate relationships. *Journal of Social and Clinical Psychology, 14*, 53–60.

Labov, W. (1980). The social origins of sound change. In W. Labov (Ed.), *Locating language in time and space* (pp. 251–265). New York: Academic Press.

Labov, W. (Ed.). (2005). *Atlas of North American English*. New York: Walter De Gruyter.

Leaper, C., & Ayres, M. M. (2007). A meta-analytic review of gender variation in adults' language use: Talkativeness, affiliative speech, and assertive speech. *Personality and Social Psychology Review, 11*(4), 328–363.

Li, P., & Gleitman, L. (2002). Turning the tables: Language and spatial reasoning. *Cognition, 83*, 265–294.

Liptak, A. (2008). Hate speech or free speech? What much of West bans is protected in U.S. *New York Times*. Retrieved May 31, 2011, from http://www.nytimes.com/2008/06/11/world/americas/11iht-hate.4.13645369.html

Martin, J. N., Krizek, R. L., Nakayama, T. K., & Bradford, L. (1999). What do White people want to be called? A study of self-labels for White Americans. In T. K. Nakayama & J. N. Martin (Eds.), *Whiteness: The communication of social identity* (pp. 27–50). Thousand Oaks, CA: Sage.

Media Awareness Network (n.d.). Criminal code of Canada: Hate provisions—summary. Retrieved May 30, 2011, from http://www.media-awareness.ca/english/resources/legislation/canadian_law/federal/criminal_code/criminal_code_hate.cfm

Mehl, M. R., & Pennebaker, J. W. (2003). The sounds of social life: A psychometric analysis of students' daily social environments and natural conversations. *Journal of Personality and Social Psychology, 84*, 857–70.

Mey, J. L. (2001). *Pragmatics: An introduction* (2nd ed.). Oxford, UK: Blackwell Publishing.

Mulac, A., Bradac, J. J., & Gibbons, P. (2001). Empirical support for the gender-as-culture hypothesis: An intercultural analysis of male/female language differences. *Human Communication Research, 27*, 121–152.

Nofsinger, R. (1999). *Everyday conversation*. Prospect Heights, IL: Waveland.

Orbe, M. P. (1998). *Constructing co-cultural theory: An explication of culture, power, and communication*. Thousand Oaks, CA: Sage.

Paramasivam, S. (2007). Managing disagreement while managing not to disagree: Polite disagreement in negotiation discourse. *Journal of Intercultural Communication Research, 36*(2), 91–116.

Pennebaker, J. W., & Stone, L. D. (2003). Words of wisdom: Language use across the life span. *Journal of Personality and Social Psychology, 82*, 291–301.

Philips, S. U. (1990). Some sources of cultural variability in the regulation of talk. In D. Carbaugh (Ed.), *Cultural communication and intercultural contact* (pp. 329–344). Hillsdale, NJ: Erlbaum.

Piaget, J. (1952). *The origins of intelligence in children*. New York: International Universities Press.

Pinker, S. (2007). *The stuff of thought: Language as a window into human nature*. New York: Viking.

Pinto, D., & Raschio, R. (2007) A comparative study of requests in heritage speaker Spanish, L1 Spanish, and L1 English. *International Journal of Bilingualism, 11*(2), 135–155.

Preston, D. R. (2003). Where are the dialects of American English at anyhow? *American Speech, 78*, 235–254.

"Prison ferme pour deux négationnistes." (2008, June 20). *Le soir*. Retrieved May 16, 2011, from http://archives.lesoir.be/?action=nav&gps=608066

Ramírez-Esparza, N., Gosling, S. D., Benet-Martínez, V., Potter, J. D., & Pennebaker, J. W. (2006). Do bilinguals have two personalities? A special case of cultural frame switching. *Journal of Research in Personality, 40*, 99–120.

Reid, S. A., Keerie, N., & Palomares, N. A. (2003). Language, gender salience, and social influence. *Journal of Language and Social Psychology, 22*, 210–233.

Rose, C. (1995). Bargaining and gender. *Harvard Journal of Law and Public Policy, 18*, 547–65.

Ruben, D. L. (2003). Help! My professor (or doctor or boss) doesn't talk English! In J. N. Martin, T. K. Nakayama, & L. A. Flores (Eds.), *Readings in intercultural communication* (2nd ed., pp. 127–138). Boston: McGraw-Hill.

Sacks, H., Schegloff, E., & Jefferson, G. (1978). A simplest systematics for the organization of turn-taking for conversation. In J. Schenkein (Ed.), *Studies in the organization of conversational interaction* (pp. 7–55). New York: Academic Press.

Sagrestano, L. M., Heavey, C. L., & Christensen, A. (1998). Theoretical approaches to understanding sex differences and similarities in conflict behavior. In D. J. Canary & K. Dindia (Eds.), *Sex differences and similarities in communication: Critical essays and empirical investigations on sex and gender in interaction* (pp. 287–302). Mahwah, NJ: Erlbaum.

Sbisa, M. (2002). Speech act in context, *Language & Communication, 22*, 421–436.

Schegloff, E. A. (2000) Overlapping talk and the organization of turn-taking for conversation, *Language in Society, 29*, 1–63.

Scheibel, D. (1995). Making waves with Burke: Surf Nazi culture and the rhetoric of localism. *Western Journal of Communication, 59*(4), 253–269.

Sellers, J. G., Woolsey, M. D., & Swann, J. B. (2007). Is silence more golden for women than men? Observers derogate effusive women and their quiet partners. *Sex Roles, 57*(7–8), 477–482.

Shutiva, C. (2004). Native American culture and communication through humor. In A. González, M. Houston, & V. Chen (Eds.), *Our voices: Essays in culture, ethnicity, and communication* (4th ed.). Los Angeles: Roxbury.

Weger, H., Jr. (2005). Disconfirming communication and self-verification in marriage: Associations among the demand/withdraw interaction pattern, feeling understood, and marital satisfaction. *Journal of Social and Personal Relationships, 22*, 19–31.

Wiest, L. R., Abernathy, T. V., Obenchain, K. M., & Major, E. M. (2006). Researcher study thyself: AERA participants' speaking times and turns by gender. *Equity & Excellence in Education, 39*(4), 313–323.

Wolfram, W., Adger, C. T., & Christian, D. (1999). *Dialects in schools and communities*. Mahwah, NJ: Erlbaum.

Wood, J. T. (2002). *Gendered lives: Communication, gender and cultures*. Belmont, CA: Wadsworth.

Wood, J. T., & Dindia, K. (1998). What's the differences? A dialogue about differences and similarities between men and women. In D. J. Canary & K. Dindia (Eds.), *Sex differences and similarities in communication: Critical essays and empirical investigations on sex and gender in interaction* (pp. 19–39). Mahwah, NJ: Erlbaum.

Chapter 6

Abu-Ghazzeh, T. M. (2000). Environmental messages in multiple family housing: Territory and personalization. *Landscape Research, 25*, 97–114.

Als, H. (1977). The newborn communicates. *Journal of Communication, 2*, 66–73.

Axtell, R. (1993). *Do's and taboos around the world*. New York: Wiley.

Becker, F. D. (1973). Study of special markers. *Journal of Personality and Social Psychology, 26*, 429–445.

Birdwhistell, R. L. (1985). Kinesics and context: Essays in body motion communication. Philadelphia: University of Philadelphia Press.

Boone, R. T., & Cunningham, J. G. (1998). Children's decoding of emotion in expressive body movement: The development of cue attunement. *Developmental Psychology, 34*, 1007–1016.

Briton, N. J., & Hall, J. A. (1995). Beliefs about female and male nonverbal communication. *Sex Roles, 32*, 79–90.

Burgoon, J. K., Buller, D. B., & Woodall, W. G. (1996). *Nonverbal communication: The unspoken dialogue*. New York: Harper & Row.

Burgoon, J. K., & Guerrero, L. K. (1994). Nonverbal communication. In M. Burgoon, F. G. Hunsaker, & E. J. Dawson (Eds.), *Human communication* (pp. 122–171). Thousand Oaks, CA: Sage.

Capella, J. (1985). The management of conversations. In M. L. Knapp & G. R. Miller (Eds.), *Handbook of interpersonal communication* (pp. 393–435). Beverly Hills, CA: Sage.

Carvajal, D. (2006, February 7). Primping for the cameras in the name of research. *New York Times*. Retrieved February 23, 2006, from http://www.nytimes.com/2006/02/07/business/07hair.html?ex=1139979600&en=f5f94cb9d81a9fa8&ei=5070&emc=eta1

Chartrand T. L., & Bargh J. A. (1999). The chameleon effect: The perception-behavior link and social interaction. *Journal of Personality and Social Psychology, 76*, 893–910.

Chiang, L. H. (1993, October). Beyond the language: Native Americans' nonverbal communication. Paper presented at the Annual Meeting of the Midwest Association of Teachers of Educational Psychology, Anderson, IN: October 1–2.

Cicca, A. H., Step, M., & Turkstra, L. (2003, December 16). Show me what you mean: Nonverbal communication theory and application. *ASHA Leader, 34*, 4–5.

Dié, L. (2008, November, 9). Obama: Speech patterns analyzed. *News Flavor: U. S. Politics*. Retrieved May 31, 2011, from http://newsflavor.com/category/politics/us-politics/

Dijksterhuis, A., & Smith, P. K. (2005). What do we do unconsciously? And how? *Journal of Consumer Psychology 15*(3), 225–229.

Duke, L. (2002). Get real! Cultural relevance and resistance to the mediated feminine ideal. *Psychology and Marketing, 19*, 211–234.

Eibl-Eibesfeld, I. (1972). Similarities and differences between cultures in expressive movement. In R. A. Hinde (Ed.), *Nonverbal communication* (pp. 297–314). Cambridge: Cambridge University Press.

Ekman, P. (2003). *Emotions revealed: Recognizing faces and feelings to improve communication and emotional life*. New York: Times Books.

Ekman, P., & Friesen, W. V. (1969). The repertoire of nonverbal behavior: Categories, origins, usage and coding. *Semiotica, 1*, 49–98.

Ekman, P., & Friesen, W. V. (1986). A new pan-cultural expression of emotion. *Motivation and Emotion, 10*(2), 159–168.

Elfenbein, H. A. (2006). Learning in emotion judgments: Teaching and the cross-cultural understanding of facial expressions. *Journal of Nonverbal Communication, 30*, 21–36.

Elfenbein, H. A., Maw, D. F., White, J., Tan, H. H., & Aik, V. C. (2007). Reading your counter-part: The benefit of emotion recognition accuracy for effectiveness in negotiation. *Journal of Nonverbal Behavior, 31*, 205–223.

Eskritt, M., & Lee, K. (2003) Do actions speak louder than words? Preschool children's use of the verbal-nonverbal consistency principle during inconsistent communication. *Journal of Nonverbal Behavior, 27*, 25–41.

Field, T. (2002). Infants' need for touch. *Human Development, 45*, 100–104.

Fussell, P. (1992). *Class: A guide through the American status system.* New York: Touchstone Books.

Givens, D. B. (2005). *The nonverbal dictionary of gestures, signs, and body language cues.* Spokane, WA: Center for Nonverbal Studies Press.

Grammer, K., Fink, B., Joller, A., & Thornhill, R. (2003). Darwinian aesthetics: Sexual selection and the biology of beauty. *Biological Reviews, 78*, 385–408.

Guerrero, L. K., & Andersen, P. A. (1991). The waxing and waning of relational intimacy: Touch as a function of relational stage, gender, and touch avoidance. *Journal of Social and Personal Relationships, 8*, 147–165.

Guerrero, L. K., & Andersen, P. A. (1994). Patterns of matching and initiation: Touch behavior and touch avoidance across romantic relationship stages. *Journal of Nonverbal Behavior, 18*, 137–153.

Guerrero, L. K., & Ebesu, A. S. (1993, May). While at play: An observational analysis of children's touch during interpersonal interaction. Paper presented at the annual conference of the International Communication Association, Washington, D.C.

Gundersen, D. F. (1990). Uniforms: Conspicuous invisibility. In J. A. Devito & M. L. Hecht (Eds.), *The nonverbal communication reader* (pp. 172–178). Prospect Heights, IL: Waveland.

Hall, E. T. (1966). *The hidden dimension.* New York: Doubleday.

Hall, E. T. (1983). *The dance of life.* Garden City, NY: Doubleday.

Hall, E. T., & Hall, M. R. (1987). *Hidden differences: Doing business with the Japanese.* Garden City, NY: Anchor.

Hall, E. T., & Hall, M. R. (1990). *Understanding cultural differences: Germans, French and Americans.* Yarmouth, ME: Intercultural Press.

Hanzal, A., Segrin, C., & Dorros, S. M. (2008). The role of marital status and age on men's and women's reactions to touch from a relational partner. *Journal of Nonverbal Behavior, 32*, 21–35.

Isaacson, L. A. (1998). Student dress codes. *ERIC Digest, 117*. Retrieved June 15, 2006, from http://eric.uoregon.edu/publications/digests/digest117.html

Johnson, A. G. (2001). *Privilege, power, and difference.* Boston: McGraw-Hill.

Jones, S. E., & LeBaron, C. D. (2002). Research on the relationship between verbal and nonver-bal communication: Emerging integration. *Journal of Communication, 52*, 499–521.

Kemmer, S. (1992). Are we losing our touch? *Total Health, 14*, 46–49.

Knapp, M. L., & Hall, J. A. (1992). *Nonverbal communication in human interaction* (3rd ed.). New York: Holt, Rinehart and Winston.

Knapp, M. L., & Hall, J. A. (2001). *Nonverbal communication in human interaction.* Belmont, CA: Wadsworth.

Kraus, M., & Keltner, D. (2009). Signs of socio-economic status: A thin-slicing approach. *Psychological Science, 20*, 99–106.

Manusov, V. (1995). Reacting to changes in nonverbal behaviors: Relational satisfaction and adaptation patterns in romantic dyads. *Human Communication Research, 21*, 456–477.

Manusov, V., & Patterson, M. (2006). *Handbook of nonverbal communication.* Thousand Oaks, CA: Sage

Mast, M. S., & Hall, J. A., (2004). Who is the boss and who is not? Accuracy of judging status. *Journal of Nonverbal Behavior, 28*, 145–165.

Matsumoto, D. (2006). Culture and nonverbal behavior. In *Handbook of nonverbal communication*, V. Manusov & M. Patters (eds.). Thousand Oaks, CA: Sage.

Mehrabian, A. (2007). *Nonverbal communication.* Chicago, IL: Aldine de Gruyter.

Mehrabian, A., & Weiner, M. (1967). Decoding of inconsistent communication. *Journal of Personality and Social Psychology, 6*, 109–104.

Mehrabian, A., & Ferris, S. R. (1967). Influence of attitudes from nonverbal communication in two channels. *Journal of Consulting Psychology, 31*, 248–252.

Mehrabian, A. (1971). *Nonverbal communication.* Chicago: Aldine-Atherton.

Meltzoff, A. N., & Prinz, W. (2002). *The imitative mind: Development, evolution, and brain bases.* Cambridge, England: Cambridge University Press.

Montepare, J. M., Goldstein, S. B., & Clausen, A. (1987). The identification of emotions from gait information. *Ethology and Sociobiology, 6*, 237–247.

Newport, F. (1999). Americans agree that being attractive is a plus in American society. *Gallup Poll Monthly, 408*, 45–49.

Parasuram, T. V. (2003, October 23). Sikh shot and injured in Arizona hate crime. *Sikh Times.* Retrieved February 24, 2006, from http://www.sikhtimes.com/news_052103a.html

Patterson, M. L. (1982). A sequential functional model of nonverbal exchange. *Psychological Bulletin, 89*, 231–249.

Patterson, M. L. (1983). *Nonverbal behavior.* New York: Springer.

Patterson, M. L. (2003). Commentary. Evolution and nonverbal behavior: Functions and mediating processes. *Journal of Nonverbal Behavior, 27*, 201–207.

Richards, V., Rollerson, B., & Phillips, J. (1991). Perceptions of submissiveness: Implications for victimization. *Journal of Psychology, 125*(4), 407–411.

Richeson, J. A., & Shelton, J. N. (2005). Brief report: Thin slices of racial bias. *Journal of Non-verbal Behavior, 29*, 75–86.

Samovar, L. & Porter, R. (2004). *Communication between cultures.* Thomson, Wadsworth.

Schwartz, L. M., Foa, U. G., & Foa, E. B. (1983) Multichannel nonverbal communication: Evidence for combinatory rules. *Journal of Personality and Social Psychology, 45*, 274–281.

Segerstrale, U., & Molnár, P. (1997) (Eds.), *Nonverbal communication: Where nature meets culture* (pp. 27–46). Mahwah, NJ: Erlbaum.

Shelp, S. (2002). Gaydar: Visual detection of sexual orientation among gay and straight men. *Journal of Homosexuality, 44*, 1–14.

Tiedens, L., & Fragale, A. (2003). "Power moves: Complementarity in dominant and submissive nonverbal behavior." *Journal of Personality and Social Psychology, 84*, 558–568.

Watson, O. & Graves, T. (1966). Quantitative research in proxemic behavior. *American Anthropologist, 68*, 971–985.

Wise, T. (2005, October 23). Opinions on NBA dress code are far from uniform. *Washington Post*, p. A01. Retrieved February 24, 2006, from http://www.washingtonpost.com/wp-dyn/content/ article/2005/10/22/AR2005102201386.html

Wolburg, J. M. (2001). Preserving the moment, commodifying time, and improving upon the past: Insights into the depiction of time in American advertising. *Journal of Communication, 51*, 696–720.

Young, R. L. (1999). *Understanding misunderstandings.* Austin, TX: University of Texas Press.

Zezima, K. (2005, December 3). Military, police now more strict on tattoos. *The San Diego Un-ion-Tribune.* Retrieved February 22, 2006, from http://www.signonsandiego.com/uniontrib/20051203/news_1n3tattoo.html

Chapter 7

Adler, P. (1975). The transitional experience: An alternative view of culture shock. *Journal of Humanistic Psychology, 15*, 13–23.

Alexie, S. (2003). *Ten little Indians.* New York: Grove Press.

Allen, B. (2003). *Difference matters: Communicating social identity.* Waveland Press.

Anderson, E. (2010, August 26). One town's post-Katrina diaspora. *msnbc.msn.com.* Retrieved September 7, 2011 from http://www.msnbc.msn.com/id/38851079/ns/us_news-katrina_five_years_later/t/one-towns-post katrina-diaspora/

Anzaldúa, G. (1999). *Borderlands/La frontera: The new mestiza.* San Francisco: Aunt Lute Books.

Bahk, M., & Jandt, F. E. (2004). Being white in America: Development of a scale. *Howard Journal of Communications, 15*, 57–68.

Bellah, R. N., Madsen, R., Sullivan, W. M., Swidler, A., & Tipton, S. M. (1996). *Habits of the heart: Individualism and commitment in American life.* Los Angeles: University of California Press.

Bennett, J. M. (1998). Transition shock: Putting culture shock in perspective. In M. J. Bennett (Ed.), *Basic concepts in intercultural communication: Selected readings* (pp. 215–224). Yarmouth, ME: Intercultural Press. First published in 1977, in N. C. Jain (Ed.), *International and Intercultural Communication Annual, 4*, 45–52.

Bercovitch, J., & Derouen, K. (2004). Mediation in internationalized ethnic conflicts, *Armed Forces & Society, 30*, 147–170.

Bernal, V. (2005). Eritrea on-line: Diaspora, cyberspace, and the public sphere. *American Ethnologist, 32*, 660–675.

Berry, J. W. (2005). Acculturation: Living successfully in two cultures. *International Journal of Intercultural Relations, 29*, 697–712.

Bertrand, O. (2011). What goes around, comes around: Effects of offshore outsourcing on the export performance of firms. *International Business Studies, 42*(2), 334–344.

Bhatia, S. (2008). 9/11 and the Indian diaspora: Narratives of race, place and immigrant identity. *Journal of Intercultural Studies, 29*(1), 21–39.

Blair, C., Brown, J. R., & Baxter, L. A. (1994). Disciplining the feminine. *Quarterly Journal of Speech, 80*, 383–409.

Bond, M. (1991). *Beyond the Chinese face.* Hong Kong: Oxford University Press.

Bond, M. (Ed.) (1996). *The handbook of Chinese psychology.* Hong Kong: Oxford University Press.

Broome, B. J. (2004). Building a shared future across the divide: Identity and conflict in Cyprus. In M. Fong and R. Chuang (Eds.), *Communicating ethnic and cultural identity* (pp. 275–294). Lanham, MD: Rowman and Littlefield, Publishers.

Budelman, R. (n.d.). *Indian Cultural Tips.* Retrieved June 13, 2006, from http://www.stylusinc.com/business/india/americans_independant.htm

Chinese Culture Connection (1987). Chinese values and the search for culture-free dimensions of culture. *Journal of Cross-Cultural Psychology, 18*, 143–164.

Chisholm, G. C. (2008). Relations between African-Americans and Whites in the United States. *Human Development, 29*(3), 15–18.

Clark-Ibanez, M. K., & Felmlee, D. (2004). Interethnic relationships: The role of social network diversity. *Journal of Marriage and Family, 66*, 229–245.

Cowan, G. (2005). Interracial interactions at racially diverse university campuses. *Journal of Social Psychology, 14*, 49–63.

Deggans, E. (2004, October 24). TV reality not often apoken of: Race. *St. Petersburg Times.*

Dunbar, R. A. (1997). Bloody footprints: Reflections on growing up poor white. In M. Wray & A. Newitz (Eds.), *White trash: Race and class in America* (pp. 73–86). New York: Routledge.

Dyson, M. E. (2009). An American man, an American moment. *Ebony, 64*(3), 90–94.

Ewing, K. P. (2004). Migration, identity negotiation, and self-experience. In J. Friedman & S. Randeria, (Eds.), *Worlds on the move: Globalization, migration, and cultural security* (pp. 117–140). London: I. B. Tauris.

Fiebert, M. S., Nugent, D., Hershberger, S. L., & Kasdan, M. (2004). Dating and commitment choices as a function of ethnicity among American college students in California. *Psychological Reports, 94*, 1293–1300.

Finn, H. K. (2003). The case for cultural diplomacy. *Foreign Affairs, 82*, 15.

Flores, L. A. (1996). Creating discursive space through a rhetoric of difference: Chicana feminists craft a homeland. *Quarterly Journal of Speech, 82,* 142–156.

Gudykunst, W. B., & Lee, C. M. (2002). Cross-cultural communication theories. In W. B. Gudykunst & B. Mody (Eds.), *Handbook of international and intercultural communication* (2nd ed., pp. 25–50). Thousand Oaks, CA: Sage.

Hall, B. J. (1997). Culture, ethics and communication. In F. L. Casmir (Ed.), *Ethics in intercultural and international communication* (pp. 11–41). Mahwah, NJ: Erlbaum.

Hall, E. T., & Hall, M. (1990). *Understanding cultural differences: Germans, French and Americans.* Yarmouth, ME: Intercultural Press.

Halualani, R. T. (2008). How do multicultural university students define and make sense of intercultural contact? A qualitative study. *International Journal of Intercultural Relations, 32,* 1–16.

Hecht, M., Sedano, M., & Ribeau, S. (1993). Understanding culture, communication, and research: Application to Chicanos and Mexican Americans. *International Journal of Intercultural Relations, 17,* 157–165.

Hecht, M. L., Jackson R. L., II, & Ribeau, S. (2002). *African American Communication: Exploring identity and culture* (2nd ed.). Hillsdale, NJ: Erlbaum.

Hegde, R. S. (1998). Swinging the trapeze: The negotiation of identity among Asian Indian immigrant women in the United States. In D. V. Tanno & A. González (Eds.), *Communication of identity across cultures* (pp. 34–55). Thousand Oaks, CA: Sage.

Hegde, R. S. (2000). Hybrid revivals: Defining Asian Indian ethnicity through celebration. In A. González, M. Houston, V. Chen (Eds.), *Our voices: Essays in culture, ethnicity and communication* (pp. 133–138). Los Angeles: Roxbury.

Hemmingsen, J. (2002) Klamath talks begin. *Indian Country Today, 21,* A1.

Herbert, B. (2005, June 6). *New York Times.* Retrieved October 7, 2005, from http://www.commondreams.org/views05/0606-27.htm

Ho, M. K. (1987). *Family therapy with ethnic minorities.* Newbury Park, CA: Sage.

Hofstede, G. (1997). *Cultures and organizations: Software of the mind* (Rev. ed.). New York: McGraw-Hill.

Hofstede, G. (1998). *Masculinity and femininity.* Thousand Oaks, CA: Sage.

Hofstede, G. (2001). *Culture's consequences* (2nd ed.). Thousand Oaks, CA: Sage.

Hulse, E. (1996). Example of the English Puritans. *Reformation Today, 153.* Retrieved June 13, 2006, from http://www.puritansermons.com/banner/hulse1.htm

Institute of International Education (2010a). *Open Doors 2010: International students in the U.S.* Retrieved February 7, 2011, from http://www.iie.org/en/Research-and-Publications/Open-Doors

Institute of International Education (2010b). *Open Doors 2010: American students studying abroad.* Retrieved February, 7, 2011, from http://www.iie.org/en/Research-and-Publications/Open-Doors

Johnson, A. G. (2006). *Privilege, power and difference.* Thousand Oaks, CA: Sage.

Johnson, B. R., & Jacobson, C. K. (2005). Context in contact: An examination of social settings on Whites' attitudes toward interracial marriage. *Journal of Social Psychology, 68,* 387–399.

Jung, E., Hecht, M. L., & Wadsworth, B. C. (2007). The role of identity in international students' psychological well-being in the United States: A model of depression level, identity gaps, discrimination, and acculturation. *International Journal of Intercultural Relations, 31,* 605–624.

Kashima, E. S., & Loh, E. (2006) International students' acculturation: Effects of international, conational, and local ties and need for closure. *International Journal of Intercultural Relations, 30,* 471–486.

Kreager, D. A. (2008). Guarded borders: Adolescent interracial romance and peer trouble at school. *Social Forces, 87*(2), 887–910.

Kikoski, J. F., & Kikoski, C. K. (1999). *Reflexive communication in the culturally diverse workplace.* Westport, CT: Praeger.

Kim, Y. Y. (2005). Adapting to a new culture: An integrative communication theory. In W. B. Gudykunst (Ed.), *Theorizing about intercultural communication* (pp. 375–400). Thousand Oaks, CA: Sage.

Koinova, M. (2010). Diasporas and secessionist conflicts: The mobilization of the Armenian, Albanian, and Chechen diasporas. *Ethnic and Racial Studies, 34,* 333–356.

Kluckhohn, F., & Strodtbeck, F. (1961). *Variations in value orientations.* Chicago: Row, Peterson & Co.

Kohls, R. L. (2001). *Survival kit for overseas living* (4th ed.). Yarmouth, ME: Nicholas Brealey/Intercultural Press.

Levin, S., Taylor, P. L., & Caudle, E. (2007). Interethnic and interracial dating in college: A longitudinal study. *Journal of Social and Personal Relationships, 24*(3), 323–341.

Lee, J. J., & Rice, C. (2007). Welcome to America? International student perceptions of discrimination. *Higher Education, 53,* 381–409.

Lin, C. (2006). Culture shock and social support: An investigation of a Chinese student organization on a U.S. campus. *Journal of Intercultural Communication Research, 35*(2), 117–137.

Loewen, J. W. (1995). *Lies my teacher told me.* New York: Simon & Schuster.

Martin, J. N., & Nakayama, T. K. (2008). *Experiencing intercultural communication: An introduction* (3rd ed.). Boston: McGraw-Hill.

Martin, J. N., Trego, A., & Nakayama, T. K., (2010). The relationship between college students' racial attitudes and friendship diversity. *Howard Journal of Communications, 21*(2), 97–118.

Matsumoto, D. (2002). *The new Japan: Debunking seven cultural stereotypes.* Yarmouth, ME: Intercultural Press.

McGoldrick, M., Giordano, J., & Pearce, J. K. (Eds.). (1996). *Ethnicity and family therapy* (2nd ed.). New York: Guilford Press.

McKinnon, S. (2004, September 1). Spotted owl habitat plan ruffles feathers. *Arizona Republic,* B1.

Melmer, D. (2004). Buffalo and Lakota are kin. *Indian Country Today, 23,* B1.

Numbers. (2008, February 4). *Time,* 18.

Orbe, M. P. (1998). *Constructing co-cultural theory: An explication of culture, power, and communication.* Thousand Oaks, CA: Sage.

Passel, J. S., & Cohn, D. V. (2008, February 11). U.S. populations projections: 2005–2050. Retrieved March 20, 2009, from http://pewhispanic.org/files/reports/85.pdf

Pendery, D. (2008). Identity development and cultural production in the Chinese diaspora to the United States, 1850–2004: new perspectives, *Asian Ethnicity, 9*(3), 201–218.

Porter, T. (2002). The words that come before all else. *Native Americas, 19,* 7–10.

Rabbi: My radio show pulled because of racism (2005, September 27). *The Associated Press.* Retrieved October 10, 2005, from http://www.newsmax.com/archives/ic/2005/9/22/173035.shtml

Reiter, M. J., & Gee, C. B. (2009). Open communication and partner support in intercultural and interfaith romantic relationship: A relational maintenance approach. *Journal of Social and Personal Relationships. 25*(4), 539–599.

Root, M. P. P. (2001). *Love's revolution: Interracial marriage.* Philadelphia, PA: Temple University Press.

Rosenstone, R. A. (2005). My wife, the Muslim. *Antioch Review, 63,* 234–246.

Schneider, S. C., & Barsoux, J. L. (2003). *Managing across cultures.* New York: Prentice Hall.

Shelden, R. G. (2004). The imprisonment crisis in America: An introduction. *Review of Policy Research, 21,* 5–13.

Shim, Y-J., Kim, M-S., & Martin, J. N. (2008) *Changing Korea: Understanding culture and communication.* New York: Peter Lang.

Simpson, J. L. (2008). The color-blind double bind. Communication Theory, 18(1), 880,139–159.

Snyder, M. (2001). Self-fulfilling stereotypes. In P. S. Rothenberg (Ed.), *Race, class & gender in the U.S.* (5th ed., pp. 511–517). New York: Worth.

Stewart, E. C., & Bennett, M. J. (1991). *American cultural patterns: A cross-cultural perspective.* Yarmouth, ME: Intercultural Press.

Tai, S. H. C., & Lau, L. B. Y. (2009). Export of American fantasy world to the Chinese. *International Journal of Case Studies in Management* (Online), 7(2), 1. Retrieved July 28, 2011 from http://login.ezproxy1.lib.asu.edu/login?url=http://search.proquest.com/docview/197457950?accountid=4485

Taylor, P., Funk, C., & Craighill, P. (2006). *Guess who's coming to dinner.* Pew Research Center Social Trends Report. Washington, DC: Pew Research Center.

Ting-Toomey, S. (1999). *Communicating across cultures.* New York: Guilford.

Tourism Highlights (2010). Retrieved February 7, 2011, from http://www.unwto.org/facts/eng/pdf/highlights/UNWTO_Highlights10_en_HR.pdf

Triandis, H. (1995). *Individualism and collectivism.* Boulder, CO: Westview Press.

Trompenaars, F., & Hampden-Turner, C. (1997). *Riding the waves of culture: Understanding diversity in global business.* Boston: McGraw-Hill.

United Nations High Commissioner for Refugees (2009). *UNHCR Statistical Yearbook 2009.* Retrieved February 7, 2011, from http://www.unhcr.org/4ce530889.html

Ward, C. (2008). Thinking outside the Berry boxes: New perspectives on identity, acculturation and intercultural relations. *International Journal of Intercultural Relations, 32,* 105–114.

Waterston, A. (2005). Bringing the past into the present: Family narratives of Holocaust, exile, and diaspora: The story of my story: An anthropology of violence, dispossession, and diaspora. *Anthropological Quarterly, 78,* 43–61.

Wells, S. (2002). *The journey of man: A genetic odyssey.* Princeton, NJ: Princeton University Press.

Yamato, G. (2001). Something about the subject makes it hard to name. In M. L. Andersen & P. H. Collins (Eds.), *Race, class, and gender: An anthology* (4th ed., pp. 90–94). Belmont, CA: Wadsworth.

Yen, H. (2011, February 3). Census estimates show big gains for US minorities. Yahoo News. Retrieved February 6, 2011, from http://news.yahoo.com/s/ap/20110203/ap_on_re_us/us_census2010_population

Zuni eagle aviary is a beautiful sign (2002, July 31). [Editorial.] Retrieved March 20, 2009, from http://www.highbeam.com/doc/1P179291291.html

Chapter 9

Adams, K., & Galanes, G. J. (2003). *Communicating in groups: Applications and skills.* Boston: McGraw-Hill.

Allen, T. H., & Plax, T. G. (2002). Exploring consequences of group communication in the classroom. In L. R. Frey (Ed.), *New directions in group communication* (pp. 219–234). Thousand Oaks, CA: Sage.

Alsop, R. (2003, September 9). Playing well with others. *Wall Street Journal* (Eastern Edition), p. R11.

Arrow, H., McGrath, J. E., & Berdahl, J. L. (2000). *Small groups as complex systems.* Thousand Oaks, CA: Sage.

Baldoni, J. (2004). Powerful leadership communication. *Leader to Leader, 32,* 20–21.

Bantz, C. R. (1993). Cultural diversity and group cross-cultural team research. *Journal of Applied Communication Research, 21,* 1–20.

Barge, J. K. (1989). Leadership as medium: A leaderless group discussion model. *Communication Quarterly, 37,* 237–247.

Barnard, C. (1938). *The functions of an executive.* Cambridge, MA: Harvard University Press.

Barnlund, D. C., & Haiman, S. (1960). *The dynamics of discussion.* Boston: Houghton-Mifflin.

Benne, K. D., & Sheats, P. (1948). Functional roles of group members. *Journal of Social Issues, 4,* 41–49.

Bensimon, E. M. & Neumann, A. (1994). *Redesigning collegiate leadership: Teams and teamwork in higher education*. Baltimore, MD: Johns Hopkins University Press.

Bock, W. (2006). Three star leadership. Retrieved March 30, 2011, from http://www.threestarleadership.com/articles/ 4mistakes.htm

Bonito, J. A., DeCamp, M. H. & Ruppel, E. K. (2008). The process of information sharing in small groups: Application of a local model. *Communication Monographs, 75*, 171–192.

Bono, J. E., & Judge, T. A. (2004). Personality and transformational and transactional leadership: A meta-analysis. *Journal of Applied Psychology, 89*(5), 901–910.

Bormann, E. G. (1975). *Discussion and group methods* (2nd ed.). New York: Harper & Row.

Bowers, C. A., Pharmer, J. A., & Salas, E. (2000). When member homogeneity is needed in work teams: A meta-analysis. *Small Group Research, 31*, 305–327.

Broome, B. J., & Chen, M. (1992). Guidelines for computer-assisted problem solving: Meeting the challenges of complex issues, *Small Group Research, 23*, 216–236.

Broome, B. J., & Fulbright, L. (1995). A multistage influence model of barriers to group problem solving: A participant-generated agenda for small group research, *Small Group Research, 26*, 24–55.

Brown, S. (2007, April 12). It's teamwork, not solos, that make for discoveries, research finds. *The Chronicle of Higher Education*. Retrieved April 17, 2011, from http://chronicle.com/article/Its-Teamwork-Not-Solos-That/38549/

Cady, S. H., & Valentine, J. (1999). Team innovation and perceptions of consideration: What difference does diversity make? *Small Group Research, 30*, 730–750.

Connaughton, S. L., & Shuffler, M. (2007). Multinational and multicultural distributed teams: A review and future agenda. *Small Group Research, 38*(1), 387–412.

Covey, S. R. (1989). *The seven habits of highly effective people: Restoring the character ethic*. New York: Simon and Schuster.

Cox, T. (1994). *Cultural diversity in organizations: Theory, research and practice*. San Francisco: Berrett-Kochler.

Cragan, J. F., & Wright, D. W. (1999). *Communication in small groups: Theory, process, skills* (5th ed.). Belmont, CA: Wadsworth.

Crown, D. F. (2007). The use of group and groupcentric individual goals for culturally heterogeneous and homogeneous task groups: An assessment of European work teams. *Small Group Research, 38*(4), 489–508.

Daft, R. L. (2010). *The leadership experience* (5th ed.). Mason, OH: Thomson Higher Education.

Denhardt, R. B. & Denhardt, J. V. (2004). *The dance of leadership*. Armonk, NJ: M. E. Sharpe.

Engleberg, I. N., & Wynn, D. R. (2010). *Working in groups: Communication principles and strategies* (5th ed.). Boston: Allyn-Bacon.

Eysenbach, G., Powell, J., Englesakis, M., Rizo, C., & Stern, A. (2004). Health related virtual communities and electronic support groups: Systematic review of the effects of online peer to peer interactions. *BMJ Journal*. Retrieved April 2, 2011, from http://www.bmj.com/content/328/7449/1166.short

Fisher, B. A. (1970). *Decision emergence: Phases in group decision-making*. Speech Monographs, 37, 53–66.

Fisher, B. A. (1980). *Small group decision making: Communication and the group process* (2nd ed.). New York: McGraw-Hill.

Fisher, B. A. & Ellis, D. G. (1993). *Small group decision making: Communication and the group process*. Boston: McGraw Hill.

Foels, R., Driskell, J. E., Mullen, B., & Salas, E. (2000). The effects of democratic leadership on group member satisfaction: An integration. *Small Group Research, 31*, 676–701.

French, J. R., Jr., & Raven, B. H. (1959). The bases of social power. In D. Cartwright (Ed.), *Studies in social power* (pp. 150–167). Ann Arbor, MI: Institute for Social Research.

Frey, L. R. (1994). The call of the field: Studying communication in natural groups. In L. R. Frey (Ed.), *Group communication in context: Studies of natural groups* (pp. ix–xiv). Hillsdale, NJ: Erlbaum.

Gagné, M., & Zuckerman, M. (1999). Performance and learning goal orientations as moderators of social loafing and social facilitation. *Small Group Research, 30*, 524–541.

Gastil, J. (1994). A meta-analytic review of the productivity and satisfaction of democratic and autocratic leadership. *Small Group Research, 25*, 384–399.

Gladwell, M. (2008). *Outliers*. NY: Little, Brown and Company.

Gokhale, A. (1995). Collaborative learning enhances critical thinking. *Journal of Technology Education, 7*, 22–30.

Gollent, M. (2007, June 6). Why are leadership skills important—for everyone? Retrieved March 30, 2011, from http:// ezinearticles.com/?why-are-leadership-skills-important—for- everyone?&id=591333

Gouran, D. S., Hirokawa, R., & Martz, A. (1986). A critical analysis of factors related to the decisional processes involved in the *Challenger* disaster. *Central States Speech Journal*, 119–135.

Greenleaf, R. (1970/1991). *The servant as leader*. Indianapolis: The Robert K. Greenleaf Center, 1–37.

Greenleaf, R. K. (2002). *Servant leadership: A journey into the nature of legitimate power and greatness*. 25th anniversary edition. New York: Paulist Press.

Groutage, H. (1999, October 10). Mother of slain student calls for tolerance. *Salt Lake Tribune*, p. A4.

Hansen, R. S. & Hansen, K. (2003, November 17). What do employers *really* want? *QuintZine, 4*(23). Retrieved March 25, 2011, from http://www.quint-careers.com/job_skills_values.html

Hargrove, R. (1998). *Mastering the art of creative collaboration*. New York: BusinessWeek Books.

Haslett, B. B., & Ruebush, J. (1999). What differences do individual differences in groups make? The effects of individuals, culture, and group composition. In L. R. Frey, D. S. Gouran, & M. S. Poole (Eds.), *The handbook of group communication theory and research* (pp. 115–138). Thousand Oaks, CA: Sage.

Henningsen, D. D., & Henningsen, M. L. M. (2006). Examining the symptoms of groupthink and retrospective sensemaking. *Small Group Research, 37*(1), 36–64.

Hirokawa, R. Y., & Salazar, A. J. (1999). Task-group communication and decision-making performance. In L. R. Frey, D. S. Gouran, & M. S. Poole (Eds.), The *handbook of group communication theory and research* (pp. 167–191). Thousand Oaks, CA: Sage.

Hughes, L. (2003). How to be an effective team player. *Women in Business, 55*, 22.

Ilgen, D. R., Hollenbeck, J. R., Johnson, M., & Jundt, D. (2005). Teams in organizations: From input-process-output models to IMOI models. *Annual Review of Psychology, 56*, 517–543.

Judge, T. A., Bono, J. E., Ilies, R., & Gerhardt, M. W. (2002). Personality and leadership: A qualitative and quantitative review. *Journal of Applied Psychology, 87*, 765–780.

Judge, T. A., & Cable, D. M. (2004). The effect of physical height on workplace success and income: Preliminary test of a theoretical model. *Journal of Applied Psychology, 89*, 428–441.

Judge, T. A., Colbert, A. E., & Ilies, R. (2004). Intelligence and leadership: A quantitative review and test of theoretical propositions. *Journal of Applied Psychology, 89*, 542–552.

Jung, D. I., & Sosik, J. J. (2002). Transformational leadership in work groups: The role of empowerment, cohesiveness, and collective-efficacy on perceived group performance. *Small Group Research, 33*, 313–336.

Kent, M. V. (1994). The presence of others. In A. P. Hare, H. H. Blumberg, M. F. Davies, & M. V. Kent. *Small group research: A handbook* (pp. 81–106). Norwood, NJ: Ablex.

Keyton, J., Harmon, N., & Frey, L. R. (1996, November). Grouphate: Implications for teaching group communication. Paper presented at the annual meeting of the National Communication Association, San Diego, CA.

Keyton, J. (1999). Relational communication in groups. In L. R. Frey, D. S. Gouran, & M. S. Poole (Eds.), *Handbook of group communication theory and research* (pp. 199–222). Thousand Oaks, CA: Sage.

Keyton, J. (2000). Introduction: The relational side of groups. *Small Group Research, 34*, 387–396.

King, N., & Anderson, N. (1990). Innovation in working groups. In M. A. West & J. F. Farr (Eds.), *Innovation and creativity at work: Psychological and organizational strategies* (pp. 110–135). Chichester, UK: Wiley.

Klocke, U. (2007). How to improve decision making in small groups: Effects of dissent and training interventions. *Small Group Research, 38*(3), 437–468.

Komives, S. R., Lucas, N. & McMahon, T. (1998). Exploring leadership for college students who want to make a difference. San Francisco: Jossey-Bass Publishers.

Landy, F. J., & Conte, J. M. (2010). *Work in the 21st Century: An Introduction to Industrial & Organizational Psychology* (3rd ed.). Hoboken: John Wiley & Sons.

Larson, J. R. (2007). Deep diversity and strong synergy: Modeling the impact of variability in members' problem solving strategies on group problem-solving performance, *Small Group Research, 38*(3), 413–436.

Levine, K. J., Muenchen, R. A. & Brooks, A. M. (2010). Measuring transformational and charismatic leadership: Why isn't charisma measured? *Communication Monographs, 77*(4), 576–591.

Lewin, K., Lippit, R., & White, R. K. (1939). Patterns of aggressive behavior in experimentally created "social climates." *Journal of Social Psychology, 10*, 271–279.

Lewis, L. K., Isbell, M. G., & Koschmann, M. A. (2010). Collaborative tensions: Practitioners' experiences of interorganizational relationships. *Communication Monographs, 77*(4), 462-481.

Li, D. C. S. (2007). Computer-mediated communication and group decision making: A functional perspective. *Small Group Research 38*(5), 593–614.

Littlejohn, S. W. (2002). *Theories of human communication* (7th ed.). Belmont, CA: Wadsworth.

Lowry, P. B., Roberts, T. L., Romano, N. C., Cheney, P. D., & Hightower R. T. (2006). The impact of group size and social presence on small-group communication: Does computer-mediated communication make a difference? *Small Group Research, 37*(6), 631–661.

MacNeil, A., & McClanahan, A. (2005). Shared leadership, The Connexions Project. Retrieved May 21, 2008, from http://cnx.org/content/m12923/latest/

Matha, B. & Boehm, M. (2008). Beyond the Babble: Leadership communication that drives results. San Francisco, CA: Jossey-Bass.

Maznevski, M., & Chudoba, C. (2000). Bridging space over time: Global virtual team dynamics and effectiveness. *Organization Science, 11*(5), 473–492.

McLeod, P. L., Lobel, S. A., & Cox, T. H. (1996). Ethnic diversity and creativity in small groups. *Small Group Research, 27*, 248–264.

Meade, R. (1985). Experimental studies of authoritarian and democratic leadership in four cultures: American, Indian, Chinese and Chinese-American. *High School Journal, 68*, 293–295.

Moore, R. M., III. (2000). Creativity of small groups and of persons working alone. *Journal of Social Psychology, 140*, 143–144.

Myers, S. A., & Goodboy, A. K. (2005). A study of grouphate in a course on small group communication. *Psychological Reports, 97*(2), 381–386.

Northouse, P. G. (2010). *Leadership: Theory and practice*. Thousand Oaks, CA: Sage.

Oetzel, J. G. (1998). Explaining individual communication processes in homogeneous and heterogeneous group through individual-collectivism and self-construal, *Human Communication Research, 25,* 202–224.

Oetzel, J. G. (2001). Self-construals, communication processes, and group outcomes in homogeneous and heterogeneous groups, *Small Group Research, 32,* 19–54.

Oetzel, J. G. (2005). Effective intercultural workgroup communication theory. In W. B. Gudykunst (Ed.), *Theorizing about intercultural communication* (pp. 351–371). Thousand Oaks, CA: Sage.

Paletz, S. B. F., Peng, K., Erez, M., & Maslach, C. (2004). Ethnic composition and its differential impact on group processes in diverse teams. *Small Group Research, 35,* 128–158.

Pavitt, C. (1999). Theorizing about the group communication-leadership relationship. In L. R. Frey, D. S. Gouran, & M. S. Poole (Eds.), *Handbook of group communication theory and research* (pp. 313–334). Thousand Oaks, CA: Sage.

Peterson, R. S., & Behfar, K. J. (2003). The dynamic relationship between performance feedback, trust, and conflict in groups: A longitudinal study. *Organizational Behavior and Human Decision Processes, 92,* 102–112.

Polzer, J. T., Milton, L. P., & Swann, W. B., Jr. (2002). Capitalizing on diversity: Interpersonal congruence in small work groups. *Administrative Science Quarterly, 47,* 296–324.

Poole, M. S. (1983). Decision development in small groups: A study of multiple sequences in decision-making. *Communication Monographs, 50,* 206–232.

Poole, M. S. (1999). Group communication theory. In L. R. Frey, D. S. Gouran, & M. S. Poole (Eds.), *Handbook of group communication theory and research* (pp. 37–70). Thousand Oaks, CA: Sage.

Poole, M. S. & Garner, J. T. (2006). Workgroup conflict and communication. In J. G. Oetzel & S. Ting-Toomey (Eds.), *The Sage handbook of conflict communication* (pp. 267–292). Thousand Oaks, CA: Sage.

Propp, K. M. (1999). Collective information processing in groups. In L. R. Frey, D. S. Gouran, & M. S. Poole (Eds.), *Handbook of group communication theory and research* (pp. 225–250). Thousand Oaks, CA: Sage.

Putnam, L. L., & Stohl, C. (1996). Bona fide groups: An alternative perspective for communication and small group decision-making. In R. Y. Hirokawa & M. S. Poole (Eds.), *Communication and group decision-making* (2nd ed., pp. 147–178). Thousand Oaks, CA: Sage.

Rauch, C. F., Jr., & Behling, O. (1984). Functionalism: Basis for alternative approach to the study of leadership. In J. G. Hunt, D.-M. H. Hosking, C. A. Schriesheim, & R. Stewart (Eds.), *Leaders and managers: International perspectives on managerial behavior and leadership* (pp. 45–62). New York: Pergamon.

Reeves, R., (2004, March). Enough of the 't'-word. *Management Today, 29.*

Riddle, B. L., Anderson, C. M., & Martin, M. M. (2000). Small group socialization scale: Development and validity. *Small Group Research, 31,* 554–572.

Rost, J. C. (2008). Leadership definition. In a. Marturano & J. Gosling (Eds.), *Leadership: The key concepts* (pp. 96–99). New York: Routledge.

Rothwell, J. D. (1995). *In mixed company: Small group communication* (2nd ed.). Fort Worth, TX: Harcourt Brace.

Rowold, J. & Heinitz, K. (2007). Transformational and charismatic leadership: Assessing the convergent, divergent and criterion validity of the MLQ and the CKS. *The Leadership Quarterly, 18,* 121–133.

Salazar, A. J. (1997). Communication effects in small group decision-making: Homogeneity and task as moderators of the communication performance relationship. *Western Journal of Communication, 61,* 35–65.

Sargent, L. D., & Sue-Chan, C. (2001). Does diversity affect group efficacy? *Small Group Research, 32,* 426–450.

Savič, B. S., & Pagon, M. (2008). Individual involvement in health care organizations: Differences between professional groups, leaders and employees. *Stress and Health, 24,* 71–84.

Schiller, S. Z., & Mandviwalla, M. (2007). Virtual team research: An analysis of theory use and a framework for theory appropriation. *Small Group Research, 38*(1), 12–59.

Schultz, B. G. (1999). Improving group communication performance. In L. R. Frey, D. S. Gouran, & M. S. Poole (Eds.), *Handbook of group communication theory and research* (pp. 371–394). Thousand Oaks, CA: Sage.

Scott, C. R. (1999). Communication technology and group communication. In L. R. Frey, D. S. Gouran, & M. S. Poole (Eds.), *The handbook of group communication theory research* (pp. 432–472). Thousand Oaks, CA: Sage.

Sell, J., Lovaglia, M. J., Mannix, E. A., Samuelson, C. D., & Wilson, R. K. (2004). Investigating conflict, power, and status within and among groups. *Small Group Research, 35,* 44–72.

Smith, P. G. (2001). Communication holds global teams together. *Machine Design, 73,* 70–73.

Stogdill, R. M. (1974). *Handbook of leadership: A survey of theory and research.* New York: Free Press.

Support Groups: Do I Really Need One? (n.d.) Adoption.com. Retrieved April 2, 2011 from http://library.adoption.com/articles/support-groups-.html

Uhl-Bien, M. (2006). Relational leadership theory: Exploring the social processes of leadership and organizing. *The Leadership Quarterly, 17,* 654–676.

Valenti, M. A., & Rockett, R. (2008). The effects of demographic differences on forming intragroup relationships. *Small Group Research, 39*(2), 179–202.

van Knippenberg, D., De Dreu, C. K. W., & Homan, A. C. (2004). Work group diversity and group performance: An integrative model and research agenda. *Journal of Applied Psychology, 89*(6), 1008–1022.

van Swol, L. M. (2009). Discussion and perception of information in groups and judge-advisor systems. *Communication Monographs, 76*(1), 99-120.

Wellen, J. M., & Neale, M. (2006). Deviance, self-typicality and group cohesion: The corrosive effects of the bad apples on the barrel. *Small Group Research, 37*(2), 165–186.

Wheelan, S. A., Davidson, B., & Tilin, F. (2003). Group development across time: Reality or illusion? *Small Group Research, 34,* 223–245.

Chapter 10

Aeberhard-Hodges, J. (1996). Sexual harassment in employment: Recent judicial and arbitral trends. *International Labor Review, 135*(5), 499–533.

Alberts, J. K., Lutgen-Sandvik, P., & Tracy, S. J. (2005, May). Bullying in the workplace: A case of escalated incivility. *Organizational Communication Division.* The International Communication Association Convention, New York, NY.

Alberts, J. K., Tracy, S., & Trethewey, A. (2011). An integrative theory of the division of domestic labor: Threshold level, social organizing, and sensemaking. *Journal of Family Communication, 11,* 271–238.

American Management Association. (2005, May 18). *2005 electronic monitoring & surveillance survey: Many companies monitoring, recording, videotaping, and firing employees.* Retrieved June 16, 2006, from http://www.amanet.org/press/amanews/ems05.htm

Barley, S. R., & Kunda, G. (1992). Design and devotion: Surges of rational and normative ideologies of control in managerial discourse. *Administrative Science Quarterly, 37,* 363–399.

Berger, C. (1979). Beyond initial interaction. In H. Giles & R. St. Clair (Eds.), *Language and psychology* (pp. 122–144). Oxford, UK: Basil Blackwell.

Bertalanffy, L. von. (1968). *General systems theory.* New York: Braziller.

Belous, R. (1989). *The contingent economy: The growth of the temporary, part-time and subcontracted workforce.* Washington, DC: The National Planning Association.

Blau, P. M., & Meyer, M. W. (1987). *Bureaucracy in modern society* (3rd ed). New York: Random House.

Brown, M. (1989, Winter). Ethics in organizations. *Issues in Ethics, 2*(1). Santa Clara University: Markkula Center for Applied Ethics. Retrieved March 15, 2006, from http://www.scu.edu/ethics/publications/iie/v2n1/homepage.html

Bullis, C., & Tompkins, P. K. (1989). The forest ranger revisited: A study of control practices and identification. *Communication Monographs, 56,* 287–306.

Canary, D., & Lakey, S. L. (2012). *Strategic conflict.* New York:, Routledge.

Casey, M. K. (1998). *Communication, stress and burnout: Use of resource replacement strategies in response to conditional demands in community-based organizations.* Unpublished doctoral dissertation, Michigan State University, East Lansing, MI.

Chambers, B., Moore, A. B., & Bachtel, D. (1998). *Role conflict, role ambiguity and job satisfaction of county extension agents in the Georgia Cooperative Extension Service.* AERC Proceedings. Retrieved September 15, 2006, from http://www.edst.educ.ubc.ca/aercd1998/98chambers.htm

Cheney, G. (1995). Democracy in the workplace: Theory and practice from the perspective of communication. *Journal of Applied Communication Research, 23,* 167–200.

Cheney, G., Christensen, L. T., Zorn, T. E., Jr., & Ganesh, S. (2004). *Organizational communication in an age of globalizations: Issues, reflections, practices.* Prospect Heights, IL: Waveland.

Chiles, A., & Zorn, T. (1995). Empowerment in organizations: Employees' perceptions of the influences on empowerment. *Journal of Applied Communication Research, 23,* 1–25.

Chilton, K., & Weidenbaum, M. (1994, November). *A new social contract for the American workplace: From paternalism to partnering.* St. Louis, MO: Center for the Study of American Business.

Clair, R. (1996). The political nature of a colloquialism, "A real job": Implications for organizational assimilation. *Communication Monographs, 63,* 249–267.

Conrad, C., & Poole, M. S. (2005). *Strategic organizational communication* (6th ed.). Belmont, CA: Wadsworth.

Conrad, C., & Witte, K. (1994). Is emotional expression repression oppression? *Communication Yearbook, 17,* 417–428. Thousand Oaks: Sage.

Coy, P., Conlin, M., & Herbst, M. (2010, Jan. 7). The disposable worker. *Bloomberg Business Week.* Retrieved September 17, 2011 from http://www.businessweek.com/magazine/content/10_03/b4163032935448.htm.

Daniels, T. D., Spiker, B. K., & Papa, M. J. (1996). *Perspectives on organizational communication* (4th ed.). Madison, WI: Brown & Benchmark.

Dansereau, F. D., & Markham, S. E. (1987). Superior– subordinate communication: Multiple levels of analysis. In F. Jablin, L. Putnam, K. Roberts, & L. Porter (Eds.), *Handbook of organizational communication* (pp. 343–386). Newbury Park, CA: Sage.

Deetz, S. (1992). *Democracy in an age of corporate colonization: Developments in communication and the politics of everyday life.* Albany, NY: SUNY Press.

DiTecco, D., Cwitco, G., Arsenault, A., & Andre, M. (1992). Operator stress and monitoring practices. *Applied Ergonomics, 23*(1), 29–34.

Dockery, T. M., & Steiner, D. D. (1990). The role of the initial interaction in leader-member exchange. *Group and Organization Studies, 15,* 395–413.

Eisenberg, E., Goodall, H. L., & Trethewey, A. (2010). *Organizational communication: Balance, creativity and constraint.* Boston, MA: Bedford/St. Martin's.

Eisenberg, E. M., Monge, P. R., & Farace, R. V. (1984). Coorientation on communication rules in managerial dyads. *Human Communication Research, 11,* 261–271.

Equal Employment Opportunity Commission. (1980). Guidelines on discrimination because of sex (Sect. 1604.11). *Federal Register, 45,* 74676–74677.

Everbach, T. (2007). The culture of a women-led newspaper: An ethnographic study of the Sarasota Herald-Tribune. *Journalism and Mass Communication Quarterly, 83,* 477–493.

Fishman, C. (2006). *The Wal-Mart effect.* NY: Penguin Press.

Follett, M. P. (1942). *Dynamic administration.* New York: Harper & Row.

Ganesh, S., Zoller, H. & Cheney, G. (2005). Transforming resistance, broadening our boundaries: Critical organization meets globalization from below. *Communication Monographs, 72*(2), 169–191.

Glisson, C., & Durick, M. (1988). Predictors of job satisfaction and organizational commitment in human service organizations. *Administrative Quarterly, 33,* 61–81.

Golembiewski, R. T., Boudreau, R. A., Sun, B. C., & Luo, H. (1998). Estimates of burnout in public agencies: Worldwide how many employees have which degrees of burnout, and with what consequences? *Public Administration Review, 58,* 59–65.

Gossett, L. (2001). The long-term impact of short-term workers. *Management Communication Quarterly, 15*(1), 115–120.

Graen, G., & Graen, J. (2006). *Sharing network leadership.* Greenwich, CT: Information Age Publishing.

Gruber, J. E., & Smith, M. D. (1995). Women's responses to sexual harassment: A multivariate analysis. *Basic and Applied Social Psychology, 17,* 543–562.

Hewlitt, S. (2007). *Off-ramps and on-ramps: Keeping talented women on the road to success.* Harvard, MA: Harvard Business School Publishing.

Highgate, P., & Upton, J. (2005). War, militarism, and masculinities. In M.S. Kimmel, J. Hearn, & R. W. Connell (Eds.), *Handbook of studies on men and masculinities* (pp. 432–447). Thousand Oaks, CA: Sage.

Hochschild, A. (1983). *The managerial heart.* Berkeley: University of California Press.

Howard-Grenville, J. A. (2006). Inside the "black box": How organizational culture and subcultures inform interpretations and actions on environmental issues. *Organization & Environment, 19*(1), 46–73.

Igbaria, M., & Guimaraes, T. (1993). Antecedents and consequences of job satisfaction among information center employees. *Journal of Management Information Systems, 9*(4), 145–155.

Jablin, F. M. (1979). Superior-subordinate communication: The state of the art. *Psychological Bulletin, 86,* 1201–1222.

Jablin, F. M., & Krone, K. J. (1987). Organizational assimilation. In C. R. Berger & S. H. Chafee (Eds.), *Handbook of communication science* (pp. 711–746). Newbury Park, CA: Sage.

Jablin, F. M., & Sias, P. M. (2001). Communication competence. In F. M. Jablin & L. Putnam (Eds.), *The new handbook of organizational communication* (pp. 819–864). Thousand Oaks, CA: Sage.

Jenner, L. (1994). *Work-family programs: Looking beyond written programs. HR Focus, 71,* 19–20.

Kirby, E. L., & Krone, K. J. (2002). "The policy exists but you can't really use it": Communication and the structuration of work-family polices. *Journal of Applied Communication Research, 30,* 50–77.

Koniarek, J., & Dudek, B. (1996). Social support as a barrier in the stress–burnout relationship. *International Journal of Stress Management, 3,* 99–106.

Kram, K. E., & Isabella, L. A. (1985). Mentoring alternatives: The role of peer relationships in career development. *Academy of Management Journal, 28,* 110–132.

Kreps, G. (1991). *Organizational communication: Theory and practice* (2nd ed.). New York: Longman.

Krugman, P. (2002). *The great unraveling: Losing our way in the new century.* New York: W. W. Norton.

Larson, J., Jr. (1989). The dynamic interplay between employees: Feedback-seeking strategies and supervisors' delivery of performance feedback. *Academy of Management Review, 14,* 408–422.

Lipson, S. (2011, January 2). Perma-lancing. *The Fiscal Times.* Retrieved July 13, 2011, from http://www .thefiscaltimes.com/Articles/2011/01/02/Permalanc-ing-The-New-Disposable-Workforce.aspx

Lutgen-Sandvik, P., Tracy, S., & Alberts, J. (2005, February*). Burned by bullying in the American workplaces: A first time study of U.S. prevalence and delineation of bullying "degree."* Presented at the Western States Communication Convention, San Francisco, CA.

Martin, J. (2002). *Organizational culture: Mapping the terrain.* Thousand Oaks, CA: Sage.

Maslach, C. (2003). Job burnout: New directions in research and intervention. *Current Directions in Psychological Science, 12*(5), 189–192.

Maslach, C., & Leiter, M. (1997). *The truth about burnout: How organizations cause personal stress and what to do about it.* San Francisco: Josey-Bass.

McGrath J. E. (1976). Stress and behavior in organizations. In M. D. Dunnette (Ed.), *Handbook of industrial and organizational psychology.* Palo Alto, CA: Consulting Psychologists Press.

McNamara, C. (2008). *Field guide to leadership and supervision.* Minneapolis, MN: Authenticity Publishing.

Miller, K. (2009). *Organizational communication: Approaches and processes* (5th ed.). Belmont, CA: Wadsworth.

Miller, V. D., & Jablin, F. (1991). Information seeking during organizational entry: Influence, tactics and a model of the process. *Academy of Management Review, 16,* 522–541.

Morgan, H., & Milliken, F. J. (1992). Keys to action: Understanding differences in organizations' responsiveness to work-and-family issues. *Human Resource Management, 31,* 227–248.

MSNBC.com News Service. (2011, July 14). FBI probes Murdoch empire over 9/11 hacking claims. Retrieved August 9, 2011, from http://www.msnbc .msn.com/id/43750733/ns/world_news- europe/t/fbi-probes-murdoch-empire-over-hacking-claims/

Prokokos, A., & Padavik, I. (2002). "There ought to be a law against bitches": Masculinity lessons in police academy training. *Gender, Work and Organization, 9*(4), 439–459.

Putnam, L. L., Phillips, N., & Chapman, P. (1996). Metaphors of communication and organization. In S. R. Clegg, C. Hardy, & W. R. Nord (Eds.), *Handbook of organization studies* (pp. 375–408). London: Sage.

Rapoport, R., & Bailyn, L. (1996). *Relinking life and work.* New York: Ford Foundation.

Rawlins, W. K. (1994). Being there and growing apart: Sustaining friendships during adulthood. In D. Canary & L. Stafford, *Communication and relational maintenance* (pp. 275–294). San Diego, CA: Academic.

Richardsen, A. M., & Martinussen, M. (2004). The Maslach burnout inventory: Factorial validity and consistency across occupational groups in Norway. *Journal of Occupational and Organizational Psychology, 77,* 1–20.

Richmond, V. P., McCroskey, J. C., & Davis, L. M. (1986). The relationship of supervisor use of power and affinity-seeking strategies with subordinate satisfaction. *Communication Quarterly, 34,* 178–193.

Rizzo, J. R., House, R. J., & Lirtzman, S. L. (1970). Role conflict and ambiguity in complex organizations. *Administrative Science Quarterly, 15,* 150–163.

Roberts, B. S., & Mann, R. A. (2000, December 5). *Sexual harassment in the workplace: A primer.* Retrieved September 12, 2006, from http://www3 .uakron.edu/lawrev/robert1.html

Roy, D. F. (1995). Banana time: Job satisfaction and informal interaction. In S. R. Corman, S. P. Banks, C. R. Bantz, & M. E. Mayer (Eds.), *Foundations of Organizational Communication: A Reader* (pp. 111–120). White Plains, NY: Longman.

Rudman, L.A., Borgida, E., & Robertson, B. A. (1995). Suffering in silence: Procedural justice versus gender socialization issues in university sexual harassment grievance procedures. *Basic and Applied Social Psychology, 17,* 519–541.

Schein, E. H. (2002). *Organizational culture and leadership.* San Francisco, CA: Josey-Bass.

Schor, J. B. (1992). *The overworked American: The unexpected decline of leisure.* New York: BasicBooks.

Scott, C., & Myers, K. (2005). The emotion of socialization and assimilation: Learning emotion management at the firehouse. *Journal of Applied Communication Research, 33*(1), 67–92.

Shuler, S., & Sypher, B. D. (2000). Seeking emotion labor: When managing the heart enhances the work experience. *Management Communication Quarterly, 14,* 50–89.

Sias, P. M. (2005). Workplace relationship quality and employee information experiences. *Communication Studies, 56*(4), 375–395.

Sias, P. M., & Cahill, D. J. (1998). From coworkers to friends: The development of peer friendships in the workplace. *Western Journal of Communication, 62,* 273–279.

Sias, P. M., & Jablin, F. M. (1995). Differential superior–subordinate relations: Perceptions of fairness, and coworker communication. *Human Communication Research, 22,* 5–38.

Sias, P. M., Smith, G., & Avdeyeva, T. (2003). Sex and sex-composition differences and similarities in peer workplace friendship development. *Communication Studies, 54,* 322–340.

Sigal, J., Braden-Maguire, J., Patt, I., Goodrich, C., & Perrino, C. S. (2003). Effect of coping response, setting, and social context on reactions to sexual harassment. *Sex Roles, 48*(3–4), 157–166.

Solomon, C. (1994). Work/family's failing grade: Why today's initiatives aren't enough. *Personnel Journal, 73*(5), 72–87.

Stanton, J. M., & Julian, A. L. (2002). The impact of electronic monitoring on quality and quantity of performance. *Computers in Human Behavior, 18*(1), 85–113.

Taylor, J. R., & Van Every, J. F. (1993). *The vulnerable fortress: Bureaucratic organizations and management in the information age.* Toronto, Canada: University of Toronto Press.

Thurnell, R., & Parker, A. (2008). Men, masculinities and firefighting: Occupational identity, shop-floor culture and organisational change. *Emotion, Space and Society, 1*(2), 127–134.

Tracy, S. J. (2000). Becoming a character for commerce: Emotion labor, self-subordination and discursive construction of identity in a total institution. *Management Communication Quarterly, 14,* 90–128.

Tracy, S. J. (2005). Locking up emotion: Moving beyond dissonance for understanding emotion labor discomfort. *Communication Monographs, 72,* 261–238.

Trethewey, A., & Corman, S. (2001). Anticipating k-commerce: E-Commerce, knowledge management, and organizational communication. *Management Communication Quarterly, 14,* 619–628.

U.S. Department of Labor. (2008, October). Fact finding. *Report from the commission on the future of worker-management relations.* Retrieved November 12, 2008, from http://www .dol.gov/_sec/media/reports/dunlop/summary/htm

U.S. General Accounting Office. (2000, June). *Contingent Workers: Income and benefits lag behind those of rest of workforce.* Retrieved November 12, 2008, from http://www.gao.gov/cgi-bin/getrpt?GAO/HEHS-00-76

Vault. (2003). *Vault office romance survey.* Retrieved March 10, 2006, from http://www.vault.com/nr/newsmain.jsp>nr_page=3dch_id=420d.article_id=16 513021

Waldron, V. R. (1994). Once more, with feeling: Reconsidering the role of emotion in work. In S. Deetz (Ed.), *Communication Yearbook, 17,* 388–416). Thousand Oaks, CA: Sage.

Wayne, S. G., & Ferris, G. R. (1990). Influence tactics, affect and exchange quality in supervisor-subordinate interactions: A laboratory experiment and field study. *Journal of Applied Psychology, 75,* 487–499.

Westman, M., & Etzion, D. (2005). The crossover of work- family conflict from one spouse to the other. *Journal of Applied Social Psychology, 35*(9), 1936–1957.

Whetton, D. A., & Cameron, K. S. (2002). *Developing managerial skills* (6th ed.). Upper Saddle River, NJ: Prentice Hall.

Zuckerman, M. B. (2011, June 20). Why the job situation is worse than it looks. *U.S. News and World Report.* Retrieved September, 17, 2011 from http://www .usnews.com/opinion/mzuckerman/articles/2011/06/20/why-the-jobs-situation-is-worse-than-it-looks

Chapter 11

Akhavan-Majid, R. (2004). Mass media reform in China: Toward a new analytical perspective. *Gazette: The International Journal for Communication Studies, 66,* 553–565.

American Academy of Pediatrics. (2002). Some things you should know about media violence and media literacy. Retrieved June 1, 2006, from http://www .aap.org/advocacy/childhealthmonth/media.htm

Anderson, C. A., & Bushman, B. J. (2002, March 29). The effects of media violence on society. *Science, 295,* 2377–2378. Retrieved May 1, 2006, from http://www.psychology.iastate.edu/faculty/caa/abstracts/2000-2004/02AB2 .pdf

Aoyagi, C. (2004, July 2–15). TV networks' current fascination with Hawaii often doesn't translate into more roles for APAs. *Pacific Citizen, 139,* 1.

Aubin, B. (2004, March 1). Why Quebecers feel especially betrayed. *Macleans.* Retrieved May 10, 2006, from http://www.macleans.ca/topstories/politics/article.jsp?content= 20040301_76248_76248

Belkin, L. (2010, December 14). Wanted: More girls on screen. *New York Times.* Retrieved July 19, 2011, from http:// parenting.blogs.nytimes.com/2010/12/14/wanted-more-girls-on-screen/

Berelson, B. (1971). *Content analysis in communication research.* New York: Hafner Publishing Co. (Originally published in 1952.)

Billings, A. C., & Eastman, S. T. (2003). Framing identities: Gender, ethnic, and national parity in network announcing of the 2002 Olympics. *Journal of Communication, 53,* 569–586.

Bissell, K. L., & Zhou, P. (2004). Must-see TV or ESPN: Entertainment and sports media exposure and body-image distortion in college women. *Journal of Communication, 54,* 5–21.

Boorstin, D. J. (1965). *The Americans: The national experience.* New York: Random House.

Bryant, J., & Miron, D. (2004). Theory and research in mass communication. *Journal of Communication, 54,* 662–704.

Bushman, B. J., & Gibson, B. (2011). Violent video games cause an increase in aggression long after the game has been turned off. *Social Psychological and Personality Science, 2,* 29–32.

Cablevision. (2000, November 4). NBC to acquire Bravo from Cablevision Systems Corporation. Retrieved June 24, 2006, from http://www.cablevision.com/index.jhtml?id=2002_11_04

Cernetig, M. (2004, January 13). Radio-Canada satire strikes nerve. *Toronto Star.* Retrieved June 24, 2006, from http://www.ondespubliques.ca/index_f.php?page=96342876

Chalaby, J. K. (2003). Television for a new global order: Transnational television networks and the formation of global systems. *Gazette: The International Journal for Communication Studies, 65,* 457–472.

Chapman, J. (2005). *Comparative media history.* Malden, MA: Polity Press.

Cho, H., & Boster, F. J. (2008). Effect of gain versus loss frame antidrug ads on adolescents. *Journal of Communication, 58,* 428–446.

Cohen, J. (2002). Television viewing preferences: Programs, schedules, and the structure of viewing choices made by Israeli adults. *Journal of Broadcasting & Electronic Media, 46,* 204–221.

comScore. (2011, June 8). Television and fixed Internet found to be most important information sources in Japan following earthquake and tsunami. Press release. Retrieved July 14, 2011, from http://www.comscore.com/Press_Events/Press_Releases/2011/6/Television_and_Fixed_Internet_ Found _to_be_Most_Important_Information_Sources_in_Japan_Following _Earthquake_and_Tsunami

Dayan, D., & Katz, E. (1992). *Media events: The live broadcasting of history.* Cambridge, MA: Harvard University Press.

DeLuca, K. M., & Peeples, J. (2002). From public sphere to public screen: Democracy, activism, and the "violence" of Seattle. *Critical Studies in Media Communication, 19,* 125–151.

de Moraes, L. (2004, October 21). No more Miss America pageantry for ABC. *Washington Post,* p. C7. Retrieved June 24, 2006, from http://www .washingtonpost.com/wp-dyn/articles/A50114-2004Oct20.html

Dixon, T. L., & Linz, D. (2002). Television news, prejudicial pretrial publicity, and the depiction of race. *Journal of Broadcasting & Electronic Media, 46,* 112–136.

Durham, M. G. (2004). Constructing the "new ethnicities": Media, sexuality, and diaspora identity in the lives of South Asian immigrant girls. *Critical Studies in Media Communication, 21,* 140–161.

Dwyer, D., & Jones, L. (2010, May 20). Rape kit testing backlog thwarts justice for victims. *ABC News.* Retrieved July 14, 2011, from http://abcnews.go.com/Politics/sexual-assault-victims-congress-solve-rape-kit-backlog/story?id =10701295

Fahmy, S. (2004). Picturing Afghan women: A content analysis of AP wire photographs during the Taliban regime and after the fall of the Taliban regime. *Gazette: The International Journal for Communication Studies, 66,* 91–112.

Federal Communications Commission. (2003, July 8). V-chip: Viewing television responsibly. Retrieved June 24, 2006, from http://www.fcc.gov/vchip/

Gerbner, G. (2002). *Against the mainstream: The selected works of George Gerbner.* M. Morgan (ed.). New York: Peter Lang.

Glaister, D. (2005, January 15). Wives or sluts? US viewers in love-hate match with TV hit. *Guardian.* Retrieved June 24, 2006, from http://www.guardian .co.uk/usa/story/0,12271,1391061,00.html

Hanke, R. (1990). Hegemonic masculinity in *thirtysomething. Critical Studies in Mass Communication, 7,* 231–248.

Hightower, K. & Sedensky, M. (2011, July 10). Anger over Casey Anthony verdict pours out online. *USA Today.* Retrieved August 1, 2011, from http://www.usatoday.com/news/topstories/2011-07-09-2575323558_x.htm

Jhally, S., & Lewis, J. (1992). *Enlightened racism: The Cosby show, audiences, and the myth of the American dream.* Boulder, CO: Westview Press.

Kennedy, M. G., O'Leary, A., Beck, V., Pollard, K., & Simpson, P. (2004). Increases in calls to the CDC National STD and AIDS Hotline following AIDS-related episodes in a soap opera. *Journal of Communication, 54,* 287–301.

Krauss, C. (2004, December 27). A twisted sitcom makes the Simpsons look like saints. *New York Times,* A4.

Law, C., & Labre, M. P. (2002). Cultural standards of attractiveness: A thirty-year look at changes in male images in magazines. *Journalism and Mass Communication Quarterly, 79,* 697–711.

Lazarsfeld, P. F., Berelson, B., & Gaudet, H. (1948). *The people's choice: How the voter makes up his mind in a presidential campaign.* New York: Columbia University Press.

Lemire, C. (2005, August 10). Even trashing "Deuce Bigalow" a tired cliché. MSNBC. Retrieved June 24, 2006, from http://msnbc.msn.com/id/8887672

Lowry, D. T., Nio, T. C. J., & Leitner, D. W. (2003). Setting the public fear agenda: A longitudinal analysis of network TV crime reporting, public perceptions of crime and FBI crime statistics. *Journal of Communication, 53,* 61–73.

McChesney, R. (1998). Making media democratic. *Boston Review, 23,* 4–10, 20. Retrieved June 24, 2006, from http://www.bostonreview.net/BR23.3/mcchesney.html

McQuail, D. et al. (1972). The television audience: a revised perspective. In McQuail, D. (ed.)., *Sociology of Mass Communication* (pp. 135–165). New York: Penguin.

McQuail, D. (1987). *Mass communication theory: An introduction* (2nd ed.). Newbury Park, CA: Sage Publications.

Meyers, M. (2004). African American women and violence: Gender, race, and class in the news. *Critical Studies in Media Communication, 21,* 95–118.

Morgan, M., & Signorielli, N. (1990). Cultivation analysis: Conceptualization and methodology. In N. Signorielli & M. Morgan (Eds.), *Cultivation analysis: New directions in media effects research* (pp. 13–34). Newbury Park, CA: Sage Publications.

Nathanson, A. (2004). Factual and evaluative approaches to modifying children's responses to violent television. *Journal of Communication, 54,* 321–336.

Niederdeppe, J., Fowler, E. F., Goldstein, K. & Pribble, J. (2010). Does local television news coverage cultivate fatalistic beliefs about cancer prevention? *Journal of Communication, 60:* 230-253.

Nielsen Media Research. (2005, September 29) Nielsen reports Americans watch TV at record levels. Retrieved June 26, 2006, from http://www.nielsenmedia .com/newsreleases/2005/AvgHoursMinutes92905.pdf

Peter, J. (2003). Country characteristics as contingent conditions of agenda setting: The moderating influence of polarized elite opinion. *Communication Research, 30,* 683–712.

Romer, D., Jamieson, K. H., & Aday, S. (2003). Television news and the cultivation of fear of crime. *Journal of Communication, 53,* 88–104.

Rubin, S. (2010, October 6). Rape kit backlog hits primetime on "SVU." *Ms. Magazine.* Retrieved July 14, 2011, from http://msmagazine.com/blog/blog/2010/10/06/rape-kit-backlog-hits-primetime-on-svu/

Shugart, H. (2008). Managing masculinities: The metrosexual moment. *Communication and Critical/Cultural Studies, 5,* 280–300.

Slater, M. D., Henry, K. L., Swaim, R. C., & Anderson, L. L. (2003). Violent media content and aggressiveness in adolescents: A downward spiral model. *Communication Research, 30,* 713–736.

Sproule, J. M. (1989). Progressive propaganda critics and the magic bullet myth. *Critical Studies in Mass Communication, 6,* 225–246.

Trujillo, N. (1991). Hegemonic masculinity on the mound: Media representations of Nolan Ryan and American sports culture. *Critical Studies in Mass Communication, 8,* 290–308.

TV Parental Guidelines Monitoring Board. (n.d.) Understanding the TV ratings. Retrieved June 24, 2006, from http://www.tvguidelines.org/ratings.htm

Wardle, C., & West, E. (2004). The press as agents of nationalism in the Queen's Golden Jubilee: How British newspapers celebrated a media event. *European Journal of Communication, 19,* 195–219.

Washington State Department of Health. (n.d.) *Media literacy: fast facts.* Retrieved June 24, 2006, from http://depts.washington.edu/thmedia/view.cgi?section =medialiteracy&page=fastfacts

Wolf, N. (2002). *The beauty myth: How images of beauty are used against women.* New York: HarperCollins. Originally published 1991.

Photo Credits

Index